D0903526

DICTIONARY OF CANADIAN BIOGRAPHY

DICTIONARY OF CANADIAN BIOGRAPHY

DICTIONNAIRE BIOGRAPHIQUE DU CANADA

GENERAL EDITORS

GEORGE W. BROWN

1959–1963

DAVID M. HAYNE

1965–1969

FRANCESS G. HALPENNY

1969–

DIRECTEURS GÉNÉRAUX ADJOINTS

MARCEL TRUDEL

1961–1965

ANDRÉ VACHON

1965–1971

JEAN HAMELIN

1973–

UNIVERSITY OF TORONTO PRESS

LES PRESSES DE L'UNIVERSITÉ LAVAL

DICTIONARY

OF CANADIAN

BIOGRAPHY

INDEX

VOLUMES I TO IV

1000 to 1800

UNIVERSITY OF TORONTO PRESS

Toronto   Buffalo   London

STAFF OF THE DICTIONARY

This volume has been prepared under the direction of
MARY McD. MAUDE and MICHEL PAQUIN
with the assistance, in Toronto, of
MARGARET FILSHIE, JANE E. GRAHAM, HEDDI KEIL,
DEBORAH MARSHALL, and STUART R. J. SUTHERLAND
and, in Quebec, of
MARIE-CÉLINE BLAIS, HUGUETTE FILTEAU,
HÉLÈNE LIZOTTE, and GASTON TISDEL

25.00·23.09
© University of Toronto Press and
Les Presses de l'université Laval, 1981
Printed in Canada

ISBN 0-8020-3326-1

Canadian Cataloguing in Publication Data
Main entry under title:

Dictionary of Canadian biography: index,
volumes I to IV, 1000 to 1800

Issued also in French.

ISBN 0-8020-3326-1

1. Dictionary of Canadian biography – Indexes.
2. Canada – Biography – Indexes.

FC25.D522   920′.071   c81-095157-6
F1005.D522

Contents

Introduction

The *Index, volumes I to IV* is the seventh work published by the *Dictionary of Canadian biography/Dictionnaire biographique du Canada*. Long hoped for by users of the DCB, both specialists and general readers, the *Index* is a guide to the contents of the first four volumes, which include persons who died between 1000 and 1800. By bringing together various finding aids, it endeavours to facilitate the use of volumes I to IV and to permit a reader to locate rapidly biographies dealing with a certain area or a certain kind of activity. The DCB/DBC hopes to publish a second index covering volumes V to VIII (1801–1860) and a third covering volumes IX to XII (1861–1900), as the publication programme for the nineteenth century is completed.

The *Index* contains four finding aids, three of them the result of new arrangements illustrating the material in the volumes, and one a merging of the indexes that have already appeared in volumes I–IV. They reflect only the contents of the four volumes, and should not be used for qualitative or quantitative judgements of the period under scrutiny. The principles governing the preparation of the finding aids have been kept as general as possible in order to permit inclusion in a uniform treatment of the wide variety of biographies already published and of those to come. A short explanation precedes each aid.

The first section of the *Index* is a list of Subjects of Biographies, arranged alphabetically. It enables the reader to have an overview of the contents of the four volumes. The Index of Identifications permits the user to find those biographies of interest from the point of view of occupation or other kind of activity. The Geographical Index enables the reader to scan the present ten provinces (some of which have been subdivided) and two territories of Canada in which the subjects of biographies lived, as well as the different countries of the world in which Canadians had careers. Finally, the Cumulative Nominal Index brings together all the individuals mentioned in the biographies of the four volumes, thus enabling the reader to establish family relationships, among other things.

The publication of this *Index* will meet, we hope, a number of needs of the users of the *Dictionary*. It goes without saying that the staff of the DCB/DBC is already considering the next indexes to be published, and is trying to improve these finding aids which aim to make the collection more accessible.

FRANCESS G. HALPENNY

JEAN HAMELIN

SUBJECTS OF BIOGRAPHIES

VOLUME I   (1000–1700)

VOLUME II (1701–1740)

VOLUME III (1741–1770)

VOLUME IV (1771–1800)

Subjects of Biographies

ABBADIE de Saint-Castin, Bernard-Anselme d',
Baron de Saint-Castin (1689–1720) II, 3–4
Abbadie de Saint-Castin, Jean-Vincent d', Baron
de Saint-Castin (1652–1707) II, 4–7
Abbadie de Saint-Castin, Joseph d', Baron de
Saint-Castin (fl. 1720–46) III, 3
Abercrombie, James (1732–75) IV, 3–4
Abercromby, James (1706–81) IV, 4–5
Abraham, John (fl. 1672–89) I, 39
Acoutsina (fl. 1717–19) II, 7–10
Adams, John (fl. 1710–45) III, 3–4
Adams, Joseph (d. 1737) II, 10
Adhémar, Jean-Baptiste (d. 1754) III, 4–5
Adhémar, Jean-Baptiste-Amable (1736–1800) IV,
5–8
Adhémar de Lantagnac, Gaspard (1681–1756) III, 5
Adhémar de Saint-Martin, Antoine (d. 1714) II,
10–12
Aernoutsz, Jurriaen (fl. 1674) I, 39–40
Agariata (fl. 1666) I, 40–41
Agrain, Jean-Antoine d', Comte d'Agrain (d. 1722)
II, 12
Agramonte, Juan de (fl. 1511) I, 41
Ahatsistari (d. 1642) I, 41–42
Aide-Créquy, Jean-Antoine (1749–80) IV, 8–10
Aigron, dit Lamothe, Pierre (fl. 1660–85) I, 42
Ailleboust, Charles-Joseph d' (d. 1761) III, 5–7
Ailleboust d'Argenteuil, Pierre d' (1659–1711) II,
12–13
Ailleboust de Cerry, Philippe-Marie d' (1702–87)
IV, 10–11
Ailleboust de Coulonge et d'Argentenay, Louis d'
(d. 1660) I, 42–47
Ailleboust de La Madeleine, François-Jean-Daniel
d' (1702–93) IV, 11–12
Ailleboust de Manthet, Nicolas d' (d. 1709) II,
13–14
Ailleboust de Périgny, Paul d' (d. 1746) III, 7
Ailleboust Des Muceaux, Charles-Joseph d'
(d. 1700) I, 47
Ailleboust Des Muceaux, Jean-Baptiste d' (1666–
1730) II, 14
Aitken, Alexander (d. 1799) IV, 12–13
Akomápis (Ackmobish, Agmabesh), Nicholas
(fl. 1778–80) IV, 13
Alavoine, Charles (d. 1764) III, 7–8
Albanel, Charles (d. 1696) I, 47–50
Alden, John (d. 1701/2) II, 14–15
Aldridge, Christopher, Sr (d. 1745/46) III, 8–9
Aldridge, Christopher, Jr (d. 1760) III, 9–10

Alexander, William, Earl of Stirling (d. 1640) I,
50–54
Alexander, Sir William (d. 1638) I, 54–55
Aleyrac, Jean-Baptiste d' (1737–96) IV, 14
Allard de Sainte-Marie, Jean-Joseph d' (d. 1730) II,
15
Allard de Sainte-Marie, Philippe-Joseph d'
(d. 1778) IV, 14–16
Allart, Germain (1618–85) I, 55
Allemand, Pierre (d. 1691) I, 56
Allenou de Lavillangevin, René-Jean (d. 1753) III,
10–12
Allet, Antoine d' (fl. 1657–93) I, 56–57
Alline, Henry (1748–84) IV, 16–20
Allouez, Claude (1622–89) I, 57–58
Aloigny, Charles-Henri d', Marquis de LaGroye
(d. 1714) II, 15–16
Alquier de Servian, Jean d' (fl. 1710–61) III, 12
Amantacha (d. c. 1636) I, 58–59
Ameau, dit Saint-Séverin, Séverin (1620–1715) II,
16–17
Amherst, Jeffery, 1st Baron Amherst (1717/18–97)
IV, 20–26
Amiot, Charles (1636–69) I, 59–60
Amiot, Jean (d. 1648) I, 60
Amiot, Jean-Baptiste (fl. 1720–63) III, 12–13
Amiot, Jean-Baptiste (1717–69) III, 13–14
Amiot de Vincelotte, Charles-Joseph (1665–1735)
II, 17–18
Amiot, dit Villeneuve, Mathieu (d. 1688) I, 60–61
Anadabijou (fl. 1603–11) I, 61
Anandamoakin (fl. 1756–72) IV, 26–27
Anderson, Thomas (d. 1696) I, 61
Andigné de Grandfontaine, Hector d' (d. 1696) I,
61–64
André, Louis (1631–1715) II, 18
André de Leigne, Louise-Catherine (Hertel de
Rouville) (1709–66) III, 14
André de Leigne, Pierre (1663–1748) III, 14–16
Angeac, François-Gabriel d' (1708–82) IV, 27–29
Angibault, dit Champdoré, Pierre (fl. 1604–8) I, 64
Ango Des Maizerets, Louis (1636–1721) II, 18–20
Annaotaha (d. 1660) I, 64–65
Annenraes (d. 1654) I, 65–66
Aongote. See Williams, Eunice
Aouenano (fl. 1699–1701) II, 20
Aprendestiguy de Martignon, Martin d' (fl. 1656–86)
I, 66–67
Apthorp, Alexander (d. c. 1720) II, 20–21
Aradgi (fl. 1700–2) II, 21

Arbuthnot, Mariot (1711–94) IV, 29–30
Argall, Sir Samuel (d. 1626) I, 67–69
Arimph, Jean-Baptiste (fl. 1776–78) IV, 30
Armstrong, Lawrence (1664–1739) II, 21–24
Arnaud, Jean-Charles d' (fl. 1722–52) III, 16–17
Arnaud, Marie-Marguerite-Daniel, *dite* Saint-Arsène (1699–1764) III, 17–18
Arnold, William (fl. 1713–16) II, 24–25
Arnoux, André (d. 1760) III, 18–20
Arrigrand, Gratien d', Sieur de La Majour (b. 1684, d. in or after 1754) III, 20
Arsac de Ternay, Charles-Henri-Louis d' (1723–80) IV, 30–32
Asticou (fl. 1608–16) I, 69–70
Atecouando (fl. 1701–26) II, 25–26
Atecouando (fl. 1749–57) III, 20–21
Atironta (fl. 1615) I, 70
Atironta (d. 1650) I, 70–71
Atironta (d. 1672) I, 71–72
Atkinson, George (d. 1792) IV, 32–33
Auber, Claude (d. 1694) I, 72
Aubert, Thomas (fl. 1508) I, 72
Aubert de Gaspé, Ignace-Philippe (1714–87) IV, 33–34
Aubert de La Chesnaye, Charles (1632–1702) II, 26–34
Aubert de La Chesnaye, François (d. 1725) II, 34–35
Aubert de La Chesnaye, Louis (1690–1745) III, 21–23
Aubery, Joseph (1673–1756) III, 23–25
Aubry, Nicolas (fl. 1604–11) I, 72
Auchagah (fl. 1729) III, 35
Audouart, *dit* Saint-Germain, Guillaume (fl. 1648–63) I, 73
Augé, Étienne (d. 1780) IV, 34–35
Auger de Subercase, Daniel d' (1661–1732) II, 35–39
Aulneau (de La Touche), Jean-Pierre (1705–36) II, 39–40
Aumasson de Courville, Louis-Léonard, known as Sieur de Courville (fl. 1723–82) IV, 35–36
Auoindaon (fl. 1623) I, 73
Avaugour, Louis d' (1669–1732) II, 40–41
Aveneau, Claude (1650–1711) II, 41
Aylwin, Thomas (d. 1791) IV, 37–38

BABIE, Jacques (d. 1688) I, 74
Baby, *dit* Dupéront, Jacques (d. 1789) IV, 38–40
Badeaux, Jean-Baptiste (1741–96) IV, 40–41
Baffin, William (d. 1622) I, 74–75
Baillif, Claude (d. *c.* 1698) I, 75–78
Bailloquet, Pierre (1613–92) I, 78
Bailly, Guillaume (d. 1696) I, 78
Bailly, *dit* Lafleur, François (d. 1690) I, 78
Bailly de Messein, Charles-François (1740–94) IV, 41–44
Baley, Henry (d. 1701) II, 41–42

Barbel, Jacques (d. 1740) II, 42–44
Barbel, Marie-Anne (Fornel) (1704–93) IV, 44–45
Barbier, Marie, *dite* de l'Assomption (d. 1739) II, 44–45
Barnard, John (1681–1770) III, 25–26
Barolet, Claude (d. 1761) III, 26
Barrat, Claude (fl. 1681–1711) II, 45
Barrin de La Galissonière, Roland-Michel, Marquis de La Galissonière (1693–1756) III, 26–32
Barsalou, Jean-Baptiste (1706–76) IV, 45–46
Barthélemy (fl. 1687) I, 79
Barthélemy, Michel (1638–1706) II, 45–46
Basset, David (d. 1724) II, 46–47
Basset, Jean (d. 1715) II, 47
Basset Des Lauriers, Bénigne (d. 1699) I, 79
Basset Du Tartre, Vincent (fl. 1665–68) I, 79–80
Bastide, John Henry (fl. 1711–70) III, 32–34
Bâtard, Étienne (Anthony) (fl. 1750–53) III, 34–35
Batiscan (fl. 1610–29) I, 80
Batt, Isaac (d. 1791) IV, 46–48
Baudeau, Pierre (1643–1708) II, 47–48
Baudoin, Gervais (1686–1752) III, 35
Baudoin, Jean (d. 1698) I, 80
Baudouin, Gervais (d. 1700) I, 80–81
Baudouin, Michel (1691–1768) III, 36
Baudry, *dit* Des Butes, Guillaume (1657–1732) II, 48
Baudry, *dit* Saint-Martin (Baudry Desbuttes, Baudry Soulard), Jean-Baptiste (d. 1755) III, 36–37
Baudry de Lamarche, Jacques (fl. 1676–1738) II, 48
Baugy, Louis-Henri de, known as Chevalier de Baugy (d. 1720) II, 48–49
Bayly, Charles (fl. 1630–80) I, 81–84
Bayne, Daniel (d. 1769) III, 37–38
Bazil, Louis (1695–1752) III, 38–39
Bazire, Charles (1624–77) I, 84–85
Beale, Anthony (d. 1731) II, 49–52
Bean, John (fl. 1751–57) III, 39
Bear. *See* Le Pesant
Bear. *See* Saint-Aubin
Beare, James (fl. 1577–85) I, 85–86
Beatson, Patrick (1758–1800) IV, 48–49
Beaubois, Nicolas-Ignace de (1689–1770) III, 39–41
Beauharnois de Beaumont et de Villechauve, Claude de (1674–1738) II, 52–53
Beauharnois de La Boische, Charles de, Marquis de Beauharnois (d. 1749) III, 41–51
Beauharnois de La Chaussaye, François de, Baron de Beauville (d. 1746) III, 51–54
Beaussier de Lisle, Louis-Joseph (d. 1765) III, 54–55
Bécart de Granville et de Fonville, Charles (d. 1703) II, 53
Bécart de Granville et de Fonville, Paul (1695–1754) III, 55–56
Becquet, Romain (d. 1682) I, 86

Bédard, Thomas-Laurent (1747–95) IV, 49–50
Bégon de La Cour, Claude-Michel (1683–1748) III, 56
Bégon de La Picardière, Michel (1667–1747) III, 57–63
Begourat (fl. 1603) I, 86
Belcher, Jonathan (1710–76) IV, 50–54
Bellenger, Étienne (fl. 1580–84) I, 87–89
Bellot, *dit* Lafontaine (fl. 1664–67) I, 89
Belt of Wampum. *See* Kaghswaghtaniunt
Bénard, Michel (fl. 1733–60) III, 63–64
Benoist, Antoine-Gabriel-François (1715–76) IV, 54–55
Benoît, Pierre (d. 1786) IV, 55
Berbudeau, Jean-Gabriel (1709–92) IV, 55–56
Berger, Le. *See* Honatteniate
Berger, Jean (fl. 1704–9) II, 54
Bergier, Clerbaud (fl. 1680–85) I, 89–90
Bergier, Marc (d. 1707) II, 54–56
Berley, George (d. *c.* 1720) II, 56
Bermen, Laurent (fl. 1647–49) I, 90–91
Bermen de La Martinière, Claude de (1636–1719) II, 56–58
Bermen de La Martinière, Claude-Antoine de (1700–61) III, 64–65
Bernard, Philip (fl. 1786) IV, 56–57
Bernard de La Rivière, Hilaire (d. 1729) II, 58–59
Bernier, Benoît-François (Joseph-Pierre) (1720–99) IV, 57–58
Bernières, Henri de (d. 1700) I, 91–92
Berry, Sir John (1635–89/90) I, 91–93
Berthier, Isaac (Alexandre) (1638–1708) II, 59–60
Bertier, Michel (1695–1740) II, 60
Beschefer, Thierry (1630–1711) II, 61–62
Besnard, *dit* Carignant, Jean-Louis (1743–91) IV, 58–59
Best, George (d. 1583/84) I, 93–94
Bevan, William (fl. 1723–37) II, 62
Biard, Pierre (d. 1622) I, 94–96
Biencourt de Poutrincourt et de Saint-Just, Jean de (1557–1615) I, 96–99
Biencourt de Saint-Just, Charles de (d. 1623 or 1624) I, 99–102
Big Mouth. *See* Otreouti
Bigot, François (d. 1708) II, 62–63
Bigot, François (d. 1778) IV, 59–71
Bigot, Jacques (1651–1711) II, 63–64
Bigot, Vincent (1649–1720) II, 64–65
Bird, Thomas (d. 1739) II, 65
Bisaillon, Peter (d. 1742) III, 65–66
Bishop, Nathaniel (d. 1723) II, 65
Bissot, François-Joseph (1673–1737) II, 65–66
Bissot de Vinsenne, François-Marie (1700–36) II, 66–68
Bissot de Vinsenne, Jean-Baptiste (1668–1719) II, 68
Bizard, Jacques (1642–92) I, 102–3

Bjarni, Herjólfsson (fl. 986) I, 103–4
Blais, Michel (d. 1783) IV, 71–72
Blaise Des Bergères de Rigauville, Nicolas (1679–1739) II, 68–69
Blaise Des Bergères de Rigauville, Raymond (1655–1711) II, 69–71
Blanchard, Guillaume (1650–1716) II, 71
Bochart de Champigny, Jean, Sieur de Noroy et de Verneuil (d. 1720) II, 71–80
Bodega y Quadra, Juan Francisco de la (d. 1794) IV, 72–74
Boiret, Urbain (1731–74) IV, 74–75
Boisdon, Jacques (fl. 1648) I, 104
Boispineau, Jean-Jard (1689–1744) III, 66–67
Boisseau, Josias (fl. 1679–81) I, 104–6
Boisseau, Nicolas (1700–71) IV, 75–76
Boivin, François (d. 1675 or 1676) I, 106
Bolvin, Gilles (d. 1766) III, 67–68
Bonamour, Jean de (fl. 1669–72) I, 106–7
Bond, William (fl. 1672–91) I, 107
Bonfoy, Hugh (d. 1762) III, 68–69
Bonhomme, *dit* Beaupré, Noël (1684–1755) III, 69
Bonnécamps, Joseph-Pierre de (d. 1790) IV, 76–77
Bonne de Missègle, Louis de (d. 1760) III, 69–70
Bonnemere, Florent (1600–83) I, 107–8
Bonner, John (d. 1725/26) II, 80–81
Boquet, Charles (fl. 1657–81) I, 108
Boscawen, Edward (1711–61) III, 70–71
Boschenry de Drucour, Augustin de (d. 1762) III, 71–74
Bouat, François-Marie (d. 1726) II, 81–82
Boucault, Nicolas-Gaspard (fl. 1719–55) III, 74–77
Boucault de Godefus, Gilbert (fl. 1729–56) III, 77–78
Bouchard, Étienne (d. 1676) I, 108–9
Boucher, Geneviève, *dite* de Saint-Pierre (1676–1766) III, 78–79
Boucher, Pierre (d. 1717) II, 82–87
Boucher, Pierre-Jérôme (d. 1753) III, 79–80
Boucher de Boucherville, Pierre (1689–1767) III, 80–81
Boucher de Grandpré, Lambert (d. 1699) I, 109
Boucher de La Perrière, René (1668–1742) III, 81–82
Boucher de Montbrun, Jean (d. 1742) III, 82
Boucher de Niverville, Jean-Baptiste (1673–1748) III, 82–83
Bouillet de La Chassaigne, Jean (1645–1733) II, 87–88
Boulduc, Louis (d. between 1699 and 1701) II, 88–89
Bouler, Robert (d. 1734) II, 89–90
Boullard, Étienne (1658–1733) II, 90–91
Boullé, Eustache (fl. 1618–38) I, 109–10
Boullé, Hélène, *dite* de Saint-Augustin (Champlain) (1598–1654) I, 110

Boullongne, Marie-Barbe de (Ailleboust de Coulogne et d'Argentenay) (d. 1685) I, 110–11

Bourassa, *dit* La Ronde, René (d. 1778) IV, 77–78

Bourdages, Raymond (d. 1787) IV, 78–79

Bourdon, Anne, *dite* de Sainte-Agnès (1644–1711) II, 91–92

Bourdon, Jacques (d. 1724) II, 92

Bourdon, Jean, known as M. de Saint-Jean or Sieur de Saint-François (d. 1668) I, 111–13

Bourdon, Marguerite, *dite* de Saint-Jean-Baptiste (1642–1706) II, 92–93

Bourdon d'Autray, Jacques (!652–88) I, 113–14

Bourdon de Dombourg, Jean-François (1647–90) I, 114

Bourdon de Dombourg, Jean-François (b. 1720, d. after 1789) IV, 79–80

Bourdon de Romainville, Jean (b. 1627, d. after 1654) I, 114–15

Bourg, Abraham (b. 1662, d. after 1727) II, 93–94

Bourg, Joseph-Mathurin (1744–97) IV, 80–82

Bourg, *dit* Belle-Humeur, Alexandre (1671–1760) III, 83–84

Bourgeois, Jacques (Jacob) (d. 1701) II, 94

Bourgeoys, Marguerite, *dite* du Saint-Sacrement (1620–1700) I, 115–19

Bourlamaque, François-Charles de (1716–64) III, 84–87

Boutet de Saint-Martin, Martin (d. 1683?) I, 119

Boutroue d'Aubigny, Claude de (1620–80) I, 119–20

Bouvart, Martin (1637–1705) II, 94–95

Bowman, James (d. 1787) IV, 82–83

Bradley, Thomas (fl. 1484–1505) I, 120

Bradstreet, John (Jean-Baptiste) (1714–74) IV, 83–87

Brandeau, Esther (fl. 1738–39) II, 95–96

Brant, Mary. *See* Koñwatsiʔtsiaiéñni

Bras-de-fer de Chateaufort, Marc-Antoine (fl. 1635–38) I, 120–21

Brassard, Louis-Marie (1726–1800) IV, 87

Brassard Deschenaux, Joseph (1722–93) IV, 87–89

Brassier, Gabriel-Jean (1729–98) IV, 89–90

Bréard, Jacques-Michel (d. 1775) IV, 90–92

Brébeuf, Jean de (1593–1649) I, 121–26

Bréhant de Galinée, René de (d. 1678) I, 126–27

Bréhaut Delisle, Achille (Antoine-Louis?) de (fl. 1636–42) I, 127

Brendan, Saint (d. *c.* 578) I, 675

Breslay, René-Charles de (1658–1735) II, 96–97

Bressani, François-Joseph (1612–72) I, 128–29

Brewse, John (d. 1785) IV, 92–93

Breynton, John (d. 1799) IV, 93–94

Briand, Jean-Olivier (1715–94) IV, 94–103

Bricault de Valmur, Louis-Frédéric (d. 1738) II, 97

Brice, Mme de (fl. 1644–52) I, 129

Bridgar, John (fl. 1678–87) I, 129–30

Bridges, Timothy (fl. 1702–8) II, 97–98

Brigeac, Claude de (d. 1661) I, 130

Brisay de Denonville, Jacques-René de, Marquis de Denonville (1637–1710) II, 98–105

Brochet, Le. *See* Kinongé

Brooke, John (d. 1789) IV, 103–5

Brossard, Jean-François (1654–1716) II, 105

Brossard, Urbain (1633–1710) II, 105–6

Brossard, *dit* Beausoleil, Joseph (1702–65) III, 87–88

Brown, William (d. 1789) IV, 105–7

Bruce, Robert George (d. 1779) IV, 107–8

Brûlé, Étienne (d. *c.* 1633) I, 130–33

Brunet, *dit* La Sablonnière, Jean (1687–1753) III, 88

Bruslé, Michel (1673–1724) II, 106

Bruyas, Jacques (1635–1712) II, 106–8

Bruyères, John (d. before 1787) IV, 108–9

Buade, Louis de, Comte de Frontenac et de Palluau (1622–98) I, 133–42

Buisson de Saint-Cosme, Jean-François (d. 1712) II, 108–9

Buisson de Saint-Cosme, Jean-François (1667–1706) II, 109–10

Bulkeley, Richard (1717–1800) IV, 109–13

Bulteau, Guillaume (1666–1716) II, 110–11

Bunt. *See* Hotsinoñhyahta?

Burch, John (1741–97) IV, 113

Burgoyne, John (1722–92) IV, 113–15

Burton, Ralph (d. 1768) III, 88–90

Busby, Thomas (1735–98) IV, 115–16

Bushell, John (d. 1761) III, 90–91

Buteux, Jacques (1599–1652) I, 142–43

Butler, John (d. 1791) IV, 116–17

Butler, John (d. 1796) IV, 117–20

Butler, Walter (1752–81) IV, 120–21

Button, Sir Thomas (d. 1634) I, 144–45

Bylot, Robert (fl. 1610–16) I, 145

Byng, John (d. 1757) III, 91–92

Byron, John (1723–86) IV, 121–23

Byssot de La Rivière, François (d. 1673) I, 145–46

Cabazié, Pierre (d. 1715) II, 111

Cabot, John (d. *c.* 1498) I, 146–52

Cabot, Sebastian (d. 1557) I, 152–58

Cadet, Joseph-Michel (1719–81) IV, 123–28

Caën, Émery de (fl. 1603–33) I, 159

Caën, Guillaume de (fl. 1619–43) I, 159–62

Cagenquarichten (fl. 1699–1726) II, 111–12

Cahideuc, Emmanuel-Auguste de, Comte Dubois de La Motte (1683–1764) III, 92–93

Cailly, François-Joseph de (fl. 1700–62) III, 93–94

Callbeck, Phillips (d. 1790) IV, 128–29

Callet, Luc (1715–67) III, 94–95

Callière, Louis-Hector de (1648–1703) II, 112–17

Calvarin, Goulven (d. 1719) II, 117

Calvert, George, 1st Baron Baltimore (d. 1632) I, 162–63

Campbell, Colin (fl. 1699–1710) II, 117–18
Campbell, Donald (d. 1763) III, 95–96
Campbell, John (d. 1795) IV, 129–31
Campbell, Lord William (d. 1778) IV, 131–32
Campion, Étienne-Charles (d. 1795) IV, 132–33
Campot, Jacques (d. 1751) III, 96
Capitanal (d. 1634) I, 163–64
Captain Jecob. *See* Winninnewaycappo
Captain Joseph. *See* Wowurna
Captain Swan. *See* Swan
Carbonariis, Giovanni Antonio de (fl. 1489–98) I, 164
Cardeneau, Bernard (fl. 1751–64) III, 96–97
Carheil, Étienne de (1633–1726) II, 118–19
Carigouan (d. 1634) I, 164–65
Carpentier, Bonaventure (1716–78) IV, 133–34
Carrerot, André (d. 1749) III, 97–98
Carrerot, Philippe (d. 1745) III, 98
Carrerot, Pierre (d. 1732) II, 119–20
Cartier, Jacques (1491–1557) I, 165–72
Cartier, Toussaint, known as 'the hermit of Saint-Barnabé' (d. 1767) III, 98–99
Casot, Jean-Joseph (1728–1800) IV, 134–35
Castaing, Pierre-Antoine (d. 1799) IV, 135–36
Castanet, Jean-Baptiste-Marie (1766–98) IV, 136–37
Catalogne, Gédéon (de) (1662–1729) II, 120–22
Catalogne, Joseph de (1694–1735) II, 122
Caulfeild, Thomas (d. 1716/17) II, 122–23
Caumont, Pierre de (d. 1694) I, 172
Cavelier, Jean (1636–1722) II, 123–24
Cavelier de La Salle, René-Robert (1643–87) I, 172–84
Céloron de Blainville, Jean-Baptiste (d. 1735) II, 124–25
Céloron de Blainville, Pierre-Joseph (1693–1759) III, 99–101
Cendre Chaude. *See* Ogenheratarihiens
Chabanel, Noël (1613–49) I, 184–85
Chabert de Joncaire, Louis-Thomas (d. 1739) II, 125–27
Chabert de Joncaire, Philippe-Thomas (fl. 1707–66) III, 101–2
Chabert de Joncaire de Clausonne, Daniel-Marie (d. 1771) IV, 137–38
Chaboulié, Charles (d. 1708) II, 127–28
Chabrand Delisle, David (1730–94) IV, 138–40
Chachagouesse (fl. 1674–1712) II, 128
Chaigneau, Léonard (1663–1711) II, 128–29
Chambalon, Louis (d. 1716) II, 129–30
Chambly, Jacques de (d. 1687) I, 185
Champflour, François de (fl. 1636–49) I, 186
Champion de Cicé, Louis-Armand (1648–1727) II, 130
Champlain, Samuel de (d. 1635) I, 186–99
Champy, Gélase (1657–1738) II, 130–31
Chapoton, Jean-Baptiste (d. 1760) III, 102–3

Chardon, Jean-Baptiste (1671–1743) III, 103
Charest, Étienne (1718–83) IV, 140–41
Charité (fl. 1628–29) I, 199–200
Charlevoix, Pierre-François-Xavier de (1682–1761) III, 103–10
Charly Saint-Ange, Jean-Baptiste (1668–1728) II, 131–32
Charly Saint-Ange, Louis (b. 1703, d. 1767 or 1768) III, 110–11
Charly Saint-Ange, Marie-Catherine, *dite* du Saint-Sacrement (1666–1719) II, 132
Charon de La Barre, François (1654–1719) II, 132–35
Charron de La Barre, Claude (d. 1687) I, 200–1
Chartier, Louis (1633–60) I, 201
Chartier, Michel (d. 1750) III, 111–12
Chartier de Lotbinière, Eustache (1688–1749) III, 112–15
Chartier de Lotbinière, Eustache (b. 1716, d. after 1785) IV, 141–43
Chartier de Lotbinière, Louis-Théandre (fl. 1641–80) I, 201–3
Chartier de Lotbinière, Michel, Marquis de Lotbinière (1723–98) IV, 143–45
Chartier de Lotbinière, René-Louis (d. 1709) II, 135–39
Chassin de Thierry, François-Nicolas de (d. 1755) III, 115–16
Chastellain, Pierre (1606–84) I, 203–4
Chauchetière, Claude (1645–1709) II, 139–40
Chaudière Noire (d. 1697) I, 204–5
Chaudillon, Antoine (1643–1707) II, 140–41
Chaumonot, Pierre-Joseph-Marie (1611–93) I, 205–7
Chaumont, Alexandre de (d. 1710) II, 141
Chaussegros de Léry, Gaspard-Joseph (1682–1756) III, 116–19
Chaussegros de Léry, Gaspard-Joseph (1721–97) IV, 145–47
Chauvigny, Marie-Madeleine de (Gruel de La Peltrie) (1603–71) I, 207–8
Chauvin de La Pierre, Pierre (fl. 1603–11) I, 208–9
Chauvin de Tonnetuit, Pierre de (d. 1603) I, 209–10
Chauvreulx, Claude-Jean-Baptiste (d. *c.* 1760) III, 119–21
Chavigny Lachevrotière, François de (1650–1725) II, 141–42
Chefdostel, Thomas (fl. 1597–1603) I, 210
Cherououny (d. 1627) I, 210–11
Cherrier, François-Pierre (d. 1793) IV, 147–49
Cheval, *dit* Saint-Jacques, and *dit* Chevalier, Jacques-Joseph (d. 1757) III, 121
Chevalier, Jean-Baptiste (d. 1746 or 1747) III, 121–22
Chevalier, Jean-Charles (Jean-Baptiste) (1694–1760) III, 122
Chevalier, *dit* Beauchêne, Robert (1686–1731) II, 142–43

Chew, Joseph (d. 1798) IV, 149
Chèze, François (1683–1740) II, 143
Chichikatelo (d. 1701) II, 143–44
Chihwatenha (d. 1640) I, 211–12
Chingouessi (fl. 1695–1701) II, 144
Cholenec, Pierre (1641–1723) II, 144–45
Chomedey de Maisonneuve, Paul de (1612–76) I, 212–22
Chomina (fl. 1618–29) I, 222–23
Chouart Des Groseilliers, Médard (fl. 1618–84) I, 223–28
Christie, Gabriel (1722–99) IV, 149–51
Church, Benjamin (1639–1717/18) II, 145–46
Cirier, Antoine (1718–98) IV, 151–52
Clairambault d'Aigremont, François (d. 1728) II, 146–48
Claparède, Jean (fl. 1714–58) III, 123
Clark, George (d. 1759) III, 123–24
Clark, Robert (d. 1794) IV, 152–53
Clarke, Richard (fl. 1572–96) I, 228–30
Claude, Joseph (d. 1796) IV, 153–54
Claus, Christian Daniel (1727–87) IV, 154–55
Claverie, Pierre (1719–56) III, 124–25
Clément Du Vuault de Valrennes, Philippe (1647–1707) II, 148–49
Clerke, Charles (1741–79) IV, 155–56
Cleveland, Aaron (1715–57) III, 125–26
Clinton, George (d. 1761) III, 126
Closse, Raphaël-Lambert (d. 1662) I, 230–32
Cloutier, Zacharie (d. 1677) I, 232
Coats, William (d. 1752) III, 127–28
Cobb, Silvanus (1709/10–62) III, 128–30
Cobbie, Walsall (fl. 1676–82) I, 232–33
Cocking, Matthew (1743–99) IV, 156–58
Coghlan, Jeremiah (fl. 1756–88) IV, 158–60
Cole, John (d. 1799) IV, 160
Colin, Michel (d. 1616) I, 233
Collet, Mathieu-Benoît (d. 1727) II, 149–52
Collier, Sir George (1738–95) IV, 160–61
Collier, John (d. 1769) III, 130–31
Collier Pendu, Le. See Kaghswaghtaniunt
Collins, John (fl. 1706–20) II, 152–53
Collins, John (d. 1795) IV, 161–62
Colston, William (fl. 1610–12) I, 233–34
Colvill, Alexander, 7th Baron Colvill (1717/18–70) III, 131–33
Côme de Mantes (fl. 1632–58) I, 234
Constantin, Justinien (1716–60) III, 133–34
Constantin, Nicolas-Bernardin (1664–1730) II, 153
Constantin (Lavallée Constantin), Pierre (fl. 1696–1750) III, 134–35
Cook, James (1728–79) IV, 162–67
Cope, Henry (d. 1742) III, 135–36
Cope, Jean-Baptiste (fl. 1750–58) III, 136–37
Coquart, Claude-Godefroy (1706–65) III, 137–38
Corbin, André (d. 1777) IV, 167–68
Corbin, David (d. 1755) III, 138–39

Cornwallis, Edward (1712/13–76) IV, 168–71
Corolère, Jean (fl. 1750–52) III, 139–40
Coron, Charles-François (1704–67) III, 140–41
Corpron, Jean (fl. 1755–65) III, 141–42
Corriveau, Marie-Josephte, known as La Corriveau (1733–63) III, 142–43
Corte-Real, Gaspar (d. c. 1501) I, 234–36
Corte-Real, Miguel (d. c. 1502) I, 236
Cosby, Alexander (d. 1742) III, 143–44
Cotté, Gabriel (d. 1795) IV, 171–72
Cotton, Barthélemy (1692–1780) IV, 172–73
Cotton, Michel (b. 1700, d. after 1747) III, 144–45
Couagne, Charles de (1651–1706) II, 153–54
Couagne, Jean-Baptiste de (1687–1740) II, 154
Couagne, Jean-Baptiste de (fl. 1720–95) IV, 173–74
Couagne, Michel de (1727–89) IV, 174–75
Couagne, René de (d. 1767) III, 145–46
Couagne, Thérèse de (Poulin de Francheville) (1697–1764) III, 146–47
Couc, Elizabeth? (La Chenette, Techenet; Montour) (d. c. 1750) III, 147–48
Coughlan, Laurence (d. c. 1784) IV, 175–77
Couillard de Lespinay, Guillaume (d. 1663) I, 236–37
Couillard de Lespinay, Jean-Baptiste (d. 1735) II, 154–55
Couillard de Lespinay, Louis (1629–78) I, 237–38
Couillard de Lespinay, Louis (d. 1728) II, 155–56
Coulon de Villiers, François (1712–94) IV, 177–78
Coulon de Villiers, Louis (1710–57) III, 148–49
Coulon de Villiers, Nicolas-Antoine (1683–1733) II, 156
Coulon de Villiers, Nicolas-Antoine (1708–50) III, 149–50
Coulon de Villiers de Jumonville, Joseph (1718–54) III, 150–51
Courreaud de La Coste, Pierre (d. 1779) IV, 178–79
Courseron, Gilbert (fl. 1621) I, 238
Couture, Guillaume (d. 1701) II, 157–59
Couturier, dit Les Bourguignon, Pierre (d. 1715) II, 159–60
Couvert, Michel-Germain de (1653–1715) II, 160–61
Cox, Nicholas (d. 1794) IV, 179–80
Cramahé, Hector Theophilus (1720–88) IV, 787–93
Crespel, Emmanuel (1703–75) IV, 180–82
Crespieul, François de (1639–1702) II, 161–62
Crevier de Saint-François, Jean (1642–93) I, 238–39
Crisafy, Antoine de, Marquis de Crisafy (d. 1709) II, 162–63
Crisafy, Thomas (d. 1696) I, 239
Crochet, Le. See Kiotseaeton
Croft, Thomas (1442–88) I, 239–40
Crout, Henry (fl. 1612–17) I, 240–41
Crowe, Josias (d. 1714) II, 163–64
Crowne, William (1617–82) I, 241–42
Cruse, Thomas (fl. 1634–77) I, 242–43

Crusoe, Robinson (d. 1755) III, 151
Cugnet, François-Étienne (1688–1751) III, 151–55
Cugnet, François-Joseph (1720–89) IV, 182–87
Cuillerier, Marie-Anne-Véronique (1680–1751) III, 155–56
Cuillerier, René (d. *c.* 1712) II, 164–65
Cumings, Archibald (fl. 1698–1726) II, 165
Cunningham, John (1575–1651) I, 243
Cuny Dauterive, Philippe-Antoine de (1709–79) IV, 187
Curatteau, Jean-Baptiste (1729–90) IV, 187–89
Curot, Maire-Louise, *dite* de Saint-Martin (1716–88) IV, 189–90
Cusson, Jean (d. 1718) II, 165–66
Cuthbert, James (d. 1798) IV, 190–91

DABLON, Claude (d. 1697) I, 244
Daccarrette, Michel (d. 1745) III, 156–57
Daccarrette, Michel (1730–67) III, 157–58
Dagneau Douville, Alexandre (1698–1774) IV, 191–92
Dagneau Douville de Quindre, Louis-Césaire (d. 1767) III, 158–59
Daine, François (d. 1765) III, 159–61
Dalmas, Antoine (1636–93) I, 244–45
Damours de Chauffours, Louis (d. 1708) II, 166–67
Damours de Chauffours, Mathieu (1618–95) I, 245
Damours de Clignancour, René (fl. 1660–1710) II, 167–68
Damours de Freneuse, Mathieu (d. 1696) I, 245–46
Dandonneau, *dit* Lajeunesse, Pierre (d. 1702) II, 168
Daneau de Muy, Charlotte, *dite* de Sainte-Hélène (1694–1759) III, 161
Daneau de Muy, Jacques-Pierre (d. 1758) III, 161–63
Daneau de Muy, Nicolas (1651–1708) III, 168–69
Dangé, François (fl. 1662–63) I, 246
Daniel, Antoine (1601–48) I, 246–47
Daniel, Charles (d. 1661) I, 247–48
Daniélou, Jean-Pierre (1696–1744) III, 163
Danks, Benoni (d. 1776) IV, 192–94
Danré de Blanzy, Louis-Claude (fl. 1710–70) III, 163–64
Darby, Nicholas (d. 1785) IV, 194–95
Dargent, Joseph (1712 –47) III, 164–65
Dasilva, *dit* Portugais, Nicolas (1698–1761) III, 165
Daudin, Henri (d. 1756) III, 165–66
Daumont de Saint-Lusson, Simon-François (fl. 1663–77) I, 248–50
Dauphin de La Forest, François (d. 1714) II, 169–70
Dauphin de Montorgueuil (d. 1694) I, 250
Davers, Sir Robert (d. 1763) III, 166–67
David, Claude (1621–87) I, 250–51
David, Jacques (d. 1726) II, 170–71
Davidson, William (d. 1790) IV, 195–97
Davion, Albert (d. 1726) II, 171
Davis, John (d. 1605) I, 251–52

Davis, Joseph (fl. 1692–1715) II, 171–72
Davis, Marie-Anne, *dite* de Saint-Benoît (d. 1749) III, 167–68
Davis, Silvanus (d. 1703) II, 172
Davison, George (d. 1799) IV, 197–99
Davost, Ambroise (1586–1643) I, 252–53
Day, John (d. 1775) IV, 199
Dazemard de Lusignan, Paul-Louis (1691–1764) III, 168–69
Déat, Antoine (1696–1761) III, 169–70
Decoste, Jean-Baptiste (1703–78) IV, 200
Degeay, Jacques (1717–74) IV, 200–1
Deguire, *dit* Desrosiers, Joseph (1704–89) IV, 201–2
Deguise, *dit* Flamand, Girard-Guillaume (d. 1752) III, 170
Deguise, *dit* Flamand, Jacques (1697–1780) IV, 202–4
Dejordy de Villebon, Charles-René (d. 1761) III, 170–71
Dekanahwideh, I, 253–55
Delaborde, Jean (d. 1754) III, 172
Delaunay, Charles (1648–1737) II, 173
DeLaune, William (d. 1761) III, 172–73
Delezenne, Ignace-François (d. 1790) IV, 204–7
Delhalle, Constantin (d. 1706) II, 173–74
Delort, Guillaume (d. before 1749) III, 173–74
Demosny, Jean (Jean-Baptiste) (1643–87) I, 255–56
Denis de Saint-Simon, Antoine-Charles (1734–85) IV, 207–8
Denison, Robert (1697–1765) III, 174–75
Denson, Henry Denny (d. 1780) IV, 208–9
Denys, Jean (fl. 1506) I, 256
Denys, Joseph (1657–1736) II, 174–76
Denys, Nicolas (1598–1688) I, 256–59
Denys de Bonaventure, Simon-Pierre (1659–1711) II, 176–78
Denys de Bonnaventure, Claude-Élisabeth (1701–60) III, 175–76
Denys de Fronsac, Richard (d. 1691) I, 259–61
Denys de La Ronde, Louis (1675–1741) III, 176–80
Denys de La Ronde, Pierre (1631–1708) II, 178–79
Denys de La Trinité, Simon (b. 1599, d. between 1678 and 1680) I, 261–62
Denys de Saint-Simon, Charles-Paul (1688–1748) III, 180
Denys de Saint-Simon, Paul (1649–1731) II, 179
Denys de Vitré, Charles (1645–1703) II, 179–80
Denys de Vitré, Théodose-Matthieu (d. 1775) IV, 209–10
Depéret, Élie (1691–1757) III, 180–81
De Peyster, Abraham (1753–98) IV, 210–11
Dermer, Thomas (d. 1621) I, 262
Derré de Gand, François (d. 1641) I, 262–63
Desandrouins, Jean-Nicolas (1729–92) IV, 211–12
Deschamps de Boishébert, Henri-Louis (1679–1736) II, 180–81

Deschamps de Boishébert et de Raffetot, Charles (1727–97) IV, 212–15

Deschamps de La Bouteillerie, Jean-Baptiste-François (d. 1703) II, 181

Deschevery, *dit* Maisonbasse, Jean-Baptiste (d. 1744 or 1745) III, 181–82

Descouts, Martin (fl. 1682–1745) III, 182

Desdames, Thierry (fl. 1622–46) I, 263–64

Desdevens de Glandons, Maurice (b. 1742, d. after 1799) IV, 215–16

Des Friches de Meneval, Louis-Alexandre (fl. 1687–1703) II, 182–84

Deshayes, Jean (d. 1706) II, 184–85

Des Herbiers de La Ralière, Charles (d. 1752) III, 182–84

Desjordy de Cabanac, Joseph (1657–1713) II, 185–86

Desjordy Moreau de Cabanac, François (1666–1726) II, 186–87

Des Landes, Joseph (1691–1742) III, 184

Deslongrais, Nicolas (fl. 1734–58) III, 184–85

Desportes, Hélène (Hébert; Morin) (d. 1675) I, 264

Dessailliant, *dit* Richeterre, Michel (fl. 1701–23) II, 187–88

Dethunes, Exupère (d. 1692) I, 264–65

Devau, *dit* Retor, Claude (d. 1784) IV, 216

Dièreville (fl. 1699–1711) II, 188–89

Dieskau, Jean-Armand, Baron de Dieskau (1701–67) III, 185–86

Dimock, Shubael (1707–81) IV, 216–17

Dixon, George (fl. 1776–91) IV, 217–19

Dizy, *dit* Montplaisir, Marguerite (Desbrieux) (fl. 1663–1730) II, 189–90

Dizy, *dit* Montplaisir, Michel-Ignace (d. 1723) II, 190

Dizy de Montplaisir, Pierre (d. 1761) III, 187

Doggett, John (1723/24–72) IV, 219–20

Dolbeau, Jean (1586–1652) I, 265–66

Dolebeau, Jean (1608–43) I, 266

Dollard Des Ormeaux, Adam (1635–60) I, 266–75

Dollier de Casson, François (1636–1701) II, 190–97

Donnacona (d. *c.* 1593) I, 275–77

Doreil, André (Jean-Baptiste) (fl. 1749–59) III, 187–89

Dorrill, Richard (d. 1762) III, 189

Dosquet, Pierre-Herman (1691–1777) IV, 220–22

Douay, Anastase (fl. 1684–99) II, 197

Doublet, François (d. before 1678) I, 277

Doucet, Pierre (b. 1750, d. in or after 1799) IV, 222–23

Doucett, John (d. 1726) II, 198–99

Douglas, Sir Charles (d. 1789) IV, 223–24

Douglas, François-Prosper, Chevalier de Douglas (1725–81) IV, 224–25

Downing, John (fl. 1647–82) I, 277–78

Downing, William (d. 1681) I, 277–78

Drachart, Christian Larsen (1711–78) IV, 225

Drake, Sir Bernard (d. 1586) I, 278–80

Drake, Sir Francis (d. 1595/96) I, 280

Drake, Francis William (d. 1788 or 1789) IV, 226

Draper, Thomas (fl. 1670–81) I, 280–81

Drouin, Robert (1607–85) I, 281

Drué, Juconde (b. 1664, d. after 1726) II, 199–200

Druillettes, Gabriel (1610–81) I, 281–82

Druillon de Macé, Pierre-Jacques (d. 1780) IV, 226–27

Dubois Berthelot de Beaucours, Josué (Jean-Maurice-Josué) (d. 1750) III, 189–92

Dubois Davaugour, Pierre (d. 1664) I, 282–85

Dubois de Cocreaumont et de Saint-Maurice, Jean-Baptiste (fl. 1665–66) I, 285–86

Dubok (fl. 1645–46) I, 286

Du Bos, Nicolas (d. 1699) I, 286

Dubreil de Pontbriand, Henri-Marie (1708–60) III, 192–99

Dubreuil, Jean-Étienne (d. 1734) II, 201

Du Calvet, Pierre (1735–86) IV, 227–32

Ducharme, Laurent (fl. 1723–87) IV, 233

Du Chesne, Adrien (fl. 1631–56) I, 287

Duchesneau de La Doussinière et d'Ambault, Jacques (d. 1696) I, 287–90

Dudevant, Arnauld-Germain (b. 1751, d. *c.* 1798) IV, 233–34

Dudley, William (1686–1743) III, 200–1

Dudouyt, Jean (d. 1688) I, 290–91

Dufournel, Louis-Gaspard (1662–1757) III, 201–3

Dufrost de La Jemerais, Christophe (1708–36) II, 201–2

Dufrost de Lajemmerais, Marie-Marguerite (Youville) (1701–71) IV, 234–39

Dugas, Joseph (1714–79) IV, 239–40

Dugay, Jacques (d. 1727) II, 202–3

Du Gua de Monts, Pierre (d. 1628) I, 291–95

Dugué de Boisbriand, Michel-Sidrac (d. 1688) I, 295

Dugué de Boisbriand, Pierre (1675–1736) II, 203–4

Du Jaunay, Pierre (d. 1780) IV, 240–42

Du Laurent, Christophe-Hilarion (d. 1760) III, 203–4

Dumas, Jean-Daniel (1721–94) IV, 242–43

Dumas Saint-Martin, Jean (1725–94) IV, 243–44

Duncan, Charles (fl. 1786–92) IV, 244–45

Duparc, Jean-Baptiste (1676–1742) III, 204–5

Du Peron, François (1610–65) I, 295–96

Du Perron, Thalour (d. 1663) I, 296

Dupleix Silvain, Jean-Baptiste (b. 1721, d. in or after 1796) IV, 245–46

Duplessis (Gastineau Duplessis; Radisson, *dit* Duplessis), Marguerite (fl. 1726–40) III, 205

Duplessis, Pacifique (d. 1619) I, 296

Du Plessis-Bochart, Charles (fl. 1633–36) I, 296–97

Dupont, Siméon (1671–1732) II, 204

Dupont de Neuville, Nicolas (d. 1716) II, 204–5

Du Pont de Renon, Michel (d. 1719) II, 205

Du Pont Duchambon, Louis (d. 1775) IV, 246–49
Du Pont Duchambon de Vergor, Louis (b. 1713, d. after 1775) IV, 249–51
Du Pont Duvivier, François (father) (1676–1714) II, 205–6
Du Pont Duvivier, François (son) (1705–76) IV, 251–55
Du Pont Duvivier, Joseph (d. 1760) IV, 783–84
Duprac, Jean-Robert (d. 1726) II, 206
Dupré, François (d. 1720) II, 206–7
Dupuy, Claude-Thomas (1678–1738) II, 207–13
Dupuy, Zacharie (d. 1676) I, 297–98
Dupuy de Lisloye, Paul (d. 1713) II, 213–14
Duquesne de Menneville, Ange, Marquis Duquesne (d. 1778) IV, 255–58
Duquet de La Chesnaye, Pierre (1643–87) I, 298
Durand, Justinien (d. 1746 or 1748) III, 207–8
Durand de La Garenne (d. 1715) II, 214–15
Durell, Philip (1707–66) III, 208–10
Duret de Chevry de La Boulaye, Charles (fl. 1677–90) I, 298–99
Durocher, Joseph (1706–56) III, 210–11
Dutch Bastard. See Flemish Bastard
Du Thet, Gilbert (d. 1613) I, 299
Dutisné, Claude-Charles (d. 1730) II, 215–16
Duval, Jean (d. 1608) I, 299–300

Eagleson, John (fl. 1765–90) IV, 258–59
Easton, Peter (fl. 1610–20) I, 300–1
Echevete, Matias de (d. 1599) I, 301
Edgcombe, Leonard (d. 1696) I, 301–2
Edwards, Richard (d. 1795) IV, 259–60
Egushwa (fl. 1730–1800) IV, 260–61
Eirikr Thorvaldsson (fl. 982–985) I, 676
Eirikr upsi Gnupsson (d. 1146) I, 675–76
Élie, Jacques (d. 1710) II, 216–17
Eliot, Hugh (fl. 1480–1510) I, 302
Ellice, Robert (1747–90) IV, 261–62
Elliot, Robert (fl. 1740–65) III, 211–12
Énault de Barbaucannes, Philippe (b. 1651, d. after 1708) II, 217
Enjalran, Jean (1639–1718) II, 217–18
Erad, Johann Burghard (d. 1757) III, 212
Erhardt, John Christian (d. 1752) III, 212–13
Ermatinger, Lawrence (d. 1789) IV, 262–63
Erouachy (fl. 1618–29) I, 302–3
Espérance (fl. 1628–29) I, 199–200
Espiet de Pensens, Jacques d' (d. 1737) II, 218–20
Estèbe, Guillaume (b. 1701, d. after 1779) IV, 263–64
Estienne Du Bourgué de Clérin, Denis d' (d. 1719) II, 220–21
Estourmel, Constantin-Louis d' (1691–1765) III, 213–14
Evison, Robert (fl. 1746–49) III, 214
Eyre, William (d. 1765) III, 214–15

Fagundes, João Alvares (fl. 1521) I, 303–4
Falkingham, Edward (d. 1757) III, 215–16
Fautoux, Léon (d. 1748) III, 216
Feltz, Charles-Elemy-Joseph-Alexandre-Ferdinand (d. 1776) IV, 264–66
Fernandes, João (fl. 1486–1505) I, 304–5
Ferrar, Constance (fl. 1629) I, 305
Ferrer Maldonado, Lorenzo (d. 1625) I, 676–77
Fézeret, René (d. 1720) II, 221
Filiastre, Luc (1646–1721) II, 221–23
Fillion, Michel (d. 1689) I, 305–6
Fillis, John (d. 1792) IV, 266–67
Fisher, Richard (fl. 1593) I, 306–7
Fléché, Jessé (d. 1611?) I, 307
Flemish Bastard (fl. 1650–87) I, 307–8
Fletcher, John (d. 1697) I, 308–9
Fletcher, Robert (fl. 1766–85) IV, 267–68
Fleury de La Gorgendière, Joseph de (1676–1755) III, 216–18
Fleury Deschambault, Jacques de (1672–98) I, 309
Fleury Deschambault, Jacques-Alexis de (d. 1715) II, 223–24
Fleury Deschambault, Joseph (1709–84) IV, 268–70
Floquet, Pierre-René (1716–82) IV, 270–71
Foi (fl. 1628) I, 199–200
Fonte, Bartholomew de (fl. 1640) I, 677
Fonteneau, Jean, known as Jean Alphonse (1484–1544) I, 309–10
Forant, Isaac-Louis de (d. 1740) II, 224–26
Forbes, John (1707–59) III, 218–19
Fordyce, John (d. 1751) III, 219–20
Forestier, Antoine (1646–1717) II, 226
Forestier, Antoine-Bertrand (1687–1742) III, 220–21
Forestier, Marie, dite de Saint-Bonaventure-de-Jésus (d. 1698) I, 310
Forget, Antoine (1672–1749) III, 221
Forget Duverger, Jacques-François (fl. 1753–64) III, 221–22
Fork. See Nissowaquet
Fornel, Joachim (b. 1697, d. after 1753) III, 222–24
Fornel, Louis (d. 1745) III, 224–25
Forrester, Andrew (fl. 1629–33) I, 310–11
Fortier, Michel (1709–76) IV, 271–72
Fotherby, Charles (d. 1720) II, 226–27
Foucault, François (1690–1766) III, 225–27
Foucault, Nicolas (d. 1702) II, 227
Foucault, Simon (1699–1744) III, 227
Foucher (fl. 1626–29) I, 311
Foucher, François (1699–1770) III, 227–28
Foureur, dit Champagne, Louis (1720–89) IV, 272
Fox, Luke (1586–1635) I, 311–12
Francheville, Pierre (d. 1713) II, 227–28
Francklin, Michael (1733–82) IV, 272–76
François, Claude, known as Brother Luc (1614–85) I, 312–15

Franquelin, Jean-Baptiste-Louis (fl. 1671–1712) II, 228–31

Franquet, Louis (d. 1768) III, 228–32

Fraser, Alexander (d. 1799) IV, 276

Frémin, Jacques (1628–91) I, 315

French, John (d. 1687) I, 315

Frobisher, Benjamin (d. 1787) IV, 276–78

Frobisher, Sir Martin (d. 1594) I, 316–19

Fuca, Juan de (1536–1602) I, 677

Fullartine, John (d. 1738) II, 231–33

GADOIS, Pierre (1632–1714) II, 233–34

Gadois, *dit* Mauger, Jacques (d. 1750) III, 232–33

Gadoys, Pierre (d. 1667) I, 319

Gage, Thomas (d. 1787) IV, 278–82

Gagnon, Mathurin (1606–90) I, 319–20

Gaillard, Guillaume (d. 1729) II, 234–35

Gaillard, Mathieu (fl. 1683–94) I, 320

Galaup, Jean-François de, Comte de Lapérouse (1741–88) IV, 282–83

Galiffet de Caffin, François de (1666–1746) III, 233

Gallard, Charlotte (1648–1725) II, 235–36

Galleran, Guillaume (d. 1636) I, 320

Gamelain de La Fontaine, Michel (b. 1640, d. *c.* 1676) I, 320–21

Gamelin, Ignace (father) (1663–1739) II, 236

Gamelin, Ignace (son) (1698–1771) IV, 283–85

Gamelin, Pierre-Joseph (1736–96) IV, 285–87

Gamelin Maugras, Pierre (1697–1757) III, 233–34

Gandeacteua (d. 1673) I, 321–22

Ganet, François (d. 1747) III, 234–35

Gannenstenhawi. *See* Williams, Eunice

Gannes de Falaise, Louis de (1658–1714) II, 236

Gannes de Falaise, Michel de (d. 1752) III, 235–36

Garakontié (d. 1677 or 1678) I, 322–23

Gargot de La Rochette, Nicolas (1619–64) I, 323–24

Garland, Thomas (fl. 1678–87) I, 324

Garnier, Charles (d. 1649) I, 324–25

Garnier, Julien (1643–1730) II, 237–38

Garreau, Léonard (d. 1656) I, 325

Garreau, *dit* Saint-Onge, Pierre (1722–95) IV, 287–88

Gaschet, René (d. 1744) III, 236–37

Gastineau Duplessis, Jean-Baptiste (1671–1750) III, 237–38

Gaudais-Dupont, Louis (fl. 1663) I, 325–26

Gaudé, Françoise (1671–1751) III, 238–39

Gaudron de Chevremont, Charles-René (b. 1702, d. before 1745) III, 239–40

Gaufin, Valérien (1699–1759) III, 240–41

Gaulin, Antoine (1674–1740) II, 238

Gaultier, Jean-François (1708–56) III, 675–81

Gaultier de Comporté, Philippe (1641–87) I, 326

Gaultier de La Vérendrye, Jean-Baptiste (1713–36) II, 238–40

Gaultier de La Vérendrye, Louis-Joseph (1717–61) III, 241–44

Gaultier de La Vérendrye et de Boumois, Pierre (1714–55) III, 244–45

Gaultier de Varennes, Jacques-René (d. 1757) III, 245–46

Gaultier de Varennes, Jean-Baptiste (1677–1726) II, 240–41

Gaultier de Varennes, René (d. 1689) I, 326–28

Gaultier de Varennes et de La Vérendrye, Pierre (1685–1749) III, 246–54

Gaultier Du Tremblay, François (1715–94) IV, 288–89

Gautier, *dit* Bellair, Joseph-Nicolas (1689–1752) III, 254–55

Gawèhe (d. 1766) III, 255–56

Gay, Robert-Michel (1663–1725) II, 241

Gay Desenclaves, Jean-Baptiste de (b. 1702, d. after 1764) III, 256–57

Genaple de Bellefonds, François (d. 1709) II, 241–43

Gendron, François (1618–88) I, 328

Geneviève-Agnès de Tous-Les-Saints. *See* Skanudharoua

Geoffroy, Louis (d. 1707) II, 243–44

Georgemé, Séraphin (d. 1705) II, 244–45

Germain, Charles (1707–79) IV, 289–90

Germain, Joseph-Louis (1633–1722) II, 245–46

Gerrish, Benjamin (1717–72) IV, 290–91

Gerrish, Joseph (1709–74) IV, 291–92

Gervaise, Louis (1708–63) III, 257–58

Geyer, George (fl. 1672–97) I, 328–29

Giard, Antoine (b. 1682, d. 1746 or 1747) III, 258

Gibbons, Richard (d. 1794) IV, 292–93

Gibbons, William (fl. 1612–14) I, 329

Gibsone, Sir John (1637–1717) II, 246

Giffard, Marie-Françoise, *dite* Marie de Saint-Ignace (1634–57) I, 329–30

Giffard de Moncel, Robert (1587–1668) I, 330–31

Gilbert, Sir Humphrey (d. 1583) I, 331–36

Gill, Joseph-Louis, known as Magouaouidombaouit (1719–98) IV, 293–94

Gill, Michael (d. 1720) II, 246–47

Gillam, Benjamin (1662/63–1706) II, 247

Gillam, Zachariah (1636–82) I, 336–38

Gilmore, Thomas (d. 1773) IV, 294–95

Girard, Jacques (d. 1782) IV, 295–97

Gladwin, Henry (d. 1791) IV, 297

Glandelet, Charles de (1645–1725) II, 247–49

Glapion, Augustin-Louis de (1719–90) IV, 297–99

Glasier, Beamsley Perkins (d. 1784) IV, 299–301

Gledhill, Samuel (b. 1677, d. 1735 or 1736) II, 249–51

Glikhikan (d. 1782) IV, 301–2

Gloria, Jean (d. 1665) I, 338

Gobin, Jean (1646–1703) II, 251–52

Godefroy, Jean-Paul (d. *c.* 1668) I, 339–40

Godefroy de Linctot, Daniel-Maurice (d. before 1783) IV, 302–3

Godefroy de Lintot, Jean (d. 1681) I, 340–41
Godefroy de Lintot, Michel (d. 1709) II, 252
Godefroy de Normanville, Thomas (d. 1652) I, 341
Godefroy de Saint-Paul, Jean-Amador (d. 1730) II, 252
Godefroy de Tonnancour, Charles-Antoine (1698–1757) III, 258–59
Godefroy de Tonnancour, Charles-Antoine (1755–98) IV, 303–4
Godefroy de Tonnancour, Louis-Joseph (d. 1784) IV, 304–5
Godefroy de Tonnancour, René (d. 1738) II, 252–53
Godefroy de Vieuxpont, Jacques (d. 1661) I, 341
Godefroy de Vieuxpont, Joseph (b. 1645, d. c. 1716) II, 253–54
Godet, Rolland (fl. 1651–53) I, 341–42
Godet Des Maretz, Claude de (d. c. 1627) I, 342
Godin, dit Bellefontaine, dit Beauséjour, Joseph (b. 1697, d. after 1774) IV, 305–6
Goffe, Edmund (d. 1740) II, 254
Goguet, Denis (1704–78) IV, 306–7
Gohin, Pierre-André, Comte de Montreuil (b. 1722, d. after 1793) IV, 307–8
Goldthwait, Benjamin (1704–61) III, 259–60
Gomes, Estevão (d. 1538) I, 342–43
Gonʔaongote. See Williams, Eunice
Gonsales, João (fl. 1501–3) I, 343
Goreham, Joseph (1725–90) IV, 308–10
Gorham, John (1709–51) III, 260–61
Gorrell, James (d. c. 1769) III, 261–62
Gorst, Thomas (fl. 1668–87) I, 343
Gosselin, Jean-Baptiste (d. 1749) III, 262–64
Gotteville de Belile, Robert-David (fl. 1696–1724) II, 254–55
Gouentagrandi (fl. 1689–1738) II, 255–56
Goupil, René (1608–42) I, 343–44
Gourdeau de Beaulieu et de La Grossardière, Jacques (d. 1720) II, 256–57
Goutin, François-Marie de (d. 1752) III, 264–65
Goutin, Mathieu de (d. 1714) II, 257–58
Goyer, Olivier (1663–1721) II, 258–59
Grande Gueule, La. See Otreouti
Grande Terre, La. See Ohonsiowanne
Grandmaison, Éléonore de (Boudier de Beauregard; Chavigny de Berchereau; Gourdeau de Beaulieu; Cailhault de La Tesserie) (d. 1692) I, 344–45
Grand Sauteux, Le. See Minweweh
Grant, Cuthbert (d. 1799) IV, 310
Grant, James (fl. 1777–99) IV, 311
Grape. See Chomina
Grasset de Saint-Sauveur, André (1724–94) IV, 311–12
Gravé Du Pont, François (fl. 1599–1629) I, 345–46
Gravé Du Pont, Robert (d. 1621) I, 346–47
Gravier, Jacques (1651–1708) II, 259–60
Graydon, John (d. 1726) II, 260–61

Gray Lock (fl. 1675–1740) III, 265–67
Great Mohawk. See Togouiroui
Great World. See Ohonsiowanne
Green, Bartholomew (1699–1751) III, 267
Green, Benjamin (1713–72) IV, 312–13
Grenouille, La. See Oumasasikweie
Greysolon de La Tourette, Claude (fl. 1683–1716) II, 261
Greysolon Dulhut, Daniel (d. 1710) II, 261–64
Gridley, Richard (1710/11–96) IV, 313–14
Grillot de Poilly, François-Claude-Victor (1726–61) III, 267–68
Grimington, Michael (father) (d. 1710) II, 264–67
Grimington, Michael (son) (fl. 1698–1719) II, 267
Grisé, Antoine (1728–85) IV, 315
Groston de Saint-Ange, Robert (fl. 1692–1738) II, 267–68
Groston de Saint-Ange et de Bellerive, Louis (d. 1774) IV, 315–16
Guen, Hamon (1687–1761) III, 268–69
Guenet, Marie, dite de Saint-Ignace (1610–46) I, 347–49
Guesdron, Julien (1667–1735) II, 268
Gugy, Conrad (d. 1786) IV, 316–17
Guichart (Guichart de Kersident), Vincent-Fleuri (1729–93) IV, 317–18
Guignas, Michel (1681–1752) III, 269
Guillemot, dit Du Plessis-Kerbodot, Guillaume (d. 1652) I, 349
Guillet de Chaumont, Nicolas-Auguste (d. 1765) III, 269–70
Guillimin, Charles (1676–1739) II, 268–69
Guillimin, Guillaume (1713–71) IV, 318–19
Guillimin, Marie-Françoise, dite de Saint-Antoine (1720–89) IV, 319–20
Guillot, dit Larose, François (b. 1727, d. before 1785) IV, 320–21
Guillouet d'Orvilliers, Claude (1668–1728) II, 269–70
Guillouet d'Orvilliers, Rémy (d. 1713) II, 270–71
Guion, François (b. 1666, d. c. 1701) II, 271
Guiton de Monrepos, Jacques-Joseph (fl. 1740–64) III, 270–71
Guy, John (d. c. 1629) I, 349–51
Guy, Nicholas (fl. 1612–31) I, 351
Guy, Pierre (1701–48) III, 271–72
Guyart, Marie, dite de l'Incarnation (Martin) (1599–1672) I, 351–59
Guyart de Fleury, Jean-Baptiste (fl. 1740–61) III, 272
Guyon, Jean (1659–87) I, 359
Guyon, Louise (Thibault; Damours de Freneuse) (fl. 1668–1711) III, 681–82
Guyon Du Buisson, Jean (father) (d. 1663) I, 359
Guyon Du Buisson, Jean (son) (1619–94) I, 359–60
Guyotte, Étienne (d. 1701) II, 271–72
Gyles, John (d. 1755) III, 272–73

HACHÉ-GALLANT, Michel (d. 1737) II, 272
Haimard, Pierre (1674–1724) II, 272–73
Haldimand, Sir Frederick (1718–91) IV, 793–94
Haldimand, Peter Frederick (d. 1765) III, 273–74
Hale, Robert (1702/3–67) III, 274–75
Halhead, Edward (fl. 1749–52) III, 275–76
Hall, James (d. 1612) I, 360
Hamare de La Borde, Jean-Baptiste-Julien (b. 1693, d. after 1729) II, 273–74
Hamelin de Bourgchemin et de L'Hermitière, Jacques-François (b. 1664, d. before 1698) I, 360–61
Hamilton, Andrew (fl. 1688–89) I, 361
Hamilton, Henry (d. 1796) IV, 321–25
Hamilton, Otho (d. 1770) III, 276–77
Handasyde, Thomas (d. 1712) II, 274
Handfield, John (fl. 1719/20–60) III, 277–78
Hanna, James (d. 1787) IV, 325–26
Hantraye, Claude (d. 1777) IV, 326
Hardy, Sir Charles (d. 1780) IV, 326–27
Hardy, Elias (d. 1798) IV, 327–29
Harrison, Edward (d. 1794) IV, 329–31
Harrison, John (fl. 1710–21) II, 274–75
Hart, Aaron (d. 1800) IV, 331–33
Havard de Beaufort, François-Charles, known as L'Avocat (fl. 1737–42) III, 278–79
Haven, Jens (1724–96) IV, 333–34
Haviland, William (1718–84) IV, 334–36
Havy, François (1709–66) III, 280–83
Hawkeridge, William (fl. 1610–31) I, 362
Hay, Lord Charles (d. 1760) III, 283–84
Hay, Charles (fl. 1770–83) IV, 336
Hay, Jehu (d. 1785) IV, 336–37
Hayes, Edward (d. c. 1613) I, 362–65
Hayman, Robert (d. 1629) I, 365–66
Hazeur, François (d. 1708) II, 275–77
Hazeur, Jean-François (d. 1733) II, 277
Hazeur, Joseph-Thierry (1680–1757) III, 284–85
Hazeur de L'Orme, Pierre (1682–1771) IV, 337–39
Hearne, Samuel (1745–92) IV, 339–42
Heavy. See Le Pesant
Hébert, Guillemette (Couillard de Lespinay) (d. 1684) I, 366–67
Hébert, Joseph (b. 1636, b. 1661 or 1662) I, 367
Hébert, Louis (d. 1627) I, 367–68
Henday, Anthony (fl. 1750–62) III, 285–87
Hendrick. See Theyanoguin
Hennepin, Louis (baptized Antoine) (b. 1626, d. c. 1705) II, 277–82
Henry, Anthony (1734–1800) IV, 342–43
Heron, Patrick (fl. 1709–52) III, 287–88
Hertel de La Fresnière, Jacques (d. 1651) I, 368–69
Hertel de La Fresnière, Joseph-François (d. 1722) II, 282–84
Hertel de La Fresnière, Zacharie-François (d. 1752) III, 288–89
Hertel de Moncours, Pierre (1687–1739) II, 284

Hertel de Rouville, Jean-Baptiste (1668–1722) II, 284–86
Hertel de Rouville, René-Ovide (1720–92) IV, 343–47
Hertel de Saint-François, Étienne (1734–60) III, 289–90
Hertel de Saint-François, Joseph-Hippolyte (1738–81) IV, 347–48
Hervieux, Louis-François (1711–48) III, 290
Hey, William (d. 1797) IV, 348–50
Hiché, Henry (d. 1758) III, 290–92
Hicks, John (1715–90) IV, 350–51
Higgins, David (d. 1783) IV, 352–53
Hill, John (d. 1735) II, 286–87
Hill, Samuel (b. 1668, d. c. 1732) II, 287
Hill, William (fl. 1634–38) I, 369
Hillaire de La Rochette, Alexandre-Robert (d') (fl. 1755–72) IV, 353–54
Hilton, Winthrop (d. 1710) II, 287–88
Hinton, William (d. c. 1688) I, 369–70
Hiriberry, Joannis de (fl. 1718–22) II, 288
Hobby, Sir Charles (d. 1715) II, 288–90
Hocquart, Gilles (1694–1783) IV, 354–65
Hodiesne, Gervais (1692–1764) III, 292
Holdsworth, Arthur (1668–1726) II, 290–91
Holmes, Charles (d. 1761) III, 293–94
Holmes, William (d. 1792) IV, 365–66
Honatteniate (d. 1650) I, 370–71
Hope, Henry (d. 1789) IV, 366–68
Hopkins, Samuel (fl. 1715–31) II, 291–92
Hopson, Peregrine Thomas (d. 1759) III, 294–95
Hore, Richard (fl. 1536–40) I, 371–72
Horné, dit Laneuville, Jacques de (1664–1730) II, 292
Hot Ash (Hot Powder). See Ogenheratarihiens
Hotsinoñhyahta? (fl. 1748–74) IV, 368
Houdin, Jean-Michel, known as Father Potentien (b. 1706, d. c. 1766) III, 295–97
How, Edward (d. 1750) III, 297–98
Howard, Joseph (d. 1797) IV, 369–70
Huault de Montmagny, Charles (d. c. 1653) I, 372–74
Hubert, Jean-François (1739–97) IV, 370–75
Hudson, Henry (d. c. 1611) I, 374–79
Hudson, John (d. c. 1611) I, 379
Huet, Paul (d. 1665) I, 379
Huguet, Joseph (1725–83) IV, 375–76
Huppé, dit Lagroix, Joseph (b. 1696, d. in or after 1776) IV, 376–77
Hutchins, Thomas (d. 1790) IV, 377–78

IGNACE de Paris (d. 1662) I, 379–80
Imbault, Maurice (b. 1686, d. after 1759) III, 298–99
Imbert, Bertrand (1714–75) IV, 378–79
Imbert, Jacques (d. 1765) III, 299–300
Ingram, David (fl. 1568–83) I, 380–81

Iroquet (fl. 1609–15) I, 381–82

Irving, Paulus Æmilius (1714–96) IV, 379–80

Irwin, Marie, *dite* de la Conception (1626–87) I, 382

Isabeau, Michel-Philippe (d. *c.* 1724) II, 292

Isbister, Joseph (d. 1771) IV, 380–81

Isbister, William (fl. 1739–51) III, 300–1

Isham, James (d. 1761) III, 301–4

JACAU de Fiedmont, Louis-Thomas (d. 1788) IV, 382–83

Jackson, John (d. 1717) II, 293–94

Jacob, Étienne (fl. 1665–1726) II, 294

Jacobs, Ferdinand (d. 1783) IV, 383–84

Jacobs, Samuel (d. 1786) IV, 384–86

Jacquelin, Françoise-Marie (Sainte-Étienne de La Tour) (1602–45) I, 383–84

Jacquet, François (fl. 1731–77) IV, 386–87

Jacquiés, *dit* Leblond, Jean (b. 1688, d. after 1724) II, 294–95

Jacquin, *dit* Philibert, Nicolas (1700–48) III, 304–5

Jacrau, Joseph-André-Mathurin (d. 1772) IV, 387–88

Jadis, Charles Newland Godfrey (b. 1730, d. in or after 1788) IV, 388–89

Jago, John (b. 1684, d. after 1724) II, 295

Jalobert, Macé (fl. 1528–55) I, 384

James, Thomas (d. *c.* 1635) I, 384–85

Jamet, Denis (d. 1625) I, 385–86

Jamet, John (d. 1763) III, 305–6

Janson, *dit* Lapalme, Dominique (1701–62) III, 306–8

Jarret de Verchères, Marie-Madeleine (Tarieu de La Pérade) (1678–1747) III, 308–13

Jarret de Verchères, Pierre (d. 1708) II, 295–96

Jarvis, Edward (d. *c.* 1800) IV, 389–90

Jautard, Valentin (d. 1787) IV, 390–92

Jay, John (d. 1528) I, 386–87

Jeanneau, Étienne (d. 1743) III, 313–14

Jeanson, Guillaume (b. 1721, d. after 1777) IV, 392

Jeantot, Jean (d. 1748) III, 314

Jérémie, *dit* Lamontagne, Catherine (Aubuchon; Lepallieur de Laferté) (d. 1744) III, 314–15

Jérémie, *dit* Lamontagne, Nicolas (d. 1732) II, 296–300

Jérémie, *dit* Lamontagne, Noël (d. between 1694 and 1697) I, 387

Jérôme. *See* Atecouando

Joannès de Chacornacle (1672–1707) II, 300

Joe (fl. 1771–89) IV, 392–93

Jogues, Isaac (1607–46) I, 387–90

Johnson, George (1564–1605) I, 390–92

Johnson, Guy (d. 1788) IV, 393–94

Johnson, William. *See* Tekawironte

Johnson, Sir William (d. 1774) IV, 394–98

Johnston, Alexander (d. 1778) IV, 398–99

Johnston, James (d. 1800) IV, 399–400

Johnstone, James, known as Chevalier de Johnstone (b. 1719, d. after 1791) IV, 400–1

Jolliet, Louis (d. 1700) I, 392–98

Jolliet de Mingan, Jean-Baptiste (d. between 1732 and 1735) II, 300–1

Jones, Henry (fl. 1725–50) III, 315–16

Jones, John (1737–1800) IV, 401–2

Jordan, Jacob (1741–96) IV, 402–4

Jourdain, *dit* Labrosse, Paul-Raymond (d. 1769) III, 316–17

Joybert de Soulanges et de Marson, Louise-Élisabeth de (Rigaud de Vaudreuil, Marquise de Vaudreuil) (1673–1740) II, 301–2

Joybert de Soulanges et de Marson, Pierre de (d. 1678) I, 398–400

Juchereau de La Ferté, Denis-Joseph (d. 1709) II, 302–3

Juchereau de La Ferté, Jean (d. 1685) I, 400

Juchereau de La Ferté, Jeanne-Françoise, *dite* de Saint-Ignace (1650–1723) II, 303–4

Juchereau de Maur, Jean (d. 1672) I, 401

Juchereau de Maur, Paul-Augustin (1658–1714) II, 304–5

Juchereau de Saint-Denis, Charlotte-Françoise, known as Comtesse de Saint-Laurent (Viennay-Pachot; Dauphin de La Forest) (d. 1732) II, 305

Juchereau de Saint-Denis, Louis (1676–1744) III, 317–18

Juchereau de Saint-Denis, Nicolas (d. 1692) I, 401–2

Juchereau de Saint-Denys, Charles (1655–1703) II, 305–7

Juchereau Des Chatelets, Noël (d. 1648) I, 402–3

Juchereau Duchesnay, Ignace (1658–1715) II, 307

Juchereau Duchesnay, Marie-Joseph, *dite* de l'Enfant-Jésus (1699–1760) III, 318–19

KAGHSWAGHTANIUNT (d. *c.* 1762) III, 319–20

Kaieñ?kwaahtoñ (d. 1786) IV, 404–6

Kakȣenthiony (d. 1756) III, 320–21

Kalm, Pehr (1716–79) IV, 406–8

Kanon, Jacques (fl. 1756–61) III, 321–22

Karaghtadie (d. 1759) III, 322–23

Kayahsota? (Kayashoton) (fl. 1725–94) IV, 408–10

Keen, William (d. 1754) III, 323–24

Kellogg, Joseph (1691–1756) III, 324–26

Kelsey, Henry (d. 1724) II, 307–15

Kempthorne, Thomas (d. 1736) II, 315–16

Kendrick, John (d. 1794) IV, 410–12

Kerrivan, Peter IV, 784–85

Kiala (fl. 1733–34) II, 316–17

Kilby, Thomas (1699–1746) III, 326–27

Kilpatrick, Robert (d. 1741) III, 327

King, James (1750–84) IV, 412–13

King Hendrick. *See* Theyanoguin

Kingminguse (fl. 1776–92) IV, 413

King of Kanadesaga. *See* Kaieñ?kwaahtoñ

Kinongé (fl. 1660–1713) II, 317–18

Kinousaki (d. 1752) III, 328
Kiotseaeton (fl. 1645–46) I, 403–4
Kirke, Sir David (d. 1654) I, 404–7
Kirke, Sir Lewis (d. before 1683) I, 407
Kirke, Thomas (fl. 1628–42) I, 407–8
Kisensik (fl. 1756–58) III, 328
Knaut, Philip Augustus (1716–81) IV, 414
Kneller, Henry (d. 1776) IV, 414–15
Knight, James (d. c. 1720) II, 318–20
Knight, John (d. 1606) I, 408
Knox, John (d. 1778) IV, 415–16
Kondiaronk (d. 1701) II, 320–23
Koñwatsiˀtsiaiéñni (d. 1796) IV, 416–19
Koutaoiliboe (fl. 1700–12) II, 323–24
Koyah (d. 1795) IV, 419–20

LABORDE, Jean (1710–81) IV, 420–23
La Bretonnière, Jacques-Quintin de (1689–1754)
    III, 329
La Brosse, Jean-Baptiste de (1724–82) IV, 423–25
La Cetière, Florent de (d. 1728) II, 325
La Chasse, Pierre de (d. 1749) III, 329–31
La Colle (fl. 1736–42) III, 331
La Colombière, Joseph de (1651–1723) II, 325–27
La Corne, Louis (Jean-Louis, Louis-François, Louis-
    Luc, Pierre) de, known as the Chevalier de La
    Corne (1703–61) III, 31–32
La Corne, Luc de, known as Chaptes de La Corne
    or La Corne Saint-Luc (d. 1784) IV, 425–29
La Corne de Chaptes, Jean-Louis de (1666–1732) II,
    327–28
La Corne de Chaptes, Joseph-Marie (Jean-Marie) de
    (d. 1779) IV, 429–31
La Corne de Chaptes, Marie-Madeleine de, dite du
    Saint-Sacrement (1700–62) III, 332–33
La Corne Dubreuil, François-Josué de (1710–53) III,
    333
La Court de Pré-Ravillon et de Granpré (fl. 1591)
    I, 408–9
La Croix, Hubert-Joseph de (1703–60) III, 334
La Croix de Chevrières de Saint-Vallier, Jean-
    Baptiste de (1653–1727) II, 328–34
Ladan, Adrien (1647–1722) II, 334–35
La Faye, Louis-François de (1657–1729) II, 335–36
La Ferrière. See Erouachy
Lafitau, Joseph-François (d. 1746) III, 334–38
Lafontaine de Belcour, Jacques de (1704–65) III,
    338–41
La Forest, Marc-Antoine de (d. 1738) II, 336
La Forière. See Erouachy
La Fourche. See Nissowaquet
La France, Joseph (fl. 1723–42) III, 341–42
La Frenaye, François de (baptized Pierre-Antoine)
    (1677–1705) II, 336–37
La Frenaye de Brucy, Antoine de (d. 1684) I, 409–10
Lagarde, Pierre-Paul-François de (1729–84) IV,
    431–32

La Goudalie, Charles de (d. c. 1753) III, 342–43
La Grande Gueule. See Otreouti
La Grande Terre. See Ohonsiowanne
Lagrené, Pierre de (1659–1736) II, 337
La Grenouille. See Oumasasikweie
Lajoüe, François de (d. c. 1719) II, 337–39
Lajus, François (1721–99) IV, 432
Lajus, Jordain (1673–1742) III, 344–45
La Lande, Jean de (d. 1646) I, 410–11
Lalemant, Charles (1587–1674) I, 411–12
Lalemant, Gabriel (1610–49) I, 412–13
Lalemant, Jérôme (1593–1673) I, 413–15
La Maisonfort Du Boisdecourt, Alexandre de,
    Marquis de La Maisonfort (fl. 1699–1752) III,
    345–46
Lamaletie, Jean-André (fl. 1718–74) IV, 433–34
La Marche, Dominique de (d. 1738) II, 339
Lamarre, dit Bélisle, Henri (d. 1740) II, 339–40
Lambert, Eustache (d. 1673) I, 415
Lambert, dit Saint-Paul, Paul (1691–1749) III,
    346–47
Lamberville, Jacques de (1641–1710) II, 340–42
Lamberville, Jean de (1633–1714) II, 342–44
Lamorinie, Jean-Baptiste de (fl. 1705–64) III, 347
La Motte de Lucière, Dominique (1636–1700) I,
    415–16
Lamotte de Saint-Paul, Pierre (fl. 1665–70) I, 416
La Nasse. See Manitougatche
Landon, Simple (1641–1712) II, 344–45
Landriaux, Louis-Nicolas (d. 1788) IV, 434–35
Landriève des Bordes, Jean-Marie (1712–78) IV,
    435–36
Landron, Jean-François (b. 1686, d. between 1756
    and 1760) III, 347–48
Landry, Alexis (d. 1798) IV, 436–37
Lane, Daniel (d. 1686 or 1687) I, 416–17
Langlois, Marie-Thérèse, dite de Saint-Jean-Baptiste
    (1684–1743) III, 348–49
Langlois, Noël (d. 1684) I, 417
Langman, Edward (1716–84) IV, 437–38
Langoissieux, Charles (d. 1645) I, 417
Lannelongue, Jean-Baptiste (1712–68) III, 349–50
Lanouguère, Thomas de (1644–78) I, 417–18
Lanoullier de Boisclerc, Jean-Eustache (d. 1750) III,
    350–52
Lanoullier de Boisclerc, Nicolas (d. 1756) III,
    352–54
La Place, Louis-Hyacinthe de (1673–1737) II, 345
La Place, Simon-Gérard de (d. 1699) I, 338–39
La Poippe (d. 1684) I, 418–19
Laporte de Lalanne, Jean (Armand) de (fl. 1720–58)
    III, 354–55
La Porte de Louvigny, Louis de (d. 1725) II, 345–47
La Ralde, Raymond de (fl. 1621–32) I, 419
Larcher, Nicolas (1722–88) IV, 438–39
Largillier, Jacques, known as Le Castor (d. 1714) II,
    347

La Ribourde, Gabriel de (d. 1680) I, 420
La Richardie, Armand de (1686–1758) III, 355–56
Larkin, George (d. 1703 or 1704) II, 348
La Roche Daillon, Joseph de (d. 1656) I, 420–21
La Roche de Mesgouez, Troilus de, Marquis de La Roche-Mesgouez (d. 1606) I, 421–22
La Rochefoucauld de Roye, Jean-Baptiste-Louis-Frédéric de, Marquis de Roucy, Duc d'Anville (1709–46) III, 356
La Roque, Marguerite de (fl. 1536) I, 425–26
La Rocque de Roberval, Jean-François de (d. 1560) I, 422–25
Lartigue, Joseph (d. 1743) III, 356–57
Larue, Guillaume de (d. 1717) II, 348
La Salle, Nicolas de (d. 1710) II, 348–49
Lascaris d'Urfé, François-Saturnin (1641–1701) II, 349–50
La Tête Blanche. See Gray Lock
Latham, Robert (d. 1713) II, 350–51
Latouche MacCarthy, Charles (1706–65) III, 357–58
Latour, Bertrand de (1701–80) IV, 439–41
La Tourasse, Charles, known as Chevalier (d. 1696) I, 426–27
Laumet, dit de Lamothe Cadillac, Antoine (1658–1730) II, 351–57
Laure, Pierre-Michel (1688–1738) II, 357–58
Laurent, Paul (fl. 1753–63) III, 358–59
Lauson, Gilles (1631–87) I, 427
Lauson, Jean de (father) (d. 1666) I, 427–29
Lauson, Jean de (son) (d. 1661) I, 429–31
Lauson de Charny, Charles de (fl. 1652–89) I, 431–32
Lauverjat, Étienne (1679–1761) III, 359–60
Lauzon, Pierre de (d. 1742) III, 360–61
Laval, François de (1623–1708) II, 358–72
Laviolette (fl. 1634–36) I, 432
Lawrence, Charles (d. 1760) III, 361–66
Leake, Sir John (1656–1720) II, 372–73
Le Baillif, Georges (fl. 1620–25) I, 433
Lebeau, Claude (fl. 1724–31) II, 373–74
Le Ber, Jacques (d. 1706) II, 374–76
Le Ber, Jeanne (1662–1714) II, 376–77
Le Ber, Pierre (d. 1707) II, 377–78
Le Berger. See Honatteniate
Le Blanc, Jean. See Outoutagan
Le Blanc, Pierre (d. 1799) IV, 441
Leblanc, dit Le Maigre, Joseph (1697–1772) III, 366–67, and IV, 441
Leblond de Latour, Jacques (1671–1715) II, 378–80
Le Borgne, Emmanuel (1610–75) I, 433–35
Le Borgne de Belle-Isle, Alexandre (d. c. 1693) I, 435–36
Le Borgne de l'Île. See Tessouat (d. 1636); Tessouat (d. 1654)
Le Brochet. See Kinongé
Le Cadet. See Chomina
Le Caron, Joseph (d. 1632) I, 436–38

Lechasseur, Jean (d. 1713) II, 380
Leclerc, Jean-Baptiste (d. 1739) II, 380–81
Le Clercq, Chrestien (b. 1641, d. in or after 1700) I, 438–41
Le Collier Pendu. See Kaghswaghtaniunt
Le Comte Dupré, Georges-Hippolyte, known as Saint-Georges Dupré (1738–97) IV, 441–43
Le Comte Dupré, Jean-Baptiste (d. 1765) III, 367
Le Conte Dupré, Louis (1654–1715) II, 381
Le Coq, Robert (d. 1650) I, 441
Le Coq de La Saussaye, René (fl. 1612–13) I, 441–42
Le Courtois de Surlaville, Michel (fl. 1714–96) IV, 443–44
Le Coutre de Bourville, François (fl. 1690–1744) III, 367–69
Le Creux Du Breuil, Nicolas (fl. 1632–52) I, 442
Le Crochet. See Kiotseaeton
Le Dorz, Bénin (fl. 1718–36) II, 381–82
Ledru, Jean-Antoine (b. 1752, d. in or after 1796) IV, 444–45
Leduc, Anne-Françoise, dite Saint-Joseph (1664–1750) III, 369
Lee, Fitzroy Henry (1698/99–1750) III, 369–70
Lefebvre, Jean (1714–60) III, 370–71
Lefebvre, Thomas (d. 1715?) II, 382
Lefebvre, dit Laciseraye, Michel (1654–1708) II, 382–83
Lefebvre Angers, Marie-Angélique, dite Saint-Simon (1710–66) III, 371
Lefebvre de Bellefeuille, François (1708–80) IV, 445–46
Lefebvre de Bellefeuille, Jean-François (b. 1670, d. c. 1744) III, 371–72
Le Febvre de La Barre, Joseph-Antoine (1622–88) I, 442–46
Lefebvre Duplessis Faber, François (1689–1762) III, 372–73
Le Fevre, François (d. 1718) II, 383
Legardeur de Beauvais, René (d. 1742) III, 373–74
Le Gardeur de Courtemanche, Augustin (1663–1717) II, 383–84
Legardeur de Croisille, Charles (1677–1749) III, 374
Legardeur de Croisille et de Montesson, Joseph-Michel (d. c. 1776) IV, 446–47
Legardeur de Repentigny, Jean-Baptiste (1632–1709) II, 384–85
Legardeur de Repentigny, Louis (1721–86) IV, 447–48
Legardeur de Repentigny, Marie-Jeanne-Madeleine, dite de Sainte-Agathe (d. 1739) II, 385
Legardeur de Repentigny, Pierre (grandfather) (d. 1648) I, 446–47
Legardeur de Repentigny, Pierre (grandson) (1657–1736) II, 385–86
Legardeur de Repentigny, Pierre-Jean-Baptiste-François-Xavier (1719–76) IV, 448–49

Legardeur de Saint-Pierre, Jacques (1701–55) III, 374–76

Legardeur de Saint-Pierre, Jean-Paul (b. 1661, d. 1722 or 1723) II, 386–87

Legardeur de Tilly, Charles (d. 1695) I, 447–48

Legardeur (de Moncarville et) de Tilly, Jean-Baptiste (1698–1757) III, 376–77

Legardeur de Tilly, Pierre-Noël (d. 1720) II, 387

Léger de La Grange, Jean (b. 1663, d. *c.* 1736) II, 387–88

Legge, Francis (d. 1783) IV, 449–52

Le Gouès de Sourdeval, Sébastien (1657–1710) II, 388–89

Le Grand Agnier. *See* Togouiroui

Le Grand Sauteux. *See* Minweweh

Le Guerne, François (1725–89) IV, 452–53

Leifr *heppni* Eiriksson (Leif the Lucky) (d. *c.* 1020) I, 448–49

Leigh, Charles (1572–1605) I, 449–52

Le Jeune, Olivier (d. 1654) I, 452

Le Jeune, Paul (1591–1664) I, 453–58

Le Loutre, Jean-Louis (1709–72) IV, 453–58

Le Maistre, Jacques (d. 1661) I, 458

Lemaître, *dit* Jugon, François (b. 1707, d. *c.* 1751) III, 377–78

Le Marchand de Lignery, Constant (d. 1731) II, 389–90

Le Marchand de Lignery, François-Marie (1703–59) III, 378–79

Le Mercier, François-Joseph (1604–90) I, 458–60

Le Mercier, François-Marc-Antoine (b. 1722, d. *c.* 1798) IV, 458–61

Lemire, Jean (1626–85) I, 460

Lemoine, *dit* Monière, Alexis (1680–1754) III, 379

Lemoine Despins, Jacques-Joseph (1719–87) IV, 461–62

Lemoine Despins, Marguerite-Thérèse (1722–92) IV, 462–63

Le Moyne, Simon (1604–65) I, 460–62

Le Moyne de Bienville, François (1666–91) I, 463

Le Moyne de Bienville, Jean-Baptiste (d. 1767) III, 379–84

Le Moyne de Châteauguay, Louis (1676–94) I, 463

Le Moyne de Longueuil, Charles, Baron de Longueuil (father) (d. 1729) II, 401–3

Le Moyne de Longueuil, Charles, Baron de Longueuil (son) (1687–1755) III, 384–85

Le Moyne de Longueuil, Paul-Joseph, known as Chevalier de Longueuil (1701–78) IV, 463–65

Le Moyne de Longueuil et de Châteauguay, Charles (1626–85) I, 463–65

Le Moyne de Maricourt, Paul (1663–1704) II, 403–5

Le Moyne de Martigny et de La Trinité, Jean-Baptiste (d. 1709) II, 405–6

Le Moyne de Sainte-Hélène, Jacques (1659–90) I, 465–67

Le Moyne de Saint-Marie, Marguerite, *dite* du Saint-Esprit (1664–1746) III, 385–86

Le Moyne de Serigny et de Loire, Joseph (d. 1734) II, 406–8

Le Moyne d'Iberville et d'Ardillières, Pierre (d. 1706) II, 390–401

Leneuf de La Poterie, Jacques (b. 1606, d. after 1685) I, 467

Leneuf de La Vallière de Beaubassin, Alexandre (1666–1712) II, 408–9

Leneuf de La Vallière de Beaubassin, Michel (father) (d. 1705) II, 409–11

Leneuf de La Vallière de Beaubassin, Michel (son) (d. 1740) II, 411–12

Leneuf Du Hérisson, Michel (d. *c.* 1672) I, 467–68

Lenoir, *dit* Rolland, François (d. 1707) II, 412–13

Le Normant de Mézy, Jacques-Ange (d. 1741) III, 386–89

Le Normant de Mézy, Sébastien-François-Ange (1702–91) IV, 465–68

Léonard de Chartres (d. 1654) I, 468–69

Lepage de Sainte-Claire, Louis (1690–1762) III, 390–91

Lepallieur de Laferté, Michel (d. 1733) II, 413–14

Le Pape Du Lescöat, Jean-Gabriel-Marie (1689–1733) II, 414

Le Pesant (fl. 1703–12) II, 414–15

Le Picard Du Mesnil de Norrey, Jacques (d. 1713) II, 415–17

Le Porc-épic. *See* Noro

Le Poupet de La Boularderie, Antoine (1705–71) IV, 468–69

Le Poupet de La Boularderie, Louis-Simon (d. 1738) II, 417–18

Le Prévost, Pierre-Gabriel (d. 1756) III, 391–92

Le Prévost Duquesnel, Jean-Baptiste-Louis (d. 1744) III, 392–93

Le Raisin. *See* Chomina

Le Rat. *See* Kondiaronk

Le Rouge, Jean (1639–1712) II, 418–19

Le Roux, Thomas-François (1730–94) IV, 469–70

Leroux, Valentin (1642–1708) II, 419

Le Roy, Henri (1639–1708) II, 419–21

Le Roy de La Potherie, *dit* Bacqueville de La Potherie, Claude-Charles (1633–1736) II, 421–23

Le Roy Desmarest, Claude-Joseph (d. 1737) II, 424

Lescarbot, Marc (d. 1642) I, 469–72

L'Espérance, Charles-Gabriel-Sébastien de, Baron de L'Espérance (1725–91) IV, 470–71

L'Espérance, Charles-Léopold-Ébérard de (d. 1738) II, 424–25

Lespinay, Jean-Michel de (d. 1721) II, 425–26

Lessard, Étienne de (1623–1703) II, 426

Lestage (Lestage Desperoux), Pierre de (1682–1743) III, 393–94

Lestringant de Saint-Martin, Alexandre-Joseph (d. 1722) II, 426–27

Le Sueur, Jacques-François (d. 1760) III, 394–95

Le Sueur, Jean, known as Abbé de Saint-Sauveur (d. 1668) I, 472

Le Sueur, Pierre (d. 1704) II, 427–29

Le Sueur, Pierre (1684–1752) III, 395–96

Le Tac, Xiste (d. 1718) II, 429–30

Letardif, Olivier (d. 1665) I, 473

Levasseur, François-Noël (d. 1794) IV, 471–73

Levasseur, Louis (1671–1748) III, 396–97

Levasseur, Michel (fl. 1699–1709) II, 430

Levasseur, Noël (1680–1740) II, 430–32

Levasseur, Pierre-Noël (1690–1770) III, 397–98

Levasseur, René-Nicolas (d. 1784) IV, 473–75

Levasseur, dit Delor, Jean-Baptiste-Antoine (d. 1775) IV, 475–76

Levasseur, dit Lavigne, Jean (1622–86) I, 473–74

Levasseur, dit L'Espérance, Pierre (b. 1629, d. after 1681) I, 474

Levasseur de Neré, Jacques (d. after 1723) II, 432–33

Léveillé, Mathieu (d. 1743) III, 398–99

Leverett, John (1616–78/79) I, 474–75

Le Verrier de Rousson, François (d. 1732) II, 433

Le Verrier de Rousson, Louis (b. 1705, d. in or after 1789) IV, 476

Lévesque, François (1732–87) IV, 476 –77

Le Vieux de Hauteville, Nicolas (fl. 1651–58) I, 475

Lévis, François de, Duc de Lévis (1719–87) IV, 477–82

Levrault de Langis Montegron, Jean-Baptiste (d. 1760) III, 399–400

Lewis, William (fl. 1777–87) IV, 482–84

L'Hermitte, Jacques (d. 1725) II, 433–35

Liégeois, Jean (d. 1655) I, 475–76

Liénard de Beaujeu, Daniel-Hyacinthe-Marie (1711–55) III, 400–2

Liénard de Beaujeu, Louis (1683–1750) III, 402–3

Liette, Pierre-Charles de (fl. 1687–1721) II, 435–36

Little, Otis (b. 1711/12, d. c. 1754) III, 403–5

Little Abraham. See Teiorhéñhsere?

Livingston, John (1680–1719/20) II, 436–38

Livius, Peter (1739–95) IV, 484–86

Lloyd, Thomas (d. 1710) II, 438–39

Lockman, Leonard (d. 1769) III, 405

Lombard de Combles, Jean-Claude-Henri de (1719–56) III, 405–6

Lom d'Arce de Lahontan, Louis-Armand de, Baron de Lahontan (b. 1666, d. before 1716) II, 439–45

Lomeron, David (b. 1591, d. after 1636) I, 476

Long, John (fl. 1768–91) IV, 486

Long Coat. See Anandamoakin

Longland, John (d. 1757) III, 406–7

Longley, Lydia, dite Sainte-Madeleine (1674–1758) III, 407–8

Loppinot, Jean-Chrysostome (fl. 1699–1712) II, 445

Lorimier de La Rivière, Claude-Nicolas de (d. 1770) III, 408–9

Lorimier de La Rivière, Guillaume de (d. 1709) II, 445–46

Loring, Joshua (1716–81) IV, 486–88

Lorit, dit Gargot, François (d. 1702) II, 446–47

Lottridge, John (d. 1763) III, 409–10

Louet, Jean-Claude (1681–1739) II, 447

Louis de Sainte-Foi. See Amantacha

Loyard, Jean-Baptiste (1678–1731) II, 447–48

Lozeau, Jean-Baptiste (d. c. 1745) III, 410–11

Lucas, Francis (d. 1770) III, 411–12

Lucas, Richard (fl. 1678–86) I, 476–77

Lupien, dit Baron, Pierre (d. 1744) III, 412–13

Lydall, William (fl. 1674–92) I, 477

Lÿdius, John Hendricks (d. 1791) IV, 488–90

Lyon, James (1735–94) IV, 490

Lyon de Saint-Ferréol, Jean (b. 1692, d. after 1744) III, 413–14

Lyonne, Martin de (1614–61) I, 477–78

Mabane, Adam (d. 1792) IV, 491–94

Macard, Charles (1656–1732) II, 448–49

Macaulay, Robert (1744–1800) IV, 494

McCarty, Charles Justin (James) (d. c. 1790) IV, 494–95

McCarty, Richard (d. 1781) IV, 495–96

McCliesh, Thomas (fl. 1698–1746) III, 414–15

MacDonald, James (1736–85) IV, 496–97

Macé, Catherine (1616–98) I, 478

Mackay, John (fl. 1785–87) IV, 498–99

McKee, Alexander (d. 1799) IV, 499–500

Mackellar, Patrick (1717–78) IV, 500–1

McLane, David (d. 1797) IV, 501–3

Maclean, Allan (1725–98) IV, 503–4

McLean, Francis (d. 1781) IV, 504–5

McLean, Neil (d. 1795) IV, 505

MacLeod, Normand (d. 1796) IV, 505–6

Madoc (Madogab Owain Gwynedd) (fl. 1170) I, 677–78

Madry, Jean (d. 1669) I, 478–79

Magnan, Pierre (d. 1627) I, 479

Magon de Terlaye, François-Auguste (1724–77) IV, 506–7

Magouaouidombaouit. See Gill, Joseph-Louis

Maheut, Louis (d. 1683) I, 479–80

Maillard, Pierre (d. 1762) III, 415–19

Maillet, Marie (1610–77) I, 480

Maillou, dit Desmoulins, Jean-Baptiste (1668–1753) III, 419–21

Mainwaring, Sir Henry (1587–1653) I, 481

Maisonnat, Marie-Madeleine (Winniett) (b. 1695, d. after 1770) II, 421–22

Maisonnat, dit Baptiste, Pierre (b. 1663, d. in or after 1714) II, 449–50

Makheabichtichiou (d. 1640 or 1641) I, 481–82

Malapart, André (fl. 1629–49) I, 482

Malepart de Beaucourt, François (1740–94) IV, 507–9

Malepart de Grand Maison, *dit* Beaucour, Paul (d. 1756) III, 422–23

Maleray de Noiré de La Mollerie, Jacques (1657–1704) II, 450–51

Malherbe, François (1627–96) I, 483

Malhiot, Jean-François (1692–1756) III, 422

Mallet, Denis (d. 1704) II, 451–52

Mallet, Pierre-Antoine (b. 1700, d. in or after 1751) III, 423–24

Manach, Jean (Jacques) (d. 1766) III, 424–26

Mance, Jeanne (d. 1673) I, 483–87

Mangeant, *dit* Saint-Germain, François (fl. 1713–44) III, 426–27

Manitougatche (d. 1634) I, 487–88

March, John (1658–1712) II, 452–53

Marchand, Étienne (1707–74) IV, 509–10

Marcol, Gabriel (1692–1755) III, 427–28

Marest, Joseph-Jacques (1653–1725) II, 453–54

Marest, Pierre-Gabriel (1662–1714) II, 454–55

Mareuil, Jacques de (fl. 1693–94) I, 488–89

Mareuil, Pierre de (1672–1742) III, 428–29

Margane de Batilly, François-Marie (1672–1704) II, 455–56

Margane de Lavaltrie, François (1685–1750) III, 429–30

Marguerie de La Haye, Francois (d. 1648) I, 489–90

Mariauchau d'Esgly, François (d. 1730) II, 456–57

Mariauchau d'Esgly, François-Louis (d. 1736) II, 457

Mariauchau d'Esgly, Louis-Philippe (1710–88) IV, 510–12

Marie (d. 1759) III, 430–31

Marie-Joseph-Angélique (d. 1734) II, 457–58

Marin de La Malgue, Charles-Paul (1633–1713) II, 458

Marin de La Malgue, Joseph (d. 1774) IV, 512–14

Marin de La Malgue, Paul (d. 1753) III, 431–32

Marin de La Perrière, Claude (d. 1752) III, 432

Marot, Bernard (fl. 1610–50) I, 490

Marquette, Jacques (1637–75) I, 490–93

Marrant, John (1755–91) IV, 514–16

Marsh, John (d. 1688/89) I, 493

Marsolet de Saint-Aignan, Nicolas (d. 1677) I, 493–95

Marston, Benjamin (1730–92) IV, 516–17

Martel, Pierre-Michel (Philippe-Michel) (1719–89) IV, 517

Martel, Raymond (1663–1708) II, 458–59

Martel de Belleville, Jean-Urbain (b. 1708, d. in or before 1764) III, 432–33

Martel de Brouague, François (1692–1761) III, 433–35

Martel de Magos, Jean (d. 1729) II, 459–60

Marten, Humphrey (d. before 1792) IV, 517–19

Martin, Abraham, known as L'Écossais or Maître Abraham (1589–1664) I, 495–96

Martin, Barthélemy (fl. 1749–65) III, 435

Martin, Charles-Amador (1648–1711) II, 460–61

Martin, Christopher (fl. 1661–78) I, 496

Martin, George (d. 1724) II, 461

Martin, Mathieu (fl. 1689–1724) II, 462

Martin de Lino, Antoine (1690–1733) II, 462

Martin de Lino, Jean-François (1686–1721) II, 462–64

Martin de Lino, Mathieu-François (1657–1731) II, 464–65

Martinet de Fonblanche, Jean (1645–1701) II, 465–66

Martínez Fernández y Martínez de la Sierra, Esteban José (1742–98) IV, 519–21

Mascarene, Paul (d. 1760) III, 435–40

Mascle de Saint-Julhien, Jean (1693–1759) III, 440–41

Mason, John (1586–1635) I, 496–97

Massé, Énemond (1575–1646) I, 497–98

Mathevet, Jean-Claude (1717–81) IV, 521–22

Mathews, David (d. 1800) IV, 522–23

Matonabbee (d. 1782) IV, 523–24

Maufils, Marie-Madeleine, *dite* de Saint-Louis (d. 1702) II, 466

Maugenest, Germain (d. 1792) IV, 524–25

Mauger, Joshua (d. 1788) IV, 525–29

Maugue, Claude (d. 1696) I, 498

Maugue-Garreau, Marie-Josèphe, *dite* de L'Assomption (d. 1785) IV, 529–30

Maumousseau, Françoise (1657–1704) II, 466–67

Maupassant, Eustache (d. 1692) I, 498–99

Maurès de Malartic, Anne-Joseph-Hippolyte de, Comte de Malartic (1730–1800) IV, 530–31

Maurin, François (fl. 1756–65) III, 441–42

May, Henry (fl. 1591–94) I, 499

Melanson, Charles (b. 1643, d. before 1700) I, 499–500

Membertou (d. 1611) I, 500–1

Membré, Zénobe (1645–89) I, 501–2

Ménage, Pierre (d. 1715) II, 467

Ménard, René (b. 1605, d. *c.* 1661) I, 502

Menou d'Aulnay, Charles de (d. 1650) I, 502–6

Mercier, Jean-François (b. 1699, d. 1769 or 1770) III, 442–43

Mercier, Jean-Pierre (1694–1753) III, 443–44

Meriel, Henri-Antoine (1661–1713) III, 467–68

Merlac, André-Louis de (fl. 1667–98) I, 506–7

Mermet, Jean (1664–1716) II, 468–69

Mésaiger, Charles-Michel (d. 1766) III, 444

Mesplet, Fleury (1734–94) IV, 532–35

Messamouet (fl. 1604–7) I, 507

Messier, Martine (Primot) (b. 1607, d. after 1672) I, 507–8

Messier, *dit* Saint-Michel, Michel (1640–1725) II, 469–70

Meulles, Jacques de (d. 1703) II, 470–73

Michel de Villebois de La Rouvillière, Honoré (1702–52) III, 444–46

Michipichy (fl. 1695–1706) III, 446

Middleton, Christopher (d. 1770) III, 446–50

Migeon de Branssat, Jean-Baptiste (1636–93) I, 508

Migeon de Branssat, Marie-Anne, *dite* de la Nativité (d. 1771) IV, 535–36

Migeon de La Gauchetière, Daniel (d. 1746) III, 450

Mikak (Micoc, Mykok) (d. 1795) IV, 536–37

Mikinak (d. 1755) III, 450–51

Millet, Pierre (1635–1708) II, 473–74

Mills, Sir Thomas (d. 1793) IV, 537–38

Milly, François (d. before 1749) III, 451–52

Miniac, Jean-Pierre de (d. 1771) IV, 538–40

Minweweh (d. 1770) III, 452–53

Miristou (d. 1628) I, 508–9

Miscomote (d. 1721) II, 474

Miscouaky (fl. 1700–13) II, 474–75

Missenden, Samuel (fl. 1685–88) I, 509–10

Mitchell, George (d. 1755) III, 453

Mitchell, Thomas (fl. 1743–51) III, 453–54

Mius d'Entremont, Philippe, Baron de Pobomcoup (d. 1700 or 1701) I, 510

Miville, Pierre, known as Le Suisse (d. 1669) I, 511

Mog (d. 1724) II, 475–77

Mohier, Gervais (1599–1662) I, 511

Moireau, Claude (d. 1703) II, 477–78

Monbeton de Brouillan, Jacques-François de (1651–1705) II, 478–82

Monbeton de Brouillan, *dit* Saint-Ovide, Joseph de (1676–1755) III, 454–57

Monckton, Robert (1726–82) IV, 540–42

Monic, Joseph de (d. 1707) II, 482–83

Monk, James (d. 1768) III, 457–58

Monseignat, Charles de (d. 1718) II, 483–86

Montcalm, Louis-Joseph de, Marquis de Montcalm (1712–59) III, 458–69

Montgolfier, Étienne (1712–91) IV, 542–45

Montgomery, Richard (1736–75) IV, 545–50

Montgomery, William (1765–1800) IV, 550–52

Montigny, François de (1669–1742) III, 469–70

Montresor, John (1736–99) IV, 552–53

Monts, Sieur de (fl. 1662) I, 511–12

Moody, John (d. 1736) II, 486–87

Moody, Samuel (1675/76–1747) III, 470–71

Moor, William (d. 1765) III, 471–72

Moore, Frances (Brooke) (d. 1789) IV, 553–56

Moore, Thomas (fl. 1671–1713) II, 487–88

Moore, William (fl. 1779–98) IV, 556–58

Moreau, Edme (fl. 1706–47) III, 472–73

Moreau, Jean-Baptiste (d. 1770) III, 473–74

Moreau de Brésoles, Judith (1620–87) I, 512–13

Morel, Thomas (1636–87) I, 513

Morel de La Durantaye, Olivier (1640–1716) II, 488–89

Morillon Du Bourg (d. 1670) I, 513–14

Morin, Germain (d. 1702) II, 489

Morin, Marie (1649–1730) II, 489–92

Morin de Fonfay, Jean-Baptiste (fl. 1737–93) IV, 558–59

Morpain, Pierre (d. 1749) III, 474–76

Morris, Charles (1711–81) IV, 559–63

Motin, Jeanne (Menou d'Aulnay; Saint-Étienne de La Tour) (d. c. 1666) I, 514

Mouchy, Nicolas de (fl. 1663–72) I, 514

Mouet de Langlade, Charles-Michel (d. c. 1800) IV, 563–64

Moulton, Ebenezer (1709–83) IV, 564–65

Moulton, Jeremiah (1688–1765) III, 476–77

Mounier, François (d. 1769) III, 477–78

Mounier, Jean-Mathieu (fl. 1715–74) IV, 565–66

Muiron, David-Bernard (1684–1761) III, 478–79

Munk, Jens Eriksen (1579–1628) I, 514–15

Munro, John (1728–1800) IV, 566–67

Muquinna (d. 1795) IV, 567–69

Murderer. *See* Cherououny

Murray, Alexander (d. 1762) III, 479–80

Murray, James (d. 1794) IV, 569–78

Murray, Walter (d. 1772) IV, 579

Myatt, Joseph (d. 1730) II, 492–93

Napper, James (d. 1737) II, 493

Nau, Luc-François (1703–53) III, 480–81

Navarre, Robert (d. 1791) IV, 579–80

Navières, Joseph (1709–56) III, 481–82

Negabamat (d. 1666) I, 516

Neilson, Samuel (1771–93) IV, 580–81

Nelson, John (1654–1734) II, 493–94

Nesbitt, William (d. 1784) IV, 581–82

Nescambiouit (d. 1727) II, 494–96

Neveu, Jean-Baptiste (d. 1754) III, 482

Newton, John (d. 1750) III, 482–83

Nicholas (Nickus). *See* Karaghtadie

Nicholas of Lynne (fl. 1360) I, 678–79

Nicholson, Francis (1655–1727/28) II, 496–99

Nick'a'thu'tin. *See* Primeau, Louis

Nicolas. *See* Orontony

Nicollet de Belleborne, Jean (d. 1642) I, 516–18

Nissowaquet (d. 1797) IV, 582–83

Nixon, John (d. 1692) I, 518–20

Noble, Arthur (d. 1746/47) III, 483–84

Nodogawerrimet (d. 1765) III, 484–85

Noël, Jacques (fl. 1585–88) I, 520

Nolan Lamarque, Charles (1694–1754) III, 485–86

Normandin, Daniel (d. 1729) II, 499

Normant Du Faradon, Louis (1681–1759) III, 486–88

Noro (fl. 1700–1) II, 499–500

Norris, Sir John (d. 1749) III, 488–89

Norton, Moses (d. 1773) IV, 583–85
Norton, Richard (1701–41) III, 489–90
Nouchet, Joseph (1690–1750) III, 490–91
Nouchet, Joseph-Étienne (1724–58) III, 491
Nouë, Anne de (1587–1646) I, 521
Nouvel, Henri (d. 1701 or 1702) II, 500–2
Noyelles de Fleurimont, Nicolas-Joseph de (1695–1761) III, 491–93
Noyon, Jacques de (1668–1745) III, 493–94
Noyrot, Philibert (1592–1629) I, 521–22
Nutt, John (fl. 1620–32) I, 522

OAKES, Forrest (d. 1783) IV, 585–86
Ogenheratarihiens (d. 1687) I, 522–23
Ogilvie, John (1724–74) IV, 586–87
Ohonsiowanne (fl. 1699–1704) II, 502
Ohquandageghte (fl. 1757–73) IV, 587–88
Oionhaton (fl. 1628–55) I, 523–24
Olabaratz, Joannis-Galand d' (d. 1778) IV, 588–89
Old Belt. See Kaghswaghtaniunt
Old King (Old Smoke). See Kaieñʔkwaahtoñ
Oliva, Frédéric-Guillaume (d. 1796) IV, 589–90
Olivier, Abel (d. 1768) III, 494
Olivier, dit Le Picard, Marc-Antoine (fl. 1688–96) I, 524
Olivier de Vézin, Pierre-François (b. 1707, d. in or after 1776) IV, 590–91
Ondaaiondiont (d. 1649) I, 524–25
Ononwarogo (d. 1764) III, 494–95
Orillat, Jean (1733–79) IV, 591–93
Orontony (fl. 1739–50) III, 495–96
Osborn, Sir Danvers (1715–53) III, 496–97
Osborn, Elizabeth (Myrick; Paine; Doane) (1715–98) IV, 593–94
Osborn, Henry (d. 1771) IV, 594–95
Otreouti (fl. 1659–88) I, 525–26
Ottrowana (fl. 1746–74) IV, 595–96
Ouachala (fl. 1716–27) II, 502–3
Ouagimou (fl. 1604–10) I, 526–27
Ouangote. See Williams, Eunice
Ouenemek (fl. 1695–1717) II, 503–4
Oumasasikweie (d. c. 1636) I, 527–28
Ounanguissé (fl. 1695–1716) II, 504
Ourehouare (d. 1698) I, 528
Outlaw, John (d. between 1696 and 1698) I, 528–29
Outoutagan (fl. 1698–1712) II, 504–6
Owen, William (1737–78) IV, 596–97
Ozon, Potentien (d. 1705) II, 506

PADANUQUES, Jacques (d. 1744) III, 497–98
Pagé, dit Carcy, Jacques (1682–1742) III, 498–99
Paillard, Léonard, known as Le Poitevin (1647–1729) II, 506–7
Pain, Félix (1668–1741) III, 499–500
Palliser, Sir Hugh (1722/23–96) IV, 597–601
Panet, Jean-Claude (d. 1778) IV, 601–3

Panounias (d. 1607) I, 529–30
Papineau, dit Montigny, Samuel (d. 1737) II, 507
Paradis, Jean (b. 1658, d. before 1725) II, 508
Paradis, Roland (d. 1754) III, 500–1
Parat, Antoine (d. 1696) I, 530
Paris, Bernard (1708–60) III, 501
Parkhurst, Anthony (fl. 1561–83) I, 530–31
Parmenius, Stephanus (d. 1583) I, 531–32
Parmentier, Jean (1494–1529) I, 532–33
Parr, John (1725–91) IV, 603–5
Pascaud, Antoine (d. 1717) II, 508–9
Pascaud, Antoine (1729–86) IV, 605
Pasquine (fl. 1681–88) I, 533
Pastedechouan (d. 1636) I, 533–34
Pastour de Costebelle, Philippe (1661–1717) II, 509–13
Patoulet, Jean-Baptiste (d. 1695) I, 534
Patterson, Walter (d. 1798) IV, 605–11
Pattin, John (d. 1754) III, 501–2
Paumart, Jean (1583–1648) I, 534
Payen de Noyan, Pierre (1663–1707) II, 513
Payen de Noyan, Pierre-Benoît (d. 1765) III, 502–3
Payen de Noyan et de Chavoy, Pierre-Jacques (1695–1771) IV, 611–12
Payne, Samuel (b. 1696, d. after 1732) II, 513–14
Peachey, James (d. 1797) IV, 612–14
Péan, Michel-Jean-Hugues (d. 1782) IV, 614–17
Péan de Livaudière, Jacques-Hugues (1682–1747) III, 503–4
Pearson, Bartholomew (fl. 1612–34) I, 534–35
Peaseley, William (b. 1714, d. after 1756) III, 504
Pécaudy de Contrecœur, Antoine (1596–1688) I, 535–36
Pécaudy de Contrecœur, Claude-Pierre (1705–75) IV, 617–18
Pécaudy de Contrecœur, François-Antoine (d. 1743) III, 505
Peiras, Jean-Baptiste de (d. 1701) II, 514
Pélerin, Ambroise (1656–1708) II, 514–15
Pélissier, Christophe (b. 1728, d. before 1800) IV, 618–19
Pellegrin, Gabriel (1713–88) IV, 619–21
Pelletier, Didace (1657–99) I, 536
Pemoussa (d. 1716 or 1717) II, 515–16
Pennisseaut, Louis (b. 1724, d. after 1771) IV, 621–22
Pepperrell, William (d. 1733/34) II, 516
Pepperrell, Sir William (1696–1759) III, 505–9
Peré, Jean (fl. 1660–99) I, 536–37
Pérez Hernández, Juan Josef (d. 1775) IV, 622–23
Peronne de Mazé, Louis (fl. 1661–65) I, 537
Peronne Dumesnil, Jean (d. before 1667) I, 537–39
Pérot, Gilles (d. 1680) I, 539
Perrault, François (d. 1745) III, 509–10
Perrault, Jacques, known as Perrault l'aîné (1718–75) IV, 623–24

Perrault, Julien (d. 1647) I, 539
Perrault, Paul (d. 1765) III, 510–11
Perreault, Hyacinthe (1654–1700) I, 539–40
Perrin, Antoine (d. *c.* 1738) II, 516
Perrot, François-Marie (1644–91) I, 540–42
Perrot, Nicolas (d. 1717) II, 516–20
Perrot de Rizy, Pierre (1672–1740) II, 520
Perthuis, Charles (1664–1722) II, 520–21
Perthuis, Jean-Baptiste-Ignace (b. 1716, d. after 1767) III, 511–12
Perthuis, Joseph (1714–82) IV, 624–25
Peter. *See* Kingminguse
Peters, Hendrick. *See* Theyanoguin
Peters, Joseph (1729–1800) IV, 625–26
Peters, Pauly (Paulus Petersen). *See* Sahonwagy
Peters, Thomas (d. 1792) IV, 626–28
Petit, Jean (1663–1720) II, 521
Petit, Louis (1629–1709) II, 521–22
Petit, Pierre (d. 1737) II, 522–23
Petit de Levilliers, Charles (d. 1714) II, 523–24
Petitpas, Barthélemy (1687–1747) III, 512–13
Petitpas, Claude (d. before 1733) II, 524
Pettrequin, Jean (d. 1764) III, 513
Peuvret de Gaudarville, Alexandre (d. 1702) II, 524–25
Peuvret Demesnu, Jean-Baptiste (1632–97) I, 542–43
Pézard de La Tousche Champlain, Étienne (b. 1624, d. *c.* 1696) I, 543
Philippe de Hautmesnil de Mandeville, François (d. 1728) II, 525–26
Philipps, Erasmus James (1705–60) III, 514–15
Philipps, Richard (d. 1750) III, 515–18
Phipps, Thomas (fl. 1679–86) I, 543–44
Phips, Sir William (1650/51–94/95) I, 544–46
Phlem, *dit* Yvon, Yves (d. 1749) III, 518–20
Piat, Irénée (1594–1674) I, 546–47
Picard, Louis-Alexandre (d. 1799) IV, 628–30
Pichon, Thomas, known as Thomas Tyrell (1700–81) IV, 630–32
Pichot de Querdisien Trémais, Charles-François (d. 1784) IV, 632–33
Picoté de Belestre, François-Marie (1716–93) IV, 633–36
Picoté de Belestre, Pierre (d. 1679) I, 547
Picquet, François (1708–81) IV, 636–38
Pierre (d. 1747) III, 520
Pierron, Jean (1631–1700) I, 547
Pieskaret (d. 1647) I, 547–48
Pigarouich (fl. 1639–44) I, 548–49
Pijart, Claude (1600–83) I, 549
Pijart, Pierre (1608–76) I, 549–50
Pike. *See* Kinongé
Pilgrim, Robert (d. 1750) III, 520–21
Pillard, Louis (d. 1768) III, 521
Pinard, Louis (d. 1695) I, 550

Pinaud, Nicolas (d. 1722) II, 526
Pinguet de Vaucour, Jacques-Nicolas (1692–1749) III, 521–22
Piot de Langloiserie, Charles-Gaspard (d. 1715) II, 526–27
Piot de Langloiserie, Marie-Marguerite, *dite* Saint-Hippolyte (1702–81) IV, 638
Plante, Charles (1680–1744) III, 522–23
Plessy, *dit* Bélair, Jean-Louis (1678–1743) III, 523–24
Pollet, Arnould-Balthazar (1702–56) III, 524
Pollet de La Combe-Pocatière, François (d. 1672) I, 550–51
Pommereau, Jean-Baptiste (1702–42) III, 524–25
Pommier, Hugues (d. 1686) I, 551
Poncet de La Rivière, Joseph-Antoine (1610–75) I, 551–52
Pontiac (d. 1769) III, 525–31
Porc-épic, Le. *See* Noro
Porlier, Pierre-Antoine (1725–89) IV, 638–39
Pote, William (b. 1718, d. before 1755) III, 531–32
Potier, Pierre-Philippe (d. 1781) IV, 640–41
Potier Dubuisson, Robert (1682–1744) III, 532–33
Potot de Montbeillard, Fiacre-François (1723–78) IV, 641–42
Pottier, Jean-Baptiste (d. 1711) II, 527–28
Potts, John (d. 1764) III, 533–34
Pouchot (Pouchot de Maupas), Pierre (1712–69) III, 534–37
Poudre Chaude. *See* Ogenheratarihiens
Poulain, Guillaume (d. 1623) I, 552
Poulet, Georges-François, known as M. Dupont (fl. 1714–18) II, 528–29
Poulin, Pierre (b. 1684, d. after 1744) III, 537–38
Poulin de Courval, François-Louis (1728–69) III, 538–39
Poulin de Courval, Jean-Baptiste (1657–1727) II, 529
Poulin de Courval, Louis-Jean (1696–1743) III, 539
Poulin de Courval Cressé, Louis-Pierre (1728–64) III, 539–40
Poulin de Francheville, François (1692–1733) II, 529–30
Poulin de La Fontaine, Maurice (d. between 1670 and 1676) I, 552–53
Poulous (Powless). *See* Sahonwagy
Pourroy de Lauberivière, François-Louis de (1711–40) II, 530–31
Power, Richard (d. 1681) I, 553
Prat, Louis (1662–1726) II, 531–32
Preissac de Bonneau, Louis de (b. 1724, d. after 1789) IV, 642
Pressart, Colomban-Sébastien (1723–77) IV, 642–43
Pressé, Hyacinthe-Olivier (fl. 1735–46) III, 540–41
Prévost, Martin (d. 1691) I, 553–54

Prevost de La Croix, Jacques (1715–91) IV, 643–47
Price, Benjamin (d. 1768) III, 541–42
Primeau, Louis (fl. 1749–1800) IV, 647
Pringle, Robert (d. 1793) IV, 647–48
Prouville, Alexandre de, Marquis de Tracy (d. 1670) I, 554–57
Provost, François (1638–1702) II, 532–33
Prud'homme, Louis (d. 1671) I, 557
Puiseaux, Pierre de (d. *c.* 1647) I, 557–58
Pynne, William (fl. 1689–1713) II, 533–34

QUARANTE SOLS. *See* Michipichy
Quen, Jean de (d. 1659) I, 558–59
Quentin, Claude (1597–1676) I, 560
Quentin, Jacques (1572–1647) I, 560
Quéré de Tréguron, Maurice (d. 1754) III, 542–43
Quesneville, Jean (d. 1701) II, 534
Quiniard, *dit* Duplessis, Antoine-Olivier (d. 1738) II, 534–35
Quintal, Augustin (1683–1776) IV, 649–50

RABY, Augustin (d. 1782) IV, 650
Radisson, Pierre-Esprit (d. 1710) II, 535–40
Raffeix, Pierre (1635–1724) II, 540
Rageot, Gilles (d. 1692) I, 560–61
Rageot de Saint-Luc, Charles (d. 1702) II, 540–41
Rageot de Saint-Luc, Nicolas (d. 1703) II, 541
Ragueneau, Paul (1608–80) I, 561–64
Raimbault, Pierre (1671–1740) II, 541–42
Raimbault de Piedmont, Joseph-Charles (1693–1737) II, 542
Raisin, Marie (d. 1691) I, 564
Rale, Sébastien (1657–1724) II, 542–45
Ralluau, Jean (fl. 1604–15) I, 564–65
Ramezay, Claude de (1659–1724) II, 545–49
Ramezay, Jean-Baptiste-Nicolas-Roch de (1708–77) IV, 650–53
Ramezay, Louise de (1705–76) IV, 653–55
Ramezay, Marie-Charlotte de, *dite* de Saint-Claude de la Croix (1697–1767) III, 543–44
Randin, Hugues (b. 1628, d. *c.* 1680) I, 565
Rankin, John (fl. 1741–48) III, 544
Ransonnet, Sylvestre-François-Michel (fl. 1726–43) III, 544–45
Rastell, John (fl. 1510–40) I, 565–66
Rat, Le. *See* Kondiaronk
Rattier, Jean (d. 1703) II, 549
Raudot, Antoine-Denis (1679–1737) II, 549–54
Raudot, Jacques (1638–1728) II, 554–61
Raymbaut, Charles (1602–42) I, 566–67
Raymond, Jean-Louis de, Comte de Raymond (d. 1771) IV, 655–57
Rayner, John (fl. 1661–62) I, 567
Razilly, Isaac de (1587–1635) I, 567–69
Récher, Jean-Félix (1724–68) III, 545–47
Reconciled. *See* Cherououny

Red Head. *See* Kakȣenthiony; Ononwarogo
Regnard Duplessis, Georges (d. 1714) II, 561
Regnard Duplessis, Marie-Andrée, *dite* de Sainte-Hélène (1687–1760) III, 547–49
Regnard Duplessis de Morampont, Charles-Denis (b. 1704, d. after 1759) III, 549
Rémy (de Saint-Rémy), Pierre (1636–1726) II, 561–62
Rémy de Courcelle, Daniel de (1626–98) I, 569–72
Renaud, Jean (d. 1794) IV, 657–58
Renaud, *dit* Cannard, Pierre (d. 1774) IV, 658–59
Renaud d'Avène de Desmeloizes, François-Marie (d. 1699) I, 572–73
Renaud d'Avène des Méloizes, Angélique (Péan) (1722–92) IV, 659–60
Renaud d'Avène Des Méloizes, Nicolas-Marie (1696–1743) III, 549–51
Renaud Dubuisson, Jacques-Charles (1666–1739) II, 562–63
Renaud Dubuisson, Louis-Jacques-Charles (b. 1709, d. *c.* 1765) III, 551–52
Render, Thomas (fl. 1729–34) II, 563–64
René, Patrice (1667–1742) III, 552
Resche, Pierre-Joseph (1695–1770) III, 553–54
Révol, Pierre (d. 1759) III, 554–55
Rhoades, John (fl. 1674–76) I, 573
Rice, Jacob (1683–1728) II, 564
Richard, *dit* Lafleur, Guillaume (1641–90) I, 573–74
Richards, Michael (1673–1722) II, 564–65
Rigaud de Vaudreuil, François-Pierre de (1703–79) IV, 660–62
Rigaud de Vaudreuil, Joseph-Hyacinthe de (1706–64) III, 555–56
Rigaud de Vaudreuil, Louis-Philippe de, Marquis de Vaudreuil (1691–1763) III, 556–57
Rigaud de Vaudreuil, Philippe de, Marquis de Vaudreuil (d. 1725) II, 565–74
Rigaud de Vaudreuil de Cavagnial, Pierre de, Marquis de Vaudreuil (1698–1778) IV, 662–74
Ritchie, John (d. 1790) IV, 674–75
Riverin, Denis (d. 1717) II, 574–76
Riverin, Joseph (1699–1756) III, 557–58
Rivet Cavelier, Pierre (d. 1721) II, 576–77
Robert, Clément (d. 1730 or 1736) II, 577
Roberts, Benjamin (fl. 1758–75) IV, 675–76
Roberts, Lewis (1596–1641) I, 574
Robertson, Charles (d. 1763) III, 558–59
Robichaux, Louis (1704–80) IV, 676–77
Robinau de Bécancour, Pierre, Baron de Portneuf (1654–1729) II, 577–79
Robinau de Bécancour, René, Baron de Portneuf (d. 1699) I, 574–76
Robinau de Neuvillette, Daniel (d. 1702) II, 579
Robinau de Portneuf, Philippe-René (d. 1759) III, 559–60
Robinau de Portneuf, Pierre (1708–61) III, 560–61

Robinau de Portneuf, René (1659–1726) II, 579–80
Robinau de Villebon, Joseph (1655–1700) I, 576–78
Robinson, Christopher (1763–98) IV, 677–78
Robinson, Sir Robert (d. 1705) II, 580–81
Robson, Joseph (fl. 1733–63) III, 561–62
Robutel de La Noue, Zacharie (1665–1733) II, 581
Rocbert de La Morandière, Étienne (b. 1668, d. 1753 or 1754) III, 562–63
Rocbert de La Morandière, Marie-Élisabeth (Bégon de La Cour) (1696–1755) III, 563–65
Rodrigue, Antoine (1722–89) IV, 678–79
Rodrigue, Jean-Baptiste (d. 1733) II, 581–82
Roger, Guillaume (1632–1702) II, 582
Rogers, Robert (1731–95) IV, 679–83
Rollet, Marie (Hébert; Hubou) (d. 1649) I, 578
Rollo, Andrew, 5th Baron Rollo (1703–65) III, 565
Roma, Jean-Pierre (fl. 1715–57) III, 566–67
Romieux, Pierre (fl. 1659–75) I, 578–79
Rondeau, Jacques-Philippe-Urbain (d. c. 1749) III, 567–68
Roope, John (d. 1719) II, 582–83
Roquemont de Brison, Claude (d. 1628) I, 579
Roscboom, Johannes (d. 1745) III, 568–69
Ross, John (fl. 1762–89) IV, 683–84
Ross, Malchom (d. 1799) IV, 684–85
Roubaud, Pierre-Joseph-Antoine (b. 1724, d. after 1789) IV, 685–87
Rouer d'Artigny, Louis (1667–1744) III, 569–70
Rouer de Villeray, Benjamin (1701–60) III, 570–71
Rouer de Villeray, Louis (1629–1700) I, 579–83
Rouer de Villeray et de La Cardonnière, Augustin (d. 1711) II, 583–84
Rouffio, Joseph (b. 1730, d. after 1764) III, 571–72
Rouillard, Ambroise (baptized Louis-Joseph) (1693–1768) III, 572
Rous, John (d. 1760) III, 572–74
Rousseau de Villejouin, Gabriel (1709–81) IV, 688–89
Roussel, Timothée (d. 1700) I, 583
Rowley, Thomas (fl. 1612–28) I, 584
Roy, Louis (1771–99) IV, 689–90
Roy, Marguerite, dite de la Conception (1674–1749) III, 574–75
Roy, dit Châtellerault, Michel (1649–1709) II, 584
Roybon d'Allonne, Madeleine de (d. 1718) II, 584–85
Ruette d'Auteuil, Denis-Joseph (1617–79) I, 584–85
Ruette d'Auteuil de Monceaux, François-Madeleine-Fortuné (d. 1737) II, 585–88
Rut, John (fl. 1512–28) I, 585–86

SABATIER, Antoine (d. 1747) III, 575–76
Sabrevois, Jacques-Charles de (d. 1727) II, 588–89
Sabrevois de Bleury, Clément de (d. 1781) IV, 690–91
Saccardy, Vincent (d. 1691) I, 586–87
Saffray de Mézy, Augustin de (d. 1665) I, 587–90
Sagard, Gabriel (baptized Théodat) (fl. 1614–36) I, 590–92
Sagean, Mathieu (fl. 1700–11) II, 589–90
Saguima (fl. 1707–12) III, 576–77
Sahonwagy (Sahonwadi) (fl. 1753–87) IV, 691–92
Saillant (Saillant de Collégien), Jean-Antoine (1720–76) IV, 692–93
Sailly, Louis-Arthus de (d. 1668) I, 592
Saint-Aubin, Ambroise (d. 1780) IV, 693
Saint-Clair, Pierre de (d. 1736) II, 590
Saint-Étienne de La Tour, Agathe de (Bradstreet; Campbell) (b. 1690, d. in or after 1743) II, 590–91
Saint-Étienne de La Tour, Charles de (father) (1593–1666) I, 592–96
Saint-Étienne de La Tour, Charles de (son) (d. 1731) II, 591–92
Saint-Étienne de La Tour, Claude de (fl. 1609–36) I, 596–98
St Leger, Barrimore Matthew (d. 1789) IV, 694–95
Saint-Ours, François-Xavier de (1717–59) III, 577–78
Saint-Ours, Pierre de (1640–1724) II, 592–93
Saint-Ours Deschaillons, Jean-Baptiste de (1669–1747) III, 578–79
Saint-Pé, Jean-Baptiste de (1686–1770) III, 579–80
Saint-Père, Agathe de (Legardeur de Repentigny) (b. 1657, d. 1747 or 1748) III, 580–81
Saint-Père, Jean de (d. 1657) I, 598–99
Salignac de La Mothe-Fénelon, François de (1641–79) I, 599–601
Sallaberry, Michel de (1704–68) III, 582–83
Salter, Malachy (d. 1781) IV, 695–97
Salusbury, John (1707–62) III, 583–84
Sanford, Esbon (1645/46–82) I, 601
Sanguinet, Simon (1733–90) IV, 697–98
Saquima (Saquin). See Saguima
Sarcel de (Du) Prévert, Jean (d. 1622) I, 601–2
Sarrazin, Michel (1659–1734) II, 593–600
Sauguaaram (fl. 1724–51) III, 584–85
Saul, Thomas (fl. 1750–60) III, 585–86
Saunders, Sir Charles (d. 1775) IV, 698–702
Saurel, Pierre de (1628–82) I, 602–3
Savage, Arthur (fl. 1720–31) II, 600–1
Savage, Thomas (d. 1705) II, 601
Savignon (fl. 1610–11) I, 603
Savonnières de La Troche, Marie de, dite de Saint-Joseph (de Saint-Bernard) (1616–52) I, 603–4
Sayward, Mary (baptized Marie-Geneviève), dite Marie des Anges (1681–1717) II, 601–2
Scatchamisse (d. 1712) II, 602
Schindler, Joseph (Jonas) (d. 1792) IV, 702–3
Schuyler, Johannes (1668–1747) III, 586–87
Schuyler, Peter (1657–1723/24) II, 602–4
Schuyler, Peter (1710–62) III, 587–89
Schwartz, Otto William (1715–85) IV, 703–4

Scolvus, John (fl. 1476) I, 679
Scott, George (d. 1767) III, 589–90
Scott, Joseph (d. 1800) IV, 704–5
Scroggs, John (fl. 1718–24) II, 604
Seccombe, John (1708–92) IV, 705–6
Secoudon (d. before 1616) I, 604
Sedgwick, Robert (1611–56) I, 604–5
Segipt (fl. 1629–32) I, 605
Seneca King. See Kaieñ?kwaahtoñ
Senet, dit Laliberté, Nicolas (d. 1732) II, 604
Senezergues de La Rodde, Étienne-Guillaume de
    (1709–59) III, 590–91
Sergeant, Henry (fl. 1683–89) I, 605–6
Serreau de Saint-Aubin, Jean (1621–1705) II, 604–5
Sevestre, Charles (d. 1657) I, 606–7
Shaw, William (fl. 1759–89) IV, 706–7
Sheepscot Jo. See Wowurna
Shepard, Thomas (fl. 1668–81) I, 607
Short, Richard (fl. 1754–66) III, 591–92
Shuldham, Molyneux, 1st Baron Shuldham (d. 1798)
    IV, 707–8
Silly, Jean-Baptiste de (fl. 1728–30) II, 605–6
Silver, Mary (baptized Adélaïde) (1694–1740) II,
    606–7
Silvy, Antoine (1638–1711) II, 607–9
Simon de Longpré, Marie-Catherine de, dite de
    Saint-Augustin (1632–68) I, 607–10
Simonet d'Abergemont, Jacques (d. 1742) III,
    592–93
Simonnet, François (1701–78) IV, 708–10
Singleton, George (d. 1789) IV, 710–11
Skanudharoua (Geneviève-Agnès de Tous-les-Saints)
    (1642–57) I, 610–11
Skeffington, George (fl. 1700–29) II, 609
Skrimsher, Samuel (d. 1755) III, 593–94
Slade, John (1719–92) IV, 711–14
Slave Woman. See Thanadelthur
Smart, Thomas (d. 1722) II, 609–10
Smith, Francis (fl. 1737–47) III, 594
Smith, James (fl. 1708–15) II, 610–11
Smith, Joseph (d. 1765) III, 594–95
Smith, William (1728–93) IV, 714–18
Smithsend, Nicholas (fl. 1685–98) I, 611
Smithsend, Richard (fl. 1685–91) I, 611–12
Smiths John (Smits Jan). See Flemish Bastard
Snorri Thorfinnsson (b. c. 1005–13) I, 612
Solomons, Lucius Levy (1730–92) IV, 718–19
Sorbier de Villars, François (1720–88) IV, 719–20
Souart, Gabriel (d. 1691) I, 612–13
Soubras, Pierre-Auguste de (d. 1725) II, 611–12
Soullard, Jean (1642–1710) II, 612
Soumande, Louis (1652–1706) II, 612–13
Soumande, Louise, dite de Saint-Augustin
    (1664–1708) II, 613
Soupiran, Simon (father) (1670–1724) II, 613–14
Soupiran, Simon (son) (1704–64) III, 595–96
Souste, André (d. 1776) IV, 720–21

Southack, Cyprian (1662–1745) III, 596–97
Sower, Christopher (1754–99) IV, 721–22
Spagniolini, Jean-Fernand (1704–64) III, 597–98
Spurrell, George (d. 1770) III, 598–99
Staunton, Richard (fl. 1694–1741) III, 599–600
Sterling, James (fl. 1759–83) IV, 722
Stewart, James, 4th Lord Ochiltree (d. 1659) I,
    613–14
Stobo, Robert (1726–70) III, 600–2
Stourton, Erasmus (1603–58) I, 614
Strouds, Gilles William (d. 1757) III, 602
Stuart, William (d. 1719) II, 614–16
Studholme, Gilfred (1740–92) IV, 723–24
Suckling, George (fl. 1752–80) IV, 724–26
Suève, Edmond de (d. 1707) II, 616–17
Sullivan, Timothy, known as Timothée Silvain
    (d. 1749) III, 602–4
Sutherland, George (fl. 1774–99) IV, 726–27
Sutherland, James (d. 1797) IV, 727–28
Sutherland, Patrick (d. c. 1766) III, 604–5
Swan (fl. 1715–19) II, 617
Swanton, Robert (d. 1765) III, 605–6
Swatana (d. 1748) III, 606–8

TACHÉ, Jean (1698–1768) III, 608–9
Taffanel de La Jonquière, Jacques-Pierre de, Marquis
    de La Jonquière (1685–1752) III, 609–12
Tailhandier, dit La Beaume, Marien (b. 1665, d. 1738
    or 1739) II, 617–18
Talbot, Jacques (1678–1756) III, 612–13
Talon (Talon Du Quesnoy), Jean (d. 1694) I, 614–32
Tanaghrisson (d. 1754) III, 613–15
Tanfield, Sir Francis (b. 1565, d. after 1630) I, 632
Tantouin de La Touche, Louis (d. 1722) II, 618–19
Taondechoren (fl. 1640–77) I, 632–33
Taratouan (d. 1637) I, 633
Tarbell, John (b. 1695, d. after 1740) III, 615
Tareha (fl. 1691–95) I, 633–34
Tarieu de La Naudière, Charles-François (1710–76)
    IV, 728–30
Tarride Duhaget, Robert (d. 1757) III, 615–16
Taschereau, Thomas-Jacques (1680–1749) III,
    616–17
Taverner, William (d. 1768) III, 617–20
Taylour, Joseph (d. 1734) II, 619
Teganissorens (fl. 1682–1721) II, 619–23
Tehorenhaegnon (fl. 1628–37) I, 634–35
Teiorhéñhsere? (Tayorheasere) (d. 1780) IV,
    730–31
Tekakwitha (Kateri) (1656–80) I, 635–36
Tekanoet (fl. 1680–1701) II, 623–24
Tekarihoken (fl. 1726–28) II, 624–25
Tekawirõnte (d. 1777) IV, 731
Temple, Sir Thomas (1613/14–74) I, 636–37
Teouatiron (d. 1640 or 1641) I, 637–38
Terriot, Pierre (d. 1725) II, 625
Terroux, Jacques (fl. 1725–77) III, 620; IV, 731

Tessier, *dit* Lavigne, Paul (1701–73) IV, 731–33
Tessouat (fl. 1603–13) I, 638–39
Tessouat (d. 1636) I, 639
Tessouat (d. 1654) I, 640–41
Testard de La Forest, Gabriel (1661–97) I, 641
Testard de Montigny, Jacques (1663–1737) II, 625–27
Testard de Montigny, Jean-Baptiste-Philippe (1724–86) IV, 733–34
Testu de La Richardière, Richard (1681–1741) III, 620–22
Tête Blanche, La. *See* Gray Lock
Tétro, Jean-Baptiste (d. before 1730) II, 627
Teyohaqueande (fl. 1756–83) IV, 734–35
Thanadelthur (d. 1717) II, 627–28
Thaumur de La Source, Dominique-Antoine-René (d. 1731) II, 628
Thavenet, Marguerite de (Hertel de La Fresnière) (1646–1708) II, 628–29
Thérèse. *See* Oionhaton
Thevet, André (1502–90) I, 679–80
Theyanoguin (d. 1755) III, 622–24
Thiboult, Thomas (d. 1724) II, 629
Thirkill, Lancelot (fl. 1498–1501) I, 641
Thomas, Jean (fl. 1635) I, 642
Thompson, Edward (fl. 1725–49) III, 624–25
Thompson, Joseph (fl. 1674–79) I, 642
Thorfinnr *karlsefni* Thordarson (fl. 1000–20) I, 642–43
Thorne, Robert (father) (d. 1519) I, 643–44
Thorne, Robert (son) (1492–1532) I, 643–44
Thubières de Levy de Queylus, Gabriel (1612–77) I, 644–49
Thury, Louis-Pierre (d. 1699) I, 649
Tibaudeau, Pierre (1631–1704) II, 629–30
Tibierge (fl. 1695–1703) II, 620
Tibierge, Marie-Catherine, *dite* de Saint-Joachim (1681–1757) III, 625–26
Tisquantum (d. 1622) I, 649–50
Tisserant de Moncharvaux, Jean-Baptiste-François (d. 1767) III, 626–27
Togouiroui (d. 1690) I, 650–51
Tomah, Pierre (fl. 1775–80) IV, 735–36
Tonatakout (fl. 1700–34) II, 631
Tonge, Winckworth (1727/28–92) IV, 736–38
Tonsahoten (d. 1688) I, 651
Tonty, Alphonse (de), Baron de Paludy (d. 1727) II, 631–33
Tonty, Henri (de) (d. 1704) II, 633–36
Tonty de Liette, Charles-Henri-Joseph de (1697–1749) III, 627
Toosey, Philip (d. 1797) IV, 738–39
Totiri (fl. 1642–46) I, 651–52
Tournois, Jean-Baptiste (b. 1710, d. after 1761) III, 627–28
Townsend, Isaac (d. 1765) III, 628–29
Tremblay, Henri-Jean (1664–1740) III, 683–85

Trevanion, Sir Nicholas (d. 1737) II, 636–37
Treworgie, John (fl. 1635–60) I, 652–53
Trotain, *dit* Saint-Seürin, François (d. 1731) II, 637
Trottier, Marguerite, *dite* Saint-Joseph (1678–1744) III, 629–30
Trottier Desauniers, Pierre (b. 1700, d. after 1755) III, 631–32
Trottier Dufy Desauniers, Thomas-Ignace (d. 1777) IV, 739–40
Trouvé, Claude (d. 1704) II, 637–39
Troyes, Pierre de, known as Chevalier de Troyes (d. 1688) I, 653–54
Tuglavina (d. 1798) IV, 740
Turc de Castelveyre, Louis, known as Brother Chrétien (1687–1755) III, 632–34
Turnor, Philip (d. 1799 or 1800) IV, 740–42
Tutty, William (d. 1754) III, 634–35
Tyng, Edward (father) (fl. 1680–91) I, 654
Tyng, Edward (son) (1683–1755) III, 635–36

UMFREVILLE, Edward (fl. 1771–89) IV, 742–43

VACHON, Paul (father) (1656–1729) II, 640–41
Vachon, Paul (son) (d. 1703) II, 639–40
Vachon de Belmont, François (1645–1732) II, 641–42
Vaillant de Gueslis, François (1646–1718) II, 642–43
Vallée, François-Madeleine (fl. 1710–42) III, 636–37
Vallette de Chévigny, Médard-Gabriel (fl. 1712–54) III, 637–38
Vallier, François-Elzéar (1707–47) III, 638–39
Vancouver, George (1757–98) IV, 743–48
Vane, George (d. 1722) II, 643–44
Varin, *dit* La Pistole, Jacques (d. 1791) IV, 748–49
Varin de La Marre, Jean-Victor (b. 1699, d. before 1786) IV, 749–51
Varlet, Dominique-Marie (1678–1742) III, 639–41
Vaughan, David (fl. 1713–19) II, 644
Vaughan, George (1676–1724) II, 644–45
Vaughan, Sir William (1575–1641) I, 654–57
Vaughan, William (1703–46) III, 641–42
Vauquelin, Jean (1728–72) IV, 751–52
Véniard de Bourgmond, Étienne de (fl. 1695–1725) II, 645–47
Verner, Hugh (fl. 1678–97) I, 657
Véron de Grandmesnil, Étienne (father) (1649–1721) II, 647–48
Véron de Grandmesnil, Étienne (son) (1679–1743) III, 642–43
Véronneau, Agathe (1707–64) III, 643
Verrazzano, Giovanni da (d. *c.* 1528) I, 657–60
Verreau, Barthélemy (1678–1718) II, 648
Verrier, Étienne (1683–1747) III, 643–46
Verrier, Louis-Guillaume (1690–1758) III, 646–48
Verville, Jean-François de (d. 1729) II, 648–50

Vetch, Samuel (1668–1732) II, 650–52
Veyssière, Leger-Jean-Baptiste-Noël, known as Father Emmanuel (1728–1800) IV, 752–54
Vézina, Charles (1685–1755) III, 648–49
Viel, Nicolas (d. 1625) I, 661
Viennay-Pachot, François (d. 1698) I, 661
Vienne, François-Joseph de (d. *c.* 1775) IV, 754–55
Vignal, Guillaume (d. 1661) I, 661–62
Vignau, Nicolas de (fl. 1611–13) I, 662–63
Vilermaula, Louis-Michel de (d. 1757 or 1758) III, 649
Villain, Jean-Baptiste (fl. 1666–70) I, 663
Villedonné, Étienne de (d. 1726) II, 652–53
Villeneuve, Robert de (fl. 1685–92) I, 663–64
Villes, Jean-Marie de (1670–1720) II, 653
Villieu, Claude-Sébastien de (fl. 1690–1705) II, 653–54
Villieu, Sébastien de (1693–1715) II, 654–55
Vimont, Barthélemy (1594–1667) I, 665
Vincent (fl. 1740–45) III, 650
Vincent, Robert (d. 1765) III, 650–51
Volant de Radisson, Étienne (d. 1735) II, 655
Volant de Saint-Claude, Claude (1654–1719) II, 655–56
Volant de Saint-Claude, Pierre (1654–1710) II, 655–56
Voyer d'Argenson, Pierre de (d. *c.* 1709) II, 656–58
Vuil, Daniel (d. 1661) I, 665–66

WABAKININE (d. 1796) IV, 755–56
Wabbicommicot (d. 1768) III, 651–52
Waddens, Jean-Étienne (d. 1782) IV, 757
Waggoner, Rowland (d. 1740) II, 658
Waldo, Samuel (1695–1759) III, 652–54
Wales, William (d. 1798) IV, 757–58
Walker, Sir Hovenden (d. 1725 or 1728) II, 658–62
Walker, Nehemiah (fl. 1670–87) I, 666
Walker, Richard (fl. 1637–80) I, 666–67
Walker, Thomas (d. 1788) IV, 758–60
Walker, William (d. 1792) IV, 760–61
Walley, John (1644–1711/12) II, 662
Wapinesiw (fl. 1755–72) IV, 761
Wappisis (d. 1755) III, 654–55
Ward, Richard (fl. 1698–1720) II, 662–63
Warren, Sir Peter (d. 1752) III, 655–59
Washington, John (fl. 1719–24) II, 663
Wasson (fl. 1763–76) IV, 761–62
Watson, Charles (1714–57) III, 659
Watts, Richard (1688–1739/40) II, 663–64
Wawatam (fl. 1762–64) III, 659–60
Waxaway (fl. 1694–1710) II, 664
Waymouth, George (fl. 1601–12) I, 667–68

Webb, James (d. 1761) III, 660–61
Webber, John (1751–93) IV, 762–63
Wenemouet (d. 1730) II, 664–66
Wenman, Richard (d. 1781) IV, 763–64
Wheelwright, Esther, *dite* de l'Enfant-Jésus (1696–1780) IV, 764–66
Whetstone, Sir William (d. 1711) II, 666
Whitbourne, Sir Richard (fl. 1579–1628) I, 668–69
White, John (fl. 1577–93) I, 669–70
White, John (d. 1800) IV, 766–67
White, Richard (fl. 1726–49) III, 661
White, Thomas (1719–56) III, 661–62
White Head. *See* Theyanoguin
White Thunder. *See* Kaghswaghtaniunt
Whitmore, Edward (d. 1761) III, 662–63
Wigate, John (fl. 1741–46) III, 663
Wikinanish (fl. 1788–93) IV, 767–68
Wilkins, John (fl. 1748–75) IV, 768–69
Willard, Abijah (1724–89) IV, 769–70
William of Canajoharie. *See* Tekawirõnte
Williams, Eunice (Marie, Marguerite) (1696–1785) IV, 770–71
Williams, Griffith (d. 1790) IV, 771–72
Williams, John (fl. 1711–18) II, 667–68
Williams, John (1664–1729) II, 667
Williamson, George (d. 1781) IV, 772–73
Willoughby, Thomas (b. 1593, d. after 1621) I, 670–71
Wilmot, Montagu (d. 1766) III, 663–65
Winniett, William (d. 1741) III, 665–66
Winninnewaycappo (d. 1799) IV, 773–74
Winslow, John (1703–74) IV, 774–75
Wolfe, James (1727–59) III, 666–74
Wood, Thomas (1711–78) IV, 775–76
Wooster, Hezekiah Calvin (1771–98) IV, 776–77
Wowurna (fl. 1670–1738) II, 668–70
Wroth, Robert (d. *c.* 1735) II, 670
Wyet, Sylvester (fl. 1594) I, 671–72
Wynne, Edward (fl. 1621–26) I, 672

YONGE, James (1646/47–1721) II, 670–72
York, Jack (fl. 1800) IV, 777–79
You de La Découverte, Pierre (1658–1718) II, 672–73
Young, James (fl. 1688–93) I, 672–73
Young, Thomas (fl. 1634–40) I, 673
Youville, Charles-Marie-Madeleine d' (1729–90) IV, 779–80
Youville, Marie-Marguerite d'. *See* Dufrost de Lajemmerais

ZENO, Antonio (d. *c.* 1403) I, 680–81
Zeno, Nicolò (d. *c.* 1402) I, 680–81
Zouberbuhler, Sebastian (d. 1773) IV, 780–81

INDEX OF IDENTIFICATIONS

CATEGORIES

Agriculture

Armed forces

Artisans

Arts

Authors

Blacks

Business

Educators

Engineers

Europeans

Explorers

Fur-traders

Indian affairs

Journalists

Legal and judicial

Mariners

Miscellaneous

Medicine

Native peoples

Office-holders

Politicians

Religious

Scientists

Surveyors

Women

Index of Identifications

Like the network of cross-references within individual biographies, this index is designed to assist readers in following their interests through the volumes of the *Dictionary*. Most of the groupings are for occupations carried out within Canada, but some have been established to help readers who approach the past from other perspectives. Women appear in one grouping, as do blacks, a reflection of the interest in their history, but they may also be found under the occupations in which they engaged. Native peoples are given by tribe. There are also lists for European ethnic groups other than British or French.

Because volumes I to IV cover a long period, from 1000 to 1800, during which occupations were not greatly specialized, the occupational categories used are general, and some cover several related activities. Nevertheless, some of the categories require explanation so that users will be better able to find biographies of particular interest. Under "agriculture" is to be found a variety of people known to have been engaged in the development of land. "Seigneurs" form a readily identifiable sub-group, but those who speculated in seigneuries will be found under "business"; "improvers" include land agents, gentlemen farmers, and colonizers. Under "settlers" are brought together those habitants or small landowners who were the first to establish themselves in an area. "Arts" includes both fine and performing arts. A distinction between fine arts and "artisans" was difficult to make in some instances; silversmiths, for example, appear under "arts" and potters under "artisans."

Although most engineers in these volumes are military officers and so will be found listed under "armed forces," it was decided to include them also under "engineers" along with civilian engineers from the early French régime and those employed by the Hudson's Bay Company. Related occupations in this period, those of surveyor, hydrographer, and cartographer, are found under "surveyors." Readers interested in architecture, town planning, or construction in general should investigate the biographies of engineers as well as those of masons ("artisans") and contractors ("business"). Those wishing to pursue the early history of education and medicine should consult, as well as "education" and "medicine," the category "religious." Under "Roman Catholics" are found the individuals involved in establishing the medical and educational institutions of French Canada. "Mariners" includes civilian captains, pilots, navigators, and privateers; naval officers appear as a sub-group of "armed forces."

Certain very large categories have been divided according to the two main political eras, the British and French régimes. Thus "office-holders" are grouped according to the régime under which they served; the sub-group entitled "colonial administrators" contains high-ranking officials: governors, lieutenant governors, administrators, and intendants. "Business" is similarly subdivided by régime. This grouping has the advantage of separating those operating within different institutional frameworks, but it also reveals interesting patterns. For instance, a New Englander trading to both Newfoundland and Canada in the late 17th century will be found under both régimes. Fur-traders, although they might have appeared under "business," are given a separate listing since they are so numerous.

The DCB/DBC attempts by its assignments to encourage research in new areas as well as familiar ones, but its selection of individuals to receive biographies reflects the survival of documentation and the areas historians have chosen to investigate. This index should not, therefore, be used for quantitative judgements about the centuries covered; it is merely a guide to what is contained in volumes I to IV.

AGRICULTURE

"Improvers"

I (1000–1700)
Alexander, William, Earl of Stirling
Alexander, Sir William
Calvert, Sir George
Colston, William

Crowne, William
Denys, Nicolas
Denys de Fronsac, Richard
Guy, John
Hayes, Edward
Hayman, Robert
Johnson, George

Kirke, Sir David
Le Coq de La Saussaye, René
Le Creux Du Breuil, Nicolas
Leigh, Charles
Mason, John
Parkhurst, Anthony
Razilly, Isaac de

Saint-Étienne de La Tour, Charles de
Stewart, James, 4th Lord Ochiltree
Vaughan, Sir William
Wynne, Edward

II (1701–1740)
Aubert de La Chesnaye, François
Gotteville de Belile, Robert-David
Le Moyne d'Iberville et d'Ardillières,
 Pierre
Le Poupet de La Boularderie, Louis-
 Simon

IV (1771–1800)
Clark, Robert
Davidson, William
Davison, George
Denson, Henry Denny
Glasier, Beamsley Perkins
Hicks, John
Higgins, David
Le Poupet de La Boularderie, Antoine
Owen, William
Tonge, Winckworth
Toosey, Philip

Seigneurs

I (1000–1700)
Amiot, dit Villeneuve, Mathieu
Aprendestiguy, Martin d'
Bazire, Charles
Becquet, Romain
Bourdon, Jean
Bourdon d'Autray, Jean
Bourdon de Dombourg, Jean-François
Byssot de La Rivière, François
Chambly, Jacques de
Couillard de Lespinay, Louis
Crevier de Saint-François, Jean
Damours de Chauffours, Mathieu
Damours de Freneuse, Mathieu
Dugué de Boisbriand, Michel-Sidrac
Duquet de La Chesnaye, Pierre
Giffard de Moncel, Robert
Godefroy de Lintot, Jean
Grandmaison, Éléonore de (Boudier
 de Beauregard; Chavigny de Ber-
 chereau; Gourdeau de Beaulieu;
 Cailhault de La Tesserie)
Hamelin de Bourgchemin et de L'Her-
 mitière, Jacques-François
Jolliet, Louis
Joybert de Soulanges et de Marson,
 Pierre de
Juchereau de Maur, Jean
Juchereau de Saint-Denis, Nicolas
Lanouguère, Thomas de
Lauson, Jean de (father)
Le Borgne de Belle-Isle, Alexandre
Le Moyne de Longueuil et de
 Châteauguay, Charles
Leneuf de La Poterie, Jacques
Leneuf Du Hérisson, Michel

Marsolet de Saint-Aignan, Nicolas
Migeon de Branssat, Jean-Baptiste
Pécaudy de Contrecœur, Antoine
Perrot, François-Marie
Peuvret Desmenu, Jean-Baptiste
Pézard de La Tousche Champlain,
 Étienne
Puiseaux, Pierre de
Saurel, Pierre de
Viennay-Pachot, François

II (1701–1740)
Amiot de Vincelotte, Charles-Joseph
Aubert de La Chesnaye, Charles
Aubert de La Chesnaye, François
Barbel, Jacques
Beauharnois de Beaumont et de
 Villechauve, Claude de
Bermen de La Martinière, Claude de
Bissot, François-Joseph
Blaise Des Bergères de Rigauville,
 Nicolas
Bouat, François-Marie
Boucher, Pierre
Chartier de Lotbinière, René-Louis
Chavigny Lachevrotière, François de
Couillard de Lespinay, Jean-Baptiste
Couillard de Lespinay, Louis
Damours de Chauffours, Louis
Damours de Clignancour, René
Denys de Vitré, Charles
Deschamps de Boishébert, Henri-Louis
Deschamps de La Bouteillerie, Jean-
 Baptiste-François
Dollier de Casson, François
Dupont de Neuville, Nicolas
Dupuy de Lisloye, Paul
Dutisné, Claude-Charles
Énault de Barbaucannes, Philippe
Fleury Deschambault, Jacques-Alexis
 de
Gaillard, Guillaume
Genaple de Bellefonds, François
Godefroy de Lintot, Michel
Godefroy de Saint-Paul, Jean-Amador
Godefroy de Tonnancour, René
Haimard, Pierre
Hazeur, François
Hertel de La Fresnière, Joseph-François
Juchereau de Maur, Paul-Augustin
Juchereau Duchesnay, Ignace
Laumet, dit de Lamothe Cadillac,
 Antoine
Le Ber, Jacques
Lechasseur, Jean
Lefebvre, Thomas
Legardeur de Repentigny, Pierre
Le Moyne de Martigny et de La Trinité,
 Jean-Baptiste
Leneuf de La Vallière de Beaubassin,
 Michel (father)
Le Picard Du Mesnil de Norrey,
 Jacques
Lessard, Étienne de

Martel, Raymond
Martel de Magos, Jean
Martin, Mathieu
Martin de Lino, Mathieu-François
Messier, dit Saint-Michel, Michel
Morel de La Durantaye, Olivier
Petit, Jean
Petit, Pierre
Pinaud, Nicolas
Poulin de Courval, Jean-Baptiste
Poulin de Francheville, François
Ramezay, Claude de
Regnard Duplessis, Georges
Robinau de Bécancour, Pierre, Baron
 de Portneuf
Rouer de Villeray et de La Cardonnière,
 Augustin
Roybon d'Allonne, Madeleine de
Saint-Étienne de La Tour, Agathe de
 (Bradstreet; Campbell)
Saint-Ours, Pierre de
Serreau de Saint-Aubin, Jean
Suève, Edmond de
Thavenet, Marguerite de (Hertel de La
 Fresnière)
Vachon de Belmont, François

III (1741–1770)
Ailleboust de Périgny, Paul d'
Bécart de Granville et de Fonville, Paul
Boucault, Nicolas-Gaspard
Boucher de Boucherville, Pierre
Boucher de La Perrière, René
Boucher de Niverville, Jean-Baptiste
Charly Saint-Ange, Louis
Chartier, Michel
Chartier de Lotbinière, Eustache
Claverie, Pierre
Daneau de Muy, Jacques-Pierre
Fleury de La Gorgendière, Joseph de
Fornel, Louis
Foucault, François
Hertel de La Fresnière, Zacharie-
 François
Hiché, Henry
Lefebvre de Bellefeuille, Jean-François
Lefebvre Duplessis Faber, François
Legardeur de Croisille, Charles
Lepage de Sainte-Claire, Louis
Lestage, Pierre de
Liénard de Beaujeu, Daniel-Hyacinthe-
 Marie
Margane de Lavaltrie, François
Migeon de La Gauchetière, Daniel
Neveu, Jean-Baptiste
Péan de Livaudière, Jacques-Hugues
Pécaudy de Contrecœur, François-
 Antoine
Poulin de Courval, Louis-Jean
Poulin de Courval Cressé, Louis-Pierre
Renaud d'Avène Des Méloizes,
 Nicolas-Marie
Rouer d'Artigny, Louis
Taschereau, Thomas-Jacques

IV (1771–1800)
Aubert de Gaspé, Ignace-Philippe
Blais, Michel
Brassard Deschenaux, Joseph
Bruyères, John
Charest, Étienne
Chartier de Lotbinière, Michel,
    Marquis de Lotbinière
Chaussegros de Léry, Gaspard-Joseph
Christie, Gabriel
Cugnet, François-Joseph
Cuthbert, James
Deguire, *dit* Desrosiers, Joseph
Delezenne, Ignace-François
Du Calvet, Pierre
Estèbe, Guillaume
Fraser, Alexander
Godefroy de Tonnancour, Charles-
    Antoine
Godefroy de Tonnancour, Louis-
    Joseph
Goguet, Denis
Gugy, Conrad
Harrison, Edward
Hart, Aaron
Howard, Joseph
Jordan, Jacob

Lefebvre de Bellefeuille, François
Legardeur de Croisille et de Montesson,
    Joseph-Michel
Le Moyne de Longueuil, Paul-Joseph
Payen de Noyan et de Chavoy, Pierre-
    Jacques
Pécaudy de Contrecœur, Claude-Pierre
Perthuis, Joseph
Ramezay, Louise de
Sabrevois de Bleury, Clément de
Simonnet, François
Tarieu de La Naudière, Charles-
    François

Settlers

I (1000–1700)
Crout, Henry
Drouin, Robert
Foucher
Gadoys, Pierre
Guy, Nicholas
Hébert, Louis
Melanson, Charles
Pearson, Bartholemew
Prévost, Martin

II (1701–1740)
Blanchard, Guillaume
Bourg, Abraham
Bourgeois, Jacques
Brossard, Jean-François
Chaudillon, Antoine
Couture, Guillaume
Cuillerier, René
Dandonneau, *dit* Lajeunesse, Pierre
Haché-Gallant, Michel
Lorit, *dit* Gargot, François
Papineau, *dit* Montigny, Samuel
Roy, *dit* Châtellerault, Michel
Terriot, Pierre
Tibaudeau, Pierre
Trotain, *dit* Saint-Seürin, François

III (1741–1770)
Brossard, *dit* Beausoleil, Joseph
Denison, Robert
Giard, Antoine
Mercier, Jean-François

IV (1771–1800)
Jeanson, Guillaume
Le Blanc, Pierre
Leblanc, *dit* Le Maigre, Joseph

ARMED FORCES

American

Army: officers

IV (1771–1800)
McCarty, Richard
Montgomery, Richard
Pélissier, Christophe

British

Army: officers

I (1000–1700)
Crowne, William
Ferrar, Constance
Forrester, Andrew
Leverett, John
Walker, Richard

II (1701–1740)
Armstrong, Lawrence
Caulfeild, Thomas
Doucett, John
Gibsone, Sir John
Gledhill, Samuel
Handasyde, Thomas
Hill, John
Latham, Robert
Lloyd, Thomas

Moody, John
Nicholson, Francis
Richards, Michael
Roope, John
Vane, George
Vetch, Samuel
Washington, John
Williams, John
Wroth, Robert

III (1741–1770)
Aldridge, Christopher (father)
Aldridge, Christopher (son)
Bastide, John Henry
Burton, Ralph
Campbell, Donald
Cope, Henry
Cosby, Alexander
DeLaune, William
Elliot, Robert
Eyre, William
Forbes, John
Gorrell, James
Haldimand, Peter Frederick
Hamilton, Otho
Handfield, John
Hay, Lord Charles
Heron, Patrick
Hopson, Peregrine Thomas
Jamet, John

Lawrence, Charles
Mascarene, Paul
Murray, Alexander
Philipps, Erasmus James
Philipps, Richard
Rollo, Andrew, 5th Baron Rollo
Robertson, Charles
Scott, George
Sutherland, Patrick
Whitmore, Edward
Wilmot, Montagu
Wolfe, James

IV (1771–1800)
Abercrombie, James
Abercromby, James
Amherst, Jeffery, 1st Baron Amherst
Bradstreet, John
Brewse, John
Bruce, Robert George
Bruyères, John
Burgoyne, John
Butler, John (d. 1796)
Butler, Walter
Campbell, John
Christie, Gabriel
Claus, Christian Daniel
Cornwallis, Edward
Cox, Nicholas
Cramahé, Hector Theophilus

33

ARMED FORCES

Cuthbert, James
Danks, Benoni
De Peyster, Abraham
Fraser, Alexander
Gage, Thomas
Gerrish, Joseph
Gladwin, Henry
Glasier, Beamsley Perkins
Goreham, Joseph
Gridley, Richard
Gugy, Conrad
Haldimand, Sir Frederick
Hamilton, Henry
Haviland, William
Hay, Jehu
Hope, Henry
Irving, Paulus Æmilius
Jadis, Charles Newland Godfrey
Johnson, Guy
Knox, John
Legge, Francis
Mackellar, Patrick
Maclean, Allan
McLean, Francis
McLean, Neil
MacLeod, Normand
Mills, Sir Thomas
Monckton, Robert
Montgomery, Richard
Montgomery, William
Montresor, John
Morris, Charles
Munro, John
Murray, James
Parr, John
Patterson, Walter
Peachey, James
Pringle, Robert
Roberts, Benjamin
Robinson, Christopher
Rogers, Robert
Ross, John
St Leger, Barrimore Matthew
Shaw, William
Singleton, George
Studholme, Gilfred
Tonge, Winckworth
Wilkins, John
Willard, Abijah
Williams, Griffith
Williamson, George
Winslow, John

Army: soldiers

IV (1771–1800)
Busby, Thomas
Henry, Anthony
Jones, John
Munro, John
Peters, Joseph
Peters, Thomas
Scott, Joseph

Militia: officers

I (1000–1700)
Phips, Sir William

II (1701–1740)
Alden, John
Church, Benjamin
Collins, John
Davis, Silvanus
Goffe, Edmond
Hilton, Winthrop
Hobby, Sir Charles
Livingston, John
March, John
Savage, Thomas
Schuyler, Peter
Vaughan, George
Walley, John

III (1741–1770)
Cobb, Silvanus
Couagne, René de
Denison, Robert
Dudley, William
Gervaise, Louis
Goldthwait, Benjamin
Gorham, John
Gyles, John
Hale, Robert
How, Edward
Little, Otis
Lottridge, John
Monk, James
Moulton, Jeremiah
Noble, Arthur
Pepperrell, Sir William
Schuyler, Johannes
Schuyler, Peter
Stobo, Robert
Vaughan, William
Waldo, Samuel
Winniett, William

IV (1771–1800)
Adhémar, Jean-Baptiste-Amable
Baby, *dit* Dupéront, Jacques
Blais, Michel
Butler, John (d. 1791)
Butler, John (d. 1796)
Callbeck, Phillips
Danks, Benoni
Denson, Henry Denny
Doggett, John
Doucet, Pierre
Fleury Deschambault, Joseph
Gerrish, Benjamin
Godefroy de Tonnancour, Louis-
    Joseph
Guillot, *dit* Larose, François
Harrison, Edward
Hay, Jehu
Johnston, Alexander

Johnstone, James
Knaut, Philip Augustus
Le Comte Dupré, Georges-Hippolyte
McKee, Alexander
Picard, Louis-Alexandre
Ritchie, John
Shaw, William
Trottier Dufy Desauniers, Thomas-
    Ignace

Navy: officers

I (1000–1700)
Argall, Sir Samuel
Berry, Sir John
Best, George
Button, Sir Thomas
Lydall, William

II (1701–1740)
Bouler, Robert
Bridges, Timothy
Crowe, Josias
Fotherby, Charles
Graydon, John
Kempthorne, Thomas
Leake, Sir John
Martin, George
Robinson, Sir Robert
Smart, Thomas
Taylour, Joseph
Trevanion, Sir Nicholas
Walker, Sir Hovenden
Whetstone, Sir William

III (1741–1770)
Bonfoy, Hugh
Boscawen, Edward
Byng, John
Clinton, George
Colvill, Alexander, 7th Baron Colvill
Dorrill, Richard
Durell, Philip
Falkingham, Edward
Holmes, Charles
Latouche MacCarthy, Charles
Lee, Fitzroy Henry
Lucas, Francis
Middleton, Christopher
Norris, Sir John
Rankin, John
Rous, John
Short, Richard
Swanton, Robert
Townsend, Isaac
Warren, Sir Peter
Watson, Charles
Webb, James

IV (1771–1800)
Arbuthnot, Mariot
Byron, John
Campbell, Lord William

Clerke, Charles
Collier, Sir George
Cook, James
Dixon, George
Douglas, Sir Charles
Drake, Francis William
Duncan, Charles
Edwards, Richard
Hardy, Sir Charles
King, James
Loring, Joshua
Osborn, Henry
Owen, William
Palliser, Sir Hugh
Saunders, Sir Charles
Shuldham, Molyneux, 1st Baron
    Shuldham
Vancouver, George

Danish

Navy: officers

I (1000–1700)
Munk, Jens Eriksen

Dutch

Navy: officers

I (1000–1700)
Aernoutsz, Juriaen

French

Army: officers

I (1000–1700)
Andigné de Grandfontaine, Hector d'
Basset Du Tartre, Vincent
Bizard, Jacques
Boucher de Grandpré, Lambert
Boullé, Eustache
Bourdon d'Autray, Jacques
Bourdon de Romainville, Jean
Bréhaut Delisle, Achille de
Chambly, Jacques de
Closse, Raphaël-Lambert
Crisafy, Thomas
Damours de Chauffours, Mathieu
Daumont de Saint-Lusson, Simon-
    François
Dollard Des Ormeaux, Adam
Dubois de Cocreaumont et de Saint-
    Maurice, Jean-Baptiste
Dugué de Boisbriand, Michel-Sidrac
Dupuy, Zacharie
Duret de Chevry de La Boulaye,
    Charles
Gaultier de Comporté, Philippe
Gaultier de Varennes, René

Godet Des Maretz, Claude de
Joybert de Soulanges et de Marson,
    Pierre de
La Frenaye de Brucy, Antoine de
La Motte de Lucière, Dominique
Lamotte de Saint-Paul, Pierre
Lanouguère, Thomas de
La Tourasse, Charles
Le Moyne de Bienville, François
Le Moyne de Châteauguay, Louis
Le Moyne de Sainte-Hélène, Jacques
Mareuil, Jacques de
Mius d'Entremont, Philippe, Baron de
    Pobomcoup
Pécaudy de Contrecœur, Antoine
Peronne de Mazé, Louis
Picoté de Belestre, Pierre
Pollet de La Combe-Pocatière,
    François
Prouville, Alexandre de, Marquis de
    Tracy
Randin, Hugues
Renaud d'Avène de Desmeloizes,
    François-Marie
Robinau de Villebon, Joseph
Saurel, Pierre de
Testard de La Forest, Gabriel
Troyes, Pierre de, known as Chevalier
    de Troyes

II (1701–1740)
Abbadie de Saint-Castin, Bernard-
    Anselme d'
Abbadie de Saint-Castin, Jean-Vincent
    d', Baron de Saint-Castin
Agrain, Jean-Antoine d', Comte
    d'Agrain
Ailleboust d'Argenteuil, Pierre d'
Ailleboust de Manthet, Nicolas d'
Ailleboust Des Muceaux, Jean-
    Baptiste d'
Allard de Sainte-Marie, Jean-Joseph d'
Aloigny, Charles-Henri d', Marquis de
    La Groye
Auger de Subercase, Daniel d'
Baugy, Louis-Henri de, known as
    Chevalier de Baugy
Berthier, Isaac (Alexandre)
Bissot de Vinsenne, François-Marie
Bissot de Vinsenne, Jean-Baptiste
Blaise Des Bergères de Rigauville,
    Nicolas
Blaise Des Bergères de Rigauville,
    Raymond
Boucher, Pierre
Bouillet de La Chassaigne, Jean
Brisay de Denonville, Jacques-René
    de, Marquis de Denonville
Callière, Louis-Hector de
Catalogne, Joseph de
Catalogne, Gédéon (de)
Céloron de Blainville, Jean-Baptiste
Chabert de Joncaire, Louis-Thomas

Chaumont, Alexandre de
Clément Du Vuault de Valrennes,
    Philippe
Couagne, Jean-Baptiste de
Couillard de Lespinay, Jean-Baptiste
Coulon de Villiers, Nicolas-Antoine
Crisafy, Antoine de, Marquis de
    Crisafy
Daneau de Muy, Nicolas
Dauphin de La Forest, François
Denys de Bonaventure, Simon-Pierre
Deschamps de Boishébert, Henri-Louis
Des Friches de Meneval, Louis-
    Alexandre
Desjordy de Cabanac, Joseph
Desjordy Moreau de Cabanac,
    François
Dufrost de La Jemerais, Christophe
Dugué de Boisbriand, Pierre
Du Pont de Renon, Michel
Du Pont Duvivier, François
Dupuy de Lisloye, Paul
Dutisné, Claude-Charles
Espiet de Pensens, Jacques d'
Estienne Du Bourgué de Clérin,
    Denis d'
Gannes de Falaise, Louis de
Godefroy de Lintot, Michel
Gotteville de Belile, Robert-David
Greysolon Dulhut, Daniel
Groston de Saint-Ange, Robert
Guillouet d'Orvilliers, Claude
Guillouet d'Orvilliers, Rémy
Hertel de La Fresnière, Joseph-François
Hertel de Moncours, Pierre
Hertel de Rouville, Jean-Baptiste
Jarret de Verchères, Pierre
Joannès de Chacornacle
Juchereau de La Ferté, Denis-Joseph
Juchereau de Saint-Denys, Charles
La Corne de Chaptes, Jean-Louis de
La Porte de Louvigny, Louis de
Laumet, *dit* de Lamothe Cadillac,
    Antoine
Le Gardeur de Courtemanche,
    Augustin
Legardeur de Repentigny, Jean-
    Baptiste
Legardeur de Repentigny, Pierre
Legardeur de Saint-Pierre, Jean-Paul
Legardeur de Tilly, Pierre-Noël
Le Marchand de Lignery, Constant
Le Moyne de Longueuil, Charles,
    Baron de Longueuil
Le Moyne de Maricourt, Paul
Le Moyne de Martigny et de La Trinité,
    Jean-Baptiste
Le Moyne d'Iberville et d'Ardillières,
    Pierre
Leneuf de La Vallière de Beaubassin,
    Michel (father)
Leneuf de La Vallière de Beaubassin,
    Michel (son)

35

Le Picard Du Mesnil de Norrey,
  Jacques
Le Poupet de La Boularderie, Louis-
  Simon
L'Espérance, Charles-Léopold-
  Ébérard
Lespinay, Jean-Michel de
Lestringant de Saint-Martin,
  Alexandre-Joseph
Levasseur de Neré, Jacques
Le Verrier de Rousson, François
L'Hermitte, Jacques
Liette, Pierre-Charles de
Lom d'Arce de Lahontan, Louis-
  Armand de, Baron de Lahontan
Lorimier de La Rivière, Guillaume de
Maleray de Noiré de La Mollerie,
  Jacques
Margane de Batilly, François-Marie
Mariauchau d'Esgly, François
Mariauchau d'Esgly, François-Louis
Marin de La Malgue, Charles-Paul
Monbeton de Brouillan, Jacques-
  François de
Monic, Joseph de
Morel de La Durantaye, Olivier
Pastour de Costebelle, Philippe
Payen de Noyan, Pierre
Petit de Levilliers, Charles
Philippe de Hautmesnil de Mandeville,
  François
Piot de Langloiserie, Charles-Gaspard
Provost, François
Ramezay, Claude de
Renaud Dubuisson, Jacques-Charles
Rigaud de Vaudreuil, Philippe de,
  Marquis de Vaudreuil
Robinau de Bécancour, Pierre, Baron
  de Portneuf
Robinau de Neuvillette, Daniel
Robinau de Portneuf, René
Robutel de La Noue, Zacharie
Sabrevois, Jacques-Charles de
Saint-Étienne de La Tour, Charles de
Saint-Ours, Pierre de
Suève, Edmond de
Testard de Montigny, Jacques
Tonty, Alphonse (de), Baron de Paludy
Tonty, Henri (de)
Véniard de Bourgmond, Étienne de
Verville, Jean-François de
Villedonné, Étienne de
Villieu, Claude-Sébastien de
You de La Découverte, Pierre

III (1741–1770)
Abbadie de Saint-Castin, Joseph d',
  Baron de Saint-Castin
Adhémar de Lantagnac, Gaspard
Ailleboust, Charles-Joseph d'
Ailleboust de Périgny, Paul d'
Alquier de Servian, Jean d'
Arnaud, Jean-Charles d'

Aubert de La Chesnaye, Louis
Bécart de Granville et de Fonville, Paul
Bégon de La Cour, Claude-Michel
Bermen de La Martinière, Claude-
  Antoine de
Bonne de Missègle, Louis de
Boucher, Pierre-Jérôme
Boucher de Boucherville, Pierre
Boucher de La Perrière, René
Boucher de Niverville, Jean-Baptiste
Bourlamaque, François-Charles de
Cailly, François-Joseph
Céloron de Blainville, Pierre-Joseph
Chabert de Joncaire, Philippe-Thomas
Chassin de Thierry, François-Nicolas
  de
Chaussegros de Léry, Gaspard-Joseph
Coulon de Villiers, Louis
Coulon de Villiers, Nicolas-Antoine
Coulon de Villiers de Jumonville,
  Joseph
Daneau de Muy, Jacques-Pierre
Dazemard de Lusignan, Paul-Louis
Dejordy de Villebon, Charles-René
Denys de Bonnaventure, Claude-
  Élisabeth
Denys de La Ronde, Louis
Dieskau, Jean-Armand, Baron de
  Dieskau
Dubois Berthelot de Beaucours, Josué
Franquet, Louis
Galiffet de Caffin, François de
Gannes de Falaise, Michel de
Gaultier de La Vérendrye, Louis-
  Joseph
Gaultier de La Vérendrye de Boumois,
  Pierre
Gaultier de Varennes, Jacques-René
Gaultier de Varennes et de La Véren-
  drye, Pierre
Goutin, François-Marie de
Grillot de Poilly, François-Claude-
  Victor
Hertel de La Fresnière, Zacharie-
  François
Hertel de Saint-François, Étienne
Juchereau de Saint-Denis, Louis
La Corne, Louis de, known as
  Chevalier de La Corne
La Corne Dubreuil, François-Josué de
Le Coutre de Bourville, François
Lefebvre Duplessis Faber, François
Legardeur de Beauvais, René
Legardeur de Croisille, Charles
Legardeur de Saint-Pierre, Jacques
Le Marchand de Lignery, François-
  Marie
Le Moyne de Bienville, Jean-Baptiste
Le Moyne de Longueuil, Charles,
  Baron de Longueuil
Levrault de Langis Montegron, Jean-
  Baptiste
Liénard de Beaujeu, Daniel-Hyacinthe-
  Marie

Liénard de Beaujeu, Louis
Lombard de Combles, Jean-Claude-
  Henri de
Lorimier de La Rivière, Claude-Nicolas
  de
Marin de La Malgue, Paul
Mascle de Saint-Julhien, Jean
Migeon de La Gauchetière, Daniel
Monbeton de Brouillan, dit Saint-
  Ovide, Joseph de
Montcalm, Louis-Joseph de, Marquis
  de Montcalm
Noyelles de Fleurimont, Nicolas-
  Joseph de
Payen de Noyan, Pierre-Benoît
Péan de Livaudière, Jacques-Hugues
Pécaudy de Contrecœur, François-
  Antoine
Pouchot, Pierre
Regnard Duplessis de Morampont,
  Charles-Denis
Renaud d'Avène Des Méloizes,
  Nicolas-Marie
Renaud Dubuisson, Louis-Jacques-
  Charles
Rigaud de Vaudreuil, Joseph-
  Hyacinthe de
Robinau de Portneuf, Pierre
Rouer de Villeray, Benjamin
Saint-Ours, François-Xavier de
Saint-Ours Deschaillons, Jean-Baptiste
  de
Senezergues de La Rodde, Étienne-
  Guillaume de
Tarride Duhaget, Robert
Tisserant de Moncharvaux, Jean-
  Baptiste-François
Tonty de Liette, Charles-Henri-Joseph
  de
Verrier, Étienne

IV (1771–1800)
Ailleboust de La Madeleine, François-
  Jean-Daniel d'
Aleyrac, Jean-Baptiste d'
Allard de Sainte-Marie, Philippe-
  Joseph d'
Angeac, François-Gabriel d'
Aubert de Gaspé, Ignace-Philippe
Benoist, Antoine-Gabriel-François
Bernier, Benoît-François
Bourdon de Dombourg, Jean-François
Chabert de Joncaire de Clausonne,
  Daniel-Marie
Chartier de Lotbinière, Michel,
  Marquis de Lotbinière
Chaussegros de Léry, Gaspard-Joseph
Couagne, Michel de
Coulon de Villiers, François
Dagneau Douville, Alexandre
Denis de Saint-Simon, Antoine-Charles
Desandrouins, Jean-Nicolas

36

Deschamps de Boishébert et de Raffe-
  tot, Charles
Douglas, François-Prosper, Chevalier
  de Douglas
Druillon de Macé, Pierre-Jacques
Dumas, Jean-Daniel
Du Pont Duchambon, Louis
Du Pont Duchambon de Vergor, Louis
Du Pont Duvivier, François
Du Pont Duvivier, Joseph
Godefroy de Linctot, Daniel-Maurice
Gohin, Pierre-André, Comte de
  Montreuil
Groston de Saint-Ange et de Bellerive,
  Louis
Hertel de Saint-François, Joseph-
  Hippolyte
Jacau de Fiedmont, Louis-Thomas
Johnstone, James, known as Chevalier
  de Johnstone
La Corne, Luc de
Le Courtois de Surlaville, Michel
Legardeur de Croisille et de Montesson,
  Joseph-Michel
Legardeur de Repentigny, Louis
Legardeur de Repentigny, Pierre-Jean-
  Baptiste-François-Xavier
Le Mercier, François-Marc-Antoine
Le Moyne de Longueuil, Paul-Joseph
Le Poupet de la Boularderie, Antoine
L'Espérance, Charles-Gabriel-
  Sébastien de, Baron de L'Espérance
Le Verrier de Rousson, Louis
Lévis, François de, Duc de Lévis
Marin de La Malgue, Joseph
Maurès de Malartic, Anne-Joseph-
  Hippolyte de, Comte de Malartic
Mouet de Langlade, Charles-Michel
Payen de Noyan et de Chavoy, Pierre-
  Jacques
Péan, Michel-Jean-Hugues
Pécaudy de Contrecœur, Claude-Pierre
Picoté de Belestre, François-Marie
Potot de Montbeillard, Fiacre-François
Preissac de Bonneau, Louis de
Ramezay, Jean-Baptiste-Nicolas-Roch
  de
Raymond, Jean-Louis de, Comte de
  Raymond
Rigaud de Vaudreuil, François-Pierre
  de
Rigaud de Vaudreuil de Cavagnial,
  Pierre de, Marquis de Vaudreuil
Rousseau de Villejouin, Gabriel
Tarieu de La Naudière, Charles-
  François
Testard de Montigny, Jean-Baptiste-
  Philippe

Army: soldiers

I (1000–1700)
Brigeac, Claude de

Godet, Rolland
Hertel de La Fresnière, Jacques
Malapart, André
Olivier, *dit* Le Picard, Marc-Antoine
Peuvret Demesnu, Jean-Baptiste
Richard, *dit* Lafleur, Guillaume

II (1701–1740)
Ameau, *dit* Saint-Séverin, Séverin
Barbel, Jacques
Boulduc, Louis
Chevalier, *dit* Beauchêne, Robert
Horné, *dit* Laneuville, Jacques de
Legardeur de Repentigny, Jean-
  Baptiste
Lenoir, *dit* Rolland, François
Martel de Magos, Jean
Normandin, Daniel
Papineau, *dit* Montigny, Samuel
Roy, *dit* Châtellerault, Michel
Sageau, Mathieu
Senet, *dit* Laliberté, Nicolas
Serreau de Saint-Aubin, Jean
Trotain, *dit* Saint-Seürin, François

III (1741–1770)
Corolère, Jean
Guillet de Chaumont, Nicolas-Auguste
Guyart de Fleury, Jean-Baptiste
Havard de Beaufort, François-Charles,
  known as L'Avocat
Malepart de Grand Maison, *dit*
  Beaucour, Paul
Noyon, Jacques de

IV (1771–1800)
Gaultier Du Tremblay, François
Guillot, *dit* Larose, François
Jeanson, Guillaume

Militia: officers

II (1701–1740)
Amiot de Vincelotte, Charles-Joseph
Charly Saint-Ange, Jean-Baptiste
Chartier de Lotbinière, René-Louis
Couture, Guillaume
Dizy, *dit* Montplaisir, Michel-Ignace
Godefroy de Saint-Paul, Jean-Amador
Godefroy de Vieuxpont, Joseph
Guillimin, Charles
Juchereau Duchesnay, Ignace
Le Ber, Jacques
Legardeur de Repentigny, Jean-
  Baptiste
Messier, *dit* Saint-Michel, Michel
Perrot de Rizy, Pierre
Véron de Grandmesnil, Étienne

III (1741–1770)
Bazil, Louis
Boucher de Montbrun, Jean
Constantin, Pierre

Couagne, René de
Dagneau Douville de Quindre, Louis-
  Césaire
Dizy de Montplaisir, Pierre
Gastineau Duplessis, Jean-Baptiste
Gervaise, Louis
Giard, Antoine
Guy, Pierre
Jeanneau, Étienne
Le Comte Dupré, Jean-Baptiste
Lestage, Pierre de
Morpain, Pierre
Perrault, Paul
Riverin, Joseph
Taché, Jean

IV (1771–1800)
Blais, Michel
Charest, Étienne
Cirier, Antoine
Deguire, *dit* Desrosiers, Joseph
Dugas, Joseph
Gamelin, Ignace
Gamelin, Pierre-Joseph
Godin, *dit* Bellefontaine, *dit*
  Beauséjour, Joseph
Trottier Dufy Desauniers, Thomas-
  Ignace

Navy: officers

I (1000–1700)
Chauvin de Tonnetuit, Pierre de
Dauphin de Montorgueil
Gargot de La Rochette, Nicolas
Gravé Du Pont, François
Gravé Du Pont, Robert
Hamelin de Bourgchemin et de L'Her-
  mitière, Jacques-François
La Poippe, Sieur de
Razilly, Isaac de

II (1701–1740)
Beauharnois de Beaumont et de
  Villechauve, Claude de
Forant, Isaac-Louis de
Gotteville de Belile, Robert-David
Le Moyne de Serigny et de Loire,
  Joseph
Leneuf de La Vallière de Beaubassin,
  Alexandre
Saint-Clair, Pierre de
Villieu, Sébastien de

III (1741–1770)
Barrin de La Galissonière, Roland-
  Michel, Marquis de La Galissonière
Beauharnois de La Boische, Charles de,
  Marquis de Beauharnois
Beaussier de Lisle, Louis-Joseph
Boschenry de Drucour, Augustin de
Cahideuc, Emmanuel-Auguste de,
  Comte Dubois de La Motte

ARTISANS

Claverie, Pierre
Denys de La Ronde, Louis
Des Herbiers de La Ralière, Charles
Estourmel, Constantin-Louis d'
Kanon, Jacques
La Maisonfort Du Boisdecourt,
  Alexandre de, Marquis de
  La Maisonfort
La Rochefoucauld de Roye, Jean-
  Baptiste-Louis-Frédéric de, Marquis
  de Roucy, Duc d'Anville
Legardeur de Tilly, Jean-Baptiste
Le Prévost Duquesnel, Jean-Baptiste-
  Louis

Morpain, Pierre
Poulin de Courval, François-Louis
Rigaud de Vaudreuil, Louis-Philippe
  de, Marquis de Vaudreuil
Sallaberry, Michel de
Taffanel de La Jonquière, Jacques-
  Pierre de, Marquis de La Jonquière
Testu de La Richardière, Richard

IV (1771–1800)
Arsac de Ternay, Charles-Henri-
  Louis d'
Duquesne de Menneville, Ange,
  Marquis Duquesne

Galaup, Jean-François de, Comte de
  Lapérouse
Pellegrin, Gabriel
Vauquelin, Jean

Spanish

Navy: officers

IV (1771–1800)
Bodega y Quadra, Juan Francisco de la
Martínez Fernández y Martínez de la
  Sierra, Esteban José
Pérez Hernández, Juan Josef

ARTISANS

I (1000–1700)
Baillif, Claude
Bailly, *dit* Lafleur, François
Boivin, François
Cloutier, Zacharie
Couillard de Lespinay, Guillaume
Duval, Jean
Echevete, Matias de
Guyon Du Buisson, Jean (father)
Lauson, Gilles
Lemire, Jean
Levasseur, *dit* Lavigne, Jean
Levasseur, *dit* L'Espérance, Pierre
Miville, Pierre, known as Le Suisse
Pelletier, Didace
Prud'homme, Louis

II (1701–1740)
Baudry, *dit* Des Butes, Guillaume
Brossard, Urbain
Chaboulié, Charles
Couture, Guillaume
Dubreuil, Jean-Étienne
Duprac, Jean-Robert
Fézeret, René
Gadois, Pierre
Genaple de Bellefonds, François
Larue, Guillaume de
Latham, Robert
Leclerc, Jean-Baptiste

Lefebvre, *dit* Laciseraye, Michel
Le Rouge, Jean
Mallet, Denis
Martin, Mathieu
Ménage, Pierre
Paillard, Léonard, known as
  Le Poitevin
Raimbault, Pierre
Soullard, Jean
Vachon, Paul (father)

III (1741–1770)
Amiot, Jean-Baptiste (d. after 1763)
Baudry, *dit* Saint-Martin, Jean-Baptiste
Bushell, John
Campot, Jacques
Cheval, *dit* Saint-Jacques, and *dit*
  Chevalier, Jacques-Joseph
Claparède, Jean
Corbin, David
Coron, Charles-François
Cotton, Michel
Dasilva, *dit* Portugais, Nicolas
Deguise, *dit* Flamand, Girard-
  Guillaume
Durocher, Joseph
Green, Bartholomew
Jourdain, *dit* Labrosse, Paul-Raymond
Lozeau, Jean-Baptiste
Lupien, *dit* Baron, Pierre

Maillou, *dit* Desmoulins, Jean-Baptiste
Mercier, Jean-François
Moreau, Edme
Pagé, *dit* Carcy, Jacques
Pettrequin, Jean

IV (1771–1800)
Brown, William
Cirier, Antoine
Corbin, André
Cotton, Barthélemy
Deguise, *dit* Flamand, Jacques
Devau, *dit* Retor, Claude
Fletcher, Robert
Foureur, *dit* Champagne, Louis
Gilmore, Thomas
Henry, Anthony
Huppé, *dit* Lagroix, Joseph
Jacquet, François
Joe
Lewis, William
Mesplet, Fleury
Moore, William
Neilson, Samuel
Renaud, *dit* Cannard, Pierre
Roy, Louis
Schindler, Joseph
Souste, André
Sower, Christopher
Tessier, *dit* Lavigne, Paul

ARTS

I (1000–1700)
Dangé, François
François, Claude, known as Brother
  Luc
Guyon, Jean

Jolliet, Louis
Mareuil, Jacques de
Olivier, *dit* Le Picard, Marc-Antoine
Pommier, Hugues
Villain, Jean-Baptiste
White, John

II (1701–1740)
Baudry, *dit* Des Butes, Guillaume
Bergier, Jean
Chaboulié, Charles
Chauchetière, Claude

Dessailliant, *dit* Richeterre, Michel
Drué, Juconde
Jacquiés, *dit* Leblond, Jean
Le Ber, Pierre
Leblond de Latour, Jacques
Levasseur, Michel
Levasseur, Noël
Mallet, Denis
Martin, Charles-Amador
Maufils, Marie-Madeleine, *dite* de
Saint-Louis
Payne, Samuel
Soullard, Jean

III (1741–1770)
Bolvin, Gilles
Coron, Charles-François

Cotton, Michel
Deschevery, *dit* Maisonbasse, Jean-
Baptiste
Gadois, *dit* Mauger, Jacques
Jourdain, *dit* Labrosse, Paul-Raymond
Lambert, *dit* Saint-Paul, Paul
Landron, Jean-François
Levasseur, Pierre-Noël
Malepart de Grand Maison, *dit*
Beaucour, Paul
Pagé, *dit* Carcy, Jacques
Paradis, Roland
Resche, Pierre-Joseph
Short, Richard
Terroux, Jacques
Vézina, Charles

IV (1771–1800)
Aide-Créquy, Jean-Antoine
Alline, Henry
Cirier, Antoine
Delezenne, Ignace-François
Foureur, *dit* Champagne, Louis
Levasseur, François-Noël
Levasseur, *dit* Delor, Jean-Baptiste-
Antoine
Lyon, James
Malepart de Beaucourt, François
Moore, William
Peachy, James
Picard, Louis-Alexandre
Schindler, Joseph
Varin, *dit* La Pistole, Jacques
Webber, John

AUTHORS

I (1000–1700)
Best, George
Fisher, Richard
Gorst, Thomas
Lescarbot, Marc
Roberts, Lewis
Sagard, Gabriel
Thevet, André

II (1701–1740)
Chevalier, *dit* Beauchêne, Robert
Dièreville
Dollier de Casson, François
Hennepin, Louis
Jérémie, *dit* Lamontagne, Nicolas
Juchereau de La Ferté, Jeanne-
Françoise, *dite* de Saint-Ignace
Lebeau, Claude
Le Roy de La Potherie, *dit* Bacqueville
de La Potherie, Claude-Charles
Lom d'Arce de Lahontan, Louis-
Armand de, Baron de Lahontan
Morin, Marie

Williams, John (1664–1729)
Yonge, James

III (1741–1770)
Charlevoix, Pierre-François-Xavier de
Daneau de Muy, Charlotte, *dite* de
Sainte-Hélène
Gyles, John
Lafitau, Joseph-François
Pouchot, Pierre
Récher, Jean-Félix
Regnard Duplessis, Marie-Andrée, *dite*
de Sainte-Hélène
Rocbert de La Morandière, Marie-
Élisabeth (Bégon de La Cour)

IV (1771–1800)
Alline, Henry
Aumasson de Courville, Louis-Léonard
Badeaux, Jean-Baptiste
Burgoyne, John
Crespel, Emmanuel
Gilmore, Thomas

Guichart, Vincent-Fleuri
Hearne, Samuel
Jautard, Valentin
Johnstone, James, known as Chevalier
de Johnstone
Kalm, Pehr
Knox, John
La Brosse, Jean-Baptiste de
Latour, Bertrand de
Lewis, William
Magon de Terlaye, François-Auguste
Marrant, John
Mathevet, Jean-Claude
Moore, Frances (Brooke)
Moore, William
Ogilvie, John
Pichon, Thomas
Potier, Pierre-Philippe
Rogers, Robert
Sanguinet, Simon
Smith, William
Umfreville, Edward
Vienne, François-Joseph de
Williams, Griffith

BLACKS

I (1000–1700)
Le Jeune, Olivier

II (1701–1740)
Marie-Joseph-Angélique

III (1741–1770)
Léveillé, Mathieu

IV (1771–1800)
Joe
Marrant, John
Peters, Thomas
York, Jack

BUSINESS

British Régime

I (1000–1700)
Cruse, Thomas
Downing, John
Downing, William
Eliot, Hugh
Hinton, William
Hore, Richard
Jay, John
Leigh, Charles
Martin, Christopher
Parkhurst, Anthony
Rhoades, John
Roberts, Lewis
Rowley, Thomas
Sedgwick, Robert
Treworgie, John
Whitbourne, Sir Richard
Willoughby, Thomas

II (1701–1740)
Arnold, William
Campbell, Colin
Collins, John
Cumings, Archibald
Gill, Michael
Gledhill, Samuel
Holdsworth, Arthur
Pepperrell, William
Skeffington, George

III (1741–1770)
Adams, John
Bayne, Daniel
Cope, Henry
Erhardt, John Christian
Gautier, *dit* Bellair, Joseph-Nicolas
Gorham, John
Hale, Robert
Keen, William
Kilby, Thomas
Leblanc, *dit* Le Maigre, Joseph
Lucas, Francis
Pepperrell, Sir William
Price, Benjamin
Saul, Thomas
Taverner, William
Waldo, Samuel
Winniett, William

IV (1771–1800)
Adhémar, Jean-Baptiste-Amable
Augé, Étienne
Aylwin, Thomas
Beatson, Patrick
Besnard, *dit* Carignant, Jean-Louis
Bourdages, Raymond

Bradstreet, John
Busby, Thomas
Butler, John (d. 1791)
Campion, Étienne-Charles
Clark, Robert
Coghlan, Jeremiah
Cotté, Gabriel
Cuthbert, James
Darby, Nicholas
Davidson, William
Davison, George
Day, John
Delezenne, Ignace-François
Doggett, John
Doucet, Pierre
Du Calvet, Pierre
Dumas Saint-Martin, Jean
Ellice, Robert
Ermatinger, Lawrence
Fillis, John
Fletcher, Robert
Fortier, Michel
Francklin, Michael
Frobisher, Benjamin
Gamelin, Pierre-Joseph
Gerrish, Benjamin
Gerrish, Joseph
Godefroy de Tonnancour, Louis-
  Joseph
Godin, *dit* Bellefontaine, *dit*
  Beauséjour, Joseph
Green, Benjamin
Gridley, Richard
Guillot, *dit* Larose, François
Harrison, Edward
Hart, Aaron
Hay, Charles
Henry, Anthony
Higgins, David
Howard, Joseph
Jacobs, Samuel
Jadis, Charles Newland Godfrey
Johnston, James
Jordan, Jacob
Knaut, Philip Augustus
Landry, Alexis
Le Comte Dupré, Georges-Hippolyte
Lemoine Despins, Jacques-Joseph
Lévesque, François
Macaulay, Robert
McLane, David
McLean, Neil
MacLeod, Normand
Marston, Benjamin
Mauger, Joshua
Mesplet, Fleury
Mounier, Jean-Mathieu
Munro, John

Oakes, Forrest
Orillat, Jean
Pélissier, Christophe
Perrault, Jacques
Renaud, Jean
Ritchie, John
Robichaux, Louis
Salter, Malachy
Sanguinet, Simon
Schindler, Joseph
Scott, Joseph
Singleton, George
Slade, John
Solomons, Lucius Levy
Sterling, James
Walker, Thomas
Wenman, Richard
Zouberbuhler, Sebastian

French Régime

I (1000–1700)
Ailleboust Des Muceaux, Charles-
  Joseph d'
Amiot, Charles
Bazire, Charles
Bellenger, Étienne
Bergier, Clerbaud
Boisdon, Jacques
Boisseau, Josias
Bourdon, Jean
Byssot de La Rivière, François
Caën, Guillaume de
Charron de La Barre, Claude
Chauvin de La Pierre, Pierre
Closse, Raphaël-Lambert
Damours de Chauffours, Mathieu
Daniel, Charles
Denys, Nicolas
Denys de Fronsac, Richard
Derré de Gand, François
Doublet, François
Gagnon, Mathurin
Gloria, Jean
Godefroy, Jean-Paul
Jolliet, Louis
Juchereau de La Ferté, Jean
Juchereau de Saint-Denis, Nicolas
Juchereau Des Chatelets, Noël
La Court de Pré-Ravillon et de Granpré
La Ralde, Raymond de
Le Borgne, Emmanuel
Legardeur de Repentigny, Pierre
Legardeur de Tilly, Charles
Le Moyne de Longueuil et de
  Châteauguay, Charles
Leneuf Du Hérisson, Michel
Lomeron, David

Migeon de Branssat, Jean-Baptiste
Peré, Jean
Picoté de Belestre, Pierre
Robinau de Bécancour, René, Baron de Portneuf
Sailly, Louis-Arthus de
Saint-Étienne de La Tour, Charles de
Sarcel de Prévert, Jean
Sevestre, Charles
Viennay-Pachot, François

II (1701–1740)
Ailleboust Des Muceaux, Jean-Baptiste d'
Alden, John
Aubert de La Chesnaye, Charles
Aubert de La Chesnaye, François
Barbel, Jacques
Basset, David
Bernard de La Rivière, Hilaire
Bissot, François-Joseph
Carrerot, Pierre
Chambalon, Louis
Charly Saint-Ange, Jean-Baptiste
Charon de La Barre, François
Chartier de Lotbinière, René-Louis
Couagne, Charles de
Couturier, dit Le Bourguignon, Pierre
David, Jacques
Davis, Silvanus
Delaunay, Charles
Denys de Bonaventure, Simon-Pierre
Denys de La Ronde, Pierre
Denys de Vitré, Charles
Énault de Barbaucannes, Philippe
Gaillard, Guillaume
Gamelin, Ignace
Gill, Michael
Gobin, Jean
Godefroy de Saint-Paul, Jean-Amador
Gourdeau de Beaulieu et de La Grossardière, Jacques
Guillimin, Charles
Haimard, Pierre
Hazeur, François
Hiriberry, Joannis
Isabeau, Michel-Philippe
Jolliet de Mingan, Jean-Baptiste
Juchereau de Maur, Paul-Augustin
Juchereau de Saint-Denis, Charlotte-Françoise, known as Comtesse de Saint-Laurent (Viennay-Pachot; Dauphin de La Forest)
Juchereau de Saint-Denys, Charles
Lajoüe, François de
Le Ber, Jacques
Le Conte Dupré, Louis
Lefebvre, dit Laciseraye, Michel
Le Gardeur de Courtemanche, Augustin
Léger de La Grange, Jean
Le Goüès de Sourdeval, Sébastien
Lenoir, dit Rolland, François

Le Poupet de La Boularderie, Louis-Simon
Macard, Charles
Martel, Raymond
Martel de Magos, Jean
Martin de Lino, Jean-François
Martin de Lino, Mathieu-François
Monseignat, Charles de
Nelson, John
Pascaud, Antoine
Peiras, Jean-Baptiste de
Pepperrell, William
Perrot de Rizy, Pierre
Perthuis, Charles
Petit, Pierre
Pinaud, Nicolas
Poulin de Courval, Jean-Baptiste
Prat, Louis
Quesneville, Jean
Regnard Duplessis, Georges
Riverin, Denis
Rivet Cavelier, Pierre
Rodrigue, Jean-Baptiste
Ruette d'Auteuil de Monceaux, François-Madeleine-Fortuné
Sarrazin, Michel
Tibaudeau, Pierre
Tibierge
Tonty, Alphonse (de), Baron de Paludy
Vetch, Samuel
Volant de Radisson, Étienne
You de La Découverte, Pierre

III (1741–1770)
Amiot, Jean-Baptiste (1717–63)
André de Leigne, Pierre
Arrigrand, Gratien d', Sieur de La Majour
Barolet, Claude
Bazil, Louis
Boucault, Nicolas-Gaspard
Boucault de Godefus, Gilbert
Brunet, dit La Sablonnière, Jean
Campot, Jacques
Cardeneau, Bernard
Carrerot, André
Carrerot, Philippe
Charly Saint-Ange, Louis
Cheval, dit Saint-Jacques, and dit Chevalier, Jacques-Joseph
Claparède, Jean
Claverie, Pierre
Constantin, Pierre
Corpron, Jean
Couagne, René de
Couagne, Thérèse de (Poulin de Francheville)
Cugnet, François-Étienne
Daccarrette, Michel (father)
Daccarrette, Michel (son)
Dagneau Douville de Quindre, Louis-Césaire
Dasilva, dit Portugais, Nicolas

Delort, Guillaume
Deschevery, dit Maisonbasse, Jean-Baptiste
Deslongrais, Nicolas
Durocher, Joseph
Fautoux, Léon
Fleury de La Gorgendière, Joseph de
Fornel, Louis
Foucault, François
Foucher, François
Gadois, dit Mauger, Jacques
Gamelin Maugras, Pierre
Ganet, François
Gastineau Duplessis, Jean-Baptiste
Gautier, dit Bellair, Joseph-Nicolas
Gervaise, Louis
Guy, Pierre
Havy, François
Hervieux, Louis-François
Hiché, Henry
Imbert, Jacques
Jacquin, dit Philibert, Nicolas
Janson, dit Lapalme, Dominique
Jeanneau, Étienne
Landron, Jean-François
Lannelongue, Jean-Baptiste
Lanoullier de Boisclerc, Nicolas
Lartigue, Joseph
Le Comte Dupré, Jean-Baptiste
Lefebvre, Jean
Lefebvre de Bellefeuille, Jean-François
Lemaître, dit Jugon, François
Lemoine, dit Monière, Alexis
Lestage, Pierre de
Lupien, dit Baron, Pierre
Maillou, dit Desmoulins, Jean-Baptiste
Malhiot, Jean-François
Mangeant, dit Saint-Germain, François
Margane de Lavaltrie, François
Martel de Belleville, Jean-Urbain
Martel de Brouague, François
Martin, Barthélemy
Maurin, François
Milly, François
Mounier, François
Muiron, David-Bernard
Neveu, Jean-Baptiste
Nolan Lamarque, Charles
Nouchet, Joseph
Perrault, François
Perthuis, Jean-Baptiste-Ignace
Plessy, dit Bélair, Jean-Louis
Pommereau, Jean-Baptiste
Poulin de Courval, Louis-Jean
Révol, Pierre
Riverin, Joseph
Roma, Jean-Pierre
Rouer d'Artigny, Louis
Rouffio, Joseph
Saint-Père, Agathe de (Legardeur de Repentigny)
Sallaberry, Michel de

Simonet d'Abergemont, Jacques
Strouds, Gilles William (rebaptized
 Louis-Claude-Joseph)
Taché, Jean
Taschereau, Thomas-Jacques
Terroux, Jacques
Trottier Desauniers, Pierre
Vallette de Chévigny, Médard-Gabriel
Véron de Grandmesnil, Étienne

IV (1771–1800)
Ailleboust de Cerry, Philippe-Marie d'
Ailleboust de La Madeleine, François-
 Jean-Daniel d'
Augé, Étienne
Barbel, Marie-Anne (Fornel)
Barsalou, Jean-Baptiste
Bréard, Jacques-Michel
Cadet, Joseph-Michel
Castaing, Pierre-Antoine
Charest, Étienne
Cherrier, François-Pierre

Courreaud de La Coste, Pierre
Deguise, *dit* Flamand, Jacques
Delezenne, Ignace-François
Dugas, Joseph
Dumas Saint-Martin, Jean
Dupleix Silvain, Jean-Baptiste
Du Pont Duchambon, Louis
Du Pont Duvivier, François
Estèbe, Guillaume
Fleury Deschambault, Joseph
Fortier, Michel
Gamelin, Ignace
Godefroy de Linctot, Daniel-Maurice
Godefroy de Tonnancour, Louis-
 Joseph
Goguet, Denis
Grasset de Saint-Sauveur, André
Guillimin, Guillaume
Hillaire de La Rochette, Alexandre-
 Robert
Imbert, Bertrand
Laborde, Jean

La Corne, Luc de
Lamaletie, Jean-André
Larcher, Nicolas
Lemoine Despins, Jacques-Joseph
Lÿdius, John Hendricks
Morin de Fonfay, Jean-Baptiste
Mounier, Jean-Mathieu
Olabaratz, Joannis-Galand d'
Pascaud, Antoine
Pennisseaut, Louis
Perrault, Jacques
Ramezay, Louise de
Renaud, *dit* Cannard, Pierre
Rodrigue, Antoine
Sabrevois de Bleury, Clément de
Sanguinet, Simon
Souste, André
Tessier, *dit* Lavigne, Paul
Trottier Dufy Desauniers, Thomas-
 Ignace
Vienne, François-Joseph de

EDUCATION

I (1000–1700)
Boutet de Saint-Martin, Martin
Brice, Madame de
Jolliet, Louis

II (1701–1740)
Ameau, *dit* Saint-Séverin, Séverin
Chaigneau, Léonard
Charon de La Barre, François
Chauchetière, Claude
Germain, Joseph-Louis

La Faye, Louis-François de
Tétro, Jean-Baptiste
Vachon de Belmont, François
Watts, Richard

III (1741–1770)
Charlevoix, Pierre-François-Xavier de
Des Landes, Joseph
Forget, Antoine
Guignas, Michel
Halhead, Edward

Jeantot, Jean
Mésaiger, Charles-Michel
Talbot, Jacques

IV (1771–1800)
Bonnécamps, Joseph-Pierre de
Brassier, Gabriel-Jean
La Brosse, Jean-Baptiste
Peters, Joseph
Sahonwagy
Simonnet, François

ENGINEERS

I (1000–1700)
Bourdon, Jean
Pasquine
Randin, Hugues
Saccardy, Vincent
Villeneuve, Robert de

II (1701–1740)
Catalogne, Gédéon (de)
Couagne, Jean-Baptiste de
Latham, Robert
Levasseur de Neré, Jacques
L'Hermitte, Jacques
Richards, Michael
Roope, John
Vane, George

Verville, Jean-François de
Washington, John

III (1741–1770)
Bastide, John Henry
Boucher, Pierre-Jérôme
Chaussegros de Léry, Gaspard-Joseph
Dubois Berthelot de Beaucours, Josué
Evison, Robert
Franquet, Louis
Eyre, William
Grillot de Poilly, François-Claude-
 Victor
Lombard de Combles, Jean-Claude-
 Henri de

Pouchot, Pierre
Robson, Joseph
Verrier, Étienne

IV (1771–1800)
Brewse, John
Bruce, Robert George
Chartier de Lotbinière, Michel,
 Marquis de Lotbinière
Chaussegros de Léry, Gaspard-Joseph
Desandrouins, Jean-Nicolas
Gridley, Richard
Mackellar, Patrick
Montresor, John
Pringle, Robert

EUROPEANS (non-British, non-French)

Belgians

II (1701–1740)
Hennepin, Louis
Jacquiés, *dit* Leblond, Jean

III (1741–1770)
Tournoix, Jean-Baptiste

Dutch

I (1000–1700)
Aernoutsz, Jurriaen

IV (1771–1800)
Lÿdius, John Hendricks

Germans

III (1741–1770)
Dieskau, Jean-Armand, Baron de
   Dieskau
Erad, Johann Burghard
Erhardt, John Christian
Lockman, Leonard

IV (1771–1800)
Claus, Christian Daniel
Feltz, Charles-Elemy-Joseph-
   Alexandre-Ferdinand
Henry, Anthony
Knaut, Philip Augustus
Oliva, Frédéric-Guillaume
Schwartz, Otto William

Greeks

I (1000–1700)
Fuca, Juan de

Greenlanders

I (1000–1700)
Leifr *heppni* Eiriksson

Hungarians

I (1000–1700)
Parmenius, Stephanus

Icelanders

I (1000–1700)
Bjarni Herjólfsson
Eirikr *upsi* Gnupsson
Eirikr Thorvaldsson
Snorri Thorfinnsonn
Thorfinnr *karlsefni* Thordarson

Italians

I (1000–1700)
Bressani, François-Joseph
Cabot, John
Cabot, Sebastian
Carbonariis, Giovanni Antonio de
Verrazzano, Giovanni da
Zeno, Nicolò
Zeno, Antonio

Portuguese

I (1000–1700)
Corte-Real, Gaspar
Corte-Real, Miguel
Fagundes, João Alvares
Fernandes, João
Gomes, Estevão
Gonsales, João

II (1701–1740)
Rodrigue, Jean-Baptiste

Scandinavians

I (1000–1700)
Munk, Jens Eriksen

IV (1771–1800)
Drachart, Christian Larsen

Haven, Jens
Kalm, Pehr

Sicilians

I (1000–1700)
Crisafy, Thomas

II (1701–1740)
Crisafy, Antoine de, Marquis de
   Crisafy

Spaniards

I (1000–1700)
Agramonte, Juan de
Ferrer Maldonado, Lorenzo

IV (1771–1800)
Bodega y Quadra, Juan Francisco de la
Martínez Fernández y Martínez de la
   Sierra, Esteban José
Pérez Hernández, Juan Josef

Swiss

I (1000–1700)
Bizard, Jacques
Miville, Pierre, known as Le Suisse

III (1741–1770)
Haldimand, Peter Frederick
Terroux, Jacques
Vilermaula, Louis-Michel de

IV (1771–1800)
Ermatinger, Lawrence
Gugy, Conrad
Haldimand, Sir Frederick
Waddens, Jean-Étienne
Webber, John
Zouberbuhler, Sebastian

EXPLORERS

I (1000–1700)
Agramonte, Juan de
Allemand, Pierre
Allouez, Claude
Baffin, William
Barthélemy

Bellenger, Étienne
Bjarni, Herjólfsson
Bourdon, Jean
Bourdon d'Autray, Jacques
Bradley, Thomas
Buteux, Jacques

Button, Sir Thomas
Cabot, John
Cabot, Sebastian
Cartier, Jacques
Cavelier de La Salle, René-Robert
Champlain, Samuel de

FUR-TRADERS

Chouart Des Groseilliers, Médard
Corte-Real, Gaspar
Corte-Real, Miguel
Cunningham, John
Daumont de Saint-Lusson, Simon-
  François
Davis, John
Denys, Jean
Dermer, Thomas
Drake, Sir Francis
Du Gua de Monts, Pierre
Duquet de La Chesnaye, Pierre
Eirikr Thorvaldsson
Fagundes, João Alvares
Fernandes, João
Ferrer Maldonado, Lorenzo
Fonte, Bartholomew de
Fox, Luke
Frobisher, Sir Martin
Fuca, Juan de
Gibbons, William
Gilbert, Sir Humphrey
Gomes, Estevão
Gonsales, João
Guy, John
Hall, James
Hayes, Edward
Hudson, Henry
Hudson, John
James, Thomas
Jolliet, Louis
Knight, John
La Motte de Lucière, Dominique
Leifr *heppni* Eiriksson
Lescarbot, Marc
Madoc
Mason, John
Munk, Jens Eriksen

Nicollet de Belleborne, Jean
Noël, Jacques
Parkhurst, Anthony
Parmenius, Stephanus
Rallau, Jean
Rastell, John
Rut, John
Thirkill, Lancelot
Thorfinnr *karlsefni* Thordarson
Thorne, Robert (father)
Thorne, Robert (son)
Verrazzano, Giovanni da
Waymouth, George
Zeno, Nicolò
Zeno, Antonio

II (1701–1740)
Cavelier, Jean
Couture, Guillaume
Dufrost de La Jemerais, Christophe
Gaultier de La Vérendrye, Jean-
  Baptiste
Greysolon Dulhut, Daniel
Hennepin, Louis
Kelsey, Henry
Knight, James
Le Moyne d'Iberville et d'Ardillières,
  Pierre
Le Sueur, Pierre
Perrot, Nicolas
Radisson, Pierre-Esprit
Stuart, William
Tonty, Henri (de)
Véniard de Bourgmond, Étienne de

III (1741–1770)
Bean, John
Boucher de Montbrun, Jean

Coats, William
Fornel, Louis
Gaultier de La Vérendrye, Louis-
  Joseph
Gaultier de La Vérendrye de Boumois,
  Pierre
Gaultier de Varennes et de La Véren-
  drye, Pierre
Henday, Anthony
Juchereau de Saint-Denis, Louis
Legardeur de Saint-Pierre, Jacques
Le Moyne de Bienville, Jean-Baptiste
Longland, John
Mallet, Pierre-Antoine
Middleton, Christopher
Mitchell, Thomas
Moor, William
Pattin, John
Smith, Francis
Smith, Joseph
Wigate, John

IV (1771–1800)
Bodega y Quadra, Juan Francisco de la
Clerke, Charles
Cocking, Matthew
Cook, James
Duncan, Charles
Gaultier Du Tremblay, François
Hearne, Samuel
King, James
Marin de La Malgue, Joseph
Martínez Fernández y Martínez de la
  Sierra, Esteban José
Pérez Hernández, Juan Josef
Turnor, Philip
Vancouver, George

FUR-TRADERS

I (1000–1700)
Abraham, John
Aigron, *dit* Lamothe, Pierre
Allemand, Pierre
Amiot, Charles
Aprendestiguy, Martin d'
Babie, Jacques
Bayly, Charles
Bridgar, John
Cobbie, Walsall
Crevier de Saint-François, Jean
David, Claude
Du Gua de Monts, Pierre
Dugué de Boisbriand, Michel-Sidrac
Gamelain de La Fontaine, Michel
Geyer, George
Godefroy de Lintot, Jean
Godefroy de Vieuxpont, Jacques
Godet Des Maretz, Claude de

Gorst, Thomas
Hamilton, Andrew
Gravé Du Pont, Robert
Jérémie, *dit* Lamontagne, Noël
Juchereau de Saint-Denis, Nicolas
Kirke, Sir Lewis
Lambert, Eustache
Laviolette
Lydall, William
Marsh, John
Marsolet de Saint-Aignan, Nicolas
Missenden, Samuel
Nixon, John
Noël, Jacques
Peré, Jean
Phipps, Thomas
Picoté de Belestre, Pierre
Power, Richard
Saint-Étienne de La Tour, Claude

Sergeant, Henry
Smithsend, Nicholas
Smithsend, Richard
Thomas, Jean
Thompson, Joseph
Verner, Hugh
Vuil, Daniel

II (1701–1740)
Adams, Joseph
Ailleboust de Manthet, Nicolas d'
Apthorp, Alexander
Baley, Henry
Baugy, Louis-Henri de, known as
  Chevalier de Baugy
Beale, Anthony
Berley, George
Bevan, William
Bird, Thomas

Bishop, Nathaniel
Bouat, François-Marie
Céloron de Blainville, Jean-Baptiste
Chambalon, Louis
Charly Saint-Ange, Jean-Baptiste
Couagne, Charles de
Damours de Chauffours, Louis
Damours de Clignancour, René
Dauphin de La Forest, François
Davis, Joseph
Delaunay, Charles
Dizy, *dit* Montplaisir, Michel-Ignace
Énault de Barbaucannes, Philippe
Fullartine, John
Gaultier de La Vérendrye, Jean-
  Baptiste
Gillam, Benjamin
Godefroy de Saint-Paul, Jean-Amador
Godefroy de Vieuxport, Joseph
Gourdeau de Beaulieu et de La Grossar-
  dière, Jacques
Greysolon de La Tourette, Claude
Greysolon Dulhut, Daniel
Grimington, Michael (father)
Grimington, Michael (son)
Hamare de La Borde, Jean-Baptiste-
  Julien
Hopkins, Samuel
Jérémie, *dit* Lamontagne, Nicolas
Jolliet de Mingan, Jean-Baptiste
Kelsey, Henry
Knight, James
Largillier, Jacques, known as
  Le Castor
Lefebvre, Thomas
Le Moyne d'Iberville et d'Ardillières,
  Pierre
Le Sueur, Pierre
Messier, *dit* Saint-Michel, Michel
Moore, Thomas
Myatt, Joseph
Napper, James
Perrot, Nicolas
Radisson, Pierre-Esprit
Render, Thomas
Saint-Étienne de La Tour, Charles de
Scroggs, John
Stuart, William
Tonty, Alphonse (de), Baron de Paludy

Tonty, Henri (de)
Vaughan, David
Waggoner, Rowland
Ward, Richard
You de La Découverte, Pierre

III (1741–1770)
Bean, John
Bisaillon, Peter
Boucher de Montbrun, Jean
Campot, Jacques
Chabert de Joncaire, Philippe-Thomas
Chevalier, Jean-Baptiste
Clark, George
Coats, William
Evison, Robert
Fleury de La Gorgendière, Joseph de
Gamelin Maugras, Pierre
Gastineau Duplessis, Jean-Baptiste
Gaultier de La Vérendrye, Louis-
  Joseph
Gaultier de Varennes et de La Véren-
  drye, Pierre
Henday, Anthony
Isbister, William
Isham, James
Kellogg, Joseph
La France, Joseph
Longland, John
McCliesh, Thomas
Mallet, Pierre-Antoine
Marin de La Perrière, Claude
Middleton, Christopher
Mitchell, Thomas
Moor, William
Newton, John
Norton, Richard
Noyon, Jacques de
Pattin, John
Pilgrim, Robert
Potts, John
Robson, Joseph
Roseboom, Johannes
Skrimsher, Samuel
Smith, Francis
Smith, Joseph
Spurrell, George
Staunton, Richard
Thompson, Edward

White, Richard
White, Thomas

IV (1771–1800)
Ailleboust de La Madeleine, François-
  Jean-Daniel d'
Atkinson, George
Baby, *dit* Dupéront, Jacques
Batt, Isaac
Bourassa, *dit* La Ronde, René
Campion, Étienne-Charles
Cocking, Matthew
Cole, John
Cotté, Gabriel
Couagne, Jean-Baptiste de
Dagneau Douville, Alexandre
Dixon, George
Ducharme, Laurent
Duncan, Charles
Grant, Cuthbert
Grant, James
Hanna, James
Hearne, Samuel
Holmes, William
Howard, Joseph
Hutchins, Thomas
Isbister, Joseph
Jacobs, Ferdinand
Jarvis, Edward
Kendrick, John
Knaut, Philip Augustus
Long, John
McCarty, Richard
McKee, Alexander
MacLeod, Normand
Marten, Humphrey
Maugenest, Germain
Mouet de Langlade, Charles-Michel
Norton, Moses
Oakes, Forrest
Primeau, Louis
Ross, Malchom
Schwartz, Otto William
Sutherland, George
Sutherland, James
Turnor, Philip
Umfreville, Edward
Waddens, Jean-Étienne
Walker, William

INDIAN AFFAIRS

I (1000–1700)
Amiot, Jean
Amiot, *dit* Villeneuve, Mathieu
Brûlé, Étienne
Du Chesne, Adrien
Godefroy, Jean-Paul
Godefroy de Lintot, Jean
Godefroy de Normanville, Thomas

Godefroy de Vieuxpont, Jacques
Hertel de La Fresnière, Jacques
Lambert, Eustache
Le Moyne de Longueuil et de
  Châteauguay, Charles
Letardif, Olivier
Marguerie de La Haye, François
Marsolet de Saint-Aignan, Nicolas

Nicollet de Belleborne, Jean
Vignau, Nicolas de

II (1701–1740)
Bissot de Vinsenne, Jean-Baptiste
Boucher, Pierre
Bruyas, Jacques
Chabert de Joncaire, Louis-Thomas

45

JOURNALISTS

Couture, Guillaume
Godefroy de Saint-Paul, Jean-Amador
Godefroy de Vieuxpont, Joseph
Hertel de La Fresnière, Joseph-François
Jérémie, *dit* Lamontagne, Nicolas
Lamberville, Jean de
Lefebvre, Thomas
Le Gardeur de Courtemanche,
   Augustin
Legardeur de Saint-Pierre, Jean-Paul
Le Moyne de Longueuil, Charles,
   Baron de Longueuil
Le Moyne de Maricourt, Paul
Liette, Pierre-Charles de
Perrot, Nicolas
Petitpas, Claude

III (1741–1770)
Chabert de Joncaire, Philippe-Thomas

Couc, Elizabeth (La Chenette,
   Techenet; Montour)
Gamelin Maugras, Pierre
Gyles, John
Kellogg, Joseph
Legardeur de Saint-Pierre, Jacques
Lottridge, John
Petitpas, Barthélemy
Schuyler, Johannes

IV (1771–1800)
Baby, *dit* Dupéront, Jacques
Butler, John (d. 1796)
Campbell, John
Chabert de Joncaire de Clausonne,
   Daniel-Marie
Chew, Joseph
Claus, Christian Daniel

Couagne, Jean-Baptiste de
Dagneau Douville, Alexandre
Francklin, Michael
Godefroy de Linctot, Daniel-Maurice
Godin, *dit* Bellefontaine, *dit* Beau-
   séjour, Joseph
Goreham, Joseph
Hay, Jehu
Hertel de Saint-François, Joseph-
   Hippolyte
Johnson, Guy
Johnson, Sir William
La Corne, Luc de
Lӱdius, John Hendricks
McKee, Alexander
MacLeod, Normand
Mouet de Langlade, Charles-Michel
Roberts, Benjamin

JOURNALISTS

IV (1771–1800)
Brown, William
Gilmore, Thomas

Henry, Anthony
Jautard, Valentin

Mesplet, Fleury
Moore, William

LEGAL AND JUDICIAL

Judges

I (1000–1700)
Bréhaut Delisle, Achille
Chartier de Lotbinière, Louis-Théandre
Courseron, Gilbert
Damours de Chauffours, Mathieu
Damours de Freneuse, Mathieu
Denys de La Trinité, Simon
Lauson, Jean de (son)
Leneuf Du Hérisson, Michel
Letardif, Olivier
Le Vieux de Hauteville, Nicolas
Migeon de Branssat, Jean-Baptiste
Mouchy, Nicolas de
Peronne de Mazé, Louis
Poulin de La Fontaine, Maurice
Rouer de Villeray, Louis
Sailly, Louis-Arthus de
Sevestre, Charles

II (1701–1740)
Aubert de La Chesnaye, Charles
Aubert de La Chesnaye, François
Barbel, Jacques
Bermen de La Martinière, Claude de
Bouat, François-Marie

Boucher, Pierre
Cabazié, Pierre
Chartier de Lotbinière, René-Louis
Couillard de Lespinay, Jean-Baptiste
Couture, Guillaume
Denys de Saint-Simon, Paul
Denys de Vitré, Charles
Dizy, *dit* Montplaisir, Michel-Ignace
Dupont de Neuville, Nicolas
Dupuy de Lisloye, Paul
Durand de La Garenne
Espiet de Pensens, Jacques d'
Fleury Deschambault, Jacques-Alexis
   de
Gaillard, Guillaume
Gaultier de Varennes, Jean-Baptiste
Godefroy de Tonnancour, René
Goutin, Mathieu de
Guillimin, Charles
Haimard, Pierre
Hazeur, François
Hazeur, Jean-François
Jacob, Étienne
Juchereau de Saint-Denys, Charles
La Cetière, Florent de
La Colombière, Joseph de
Larue, Guillaume de

Lechasseur, Jean
Legardeur de Tilly, Pierre-Noël
Lepallieur de Laferté, Michel
Macard, Charles
Martin de Lino, Mathieu-François
Monseignat, Charles de
Morel de La Durantaye, Olivier
Peiras, Jean-Baptiste de
Petit, Jean
Raimbault, Pierre
Riverin, Denis
Roger, Guillaume
Rouer de Villeray et de La Cardonnière,
   Augustin
Sarrazin, Michel
Smith, James
Tailhandier, *dit* La Beaume, Marien

III (1741–1770)
André de Leigne, Pierre
Benard, Michel
Boucault, Nicolas-Gaspard
Carrerot, André
Chartier de Lotbinière, Eustache
Collier, John
Couagne, René de
Cugnet, François-Étienne

Daine, François
Danré de Blanzy, Louis-Claude
Delort, Guillaume
Denison, Robert
Dizy de Montplaisir, Pierre
Foucault, François
Gaudron de Chevremont, Charles-René
Gaschet, René
Goutin, François-Marie de
Guiton de Monrepos, Jacques-Joseph
Hiché, Henry
Imbert, Jacques
Lafontaine de Belcour, Jacques de
Lanoullier de Boisclerc, Nicolas
Lartigue, Joseph
Levasseur, Louis
Malhiot, Jean-François
Monk, James
Mounier, François
Nouchet, Joseph-Étienne
Pinguet de Vaucour, Jacques-Nicolas
Poulin de Courval, Louis-Jean
Rouer d'Artigny, Louis
Taschereau, Thomas-Jacques
Vallier, François-Elzéar

IV (1771–1800)
Belcher, Jonathan
Bulkeley, Richard
Butler, John (d. 1791)
Butler, John (d. 1796)
Callbeck, Phillips
Cramahé, Hector Theophilus
Cugnet, François-Joseph
Denson, Henry Denny
Doggett, John
Estèbe, Guillaume
Gamelin, Ignace
Gerrish, Joseph
Gibbons, Richard
Green, Benjamin
Guillimin, Guillaume
Hertel de Rouville, René-Ovide
Hey, William
Johnston, Alexander
Langman, Edward
Larcher, Nicolas
Livius, Peter
Mabane, Adam
McKee, Alexander
McLean, Neil
Morris, Charles
Munro, John
Nesbitt, William
Panet, Jean-Claude
Perthuis, Joseph
Ritchie, John
Sanguinet, Simon
Scott, Joseph
Smith, William
Tonge, Winckworth
Varin de La Marre, Jean-Victor

Justices of the peace

III (1741–1770)
Adams, John
Collier, John
Denison, Robert
How, Edward
Keen, William
Kilby, Thomas
Monk, James
Mounier, François
Price, Benjamin

IV (1771–1800)
Adhémar, Jean-Baptiste-Amable
Aylwin, Thomas
Baby, *dit* Dupéront, Jacques
Badeaux, Jean-Baptiste
Brassard Deschenaux, Joseph
Burch, John
Cotté, Gabriel
Coughlan, Laurence
Cuthbert, James
Danks, Benoni
Davidson, William
Davison, George
Day, John
De Peyster, Abraham
Doggett, John
Du Calvet, Pierre
Dumas Saint-Martin, Jean
Fillis, John
Gamelin, Pierre-Joseph
Gerrish, Benjamin
Gerrish, Joseph
Green, Benjamin
Gugy, Conrad
Hicks, John
Knaut, Philip Augustus
Langman, Edward
Lévesque, François
McLean, Neil
Morris, Charles
Munro, John
Murray, Walter
Nesbitt, William
Owen, William
Panet, Jean-Claude
Ritchie, John
Salter, Malachy
Scott, Joseph
Shaw, William
Tonge, Winckworth
Walker, Thomas
Wenman, Richard
Zouberbuhler, Sebastian

Lawyers

II (1701–1740)
Larkin, George

III (1741–1770)
Little, Otis

IV (1771–1800)
Aumasson de Courville, Louis-Léonard
Gibbons, Richard
Guillimin, Guillaume
Hardy, Elias
Jautard, Valentin
Kneller, Henry
McCarty, Richard
Nesbitt, William
Panet, Jean-Claude
Robinson, Christopher
Saillant, Jean-Antoine
Sanguinet, Simon
Suckling, George
White, John

Notaries

I (1000–1700)
Auber, Claude
Audouart, *dit* Saint-Germain,
  Guillaume
Basset Des Lauriers, Bénigne
Becquet, Romain
Bermen, Laurent
Closse, Raphaël-Lambert
Duquet de La Chesnaye, Pierre
Fillion, Michel
Gloria, Jean
Godet, Rolland
Maugue, Claude
Mouchy, Nicolas de
Peuvret Desmenu, Jean-Baptiste
Rageot, Gilles
Saint-Père, Jean de

II (1701–1740)
Adhémar de Saint-Martin, Antoine
Ameau, *dit* Saint-Séverin, Séverin
Barbel, Jacques
Barrat, Claude
Bernard de La Rivière, Hilaire
Bigot, François
Bourdon, Jacques
Cabazié, Pierre
Chambalon, Louis
Cusson, Jean
David, Jacques
Dubreuil, Jean-Étienne
Duprac, Jean-Robert
Genaple de Bellefonds, François
Horné, *dit* Laneuville, Jacques de
Jacob, Étienne
La Cetière, Florent de
Larue, Guillaume de
Lepallieur de Laferté, Michel
Le Roy Desmarest, Claude-Joseph
Loppinot, Jean-Chrysostome
Louet, Jean-Claude

MARINERS

Normandin, Daniel
Petit, Pierre
Pottier, Jean-Baptiste
Quiniard, *dit* Duplessis, Antoine-
  Olivier
Rageot de Saint-Luc, Charles
Rageot de Saint-Luc, Nicolas
Raimbault, Pierre
Raimbault de Piedmont, Joseph-
  Charles
Rivet Cavelier, Pierre
Roger, Guillaume
Roy, *dit* Châtellerault, Michel
Senet, *dit* Laliberté, Nicolas
Tailhandier, *dit* La Beaume, Marien
Tétro, Jean-Baptiste
Trotain, *dit* Saint-Seürin, François
Vachon, Paul (father)
Véron de Grandmesnil, Étienne
Verreau, Barthélemy

III (1741–1770)
Adhémar, Jean-Baptiste
Barolet, Claude
Boucault de Godefus, Gilbert
Bourg, *dit* Belle-Humeur, Alexandre
Coron, Charles-François
Danré de Blanzy, Louis-Claude
Du Laurent, Christophe-Hilarion
Gaschet, René
Gaudron de Chevremont, Charles-René
Guillet de Chaumont, Nicolas-Auguste
Guyart de Fleury, Jean-Baptiste
Hiché, Henry
Imbert, Jacques
Jeanneau, Étienne
Pillard, Louis
Pinguet de Vaucour, Jacques-Nicolas
Pollet, Arnould-Balthazar
Poulin, Pierre
Pressé, Hyacinthe-Olivier

Rondeau, Jacques-Philippe-Urbain
Taché, Jean

IV (1771–1800)
Aumasson de Courville, Louis-
  Léonard, known as Sieur de Cour-
  ville
Badeaux, Jean-Baptiste
Boisseau, Nicolas
Cherrier, François-Pierre
Grisé, Antoine
Guillimin, Guillaume
Hantraye, Claude
Laborde, Jean
Navarre, Robert
Nesbitt, William
Panet, Jean-Claude
Saillant, Jean-Antoine
Sanguinet, Simon
Simonnet, François
Souste, André

MARINERS

I (1000–1700)
Aigron, *dit* Lamothe, Pierre
Allemand, Pierre
Angibault, *dit* Champdoré, Pierre
Beare, James
Bond, William
Bourdon de Dombourg, Jean-François
Bylot, Robert
Caën, Émery de
Caën, Guillaume de
Chauvin de La Pierre, Pierre
Chefdostel, Thomas
Clarke, Richard
Couillard de Lespinay, Guillaume
Daniel, Charles
Denys, Jean
Denys, Nicolas
Denys de La Trinité, Simon
Desdames, Thierry
Drake, Sir Bernard
Draper, Thomas
Du Plessis-Bochart, Charles
Easton, Peter
Edgcombe, Leonard
Fisher, Richard
Fletcher, John
Fonteneau, Jean
Fox, Luke
Frobisher, Sir Martin
Garland, Thomas
Gillam, Zachariah
Godefroy, Jean-Paul
Hawkeridge, William
Hill, William
Hore, Richard
Hudson, Henry

Ingram, David
Jalobert, Macé
James, Thomas
Kirke, Sir David
Kirke, Sir Lewis
Kirke, Thomas
Knight, John
Lane, Daniel
Langlois, Noël
La Ralde, Raymond de
Legardeur de Tilly, Charles
Le Moyne de Châteauguay, Louis
Lucas, Richard
Mainwaring, Sir Henry
Marot, Bernard
Martin, Abraham
Martin, Christopher
Mason, John
May, Henry
Menou d'Aulnay, Charles de
Nutt, John
Outlaw, John
Parmentier, Jean
Phips, Sir William
Rayner, John
Roquemont de Brison, Claude
Rut, John
Sanford, Esbon
Scolvus, Jean
Shepard, Thomas
Walker, Nehemiah
Whitbourne, Sir Richard
Wyet, Sylvester
Wynne, Edward
Young, James
Young, Thomas

II (1701–1740)
Alden, John
Amiot de Vincelotte, Charles-Joseph
Baley, Henry
Basset, David
Bevan, William
Bissot, François-Joseph
Bonner, John
Chevalier, *dit* Beauchêne, Robert
Davis, Joseph
Gill, Michael
Gillam, Benjamin
Guion, François
Hill, Samuel
Kelsey, Henry
Léger de La Grange, Jean
Le Moyne d'Iberville et d'Ardillières,
  Pierre
Leneuf de La Vallière de Beaubassin,
  Michel (son)
Maisonnat, *dit* Baptiste, Pierre
Moore, Thomas
Napper, James
Paradis, Jean
Petitpas, Claude
Render, Thomas
Rodrigue, Jean-Baptiste
Scroggs, John
Serreau de Saint-Aubin, Jean
Vaughan, David
Ward, Richard

III (1741–1770)
Coats, William
Cobb, Silvanus
Daccarrette, Michel (father)

Gautier, *dit* Bellair, Joseph-Nicolas
Lannelongue, Jean-Baptiste
Lemaître, *dit* Jugon, François
Longland, John
Middleton, Christopher
Mitchell, Thomas
Moor, William
Morpain, Pierre
Olivier, Abel
Paris, Bernard
Petitpas, Barthélemy
Pilgrim, Robert
Pote, William
Rous, John

Smith, Francis
Southack, Cyprian
Spurrell, George
Testu de La Richardière, Richard
Tyng, Edward

IV (1771–1800)
Ailleboust de Cerry, Philippe-Marie d'
Beatson, Patrick
Darby, Nicholas
Denys de Vitré, Théodose-Matthieu
Dixon, George
Doggett, John
Doucet, Pierre

Dugas, Joseph
Duncan, Charles
Fortier, Michel
Hanna, James
Higgins, David
Kendrick, John
Loring, Joshua
Mauger, Joshua
Olabaratz, Joannis-Galand d'
Pellegrin, Gabriel
Raby, Augustin
Rodrigue, Antoine
Slade, John

MEDICINE

I (1000–1700)
Baudouin, Gervais
Bonamour, Jean de
Bonnemere, Florent
Bouchard, Étienne
Chartier, Louis
Demosny, Jean
Du Chesne, Adrien
Gamelain de La Fontaine, Michel
Gendron, François
Giffard de Moncel, Robert
Goupil, René
Hébert, Louis
Madry, Jean
Maheut, Louis
Mance, Jeanne
Marot, Bernard
Pinard, Louis
Romieux, Pierre
Roussel, Timothée

II (1701–1740)
Baudeau, Pierre
Bertier, Michel
Bourgeois, Jacques
Charon de La Barre, François
Chaudillon, Antoine

Dièreville
Dizy, *dit* Montplaisir, Marguerite
    (Desbrieux)
Dugay, Jacques
Énault de Barbaucannes, Philippe
Forestier, Antoine
Lamarre, *dit* Bélisle, Henri
Martinet de Fonblanche, Jean
Sarrazin, Michel
Soupiran, Simon
Tailhandier, *dit* La Beaume, Marien
Yonge, James

III (1741–1770)
Alavoine, Charles
Arnoux, André
Baudoin, Gervais
Boispineau, Jean-Jard
Chapoton, Jean-Baptiste
Descouts, Martin
Erad, Johann Burghard
Forestier, Antoine-Bertrand
Gaschet, René
Gaultier, Jean-François
Jérémie, *dit* Lamontagne, Catherine
    (Aubuchon; Lepallieur de Laferté)
La Croix, Hubert-Joseph de

Lajus, Jordain
Lockman, Leonard
Phlem, *dit* Yvon, Yves
Potts, John
Soupiran, Simon
Spagniolini, Jean-Fernand
Sullivan, Timothy, known as Timothée
    Silvain
Thompson, Edward

IV (1771–1800)
Berbudeau, Jean-Gabriel
Bourdages, Raymond
Bowman, James
Day, John
Feltz, Charles-Elemy-Joseph-
    Alexandre-Ferdinand
Hutchins, Thomas
Lajus, François
Landriaux, Louis-Nicolas
Mabane, Adam
Mackay, John
Oliva, Frédéric-Guillaume
Osborn, Elizabeth (Myrick; Paine;
    Doane)
Wood, Thomas

MISCELLANEOUS

I (1000–1700)
Colin, Michel
Dubok
Hébert, Joseph
Magnan, Pierre
Peronne Dumesnil, Jean
Snorri Thorfinnsson

II (1701–1740)
Baudry de Lamarche, Jacques
Cuillerier, René
Hill, Samuel
Williams, John (1664–1729)

III (1741–1770)
Cartier, Toussaint, known as 'the her-
    mit of Saint-Barnabé'

Davers, Sir Robert
Havard de Beaufort, François-Charles,
    known as L'Avocat

IV (1771–1800)
Kerrivan, Peter

NATIVE PEOPLES

Abenakis

I (1000–1700)
Asticou

II (1701–1740)
Abbadie de Saint-Castin, Jean-Vincent
   d', Baron de Saint-Castin
Atecouando
Mog
Nescambiouit
Waxaway
Wenemouet
Wowurna

III (1741–1770)
Abbadie de Saint-Castin, Joseph d',
   Baron de Saint-Castin
Atecouando
Gray Lock
Nodogawerrimet
Sauguaaram

IV (1771–1800)
Gill, Joseph-Louis

Algonkins

I (1000–1700)
Batiscan
Iroquet
Oumasasikweie
Pieskaret
Pigarouich
Tessouat (fl. 1603–13)
Tessouat (d. 1636)
Tessouat (d. 1654)

Cayugas

IV (1771–1800)
Ottrowana

Chipewyans

II (1701–1740)
Thanadelthur

IV (1771–1800)
Matonabbee

Comanches

III (1741–1770)
Pierre

Crees

II (1701–1740)
Auchagah
Miscomote
Scatchamisse
Swan

III (1741–1770)
Crusoe, Robinson
La Colle
Wappisis

IV (1771–1800)
Wapinesiw
Winninnewaycappo

Delawares

IV (1771–1800)
Anandamoakin
Glikhikan

Eries

I (1000–1700)
Gandeacteua

Foxes

II (1701–1740)
Kiala
Noro
Ouachala
Pemoussa

Haidas

IV (1771–1800)
Koyah

Hurons

I (1000–1700)
Ahatsistari
Amantacha
Annaotaha
Atironta (fl. 1615)
Atironta (d. 1650)
Atironta, (d. 1672)
Auoindaon
Chihouatenha
Oionhaton
Ondaaiondiont
Savignon

Skanudharoua, *dite* Geneviève-Agnès,
   de Tous-les-Saints
Taondechoren
Taratouan
Tehorenhaegnon
Teouatiron
Tonsahoten
Totiri

II (1701–1740)
Kondiaronk

III (1741–1770)
Michipichy
Orontony
Vincent

Illinois

II (1701–1740)
Chachagouesse

Inuit

II (1701–1740)
Acoutsina

IV (1771–1800)
Kingminguse
Mikak
Tuglavina

Iroquois

I (1000–1700)
Dekanahwideh
Donnacona
Ourehouare

Malecites

I (1000–1700)
Ouagimou
Secoudon

IV (1771–1800)
Akomápis, Nicholas
Benoît, Pierre
Saint-Aubin, Ambroise
Tomah, Pierre

Miamis

II (1701–1740)
Chichikatelo

Micmacs

I (1000–1700)
Membertou
Messamouet
Panounias
Segipt

III (1741–1770)
Bâtard, Étienne (Anthony)
Cope, Jean-Baptiste
Laurent, Paul
Padanuques, Jacques

IV (1771–1800)
Arimph, Jean-Baptiste
Bernard, Philip
Claude, Joseph

Mississaugas

III (1741–1770)
Wabbicommicot

IV (1771–1800)
Wabakinine

Mohawks

I (1000–1700)
Agariata
Flemish Bastard
Honatteniate
Kiotseaeton
Tekakwitha, Kateri
Togouiroui

II (1701–1740)
Tekarihoken

III (1741–1770)
Karaghtadie
Theyanoguin

IV (1771–1800)
Koñwatsi⁊tsiaiéñni (Mary Brant)
Sahonwagy
Teiorhéñhsere⁊
Tekawiroñte

Montagnais

I (1000–1700)
Anadabijou
Begourat
Capitanal
Charité
Cherououny
Chomina

Erouachy
Espérance
Foi
Makheabichtichiou
Manitougatche
Miristou
Negabamat
Pastedechouan

Nipissings

III (1741–1770)
Kisensik

Nootkas

IV (1771–1800)
Muquinna
Wikinanish

Ojibwas

III (1741–1770)
Minweweh
Wawatam

IV (1771–1800)
Wasson

Oneidas

I (1000–1700)
Ogenheratarihiens
Tareha

II (1701–1740)
Gouentagrandi

III (1741–1770)
Gawèhe
Swatana

Onondagas

I (1000–1700)
Annenraes
Chaudière Noire
Garakontié
Otreouti

II (1701–1740)
Aradgi
Ohonsiowanne
Teganissorens

III (1741–1770)
Kak8enthiony
Ononwarogo

IV (1771–1800)
Hotsinoñhyahta⁊
Ohquandageghte
Teyohaqueande

Ottawas

II (1701–1740)
Chingouessi
Koutaoiliboe
Kinongé
Le Pesant
Miscouaky
Outoutagan

III (1741–1770)
Kinousaki
Mikinak
Pontiac
Saguima

IV (1771–1800)
Egushwa
Nissowaquet

Pawnees

III (1741–1770)
Duplessis, Marguerite

Potawatomis

II (1701–1740)
Ouenemek
Ounanguissé

Senecas

II (1701–1740)
Aouenano
Cagenquarichten
Tekanoet
Tonatakout

III (1741–1770)
Kaghswaghtaniunt
Tanaghrisson

IV (1771–1800)
Kaieñ⁊kwaahtoñ
Kayahsota⁊

Wabanakis

I (1000–1700)
Tisquantum

OFFICE-HOLDERS

British Régime

Colonial administrators

I (1000–1700)
Colston, William
Guy, John
Hayman, Robert
Hill, William
Mason, John
Rayner, John
Tanfield, Sir Francis
Temple, Sir Thomas
Treworgie, John
Tyng, Edward
Walker, Richard
Whitbourne, Sir Richard
Wynne, Edward

II (1701–1740)
Armstrong, Lawrence
Bouler, Robert
Caulfeild, Thomas
Collins, John
Doucett, John
Graydon, John
Hobby, Sir Charles
Kempthorne, Thomas
Leake, Sir John
Moody, John
Nicholson, Francis
Trevanion, Sir Nicholas
Vetch, Samuel

III (1741–1770)
Bonfoy, Hugh
Burton, Ralph
Byng, John
Clinton, George
Cope, Henry
Cosby, Alexander
Dorrill, Richard
Falkingham, Edward
Hamilton, Otho
Hopson, Peregrine Thomas
Lawrence, Charles
Lee, Fitzroy Henry
Mascarene, Paul
Philipps, Richard
Webb, James
Whitmore, Edward
Wilmot, Montagu

IV (1771–1800)
Arbuthnot, Mariot
Belcher, Jonathan
Bradstreet, John

Byron, John
Campbell, Lord William
Cornwallis, Edward
Cox, Nicholas
Cramahé, Hector Theophilus
Drake, Francis William
Edwards, Richard
Francklin, Michael
Gage, Thomas
Goreham, Joseph
Haldimand, Sir Frederick
Hamilton, Henry
Hardy, Sir Charles
Hay, Jehu
Hope, Henry
Irving, Paulus-Æmilius
Legge, Francis
Monckton, Robert
Murray, James
Osborn, Henry
Palliser, Sir Hugh
Parr, John
Patterson, Walter
Shuldham, Molyneux, 1st Baron
    Shuldham

Officials, appointed

II (1701–1740)
Campbell, Colin
Cumings, Archibald
Doucett, John
Harrison, John
Savage, Arthur

III (1741–1770)
Adams, John
Aldridge, Christopher (father)
Bourg, *dit* Belle-Humeur, Alexandre
Collier, John
Cope, Henry
Cosby, Alexander
Gorham, John
Hamilton, Otho
Handfield, John
How, Edward
Kilby, Thomas
Little, Otis
Mangeant, *dit* Saint-Germain,
    François
Monk, James
Mounier, François
Osborn, Sir Danvers
Philipps, Erasmus James
Price, Benjamin
Rous, John
Salusbury, John

Saul, Thomas
Southack, Cyprian
Winniett, William

IV (1771–1800)
Baby, *dit* Dupéront, Jacques
Bruyères, John
Bulkeley, Richard
Burch, John
Busby, Thomas
Butler, John (d. 1791)
Butler, John (d. 1796)
Callbeck, Phillips
Chaussegros de Léry, Gaspard-Joseph
Coghlan, Jeremiah
Collins, John
Cox, Nicholas
Cramahé, Hector Theophilus
Cugnet, François-Joseph
Cuthbert, James
Danks, Benoni
Davison, George
Day, John
Denson, Henry Denny
De Peyster, Abraham
Doggett, John
Fleury Deschambault, Joseph
Francklin, Michael
Gerrish, Benjamin
Gerrish, Joseph
Green, Benjamin
Gugy, Conrad
Harrison, Edward
Hertel de Rouville, René-Ovide
Higgins, David
Irving, Paulus-Æmilius
Johnston, Alexander
Knaut, Philip Augustus
Kneller, Henry
La Corne, Luc de
Landry, Alexis
Langman, Edward
Le Comte Dupré, Georges-Hippolyte
Lévesque, François
Mabane, Adam
McKee, Alexander
McLean, Neil
Marston, Benjamin
Mathews, David
Mills, Sir Thomas
Morris, Charles
Munro, John
Murray, Walter
Nesbitt, William
Pécaudy de Contrecœur, Claude-Pierre
Peters, Joseph
Picoté de Belestre, François-Marie

Renaud, Jean
Ritchie, John
Robinson, Christopher
Salter, Malachy
Schwartz, Otto William
Scott, Joseph
Shaw, William
Simonnet, François
Slade, John
Smith, William
Sower, Christopher
Studholme, Gilfred
Sterling, James
Suckling, George
Tarieu de La Naudière, Charles-
 François
Tonge, Winckworth
Walker, Thomas
Wenman, Richard
White, John
Willard, Abijah
Zouberbuhler, Sebastian

French Régime

Colonial administrators

I (1000–1700)
Ailleboust de Coulonge et
 d'Argentenay, Louis d'
Ailleboust Des Muceaux, Charles-
 Joseph d'
Andigné de Grandfontaine, Hector d'
Bellot, *dit* Lafontaine
Biencourt de Poutrincourt et de Saint-
 Just, Jean de
Biencourt de Saint-Just, Charles de
Boutroue d'Aubigny, Claude de
Bras-de-fer de Chateaufort, Marc-
 Antoine
Buade, Louis de, Comte de Frontenac
 et de Palluau
Caën, Émery de
Chambly, Jacques de
Champflour, François de
Champlain, Samuel de
Chauvin de Tonnetuit, Pierre de
Chomedey de Maisonneuve, Paul de
Denys de Fronsac, Richard
Dubois Davaugour, Pierre
Duchesneau de La Doussinière et
 d'Ambault, Jacques
Du Gua de Monts, Pierre
Du Perron, Thalour
Dupuy, Zacharie
Gaultier de Varennes, René
Guillemot, Guillaume
Huault de Montmagny, Charles
Joybert de Soulanges et de Marson,
 Pierre de
La Poippe, Sieur de
La Roche de Mesgouez, Troilus de

La Rocque de Roberval, Jean-François
Lauson, Jean de (father)
Lauson de Charny, Charles de
Laviolette
Le Borgne de Belle-Isle, Alexandre
Le Febvre de La Barre, Joseph-Antoine
Leneuf de La Poterie, Jacques
Leneuf Du Hérisson, Michel
Menou d'Aulnay, Charles de
Parat, Antoine
Perrot, François-Marie
Prouville, Alexandre de, Marquis de
 Tracy
Razilly, Isaac de
Rémy de Courcelle, Daniel de
Robinau de Villebon, Joseph
Saffray de Mézy, Augustin
Saint-Étienne de La Tour, Charles de
Talon, Jean

II (1701–1740)
Auger de Subercase, Daniel d'
Bochart de Champigny, Jean
Boucher, Pierre
Bouillet de La Chassaigne, Jean
Brisay de Denonville, Jacques-René
 de, Marquis de Denonville
Callière, Louis-Hector de
Crisafy, Antoine de, Marquis de
 Crisafy
Des Friches de Meneval, Louis-
 Alexandre
Dupuy, Claude-Thomas
Forant, Isaac-Louis de
La Porte de Louvigny, Louis de
Laumet, *dit* de Lamothe Cadillac,
 Antoine
Le Moyne de Longueuil, Charles,
 Baron de Longueuil
Le Moyne de Serigny et de Loire,
 Joseph
Leneuf de La Vallière de Beaubassin,
 Michel (father)
Meulles, Jacques de
Monbeton de Brouillan, Jacques-
 François de
Monic, Joseph de
Pastour de Costebelle, Philippe
Provost, François
Ramezay, Claude de
Raudot, Antoine-Denis
Raudot, Jacques
Rigaud de Vaudreuil, Philippe de,
 Marquis de Vaudreuil
Soubras, Pierre-Auguste de
Voyer d'Argenson, Pierre de

III (1741–1770)
Barrin de La Galissonière, Roland-
 Michel, Marquis de La Galissonière
Beauharnois de La Boische, Charles de,
 Marquis de Beauharnois

Beauharnois de La Chaussaye, François
 de, Baron de Beauville
Bégon de La Cour, Claude-Michel
Bégon de La Picardière, Michel
Boschenry de Drucour, Augustin de
Dubois Berthelot de Beaucours, Josué
Galiffet de Caffin, François de
Le Moyne de Bienville, Jean-Baptiste
Le Moyne de Longueuil, Charles,
 Baron de Longueuil
Le Normant de Mézy, Jacques-Ange
Le Prévost Duquesnel, Jean-Baptiste-
 Louis
Monbeton de Brouillan, *dit* Saint-
 Ovide, Joseph de
Rigaud de Vaudreuil, Joseph-
 Hyacinthe de
Taffanel de La Jonquière, Jacques-
 Pierre de, Marquis de La Jonquière

IV (1771–1800)
Angeac, François-Gabriel d'
Bigot, François
Duquesne de Menneville, Ange,
 Marquis Duquesne
Hocquart, Gilles
Le Moyne de Longueuil, Paul-Joseph
L'Espérance, Charles-Gabriel-
 Sébastien de, Baron de L'Espérance
Raymond, Jean-Louis de, Comte de
 Raymond
Rigaud de Vaudreuil, François-Pierre
 de
Rigaud de Vaudreuil de Cavagnial,
 Pierre de, Marquis de Vaudreuil

Officials, appointed

I (1000–1700)
Audouart, *dit* Saint-Germain,
 Guillaume
Bazire, Charles
Bergier, Clerbaud
Chartier de Lotbinière, Louis-Théandre
Fillion, Michel
Gaillard, Mathieu
Gaudais-Dupont, Louis
Gaultier de Comporté, Philippe
Godet, Rolland
Hébert, Louis
Lauson, Jean de (son)
Levasseur, *dit* Lavigne, Jean
Migeon de Branssat, Jean-Baptiste
Mius d'Entremont, Philippe, Baron de
 Pobomcoup
Monts, Sieur de
Morillon Du Bourg
Mouchy, Nicolas de
Patoulet, Jean-Baptiste
Peuvret Demesnu, Jean-Baptiste
Poulin de La Fontaine, Maurice
Rageot, Gilles

53

Robinau de Bécancour, René, Baron de
Portneuf
Rouer de Villeray, Louis
Ruette d'Auteuil, Denis-Joseph
Saint-Père, Jean de

II (1701–1740)
Adhémar de Saint-Martin, Antoine
Ameau, *dit* Saint-Séverin, Séverin
Barbel, Jacques
Barrat, Claude
Bécart de Granville et de Fonville,
Charles
Bermen de La Martinière, Claude de
Bernard de La Rivière, Hilaire
Bigot, François
Boulduc, Louis
Bourdon, Jacques
Bricault de Valmur, Louis-Frédéric
Carrerot, Pierre
Cabazié, Pierre
Chartier de Lotbinière, René-Louis
Clairambault d'Aigremont, François
Collet, Mathieu-Benoît
Couillard de Lespinay, Jean-Baptiste
Cusson, Jean
David, Jacques
Denys de Saint-Simon, Paul
Dubreuil, Jean-Étienne
Dupont de Neuville, Nicolas
Duprac, Jean-Robert
Dupuy de Lisloye, Paul
Durand de La Garenne
Élie, Jacques
Fleury Deschambault, Jacques-Alexis
de
Gaultier de Varennes, Jean-Baptiste
Genaple de Bellefonds, François
Godefroy de Tonnancour, René
Goutin, Mathieu de
Haimard, Pierre
Hamare de La Borde, Jean-Baptiste-
Julien
Horné, *dit* Laneuville, Jacques de
Jacob, Étienne
La Cetière, Florent de
La Forest, Marc-Antoine de
Larue, Guillaume de
La Salle, Nicolas de
Lechasseur, Jean
Le Gouès de Sourdeval, Sébastien
Lepallieur de Laferté, Michel
Le Roy de La Potherie, *dit* Bacqueville
de La Potherie, Claude-Charles
Le Roy Desmarest, Claude-Joseph
Loppinot, Jean-Chrysostome
Lorit, *dit* Gargot, François
Louet, Jean-Claude
Martel de Magos, Jean
Martin de Lino, Jean-François
Martin de Lino, Mathieu-François
Monseignat, Charles de
Normandin, Daniel

Perrin, Antoine
Petit, Jean
Petit, Pierre
Peuvret de Gaudarville, Alexandre
Pottier, Jean-Baptiste
Poulin de Courval, Jean-Baptiste
Prat, Louis
Quesneville, Jean
Quiniard, *dit* Duplessis, Antoine-
Olivier
Rageot de Saint-Luc, Charles
Rageot de Saint-Luc, Nicolas
Raimbault, Pierre
Raimbault de Piedmont, Joseph-
Charles
Rattier, Jean
Regnard Duplessis, Georges
Riverin, Denis
Rivet Cavelier, Pierre
Robinau de Bécancour, Pierre, Baron
de Portneuf
Roger, Guillaume
Roy, *dit* Châtellerault, Michel
Ruette d'Auteuil de Monceaux,
François-Madeleine-Fortuné
Silly, Jean-Baptiste de
Soubras, Pierre-Auguste de
Tailhandier, *dit* La Beaume, Marien
Tantouin de La Touche, Louis
Tétro, Jean-Baptiste
Trotain, *dit* Saint-Seürin, François
Vachon, Paul (father)
Verreau, Barthélemy

III (1741–1770)
Adhémar, Jean-Baptiste
Barolet, Claude
Bénard, Michel
Boucault, Nicolas-Gaspard
Carrerot, André
Carrerot, Philippe
Cheval, *dit* Saint-Jacques, and *dit*
Chevalier, Jacques-Joseph
Claverie, Pierre
Corolère, Jean
Corpron, Jean
Cugnet, François-Étienne
Daine, François
Denys de Saint-Simon, Charles-Paul
Delaborde, Jean
Deslongrais, Nicolas
Dizy de Montplaisir, Pierre
Doreil, André
Du Laurent, Christophe-Hilarion
Foucault, François
Foucher, François
Gaudron de Chevremont, Charles-René
Goutin, François-Marie de
Guyart de Fleury, Jean-Baptiste
Hiché, Henry
Janson, *dit* Lapalme, Dominique
Jeanneau, Étienne
Lafontaine de Belcour, Jacques de

Lanoullier de Boisclerc, Jean-Eustache
Lanoullier de Boisclerc, Nicolas
Laporte de Lalanne, Jean de
Levasseur, Louis
Léveillé, Mathieu
Martel de Belleville, Jean-Urbain
Maurin, François
Michel de Villebois de La Rouvillière,
Honoré
Morpain, Pierre
Nouchet, Joseph
Nouchet, Joseph-Étienne
Perthuis, Jean-Baptiste-Ignace
Pillard, Louis
Pommereau, Jean-Baptiste
Potier Dubuisson, Robert
Poulin, Pierre
Poulin de Courval, Louis-Jean
Poulin de Courval Cressé, Louis-Pierre
Pressé, Hyacinthe-Olivier
Regnard Duplessis de Morampont,
Charles-Denis
Rocbert de La Morandière, Étienne
Rondeau, Jacques-Philippe-Urbain
Sabatier, Antoine
Testu de La Richardière, Richard
Vallette de Chévigny, Médard-Gabriel
Véron de Grandmesnil, Étienne
Verrier, Louis-Guillaume

IV (1771–1800)
Adhémar, Jean-Baptiste-Amable
Ailleboust de Cerry, Philippe-Marie d'
Aumasson de Courville, Louis-Léonard
Berbudeau, Jean-Gabriel
Bernier, Benoît-François
Boisseau, Nicolas
Brassard Deschenaux, Joseph
Bréard, Jacques-Michel
Cadet, Joseph-Michel
Castaing, Pierre-Antoine
Cotton, Barthélemy
Cugnet, François-Joseph
Cuny Dauterive, Philippe-Antoine de
Decoste, Jean-Baptiste
Du Calvet, Pierre
Estèbe, Guillaume
Fleury Deschambault, Joseph
Gamelin, Ignace
Gamelin, Pierre-Joseph
Godefroy de Tonnancour, Louis-
Joseph
Goguet, Denis
Grasset de Saint-Sauveur, André
Guillimin, Guillaume
Hantraye, Claude
Hertel de Rouville, René-Ovide
Laborde, Jean
La Corne, Luc de
Lamaletie, Jean-André
Landriève Des Bordes, Jean-Marie
Le Normant de Mézy, Sébastien-
François-Ange

Le Poupet de La Boularderie, Antoine
Levasseur, René-Nicolas
Martel, Pierre-Michel
Morin de Fonfay, Jean-Baptiste
Navarre, Robert
Olabaratz, Joannis-Galand d'

Olivier de Vézin, Pierre-François
Pélissier, Christophe
Perthuis, Joseph
Pichon, Thomas
Pichot de Querdisien Trémais, Charles-
    François

Prevost de La Croix, Jacques
Rodrigue, Antoine
Saillant, Jean-Antoine
Varin de La Marre, Jean-Victor
Vienne, François-Joseph de

POLITICIANS

III (1741–1770)
Denison, Robert
Philipps, Erasmus James

IV (1771–1800)
Butler, John (d. 1791)
Callbeck, Phillips
Danks, Benoni
Davidson, William
Day, John
Denson, Henry Denny
Doggett, John

Fillis, John
Francklin, Michael
Gerrish, Benjamin
Gerrish, Joseph
Gibbon, Richard
Glasier, Beamsley Perkins
Hardy, Elias
Hicks, John
Higgins, David
Jordan, Jacob
Knaut, Philip Augustus
Le Comte Dupré, Georges-Hippolyte

Nesbitt, William
Ritchie, John
Robinson, Christopher
Salter, Malachy
Schwartz, Otto William
Scott, Joseph
Shaw, William
Suckling, George
Tonge, Winckworth
Wenman, Richard
White, John
Zouberbuhler, Sebastian

RELIGIOUS

Baptists

IV (1771–1800)
Dimock, Shubael
Moulton, Ebenezer

Church of England

I (1000–1700)
Anderson, Thomas
French, John
Stourton, Erasmus

II (1701–1740)
Harrison, John
Jackson, John
Jago, John
Rice, Jacob
Watts, Richard

III (1741–1770)
Cleveland, Aaron
Fordyce, John
Houdin, Jean-Michel, known as
    Father Potentien
Jones, Henry
Kilpatrick, Robert
Moreau, Jean-Baptiste
Peaseley, William
Tutty, William
Vincent, Robert

IV (1771–1800)
Breynton, John
Brooke, John
Chabran Delisle, David
Coughlan, Laurence
Eagleson, John
Langman, Edward
Ogilvie, John
Toosey, Philip
Veyssière, Leger-Jean-Baptiste-Noël
Wood, Thomas

Congregationalists

III (1741–1770)
Barnard, John
Cleveland, Aaron
Moody, Samuel

IV (1771–1800)
Jones, John
Seccombe, John

Methodists

IV (1771–1800)
Coughlan, Laurence
McCarthy, Charles Justin
Marrant, John
Wooster, Hezekiah Calvin

Moravians

IV (1771–1800)
Drachart, Christian Larsen
Haven, Jens

New Light

IV (1771–1800)
Alline, Henry

Presbyterians

IV (1771–1800)
Eagleson, John
Lyon, James

Roman Catholics

Benedictines

II (1701–1740)
Poulet, Georges-François, known as
    M. Dupont

*Brothers Hospitallers of the Cross and
of St Joseph*

II (1701–1740)
Charon de La Barre, François

RELIGIOUS

III (1741–1770)
Hodiesne, Gervais
Jeantot, Jean
Pillard, Louis
Turc de Castelveyre, Louis, known as
  Brother Chrétien

IV (1771–1800)
Simonnet, François

Capuchins

I (1000–1700)
Côme de Mantes
Ignace de Paris
Léonard de Chartres

Congregation of Notre-Dame

I (1000–1700)
Bourgeoys, Marguerite, *dite* du Saint-
  Sacrement
Raisin, Marie

II (1701–1740)
Barbier, Marie, *dite* de L'Assomption
Charly Saint-Ange, Marie-Catherine,
  dite du Saint-Sacrement
Sayward, Mary, *dite* Marie des Anges

III (1741–1770)
Arnaud, Marie-Marguerite-Daniel, *dite*
  Saint-Arsène
La Corne de Chaptes, Marie-Madeleine
  de, *dite* du Saint-Sacrement
Lefebvre Angers, Marie-Angélique,
  dite Saint-Simon
Le Moyne de Sainte-Marie, Marguerite,
  dite du Saint-Esprit
Longley, Lydia, *dite* Sainte-Madeleine
Roy, Marguerite, *dite* de la Conception
Trottier, Marguerite, *dite* Saint-Joseph

IV (1771–1800)
Maugue-Garreau, Marie-Josephe, *dite*
  de l'Assomption
Piot de Langloiserie, Marie-
  Marguerite, *dite* Saint-Hippolyte

Dominicans

IV (1771–1800)
Ledru, Jean-Antoine (possibly)

Franciscans

I (1000–1700)
Nicholas of Lynne
Thevet, André

Hospital nuns of St Joseph

I (1000–1700)
Macé, Catherine
Maillet, Marie
Moreau de Brésoles, Judith

II (1701–1740)
Gallard, Charlotte
Maumousseau, Françoise
Morin, Marie
Silver, Mary

III (1741–1770)
Cuillerier, Marie-Anne-Véronique
Gaudé, Françoise
Leduc, Anne-Françoise, *dite* Saint-
  Joseph

*Hospital nuns of the Hôpital Général
  (Quebec)*

III (1741–1770)
Juchereau Duchesnay, Marie-Joseph,
  dite de l'Enfant-Jésus
Langlois, Marie-Thérèse, *dite* de Saint-
  Jean-Baptiste
Ramezay, Marie-Charlotte de, *dite* de
  Saint-Claude de la Croix

*Hospital nuns of the Hôtel-Dieu
  (Quebec)*

I (1000–1700)
Forestier, Marie, *dite* de Saint-
  Bonaventure-de-Jésus
Giffard, Marie-Françoise, *dite* Marie de
  Saint-Ignace
Guenet, Marie, *dite* de Saint-Ignace
Irwin, Marie, *dite* de la Conception
Simon de Longpré, Marie-Catherine
  de, *dite* de Saint-Augustin
Skanudharoua, Geneviève-Agnès, *dite*
  de Tous-les-Saints

II (1701–1740)
Bourdon, Marguerite, *dite* de Saint-
  Jean-Baptiste
Juchereau de La Ferté, Jeanne-
  Françoise, *dite* de Saint-Ignace
Maufils, Marie-Madeleine, *dite* de
  Saint-Louis
Soumande, Louise, *dite* de Saint-
  Augustin

III (1741–1770)
Regnard Duplessis, Marie-Andrée, *dite*
  de Sainte-Hélène
Tibierge, Marie-Catherine, *dite* de
  Saint-Joachim

IV (1771–1800)
Curot, Marie-Louise, *dite* de Saint-
  Martin

Jesuits

I (1000–1700)
BROTHERS
Bonnemere, Florent
Du Thet, Gilbert
Goupil, René
Liégeois, Jean
Malherbe, François
DONNÉS
Boquet, Charles
Gendron, François
La Lande, Jean de
Lambert, Eustache
Le Coq, Robert
Pinard, Louis
PRIESTS
Albanel, Charles
Allouez, Claude
Bailloquet, Pierre
Biard, Pierre
Brébeuf, Jean de
Buteux, Jacques
Chabanel, Noël
Chastellain, Pierre
Chaumonot, Pierre-Joseph-Marie
Dablon, Claude
Dalmas, Antoine
Daniel, Antoine
Davost, Ambroise
Dolebeau, Jean
Druillettes, Gabriel
Du Peron, François
Frémin, Jacques
Garnier, Charles
Garreau, Léonard
Jogues, Isaac
Lalemant, Charles
Lalemant, Gabriel
Lalemant, Jérôme
Le Jeune, Paul
Le Mercier, François-Joseph
Le Moyne, Simon
Lyonne, Martin de
Marquette, Jacques
Massé, Énemond
Ménard, René
Nouë, Anne de
Noyrot, Philibert
Perrault, Julien
Pierron, Jean
Pijart, Claude
Pijart, Pierre
Poncet de La Rivière, Joseph-Antoine
Quen, Jean de
Quentin, Claude

Quentin, Jacques
Ragueneau, Paul
Raymbaut, Charles
Vimont, Barthélemy

II (1701–1740)
DONNÉS
Couture, Guillaume
Largillier, Jacques, known as
    Le Castor
Le Sueur, Pierre
PRIESTS
André, Louis
Aulneau (de La Touche), Jean-Pierre
Avaugour, Louis d'
Aveneau, Claude
Beschefer, Thierry
Bigot, Jacques
Bigot, Vincent
Bouvart, Martin
Bruyas, Jacques
Carheil, Étienne de
Chauchetière, Claude
Cholenec, Pierre
Couvert, Michel-Germain de
Crespieul, François de
Enjalran, Jean
Garnier, Julien
Germain, Joseph-Louis
Gravier, Jacques
Lagrené, Pierre de
Lamberville, Jacques de
Lamberville, Jean de
Laure, Pierre-Michel
Loyard, Jean-Baptiste
Marest, Joseph-Jacques
Marest, Pierre-Gabriel
Mermet, Jean
Millet, Pierre
Nouvel, Henri
Raffeix, Pierre
Rale, Sébastien
Silvy, Antoine
Vaillant de Gueslis, François
Villes, Jean-Marie de

III (1741–1770)
BROTHERS
Boispineau, Jean-Jard
PRIESTS
Aubery, Joseph
Baudouin, Michel
Beaubois, Nicolas-Ignace de
Chardon, Jean-Baptiste
Charlevoix, Pierre-François-Xavier de
Coquart, Claude-Godefroy
Daniélou, Jean-Pierre
Des Landes, Joseph
Duparc, Jean-Baptiste
Guignas, Michel
La Bretonnière, Jacques-Quintin de

La Chasse, Pierre de
Lafitau, Joseph-François
Lamorinie, Jean-Baptiste de
La Richardie, Armand de
Lauverjat, Étienne
Lauzon, Pierre de
Le Sueur, Jacques-François
Marcol, Gabriel
Mareuil, Pierre de
Mésaiger, Charles-Michel
Nau, Luc-François
Saint-Pé, Jean-Baptiste de
Tournois, Jean-Baptiste

IV (1771–1800)
Bonnécamps, Joseph-Pierre de
Casot, Jean-Joseph
Du Jaunay, Pierre
Floquet, Pierre-René
Germain, Charles
Glapion, Augustin-Louis de
Huguet, Joseph
La Brosse, Jean-Baptiste de
Potier, Pierre-Philippe
Roubaud, Pierre-Joseph-Antoine

Minims

I (1000–1700)
Boullé, Eustache

Recollets

I (1000–1700)
BROTHERS
Duplessis, Pacifique
Langoissieux, Charles
Mohier, Gervais
Pelletier, Didace
Sagard, Gabriel
PRIESTS
Allart, Germain
Dethunes, Exupère
Dolebeau, Jean
François, Claude, known as Brother
    Luc
Galleran, Guillaume
Huet, Paul
Jamet, Denis
La Place, Simon-Gérard de
La Ribourde, Gabriel de
La Roche Daillon, Joseph de
Le Baillif, Georges
Le Caron, Joseph
Le Clercq, Chrestien
Maupassant, Eustache
Membré, Zénobe
Perrault, Hyacinthe
Piat, Irénée
Poulain, Guillaume
Viel, Nicolas

II (1701–1740)
Bruslé, Michel
Bulteau, Guillaume
Champy, Gélase
Constantin, Nicolas-Bernardin
Delhalle, Constantin
Denys, Joseph
Douay, Anastase
Drué, Juconde
Dupont, Siméon
Filiastre, Luc
Georgemé, Séraphin
Goyer, Olivier
Guesdron, Julien
Hennepin, Louis
Ladan, Adrien
La Frenaye, François de
La Marche, Dominique de
Landon, Simple
La Place, Louis-Hyacinthe de
Le Dorz, Bénin
Leroux, Valentin
Le Roy, Henri
Le Tac, Xiste
Martin de Lino, Antoine
Moireau, Claude
Ozon, Potentien
Pélerin, Ambroise

III (1741–1770)
Callet, Luc
Constantin, Justinien
Durand, Justinien
Foucault, Simon
Gaufin, Valérien
Houdin, Jean-Michel
Imbault, Maurice
Pain, Félix
René, Patrice
Rouillard, Ambroise

IV (1771–1800)
Carpentier, Bonaventure
Castenet, Jean-Baptiste-Marie
Chartier de Lotbinière, Eustache
Crespel, Emmanuel
Quintal, Augustin
Veyssière, Leger-Jean-Baptiste-Noël

Regulars

I (1000–1700)
Brendan, Saint

Seculars

I (1000–1700)
Aubry, Nicolas
Bernières, Henri de
Carbonariis, Giovanni Antonio de
Caumont, Pierre de

RELIGIOUS

Du Bos, Nicolas
Dudouyt, Jean
Eirikr *upsi* Gnupsson
Fléché, Jessé
Fleury d'Eschambault, Jacques
Gendron, François
Guyon, Jean
Lauson de Charny, Charles de
Le Sueur, Jean, known as Abbé de
    Saint-Sauveur
Merlac, André-Louis de
Morel, Thomas
Paumart, Jean
Pommier, Hugues
Thury, Louis-Pierre

II (1701–1740)
Ango Des Maizerets, Louis
Basset, Jean
Bergier, Marc
Boullard, Étienne
Buisson de Saint-Cosme, Jean-François
    (1660–1712)
Buisson de Saint-Cosme, Jean-François
    (1667–1706)
Calvarin, Goulven
Davion, Albert
Dupré, François
Gaulin, Antoine
Foucault, Nicolas
Francheville, Pierre
Gaultier de Varennes, Jean-Baptiste
Glandelet, Charles de
La Colombière, Joseph de
La Croix de Chevrières de Saint-
    Vallier, Jean-Baptiste de
Laval, François de
Martin, Charles-Amador
Morin, Germain
Petit, Louis
Pourroy de Lauberivière, François-
    Louis de
Soumande, Louis
Thaumur de La Source, Dominique-
    Antoine-René
Thiboult, Thomas
Vachon, Paul (son)
Volant de Saint-Claude, Pierre and
    Claude

III (1741–1770)
Allenou de Lavillangevin, René-Jean
Chartier de Lotbinière, Eustache
Chevalier, Jean-Charles
Daudin, Henri
Dubreil de Pontbriand, Henri-Marie
Dufournel, Louis-Gaspard
Forget Duverger, Jacques-François
Fornel, Joachim
Godefroy de Tonnancour, Charles-
    Antoine
Gosselin, Jean-Baptiste
Hazeur, Joseph-Thierry

Lepage de Sainte-Claire, Louis
Le Prévost, Pierre-Gabriel
Lyon de Saint-Ferréol, Jean
Maillard, Pierre
Manach, Jean
Margane de Lavaltrie, François
Mercier, Jean-Pierre
Montigny, François de
Navières, Joseph
Plante, Charles
Ransonnet, Sylvestre-François-Michel
Récher, Jean-Félix
Resche, Pierre-Joseph
Robinau de Portneuf, Philippe-René
Tremblay, Henri-Jean
Vallier, François-Elzéar
Varlet, Dominique-Marie

IV (1771–1800)
Aide-Créquy, Jean-Antoine
Bailly de Messein, Charles-François
Bédard, Thomas-Laurent
Boiret, Urbain
Bourg, Joseph-Mathurin
Brassard, Louis-Marie
Briand, Jean-Olivier
Dudevant, Arnauld-Germain
Garreau, *dit* Saint-Onge, Pierre
Girard, Jacques
Hazeur de L'Orme, Pierre
Hubert, Jean-François
Jacrau, Joseph-André-Mathurin
La Corne de Chaptes, Joseph-Marie de
Le Guerne, François
Le Loutre, Jean-Louis
Le Roux, Thomas-François
MacDonald, James
Marchand, Étienne
Mariauchau d'Esgly, Louis-Philippe
Porlier, Pierre-Antoine
Pressart, Colomban-Sébastien
Sorbier de Villars, François
Youville, Charles-Marie-Madeleine d'

*Sisters of Charity of the Hôpital
    Général (Montreal) (Grey Nuns)*

III (1741–1770)
Véronneau, Agathe

IV (1771–1880)
Dufrost de Lajemmerais, Marie-
    Marguerite (Youville)
Lemoine Despins, Marguerite-Thérèse

Sulpicians

I (1000–1700)
Allet, Antoine d'
Bailly, Guillaume
Baudoin, Jean
Bréhant de Galinée, René de
Le Maistre, Jacques

Pérot, Gilles
Salignac de La Mothe-Fénelon,
    François de
Souart, Gabriel
Thubières de Levy de Queylus, Gabriel
Vignal, Guillaume

II (1701–1740)
Barthélemy, Michel
Breslay, René-Charles de
Cavelier, Jean
Chaigneau, Léonard
Champion de Cicé, Louis-Armand
Chèze, François
Dollier de Casson, François
Gay, Robert-Michel
Geoffroy, Louis
Guyotte, Étienne
La Faye, Louis-François de
Lascaris d'Urfé, François-Saturnin
Le Fevre, François
Le Pape Du Lescöat, Jean-Gabriel-
    Marie
Meriel, Henri-Antoine
Rémy, Pierre
Robert, Clément
Trouvé, Claude
Vachon de Belmont, François

III (1741–1770)
Chauvreulx, Claude-Jean-Baptiste
Chevalier, Jean-Charles
Dargent, Joseph
Déat, Antoine
Depéret, Élie
Gay Desenclaves, Jean-Baptiste de
Guen, Hamon
La Goudalie, Charles de
Le Sueur, Pierre
Normant Du Faradon, Louis
Quéré de Tréguron, Maurice
Vilermaula, Louis-Michel de

IV (1771–1800)
Brassier, Gabriel-Jean
Curatteau, Jean-Baptiste
Degeay, Jacques
Dosquet, Pierre-Herman
Guichart, Vincent-Fleuri
Lagarde, Pierre-Paul-François de
Latour, Bertrand de
Magon de Terlaye, François-Auguste
Mathevet, Jean-Claude
Miniac, Jean-Pierre de
Montgolfier, Étienne
Picquet, François

Ursulines

I (1000–1700)
Guyart, Marie, *dite* de l'Incarnation
    (Martin)

Savonnières de La Troche, Marie de, *dite* de Saint-Joseph

II (1701–1740)
Bourdon, Anne, *dite* de Sainte-Agnès
Legardeur de Repentigny, Marie-Jeanne-Madeleine, *dite* de Sainte-Agathe

III (1741–1770)
Boucher, Geneviève, *dite* de Saint-Pierre
Daneau de Muy, Charlotte, *dite* de Sainte-Hélène
Davis, Marie-Anne, *dite* de Saint-Benoît

IV (1771–1800)
Guillimin, Marie-Françoise, *dite* de Saint-Antoine
Migeon de Branssat, Marie-Anne, *dite* de la Nativité
Wheelwright, Esther (Marie-Joseph), *dite* de l'Enfant-Jésus

SCIENTISTS

II (1701–1740)
Jérémie, *dit* Lamontagne, Nicolas
Sarrazin, Michel

III (1741–1770)
Gaultier, Jean-François
Gosselin, Jean-Baptiste

Isham, James
Jérémie, *dit* Lamontagne, Catherine (Aubuchon; Lepallieur de Laferté)
La Croix, Hubert-Joseph de
Lafitau, Joseph-François

IV (1771–1800)
Bonnécamps, Joseph-Pierre de
Hearne, Samuel
Hutchins, Thomas
Kalm, Pehr
Schindler, Joseph
Wales, William

SLAVES

I (1000–1700)
Le Jeune, Olivier

II (1701–1740)
Acoutsina
Marie-Joseph-Angélique

III (1741–1770)
Duplessis, Marguerite
Léveillé, Mathieu
Marie
Pierre

IV (1771–1800)
Joe
York, Jack

SURVEYORS

I (1000–1700)
Allemand, Pierre
Basset Des Lauriers, Bénigne
Bourdon, Jean
Guyon Du Buisson, Jean (son) Pasquine
Randin, Hugues
Saccardy, Vincent
Villeneuve, Robert de

II (1701–1740)
Bécart de Granville et de Fonville, Charles
Bernard de La Rivière, Hilaire
Catalogne, Gédéon
Couagne, Jean-Baptiste de
Deshayes, Jean

Franquelin, Jean-Baptiste-Louis
Lajoüe, François de
Le Rouge, Jean
L'Hermitte, Jacques
Volant de Radisson, Étienne

III (1741–1770)
Bonhomme, *dit* Beaupré, Noël
Boucher, Pierre-Jérôme
Haldimand, Peter Frederick
Janson, *dit* Lapalme, Dominique
Levasseur, Pierre-Noël
Maillou, *dit* Desmoulins, Jean-Baptiste
Mitchell, George
Monk, James
Pattin, John

Robson, Joseph
Southack, Cyprian
Taverner, William
Vallée, François-Madeleine
Wigate, John

IV (1771–1800)
Aitken, Alexander
Collins, John
Cook, James
Desdevens de Glandons, Maurice
Marston, Benjamin
Morris, Charles
Peachy, James
Turnor, Philip
Vancouver, George

WOMEN

I (1000–1700)

Boullé, Hélène, *dite* de Saint-Augustin (Champlain)
Boullongne, Marie-Barbe de (Ailleboust de Coulonge et d'Argentenay)
Bourgeoys, Marguerite, *dite* du Saint-Sacrement
Brice, Madame de
Charité
Desportes, Hélène (Hébert; Morin)
Espérance
Foi
Forestier, Marie, *dite* de Saint-Bonaventure-de-Jésus
Gandeacteua
Giffard, Marie-Françoise, *dite* Marie de Saint-Ignace
Grandmaison, Éléonore de (Boudier de Beauregard; Chavigny de Berchereau; Gourdeau de Beaulieu; Cailhault de La Tesserie)
Guenet, Marie, *dite* de Saint-Ignace
Guyart, Marie, *dite* de l'Incarnation (Martin)
Hébert, Guillemette (Couillard de Lespinay)
Irwin, Marie, *dite* de la Conception
Jacquelin, Françoise-Marie (Saint-Étienne de La Tour)
La Roque, Marguerite de
Macé, Catherine
Maillet, Marie
Mance, Jeanne
Messier, Martine (Primot)
Moreau de Brésoles, Judith
Motin, Jeanne (Menou d'Aulnay; Saint-Étienne de La Tour)
Oionhaton
Raisin, Marie
Rollet, Marie (Hébert)
Savonnières de La Troche, Marie de, *dite* de Saint-Joseph
Simon de Longpré, Marie-Catherine de, *dite* de Saint-Augustin
Skanudharoua, *dite* Geneviève-Agnès, de Tous-les-Saints
Tekakwitha, Kateri

II (1701–1740)

Acoutsina
Barbier, Marie, *dite* de l'Assomption
Bourdon, Anne, *dite* de Sainte-Agnès
Bourdon, Marguerite, *dite* de Saint-Jean-Baptiste
Brandeau, Esther
Charly Saint-Ange, Marie-Catherine, *dite* du Saint-Sacrement
Dizy, *dit* Montplaisir, Marguerite (Desbrieux)

Gallard, Charlotte
Gouentagrandi
Joybert de Soulanges et de Marson, Louise-Élisabeth de (Rigaud de Vaudreuil, Marquise de Vaudreuil)
Juchereau de La Ferté, Jeanne-Françoise, *dite* de Saint-Ignace
Juchereau de Saint-Denis, Charlotte-Françoise, known as Comtesse de Saint-Laurent (Viennay-Pachot; Dauphin de La Forest)
Le Ber, Jeanne
Legardeur de Repentigny, Marie-Jeanne-Madeleine, *dite* de Sainte-Agathe
Marie-Joseph-Angélique
Maufils, Marie-Madeleine, *dite* de Saint-Louis
Maumousseau, Françoise
Morin, Marie
Roybon d'Allonne, Madeleine de
Saint-Étienne de La Tour, Agathe de (Bradstreet; Campbell)
Sayward, Mary, *dite* Marie des Anges
Silver, Mary
Soumande, Louise, *dite* de Saint-Augustin
Thanadelthur
Thavenet, Marguerite de (Hertel de La Fresnière)

III (1741–1770)

André de Leigne, Louise-Catherine (Hertel de Rouville)
Arnaud, Marie-Marguerite-Daniel, *dite* Saint-Arsène
Boucher, Geneviève, *dite* de Saint-Pierre
Corriveau, Marie-Josephte, known as La Corriveau (Bouchard; Dodier)
Couagne, Thérèse de (Poulin de Francheville)
Couc, Elizabeth (La Chenette, Techenet; Montour)
Cuillerier, Marie-Anne-Véronique
Daneau de Muy, Charlotte, *dite* de Sainte-Hélène
Davis, Marie-Anne, *dite* de Saint-Benoît
Duplessis, Marguerite
Gaudé, Françoise
Guyon, Louise (Thibault; Damours de Freneuse)
Jarret de Verchères, Marie-Madeleine (Tarieu de La Pérade)
Jérémie, *dit* Lamontagne, Catherine (Aubuchon; Lepallieur de Laferté)

Juchereau Duchesnay, Marie-Joseph, *dite* de l'Enfant-Jésus
La Corne de Chaptes, Marie-Madeleine de, *dite* du Saint-Sacrement
Langlois, Marie-Thérèse, *dite* de Saint-Jean-Baptiste
Leduc, Anne-Françoise, *dite* Saint-Joseph
Lefebvre Angers, Marie-Angélique, *dite* Saint-Simon
Le Moyne de Sainte-Marie, Marguerite, *dite* du Saint-Esprit
Longley, Lydia, *dite* Sainte-Madeleine
Maisonnat, Marie-Madeleine (Winniett)
Marie
Ramezay, Marie-Charlotte de, *dite* de Saint-Claude de la Croix
Regnard Duplessis, Marie-Andrée, *dite* de Sainte-Hélène
Rocbert de La Morandière, Marie-Élisabeth (Bégon de La Cour)
Roy, Marguerite, *dite* de la Conception
Saint-Père, Agathe de (Legardeur de Repentigny)
Tibierge, Marie-Catherine, *dite* de Saint-Joachim
Trottier, Marguerite, *dite* Saint-Joseph
Véronneau, Agathe

IV (1771–1800)

Barbel, Marie-Anne (Fornel)
Curot, Marie-Louise, *dite* de Saint-Martin
Dufrost de Lajemmerais, Marie-Marguerite (Youville)
Guillimin, Marie-Françoise, *dite* de Saint-Antoine
Koñwatsiˀtsiaiéñni (Mary Brant)
Lemoine Despins, Marguerite-Thérèse
Maugue-Garreau, Marie-Josèphe, *dite* de l'Assomption
Migeon de Branssat, Marie-Anne, *dite* de la Nativité
Mikak
Moore, Frances (Brooke)
Osborn, Elizabeth (Myrick; Paine; Doane)
Piot de Langloiserie, Marie-Marguerite, *dite* Saint-Hippolyte
Ramezay, Louise de
Renaud d'Avène Des Méloizes, Angélique (Péan)
Wheelwright, Esther (Marie-Joseph), *dite* de l'Enfant-Jésus
Williams, Eunice

GEOGRAPHICAL INDEX

CANADA

Alberta

British Columbia
Mainland
Vancouver Island

Manitoba

New Brunswick

Newfoundland and Labrador
Labrador
Newfoundland

Northwest Territories

Nova Scotia
Cape Breton Island
Mainland

Ontario
Centre
East
Niagara
North
Southwest

Prince Edward Island

Quebec
Bas-Saint-Laurent–Gaspésie/
　Côte-Nord
Montréal/Outaouais
Nord-Ouest/Saguenay–Lac-Saint-Jean/
　Nouveau-Québec
Québec
Trois-Rivières/Cantons-de-l'Est

Saskatchewan

OTHER COUNTRIES

Azores
Chile
England
Ireland
Falkland Islands
France
French Guyana
India
Malagasy Republic

Malta
Mexico
Saint-Pierre and Miquelon
Senegal
Spain
United States of America
Union of Soviet Socialist Republics
West Indies

ONTARIO

I East
II Centre
III Niagara
IV Southwest
V North

63

QUEBEC

I Bas-Saint-Laurent–Gaspésie/Côte-Nord
II Québec
III Trois-Rivières/Cantons-de-l'Est
IV Montréal/Outaouais
V Nord-Ouest/Saguenay–Lac-Saint-Jean/
Nouveau-Québec

Geographical Index

The Geographical Index is divided into two sections: Canada, including the biographies that deal with particular areas of this country, and Other Countries, including biographies of those born in Canada who made an impact elsewhere.

For the purposes of this index, Canada is divided according to the present provinces and territories, listed alphabetically. (Yukon Territory does not appear here, however, since no one in these volumes reached it.) Five provinces are further subdivided. British Columbia, Newfoundland and Labrador, and Nova Scotia each have two subdivisions. Ontario and Quebec appear in five subdivisions as shown on the maps; those for Quebec are based on the administrative regions defined by the Direction générale du domaine territorial.

A biography is found in a division according to the activity of the subject as an adult. Places of birth, education, retirement, and death have not been considered. Persons whose functions may span several regions, such as a bishop or a governor, have been listed according to their seat of office and the activities described in their biographies. Merchants are listed in the area of the primary location of their business, and explorers in the areas they discovered or visited.

Place of birth determines the persons found in the second section, Other Countries. Only persons born in the territory of present-day Canada are listed in this section and they are given under the country or countries in which they had a career or in which they were active. (Persons not born in Canada who had a career elsewhere as well as in this country are found only in the first section.) Under the heading Other Countries will be found subdivisions for overseas territories of European countries, for example, Saint-Pierre and Miquelon. All West Indian islands have been grouped together.

CANADA

ALBERTA

II (1701–1740)
Swan

III (1741–1770)
Henday, Anthony

IV (1771–1800)
Grant, Cuthbert
Sutherland, George
Turnor, Philip
Wapinesiw

BRITISH COLUMBIA

Mainland

IV (1771–1800)
Dixon, George
Koyah
Pérez Hernandez, Juan Josef
Vancouver, George

Vancouver Island

I (1000–1700)
Drake, Sir Francis

IV (1771–1800)
Bodega y Quadra, Juan Francisco de la
Clerke, Charles
Cook, James
Dixon, George
Duncan, Charles
Hanna, James
Kendrick, John
King, James
Mackay, John
Martínez Fernández y Martínez de la Sierra, Estaban José
Muquinna
Pérez Hernandez, Juan Josef
Vancouver, George
Webber, John
Wikinanish

MANITOBA

I (1000–1700)
Abraham, John
Allemand, Pierre
Anderson, Thomas
Bayly, Charles
Bond, William
Bridgar, John
Button, Sir Thomas
Chouart Des Groseilliers, Médard
Edgcombe, Leonard
Fletcher, John
Garland, Thomas
Geyer, George
Gillam, Zacharie
Gorst, Thomas
Hamilton, Andrew
Le Moyne de Châteauguay, Louis
Missenden, Samuel
Munk, Jens Eriksen
Phipps, Thomas
Sanford, Esbon
Sergeant, Henry
Smithsend, Nicholas
Smithsend, Richard
Testard de La Forest, Gabriel
Verner, Hugh
Walker, Nehemiah
Young, James

II (1701–1740)
Apthorp, Alexander
Aulneau (de La Touche), Jean-Pierre
Baley, Henry
Beale, Anthony
Berley, George
Bermen de La Martinière, Claude de
Bird, Thomas
Bishop, Nathaniel
Davis, Joseph
Denys de Bonaventure, Simon-Pierre
Dufrost de La Jemerais, Christophe
Dugué de Boisbriand, Pierre
Fullartine, John
Gaultier de La Vérendrye, Jean-
  Baptiste

Gillam, Benjamin
Grimington, Michael (father)
Grimington, Michael (son)
Hopkins, Samuel
Jérémie, *dit* Lamontagne, Nicolas
Juchereau de La Ferté, Denis-Joseph
Kelsey, Henry
Knight, James
Le Moyne d'Iberville et d'Ardillières,
  Pierre
Le Moyne de Martigny et de
  La Trinité, Jean-Baptiste
Le Moyne de Serigny et de Loire,
  Joseph
Marest, Pierre-Gabriel
Napper, James
Radisson, Pierre-Esprit
Render, Thomas
Scroggs, John
Silvy, Antoine
Stuart, William
Swan
Thanadelthur
Vaughan, David
Waggoner, Rowland
Ward, Richard

III (1741–1770)
Bean, John
Clark, George
Coquart, Claude-Godefroy
Dejordy de Villebon, Charles-René
Evison, Robert
Gaultier de La Vérendrye, Louis-
  Joseph
Gaultier de La Vérendrye de Boumois,
  Pierre
Gaultier de Varennes et de La
  Vérendrye, Pierre
Henday, Anthony
Isham, James
La Corne, Louis de, known as
  Chevalier de La Corne
La France, Joseph
Lamorinie, Jean-Baptiste de

Legardeur de Saint-Pierre, Jacques
McCliesh, Thomas
Middleton, Christopher
Moor, William
Newton, John
Nolan Lamarque, Charles
Norton, Richard
Pilgrim, Robert
Potts, John
Robson, Joseph
Skrimsher, Samuel
Smith, Francis
Smith, Joseph
Staunton, Richard
Thompson, Edward
White, Richard
White, Thomas

IV (1771–1800)
Batt, Isaac
Cocking, Matthew
Cole, John
Duncan, Charles
Galaup, Jean-François de, Comte de
  Lapérouse
Gaultier Du Tremblay, François
Grant, Cuthbert
Hearne, Samuel
Hutchins, Thomas
Isbister, Joseph
Jacobs, Ferdinand
Jarvis, Edward
Marten, Humphrey
Matonabbee
Norton, Moses
Primeau, Louis
Ross, Malchom
Sutherland, George
Sutherland, James
Turnor, Philip
Umfreville, Edward
Waddens, Jean-Étienne
Wales, William
Walker, William
Wapinesiw

NEW BRUNSWICK

I (1000–1700)
Aernoutsz, Jurriaen
Aprendestiguy, Martin d'
Asticou
Biard, Pierre
Bourdon de Romainville, Jean
Chambly, Jacques de

Champlain, Samuel de
Côme de Mantes
Denys, Nicolas
Denys de Fronsac, Richard
Desdames, Thierry
Dolebeau, Jean
Frémin, Jacques

Gravé Du Pont, Robert
Ignace de Paris
Jacquelin, Françoise-Marie (Saint-
  Étienne de La Tour)
Joybert de Soulanges et de Marson,
  Pierre de
La Place, Simon-Gérard de

La Ralde, Raymond de
La Tourasse, Charles
Le Borgne, Emmanuel
Le Clercq, Chrestien
Lescarbot, Marc
Leverett, John
Lyonne, Martin de
Marot, Bernard
Menou d'Aulnay, Charles de
Messamouet
Motin, Jeanne (Menou d'Aulnay; Saint-Étienne de La Tour)
Ouagimou
Panounias
Pasquine
Perrot, François-Marie
Quentin, Claude
Ralluau, Jean
Randin, Hugues
Rhoades, John
Robinau de Villebon, Joseph
Saccardy, Vincent
Saint-Étienne de La Tour, Charles de
Saint-Étienne de La Tour, Claude de
Sarcel de Prévert, Jean
Secoudon
Sedgwick, Robert
Temple, Sir Thomas
Thury, Louis-Pierre
Tyng, Edward
Walker, Richard

II (1701–1740)
Abbadie de Saint-Castin, Bernard-Anselme d', Baron de Saint-Castin
Abbadie de Saint-Castin, Jean-Vincent d', Baron de Saint-Castin
Alden, John
Allard de Sainte-Marie, Jean-Joseph d'
Basset, David
Blanchard, Guillaume
Bruslé, Michel
Church, Benjamin
Damours de Chauffours, Louis
Damours de Clignancour, René
Denys de Bonaventure, Simon-Pierre
Énault de Barbaucannes, Philippe
Goutin, Mathieu de
Guion, François
Hilton, Winthrop
Leneuf de La Vallière de Beaubassin, Alexandre
L'Hermitte, Jacques
Loyard, Jean-Baptiste
Maisonnat, dit Baptiste, Pierre
Martel de Magos, Jean
Moireau, Claude
Monbeton de Brouillan, Jacques-François de
Petit, Louis
Rale, Sébastien
Robinau de Bécancour, Pierre, Baron de Portneuf

Robinau de Neuvillette, Daniel
Serreau de Saint-Aubin, Jean
Testard de Montigny, Jacques
Tibaudeau, Pierre
Tibierge
Villieu, Claude-Sébastien de
Wroth, Robert

III (1741–1770)
Abbadie de Saint-Castin, Joseph d', Baron de Saint-Castin
Ailleboust de Périgny, Paul d'
Aubery, Joseph
Bâtard, Étienne
Bermen de La Martinière, Claude-Antoine de
Bourg, dit Belle-Humeur, Alexandre
Brossard, dit Beausoleil, Joseph
Chartier, Michel
Cobb, Silvanus
Cope, Jean-Baptiste
Daniélou, Jean-Pierre
Elliot, Robert
Franquet, Louis
Gaultier de La Vérendrye de Boumois, Pierre
Goldthwait, Benjamin
Gorham, John
Guyon, Louise (Thibault; Damours de Freneuse)
Gyles, John
How, Edward
La Chasse, Pierre de
La Corne, Louis de, known as Chevalier de La Corne
La Goudalie, Charles de
Laurent, Paul
Lauverjat, Étienne
Levrault de Langis Montegron, Jean-Baptiste
Manach, Jean
Marin de La Malgue, Paul
Mitchell, George
Nodogawerrimet
Pote, William
Rouer de Villeray, Benjamin
Rous, John
Saint-Ours, François-Xavier de
Scott, George
Southack, Cyprian
Testu de La Richardière, Richard

IV (1771–1800)
Akomápis, Nicholas
Alline, Henry
Angeac, François-Gabriel d'
Arimph, Jean-Baptiste
Aubert de Gaspé, Ignace-Philippe
Aumasson de Courville, Louis-Léonard
Benoît, Pierre
Bourdages, Raymond
Bourg, Joseph-Mathurin

Brewse, John
Bruce, Robert George
Byron, John
Carpentier, Bonaventure
Castanet, Jean-Baptiste-Marie
Chartier de Lotbinière, Michel
Cox, Nicholas
Danks, Benoni
Davidson, William
Denis de Saint-Simon, Antoine-Charles
Denys de Vitré, Théodose-Matthieu
De Peyster, Abraham
Deschamps de Boishébert et de Raffetot, Charles
Du Calvet, Pierre
Dugas, Joseph
Dumas, Jean-Daniel
Du Pont Duchambon de Vergor, Louis
Du Pont Duvivier, François
Du Pont Duvivier, Joseph
Eagleson, John
Germain, Charles
Glasier, Beamsley Perkins
Godin, Joseph
Goreham, Joseph
Hardy, Elias
Jacau de Fiedmont, Louis-Thomas
Jacobs, Samuel
Jadis, Charles Newland Godfrey
Jeanson, Guillaume
Johnstone, James, known as Chevalier de Johnstone
La Brosse, Jean-Baptiste de
Landry, Alexis
Ledru, Jean-Antoine
Legardeur de Croisille et de Montesson, Joseph-Michel
Le Guerne, François
Le Loutre, Jean-Louis
Le Roux, Thomas-François
Lewis, William
Marston, Benjamin
Monckton, Robert
Morris, Charles
Munro, John
Owen, William
Pellegrin, Gabriel
Peters, Thomas
Pichon, Thomas
Picoté de Belestre, François-Marie
Ramezay, Jean-Baptiste-Nicolas-Roch de
Robinson, Christopher
Saint-Aubin, Ambroise
Sower, Christopher
Studholme, Gilfred
Tarieu de La Naudière, Charles-François
Tomah, Pierre
Tonge, Winckworth
Willard, Abijah
Winslow, John
Wood, Thomas

NEWFOUNDLAND AND LABRADOR

Labrador

I (1000–1700)
Bjarni, Herjólfsson
Cabot, John
Cabot, Sebastian
Corte-Real, Gaspar
Cunningham, John
Fernandes, John
Jolliet, Louis
Knight, John
Leifr *heppni* Eiriksson
Rut, John
Thorfinnr *karlsefni* Thordarson
Waymouth, George

II (1701–1740)
Deschamps de Boishébert, Henri-Louis
Juchereau de La Ferté, Denis-Joseph
Moore, Thomas
Silvy, Antoine

III (1741–1770)
Bayne, Daniel
Bazil, Louis
Constantin, Pierre
Lucas, Francis
Margane de Lavaltrie, François
Martel de Brouague, François
Pattin, John
Webb, James

IV (1771–1800)
Ailleboust de Cerry, Philippe-Marie d'
Charest, Étienne
Coghlan, Jeremiah
Darby, Nicholas
Drachart, Christian Larsen
Haven, Jens
Kingminguse
Mikak
Palliser, Sir Hugh
Perrault, Jacques
Raby, Augustin
Shuldham, Molyneux, 1st Baron Shuldham
Slade, John
Tuglavina

Newfoundland

I (1000–1700)
Aubert, Thomas
Baudoin, Jean
Bellot, *dit* Lafontaine
Berry, Sir John
Bjarni, Herjólfsson
Cabot, John

Cabot, Sebastian
Calvert, Sir George
Cartier, Jacques
Clarke, Richard
Colston, William
Corte-Real, Gaspar
Corte-Real, Miguel
Crout, Henry
Cruse, Thomas
Denys, Jean
Dermer, Thomas
Downing, John
Downing, William
Drake, Sir Bernard
Du Perron, Thalour
Easton, Peter
Echevette, Matias de
Eliot, Hugh
Fagundes, João Alvares
Fernandes, João
Gilbert, Sir Humphrey
Gomes, Estevão
Gonsales, João
Guy, John
Guy, Nicholas
Hayes, Edward
Hayman, Robert
Hill, William
Hinton, William
Hore, Richard
Ingram, David
Jay, John
Johnson, George
Kirke, Sir David
Kirke, Sir Lewis
La Poippe
La Roche de Mesgouez, Troilus de, Marquis de La Roche-Mesgouez
La Rocque de Roberval, Jean-François de
Leigh, Charles
Mainwaring, Sir Henry
Martin, Christopher
Mason, John
May, Henry
Monts, Sieur de
Nutt, John
Parat, Antoine
Parkhurst, Anthony
Parmenius, Stephanus
Parmentier, Jean
Pearson, Bartholomew
Pelletier, Didace
Pommier, Hugues
Rastell, John
Rayner, John
Roberts, Lewis
Rowley, Thomas
Rut, John

Stourton, Erasmus
Tanfield, Sir Francis
Tisquantum
Treworgie, John
Vaughan, Sir William
Verrazzano, Giovanni da
Whitbourne, Sir Richard
Willoughby, Thomas
Wyet, Sylvester
Wynne, Edward

II (1701–1740)
Ailleboust d'Argenteuil, Pierre d'
Allard de Sainte-Marie, Jean-Joseph d'
Amiot de Vincelotte, Charles-Joseph
Arnold, William
Auger de Subercase, Daniel d'
Barrat, Claude
Bouler, Robert
Bridges, Timothy
Campbell, Colin
Carrerot, Pierre
Catalogne, Gédéon (de)
Collins, John
Crowe, Josias
Cumings, Archibald
Daneau de Muy, Nicolas
Denys, Joseph
Denys de Bonaventure, Simon-Pierre
Deschamps de Boishébert, Henri-Louis
Dugué de Boisbriand, Pierre
Durand de La Garenne
Espiet de Pensens, Jacques d'
Fotherby, Charles
Gibsone, Sir John
Gill, Michael
Gledhill, Samuel
Gotteville de Belile, Robert-David
Goyer, Olivier
Graydon, John
Handasyde, Thomas
Holdsworth, Arthur
Jackson, John
Jago, John
Jérémie, *dit* Lamontagne, Nicolas
Joannès de Chacornacle
Juchereau de La Ferté, Denis-Joseph
Kempthorne, Thomas
La Forest, Marc-Antoine de
Larkin, George
Latham, Robert
Leake, Sir John
Léger de La Grange, Jean
Le Gouès de Sourdeval, Sébastien
Le Moyne d'Iberville et d'Ardillières, Pierre
Le Moyne de Maricourt, Paul
Le Moyne de Martigny et de La Trinité, Jean-Baptiste

Leneuf de La Vallière de Beaubassin,
  Alexandre
Leneuf de La Vallière de Beaubassin,
  Michel (son)
Le Poupet de La Boularderie, Louis-
  Simon
Le Tac, Xiste
L'Hermitte, Jacques
Lloyd, Thomas
Lom d'Arce de Lahontan, Louis-
  Armand de, Baron de Lahontan
Loppinot, Jean-Chrysostome
Maisonnat, *dit* Baptiste, Pierre
Monbeton de Brouillan, Jacques-
  François de
Monic, Joseph de
Moody, John
Moore, Thomas
Nescambiouit
Pastour de Costebelle, Philippe
Payen de Noyan, Pierre
Pepperrell, William
Perrot de Rizy, Pierre
Pynne, William
Rice, Jacob
Richards, Michael
Robinson, Sir Robert
Roope, John
Saint-Clair, Pierre de
Sarrazin, Michel
Serreau de Saint-Aubin, Jean
Skeffington, George
Smith, James
Taylour, Joseph
Testard de Montigny, Jacques
Trevanion, Sir Nicholas
Vane, George
Villedonné, Étienne de
Walker, Sir Hovenden
Whetstone, Sir William
Yonge, James

III (1741–1770)
Ailleboust, Charles-Joseph d'

Aldridge, Christopher (son)
Arrigrand, Gratien d', Sieur de
  La Majour
Aubert de La Chesnaye, Louis
Bonfoy, Hugh
Boucher de La Perrière, René
Byng, John
Clinton, George
Colvill, Alexander, 7th Baron Colvill
Constantin, Pierre
Cope, Henry
Daccarrette, Michel (father)
Delort, Guillaume
Denys de La Ronde, Louis
Descouts, Martin
Dorrill, Richard
Dubois Berthelot de Beaucour, Josué
Durell, Philip
Erhardt, John Christian
Falkingham, Edward
Fordyce, John
Fornel, Louis
Gaultier de Varennes et de La
  Vérendrye, Pierre
Gorham, John
Hamilton, Otho
Jones, Henry
Keen, William
Kilpatrick, Robert
La Maisonfort Du Boisdecourt,
  Alexandre de, Marquis de
  La Maisonfort
Lartigue, Joseph
Lee, Fitzroy Henry
Lefebvre de Bellefeuille, Jean-François
Le Moyne de Bienville, Jean-Baptiste
Lucas, Francis
Mascarene, Paul
Monbeton de Brouillan, *dit* Saint-
  Ovide, Joseph de
Morpain, Pierre
Norris, Sir John
Pain, Félix

Peaseley, William
Pécaudy de Contrecoeur, François-
  Antoine
Poulin de Courval, François-Louis
Rous, John
Southack, Cyprian
Sutherland, Patrick
Taverner, William
Testu de La Richardière, Richard
Tyng, Edward
Watson, Charles
Webb, James

IV (1771–1800)
Arsac de Ternay, Charles-Henri-
  Louis d'
Bradstreet, John
Brewse, John
Byron, John
Coghlan, Jeremiah
Cook, James
Coughlan, Laurence
Darby, Nicholas
Douglas, Sir Charles
Drake, Francis William
Edwards, Richard
Galaup, Jean-François de, Comte de
  Lapérouse
Goreham, Joseph
Jones, John
Kerrivan, Peter
King, James
Langman, Edward
Osborn, Henry
Palliser, Sir Hugh
Pellegrin, Gabriel
Pringle, Robert
Saunders, Sir Charles
Shuldham, Molyneux, 1st Baron
  Shuldham
Slade, John
Williams, Griffith
Winslow, John

NORTHWEST TERRITORIES

I (1000–1700)
Baffin, William
Bayly, Charles
Beare, James
Best, George
Bjarni, Herjólfsson
Bond, William
Button, Sir Thomas
Bylot, Robert
Cabot, John
Cabot, Sebastian
Corbie, Walsall
Davis, John

Draper, Thomas
Fernandes, João
Fonteneau, Jean
Fox, Luke
Frobisher, Sir Martin
Garland, Thomas
Gibbons, William
Gillam, Zacharie
Hall, James
Hawkeridge, William
Hudson, Henry
Hudson, John
James, Thomas

Lane, Daniel
Leifr *heppni* Eiriksson
Le Moyne de Châteauguay, Louis
Lucas, Richard
Marsh, John
Munk, Jens Eriksen
Nixon, John
Outlaw, John
Peré, Jean
Phipps, Thomas
Power, Richard
Romieux, Pierre
Sanford, Esbon

Sergeant, Henry
Smithsend, Nicholas
Smithsend, Richard
Thompson, Joseph
Thorfinnr *karlsefni* Thordarson
Verner, Hugh
Walker, Nehemiah
Waymouth, George
White, John

II (1701–1740)
Apthorp, Alexander
Beale, Anthony
Berley, George
Fullartine, John
Grimington, Michael (father)
Kelsey, Henry

Knight, James
Le Moyne d'Iberville et d'Ardillières,
  Pierre
Le Moyne de Martigny et de La
  Trinité, Jean-Baptiste
Le Roy de La Potherie, *dit* Bacqueville
  de La Potherie, Claude-Charles
Napper, James
Scroggs, John
Stuart, William
Thanadelthur
Vaughan, David
Villieu, Sébastien de

III (1741–1770)
Bean, John

Denys de La Ronde, Louis
Henday, Anthony
Le Moyne de Bienville, Jean-Baptiste
Middleton, Christopher
Rankin, John
Smith, Francis
Spurrell, George
Thompson, Edward
Wigate, John

IV (1771–1800)
Duncan, Charles
Hearne, Samuel
Matonabbee
Norton, Moses
Turnor, Philip

NOVA SCOTIA

Cape Breton Island

I (1000–1700)
Alexander, Sir William
Aprendestiguy, Martin d'
Champlain, Samuel de
Daniel, Charles
Denys, Nicolas
Denys de Fronsac, Richard
Denys de La Trinité, Simon
Ferrar, Constance
Fisher, Richard
Johnson, George
Le Borgne, Emmanuel
Leigh, Charles
Malapart, André
May, Henry
Menou d'Aulnay, Charles de
Noyrot, Philibert
Parmenius, Stephanus
Parmentier, Jean
Perrault, Julien
Rut, John
Stewart, James, 4th Lord Ochiltree
Verrazzano, Giovanni da
Vimont, Barthélemy

II (1701–1740)
Agrain, Jean-Antoine d', Comte
  d'Agrain
Armstrong, Lawrence
Breslay, René-Charles de
Carrerot, Pierre
Catalogne, Gédéon (de)
Catalogne, Joseph de
Couagne, Jean-Baptiste
Denys, Joseph
Du Pont de Renon, Michel
Du Pont Duvivier, François
Espiet de Pensens, Jacques d'

Forant, Isaac-Louis de
Gotteville de Belile, Robert-David
Goutin, Mathieu de
Guesdron, Julien
Hertel de Rouville, Jean-Baptiste
Isabeau, Michel-Philippe
La Forest, Marc-Antoine de
La Marche, Dominique de
Le Dorz, Bénin
Leneuf de La Vallière de Beaubassin,
  Alexandre
Leneuf de La Vallière de Beaubassin,
  Michel (father)
Leneuf de La Vallière de Beaubassin,
  Michel (son)
Le Poupet de La Boularderie, Louis-
  Simon
Le Roy Desmarest, Claude-Joseph
L'Espérance, Charles-Léopold-
  Éberard de
L'Hermitte, Jacques
Maisonnat, *dit* Baptiste, Pierre
Moore, Thomas
Pastour de Costebelle, Philippe
Pepperrell, William
Petitpas, Claude
Rodrigue, Jean-Baptiste
Ruette d'Auteuil de Monceaux,
  François-Madeleine-Fortuné
Saint-Étienne de La Tour, Charles de
Smart, Thomas
Soubras, Pierre-Auguste de
Verville, Jean-François de
Walker, Sir Hovenden

III (1741–1770)
Adhémar de Lantagnac, Gaspard
Ailleboust, Charles-Joseph d'
Aldridge, Christopher
Arnaud, Marie-Marguerite-Daniel, *dite*
  Saint-Arsène

Arrigrand, Gratien d', Sieur de La
  Majour
Barrin de La Galissonière, Roland-
  Michel, Marquis de La Galissonière
Bastide, John Henry
Bâtard, Étienne
Beaussier de Lisle, Louis-Joseph
Boscawen, Edward
Boschenry de Drucour, Augustin de
Boucher, Pierre-Jérôme
Bourg, *dit* Belle-Humeur, Alexandre
Burton, Ralph
Cailly, François-Joseph
Carrerot, André
Carrerot, Philippe
Chassin de Thierry, François-Nicolas
  de
Chauvreulx, Claude-Jean-Baptiste
Claparède, Jean
Cobb, Silvanus
Colvill, Alexander, 7th Baron Colvill
Cope, Jean-Baptiste
Daccarrette, Michel (father)
Daccarrette, Michel (son)
Delaborde, Jean
De Laune, William
Delort, Guillaume
Denison, Robert
Denys de Bonnaventure, Claude-
  Élisabeth
Denys de La Ronde, Louis
Des Herbiers de La Ralière, Charles
Deslongrais, Nicolas
Dubois Berthelot de Beaucour, Josué
Durand, Justinien
Durell, Philip
Elliot, Robert
Fautoux, Léon
Fornel, Joachim
Franquet, Louis
Ganet, François

Gannes de Falaise, Michel de
Gay Desenclaves, Jean-Baptiste de
Goldthwait, Benjamin
Gorham, John
Goutin, François-Marie de
Green, Bartholomew
Grillot de Poilly, François-Claude-
    Victor
Haldimand, Peter Frederick
Hale, Robert
Handfield, John
Hay, Lord Charles
Heron, Patrick
Hertel de Saint-François, Étienne
Holmes, Charles
Hopson, Peregrine Thomas
Kilby, Thomas
La Goudalie, Charles de
La Maisonfort Du Boisdecourt,
    Alexandre de, Marquis de
    La Maisonfort
Lannelongue, Jean-Baptiste
Lartigue, Joseph
Latouche MacCarthy, Charles
Lawrence, Charles
Leblanc, dit Le Maigre, Joseph
Le Coutre de Bourville, François
Legardeur de Tilly, Jean-Baptiste
Le Normant de Mézy, Jacques-Ange
Le Prévost Duquesnel, Jean-Baptiste-
    Louis
Levasseur, Louis
Levrault de Langis Montegron, Jean-
    Baptiste
Maillard, Pierre
Manach, Jean
Mangeant, François
Mascle de Saint-Julhien, Jean
Milly, François
Monbeton de Brouillan, dit Saint-
    Ovide, Joseph de
Monk, James
Moody, Samuel
Morpain, Pierre
Moulton, Jeremiah
Muiron, Daivd-Bernard
Murray, Alexander
Noble, Arthur
Padanuques, Jacques
Pain, Félix
Paris, Bernard
Payen de Noyan, Pierre-Benoît
Péan de Livaudière, Jacques-Hugues
Pepperrell, Sir William
Petitpas, Barthélemy
Poulin de Courval, François-Louis
Rigaud de Vaudreuil, Louis-Philippe
    de, Marquis de Vaudreuil
Rollo, Andrew, 5th Baron Rollo
Rondeau, Jacques-Philippe-Urbain
Rouer de Villeray, Benjamin
Rous, John
Roy, Marguerite, dite de la Conception
Sabatier, Antoine

Sallaberry, Michel de
Saul, Thomas
Scott, George
Southack, Cyprian
Stobo, Robert
Sutherland, Patrick
Swanton, Robert
Tarride Duhaget, Robert
Townsend, Isaac
Trottier, Marguerite, dite Saint-Joseph
Tyng, Edward
Vallée, François-Madeleine
Vaughan, William
Verrier, Étienne
Waldo, Samuel
Warren, Sir Peter
Watson, Charles
Whitmore, Edward
Wilmot, Montagu
Wolfe, James

IV (1771–1800)
Abercrombie, James
Abercromby, James
Ailleboust de Cerry, Philippe-Marie d'
Allard de Sainte-Marie, Philippe-
    Joseph d'
Alline, Henry
Amherst, Jeffery, 1st Baron Amherst
Angeac, François-Gabriel d'
Berbudeau, Jean-Gabriel
Bigot, François
Bourdon de Dombourg, Jean-François
Bradstreet, John
Brewse, John
Breynton, John
Brooke, John
Byron, John
Castaing, Pierre-Antoine
Cook, James
Couagne, Michel de
Cox, Nicolas
Cramahé, Hector-Théophilus
Deschamps de Boishébert et de
    Raffetot, Charles
Douglas, Sir Charles
Druillon de Macé, Pierre-Jacques
Dugas, Joseph
Dupleix Silvain, Jean-Baptiste
Dupont Duchambon, Louis
Du Pont Duchambon de Vergor, Louis
Du Pont Duvivier, François
Du Pont Duvivier, Joseph
Fraser, Alexander
Galaup, Jean-François de, Comte de
    Lapérouse
Gerrish, Joseph
Gibbons, Richard
Gladwin, Henry
Glasier, Beamsley Perkins
Goreham, Joseph
Green, Benjamin
Gridley, Richard
Hamilton, Henry

Hardy, Sir Charles
Haviland, William
Imbert, Bertrand
Jacau de Fiedmont, Louis-Thomas
Jacobs, Samuel
Johnstone, James, known as Chevalier
    de Johnstone
Laborde, Jean
La Brosse, Jean-Baptiste de
Lajus, François
Larcher, Nicolas
Le Courtois de Surlaville, Michel
Ledru, Jean-Antoine
Legardeur de Repentigny, Pierre-Jean-
    Baptiste-François-Xavier
Le Loutre, Jean-Louis
Le Mercier, François-Marc-Antoine
Le Normant de Mézy, Sébastien-
    François-Ange
Le Poupet de La Boularderie, Antoine
Le Roux, Thomas-François
L'Espérance, Charles-Gabriel-
    Sébastien de, Baron de
    L'Espérance
Loring, Joshua
Mackellar, Patrick
Marin de La Malgue, Joseph
Mathews, David
Mauger, Joshua
Montresor, John
Morin de Fonfay, Jean-Baptiste
Morris, Charles
Murray, James
Olabaratz, Joannis-Galand d'
Peters, Joseph
Pichon, Thomas
Prevost de La Croix, Jacques
Raymond, Jean-Louis de, Comte de
    Raymond
Rodrigue, Antoine
Rousseau de Villejouin, Gabriel
St Leger, Barrimore Matthew
Tonge, Winckworth
Vauquelin, Jean
Willard, Abijah
Williamson, George
Wood, Thomas
Zouberbuhler, Sebastian

Mainland

I (1000–1700)
Aernoutsz, Jurriaen
Alexander, William, Earl of Stirling
Alexander, Sir William
Andigné de Granfontaine, Hector d'
Angibault, dit Champdoré, Pierre
Argall, Sir Samuel
Aubry, Nicolas
Bailloquet, Pierre
Baudoin, Jean
Bergier, Clerbaud
Biard, Pierre

71

NOVA SCOTIA: MAINLAND

Biencourt de Poutrincourt et de Saint-
Just, Jean de
Biencourt de Saint-Just, Charles de
Brice, Mme de
Champlain, Samuel de
Chefdostel, Thomas
Côme de Mantes
Crowne, William
Damours de Freneuse, Mathieu
Daumont de Saint-Lusson, Simon-
François
Dauphin de Montorgueuil
Denys, Nicolas
Du Gua de Monts, Pierre
Duret de Chevry de La Boulaye,
Charles
Du Thet, Gilbert
Fléché, Jessé
Fleury d'Eschambault, Jacques
Forrester, Andrew
Gargot de La Rochette, Nicolas
Gomes, Estevão
Gravé Du Pont, François
Gravé Du Pont, Robert
Hébert, Louis
Ignace de Paris
Joybert de Soulanges et de Marson,
Pierre de
La Roche de Mesgouez, Troilus de,
Marquis de La Roche-Mesgouez
La Tourasse, Charles
Le Borgne, Emmanuel
Le Borgne de Belle-Isle, Alexandre
Le Coq de La Saussaye, René
Le Creux Du Breuil, Nicolas
Léonard de Chartres
Lescarbot, Marc
Leverett, John
Lomeron, David
Lyonne, Martin de
Marot, Bernard
Melanson, Charles
Membertou
Menou d'Aulnay, Charles de
Messamouet
Mius d'Entremont, Philippe, Baron de
Pobomcoup
Morillon Du Bourg
Motin, Jeanne (Menou d'Aulany;
Saint-Étienne de La Tour)
Parmenius, Stephanus
Pasquine
Patoulet, Jean-Baptiste
Perrot, François-Marie
Phips, Sir William
Ralluau, Jean
Razilly, Isaac de
Robinau de Villebon, Joseph
Saccardy, Vincent
Saint-Étienne de La Tour, Charles de
Saint-Étienne de La Tour, Claude de
Sarcel de Prévert, Jean
Secoudon

Sedgwick, Robert
Segipt
Temple, Sir Thomas
Thomas, Jean
Thury, Louis-Pierre
Tyng, Edward
Verrazzano, Giovanni da
Walker, Richard

II (1701–1740)
Abbadie de Saint-Castin, Bernard-
Anselme d', Baron de Saint-Castin
Alden, John
Allard de Sainte-Marie, Jean-Joseph d'
Amiot de Vincelotte, Charles-Joseph
Armstrong, Lawrence
Auger de Subercase, Daniel d'
Basset, David
Bourg, Abraham
Bourgeois, Jacques
Breslay, René-Charles de
Brossard, Jean-François
Bruslé, Michel
Buisson de Saint-Cosme, Jean-
François (1667–1706)
Caulfeild, Thomas
Chevalier, dit Beauchêne, Robert
Church, Benjamin
Damours de Chauffours, Louis
Damours de Clignancour, René
Denys de Bonaventure, Simon-Pierre
Deschamps de Boishébert, Henri-Louis
Des Friches de Meneval, Louis-
Alexandre
Dièreville
Doucett, John
Du Pont de Renon, Michel
Du Pont Duvivier, François
Élie, Jacques
Espiet de Pensens, Jacques d'
Gannes de Falaise, Louis de
Gaulin, Antoine
Geoffroy, Louis
Goffe, Edmund
Goutin, Mathieu de
Guion, François
Haché-Gallant, Michel
Harrison, John
Hilton, Winthrop
Hobby, Sir Charles
Joannès de Chacornacle
La Marche, Dominique de
Laumet, dit de Lamothe Cadillac,
Antoine
Leneuf de La Vallière de Beaubassin,
Alexandre
Leneuf de La Vallière de Beaubassin,
Michel (father)
Leneuf de La Vallière de Beaubassin,
Michel (son)
Le Poupet de La Boularderie, Louis-
Simon
L'Hermitte, Jacques

Livingston, John
Loppinot, Jean-Chrysostome
Maisonnat, dit Baptiste, Pierre
March, John
Martin, George
Martin, Mathieu
Moireau, Claude
Monbeton de Brouillan, Jacques-
François de
Nelson, John
Nescambiouit
Nicholson, Francis
Pepperrell, William
Petit, Louis
Petitpas, Claude
Robinau de Neuvillette, Daniel
Robinau de Portneuf, René
Rodrigue, Jean-Baptiste
Saint-Étienne de La Tour, Agathe de
(Bradstreet; Campbell)
Saint-Étienne de La Tour, Charles de
Savage, Arthur
Smart, Thomas
Terriot, Pierre
Tibaudeau, Pierre
Tibierge
Trouvé, Claude
Vane, George
Vaughan, George
Vetch, Samuel
Villieu, Claude-Sébastien de
Villieu, Sébastien de
Washington, John
Watts, Richard
Williams, John (fl. 1711–18)
Wroth, Robert

III (1741–1770)
Adams, John
Ailleboust, Charles-Joseph d'
Aldridge, Christopher (father)
Aldridge, Christopher (son)
Aubert de La Chesnaye, Louis
Barnard, John
Bastide, John Henry
Boscawen, Edward
Bourg, dit Belle-Humeur, Alexandre
Brossard, dit Beausoleil, Joseph
Bushell, John
Cahideuc, Emmanuel-Auguste de,
Comte Dubois de La Motte
Chauvreulx, Claude-Jean-Baptiste
Cleveland, Aaron
Cobb, Silvanus
Collier, John
Colvill, Alexander, 7th Baron Colvill
Cope, Henry
Cope, Jean-Baptiste
Cosby, Alexander
Daudin, Henri
Denison, Robert
Denys de Bonaventure, Claude-
Élisabeth

Denys de La Ronde, Louis
Descouts, Martin
Dudley, William
Du Pont Duchambon de Vergor, Louis
Durand, Justinien
Durell, Philip
Elliot, Robert
Erad, Johann Burghard
Estourmel, Constantin-Louis d'
Forbes, John
Gannes de Falaise, Michel de
Gautier, *dit* Bellair, Joseph-Nicolas
Gay Desenclaves, Jean-Baptiste de
Goldthwait, Benjamin
Gorham, John
Goutin, François-Marie de
Green, Bartholomew
Guyon, Louise (Thibault; Damours de Freneuse)
Gyles, John
Hale, Robert
Halhead, Edward
Hamilton, Otho
Handfield, John
Hay, Lord Charles
Heron, Patrick
Hiché, Henry
Holmes, Charles
Hopson, Peregrine Thomas
How, Edward
Kilby, Thomas
La Corne, Louis de, known as Chevalier de La Corne
La Goudalie, Charles de
La Rochefoucauld de Roye, Jean-Baptiste-Louis-Frédéric de, Marquis de Roucy, Duc d'Anville
Laurent, Paul
Lawrence, Charles
Leblanc, *dit* Le Maigre, Joseph
Le Marchand de Lignery, François-Marie
Liénard de Beaujeu, Daniel-Hyacinthe-Marie
Little, Otis
Lockman, Leonard
Maillard, Pierre
Maisonnat, Marie-Madeleine
Manach, Jean
Mangeant, François
Mascarene, Paul
Mitchell, George
Monk, James
Moody, Samuel
Moreau, Jean-Baptiste
Morpain, Pierre
Moulton, Jeremiah
Murray, Alexander
Noble, Arthur
Osborn, Sir Danvers
Pain, Félix
Petitpas, Barthélemy
Pettrequin, Jean

Philipps, Erasmus James
Philipps, Richard
Pote, William
Poulin de Courval, François-Louis
René, Patrice
Rollo, Andrew, 5th Baron Rollo
Rous, John
Saint-Ours, François-Xavier de
Salusbury, John
Saul, Thomas
Scott, George
Short, Richard
Southack, Cyprian
Sutherland, Patrick
Taffanel de La Jonquière, Jacques-Pierre de, Marquis de La Jonquière
Terroux, Jacques
Testu de La Richardière, Richard
Tutty, William
Tyng, Edward
Vincent
Vincent, Robert
Warren, Sir Peter
Watson, Charles
Whitmore, Edward
Wilmot, Montagu
Winniett, William
Wolfe, James

IV (1771–1800)

Abercromby, James
Alline, Henry
Arbuthnot, Mariot
Aubert de Gaspé, Ignace-Philippe
Bailly de Messein, Charles-François
Belcher, Jonathan
Bernard, Philip
Bourdon de Dombourg, Jean-François
Bourg, Joseph-Mathurin
Bradstreet, John
Brewse, John
Breynton, John
Bruce, Robert George
Bulkeley, Richard
Busby, Thomas
Byron, John
Campbell, Lord William
Chartier de Lotbinière, Michel
Chaussegros de Léry, Gaspard-Joseph
Collier, Sir George
Cornwallis, Edward
Couagne, Michel de
Cox, Nicholas
Danks, Benoni
Davidson, William
Day, John
Denson, Henry Denny
Denys de Vitré, Théodose-Matthieu
De Peyster, Abraham
Deschamps de Boishébert et de Raffetot, Charles
Dimock, Shubael
Doggett, John

Doucet, Pierre
Douglas, Sir Charles
Dugas, Joseph
Dumas, Jean-Daniel
Dupont Duvivier, Joseph
Eagleson, John
Fillis, John
Fletcher, Robert
Francklin, Michael
Gage, Thomas
Gerrish, Benjamin
Gerrish, Joseph
Gibbons, Richard
Girard, Jacques
Glasier, Beamsley Perkins
Godin, Joseph
Goreham, Joseph
Green, Benjamin
Hardy, Sir Charles
Hardy, Elias
Henry, Anthony
Hicks, John
Hope, Henry
Jadis, Charles Newland Godfrey
Jeanson, Guillaume
Knaut, Philip Augustus
Knox, John
Le Blanc, Pierre
Leblanc, *dit* Le Maigre, Joseph
Le Courtois de Surlaville, Michel
Ledru, Jean-Antoine
Legardeur de Croisille et de Montesson, Joseph-Michel
Legge, Francis
Le Loutre, Jean-Louis
Le Mercier, François-Marc-Antoine
Le Poupet de La Boularderie, Antoine
Lyon, James
Mackellar, Patrick
McLean, Francis
Marin de La Malgue, Joseph
Marrant, John
Marston, Benjamin
Mauger, Joshua
Miniac, Jean-Pierre de
Monckton, Robert
Montgomery, William
Moore, William
Morris, Charles
Moulton, Ebenezer
Munro, John
Nesbitt, William
Olabaratz, Joannis-Galand d'
Osborn, Elizabeth
Owen, William
Parr, John
Peachey, James
Pellegrin, Gabriel
Peters, Joseph
Peters, Thomas
Pichot de Querdisien Trémais, Charles-François
Picoté de Belestre, François-Marie

73

Ramezay, Jean-Baptiste-Nicolas-
  Roch de
Rigaud de Vaudreuil, François-
  Pierre de
Ritchie, John
Robichaux, Louis
Robinson, Christopher
Saint-Aubin, Ambroise
Salter, Malachy

Saunders, Sir Charles
Schwartz, Otto William
Scott, Joseph
Seccombe, John
Shaw, William
Shuldham, Molyneux, 1st Baron
  Shuldham
Studholme, Gilfred
Suckling, George

Tarieu de La Naudière, Charles-
  François
Tonge, Winckworth
Wenman, Richard
Willard, Abijah
Williamson, George
Winslow, John
Wood, Thomas
Zouberbuhler, Sebastian

ONTARIO

Centre

I (1000–1700)

Ahatsistari
Amantacha
Amiot, Jean
Annaotaha
Annenraes
Atironta (fl. 1615)
Atironta (d. 1650)
Atironta (d. 1672)
Auoindaon
Brébeuf, Jean de
Bressani, François-Joseph
Brûlé, Étienne
Chabanel, Noël
Champlain, Samuel de
Chastellain, Pierre
Chaudière Noire
Chaumonot, Pierre-Joseph-Marie
Chihwatenha
Chouart Des Groseilliers, Médard
Dablon, Claude
Daniel, Antoine
Daumont de Saint-Lusson, Simon-
  François
Davost, Ambroise
Du Peron, François
Garnier, Charles
Garreau, Léonard
Gendron, François
Iroquet
Jogues, Isaac
Lalemant, Gabriel
Lalemant, Jérôme
Lambert, Eustache
La Roche Daillon, Joseph de
Le Caron, Joseph
Le Coq, Robert
Le Mercier, François-Joseph
Le Moyne, Simon
Le Moyne de Longueuil et de
  Châteauguay, Charles
Malherbe, François
Marguerie de La Haye, François
Ménard, René

Nicollet de Belleborne, Jean
Nouë, Anne de
Ondaaiondiont
Peré, Jean
Pijart, Pierre
Poncet de La Rivière, Joseph-Antoine
Poulain, Guillaume
Ragueneau, Paul
Raymbaut, Charles
Sagard, Gabriel
Salignac de La Mothe-Fénelon,
  François de
Taondechoren
Taratouan
Tehorenhaegnon
Teouatiron
Tessouat (d. 1636)
Totiri
Viel, Nicolas

II (1701–1740)

Boucher, Pierre
Couture, Guillaume
Morel de La Durantaye, Olivier

III (1741–1770)

Pattin, John
Robinau de Portneuf, Pierre
Wabbicommicot

IV (1771–1800)

Aitken, Alexander
Long, John
Robinson, Christopher
Rogers, Robert
Singleton, George
Wabakinine
White, John

East

I (1000–1700)

Bourdon d'Autray, Jacques
Cavelier de La Salle, René-Robert
Champlain, Samuel de
Crisafy, Thomas

Dekanahwideh
Garakontié
La Frenaye de Brucy, Antoine de
La Motte de Lucière, Dominique
Lanouguère, Thomas de
La Ribourde, Gabriel de
Le Moyne de Longueuil et de
  Châteauguay, Charles
Membré, Zénobe
Ourehouare
Pécaudy de Contrecœur, Antoine
Peré, Jean
Perrot, François-Marie
Randin, Hugues
Richard, dit Lafleur, Guillaume
Salignac de La Mothe-Fénelon,
  François de
Taondechoren
Togouiroui
Villeneuve, Robert de

II (1701–1740)

Ailleboust de Manthet, Nicolas d'
Aloigny, Charles-Henri d', Marquis de
  La Groye
Barthélemy, Michel
Blaise Des Bergères de Rigauville
  Nicolas
Blaise Des Bergères de Rigauville,
  Raymond
Bochart de Champigny, Jean
Brisay de Denonville, Jacques-René
  de, Marquis de
Denonville
Chabert de Joncaire, Louis-Thomas
Champion de Cicé, Louis-Armand
Chauchetière, Claude
Chavigny Lachevrotière, François
  de
Clément Du Vuault de Valrennes,
  Philippe
Dauphin de La Forest, François
Deshayes, Jean
Desjordy de Cabanac, Joseph
Desjordy Moreau de Cabanac,
  François

Dizy, *dit* Montplaisir,
  Michel-Ignace
Dollier de Casson, François
Estienne Du Bourgué de Clérin,
  Denis d'
Greysolon Dulhut, Daniel
Guillouet d'Orvilliers, Claude
Guillouet d'Orvilliers, Rémy
Hennepin, Louis
Hertel de La Fresnière,
  Joseph-François
Joannès de Chacornacle
Juchereau de La Ferté,
  Denis-Joseph
Kondiaronk
La Corne de Chaptes Jean-Louis de
Lamberville, Jacques de
Lamberville, Jean de
La Porte de Louvigny, Louis de
Lascaris d'Urfé, François-Saturnin
Legardeur de Repentigny, Pierre
Legardeur de Saint-Pierre,
  Jean-Paul
Leneuf de La Vallière de Beaubassin,
  Michel (father)
Lom d'Arce de Lahontan, Louis-
  Armand de, Baron de Lahontan
Marin de La Malgue, Charles-Paul
Millet, Pierre
Ozon, Potentien
Petit de Levilliers, Charles
Roybon d'Allonne, Madeleine de
Sabrevois, Jacques-Charles de
Saint-Ours, Pierre de
Takanoet
Tonty, Alphonse (de), Baron de Paludy
Trouvé, Claude
You de La Découverte, Pierre

III (1741–1770)
Ailleboust de Périgny, Paul d'
Arnaud, Jean-Charles d'
Boucher de Boucherville, Pierre
Bourlamaque, François-Charles de
Charlevoix, Pierre-François-Xavier
  de
Dieskau, Jean-Armand, Baron de
  Dieskau
Dubois Berthelot de Beaucour,
  Josué
Eyre, William
Fleury de La Gorgendière, Joseph
  de
Gaudron de Chevremont, Charles-
  René
Hertel de La Fresnière, Zacharie-
  François
La Corne, Louis de, known as
  Chevalier de La Corne
Lefebvre Duplessis Faber, François
Legardeur de Beauvais, René
Liénard de Beaujeu, Daniel-Hyacinthe

Lombard de Combles, Jean-Claude-
  Henri de
Lorimier de La Rivière, Claude-
  Nicolas de
Lottridge, John
Montcalm, Louis-Joseph de, Marquis
  de Montcalm
Ononwarogo
Pattin, John
Péan de Livaudière, Jacques-Hugues
Pouchot, Pierre
Poulin de Courval Cressé, Louis-Pierre
Robinau de Portneuf, Pierre
Senezergues de La Rodde, Étienne-
  Guillaume de
Tonty de Liette, Charles-Henri-Joseph
  de

IV (1771–1800)
Aitken, Alexander
Benoist, Antoine-Gabriel-François
Bonnécamps, Joseph-Pierre de
Bradstreet, John
Butler, John
Carpentier, Bonaventure
Collins, John
Couagne, Jean-Baptiste de
Crespel, Emmanuel
Dagneau Douville, Alexandre
Desandrouins, Jean-Nicolas
Druillon de Macé, René-Jacques
Gamelin, Pierre-Joseph
Gladwin, Henry
Johnson, Sir William
Koñwatsiʔtsiaiéñni
Lagarde, Pierre-Paul-François de
Le Mercier, François-Marie-
  Antoine
Le Moyne de Longueuil, Paul-Joseph,
  known as Chevalier de Longueuil
Loring, Joshua
Macaulay, Robert
McCarty, Charles Justin
McLean, Neil
Maurès de Malartic, Anne-Joseph-
  Hippolyte de, Comte de Malartic
Munro, John
Ohquandageghte
Ottrowana
Payen de Noyan et de Chavoy,
  Pierre-Jacques
Peachey, James
Picquet, François
Rigaud de Vaudreuil de Cavagnial,
  Pierre de, Marquis de Vaudreuil
Robinson, Christopher
Rogers, Robert
Ross, John
Singleton, George
White, John
Williamson, George
Wooster, Hezekiah Calvin

Niagara

I (1000–1700)
Bréhant de Galinée, René de
Brûlé, Étienne
Cavelier de La Salle, René-Robert
La Roche Daillon, Joseph de
Villeneuve, Robert de

II (1701–1740)
Blaise Des Bergères de Rigauville,
  Nicolas
Blaise Des Bergères de Rigauville,
  Raymond
Chabert de Joncaire, Louis-Thomas
Dollier de Casson, Fançois
Hennepin, Louis
Tonty, Henri (de)

IV (1771–1800)
Aitken, Alexander
Burch, John
Butler, John
Kaieñʔkwaahtoñ
Kalm, Pehr
Ledru, Jean-Antoine
Montresor, John
Roy, Louis
Wabakinine
White, John
Wilkins, John

North

I (1000-1700)
Albanel, Charles
Allouez, Claude
Bond, William
Bridgar, John
Brûlé, Étienne
Cavelier de La Salle, René-Robert
Champlain, Samuel de
Chouart Des Groseilliers, Médard
Dablon, Claude
French, John
Jolliet, Louis
Lane, Daniel
Le Moyne de Sainte-Hélène, Jacques
Marquette, Jacques
Marsh, John
Ménard, René
Missenden, Samuel
Nixon, John
Outlaw, John
Peré, Jean
Phipps, Thomas
Poulain, Guillaume
Randin, Hugues
Raymbaut, Charles
Sergeant, Henry
Smithsend, Nicholas
Smithsend, Richard

Troyes, Pierre de, *dit* Chevalier de
  Troyes
Verner, Hugh
Vignau, Nicolas de

II (1701–1740)
Adams, Joseph
Ailleboust d'Argenteuil, Pierre d'
Ailleboust de Manthet, Nicolas d'
André, Louis
Auchagah
Aulneau (de La Touche), Jean-Pierre
Baley, Henry
Beale, Anthony
Berley, George
Bevan, William
Bird, Thomas
Bishop, Nathaniel
Charly Saint-Ange, Jean-Baptiste
Chavigny Lachevrotière, François de
Davis, Joseph
Denys de Bonaventure, Simon-Pierre
Dollier de Casson, Fançois
Dufrost de La Jemerais, Christophe
Fullartine, John
Gaultier de La Vérendrye,
  Jean-Baptiste
Greysolon de La Tourette, Claude
Greysolon Dulhut, Daniel
Grimington, Michael (father)
Grimington, Michael (son)
Hopkins, Samuel
Juchereau de La Ferté, Denis-Joseph
Kelsey, Henry
Knight, James
Largillier, Jacques, known as Le Castor
Le Moyne d'Iberville et d'Ardillières,
  Pierre
Le Moyne de Martigny et de La Trinité,
  Jean-Baptiste
Le Pesant
Le Sueur, Pierre
Lom d'Arce de Lahontan, Louis-
  Armand de, Baron de Lahontan
Messier, *dit* Saint-Michel, Michel
Miscomote
Moore, Thomas
Myatt, Joseph
Napper, James
Nouvel, Henri
Perrot, Nicolas
Radisson, Pierre-Esprit
Render, Thomas

Scatchamisse
Silvy, Antoine
Stuart, William
Tonty, Henri (de)
Vaughan, David
Waggoner, Rowland
Ward, Richard

III (1741–1770)
Boucher de Montbrun, Jean
Clark, George
Coats, William
Crusoe, Robinson
Dagneau Douville de Quindre,
  Louis-Césaire
Gaultier de La Vérendrye, Louis-
  Joseph
Gaultier de La Vérendrye de Boumois,
  Pierre
Gaultier de Varennes et de La
  Vérendrye, Pierre
Isbister, William
Jamet, John
La Colle
La Corne Dubreuil, François-Josué de
La France, Joseph
Legardeur de Saint-Pierre, Jacques
Longland, John
McCliesh, Thomas
Marin de La Perrière, Claude
Mésaiger, Charles-Michel
Mitchell, Thomas
Noyon, Jacques de
Pilgrim, Robert
Potts, John
Saint-Ours Deschaillons, Jean-Baptiste
Staunton, Richard
Thompson, Edward
Wappisis
White, Richard
White, Thomas

IV (1771–1800)
Ailleboust de La Madeleine, François-
  Jean-Daniel d'
Atkinson, George
Bourassa, *dit* La Ronde, René
Cocking, Matthew
Gaultier Du Tremblay, François
Hutchins, Thomas
Isbister, Joseph
Jarvis, Edward

La Corne, Luc de, known as Chaptes
  de La Corne or La Corne Saint-Luc
Long, John
Marten, Humphrey
Maugenest, Germain
Primeau, Louis
Sutherland, George
Sutherland, James
Turnor, Philip
Umfreville, Edward
Winninnewaycappo

Southwest

I (1000–1700)
Brûlé, Étienne
Cavelier de La Salle, René-Robert
Champlain, Samuel de
Chouart Des Groseilliers, Médard
Iroquet
La Ribourde, Gabriel de
La Roche Daillon, Joseph de
Totiri

II (1701–1740)
Dollier de Casson, François
Lom d'Arce de Lahontan, Louis-
  Armand de, Baron de Lahontan
Tonty, Henri (de)

III (1741–1770)
Campbell, Donald
Chapoton, Jean-Baptiste
Davers, Sir Robert
Gervaise, Louis
La Richardie, Armand de
Michipichy
Minweweh
Pontiac
Robertson, Charles

IV (1771–1800)
Aitken, Alexander
Egushwa
Gladwin, Henry
Glikhikan
McKee, Alexander
Navarre, Robert
Potier, Pierre-Philippe
Sahonwagy
Wasson
York, Jack

PRINCE EDWARD ISLAND

II (1701–1740)
Aubert de La Chesnaye, François
Breslay, René-Charles de
Bruslé, Michel

Catalogne, Gédéon (de)
Espiet de Pensens, Jacques d'
Gotteville de Belile, Robert-David

Haché-Gallant, Michel
Leneuf de La Vallière de Beaubassin,
  Michel (son)

III (1741–1770)
Denys de Bonnaventure, Claude-
  Élisabeth
Descouts, Martin
Deslongrais, Nicolas
Dubois Berthelot de Beaucour, Josué
Franquet, Louis
Gautier, dit Bellair, Joseph-Nicolas
Goutin, François-Marie de
Haldimand, Peter Frederick
La Goudalie, Charles de
Maillard, Pierre
Monbeton de Brouillan, dit Saint-
  Ovide, Joseph de
Pain, Félix
Potier Dubuisson, Robert
Rollo, Andrew, 5th Baron Rollo
Roma, Jean-Pierre
Tarride Duhaget, Robert

Testu de La Richardière, Richard
Verrier, Étienne

IV (1771–1800)
Allard de Sainte-Marie, Phillipe-
  Joseph d'
Alline, Henry
Berbudeau, Jean-Gabriel
Bourdon de Dombourg, Jean-François
Callbeck, Philipps
Clark, Robert
Deschamps de Boishébert et de
  Raffetot, Charles
Dugas, Joseph
Dupont Duchambon, Louis
Dupont Duchambon de Vergor, Louis
Dupont Duvivier, Joseph
Eagleson, John
Girard, Jacques

Higgins, David
Johnstone, James
La Brosse, Jean-Baptiste de
Ledru, Jean-Antoine
Legardeur de Croisille et de Montesson,
  Joseph-Michel
Le Roux, Thomas-François
MacDonald, James
Marin de La Malgue, Joseph
Mauger, Joshua
Montgomery, William
Morris, Charles
Patterson, Walter
Pellegrin, Gabriel
Pichon, Thomas
Raymond, Jean-Louis de, Comte
  de Raymond
Rousseau de Villejouin, Gabriel

QUEBEC

Bas-Saint-Laurent–Gaspésie/Côte-Nord

I (1000 –1700)
Aigron, dit Lamothe, Pierre
Albanel, Charles
Amiot, Charles
Cartier, Jacques
Champlain, Samuel de
Chauvin de Tonnetuit, Pierre de
Chomina
Couillard de Lespinay, Louis
Dalmas, Antoine
Dethunes, Exupère
Dolbeau, Jean
Doublet, François
Druillettes, Gabriel
Erouachy
Fisher, Richard
Gravé Du Pont, François
Huet, Paul
Jérémie, dit Lamontagne, Noël
Jolliet, Louis
Juchereau de Saint-Denis, Nicolas
Kirke, Sir David
Kirke, Sir Lewis
Kirke, Thomas
La Court de Pré-Ravillon et de
  Grandpré
Lambert, Eustache
La Ralde, Raymond de
La Roque, Marguerite de
Le Caron, Joseph
Le Clercq, Chrestien
Legardeur de Tilly, Charles
Leigh, Charles
Le Jeune, Paul
Le Baillif, Georges

Malherbe, François
Marsolet de Saint-Aignan, Nicolas
Maupassant, Eustache
Monts, Sieur de
Negabamat
Pastedechouan
Pelletier, Didace
Piat, Irénée
Quen, Jean de
Roquemont de Brison, Claude
Thury, Louis-Pierre
Viennay-Pachot, François
Villeneuve, Robert de
Wyet, Sylvester

II (1701-1740)
Acoutsina
André, Louis
Aubert de La Chesnaye, Charles
Bissot, François-Joseph
Bonner, John
Bruslé, Michel
Chavigny Lachevrotière, François de
Crespieul, François de
Denys, Joseph
Denys de Bonaventure, Simon-Pierre
Denys de La Ronde, Pierre
Denys de Saint-Simon, Paul
Deschamps de Boishébert,
  Henri-Louis
Gourdeau de Beaulieu et de La
  Grossardière, Jacques
Haimard, Pierre
Hazeur, François
Hazeur, Jean-François
Jérémie, dit Lamontagne, Nicolas
Jolliet de Mingan, Jean-Baptiste
Laure, Pierre-Michel

Le Gardeur de Courtemanche, Augustin
L'Hermitte Jacques
Moireau, Claude
Nouvel, Henri
Peiras, Jean-Baptiste de
Raffeix, Pierre
Rouer de Villeray et de La Cardon-
  nière, Augustin

III (1741–1770)
Boucher de Boucherville, Pierre
Cartier, Toussaint, known as 'the her-
  mit of Saint-Barnabé'
Chardon, Jean-Baptiste
Constantin, Pierre
Coquart, Claude-Godefroy
Elliot, Robert
Gaultier de Varennes, Jacques-René
Gyles, John
Haldimand, Peter Frederick
Imbault, Maurice
Jeanneau, Étienne
Lafontaine de Belcour, Jacques de
Lefebvre de Bellefeuille,
  Jean-François
Mangeant, François
Perrault, François
Pommereau, Jean-Baptiste
Révol, Pierre
Rouillard, Ambroise
Saint-Pé, Jean-Baptiste de
Sallaberry, Michel de
Scott, George
Swanton, Robert
Testu de La Richardière, Richard
Valette de Chévigny,
  Médard-Gabriel
Wolfe, James

IV (1771–1800)
Ailleboust de Cerry, Philippe-Marie d'
Bourdages, Raymond
Bourdon de Dombourg, Jean-François
Bourg, Joseph-Mathurin
Carpentier, Bonaventure
Claude, Joseph
Collins, John
Cook, James
Cox, Nicholas
Crespel, Emmanuel
Darby, Nicholas
Denis de Saint-Simon, Antoine-
 Charles
Deschamps de Boishébert et de
 Raffetot, Charles
Fortier, Michel
Goreham, Joseph
Gridley, Richard
Hardy, Sir Charles
Isbister, Joseph
La Brosse Jean-Baptiste de
Ledru, Jean-Antoine
Lefebvre de Bellefeuille, François
Legardeur de Croisille et de
 Montesson, Joseph-Michel
Le Roux, Thomas-François
Long, John
Pellegrin, Gabriel
Perthuis, Joseph
Porlier, Pierre-Antoine
Renaud, Jean
Vienne, François-Joseph de

Montréal/Outaouais

I (1000–1700)
Ailleboust de Coulonge et
 d'Argentenay, Louis d'
Ailleboust Des Muceaux, Charles-
 Joseph d'
Albanel, Charles
Allet, Antonin d'
Anadabijou
Andigné de Grandfontaine, Hector d'
Annaotaha
Babie, Jacques
Bailly, Guillaume
Bailly, dit Lafleur, François
Basset Des Lauriers, Bénigne
Bizard, Jacques
Bouchard, Étienne
Boullongne, Marie-Barbe de
 (Ailleboust de Coulonge et d'Argen-
 tenay)
Bourgeoys, Marguerite
Bréhant de Galinée, René de
Brigeac, Claude de
Brûlé, Étienne
Cartier, Jacques
Caumont, Pierre de
Cavelier de La Salle, René-Robert
Chambly, Jacques de

Champflour, François de
Champlain, Samuel de
Chartier, Louis
Chaudière Noire
Chomedey de Maisonneuve, Paul
 de
Chouart Des Groseilliers, Médard
Closse, Raphaël-Lambert
Crisafy, Thomas
Dalmas, Antoine
Dollard Des Ormeaux, Adam
Doublet, François
Du Peron, François
Dupuy, Zacharie
Flemish Bastard
Gadoys, Pierre
Gaillard, Mathieu
Gamelain de La Fontaine, Michel
Gandeacteua
Garakontié
Iroquet
Jalobert, Macé
La Frenaye de Brucy, Antoine de
La Motte de Lucière, Dominique
Lamotte de Saint-Paul, Pierre
Lanouguère, Thomas de
La Rocque de Roberval, Jean-François
 de
Lauson, Gilles
Le Caron, Joseph
Le Clercq, Chrestien
Le Jeune, Paul
Le Maistre, Jacques
Le Mercier, François-Joseph
Le Moyne de Bienville, François
Le Moyne de Longueuil et de
 Châteauguay, Charles
Le Moyne de Sainte-Hélène, Jacques
Macé, Catherine
Maillet, Marie
Mance, Jeanne
Marguerie de La Haye, François
Marsolet de Saint-Aignan, Nicolas
Messier, Martine (Primot)
Migeon de Branssat, Jean-Baptiste
Moreau de Brésoles, Judith
Mouchy, Nicolas de
Nicollet de Belleborne, Jean
Noüe, Anne de
Ogenheratarihiens
Olivier, dit Le Picard, Marc-
 Antoine
Otreouti
Oumasasikweie
Ourehouare
Pécaudy de Contrecœur, Antoine
Pelletier, Didace
Pérot, Gilles
Perrot, François-Marie
Pézard de La Tousche Champlain,
 Étienne
Picoté de Belestre, Pierre
Pieskaret

Pigarouich
Pommier, Hugues
Poncet de La Rivière, Joseph-
 Antoine
Prud'homme, Louis
Puiseaux, Pierre de
Raisin, Marie
Randin, Hugues
Richard, dit Lafleur, Guillaume
Sailly, Louis-Arthus de
Saint-Père, Jean de
Salignac de La Mothe-Fénelon,
 François de
Saurel, Pierre de
Savignon
Souart, Gabriel
Taondechoren
Taratouan
Tareha
Tekakwitha, Kateri
Tessouat (fl. 1603–13)
Tessouat (d. 1636)
Tessouat (d. 1654)
Thubières de Levy de Queylus, Gabriel
Togouiroui
Tonsahoten
Troyes, Pierre de, dit Chevalier de
 Troyes
Viel, Nicolas
Vignal, Guillaume
Vignau, Nicolas de
Villain, Jean-Baptiste
Villeneuve, Robert de
Vimont, Barthélemy

II (1701–1740)
Adhémar de Saint-Martin, Antoine
Ailleboust d'Argenteuil, Pierre d'
Ailleboust de Manthet, Nicolas d'
Ailleboust Des Muceaux, Jean-
 Baptiste d'
Aloigny, Charles-Henri d',
 Marquis de La Groye
André, Louis
Aouenano
Auger de Subercase, Daniel d'
Barbier, Marie, dite de
 l'Assomption
Barthélemy, Michel
Basset, Jean
Baudeau, Pierre
Berger, Jean
Berthier, Isaac (Alexandre)
Beschefer, Thierry
Bigot, Vincent
Blaise Des Bergères de Rigauville,
 Nicolas
Blaise Des Bergères de Rigauville,
 Raymond
Bouat, François-Marie
Boucher, Pierre
Bouillet de La Chassaigne, Jean
Bourdon, Jacques

Breslay, René-Charles de
Brisay de Denonville, Jacques-René de, Marquis de Denonville
Brossard, Urbain
Bruslé, Michel
Bruyas, Jacques
Bulteau, Guillaume
Cabazié, Pierre
Callière, Louis-Hector de
Catalogne, Gédéon (de)
Cavelier, Jean
Céloron de Blainville, Jean-Baptiste
Chabert de Joncaire, Louis-Thomas
Chaboulié, Charles
Chachagouesse
Chaigneau (Du Chaigneau), Léonard
Charly Saint-Ange, Jean-Baptiste
Charly Saint-Ange, Marie-Catherine, dite du Saint-Sacrement
Charon de La Barre, François
Chauchetière, Claude
Chaudillon, Antoine
Chèze, François
Chichikatelo
Chingouessi
Cholenec, Pierre
Clairambault d'Aigremont, François
Clément Du Vuault de Valrennes, Philippe
Constantin, Nicolas-Bernardin
Couagne, Charles de
Couture, Guillaume
Couturier, dit Le Bourguignon, Pierre
Crisafy, Antoine de, Marquis de Crisafy
Cuillerier, René
Cusson, Jean
Daneau de Muy, Nicolas
Dauphin de La Forest, François
David, Jacques
Delaunay, Charles
Denys, Joseph
Denys de Vitré, Charles
Desjordy de Cabanac, Joseph
Desjordy Moreau de Cabanac, François
Dessailliant, dit Richeterre, Michel
Dollier de Casson, François
Drué, Juconde
Dufrost de La Jemerais, Christophe
Enjalran, Jean
Estienne Du Bourgué de Clérin, Denis d'
Fézeret, René
Filiastre, Luc
Fleury Deschambault, Jacques-Alexis de
Forestier, Antoine
Francheville, Pierre
Gadois, Pierre
Gallard, Charlotte
Gamelin, Ignace

Garnier, Julien
Gay, Robert-Michel
Geoffroy, Louis
Godefroy de Saint-Paul, Jean-Amador
Godefroy de Vieuxpont, Joseph
Gouentagrandi
Greysolon de La Tourette, Claude
Greysolon Dulhut, Daniel
Guillouet d'Orvilliers, Claude
Guyotte, Étienne
Hertel de Moncours, Pierre
Jarret de Vechères, Pierre
Juchereau de Saint-Denys, Charles
Kiala
Kinongé
Kondiaronk
Koutaoiliboe
La Colombière, Joseph de
La Faye, Louis-François de
La Frenaye, François de
Lagrené, Pierre de
La Marche, Dominique de
Lamarre, dit Bélisle, Henri
Lamberville, Jacques de
Lamberville, Jean de
La Place, Louis-Hyacinthe de
La Porte de Louvigny, Louis de
Lascaris d'Urfé, François-Saturnin
Le Ber, Jacques
Le Ber, Jeanne
Le Ber, Pierre
Le Conte Dupré, Louis
Le Fevre, François
Legardeur de Repentigny, Jean-Baptiste
Legardeur de Repentigny, Pierre
Legardeur de Saint-Pierre, Jean-Paul
Le Moyne de Longueuil, Charles, Baron de Longueuil
Le Moyne de Maricourt, Paul
Le Moyne de Martigny et de La Trinité, Jean-Baptiste
Leneuf de La Vallière de Beaubassin, Michel (father)
Lenoir, dit Rolland, François
Lepallieur de Laferté, Michel
Le Pape Du Lescöat, Jean-Gabriel-Marie
Le Pesant
Le Picard du Mesnil de Norrey, Jacques
Le Sueur, Pierre
Levasseur, Noël
Le Verrier de Rousson, François
Liette, Pierre-Charles de
Lom d'Arce de Lahontan, Louis-Armand de, Baron de Lahontan
Lorimier de La Rivière, Guillaume de
Lorit, dit Gargot, François
Malleray de Noiré de La Mollerie, Jacques
Mallet, Denis

Margane de Batilly, François-Marie
Mariauchau d'Esgly, François
Marie-Joseph-Angélique
Marin de La Malgue, Charles-Paul
Martel, Raymond
Martin de Lino, Antoine
Martinet de Fonblanche, Jean
Maumousseau, Françoise
Meriel, Henri-Antoine
Messier, dit Saint-Michel, Michel
Millet, Pierre
Miscouaky
Morel de La Durantaye, Olivier
Morin, Germain
Morin, Marie
Normandin, Daniel
Noro
Nouvel, Henri
Ohonsiowanne
Ouachala
Ouenemek
Ounanguissé
Outoutagan
Paillard, Léonard, known as Le Poitevin
Papineau, dit Montigny, Samuel
Pascaud, Antoine
Payne, Samuel
Pemoussa
Perrin, Antoine
Perrot, Nicolas
Petit, Louis
Petit de Levilliers, Charles
Philippe de Hautmesnil de Mandeville, François
Piot de Langloiserie, Charles-Gaspard
Pottier, Jean-Baptiste
Poulin de Francheville, François
Quesneville, Jean
Raffeix, Pierre
Raimbault, Pierre
Raimbault de Piedmont, Joseph-Charles
Ramezay, Claude de
Rémy (de Saint-Rémy), Pierre
Rigaud de Vaudreuil, Philippe de, Marquis de Vaudreuil
Rivet Cavelier, Pierre
Robert, Clément
Robinau de Portneuf, René
Robutel de La Noue, Zacharie
Roybon d'Allonne, Madeleine de
Sabrevois, Jacques-Charles de
Saint-Ours, Pierre de
Sarrazin, Michel
Sayward, Mary, dite Marie des Anges
Schuyler, Peter
Senet, dit Laliberté, Nicolas
Silly, Jean-Baptiste de
Silver, Mary
Silvy, Antoine

Suève, Edmond de
Tailhandier, *dit* La Beaume, Marien
Tantouin de La Touche, Louis
Teganissorens
Tekanoet
Tekarihoken
Testard de Montigny, Jacques
Tétro, Jean-Baptiste
Thavenet, Marguerite de (Hertel de La Fresnière)
Tonatakout
Tonty, Alphonse (de), Baron de Paludy
Tonty, Henri (de)
Trouvé, Claude
Vachon, Paul (son)
Vachon de Belmont, François
Vaillant de Gueslis, François
Véron de Grandmesnil, Étienne
Volant de Radisson, Étienne
Volant de Saint-Claude, Pierre
Volant de Saint-Claude, Claude
You de La Découverte, Pierre

III (1741–1770)
Adhémar, Jean-Baptiste
Adhémar de Lantagnac, Gaspard
Ailleboust, Charles-Joseph d'
Ailleboust de Périgny, Paul d'
Alavoine, Charles
Arnaud, Marie-Marguerite-David, *dite* Saint-Arsène
Arnoux, André
Aubery, Joseph
Beauharnois de La Boische, Charles de, Marquis de Beauharnois
Bégon de La Cour, Claude-Michel
Bisaillon, Peter
Bolvin, Gilles
Boucault, Nicolas-Gaspard
Boucher de Boucherville, Pierre
Boucher de La Perrière, René
Boucher de Montbrun, Jean
Boucher de Niverville, Jean-Baptiste
Bourlamaque, François-Charles de
Brunet, *dit* La Sablonnière, Jean
Burton, Ralph
Campot, Jacques
Céloron de Blainville, Pierre-Joseph
Chabert de Joncaire, Philippe-Thomas
Chardon, Jean-Baptiste
Charlevoix, Pierre-François-Xavier de
Charly Saint-Ange, Louis
Chaussegros de Léry, Gaspard-Joseph
Chauvreulx, Charles-Jean-Baptiste
Cheval, *dit* Saint-Jacques, et *dit* Chevalier, Jacques-Joseph
Chevalier, Jean-Baptiste
Chevalier, Jean-Charles
Claverie, Pierre
Constantin, Justinien

Coquart, Claude-Godefroy
Corbin, David
Coron, Charles-François
Cotton, Michel
Couagne, René de
Couagne, Thérèse de (Poulin de Francheville)
Coulon de Villiers, Louis
Coulon de Villiers de Jumonville, Joseph
Cuillerier, Marie-Anne-Véronique
Daine, François
Daneau de Muy, Jacques-Pierre
Danré de Blanzy, Louis-Claude
Dargent, Joseph
Dazemard de Lusignan, Paul-Louis
Déat, Antoine
Dejordy de Villebon, Charles-René
Depéret, Élie
Deschevery, *dit* Maisonbasse, Jean-Baptiste
Dubois Berthelot de Beaucour, Josué
Dubreil de Pontbriand, Henri-Marie
Dudley, William
Du Laurent, Christophe-Hilarion
Duparc, Jean-Baptiste
Duplessis, Marguerite
Durocher, Joseph
Elliot, Robert
Eyre, William
Forestier, Antoine-Bertrand
Forget, Antoine
Foucault, Simon
Foucher, François
Franquet, Louis
Gadois, *dit* Mauger, Jacques
Galiffet de Caffin, François de
Gamelin Maugras, Pierre
Gaschet, René
Gaudé, François
Gaudron de Chevremont, Charles-René
Gaultier de La Vérendrye, Louis-Joseph
Gaultier de La Vérendrye de Boumois, Pierre
Gaultier de Varennes, Jacques-René
Gaultier de Varennes et de La Vérendrye, Pierre
Gawèhe
Gay Desenclaves, Jean-Baptiste de
Gorrell, James
Gosselin, Jean-Baptiste
Guen, Hamon
Guignas, Michel
Guillet de Chaumont, Nicolas-Auguste
Guiton de Monrepos, Jacques-Joseph
Guy, Pierre
Guyart de Fleury, Jean-Baptiste
Haldimand, Peter Frederick
Havard de Beaufort, François-Charles, known as L'Avocat
Hazeur, Joseph-Thierry

Hertel de La Fresnière, Zacharie-François
Hervieux, Louis-François
Hodiesne, Gervais
Houdin, Jean-Michel, known as Father Potenfien
Jamet, John
Janson, *dit* Lapalme, Dominique
Jarret de Verchères, Marie-Madeleine
Jeantot, Jean
Jérémie, *dit* Lamontagne, Catherine (Aubuchon; Lepallieur de La Ferté)
Jourdain, *dit* Labrosse, Paul-Raymond
Kaghswaghtaniunt
Kakᵂenthiony
Karaghtadie
Kellogg, Joseph
Kinousaki
Kisensik
La Bretonnière, Jacques-Quintin de
La Corne, Louis de, known as Chevalier de La Corne
La Corne de Chaptes, Marie-Madeleine de, *dite* du Saint-Sacrement
La Corne Dubreuil, François-Josué de
Lafitau, Joseph-François
Lafontaine de Belcour, Jacques de
La France, Joseph
La Goudalie, Charles de
Lamorinie, Jean-Baptiste de
Landron, Jean-François
Lanouillier de Boisclerc, Jean-Eustache
Laporte de Lalanne, Jean de
Lauverjat, Étienne
Lauzon, Pierre de
Le Comte Dupré, Jean-Baptiste
Leduc, Anne-Françoise, *dite* Saint-Joseph
Lefebvre Angers, Marie-Angélique, *dite* Saint-Simon
Lefebvre Duplessis Faber, François
Legardeur de Beauvais, René
Legardeur de Saint-Pierre, Jacques
Legardeur de Tilly, Jean-Baptiste
Le Marchand de Lignery, François-Marie
Lemoine, *dit* Monière, Alexis
Le Moyne de Longueuil, Charles, Baron de Longueuil
Le Moyne de Sainte-Marie, Marguerite, *dite* du Saint-Esprit
Lepage de Sainte-Claire, Louis
Lestage, Pierre
Le Sueur, Jacques-François
Le Sueur, Pierre
Levasseur, Pierre-Noël
Levrault de Langis Montegron, Jean-Baptiste
Liénard de Beaujeu, Louis

Lombard de Combles, Jean-Claude-
Henri de
Longley, Lydia, *dite* Sainte-Madeleine
Lorimier de La Rivière, Claude-Nicolas
de
Lottridge, John
Lupien, *dit* Baron, Pierre
Malhiot, Jean-François
Malepart de Grand Maison, *dit* Beau-
cour, Paul
Marcol, Gabriel
Marin de La Malgue, Paul
Maurin, François
Mesaiger, Charles-Michel
Michel de Villebois de La Rouvillière,
Honoré
Migeon de La Gauchetière, Daniel
Mikinak
Montcalm, Louis-Joseph de, Marquis
de Montcalm
Montigny, François de
Moreau, Edme
Nau, Luc-François
Neveu, Jean-Baptiste
Nolan Lamarque, Charles
Normant Du Faradon, Louis
Noyelles de Fleurimont, Nicolas-
Joseph de
Noyon, Jacques de
Paradis, Roland
Pattin, John
Péan de Livaudière, Jacques-Hugues
Pécaudy de Contrecœur, François-
Antoine
Perrault, François
Perrault, Paul
Pierre
Pillard, Louis
Plante, Charles
Plessy, *dit* Bélair, Jean-Louis
Pollet, Arnould-Balthazar
Potier Dubuisson, Robert
Pouchot, Pierre
Price, Benjamin
Quéré de Tréguron, Maurice
Rocbert de La Morandière, Étienne
Rocbert de La Morandière, Marie-
Élisabeth (Bégon de La Cour)
Rollo, Andrew, 5th Baron Rollo
Roseboom, Johannes
Rouer de Villeray, Benjamin
Rouillard, Ambroise
Roy, Marguerite, *dite* de la Conception
Saguima
Saint-Ours Deschaillons, Jean-Baptiste
Saint-Pé, Jean-Baptiste de
Saint-Père, Agathe de (Legardeur de
Repentigny)
Schuyler, Johannes
Schuyler, Peter
Senezergues de La Rodde, Étienne-
Guillaume de
Spagniolini, Jean-Fernand

Stobo, Robert
Sullivan, Timothy, known as Timothée
Silvain
Swatana
Talbot, Jacques
Tanaghrisson
Tarbell, John
Theyanoguin
Tonty de Liette, Charles-Henri-Joseph
de
Tournois, Jean-Baptiste
Trottier, Marguerite, *dite* Saint-Joseph
Turc de Castelveyre, Louis, known as
Brother Chrétien
Valette de Chévigny, Médard-Gabriel
Véronneau, Agathe
Vilermaula, Louis-Michel de
Vincent

IV (1771–1800)

Abercrombie, James
Adhémar, Jean-Baptiste-Amable
Ailleboust de La Madeleine, François-
Jean d'
Aleyrac, Jean-Baptiste d'
Amherst, Jeffery
Anandamoakin
Augé, Étienne
Aumasson de Courville, Louis-Léonard
Baby, *dit* Dupéront, Jacques
Barsalou, Jean-Baptiste
Benoist, Antoine-Gabriel-François
Bernier, Benoît-François
Besnard, *dit* Carignant, Jean-Louis
Bourassa, *dit* La Ronde, René
Bourg, Joseph-Mathurin
Brassier, Gabriel-Jean
Brooke, John
Bruyères, John
Burgoyne, John
Busby, Thomas
Butler, John
Butler, Walter
Campbell, John
Campion, Étienne-Charles
Chabert de Joncaire de Clausonne,
Daniel-Marie
Chabrand Delisle, David
Chartier de Lotbinière, Michel,
Marquis de Lotbinière
Chaussegros de Léry, Gaspard-Joseph
Cherrier, François-Pierre
Chew, Joseph
Christie, Gabriel
Cirier, Antoine
Claus, Christian Daniel
Collins, John
Cotté, Gabriel
Couagne, Jean-Baptiste de
Couagne, Michel de
Courreau de La Coste, Pierre
Crespel, Emmanuel
Cuny Dauterive, Philippe-Antoine de

Curatteau, Jean-Baptiste
Cuthbert, James
Dagneau Douville, Alexandre
Decoste, Jean-Baptiste
Degeay, Jacques
Deguire, Joseph
Delezenne, Ignace-François
Denis de Saint-Simon, Antoine-
Charles
Desandrouins, Jean-Nicolas
Deschamps de Boishébert et de Raf-
fetot, Charles
Desdevens de Glandons, Maurice
Devau, Claude
Druillon de Macé, René-Jacques
Du Calvet, Pierre
Ducharme, Laurent
Dufrost de Lajemmerais, Marie-
Marguerite (Youville)
Dumas Saint-Martin, Jean
Ellice, Robert
Ermatinger, Lawrence
Feltz, Charles-Elemy-Joseph-
Alexandre-Ferdinand
Fleury Deschambault, Joseph
Floquet, Pierre-René
Foureur, Loius
Fraser, Alexander
Frobisher, Benjamin
Gage, Thomas
Gamelin, Ignace
Gamelin, Pierre-Joseph
Gaultier Du Tremblay, François
Godefroy de Linctot, Daniel-Maurice
Gohin, Pierre-André, Comte de Mon-
treuil
Grant, James
Grasset de Saint-Sauveur, André
Grisé, Antoine
Guichart, Vincent-Fleuri
Haldimand, Sir Frederick
Hamilton, Henry
Hantraye, Claude
Harrison, Edward
Haviland, William
Hertel de Rouville, René-Ovide
Hertel de Saint-François, Joseph-
Hippolyte
Holmes, William
Hotsinoñhyahta?
Howard, Joseph
Hubert, Jean-François
Huguet, Joseph
Huppé, Joseph
Jacobs, Samuel
Jacquet, François
Jautard, Valentin
Johnson, Guy
Johnson, Sir William
Johnstone, James, known as Chevalier
de Johnstone
Jordan, Jacob
Kalm, Pehr

Kayahsota?
Knox, John
Koñwatsi?tsiaiéñni
La Brosse, Jean-Baptiste de
La Corne, Luc de, known as Chaptes de
    La Corne or La Corne Saint-Luc
Lagarde, Pierre-Paul-François de
Landriève Des Bordes, Jean-Marie
Le Comte Dupré, Georges-Hippolyte
Legardeur de Croisille et de Montesson,
    Joseph-Michel
Legardeur de Repentigny, Louis
Le Mercier, François-Marc-Antoine
Lemoine Despins, Jacques-Joseph
Lemoine Despins, Marguerite-Thérèse
Le Verrier de Rousson, Louis
Lévis, François de, Duc de Lévis
Long, John
Lÿdius, John Hendricks
McCarty, Richard
McLane, David
MacLean, Allan
MacLeod, Normand
Magon de Terlaye, François-Auguste
Malepart de Beaucourt, François
Marchand, Étienne
Marin de La Malgue, Joseph
Martel, Pierre-Michel
Mathevet, Jean-Claude
Maugenest, Germain
Maugue-Garreau, Marie-Josèphe, *dite*
    de l'Assomption
Maurès de Malartic, Anne-Joseph-
    Hippolyte de, Comte de Malartic
Mesplet, Fleury
Miniac, Jean-Pierre de
Montgolfier, Étienne
Montgomery, Richard
Moore, William
Mouet de Langlade, Charles-Michel
Munro, John
Murray, James
Nissowaquet
Ogilvie, John
Ohquandageghte
Olabaratz, Joannis-Galand d'
Orillat, Jean
Payet de Noyan et de Chavoy, Pierre-
    Jacques
Peachey, James
Pécaudy de Contrecœur, Claude-Pierre
Pennisseault, Louis
Picard, Louis-Alexandre
Picoté de Belestre, François-Marie
Picquet, François
Piot de Langloiserie, Marie-
    Marguerite, *dite* Saint-Hippolyte
Porlier, Pierre-Antoine
Potot de Montbeillard, Fiacre-François
Preissac de Bonneau, Louis de
Pressart, Colomban-Sébastien
Primeau, Louis
Quintal, Augustin

Ramezay, Louise de
Rigaud de Vaudreuil, François-Pierre
    de
Roberts, Benjamin
Robinson, Christopher
Rogers, Robert
Ross, John
Roubaud, Pierre-Joseph-Antoine
Roy, Louis
Sabrevois de Bleury, Clément de
Sahonwagy
St Leger, Barrimore Matthew
Sanguinet, Simon
Schindler, Joseph
Simonnet, François
Singleton, George
Solomons, Lucius Levy
Souste, André?
Teiorhéñhsere?
Tekawiroñte
Tessier, *dit* Lavigne, Paul
Testard de Montigny, Jean-Baptiste-
    Philippe
Teyohaqueande
Tossey, Philip
Trottier Dufy Desauniers, Thomas-
    Ignace
Varin, *dit* La Pistole, Jacques
Varin de La Marre, Jean-Victor
Vauquelin, Jean
Veyssière, Leger-Jean-Baptiste-Noël,
    known as Father Emmanuel
Waddens, Jean-Étienne
Walker, Thomas
Wheelwright, Esther, *dite* de l'Enfant-
    Jésus
Williams, Eunice (Marie, Marguerite)
Youville, Charles-Marie-Madeleine d'

Nord-Ouest/Saguenay–Lac-Saint-Jean/Nouveau-Québec

I (1000–1700)
Aigron, *dit* Lamothe, Pierre
Albanel, Charles
Allemand, Pierre
Bayly, Charles
Champlain, Samuel de
Chouart Des Groseilliers, Médard
Dablon, Claude
Dalmas, Antoine
Druillettes, Gabriel
Jolliet, Louis
La Rocque de Roberval, Jean-François
    de
Le Moyne de Sainte-Hélène, Jacques
Lydall, William
Nixon, John
Outlaw, John
Quen, Jean de
Shepard, Thomas
Smithsend, Richard

Troyes, Pierre de, *dit* Chevalier de
    Troyes
Verner, Hugh
Walker, Nehemiah

II (1701–1740)
Adams, Joseph
André, Louis
Baley, Henry
Bevan, William
Couture, Guillaume
Crespieul, François de
Denys de Saint-Simon, Paul
Fullartine, John
Hertel de La Fresnière, Joseph-François
Jérémie, *dit* Lamontagne, Nicolas
Kelsey, Henry
Knight, James
Laure, Pierre-Michel
Le Moyne d'Iberville et d'Ardillières,
    Pierre
Le Moyne de Maricourt, Paul
Le Moyne de Martigny et de La Trinité,
    Jean-Baptiste
Lenoir, *dit* Rolland, François
Moore, Thomas
Myatt, Joseph
Radisson, Pierre-Esprit
Render, Thomas
Robutel de La Noue, Zacharie
Silvy, Antoine
Ward, Richard

III (1741–1770)
Chardon, Jean-Baptiste
Clark, George
Coats, William
Coquart, Claude-Godefroy
Crusoe, Robinson
Guignas, Michel
Longland, John
McCliesh, Thomas
Mitchell, Thomas
Potts, John

IV (1771–1800)
Atkinson, George
Grant, James
Isbister, Joseph
Turnor, Philip

Québec

I (1000–1700)
Agariata
Ahatsistari
Aigron, *dit* Lamothe, Pierre
Ailleboust de Coulonge et d'Argen-
    tenay, Louis d'
Ailleboust Des Muceaux, Charles-
    Joseph d'
Albanel, Charles

Allart, Germain
Allemand, Pierre
Amantacha
Amiot, Charles
Amiot, *dit* Villeneuve, Mathieu
Anadabijou
Andigné de Grandfontaine, Hector d'
Annaotaha
Atironta (d. 1650)
Atironta (d. 1672)
Auber, Claude
Audouart, *dit* Saint-Germain, Guillaume
Baillif, Claude
Basset Du Tartre, Vincent
Batiscan
Baudoin, Gervais
Bazire, Charles
Bermen, Laurent
Bernières, Henri de
Boisdon, Jacques
Boisseau, Josias
Boivin, François
Bonamour, Jean de
Bonnemere, Florent
Boquet, Charles
Boucher de Grandpré, Lambert
Boullé, Eustache
Boullé, Hélène, *dite* de Saint-Augustin (Champlain)
Boullongne, Marie-Barbe de (Ailleboust de Coulonge et d'Argentenay)
Bourdon, Jean
Bourdon de Dombourg, Jean-François
Boutet de Saint-Martin, Martin
Boutroue d'Aubigny, Claude de
Bras-de-Fer de Chateaufort, Marc-Antoine
Brébeuf, Jean de
Bréhaut Delisle, Achille de
Bridgar, John
Buade, Louis de, Comte de Frontenac et de Palluau
Byssot de La Rivière, François
Caën, Émery de
Caën, Guillaume de
Cartier, Jacques
Caumont, Pierre de
Champlain, Samuel de
Charité
Charron de La Barre, Claude
Chartier de Lotbinière, Louis-Théandre
Chastellain, Pierre
Chaumonot, Pierre-Joseph-Marie
Chauvigny, Marie-Madeleine de (Gruel de La Peltrie)
Chauvin de La Pierre, Pierre
Cherououny
Chouart Des Groseilliers, Médard
Cloutier, Zacharie
Colin, Michel
Couillard de Lespinay, Guillaume
Couillard de Lespinay, Louis

Courseron, Gilbert
Dablon, Claude
Dalmas, Antoine
Damours de Chauffours, Mathieu
Dangé, François
Daumont de Saint-Lusson, Simon-François
Demosny, Jean
Denys de La Trinité, Simon
Derré de Gand, François
Desdames, Thierry
Desportes, Hélène (Hébert)
Dethunes, Exupère
Dolbeau, Jean
Donnacona
Drouin, Robert
Dubois Davaugour, Pierre
Dubois de Cocreaumont et de Saint-Maurice, Jean-Baptiste
Dubok
Du Bos, Nicolas
Du Chesne, Adrien
Duchesneau de La Doussinière et d'Ambault, Jacques
Dudouyt, Jean
Duplessis, Pacifique
Du Plessis-Bochart, Charles
Dupuy, Zacharie
Duquet de La Chesnaye, Pierre
Duval, Jean
Erouachy
Espérance
Fillion, Michel
Flemish Bastard
Foi
Fonteneau, Jean
Forestier, Marie, *dite* de Saint-Bonaventure-de-Jésus
Foucher
François, Claude, known as Brother Luc
Gadoys, Pierre
Gagnon, Mathurin
Galleran, Guillaume
Garakontié
Garreau, Léonard
Gaudais-Dupont, Louis
Gaultier de Comporté, Philippe
Giffard, Marie-Françoise, *dite* Marie de Saint-Ignace
Giffard de Moncel, Robert
Gloria, Jean
Godefroy, Jean-Paul
Godefroy de Normanville, Thomas
Godet, Rolland
Godet Des Maretz, Claude de
Goupil, René
Grandmaison, Éléonore de (Boudier de Beauregard; Chavigny de Berchereau; Gourdeau de Beaulieu; Cailhault de La Tesserie)
Gravé Du Pont, François
Guenet, Marie, *dite* de Saint-Ignace

Guyart, Marie, *dite* de l'Incarnation (Martin)
Guyon, Jean
Guyon Du Buisson, Jean (father)
Guyon Du Buisson, Jean (son)
Hébert, Guillemette (Couillard de Lespinay)
Hébert, Joseph
Hébert, Louis
Huault de Montmagny, Charles
Iroquet
Irwin, Marie, *dite* de la Conception
Jamet, Denis
Jérémie, *dit* Lamontagne, Noël
Jolliet, Louis
Joybert de Soulanges et de Marson, Pierre de
Juchereau de La Ferté, Jean
Juchereau de Maur, Jean
Juchereau de Saint-Denis, Nicolas
Juchereau Des Chatelets, Noël
Kirke, Sir David
Kirke, Sir Lewis
Kirke, Thomas
La Frenaye de Brucy, Antoine de
La Lande, Jean de
Lalemant, Charles
Lalemant, Gabriel
Lalemant, Jérôme
Lambert, Eustache
La Motte de Lucière, Dominique
Lamotte de Saint-Paul, Pierre
Langlois, Noël
Langoissieux, Charles
Lanouguère, Thomas de
La Ralde, Raymond de
La Ribourde, Gabriel de
La Roche Daillon, Joseph de
La Rocque de Roberval, Jean-François de
Lauson, Jean de (father)
Lauson, Jean de (son)
Lauson de Charny, Charles de
Le Baillif, Georges
Le Caron, Joseph
Le Clercq, Chrestien
Le Febvre de La Barre, Joseph-Antoine
Legardeur de Repentigny, Pierre
Legardeur de Tilly, Charles
Le Jeune, Olivier
Le Jeune, Paul
Le Mercier, François-Joseph
Lemire, Jean
Le Moyne, Simon
Le Moyne de Sainte-Hélène, Jacques
Leneuf de La Poterie, Jacques
Letardif, Olivier
Le Sueur, Jean, known as Abbé de Saint-Sauveur
Levasseur, *dit* Lavigne, Jean
Levasseur, *dit* L'Espérance, Pierre
Le Vieux de Hauteville, Nicolas
Liégeois, Jean

83

Madry, Jean
Maheut, Louis
Makheabichtichiou
Malherbe, François
Manitougatche
Mareuil, Jacques de
Marsolet de Saint-Aignan, Nicolas
Martin, Abraham, known as l'Écossais
    or Maître Abraham
Massé, Énemond
Maupassant, Eustache
Membré, Zénobe
Merlac, André-Louis de
Miristou
Miville, Pierre, known as Le Suisse
Mohier, Gervais
Monts, Sieur de
Morel, Thomas
Mouchy, Nicolas de
Negabamat
Nicollet de Belleborne, Jean
Noël, Jacques
Nouë, Anne de
Noyrot, Philibert
Oionhaton
Otreouti
Oumasasikweie
Ourehouare
Outlaw, John
Pastedechouan
Patoulet, Jean-Baptiste
Pelletier, Didace
Peré, Jean
Peronne de Mazé, Louis
Peronne Dumesnil, Jean
Perreault, Hyacinthe
Peuvret Demesnu, Jean-Baptiste
Phips, Sir William
Pigarouich
Pijart, Pierre
Pollet de La Combe-Pocatière, François
Pommier, Hugues
Poncet de La Rivière, Joseph-Antoine
Prévost, Martin
Prouville, Alexandre, Marquis
    de Tracy
Puiseaux, Pierre de
Quen, Jean de
Quentin, Claude
Rageot, Gilles
Ragueneau, Paul
Rémy de Courcelle, Daniel de
Renaud d'Avène de Desmeloizes,
    François-Marie
Richard, *dit* Lafleur, Guillaume
Robineau de Bécancour, René, Baron
    de Portneuf
Rollet, Marie (Hébert)
Romieux, Pierre
Rouer de Villeray, Louis
Roussel, Timothée
Ruette d'Auteuil, Denis-Joseph
Saffray de Mézy, Augustin de

Saint-Étienne de La Tour, Charles de
Sarcel de Prévert, Jean
Saurel, Pierre de
Savonnières de La Troche, Marie de,
    dite de Saint-Joseph
Sevestre, Charles
Simon de Longpré, Marie-Catherine
    de, *dite* de Saint-Augustin
Skanudharoua (Geneviève-Agnès
    de Tous-les-Saints)
Smithsend, Richard
Talon, Jean
Taondechoren
Taratouan
Tareha
Teouatiron
Tessouat (d. 1654)
Thubières de Levy de Queylus, Gabriel
Tonsahoten
Troyes, Pierre de, *dit* Chevalier de
    Troyes
Viennay-Pachot, François
Vignal, Guillaume
Villain, Jean-Baptiste
Villeneuve, Robert de
Vimont, Barthélemy
Vuil, Daniel
Young, Thomas

II (1701–1740)
Aloigny, Charles-Henri d', Marquis de
    La Groye
Ameau, *dit* Saint-Séverin, Séverin
Amiot de Vincelotte, Charles-Joseph
Ango Des Maizerets, Louis
Armstrong, Lawrence
Aubert de La Chesnaye, Charles
Aubert de La Chesnaye, François
Avaugour, Louis d'
Barbel, Jacques
Barbier, Marie, *dite* de l'Assomption
Basset, Jean
Baudeau, Pierre
Baugy, Louis-Henri de, known as
    Chevalier de Baugy
Beauharnois de Beaumont et de Ville-
    chauve, Claude de
Bécart de Granville et de Fonville,
    Charles
Bermen de La Martinière, Claude de
Bernard de La Rivière, Hilaire
Berthier, Isaac (Alexandre)
Bertier, Michel
Beschefer, Thierry
Bigot, Jacques
Bigot, Vincent
Bissot, François-Joseph
Bochart de Champigny, Jean
Bonner, John
Boucher, Pierre
Bouillet de La Chassaigne, Jean
Boulduc, Louis
Boullard, Étienne

Bourdon, Anne, *dite* Sainte-Agnès
Bourdon, Marguerite, *dite* de Saint-
    Jean-Baptiste
Bouvart, Martin
Brandeau, Esther
Bricault de Valmur, Louis-Frédéric
Brisay de Denonville, Jacques-René
    de, Marquis de Denonville
Buisson de Saint-Cosme, Jean-François
Bulteau, Guillaume
Callière, Louis-Hector de
Calvarin, Goulven
Carheil, Étienne de
Catalogne, Gédéon (de)
Caulfeild, Thomas
Chaboulié, Charles
Chambalon, Louis
Champy, Gélase
Charly Saint-Ange, Jean-Baptiste
Chartier de Lotbinière, René-Louis
Chauchetière, Claude
Chaumont, Alexandre de
Chavigny Lachevrotière, François de
Chingouessi
Cholenec, Pierre
Clairambault d'Aigremont François
Collet, Mathieu-Benoît
Constantin, Nicolas-Bernardin
Couagne, Jean-Baptiste de
Couillard de Lespinay, Jean-Baptiste
Couillard de Lespinay, Louis
Coulon de Villiers, Nicolas-Antoine
Couture, Guillaume
Couvert, Michel-Germain de
Crespieul, François de
Crisafy, Antoine de, Marquis de
    Crisafy
Daneau de Muy, Nicolas
David, Jacques
Davion, Albert
Davis, Silvanus
Denys, Joseph
Denys de Bonaventure, Simon-Pierre
Denys de La Ronde, Pierre
Denys de Saint-Simon, Paul
Denys de Vitré, Charles
Deschamps de Boishébert, Henri-Louis
Deschamps de La Bouteillerie, Jean-
    Baptiste-François
Deshayes, Jean
Desjordy de Cabanac, Joseph
Desjordy Moreau de Cabanac, François
Dessailliant, *dit* Richeterre, Michel
Drué, Juconde
Dubreuil, Jean-Étienne
Dupont de Neuville, Nicolas
Duprac, Jean-Robert
Dupré, François
Dupuy, Claude-Thomas
Dupuy de Lisloye, Paul
Dutisné, Claude-Charles
Élie, Jacques
Enjalran, Jean

Filiastre, Luc
Fleury Dechambault, Jacques-Alexis de
Francheville, Pierre
Franquelin, Jean-Baptiste-Louis
Gaillard, Guillaume
Gannes de Falaise, Louis de
Garnier, Julien
Gaultier de Varennes, Jean-Baptiste
Genaple de Bellefonds, François
Georgemé, Séraphin
Germain, Joseph-Louis
Glandelet, Charles de
Gobin, Jean
Godefroy de Vieuxpont, Joseph
Gouentagrandi
Gourdeau de Beaulieu et de La Grossardière, Jacques
Goyer, Olivier
Gravier, Jacques
Guesdron, Julien
Guillimin, Charles
Guillouet d'Orvilliers, Claude
Guion, François
Haimard, Pierre
Hamare de La Borde, Jean-Baptiste-Julien
Hazeur, François
Hazeur, Jean-François
Hennepin, Louis
Hertel de La Fresnière, Joseph-François
Hertel de Rouville, Jean-Baptiste
Hill, John
Hill, Samuel
Horné, dit Laneuville, Jacques de
Jacob, Étienne
Joybert de Soulanges et de Marson, Louise-Élisabeth de (Rigaud de Vaudreuil, Marquise de Vaudreuil)
Juchereau de La Ferté, Denis-Joseph
Juchereau de La Ferté, Jeanne-Françoise, dite de Saint-Ignace
Juchereau de Maur, Paul-Augustin
Juchereau de Saint-Denis, Charlotte-Françoise, known as Comtesse de Saint-Laurent (Viennay-Pachot; Dauphin de La Forest)
Juchereau Duchesnay, Ignace
La Cetière, Florent de
La Colombière, Joseph de
La Corne de Chaptes, Jean-Louis de
La Croix de Chevrières de Saint-Vallier, Jean-Baptiste de
Ladan, Adrien
Lagrené, Pierre de
Lajoüe, François de
La Marche, Dominique de
Lamarre, dit Bélisle, Henri
Lamberville, Jacques de
Landon, Simple
La Place, Louis-Hyacinthe de
La Porte de Louvigny, Louis de

Lascaris d'Urfé, François-Saturnin
Laumet, dit de Lamothe Cadillac, Antoine
Laure, Pierre-Michel
Laval, François de
Lebeau, Claude
Leblond de Latour, Jacques
Lechasseur, Jean
Lefebvre, Thomas
Le Gardeur de Courtemanche, Augustin
Legardeur de Repentigny, Marie-Jeanne-Madeleine, dite de Sainte-Agathe
Legardeur de Tilly, Pierre-Noël
Léger de La Grange, Jean
Le Moyne d'Iberville et d'Ardillières, Pierre
Le Moyne de Longueuil, Charles, Baron de Longueuil
Le Moyne de Maricourt, Paul
Le Moyne de Serigny et de Loire, Joseph
Leneuf de La Vallière de Beaubassin, Michel (father)
Lepallieur de Laferté, Michel
Le Picard Du Mesnil de Norrey, Jacques
Le Rouge, Jean
Leroux, Valentin
Le Roy, Henri
Le Roy de La Potherie, dit Bacqueville de La Potherie, Claude-Charles
Lespinay, Jean-Michel de
Lessard, Étienne de
Lestringant de Saint-Martin, Alexandre-Joseph
Le Tac, Xiste
Levasseur, Michel
Levasseur, Noël
Levasseur de Neré, Jacques
Le Verrier de Rousson, François
Livingston, John
Lom d'Arce de Lahontan, Louis-Armand de, Baron de Lahontan
Lorimier de La Rivière, Guillaume de
Louet, Jean-Claude
Macard, Charles
Mallet, Denis
March, John
Marest, Joseph-Jacques
Mariauchau d'Esgly, François
Martel, Raymond
Martel de Magos, Jean
Martin, Charles-Amador
Martin de Lino, Antoine
Martin de Lino, Jean-François
Martin de Lino, Mathieu-François
Maufils, Marie-Madeleine, dite de Saint-Louis
Ménage, Pierre
Meulles, Jacques de
Millet, Pierre
Mog

Moireau, Claude
Monic, Joseph de
Monseignat, Charles de
Moore, Thomas
Morel de La Durantaye, Olivier
Morin, Germain
Nelson, John
Nouvel, Henri
Ohonsiowanne
Ozon, Potentien
Paillard, Léonard, known as Le Poitevin
Paradis, Jean
Payen de Noyan, Pierre
Peiras, Jean-Baptiste de
Pélerin, Ambroise
Perrot de Rizy, Pierre
Perthuis, Charles
Petit, Jean
Petit, Louis
Peuvret de Gaudarville, Alexandre
Pinaud, Nicolas
Piot de Langloiserie, Charles-Gaspard
Poulet, Georges-François, known as M. Dupont
Pourroy de Lauberivière, François-Louis de
Prat, Louis
Provost, François
Quinard, dit Duplessis, Antoine-Olivier
Raffeix, Pierre
Rageot de Saint-Luc, Charles
Rageot de Saint-Luc, Nicolas
Rale, Sébastien
Ramezay, Claude de
Rattier, Jean
Raudot, Antoine-Denis
Raudot, Jacques
Regnard Duplessis, Georges
Renaud Dubuisson, Jacques-Charles
Rigaud de Vaudreuil, Philippe de, Marquis de Vaudreuil
Riverin, Denis
Rivet Cavelier, Pierre
Robinau de Portneuf, René
Rodrigue, Jean-Baptiste
Roger, Guillaume
Rouer de Villeray et de La Cardonnière, Augustin
Roy, dit Châtellerault, Michel
Ruette d'Auteuil de Monceaux, François-Madeleine-Fortuné
Saint-Ours, Pierre de
Sarrazin, Michel
Savage, Thomas
Sayward, Mary, dite Marie des Anges
Schuyler, Peter
Serreau de Saint-Aubin, Jean
Silly, Jean-Baptiste de
Silvy, Antoine
Soullard, Jean
Soumande, Louis

Soumande, Louise, *dite* de Saint-Augustin
Soupiran, Simon
Teganissorens
Tekarihoken
Thiboult, Thomas
Trouvé, Claude
Vachon, Paul (father)
Vachon, Paul (son)
Vaillant de Gueslis, François
Verreau, Barthélemy
Vetch, Samuel
Villedonné, Étienne de
Villieu, Claude-Sébastien de
Volant de Saint-Claude, Pierre
Voyer d'Argenson, Pierre de
Walker, Sir Hovenden
Walley, John
Waxaway
Williams, John (1664–1729)
Williams, John (fl. 1711–18)
Wowurna

III (1741–1770)
Adhémar de Lantagnac, Gaspard
Ailleboust, Charles-Joseph d'
Allenou de Lavillangevin, René-Jean
Alquier de Servian, Jean d'
Amiot, Jean-Baptiste (1717–69)
André de Leigne, Louise-Catherine (Hertel de Rouville)
André de Leigne, Pierre
Arnaud, Jean-Charles d'
Arnoux, André
Atecouando
Aubert de La Chesnaye, Louis
Aubery, Joseph
Barolet, Claude
Barrin de La Galissonière, Roland-Michel, Marquis de La Galissonière
Baudoin, Gervais
Baudry, *dit* Saint-Martin, Jean-Baptiste
Bayne, Daniel
Bazil, Louis
Beauharnois de La Boische, Charles de, Marquis de Beauharnois
Beauharnois de La Chaussaye, François de, Baron de Beauville
Beaussier de Lisle, Louis-Joseph
Bécart de Granville et de Fonville, Paul
Bégon de La Cour, Claude-Michel
Begon de La Picardière, Michel
Bénard, Michel
Boispineau, Jean-Jard
Bolvin, Gilles
Bonhomme, *dit* Beaupré, Noël
Bonne de Missègle, Louis de
Boucault, Nicolas-Gaspard
Boucault de Godefus, Gilbert
Boucher, Geneviève, *dite* de Saint-Pierre
Boucher de Montbrun, Jean
Bourlamaque, François-Charles de
Burton, Ralph

Callet, Luc
Campot, Jacques
Cardeneau, Bernard
Chardon, Jean-Baptiste
Charlevoix, Pierre-François-Xavier de
Chartier, Michel
Chartier de Lotbinière, Eustache
Chaussegros de Léry, Gaspard-Joseph
Chevalier, Jean-Charles
Claverie, Pierre
Colvill, Alexander, 7th Baron Colvill
Constantin, Justinien
Constantin, Pierre
Coquart, Claude-Godefroy
Corbin, David
Corolère, Jean
Corpron, Jean
Corriveau, Marie-Josephte, known as La Corriveau (Bouchard; Dodier)
Cotton, Michel
Coulon de Villiers, Nicolas-Antoine
Cugnet, François-Étienne
Daine, François
Daneau de Muy, Charlotte, *dite* de Sainte-Hélène
Daniélou, Jean-Pierre
Dasilva, *dit* Portugais, Nicolas
Davis, Marie-Anne, *dite* de Saint-Benoît
Dazemard de Lusignan, Paul-Louis
Deguise, *dit* Flamand, Girard-Guillaume
De Laune, William
Denys de La Ronde, Louis
Denys de Saint-Simon, Charles-Paul
Deschevery, *dit* Maisonbasse, Jean-Baptiste
Des Landes, Joseph
Dieskau, Jean-Armand, Baron de Dieskau
Doreil, André (Jean-Baptiste)
Dubois Berthelot de Beaucours, Josué
Dubreil de Pontbriand, Henri-Marie
Dudley, William
Dufournel, Louis-Gaspard
Du Laurent, Christophe-Hilarion
Duparc, Jean-Baptiste
Duplessis, Marguerite
Durand, Justinien
Durell, Philip
Elliot, Robert
Fleury de La Gorgendière, Joseph de
Forget Duverger, Jacques-François
Fornel, Joachim
Fornel, Louis
Foucault, François
Foucault, Simon
Foucher, François
Franquet, Louis
Galiffet de Caffin, François de
Gaschet, René
Gaudron de Chevremont, Charles-René
Gaufin, Valérien
Gaultier, Jean-François

Gaultier de La Vérendrye, Louis-Joseph
Gaultier de La Vérendrye de Boumois, Pierre
Gaultier de Varennes, Jacques-René
Gaultier de Varennes et de La Vérendrye, Pierre
Godfroy de Tonnancour, Charles-Antoine
Gosselin, Jean-Baptiste
Guignas, Michel
Guy, Pierre
Guyart de Fleury, Jean-Baptiste
Guyon, Louise (Thibault; Damours de Freneuse)
Havy, François
Hazeur, Joseph-Thierry
Hertel de Saint-François, Étienne
Hiché, Henry
Holmes, Charles
Houdin, Jean-Michel, known as Father Potentien
Imbault, Maurice
Imbert, Jacques
Jacquin, *dit* Philibert, Nicolas
Janson, *dit* Lapalme, Dominique
Jeanneau, Étienne
Jérémie, *dit* Lamontagne, Catherine (Aubuchon; Lepallieur de Laferté)
Jucherau Duchesnay, Marie-Joseph, *dite* de l'Enfant-Jésus
Kanon, Jacques
La Bretonnière, Jacques-Quintin de
La Chasse, Pierre de
La Corne, Louis de, known as Chevalier de La Corne
La Corne Dubreuil, François-Josué de
La Croix, Hubert-Joseph de
Lafitau, Joseph-François
Lafontaine de Belcour, Jacques de
Lajus, Jordain
Lambert, *dit* Saint-Paul, Paul
Lamorinie, Jean-Baptiste de
Landron, Jean-François
Langlois, Marie-Thérèse, *dite* de Saint-Jean-Baptiste
Lanoullier de Boisclerc, Jean-Eustache
Lanoullier de Boisclerc, Nicolas
Laporte de Lalanne, Jean-Armand de
La Richardie, Armand de
Latouche MacCarthy, Charles
Lauverjat, Étienne
Lauzon, Pierre de
Leduc, Anne-Françoise, *dite* Saint-Joseph
Lefebvre, Jean
Legardeur de Croisille, Charles
Legardeur de Tilly, Jean-Baptiste
Lemaître, *dit* Jugon, François
Lemoine, *dit* Monière, Alexis
Lepage de Sainte-Claire, Louis
Le Prévost, Pierre-Gabriel
Le Prévost Duquesnel, Jean-Baptiste-Louis

Le Sueur, Jacques-François
Levasseur, Louis
Levasseur, Pierre-Noël
Léveillé, Mathieu
Liénard de Beaujeu, Daniel-Hyacinthe-Marie
Liénard de Beaujeu, Louis
Lombard de Combles, Jean-Claude-Henri de
Longley, Lydia, *dite* Sainte-Madeleine
Lorimier de La Rivière, Claude-Nicolas de
Lozeau, Jean-Baptiste
Lyon de Saint-Ferréol, Jean
Maillou, *dit* Desmoulins, Jean-Baptiste
Malepart de Grand Maison, *dit* Beaucour, Paul
Mangeant, François
Marcol, Gabriel
Mareuil, Pierre de
Margane de Lavaltrie, François
Marin de La Malgue, Paul
Martel de Belleville, Jean-Urbain
Martel de Brouague, François
Martin, Barthélemy
Mercier, Jean-François
Mercier, Jean-Paul
Mesaiger, Charles-Michel
Michel de Villebois de La Rouvilliere, Honoré
Montcalm, Louis-Joseph de, Marquis de Montcalm
Montigny, François de
Mounier, François
Murray, Alexander
Nau, Luc-François
Navières, Joseph
Normant Du Faradon, Louis
Nouchet, Joseph
Nouchet, Joseph-Étienne
Noyelles de Fleurimont, Nicolas-Joseph de
Noyon, Jacques de
Olivier, Abel
Orontony
Pagé, *dit* Carcy, Jacques
Pain, Félix
Paradis, Roland
Paris, Bernard
Pattin, John
Péan de Livaudière, Jacques-Hugues
Perrault, François
Perrault, Paul
Perthuis, Jean-Baptiste-Ignace
Petitpas, Barthélemy
Phlem, *dit* Yvon, Yves
Pillard, Louis
Pinguet de Vaucour, Jacques-Nicolas
Plante, Charles
Pollet, Arnould-Balthazar
Pote, William
Poulin, Pierre
Poulin de Courval, François-Louis
Poulin de Courval, Louis-Jean

Poulin de Courval Cressé, Louis-Pierre
Price, Benjamin
Ramezay, Marie-Charlotte, *dite* de Saint-Claude de la Croix
Ransonnet, Sylvestre-François-Michel
Récher, Jean-Félix
Regnard Duplessis, Marie-Andrée, *dite* de Sainte-Hélène
Regnard Duplessis de Morampont, Charles-Denis
Renaud d'Avène des Méloizes, Nicolas-Marie
Renaud Dubuisson, Louis-Jacques-Charles
René, Patrice
Resche, Pierre-Joseph
Révol, Pierre
Rigaud de Vaudreuil, Louis-Philippe de, Marquis de Vaudreuil
Riverin, Joseph
Robinau de Portneuf, Philippe-René
Robinau de Portneuf, Pierre
Rocbert de La Morandière, Marie-Élisabeth (Bégon de La Cour)
Roma, Jean-Pierre
Roseboom, Johannes
Rouer d'Artigny, Louis
Rouer de Villeray, Benjamin
Rouffio, Joseph
Rouillard, Ambroise
Rous, John
Saguima
Saint-Ours, François-Xavier de
Saint-Ours Deschaillons, Jean-Baptiste de
Saint-Pé, Jean-Baptiste de
Saint-Père, Agathe de (Legardeur de Repentigny)
Sallaberry, Michel de
Sauguaaram
Schuyler, Peter
Scott, George
Senezergues de La Rodde, Étienne-Guillaume de
Short, Richard
Soupiran, Simon
Southack, Cyprian
Stobo, Robert
Strouds, Gilles William
Swanton, Robert
Taché, Jean
Taffanel de La Jonquière, Jacques-Pierre de, Marquis de La Jonquière
Taschereau, Thomas-Jacques
Terroux, Jacques
Testu de La Richardière, Richard
Tibierge, Marie-Catherine, *dite* de Saint-Joachim
Tisserant de Moncharvaux, Jean-Baptiste-François
Tournois, Jean-Baptiste
Tremblay, Henri-Jean
Trottier, Marguerite, *dite* Saint-Joseph
Trottier Desauniers, Pierre

Turc de Castelveyre, Louis, known as Brother Chrétien
Vallette de Chévigny, Médard-Gabriel
Vallier, François-Elzéar
Varlet, Dominique-Marie
Véron de Grandmesnil, Étienne
Verrier, Louis-Guillaume
Vézina, Charles
Vincent
Wilmot, Montagu
Wolfe, James

IV (1771–1800)
Adhémar, Jean-Baptiste-Amable
Aide-Créquy, Jean-Antoine
Ailleboust de Cerry, Philippe-Marie d'
Aleyrac, Jean-Baptiste d'
Amherst, Jeffery, 1st Baron Amherst
Angeac, François-Gabriel d'
Aubert de Gaspé, Ignace-Philippe
Aumasson de Courville, Louis-Léonard, known as Sieur de Courville
Aylwin, Thomas
Bailly de Messein, Charles-François
Barbel, Marie-Anne (Fornel)
Beatson, Patrick
Bédard, Thomas-Laurent
Bernier, Benoît-François
Bigot, François
Blais, Michel
Boiret, Urbain
Boisseau, Nicolas
Bonnécamps, Joseph-Pierre de
Bourdages, Raymond
Bowman, James
Brassard, Louis-Marie
Brassard Deschenaux, Joseph
Bréard, Jacques-Michel
Briand, Jean-Olivier
Brooke, John
Brown, William
Bruyères, John
Burgoyne, John
Butler, John
Butler, Walter
Cadet, Joseph-Michel
Campbell, John
Carpentier, Bonaventure
Casot, Jean-Joseph
Castanet, Jean-Baptiste-Marie
Charest, Étienne
Chartier de Lotbinière, Eustache
Chartier de Lotbinière, Michel, Marquis de Lotbinière
Chaussegros de Léry, Gaspard-Joseph
Christie, Gabriel
Claus, Christian Daniel
Collins, John
Corbin, André
Cotton, Barthélemy
Couagne, Michel de
Courreaud de La Coste, Pierre
Cox, Nicholas

Cramahé, Hector Theophilus
Crespel, Emmanuel
Cugnet, François-Joseph
Cuny Dauterive, Philippe-Antoine de
Curot, Marie-Louise, *dite* de Saint-
  Martin
Cuthbert, James
Dagneau Douville, Alexandre
Danks, Benoni
Davidson, George
Deguise, Jacques
Delezenne, Ignace-François
Denys de Vitré, Théodose-Matthieu
Desandrouins, Jean-Nicolas
Deschamps de Boishébert et de
  Raffetot, Charles
Desdevens de Glandons, Maurice
Dosquet, Pierre-Herman
Douglas, Sir Charles
Douglas, François-Prosper
Druillon de Macé, Pierre-Jacques
Du Calvet, Pierre
Dudevant, Arnauld-Germain
Du Jaunay, Pierre
Dumas, Jean-Daniel
Du Pont Duchambon de Vergor, Louis
Du Pont Duvivier, Joseph
Duquesne de Menneville, Ange,
  Marquis Duquesne
Estèbe, Guillaume
Feltz, Charles-Elemy-Joseph-
  Alexandre-Ferdinand
Floquet, Pierre-René
Fortier, Michel
Fraser, Alexander
Garreau, Pierre
Germain, Charles
Gilmore, Thomas
Girard, Jacques
Glapion, Augustin-Louis de
Glasier, Beamsley Perkins
Godefroy de Tonnancour, Charles-
  Antoine
Goguet, Denis
Gohin, Pierre-André, Comte de
  Montreuil
Grasset de Saint-Sauveur, André
Guillimin, Guillaume
Guillot, *dit* Larose, François
Haldimand, Sir Frederick
Hamilton, Henry
Harrison, Edward
Hay, Charles
Hay, Jehu
Hazeur de L'Orme, Pierre
Hertel de Rouville, René-Ovide
Hey, William
Hillaire de La Rochette, Alexandre-
  Robert
Hocquart, Gilles
Hope, Henry
Hubert, Jean-François
Huppé, *dit* Lagroix, Joseph

Irving, Paulus Æmilius
Isbister, Joseph
Jacau de Fiedmont, Louis-Thomas
Jacobs, Samuel
Jacquet, François
Jacrau, Joseph-André-Mathurin
Jadis, Charles Newland Godfrey
Joe
Johnston, Alexander
Johnston, James
Johnstone, James, known as Chevalier
  de Johnstone
Kalm, Pehr
Kneller, Henry
Knox, John
La Brosse, Jean-Baptiste de
La Corne, Luc de
La Corne de Chaptes, Joseph-Marie
  (Jean-Marie) de
La Garde, Pierre-Paul-François de
Lajus, François
Lamaletie, Jean-André
Landriaux, Louis-Nicolas
Landrième Des Bordes, Jean-Marie
Latour, Bertrand de
Legardeur de Croisille et de Montesson,
  Joseph-Michel
Legardeur de Repentigny, Louis
Legardeur de Repentigny, Pierre-Jean-
  Baptiste-François-Xavier
Le Guerne, François
Le Mercier, François-Marc-Antoine
Le Moyne de Longueuil, Paul-Joseph,
  known as Chevalier de Longueuil
Levasseur, François-Noël
Levasseur, René-Nicolas
Levasseur, *dit* Delor, Jean-Baptiste-
  Antoine
Le Verrier de Rousson, Louis
Lévesque, François
Lévis, François de, Duc de Lévis
Livius, Peter
Long, John
Mabane, Adam
MacDonald, James
Mackellar, Patrick
McLane, David
Maclean, Allan
Marchand, Étienne
Mariauchau d'Esgly, Louis-Philippe
Marin de La Malgue, Joseph
Martel, Pierre-Michel
Maurès de Malartic, Anne-Joseph-
  Hippolyte de, Comte de Malartic
Migeon de Branssat, Marie-Anne, *dite*
  de la Nativité
Mills, Sir Thomas
Miniac, Jean-Pierre de
Monckton, Robert
Montgomery, Richard
Montresor, John
Moore, Frances (Brooke)
Moore, William

Mouet de Langlade, Charles-Michel
Mounier, Jean-Mathieu
Murray, James
Murray, Walter
Neilson, Samuel
Oakes, Forrest
Oliva, Frédéric-Guillaume
Palliser, Sir Hugh
Panet, Jean-Claude
Pascaud, Antoine
Peachey, James
Péan, Michel-Jean-Hugues
Pélissier, Christophe
Pellegrin, Gabriel
Pennisseaut, Louis
Perrault, Jacques
Perthuis, Joseph
Picard, Louis-Alexandre
Pichot de Querdisien Trémais, Charles-
  François
Picquet, François
Potier, Pierre-Philippe
Potot de Montbeillard, Fiacre-François
Preissac de Bonneau, Louis de
Pressart, Colomban-Sébastien
Primeau, Louis
Raby, Augustin
Ramezay, Jean-Baptiste-Nicolas-
  Roch de
Ramezay, Louise de
Renaud, Jean
Renaud, *dit* Cannard, Pierre
Renaud d'Avène Des Méloizes,
  Angélique (Péan)
Rigaud de Vaudreuil, François-Pierre de
Rigaud de Vaudreuil de Cavagnial,
  Pierre de, Marquis de Vaudreuil
Robichaux, Louis
Rogers, Robert
Roubaud, Pierre-Joseph-Antoine
Roy, Louis
Saillant, Jean-Antoine
St Leger, Barrimore Matthew
Sanguinet, Simon
Saunders, Sir Charles
Smith, William
Sorbier de Villars, François
Sterling, James
Suckling, George
Tarieu de La Naudière, Charles-
  François
Teyohaqueande
Tonge, Winckworth
Toosey, Philip
Varin de La Marre, Jean-Victor
Vauquelin, Jean
Veyssière, Leger-Jean-Baptiste-Noël,
  known as Father Emmanuel
Vienne, François-Joseph de
Wheelwright, Esther, *dite* de l'Enfant-
  Jésus
Williamson, George
Youville, Charles-Marie-Madeleine d'

Trois-Rivières/Cantons-de-l'Est

I (1000–1700)
Albanel, Charles
Allouez, Claude
Amiot, Jean
Amiot, *dit* Villeneuve, Mathieu
Anadabijou
Annaotaha
Atironta (d. 1650)
Audouart, *dit* Saint-Germain,
  Guillaume
Babie, Jacques
Batiscan
Boivin, François
Boucher de Grandpré, Lambert
Bourdon, Jean
Bras-de-Fer de Chateaufort, Marc-
  Antoine
Bréhaut Delisle, Achille
Bressani, François-Joseph
Buteux, Jacques
Capitanal
Carigouan
Cartier, Jacques
Champflour, François de
Champlain, Samuel de
Cherououny
Chouart Des Groseilliers, Médard
Crevier de Saint-François, Jean
Dalmas, Antoine
David, Claude
Duplessis, Pacifique
Flemish Bastard
Frémin, Jacques
Gamelain de La Fontaine, Michel
Garreau, Léonard
Gaultier de Varennes, René
Godefroy de Lintot, Jean-Paul
Godefroy de Normanville, Thomas
Godefroy de Vieuxpont, Jacques
Guillemot, Guillaume
Hamelin de Bourgchemin et de
  L'Hermitière, Jacques-François
Hertel de La Fresnière, Jacques
Honatteniate
Huet, Paul
Jérémie, *dit* Lamontagne, Noël
Kiotseaeton
La Lande, Jean de
Langoissieux, Charles
Lanouguère, Thomas de
La Ribourde, Gabriel de
La Roche Daillon, Joseph de
Legardeur de Tilly, Charles
Le Jeune, Paul
Le Mercier, François-Joseph
Le Moyne, Simon
Le Moyne de Longueuil et de Château-
  guay, Charles
Leneuf de La Poterie, Jacques
Leneuf Du Hérisson, Michel
Laviolette

Liégeois, Jean
Madry, Jean
Magnan, Pierre
Makheabichtichiou
Malapart, André
Malherbe, François
Marguerite de La Haye, François
Marquette, Jacques
Marsolet de Saint-Aignan, Nicolas
Ménard, René
Miristou
Monts, Sieur de
Negabamat
Nicollet de Belleborne, Jean
Noüe, Anne de
Oionhaton
Olivier, *dit* Le Picard, Marc-Antoine
Pelletier, Didace
Pézard de La Tousche Champlain,
  Étienne
Pigarouich
Pijart, Pierre
Pinard, Louis
Poncet de La Rivière, Joseph-Antoine
Poulain, Guillaume
Poulin de La Fontaine, Maurice
Quen, Jean de
Quentin, Claude
Ragueneau, Paul
Raisin, Marie
Raymbaut, Charles
Robinau de Bécancour, René, Baron
  de Portneuf
Rouer de Villeray, Louis
Sevestre, Charles
Taratouan
Teouatiron
Tessouat (d. 1654)
Totiri
Vignal, Guillaume

II (1701–1740)
Adhémar de Saint-Martin, Antoine
Ameau, *dit* Saint-Séverin, Séverin
Atecouando
Baudry, *dit* Des Butes, Guillaume
Bernard de La Rivière, Hilaire
Bigot, François
Bigot, Jacques
Blaise Des Bergères de Rigauville,
  Raymond
Bochart de Champigny, Jean
Boucher, Pierre
Bouillet de La Chassaigne, Jean
Bulteau, Guillaume
Catalogne, Gédéon (de)
Chaigneau (Du Chaigneau), Léonard
Constantin, Nicolas-Bernardin
Couagne, Jean-Baptiste de
Couture, Guillaume
Crisafy, Antoine de, Marquis de
  Crisafy
Cusson, Jean

Dandonneau, *dit* Lajeunesse, Pierre
Dauphin de La Forest, François
Delhalle, Constantin
Denys, Joseph
Denys de La Ronde, Pierre
Desjordy de Cabanac, Joseph
Desjordy Moreau de Cabanac, François
Dizy, *dit* Montplaisir, Marguerite (Des-
  brieux)
Dizy, *dit* Montplaisir, Michel-Ignace
Dollier de Casson, François
Drué, Juconde
Dugay, Jacques
Dupont, Siméon
Dupré, François
Filiastre, Luc
Foucault, Nicolas
Geoffroy, Louis
Glandelet, Charles de
Godefroy de Lintot, Michel
Godefroy de Saint-Paul, Jean-Amador
Godefroy de Tonnancour, René
Godefroy de Vieuxpont, Joseph
Guesdron, Julien
Hennepin, Louis
Hertel de La Fresnière, Joseph-François
Horné, *dit* Laneuville, Jacques de
Jacquiès, *dit* Leblond, Jean
La Corne de Chaptes, Jean-Louis de
Lamarre, *dit* Bélisle, Henri
La Place, Louis-Hyacinthe de
La Porte de Louvigny, Louis de
Largillier, Jacques, known as Le Castor
Larue, Guillaume de
Lechasseur, Jean
Leclerc, Jean-Baptiste
Le Conte Dupré, Louis
Lefebvre, *dit* Laciseraye, Michel
Legardeur de Repentigny, Jean-
  Baptiste
Le Marchand de Lignery, Constant
Le Moyne de Longueuil, Charles,
  Baron de Longueuil
Le Picard Du Mesnil de Norrey,
  Jacques
Le Tac, Xiste
L'Hermitte, Jacques
Lorit, *dit* Gargot, François
Mariauchau d'Esgly, François
Martin de Lino, Antoine
Moireau, Claude
Morin, Germain
Nescambiouit
Normandin, Daniel
Pélerin, Ambroise
Perrot, Nicolas
Petit, Pierre
Pottier, Jean-Baptiste
Poulin de Courval, Jean-Baptiste
Poulin de Francheville, François
Provost, François
Radisson, Pierre-Esprit
Rale, Sébastien

89

Ramezay, Claude de
Rattier, Jean
Renaud Dubuisson, Jacques-Charles
Robinau de Bécancour, Pierre, Baron
  de Portneuf
Roy, *dit* Châtellerault, Michel
Sarrazin, Michel
Tekarihoken
Trotain, *dit* Saint-Seürin, François
Vachon, Paul (son)
Véron de Grandmesnil, Étienne
Volant de Saint-Claude, Claude
Wowurna

III (1741–1770)
Ailleboust, Charles-Joseph d'
Alavoine, Charles
André de Leigne, Louise-Catherine
  (Hertel de Rouville)
Atecouando (fl. 1749–57)
Aubery, Joseph
Bégon de La Cour, Claude-Michel
Bolvin, Gilles
Boucault, Nicolas-Gaspard
Burton, Ralph
Charlevoix, Piere-François-Xavier de
Chaussegros de Léry, Gaspard-Joseph
Coulon de Villiers, Nicolas-Antoine
Daine, François
Dizy de Montplaisir, Pierre
Dubois Berthelot de Beaucours, Josué
Dubreil de Pontbriand, Henri-Marie
Dufournel, Louis-Gaspard
Franquet, Louis
Galiffet de Caffin, François de
Gastineau Duplessis, Jean-Baptiste
Gaufin, Valérien
Gaultier de Varennes et de La
  Vérendrye, Pierre
Guignas, Michel
Guyart de Fleury, Jean-Baptiste
Haldimand, Peter Frederick
Hertel de La Fresnière, Zacharie-
  François
Houdin, Jean-Michel, known as Father
  Potentien

Imbault, Maurice
Jarret de Verchères, Marie-Madeleine
Jérémie, *dit* Lamontagne, Catherine
  (Aubuchon; Lepallieur de Laferté)
Lanoullier de Boisclerc, Jean-Eustache
Laporte de Lalanne, Jean de
Lauverjat, Étienne
Legardeur de Croisille, Charles
Le Sueur, Jacques-François
Marcol, Gabriel
Mareuil, Pierre de
Marie
Martel de Belleville, Jean-Urbain
Noyelles de Fleurimont, Nicolas-
  Joseph de
Perrault, François
Phlem, *dit* Yvon, Yves
Pillard, Louis
Pollet, Arnould-Balthazar
Poulin, Pierre
Poulin de Courval, Louis-Jean
Poulin de Courval Cressé, Louis-Pierre
Pressé, Hyacinthe-Olivier
Renaud Dubuisson, Louis-Jacques-
  Charles
Rocbert de La Morandière, Marie-
  Élisabeth (Bégon de La Cour)
Rollo, Andrew, 5th Baron Rollo
Rouillard, Ambroise
Simonet d'Abergemont, Jacques
Véron de Grandmesnil, Étienne

IV (1771–1800)
Aleyrac, Jean-Baptiste d'
Badeaux, Jean-Baptiste
Brassard, Louis-Marie
Bruyères, John
Campbell, John
Carpentier, Bonaventure
Chartier de Lotbinière, Eustache
Corbin, André
Cuthbert, James
Davison, George
Deguise, Jacques
Delezenne, Ignace-François
Desdevens de Glandons, Maurice

Devau, *dit* Retor, Claude
Estèbe, Guillaume
Garreau, *dit* Saint-Onge, Pierre
Germain, Charles
Gill, Joseph-Louis
Godefroy de Tonnancour, Charles-
  Antoine
Godefroy de Tonnancour, Louis-
  Joseph
Gugy, Conrad
Guillimin, Marie-Françoise, *dite* de
  Saint-Antoine
Guillot, *dit* Larose, François
Haldimand, Sir Frederick
Hamilton, Henry
Harrison, Edward
Hart, Aaron
Hazeur de L'Orme, Pierre
Hertel de Rouville, René-Ovide
La Brosse, Jean-Baptiste de
Lefebvre de Bellefeuille, François
Legardeur de Croisille et de Montesson,
  Joseph-Michel
Legge, Francis
Le Mercier, François-Marc-Antoine
Le Moyne de Longueuil, Paul-Joseph,
  known as Chevalier de Longueuil
Marchand, Étienne
Olivier de Vézin, Pierre-François
Payen de Noyan et de Chavoy, Pierre-
  Thomas
Pélissier, Christophe
Pellegrin, Gabriel
Perrault, Jacques
Porlier, Pierre-Antoine
Quintal, Augustin
Renaud, Jean
Rigaud de Vaudreuil, François-Pierre
  de
Rigaud de Vaudreuil de Cavagnial,
  Pierre de, Marquis de Vaudreuil
Rogers, Robert
Simonet, François
Tarieu de La Naudière, Charles-
  François
Veyssière, Leger-Jean-Baptiste-Noël,
  known as Father Emmanuel

SASKATCHEWAN

II (1701–1740)
Kelsey, Henry

III (1741–1770)
Dejordy de Villebon, Charles-René
Henday, Anthony
La Corne, Louis de, known as
  Chevalier de La Corne

La France, Joseph
Smith, Joseph

IV (1771–1800)
Batt, Isaac
Cocking, Matthew
Cole, John
Grant, Cuthbert

Hearne, Samuel
Holmes, William
Marten, Humphrey
Primeau, Louis
Ross, Malchom
Turnor, Philip
Umfreville, Edward
Waddens, Jean-Étienne
Walker, William

OTHER COUNTRIES

AZORES

III (1741–1770)
Rigaud de Vaudreuil, Louis-Philippe de, Marquis de Vaudreuil

CHILE

III (1741–1770)
Denis de Saint-Simon, Antoine-Charles

ENGLAND

I (1000–1700)
Segipt

III (1741–1700)
Denys de La Ronde, Louis
Taverner, William

IV (1771–1800)
Adhémar, Jean-Baptiste-Amable
Bailly de Messein, Charles-François
Bradstreet, John
Chabert de Joncaire de Clausonne, Daniel-Marie
Charest, Étienne
Chartier de Lotbinière, Michel, Marquis de Lotbinière
Chaussegros de Léry, Gaspard-Joseph
Darby, Nicholas
Denys de Vitré, Théodose-Matthieu
Lemoine Despins, Jacques-Joseph
Le Poupet de La Boularderie, Antoine
Mikak
Raby, Augustin

FALKLAND ISLANDS

IV (1771–1800)
Denis de Saint-Simon, Antoine-Charles

FRANCE

I (1000–1700)
Bourdon de Dombourg, Jean-François
Donnacona
Guyon, Jean
Ourehouare
Savignon

II (1701–1740)
Baudry de Lamarche, Jacques

Chevalier, *dit* Beauchêne, Robert
Joybert de Soulanges et de Marson, Louise-Élisabeth de (Rigaud de Vaudreuil, Marquise de Vaudreuil)
Le Moyne de Serigny et de Loire, Joseph
Lenoir, *dit* Rolland, François
Villieu, Sébastien de

III (1741–1770)
Ailleboust, Charles-Joseph d'
Baudoin, Michel
Boucher de Boucherville, Pierre
Carrerot, André
Charly Saint-Ange, Louis
Chartier de Lotbinière, Eustache
Coulon de Villiers, Nicolas-Antoine
Daccarrette, Michel (son)
Denys de La Ronde, Louis
Gannes de Falaise, Michel de
Gaultier de Varennes et de La Vérendrye, Pierre
Goutin, François-Marie de
Guyon, Louise (Thibault; Damours de Freneuse)
Leblanc, *dit* Le Maigre, Joseph
Lefebvre Duplessis Faber, François
Le Moyne de Bienville, Jean-Baptiste
Le Moyne de Longueuil, Charles, Baron de Longueuil
Levasseur, Louis
Marin de La Malgue, Paul
Martel de Belleville, Jean-Urbain
Martel de Brouague, François
Migeon de La Gauchetière, Daniel
Pagé, *dit* Carcy, Jacques
Paris, Bernard
Perrault, Paul
Perthuis, Jean-Baptiste-Ignace
Petitpas, Barthélemy
Poulin de Courval, François-Louis
Regnard Duplessis de Morampont, Charles-Denis
Renaud d'Avène Des Méloizes, Nicolas-Marie
Renaud Dubuisson, Louis-Jacques-Charles
Rigaud de Vaudreuil, Joseph-Hyacinthe de
Rigaud de Vaudreuil, Louis-Philippe de, Marquis de Vaudreuil
Rocbert de La Morandière, Marie-Élisabeth (Bégon de La Cour)
Rouer de Villeray, Benjamin
Testu de La Richardière, Richard
Trottier Desauniers, Pierre

IV (1771–1800)
Adhémar, Jean-Baptiste-Amable
Ailleboust de Cerry, Philippe-Marie d'
Allard de Sainte-Marie, Philippe-Joseph d'
Angeac, François-Gabriel d'
Bailly de Messein, Charles-François
Bourg, Joseph-Mathurin
Cadet, Joseph-Michel
Chabert de Joncaire de Clausonne, Daniel-Marie
Charest, Étienne
Chartier de Lotbinière, Eustache
Chartier de Lotbinière, Michel, Marquis de Lotbinière
Chaussegros de Léry, Gaspard-Joseph
Cotton, Barthélemy
Couagne, Michel de
Cugnet, François-Joseph
Denis de Saint-Simon, Antoine-Charles
Denys de Vitré, Théodose-Matthieu
Deschamps de Boishébert et de Raffetot, Charles
Dupleix Silvain, Jean-Baptiste
Du Pont Duvivier, François
Fleury Deschambault, Joseph
Gamelin, Pierre-Joseph
Godefroy de Linctot, Daniel-Maurice
Godin, Joseph
Hazeur de L'Orme, Pierre
Hertel de Rouville, René-Ovide
Hertel de Saint-François, Joseph-Hippolyte
Jacau de Fiedmont, Louis-Thomas
La Corne de Chaptes, Joseph-Marie (Jean-Marie) de
Leblanc, *dit* Le Maigre, Joseph
Legardeur de Croisille et de Montesson, Joseph-Michel
Legardeur de Repentigny, Louis
Legardeur de Repentigny, Pierre-Jean-Baptiste-François-Xavier
Lemoine Despins, Jacques-Joseph
Le Moyne de Longueuil, Paul-Joseph, known as Chevalier de Longueuil
Le Poupet de La Boularderie, Antoine
L'Espérance, Charles-Gabriel-Sébastien de, Baron de L' Espérance
Le Verrier de Rousson, Louis
Malepart de Beaucourt, François
Marchand, Étienne
Marin de La Malgue, Joseph
Martel, Pierre-Michel
Morin de Fonfay, Jean-Baptiste
Payen de Noyan et de Chavoy, Pierre-Jacques

Péan, Michel-Jean-Hugues
Perthuis, Joseph
Picoté de Belestre, François-Marie
Ramezay, Jean-Baptiste-Nicolas-Roch
   de
Renaud d'Avène Des Méloizes,
   Angélique (Péan)
Rigaud de Vaudreuil, François-Pierre
   de
Rigaud de Vaudreuil de Cavagnial,
   Pierre de, Marquis de Vaudreuil
Rodrigue, Antoine
Rousseau de Villejouin, Gabriel
Sabrevois de Bleury, Clément de
Tarieu de La Naudière, Charles-
   François
Testard de Montigny, Jean-Baptiste-
   Philippe

FRENCH GUYANA

III (1741–1770)
Perrault, Paul

IV (1771–1800)
Jacau de Fiedmont, Louis-Thomas

INDIA

IV (1771–1800)
Legardeur de Repentigny, Pierre-Jean-
   Baptiste-François-Xavier

IRELAND

II (1701–1740)
Saint-Étienne de La Tour, Agathe de
   (Bradstreet; Campbell)

III (1741–1770)
Denys de La Ronde, Louis

MALAGASY REPUBLIC

IV (1771–1800)
Marin de La Malgue, Joseph

MALTA

III (1741–1770)
Rigaud de Vaudreuil, Louis-Philippe
   de, Marquis de Vaudreuil

MEXICO

III (1741–1770)
Juchereau de Saint-Denis, Louis

SAINT-PIERRE AND
MIQUELON

III (1741–1770)
Leblanc, *dit* Le Maigre, Joseph
Perrault, Paul

Poulin de Courval, François-Louis
Taverner, William

IV (1771–1800)
Dugas, Joseph
L'Espérance, Charles-Gabriel-
   Sébastien de, Baron de L'Espérance
Rodrigue, Antoine

SENEGAL

IV (1771–1800)
Legardeur de Repentigny, Louis

SPAIN

III (1741–1770)
Mallet, Pierre-Antoine

IV (1771–1800)
Adhémar, Jean-Baptiste-Amable
Jacau de Fiedmont, Louis-Thomas

UNION OF SOVIET
SOCIALIST REPUBLICS

IV (1771–1800)
Darby, Nicholas

UNITED STATES OF
AMERICA

I (1000–1700)
Bourdon d'Autray, Jacques
Cherououny
Crevier de Saint-François, Jean
Duquet de La Chesnaye, Pierre
Hébert, Joseph
Jolliet, Louis
Le Moyne de Bienville, François
Le Moyne de Sainte-Hélène, Jacques
Membertou
Negabamat
Ogenheratarihiens
Oionhaton'
Ondaaiondiont
Ouagimou
Oumasasikweie
Panounias
Pieskaret
Robinau de Villebon, Joseph
Secoudon

II (1701–1740)
Ailleboust d'Argenteuil, Pierre d'
Ailleboust de Manthet, Nicolas d'
Amiot de Vincelotte, Charles-Joseph
Bissot de Vinsenne, François-Marie
Bissot de Vinsenne, Jean-Baptiste
Bouat, François-Marie
Buisson de Saint-Cosme, Jean-François
   (1667–1706)
Chevalier, *dit* Beauchêne, Robert

Damours de Chauffours, Louis
Delaunay, Charles
Denys de Bonaventure, Simon-Pierre
Deschamps de Boishébert, Henri-Louis
Dizy, *dit* Montplaisir, Marguerite (Des-
   brieux)
Dufrost de La Jemerais, Christophe
Dugué de Boisbriand, Pierre
Gaulin, Antoine
Gaultier de La Vérendrye, Jean-
   Baptiste
Godefroy de Saint-Paul, Jean-Amador
Godefroy de Vieuxpont, Joseph
Guion, François
Hertel de La Fresnière, Joseph-François
Hertel de Moncours, Pierre
Hertel de Rouville, Jean-Baptiste
Jarret de Verchères, Pierre
Juchereau de La Ferté, Denis-Joseph
Juchereau de Saint-Denys, Charles
Juchereau Duchesnay, Ignace
Le Gardeur de Courtemanche,
   Augustin
Legardeur de Repentigny, Pierre
Legardeur de Saint-Pierre, Jean-Paul
Le Moyne d'Iberville et d'Ardillières,
   Pierre
Le Moyne de Longueuil, Charles, Baron
   de Longueuil
Le Moyne de Maricourt, Paul
Le Moyne de Serigny et de Loire,
   Joseph
Leneuf de La Vallière de Beaubassin,
   Alexandre
Leneuf de La Vallière de Beaubassin,
   Michel (father)
Margane de Batilly, François-Marie
Mariauchau d'Esgly, François-Louis
Martin de Lino, Antoine
Philippe de Hautmesnil de Mandeville,
   François
Robinau de Portneuf, René
Sagean, Mathieu
Testard de Montigny, Jacques
Thaumur de La Source, Dominique-
   Antoine-René
Volant de Radisson, Étienne

III (1741–1770)
Amiot, Jean-Baptiste (d. after 1763)
Baudouin, Michel
Baudry, *dit* Saint-Martin, Jean-Baptiste
Bécart de Granville et de Fonville, Paul
Bermen de La Martinière, Claude-
   Antoine de
Boucher de Boucherville, Pierre
Boucher de La Perrière, René
Boucher de Montbrun, Jean
Boucher de Niverville, Jean-Baptiste
Brossard, *dit* Beausoleil, Joseph
Campot, Jacques
Carrerot, Philippe
Céloron de Blainville, Pierre-Joseph

Chabert de Joncaire, Philippe-Thomas
Chevalier, Jean-Baptiste
Corbin, David
Couc, Elizabeth (La Chenette, Techenet; Montour)
Coulon de Villiers, Louis
Coulon de Villiers, Nicolas-Antoine
Coulon de Villiers de Jumonville, Joseph
Dagneau Douville de Quindre, Louis-Césaire
Daneau de Muy, Jacques-Pierre
Dazemard de Lusignan, Paul-Louis
Dejordy de Villebon, Charles-René
Denys de La Ronde, Louis
Gamelin Maugras, Pierre
Gastineau Duplessis, Jean-Baptiste
Gaultier de La Vérendrye, Louis-Joseph
Gaultier de La Vérendrye de Boumois, Pierre
Gaultier de Varennes et de La Vérendrye, Pierre
Gervaise, Louis
Giard, Antoine
Hertel de La Fresnière, Zacharie-François
Hertel de Saint-François, Étienne
Janson, dit Lapalme, Dominique
Juchereau de Saint-Denis, Louis
La Corne, Louis de, known as Chevalier de La Corne
La Corne Dubreuil, François-Josué de
Lefebvre Duplessis Faber, François
Legardeur de Beauvais, René
Legardeur de Croisille, Charles
Legardeur de Saint-Pierre, Jacques
Le Marchand de Lignery, François-Marie
Le Moine, dit Monière, Alexis
Le Moyne de Bienville, Jean-Baptiste
Le Moyne de Longueuil, Charles, Baron de Longueuil
Levrault de Langis Montegron, Jean-Baptiste
Liénard de Beaujeu, Daniel-Hyacinthe
Lorimier de La Rivière, Claude-Nicolas de
Lupien, dit Baron, Pierre
Maillou, dit Desmoulins, Jean-Baptiste
Mallet, Pierre-Antoine
Marin de La Malgue, Paul
Marin de La Perrière, Claude
Mercier, Jean-François
Mercier, Jean-Paul
Migeon de La Gauchetière, Daniel
Noyon, Jacques de
Padanuques, Jacques
Pécaudy de Contrecœur, François-Antoine

Petitpas, Barthélemy
Renaud Dubuisson, Louis-Jacques-Charles
Robinau de Portneuf, Pierre
Saint-Ours, François-Xavier de
Saint-Ours Deschaillons, Jean-Baptiste de
Tonty de Liette, Charles-Henri-Joseph de

IV (1771–1800)
Adhémar, Jean-Baptiste-Amable
Ailleboust de la Madeleine, François-Jean-Daniel d'
Arimph, Jean-Baptiste
Aubert de Gaspé, Ignace-Philippe
Baby, dit Dupéront, Jacques
Benoist, Antoine-Gabriel-François
Bernier, Benoist-François
Besnard, dit Carignant, Jean-Louis
Bonnécamps, Joseph-Pierre de
Bourassa, dit La Ronde, René
Bradstreet, John
Campion, Étienne-Charles
Carpentier, Bonaventure
Chabert de Joncaire de Clausonne, Daniel-Marie
Chartier de Lotbinière, Eustache
Chartier de Lotbinière, Michel, Marquis de Lotbinière
Chaussegros de Léry, Gaspard-Joseph
Cotté, Gabriel
Couagne, Jean-Baptiste de
Coulon de Villiers, François
Dagneau Douville, Alexandre
Denis de Saint-Simon, Antoine-Charles
Deschamps de Boishébert et de Raffetot, Charles
Doucet, Pierre
Ducharme, Laurent
Du Jaunay, Pierre
Dumas, Jean-Daniel
Gamelin, Pierre-Joseph
Gaultier Du Tremblay, François
Gill, Joseph-Louis
Godefroy de Linctot, Daniel-Maurice
Godin, Joseph
Grant, James
Groston de Saint-Ange et de Bellerive, Louis
Hertel de Saint-François, Joseph-Hippolyte
Hubert, Jean-François
Jacau de Fiedmont, Louis-Thomas
La Corne, Luc de, known as Chaptes de La Corne or La Corne Saint-Luc
Le Blanc, Pierre
Legardeur de Croisille et de Montesson, Joseph-Michel
Legardeur de Repentigny, Louis

Legardeur de Repentigny, Pierre-Jean-Baptiste-François-Xavier
Le Moyne de Longueuil, Paul-Joseph, known as Chevalier de Longueuil
Le Poupet de La Boularderie, Antoine
Le Verrier de Rousson, Louis
Malepart de Beaucourt, François
Marin de La Malgue, Joseph
Payen de Noyan et de Chavoy, Pierre-Jacques
Pécaudy de Contrecœur, Claude-Pierre
Picoté de Belestre, François-Marie
Primeau, Louis
Ramezay, Jean-Baptiste-Nicolas-Roch de
Rigaud de Vaudreuil, François-Pierre de
Rigaud de Vaudreuil de Cavagnial, Pierre de, Marquis de Vaudreuil
Robichaux, Louis
Roy, Louis
Saint-Aubin, Ambroise
Tarieu de La Naudière, Charles-François
Testard de Montigny, Jean-Baptiste-Philippe
Tomah, Pierre

WEST INDIES

II (1701–1740)
Le Moyne de Serigny et de Loire, Joseph

III (1741–1770)
Aubert de La Chesnaye, Louis
Denys de La Ronde, Louis
Martel de Belleville, Jean-Urbain
Paris, Bernard
Petitpas, Barthélemy
Poulin de Courval, François-Louis
Renaud Dubuisson, Louis-Jacques-Charles
Rigaud de Vaudreuil, Joseph-Hyacinthe de
Rigaud de Vaudreuil, Louis-Philippe de, Marquis de Vaudreuil

IV (1771–1800)
Ailleboust de Cerry, Philippe-Marie d'
Allard de Sainte-Marie, Philippe-Joseph d'
Couagne, Michel de
Cugnet, François-Joseph
Denis de Saint-Simon, Antoine-Charles
Legardeur de Repentigny, Louis
Rousseau de Villejouin, Gabriel

CUMULATIVE NOMINAL INDEX

PUBLISHED

VOLUME I   1000–1700
VOLUME II   1701–1740
VOLUME III   1741–1770
VOLUME IV   1771–1800
VOLUME IX   1861–1870
VOLUME X   1871–1880

IN PREPARATION

VOLUME V   1801–1820
VOLUME VI   1821–1835
VOLUME VII   1836–1850
VOLUME VIII 1851–1860
VOLUME XI   1881–1890
VOLUME XII   1891–1900

Cumulative Nominal Index

Included in the index are the names of persons mentioned in volumes I to IV. They are listed by their family names, with first names and titles following. Wives are entered under their maiden name with their married name (or names) in parentheses. Persons who appear in incomplete citations in the text are fully identified when possible. Titles, nicknames, variant spellings, married and religious names are fully cross-referenced. A full explanation of the DCB/DBC editorial practices is found in the Editorial Notes of each volume. Numerals in bold face immediately following a volume number indicate the pages on which a biography appears.

An asterisk indicates that the person so identified has received a biography in a volume already published (other than I to IV), or will probably receive one in a volume yet to be completed. A death date or last floruit date constitutes a reference for the reader to the volume in which the biography will be found.

This index incorporates the results of continuing research at the DCB/DBC; the form and content of names have thus been made consistent for the published volumes and with volumes in progress.

AAOUANDIO. *See* Le Maistre, Jacques
Aaron. *See* Kanonraron
Abancourt. *See also* Jolliet
Abancourt, Marie d' (Jollyet; Guillot; Prévost), I, 392, 554
Abbadie, Jean-Jacques-Blaise d', III, 527
Abbadie de Saint-Castin, Bernard-Anselme d', Baron de Saint-Castin, II, **3–4**, xxxvii, 5, 7, 37, 38, 177, 238, 289, 437, 452; III, xxxix, 3, 330
Abbadie de Saint-Castin, Brigitte d', II, 4
Abbadie, de Saint-Castin, Isabeau d', Baronne de Saint-Castin. *See* Béarn-Bonasse
Abbadie de Saint-Castin, Jean-Jacques d', Baron de Saint-Castin (father), II, 4
Abbadie de Saint-Castin, Jean-Jacques d', Baron de Saint-Castin, II, 4, 5
Abbadie de Saint-Castin, Jean-Pierre d', II, 7
Abbadie de Saint-Castin, Jean-Vincent d', Baron de Saint-Castin, I, 63, 185, 510, 577, 649; II, **4–7**, xxxvii, 3, 145, 167, 177, 182, 394, 440, 480, 494, 579, 605, 626, 654; III, xxxix, 3; IV, xviii
Abbadie de Saint-Castin, Joseph d', Baron de Saint-Castin, II, 7, 669; III, **3**, xxxii, 359
Abbadie de Saint-Castin, Louise d', II, 4
Abbadie de Saint-Castin, Marie d' (Labaig), II, 4, 7
Abbadie de Saint-Castin, Marie-Anselme d', Baronne de Saint-Castin (Bourbon), II, 4; III, 3
Abbadie de Saint-Castin, Marie-Charlotte d', Baronne de Saint-Castin. *See* Damours de Chauffours
Abbadie de Saint-Castin, Marie-Josephe (Anastasie?) d' (Le Borgne de Belle-Isle), II, 7; III, 567
Abbadie de Saint-Castin, Marie-Mathilde d', Baronne de Saint-Castin. *See* Pidianske
Abbadie de Saint-Castin, Thérèse d' (Mius d'Entremont), II, 7
Abbadie de Saint-Castin, Ursule d' (Damours de Freneuse), II, 7
Abbot, George, I, 678
Abbott, Edward, IV, 321, 322
Abdy, Matthew, IV, 705
Abeel, Catalina (Mathews), IV, 522

Abel, Olivier. *See* Olivier
Aberchalder. *See* McDonell
Abercrombie, James, IV, **3–4**, 98
Abercromby, Alexander, IV, 4
Abercromby, Helen. *See* Meldrum
Abercromby, James, III, xxv, xxviii, xxix, 85, 273, 462, 535, 588, 591; IV, **4–5**, 3, 22, 23, 34, 85, 115, 117, 129, 174, 211, 278, 297, 335, 395, 396, 460, 479, 503, 531, 606, 634, 642, 670, 679, 680, 694, 793
Abercromby, James (brother of Sir Ralph), IV, 4
Abercromby, James (son of JAMES), IV, 4
Abercromby, Jemmy, IV, 4
Abercromby, Mary. *See* Duff
Abercromby, Sir Ralph, IV, 4
Abergemont. *See* Simonet
Aberli, Johann Ludwig, IV, 762
Abraham (Abram), Chapman, IV, 332, 718, 719
Abraham, John, I, **39**, 107, 329, 493, 529; II, 265
Abraham, Mary, I, 39
Acaret. *See* Daccarette
Accault, Michel, II, 278, 281, 635
Achard, Charles, II, 127
Aché de Serquigny, Anne-Antoine, Comte d'Aché, IV, 131
Achiendassé. *See* Lalemant, Jérôme
Achinaga, II, 263
Ackmobish. *See* Akomápis
Acosta, José de, III, 337
Acoutsina (Acountsina), II, **7–10**, 384
Acqueville, Baron d'. *See* Bernières
Acqueville, Baronne d'. *See* Le Breton
Actodin, I, 501
Adam, I, 559
Adames. *See* Adams
Adams, Avis (wife of John, father), III, 3
Adams, Clement, I, 158
Adams, James, II, 54
Adams, John (army officer), II, 644
Adams, John (father), III, 3
Adams, John (U.S. president), IV, 715
Adams, John, III, **3–4**, 143, 437, 517

Adams, Joseph, II, **10**, 62, 65, 492, 493, 563; III, 415, 661
Adams, Katherine (wife of William), II, 10
Adams, Mary (aunt), II, 10
Adams, Mary, II, 10
Adams, Robert, IV, 153
Adams, Samuel, IV, 715
Adams, Sir Thomas, III, 411
Adams, William, II, 10
Adario. *See* Kondiaronk
Addeawando (Adeawanadon, Adeawando). *See* Atecouando
Addison, Joseph, IV, 553
Adems. *See* Adams
Adhasatah. *See* Togouiroui
Adhémar, Catherine. *See* Lepallieur de Laferté; Moreau
Adhémar, Cécile. *See* Gasche
Adhémar, Jean-Baptiste, II, 11, 164; III, **4–5**, 271; IV, 5, 34, 200, 270
Adhémar, Jean-Baptiste-Amable, IV, **5–8**, 543
Adhémar, Marguerite. *See* Lemoine Despins
Adhémar, Michel, II, 11
Adhémar, *dit* Saint-Martin, Marie (Tessier, *dit* Lavigne), IV, 732
Adhémar de Lantagnac, Anne. *See* Rigaud de Vaudreuil
Adhémar de Lantagnac, Anne (La Barre), III, 5
Adhémar de Lantagnac, Antoine, III, 5
Adhémar de Lantagnac, Gaspard, II, 465, 565, 571; III, **5**, 550
Adhémar de Lantagnac, Geneviève-Françoise. *See* Martin de Lino
Adhémar de Lantagnac, Jeanne-Antoinette. *See* Truchi
Adhémar de Lantagnac, Pierre, II, 565; III, 5
Adhémar de Lantagnac, Pierre-Gaspard-Antoine, III, 5
Adhémar de Saint-Martin, Antoine, II, **10–12**, xxiv, 133, 135, 160, 190, 196, 422, 458; III, 4, 505
Adhémar de Saint-Martin, Geneviève. *See* Sageot
Adhémar de Saint-Martin, Marie. *See* Sédilot
Adhémar de Saint-Martin, Michelle. *See* Cusson
Adiawonda. *See* Atecouando
Adié, Count d'. *See* Jadis
Admyrauld, Pierre-Gabriel, IV, 433
Adonwentishon* (Catharine Brant) (1759–1837), IV, 613
Adoucourt. *See* Souart
Adrawanah. *See* Ottrowana
Adriansdatter, Katherine (Munk), I, 514
Aenon, I, 133
Aëoptahon. *See* Atironta (Jean-Baptiste)
Aernoutsz, Jurriaen, I, **39–40**, 25, 185, 399, 573
Agariata, I, **40–41**, 308, 556
Agashawa. *See* Egushwa
Agathe, I, 523
Agemantan. *See* Argimault
Agmabesh. *See* Akomápis
Agnello, I, 317
Agona, I, 168, 169, 276
Agonstot, II, 624, 634
Agrain, Jean-Antoine d', Comte d'Agrain, II, **12**
Agrain Du Mazel, Jugues d', II, 12
Agramonte, Juan de, I, **41**
Aguesseau, Henri-François d', III, 491, 639
Aguesseau, Jean-Baptiste-Paulin d', III, 639
Aguiguida, II, 646
Ahatsistari, I, **41–42**, 344, 388, 523; II, 157
Ahinsistan. *See* Pastedechouan

Ahuntsic (Auhaitsique, Ahautsic, François), I, 661
Aiandacé, I, 637
Aide-Créquy, Jean-Antoine, IV, **8–10**
Aide-Créquy, Louis, IV, 8
Aide-Créquy, Marie-Hélène. *See* Lefebvre
Aigremont. *See* Clairambault
Aigron, Marie. *See* Daquin
Aigron, Pierre, I, 42
Aigron, *dit* Lamothe, Marie-Madeleine. *See* Doucet
Aigron, *dit* Lamothe (de La Motte), Nicolas, II, 454
Aigron, *dit* Lamothe, Pierre, I, **42**, 666; II, 367, 454
Aiguillon. *See* Vignerot
Ailleboust, Antoine d', I, 42
Ailleboust, Catherine d', I, 43
Ailleboust, Charles d', I, 42
Ailleboust, Charles-Joseph d', III, **5–7**, 236; IV, 644, 656
Ailleboust, Dorothée d'. *See* Manthet d'Argentenay
Ailleboust, Françoise-Charlotte d'. *See* Alavoine
Ailleboust, Jean d', I, 42
Ailleboust, Marie-Josephte d'. *See* Bertrand
Ailleboust, Suzanne d'. *See* Hotman
Ailleboust d'Argenteuil, Jean d', II, 451
Ailleboust d'Argenteuil, Louis d', IV, 10
Ailleboust d'Argenteuil, Marie-Louise d'. *See* Denys de La Ronde
Ailleboust d'Argenteuil, Pierre d', II, **12–13**, 168, 284, 324, 415; III, 5, 7; IV, 10
Ailleboust de Cerry, Marie-Madeleine d'. *See* Chéron
Ailleboust de Cerry, Philippe-Marie d', IV, **10–11**, 620
Ailleboust de Coulonge et d'Argentenay, Louis d', I, **42–47**, 60, 79, 110, 112, 128, 217, 218, 219, 230, 231, 339, 340, 344, 349, 353, 373, 412, 431, 447, 453, 473, 480, 494, 511, 538, 580, 606, 645, 662; II, xvi, 83, 426, 489, 639
Ailleboust de Coulonge et d'Argentenay, Marie-Barbe d'. *See* Boullongne
Ailleboust de La Boulasserie, Jean-Baptiste-Alphonse d', IV, 11
Ailleboust de La Madeleine, François-Jean-Daniel d', IV, **11–12**
Ailleboust de La Madeleine, Marie-Charlotte d'. *See* Godefroy de Linctot
Ailleboust de La Madeleine et de Coulonge, Louis d', II, 67
Ailleboust de La Madeleine et de Coulonge, Nicolas d', I, 43, 45, 47
Ailleboust de Manthet, Françoise d'. *See* Denys de La Ronde
Ailleboust de Manthet, Louise-Catherine d' (Charly Saint-Ange; Payen de Noyan et de Chavoy), II, 131; III, 110; IV, 612
Ailleboust de Manthet, Madeleine d' (Jarret de Verchères; Levrault de Langis Montegron), III, 399
Ailleboust de Manthet, Nicolas d', I, 466; II, **13–14**, 131, 284, 383, 392, 406, 523, 546, 581, 603
Ailleboust de Manthet, Pierre-Joseph d', IV, 11
Ailleboust de Périgny, Ignace-René d', IV, 11
Ailleboust de Périgny, Madeleine-Louise d'. *See* Margane de Lavaltrie
Ailleboust de Périgny, Paul d', II, 284; III, **7**
Ailleboust de Périgny, Thérèse d' (Hertel de Moncours), II, 284; III, 7
Ailleboust de Saint-Vilmé, Hector-Pierre d', III, 6; IV, 10
Ailleboust Des Muceaux, Anne d'. *See* Le Picard
Ailleboust Des Muceaux, Catherine d'. *See* Legardeur de Repentigny

CUMULATIVE NOMINAL INDEX

Ailleboust Des Muceaux, Catherine d' (Daneau de Muy), II, 168

Ailleboust Des Muceaux, Charles-Joseph d', I, **47**, 44, 45, 219, 447, 508, 592, 600; II, 12, 13, 14, 92, 421; III, 7

Ailleboust Des Muceaux, Félicité d' (Guillet de Chaumont), III, 270

Ailleboust Des Muceaux, Jean-Baptiste d', II, **14**, 159, 284; III, 270; IV, 11

Ailleboust Des Muceaux, Nicolas-Marie d', IV, 11

Aillon. *See* La Roche Daillon

Ailly. *See* Albert

Ainslie*, Thomas (b. 1829, d. after 1805), IV, 74, 550, 570, 791

Ainsse*, Joseph-Louis (1744–1802), IV, 241

Ainsworth, Henry, I, 391

Aitken, Alexander, IV, **12–13**

Aitken, Catherine (?) (mother of ALEXANDER), IV, 12

Aitken, David, IV, 12

Aix de La Chaise, François d', II, 330, 369, 371

Ajac, Baron d'. *See* Lévis

Ajac, Baronne d'. *See* Maguelonne

Akins*, Thomas Beamish (1809–91), IV, xxvi

Akomápis, Nicholas, IV, **13**

Alard, Madeleine (Troyes), I, 653

Alavoine, Charles (father), III, 7

Alavoine, Charles, II, 48; III, **7–8**, 6, 430

Alavoine, Françoise-Charlotte (Ailleboust; Guyon, Marquise de Diziers), III, 6

Alavoine, Marie-Anne. *See* Lefebvre, *dit* Laciseraye

Alavoine, Marie-Françoise (Chevalier), III, 121

Alavoine, Marie-Thérèse. *See* Macard

Albanel, Charles, I, **47–50**, 35, 83, 108, 226, 227, 244, 282, 396, 402, 558, 625, 629; II, xxxiv, 161, 179, 347, 537

Albemarle, Duke of. *See* Monk

Albemarle, Earl of. *See* Keppel

Albert, Guillaume, I, 256

Albert, Marie-Louise (Demosny), I, 256

Albert d'Ailly, Honoré d', Duc de Chaulnes, II, 27

Albon. *See* Lefèvre

Alby, Comte d'. *See* Sartine

Alcalá-Galiano*, Dionisio (1762–1805), IV, 745

Alden, Elizabeth. *See* Phillips

Alden, Elizabeth (wife of JOHN), II, 15

Alden, John (father), II, 14

Alden, John, I, 576, 654; II, **14–15**, 177, 494; III, 7, 596

Alden, Priscilla. *See* Mullens

Alden, William, I, 576, 654; II, 14

Aldridge, Christopher (father), II, 668; III, **8–9**, 10, 297

Aldridge, Christopher (son), III, **9–10**, 324

Aldridge, Christopher (3rd), III, 10

Aldridge, Martha (wife of CHRISTOPHER, son), III, 10

Aldridge, Mary (Bradstreet; Bradstreet), IV, 83

Aleman, Lazaro. *See* Noremberguer

Alençon, François-Hercule, Duc d'Alençon, I, 229

Alès de Corbet, Louise d' (Brisay de Denonville), II, 98

Alexander VII, I, 111, 645

Alexander, Janet, Countess of Stirling. *See* Erskine

Alexander, William, Earl of Stirling, I, **50–54**, 25, 55, 242, 311, 407, 497, 597, 605, 613, 636; III, 653; IV, xvii

Alexander, Sir William, I, **54–55**, 25, 53, 311, 405, 499, 593, 597, 605, 613

Alexis, II, 665

Aleyrac, Jean-Baptiste d', IV, **14**

Aleyrac, Jeanne-Marie d'. *See* Vernhes

Aleyrac, Noé d', IV, 14

Alfonse, Jean. *See* Fonteneau, Jean

Alfonse, Valentine (Fonteneau), I, 309

Algimou, III, 358

Aliecte, Antoine, I, 167

Aliecte, Guillaume, I, 167

Aliés, Joseph, IV, 125

Aliomet, Isabelle (Prud'homme), I, 557

Alix, Marguerite (Boullé), I, 109, 110

Allain, Louis, II, 198; III, 254

Allain, Marguerite. *See* Bourg

Allain, Marie (Gautier, *dit* Bellair), III, 254

Allaire*, Jean-Baptiste-Arthur (1866–1943), IV, 87

Allan*, John (1746/47–1805), IV, 13, 30, 79, 81, 196, 275, 693, 723, 736

Allanby, William, IV, 607, 608

Allard, Thomas, IV, 203

Allard de Sainte-Marie, M., known as Chevalier de Sainte-Marie, IV, 15

Allard de Sainte-Marie, Angélique d'. *See* Carrerot

Allard de Sainte-Marie, Jean-Joseph d', II, **15**, 336; IV, 14

Allard de Sainte-Marie, Jeanne d'. *See* Jacau

Allard de Sainte-Marie, Marie-Anne d'. *See* Tour

Allard de Sainte-Marie, Philippe-Joseph d', II, 15; IV, **14–16**, 62, 248, 382

Allart, Germain (baptized Théodore), I, **55**, 313, 420, 439; II, 344, 345

Allde, John, I, 670

Allègre, Marguerite d' (Lascaris, Marquise d'Urfé et de Baugé), II, 349

Alleine, Joseph, III, 470

Allemagne, Antoinette d' (La Corne), II, 327

Allemand, Claude, I, 56

Allemand, Louise. *See* Douaire de Bondy

Allemand, Marie. *See* Mandet

Allemand, Pierre, I, **56**, 653; II, 526

Allemewi (Salomon), IV, 26, 27

Allen, Abigail (Belcher), IV, 50

Allen, Abigail (Bissell; Williams), II, 667

Allen, Edward, IV, 556

Allen, Ethan, IV, 120, 130, 427, 545, 546, 694, 759

Allen, George Nickleson, IV, 713

Allen, Isaac, IV, 55

Allen, Thomas, II, 667

Allen, William (author), IV, 416

Allen, William (ship's captain), I, 641; II, 266, 394

Allenou de Grandchamp, Marie, IV, 95

Allenou de Lavillangevin, René-Jean, III, **10–12**, 193, 259, 546; IV, 95, 429

Allet, Antoine d', I, **56–57**, 220, 612, 644

Alliés, Marie-Geneviève (Couillard), IV, 71

Alline, Henry, IV, **16–20**, 217, 343, 705

Alline, Rebecca. *See* Clark

Alline, William, IV, 16

Allonne. *See* Roybon

Allouez, Claude, I, **57–58**, 14, 121, 244, 249, 492, 626; II, 347, 501, 517, 607

Allsopp, Anna Marie. *See* Bondfield

Allsopp*, George (d. 1805), IV, 104, 190, 323, 369, 379, 385, 399, 538, 554, 570, 618

Allumapees, III, 607

Allyn. *See also* Allen

Allyn (Allen), Elizabeth (Gorham), III, 260
Almain, Élisabeth-Simone. *See* Lajus
Almodóvar del Río, Duke of. *See* Luján
Aloigny, Charles-Henri d', Marquis de La Groye, I, 85;
 II, **15–16**, 304, 507, 533; III, 410
Aloigny, Charlotte d', Marquise de La Groye. *See* Chasteigner
Aloigny, Geneviève d', Marquise de La Groye. *See* Macard
Aloigny, Louis d', Marquis de La Groye, II, 15
Aloperca. *See* Laborde
Alquier de Servian, Jean d', III, **12**, 86; IV, 480
Alward, Robert, I, 369
Alymph. *See* Arimph
Amantacha, I, **58–59**, 247
Amaraguened, III, 266
Amaugère, Geneviève (Bourdon), I, 114
Ambault. *See* Duchesneau
Amboise. *See also* Bergeron
Amboise, Michel d', I, 424
Ambroise. *See also* Saint-Aubin
Ambroise, Father, IV, 134
Ameau, Françoise. *See* Remogis
Ameau, Jean, II, 16
Ameau, Marguerite (Godefroy de Tonnancour), II, 253;
 III, 259; IV, 304
Ameau, *dit* Saint-Séverin, Madeleine. *See* Baudoin
Ameau, *dit* Saint-Séverin, Séverin, I, 327, 550, 575, 579;
 II, **16–17**, xvi, xvii, 253, 282, 382, 528
Amelotte, Marguerite (Chartier), I, 202
Amherst, Elizabeth, Baroness Amherst. *See* Cary
Amherst, Elizabeth. *See* Kerrill
Amherst, Jane, Lady Amherst. *See* Dalison
Amherst, Jeffery (father), IV, 20
Amherst, Jeffery, 1st Baron Amherst, III, xxii, xxv, xxvi,
 xxix, xxxviii, xli, 10, 33, 71, 72, 73, 86, 87, 89, 167, 209,
 211, 215, 230, 256, 268, 283, 320, 332, 364, 365, 371,
 409, 467, 479, 480, 501, 509, 526, 527, 528, 529, 536,
 558, 565, 588, 589, 601, 605, 654, 663, 666, 667, 668,
 669, 671, 704; IV, **20–26**, xxvii, xxxiii, xxxiv, xxxv, 3,
 4, 5, 31, 53, 79, 85, 93, 96, 109, 115, 117, 162, 211, 228,
 279, 280, 297, 298, 299, 308, 314, 331, 335, 368, 380,
 393, 396, 401, 408, 415, 421, 431, 481, 487, 491, 500,
 541, 542, 545, 552, 569, 570, 571, 586, 587, 588, 595,
 606, 637, 646, 670, 672, 673, 680, 685, 686, 700, 722,
 730, 734, 737, 768, 772, 773, 783, 793
Amherst, Jeffery (son), IV, 25
Amherst, Sackville, IV, 25
Amherst, William, III, 132; IV, 24, 26, 31, 223, 598
Amherst, William Pitt, 1st Earl Amherst, IV, 26
Amhurst, Edward, III, 277
Amiconti, Sieur, II, 523
Amiot, Anne. *See* Convent
Amiot, Augustin, III, 12
Amiot, Catherine. *See* Mouet de Mora
Amiot, Charles, I, **59–60**, 250, 387; II, 17, 155, 159, 500
Amiot, Geneviève. *See* Chavigny de Berchereau
Amiot, Jean, I, **60**, 490
Amiot, Jean-Baptiste (d. after 1763), III, **12–13**; IV, 241
Amiot, Jean-Baptiste (1717–69), III, **13–14**; IV, 123, 263,
 729
Amiot, Jean-Nicolas, IV, 702
Amiot*, Laurent (1764–1839), III, 346; IV, 206
Amiot, Louise. *See* Bazin

Amiot, Marie-Anne. *See* Cadet
Amiot, Marie-Anne (wife of JEAN-BAPTISTE, d. after
 1763), III, 12
Amiot, Marie-Anne (Perrault), III, 13
Amiot, Marie-Madeleine (Barbel), II, 43
Amiot, Philippe, I, 59, 60
Amiot, Pierre, III, 13; IV, 123
Amiot, *dit* Villeneuve, Charles, I, 61
Amiot, *dit* Villeneuve, Étienne, IV, 35
Amiot, *dit* Villeneuve, Marie. *See* Miville
Amiot, *dit* Villeneuve, Marie-Anne (Aumasson de
 Courville), IV, 35
Amiot, *dit* Villeneuve, Marie-Catherine (Maillou, *dit*
 Desmoulins), III, 420
Amiot, *dit* Villeneuve, Mathieu, I, **60–61**, 250
Amiot de Lincourt, Étienne, II, 508
Amiot de Vincelotte, Charles-Joseph, I, 60; II, **17–18**, 114,
 142, 155, 452, 520, 567; III, 177, 682
Amiot de Vincelotte, Marie-Gabrielle. *See* Philippe de
 Hautmesnil de Marigny
Amiotte, M., III, 242
Amiscouecan. *See* Chomina
Amours. *See* Damours
Amyot. *See* Amiot
Anadabijou, I, **61**, 86, 508, 638
Anandamoakin, IV, **26–27**
Anapã, IV, 567
Anceau, Anne, *dite* de Sainte-Thérèse, IV, 535
Andehoua (Jean-Armand), I, 637, 638
Anderson, Sir Edmund, I, 280
Anderson, John, IV, 273
Anderson, Thomas, I, **61**; II, 454
Andigné de Grandfontaine, Anne d', I, 62
Andigné de Grandfontaine, Gaston d', I, 62
Andigné de Grandfontaine, Hector d' (father), I, 62
Andigné de Grandfontaine, Hector d', I, **61–64**, 185, 398,
 435, 436, 510, 637, 667; II, 5, 88, 532
Andigné de La Chaise, Jeanne-Françoise d' (Cahideuc,
 Comtesse Dubois de La Motte), III, 92
Andioura, I, 429
André, IV, 375
André, Balthazar, III, 545
André, François, III, 14
André, John, IV, 721
André, Louis, I, 50; II, **18**; III, 104
André, Marie. *See* Turin
André de Leigne, Anne-Catherine, III, 15
André de Leigne, Claude. *See* Fredin
André de Leigne, Jeanne (Lanoullier de Boisclerc), III, 14,
 15, 352
André de Leigne, Louise-Catherine (Hertel de Rouville),
 II, 286; III, **14**, 15, 285; IV, 343
André de Leigne, Pierre, II, 155; III, **14–16**, 44, 75, 160,
 340, 352, 398, 519; IV, 344
Andresy, Sieur d', II, 507
Andrewes, William, I, 334
Andros, Sir Edmund, I, 537, 573, 654; II, xxxix, 6, 103,
 182, 494, 496; III, 470
Angé. *See* Dangé
Angeac, François-Gabriel d', III, 211, 418, 538; IV, **27–29**,
 79, 122, 153, 175, 223, 240, 470, 598, 678, 783
Angeac, Gabriel d', IV, 27
Angeac, Geneviève d'. *See* Lefebvre de Bellefeuille

Angeac, Marguerite d'. *See* Bertrand
Angélique de Sainte-Agnès. *See* Tibierge
Angélique de Saint-Joseph. *See* Hayot
Angélique de Saint-Martin. *See* Viger
Angélique-Denise (slave), III, 399
Angers. *See also* Lefebvre
Angers, Pierre, III, 75, 76
Angerville, Moufle d', IV, 68
Anghiera. *See* Martire
Angibault, *dit* Champdoré, Pierre, I, **64**, 69, 72, 189, 292, 293, 564
Anglesey, Earl of. *See* Villiers
Ango, Jean, I, 72, 532
Ango de La Mothe (lawyer), II, 18
Ango Des Maizerets, Louis, I, 92, 291, 506; II, **18–20**, 207, 238, 240, 248, 329, 629, 655; III, 684
Angulo. *See* Flórez
Anjou, Duc d'. *See* Philip V
Anjoult, Anne (Lefebvre), II, 382
Anna (wife of GLIKHIKAN), IV, 302
Annaotaha, I, **64–65**, 267, 272
Anne, Queen of Great Britain and Ireland, II, 3, 123, 232, 233, 286, 289, 319, 332, 339, 373, 475, 487, 497, 498, 511, 603, 661, 666; III, 428, 623; IV, xxi
Anne de Saint-Bernard. *See* Le Cointre
Anne de Sainte-Agnès. *See* Bourdon
Anne de Sainte-Thérèse. *See* Anceau
Anne of Austria, Queen of France, I, 129, 324, 328, 348, 389, 484; II, 360, 363
Annenraes, I, **65–66**, 524
Anneville, Gabrielle d' (Lagrange; Bernard de La Rivière), II, 59
Annssoet, III, 654
Anonchiara. *See* Du Peron, François
Anondounoakom. *See* Anandamoakin
Anotaha. *See* Annaotaha
An�8ennen. *See* Daniel, Antoine
Anson, George, 1st Baron Anson, III, 6, 610, 657, 658; IV, 15, 122, 382, 699, 701, 702
Antaïok. *See* Amiot, Jean
Anthoine, Dom, I, 167
Anticosti. *See* Jolliet
Antill, Edward, IV, 215
Antin, Marquis d'. *See* Pardaillan
Antonèlli, Leonardo, IV, 43, 372
Antonio, Dom, I, 228
Antrobus*, John (d. 1820), IV, 330
Anville. *See* La Rochefoucauld
Anwyl, William, III, 634, 635
Aonetta (Marie), I, 212
Aongote. *See* Williams, Eunice
Aontarisati, I, 65; II, 624
Aouandoie, I, 73
Aouenano, II, **20**, xxxix, 21, 323, 502, 631; III, xl
Aouschik. *See* Hotchig
Apānas, IV, 768
Apostolos Valerianos. *See* Fuca, Juan de
Aprendestiguy, Jeanne d'. *See* Saint-Étienne de La Tour
Aprendestiguy, Joanis d', I, 66
Aprendestiguy, Marianne d' (Bourgeois), I, 67
Aprendestiguy de Martignon, Martin d', I, **66–67**, 25, 63, 595
Apsley, Baron. *See* Bathurst

Apthorp, Alexander, II, **20–21**
Apthorp, Charles, III, 33
Aquipaguetin, II, 279
Aradgi, II, **21**, xxxvi, 20, 502, 631
Arblay, Frances d'. *See* Burney
Arbuthnot, Mariot, IV, **29–30**, 80, 111, 161, 275, 708
Arce. *See* Lom
Archambault, Anne (Chauvin), I, 557
Archambault, Françoise. *See* Toureault
Archambault, Jacques, I, 427, 463
Archambault, Jeanne (Lamarre, *dit* Bélisle), II, 340
Archambault, Marie (Lauson), I, 427
Arcos, Duke of. *See* Ponce de Léon
Ardie. *See* Hardy
Ardillières. *See* Le Moyne
Ardilliers, François-Paul, IV, 77
Ardouin, Jeanne (Badeaux), IV, 40
Arentson. *See* Aernoutsz
Argall, Mary. *See* Scott
Argall, Richard, I, 67
Argall, Sir Samuel, I, **67–69**, 24, 53, 69, 95, 98, 101, 299, 441, 470, 498, 560, 592, 596
Argenson. *See* Voyer
Argentenay. *See* Ailleboust; Manthet
Argenteuil. *See* Ailleboust
Argimault (Agemantan), Joseph, III, 418
Argyll. *See* Campbell
Argyll, Duchess of. *See* Bellenden
Arimph, Jean-Baptiste, IV, **30**
Arioo. *See* Chastellain, Pierre
Arlens. *See* Preissac
Armitinger. *See* Ermatinger
Arms, John, II, 285
Armstrong, Lawrence, II, **21–24**, 93, 96, 97, 199, 219, 238, 275, 462, 591, 643, 663, 670; III, 4, 8, 9, 83, 84, 120, 143, 144, 256, 276, 277, 287, 297, 343, 426, 427, 437, 439, 453, 500, 514, 516, 517, 596, 665; IV, xxii, xxv, 305, 453, 454
Arnald (Arnall). *See* Arnold
Arnaud, Bertrand, II, 175
Arnaud, Charles, II, 520
Arnaud, Jean, II, 195; III, 17
Arnaud, Jean-Charles d', III, **16–17**, 47, 492
Arnaud, Marie. *See* Truteau
Arnaud, Marie. *See* Willis
Arnaud, Marie-Charlotte (Potier Dubuisson), III, 533
Arnaud, Marie-Marguerite-Daniel, *dite* Saint-Arsène, III, **17–18**, 630; IV, 638
Arnauld, Antoine, known as le Grand Arnauld, II, 249
Arnauld, Henri, I, 512
Arnauld, Madeleine (Sabatier), III, 575
Arnold*, Benedict (1741–1801), IV, 114, 120, 142, 215, 223, 270, 329, 494, 503, 545, 547, 548, 549, 552, 759, 791
Arnold, Mary. *See* Holyoke
Arnold, William, II, **24–25**
Arnoldi*, Michael (1763–1807), IV, 206
Arnoldi, Peter, IV, 206
Arnoulet, Jacqueline (Le Poupet de Saint-Aubin), II, 417
Arnoult, Maître, IV, 127
Arnouville. *See* Machault
Arnoux, Alexandre, III, 18
Arnoux, André, III, **18–20**, 35

Arnoux, Blaise, III, 19
Arnoux, Charlotte. *See* Soupiran
Arnoux, Joseph, III, 19, 292
Arnoux, Lucresse. *See* Masson
Arnoux, Suzanne. *See* Levret
Aroas, III, 320
Arosen (François-Xavier), IV, 770
Arouet, François-Marie (Voltaire), II, 444; III, 92, 104, 108, 283; IV, 44, 92, 234, 391, 544
Arpentigny. *See* Aprendestiguy
Arran, Earl of. *See* Butler; Stewart
Arrigrand, Gratien d', Sieur de La Majour, II, 220; III, **20**, 234, 235, 456, 478, 479
Arrigrand, Jean-Jacques d', III, 20
Arrigrand, Marguerite d'. *See* Auger de Subercase
Arrowsmith, Aaron, IV, 742
Arsac, Charles-François d', Marquis de Ternay, IV, 31
Arsac, Louise d', Marquise de Ternay. *See* Lefebvre de Laubrière
Arsac de Ternay, Charles-Henri-Louis d', III, 132, 538; IV, **30–32**, xxvii, 24, 53, 163, 223, 282, 448, 513, 733
Arsenault, Pierre, IV, xx
Arseneau, Louise (Dugas), IV, 239, 240
Artaguiette Diron, Bernard d', III, 383
Artaguiette Diron, Jean-Baptiste-Martin d', II, 349; III, 380
Artaguiette d'Itouralde, Pierre d', II, xxviii, 67, 215, 216, 267, 457, 523; III, xxxiii, 47, 108, 383, 626, 627; IV, li
Arteaga, Ignacio de, IV, 73
Artigny. *See* Berthelot; Rouer
Arundel, Earl of. *See* Howard
Arundell, Thomas, 1st Lord Arundell of Wardour, I, 667
Ascumbuit. *See* Nescambiouit
Asenragéhaon (Jeanne), I, 610
Asfeld, Marquis d'. *See* Bidal
Askin*, John (d. 1815), IV, 592, 680, 778
Assaçambuit. *See* Nescambiouit
Assendasé (Pierre), II, 107
Asshehurst, Thomas, I, 302, 343, 386
Assichqua, II, 20
Assigny. *See* Le Moyne
Assomption. *See* Barbier; Maugue-Garreau
Assour, Marie (Byssot Du Hommée), I, 145
Assup, IV, 774
Assurowlaway. *See* Waxaway
Asticou, I, **69–70**, 101, 526
Aston, Sir Arthur, I, 672
Aston, Salusbury (Haviland), IV, 334
Atarhea. *See* Tareha
Atawenta, III, 615
Atchamissey. *See* Scatchamisse
Atecouando, II, **25–26**, xxxviii, 543; III, 21, 23
Atecouando (Jérôme), II, 26; III, **20–21**, 24
Atetkouanon. *See* Pastedechouan
Athasata. *See* Togouiroui
Athicouando (Athurnando). *See* Atecouando
Athlone, Earl of. *See* Ginkel
Atholl, Earl of. *See* Stewart
Atiaʔtawiʔtsheraʔ. *See* Anandamoakin
Atic. *See* Chomina
Atironta (fl. 1615), I, **70**
Atironta (Jean-Baptiste), I, **70–71**, 128
Atironta (Pierre), I, **71–72**

Atkins, Elizabeth (Kenwrick), IV, 410
Atkinson, George, IV, **32–33**
Atkinson, George (Sneppy), IV, 33
Atkinson, Isabella (Gledhill), II, 249
Atontinon (Marie-Barbe), I, 118
Atotarho, I, 253, 254
Atquandadeghte. *See* Ohquandageghte
Atterwana. *See* Ottrowana
Attickasish, III, 286
Au, Chevalier d'. *See* Jolliet
Auber, Anne (Baudouin), I, 80; II, 286; III, 35, 36
Auber, Claude; I, **72**, 80; II, 228, 582; III, 201
Auber, Élisabeth (Chesné; Franquelin), II, 228
Auber, Félix, I, 72
Auber, Geneviève (Roberge), II, 520
Auber, Jacqueline. *See* Lucas
Auber, Jacques, I, **72**
Auber, Marguerite (Doublet), I, 277
Auber, Marguerite (Grouvel; Fillion), I, 305
Auber, Marie. *See* Le Boucher
Auberi. *See* Aubery
Aubert, Anne, II, 26
Aubert, François, II, 129
Aubert, Jacques, II, 26
Aubert, Louis, II, 27
Aubert, Louis-François, II, 509, 575; III, 352
Aubert, Marie. *See* Goupy
Aubert, Marie (Milly), III, 451
Aubert, Pierre, II, 666
Aubert, Thomas, I, **72**, 22, 658, 660
Aubert de Courserac, Marie-Anne (Savigny; Boschenry de Drucour), III, 72, 73
Aubert de Gaspé, Catherine. *See* Tarieu de Lanaudière
Aubert de Gaspé, Ignace-Philippe, IV, **33–34**
Aubert de Gaspé, Madeleine-Angélique. *See* Legardeur de Tilly
Aubert de Gaspé, Marie-Anne. *See* Coulon de Villiers
Aubert* de Gaspé, Philippe-Joseph (1786–1871), II, 33, 58; III, 143, 677; IV, 34, 589, 590
Aubert de Gaspé, Pierre, II, 33; IV, 33
Aubert* de Gaspé, Pierre-Ignace (1758–1823), IV, 34
Aubert de La Chesnaye, Anne-Ursule. *See* Denys de La Ronde
Aubert de La Chesnaye, Catherine (Galiffet de Caffin), III, 233
Aubert de La Chesnaye, Catherine-Gertrude. *See* Couillard de Lespinay
Aubert de La Chesnaye, Charles, I, 21, 56, 84, 85, 104, 105, 178, 200, 224, 227, 289, 338, 387, 393, 396, 397, 400, 444, 445, 538, 602; II, **26–34**, 14, 43, 138, 174, 178, 190, 251, 261, 263, 273, 275, 276, 375, 381, 387, 391, 448, 459, 464, 488, 509, 522, 523, 526, 538, 657; III, 21, 22, 192, 233, 493; IV, 33
Aubert de La Chesnaye, Charles (son), II, 33
Aubert de La Chesnaye, François, II, **34–35**, 32, 33, 305; III, 22; IV, 265
Aubert de La Chesnaye, Françoise (Le Moyne de Maricourt; Dubois Berthelot de Beaucours), II, 405; III, 192
Aubert de La Chesnaye, Ignace-François, III, 21, 22
Aubert de La Chesnaye, Louis, II, 33; III, **21–23**
Aubert de La Chesnaye, Marie-Angélique. *See* Denys de La Ronde

Aubert de La Chesnaye, Marie-Angélique (Goutin), III, 264; IV, 41

Aubert de La Chesnaye, Marie-Anne-Josette. *See* Lestringant de Saint-Martin

Aubert de La Chesnaye, Marie-Charlotte, *dite* de Saint-Michel, III, 369

Aubert de La Chesnaye, Marie-Louise. *See* Juchereau de La Ferté

Aubert de La Chesnaye, Marie-Thérèse. *See* La Lande Gayon

Aubert de La Chesnaye, Marie-Ursule (Le Marchand de Lignery; Feltz), IV, 265

Aubert Duforillon, Barbe. *See* Leneuf de La Vallière et de Beaubassin

Aubert Duforillon, Louis, II, 33, 587; III, 21, 22, 291

Aubery, Joseph, II, 25, 26, 447, 495, 665; III, **23–25**, 21, 163, 266, 359, 395; IV, 424

Aubigné, Françoise d', Marquise de Maintenon, I, 631; II, 98, 132, 330, 483

Aubigny. *See* Boutroue

Aubigny, Duke of. *See* Lennox

Aubin, Michel, II, 639

Aubry, Charles, II, 208

Aubry, Charles-Philippe, III, 87, 531

Aubry, Élisabeth (Dupuy), II, 207, 208

Aubry, Jacques-Charles, II, 208

Aubry, Nicolas, I, **72**, 64, 192, 292

Aubuchon, Catherine. *See* Jérémie, *dit* Lamontagne

Aubuchon, Jacques, II, 296, 413; III, 314

Aubuchon, Jean, II, 11

Aubuchon, Marie-Anne (Chorel de Saint-Romain, *dit* d'Orvilliers), II, 267

Aubuchon, *dit* L'Espérance, Marguerite (Courreaud de La Coste), IV, 178

Aubusson. *See* Du Verger

Auchagah, II, **35**; III, 248

Aucher, Anne (Gilbert), I, 331

Au-Ciel. *See* Ogenheratarihiens

Aucoin, Marie-Josette (Jeanson), IV, 392

Audet*, Francis-Joseph (1867–1943), IV, 232, 398, 698

Audet de Piercotte de Bailleul, Marguerite (Lajus), IV, 432

Audette, *dit* Lapointe, Marie-Josette (Jacobs; Rieutord), IV, 385

Audiepvre, Michel, I, 167

Audin. *See* Daudin

Audoire, Marguerite (Morpain), III, 474

Audouart, *dit* Saint-Germain, Guillaume, I, **73**, 91, 224, 298, 430, 538; II, xvi, 91

Augé, Antoinette. *See* Barabé

Augé, Étienne, IV, **34–35**, 530

Augé, François, IV, 732

Augé, Louis, IV, 34

Augé, Louise-Françoise. *See* Dalgueuil, *dit* Labrèche

Augé, Michel, IV, 35

Auger. *See* Dangé

Auger, *dit* Le Baron, Jean, I, 109

Auger de Marillac, Charles-François, IV, 14

Auger de Subercase, Daniel d', II, **35–39**, 3, 4, 15, 117, 118, 120, 177, 180, 187, 206, 214, 258, 285, 350, 411, 434, 437, 445, 452, 461, 482, 487, 495, 497, 510, 511, 534, 583, 588, 609, 618, 626, 651, 654; III, 20, 22, 177, 190, 207, 234, 247, 264, 290, 436, 474, 505, 552, 682

Auger de Subercase, Marguerite d' (Arrigrand), III, 20

Auger de Subercase, Marie-Anne d'. *See* Du Bourget

Augier, Daniel, IV, 678

Augier, *dit* Desjardins, Christophe, I, 267

Augooshaway. *See* Egushwa

Auguel, *dit* Le Picard Du Guay, Antoine, II, 278, 281

Augusta, Princess (mother of King George III), IV, 536

Auhaitsique. *See* Ahuntsic

Auldjo*, George (d. 1846), IV, 48

Aulnay. *See* Menou

Aulneau (de La Touche), Jean-Pierre, II, **39–40**, 239; III, 46, 137, 241, 251, 361; IV, 240

Aulneau (de La Touche), Michel, II, 40

Aulquoy, Ambroise d' (Thomelin), I, 213

Aumale, Duc d'. *See* Lorraine

Aumasson de Courville, Charles-Léonard, IV, 36

Aumasson de Courville, Claude, IV, 35

Aumasson de Courville, Judith. *See* Chevreau

Aumasson de Courville, Louis-Léonard, known as Sieur de Courville, III, 124; IV, **35–36**, 249, 250, 251, 425, 455, 457, 621, 660

Aumasson de Courville, Marie-Anne. *See* Amiot, *dit* Villeneuve

Aunois, Jeanne (Lefebvre), II, 382

Auoindaon, I, **73**

Aureil. *See* Doreil

Aussillon de Sauveterre, Paul d', I, 423, 424

Austin, Elizabeth. *See* Gooch

Austin, Elizabeth (Hill), II, 287

Austin, Samuel, II, 287

Auterive. *See* Cuny

Auteuil. *See* Ruette

Autray. *See* Bourdon

Auvergne. *See* La Tour

Aux (Eau de Jolliet), Pierre d', II, 441, 602

Auxillon. *See* Aussillon

Auzon, Françoise, IV, 235

Avamy, Jeanne (Viennay-Pachot), I, 661; II, 305

Avaugour, Louis d', II, **40–41**; III, 23, 336

Avène. *See* Renaud

Aveneau, Claude, II, **41**, 144, 347, 468, 501; III, 103

Averne, Comte d', II, 485

Avet Forel, Gabrielle (Desdevens de Glandons), IV, 215

Avisse, Marie-Jeanne (Trefflé, *dit* Rottot; Soupiran), III, 596

Awanano (Awenano). *See* Aouenano

Awenemwet. *See* Wenemouet

Ayala, Pedro de, I, 147, 148, 149, 150, 151

Ayen. *See* Noailles

Ayer, Thomas, II, 285

Aylmer, Catherine (Plunket; Warren), III, 654

Aylmer, Elizabeth (Norris), III, 488

Aylmer, Matthew, 1st Baron Aylmer, III, 488, 655

Aylwin, Lucy. *See* Cushing

Aylwin, Thomas, IV, **37–38**, 725

Aylwin*, Thomas Cushing (1806–71), IV, 38

Ayolas, Juan de, I, 342, 343

Ayotte, Pierre, IV, 71

Ayres. *See* Eyre

Babie, Isabeau. *See* Robin

Babie, Jacques, I, **74**; II, 11

Babie, Jeanne. *See* Dandonneau, *dit* Lajeunesse
Babie, Jeanne (Dazemard de Lusignan), III, 168
Babie, Raymond, I, 74
Babin, Marie-Madeleine (Le Blanc), IV, 441
Babonneau, Renée, II, 490
Baby, Antoine, IV, 38
Baby*, François (1733–1820), I, 74; IV, xxxix, 38, 39, 72, 146, 147, 197, 324, 344, 495, 549
Baby*, François-Louis-Georges (1832–1906), IV, 799
Baby*, James (baptized Jacques Duperron) (1762–1833), IV, 39, 778
Baby, Louis, IV, 38
Baby, Raymond, IV, 38
Baby, Thérèse. *See* Le Comte Dupré
Baby, Véronique (Corbin), IV, 167
Baby, *dit* Dupéront, Jacques, I, 74; IV, **38–40**
Baby, *dit* Dupéront, Susanne. *See* Réaume, *dit* La Croix
Baby de Ranville, Jacques, IV, 38
Bachaddelebat, Marie (Druillon), IV, 226
Bachand, *dit* Vertefeuille, Joseph, IV, 151
Bacon, Louise (Constantin), III, 134
Bâcon, Madeleine, *dite* de la Résurrection, II, 93
Bacon, Nathaniel, III, xxiv
Bacqueville. *See* Le Roy
Badeau, Fabien, III, 138
Badeaux, Antoine-Isidore, IV, 40
Badeaux, Catherine. *See* Loisy
Badeaux, Charles, IV, 40
Badeaux, Jacques, IV, 40
Badeaux, Jean-Baptiste, IV, **40–41**, 109, 304, 320, 547
Badeaux, Jeanne. *See* Ardouin
Badeaux*, Joseph (1777–1834), IV, 40, 332
Badeaux, Marguerite. *See* Bolvin
Badeaux, Marguerite. *See* Pratte
Badelard*, Philippe-Louis-François (1728–1802), IV, 82, 106
Badelart, Marie-Charlotte. *See* Guillimin
Badon, Clémence de (La Motte), I, 415
Baffin, Mrs (wife of WILLIAM), I, 75
Baffin, William, I, **74–75**, 5, 20, 144, 145, 252, 360, 378
Bagot, Jean, II, 18, 359, 360
Bagshawe, Catherina. *See* Stratham
Baguleughe, Elizabeth (Pearson), I, 535
Bailey, Captain, I, 383
Bailey*, Jacob (1731–1808), IV, 94, 504, 763
Baillairgé*, François (1759–1830), IV, 49
Baillairgé*, Thomas (1791–1859), I, 76, 77; II, 200
Baillargeon, Anne (Dugay), II, 203
Baillargeon, Catherine (Bigot), II, 63
Baillargeon*, Charles-François (1798–1870), I, 356
Bailleul. *See* Audet
Baillie, Jane (Douglas, Lady Douglas), IV, 223
Baillif, Catherine. *See* Sainctar
Baillif, Claude, I, **75–77**, 460, 536, 664; II, 338, 418, 467; III, 419
Bailloquet, Pierre, I, **78**, 282, 345; II, 174
Bailly, Georges-Frédéric, III, 474
Bailly, Guillaume, I, **78**; II, 46
Bailly, Marie. *See* Fonteneau
Bailly, Robertus de, I, 659
Bailly, *dit* Lafleur, François, I, **78**; II, 105
Bailly de Messein, Anne. *See* Bonhomme

Bailly de Messein, Anne. *See* Marsain
Bailly de Messein, Charles-François, IV, **41–44**, 72, 80, 89, 372, 373, 374, 469, 676, 698, 799
Bailly de Messein, Félicité-Élisabeth (Le Moyne de Martigny), IV, 43
Bailly de Messein, François-Augustin, IV, 41
Bailly de Messein, Marie-Anne. *See* Goutin
Bailly de Messein, Michel, IV, 41
Bailly de Messein, Nicolas, IV, 41
Baily. *See* Bayly
Baionas, Rachel Relind (Strouds), III, 602
Baker, John, IV, 784
Baker, Samuel, III, 585
Baker, William, III, 585, 586
Baley, Henry, I, 308, 611; II, **41–42**, 203, 231, 266, 267, 311, 319, 395, 406, 407
Baley, Judith (wife of HENRY), II, 42
Balfour, George, III, 71
Balfour, Henry, III, 262
Ball*, Ingram (1752–1807), IV, 523
Ball, John, IV, 515, 627
Ballard (?), Hannah (Moulton), III, 476
Balneavis, Miss (Pringle), IV, 647
Baltimore. *See* Calvert
Baltimore, Baroness. *See* Mynne
Bangs*, Nathan (1778–1862), IV, 777
Banker (Bancker), Evert, III, 56
Banks*, Sir Joseph (1743–1820), IV, 156, 218, 536, 601, 747, 762
Bannerman, Captain, III, 136
Baptiste. *See* Maisonnat
Baptiste, Jean, III, 452
Bar (Barre), François. *See* Bigot, François
Bar, Marguerite (Messier), II, 469
Barabé, Antoinette (Augé), IV, 34
Barat. *See* Barrat
Barbaucannes. *See* Énault
Barbe, Élisabeth (Hazeur), II, 276
Barbe, Jeanne. *See* Girardin
Barbé, Jeanne (Villain), I, 663
Barbe, Sylvain, II, 276
Barbeau, *dit* Lucault, Barbe. *See* Poisson
Barbeau, *dit* Lucault, Léonard, I, 230; II, 164
Barbeau, *dit* Lucault, Marie (Cuillerier), II, 164; III, 155
Barbel, Catherine. *See* Provost
Barbel, Charles, II, 42
Barbel, Jacques, II, **42–44**, xxiii, xxiv, 58, 256, 325, 521; III, 78, 224, 299, 498, 642; IV, 44, 263
Barbel, Jacques-François, IV, 678
Barbel, Louise-Renée. *See* Toupin
Barbel, Marie-Anne. *See* Le Picard
Barbel, Marie-Anne (Fornel), III, 154, 224, 282; IV, **44–45**, 66, 386
Barbel, Marie-Madeleine. *See* Amiot
Barbequière, Jeanne (Dudevant), IV, 234
Barbequière, Louis-Hyacinthe, IV, 234
Barbier, Catherine. *See* La Vau
Barbier, Gilbert, known as Le Minime, I, 230; II, 44
Barbier, Marie, *dite* de l'Assomption, I, 117; II, **44–45**, 132, 249, 378; III, 385; IV, 529
Barbocant. *See* Énault
Barçalo. *See* Barsalou

Barcelos, Pedro de, I, 234, 305
Barclay, Henry, III, 323; IV, 586
Barclay, John, IV, 286
Barclay, Robert, IV, 286
Barclay*, Thomas (1753–1830), IV, 604
Bárdarson. *See* Herjólfr; Ivar
Bardou, Anselme (Ignace?), I, 55, 312, 420; II, 344
Barette, Guillaume, IV, 720
Bariac, Marguerite (Berthier), II, 59
Barker, Andrew, I, 74
Barker, Bethiah (Johnson; Winslow), IV, 774
Barker, Jacob, IV, 389
Barker, John, I, 365
Barkley*, Charles William (1759–1832), IV, 498
Barkley, Frances Hornby. *See* Trevor
Barley (Barlow). *See* Berley
Barlow, Richard, IV, 300
Barlow, Roger, I, 156
Barnard, Anna. *See* Woodbury
Barnard, Anne (Fox), I, 311
Barnard, Esther. *See* Travis
Barnard, John (deacon), III, 26
Barnard, John (father), III, 25
Barnard, John, III, **25–26**
Barnard, William, IV, 501
Barnoin, François de, I, 478
Barnsfare, Adam, IV, 548
Barolet, Claude, II, 129; III, **26**, 35, 194; IV, 602
Barolet, Françoise. *See* Dumontier
Barolet, Marie. *See* Dauteuil
Barolet, Marie-Françoise (Bedout), III, 26
Barolet, Marie-Louise (Panet), III, 26; IV, 602
Barolet, Pierre, III, 26
Baron. *See* Lupien
Baron, Le. *See* Le Baron
Barrat, Barbe (Nouchet), III, 490
Barrat, Claude, II, **45**
Barrat, Jeanne. *See* Quisence
Barre, Sieur de, IV, 70
Barré, Charlotte, *dite* de Saint-Ignace, I, 43, 208, 217, 230
Barré, Isaac, III, 672; IV, 571
Barrell, John, IV, 291, 292
Barrell, Joseph, IV, 411
Barrère, Rosalie (Maugenest), IV, 524
Barrière, Marie (Lannelongue), III, 349
Barrin de La Galissonière, Catherine. *See* Bégon
Barrin de La Galissonière, Marie-Catherine-Antoinette,
    Marquise de La Galissonière. *See* Lauson
Barrin de La Galissonière, Roland, III, 26, 57
Barrin de La Galissonière, Roland-Michel, Marquis de La
    Galissonière, II, 595; III, **26–32**, 22, 49, 57, 92, 99, 231,
    253, 261, 320, 322, 375, 401, 554, 564, 570, 610, 628,
    675, 678, 680; IV, 63, 76, 143, 145, 147, 169, 187, 226,
    256, 289, 365, 407, 449, 456, 633, 636, 661, 666
Barrington, John, III, 295
Barrington, William Wildman, 2nd Viscount Barrington,
    IV, xxxvii
Barrois. *See* Lothman
Barron. *See* Lupien
Barrow, Henry, I, 390
Barroy, Anna, II, 376
Barruel, Augustin de, IV, 502

Barsalou, Élisabeth. *See* Urtebise
Barsalou, Geneviève. *See* Bouchard, *dit* Dorval
Barsalou, Gérard, II, 173; III, 88, 270, 523; IV, 46
Barsalou, Jean-Baptiste, III, 88, 270; IV, **45–46**
Barsalou, Jean-François, IV, 46
Barsalou, Joseph (great-uncle), IV, 46
Barsalou, Joseph, IV, 46
Barsalou, Marie-Catherine. *See* Legras
Barsalou, Marie-Jeanne. *See* Becquet
Bartaud, Anne (Bouillet de La Chassaigne), II, 87
Barthe, Charles, IV, 204
Barthélemy, I, **79**; II, 124
Barthélemy, Michel, I, 126, 127, 647; II, **45–46**, 191, 241
Bartolozzi, Francesco, IV, 763
Barton, Françoise-Marthe (Chevalier), III, 121
Barton, Thomas, IV, 731
Bartram, John, III, 335, 606, 607; IV, 407
Basaline, Elizabeth (Mackellar), IV, 500
Basing. *See* Paulet
Basset, Bonaventure, I, 80
Basset, Catherine. *See* Gaudreau
Basset, David, I, 530; II, **46–47**
Basset, Jean (father of BÉNIGNE), I, 79
Basset, Jean, II, **47**; III, 284
Basset, Mary. *See* Laverdure
Basset Des Lauriers, Bénigne, I, **79**, 80, 201, 225, 230, 266,
    273, 465, 498, 557; II, xvi, xvii, 111, 192, 276, 377, 469,
    470
Basset Des Lauriers, Jeanne. *See* Vauvilliers
Basset Du Tartre, Vincent, I, **79–80**
Bastard, Hélène (Révol), III, 554
Bastide, John Henry, III, **32–34**, 507, 532, 645; IV, 93, 314,
    500
Bastille. *See* Le Breton-Bastille
Batailler, Angélique. *See* Roy
Batailler, Catherine (Paradis), II, 508
Batailler, Pierre, II, 508
Bâtard, Étienne (Anthony), III, **34–35**, 136, 298
Bâtard Flamand. *See* Flemish Bastard
Bathurst, Henry, 1st Baron Apsley, IV, 350
Batilly. *See* Margane
Batiscan (Batisquan), I, **80**, 222
Batoni, Pompeo, III, 166
Batt, Isaac, III, 304, 595; IV, **46–48**, 156, 160
Batt, Sarah. *See* Fowler
Batt, Thomas, IV, 309, 723
Batts, Elizabeth (Cook), IV, 163
Bau. *See* Ruau
Baubee. *See* Babie
Baudart de Vaudésir, Claude, Baron de Sainte-James,
    III, 142, 442; IV, 353
Baudeau, Pierre, II, **47–48**, 416, 594
Baudin, Madeleine (Cugnet), III, 151
Baudoin. *See also* Baudouin
Baudoin, Charles-Louis, III, 35
Baudoin, Françoise (Blais), IV, 71
Baudoin, Gervais, I, 81; III, **35**, 36
Baudoin, Jean, I, **80**, 577; II, 626; IV, xxiii
Baudoin, Madeleine (Ameau), II, 16
Baudoin, Marie-Agathe (Martel), IV, 517
Baudoin, Marie-Thérèse. *See* Guyon Fresnay
Baudoin, Marthe. *See* Marcoux

Baudoin, Marthe (Pélissier), IV, 618
Baudouin, Anne. *See* Auber
Baudouin, Gervais (father), I, 80
Baudouin, Gervais, I, **80–81**; II, 286; III, 35, 36, 237, 344; IV, 618
Baudouin, Jeanne. *See* Desrues
Baudouin, Louis, III, 35
Baudouin, Marie-Anne. *See* Roussel
Baudouin, Marie-Anne (Hertel de Rouville), II, 286; III, 15, 35; IV, 343
Baudouin, Marie-Jeanne (Dizy, *dit* Montplaisir), II, 190
Baudouin, Marie-Madeleine (Lucas Dontigny; Dizy de Montplaisir), III, 187
Baudouin, Michel, I, 81; III, **36**, 35
Baudouin, René, II, 190; III, 187
Baudry. *See also* Beaudry
Baudry, Anne (Lefebvre de Bellefeuille), III, 372; IV, 445
Baudry, Catherine (Milly), III, 451
Baudry, Françoise (Rondeau), III, 567, 568
Baudry, Jean-Baptiste, II, 48
Baudry, Jeanne. *See* Mechin
Baudry, Madeleine (Puybarau de Maisonneuve; Tailhandier, *dit* La Beaume), II, 617
Baudry, Pierre, III, 451
Baudry, Toussaint, II, 517
Baudry, *dit* Des Butes, Claude-Charles, III, 37
Baudry, *dit* Des Butes, Guillaume, II, **48**; III, 36
Baudry, *dit* Des Butes, Jean, III, 37
Baudry, *dit* Des Butes, Jeanne. *See* Soullard
Baudry, *dit* Des Butes, René, III, 37
Baudry, *dit* Des Butes, Urbain, III, 37
Baudry, *dit* La Marche, Jeanne (Dugay), II, 202
Baudry, *dit* La Marche, Madeleine. *See* Boucher
Baudry, *dit* La Marche, Urbain, II, 48, 202; III, 37
Baudry, *dit* Saint-Martin (Baudry Desbuttes, Baudry Soulard), Jean-Baptiste, III, **36–37**
Baudry, *dit* Saint-Martin, Marie-Louise. *See* Doyon
Baudry de Lamarche, Jacques, II, **48**, 632
Bauffremont, Marquise de. *See* Courtenay
Bauffremont, Joseph de, Prince de Listenois, III, 93
Baugé, Marquis de. *See* Lascaris
Baugé, Marquise de. *See* Allègre
Baugé, Jeanne de (Le Royer de La Dauversière), I, 214
Baugy, Guillaume de, II, 48
Baugy, Louis-Henri de, known as Chevalier de Baugy, I, 178, 444; II, **48–49**, 488, 634
Baulos, Marie-Anne (Pascaud), IV, 605
Baussy. *See* Lambert
Bavaria, Elector of. *See* Maximilian II
Bavin, Thomas, I, 333
Bavis, Jean, I, 74
Baxter, Joseph, II, 543, 668
Bayard, Gertrude (Kemble), IV, 279
Baye de La Giraudière (La Girodière), Charles, I, 257
Bayley (Bayly). *See* Baley
Bayly, Miss (Mansel, Lady Mansel; St Leger), IV, 694
Bayly, Charles, I, **81–84**, 39, 47, 49, 50, 107, 129, 226, 328, 337, 343, 396, 477, 518, 519, 553, 657, 666; II, 49, 487, 537
Bayly, Hannah (wife of CHARLES), I, 83, 84
Bayne, Daniel, III, **37–38**; IV, 194, 195, 599
Bayne, John, III, 38
Bazil, Charlotte. *See* Duroy

Bazil, Louis (father), III, 38
Bazil, Louis, II, 43; III, **38–39**, 224, 281
Bazil, Marie-Madeleine. *See* Moreau
Bazin, Louise (Amiot), III, 13
Bazire, Charles, I, **84–85**, 114, 238, 326; II, 16, 28, 29, 31, 174, 178, 375, 448, 533
Bazire, Charles (son), I, 84
Bazire, Geneviève. *See* Macard
Bazire, Jean, I, 84
Bazire, Jeanne. *See* Le Borgne
Bazire, Marie (Gaultier de Comporté), I, 84, 326; II, 576
Beaglehole, John Cawte, IV, 167, 746
Beale, Anthony, II, **49–52**, 10, 65, 232, 266, 311, 312, 313, 314, 319, 474, 602; III, 414, 415, 489
Beale, Frances, II, 51
Beale, Joanna (wife of ANTHONY), II, 51
Beale, Mary (wife of ANTHONY), II, 50
Beall, Joshua, III, 261
Bean, John, III, **39**
Bean, Joseph, II, 664
Bear. *See* Le Pesant
Bear, Ambroise. *See* Saint-Aubin, Ambroise
Beardsley, Samuel, IV, 108
Beare, James, I, **85–86**, 317
Béarn-Bonasse, Isabeau de (Abbadie de Saint-Castin, Baronne de Saint-Castin), II, 4
Beaton. *See* Bethune
Beatson, Elizabeth. *See* Bruce
Beatson, John (father), IV, 48
Beatson, John, IV, 48, 49
Beatson, Patrick, IV, **48–49**
Beatson, William, IV, 48, 49
Beaubassin. *See* Hertel; Leneuf
Beaubien. *See* Cuillerier; Trottier
Beaubois, Nicolas-Ignace de, II, 41, 646; III, **39–41**, 382
Beauceron. *See* Ridday
Beauchamp, Viscount. *See* Seymour
Beauchêne. *See* Chevalier
Beauclerk, Vere, 1st Baron Vere, III, 126, 323, 324; IV, 594, 595
Beaucour; Beaucourt. *See* Malepart
Beaucours. *See* Dubois
Beaudéduit, Alexandre-René, IV, 28
Beaudry. *See also* Baudry
Beaudry, Marguerite (Pillard), III, 521
Beauffremont, Marquise de. *See* Courtenay
Beaufort. *See also* Havard
Beaufort, Duc de. *See* Bourbon
Beaufort, Sieur, II, 116
Beaugny (Beaunier), Éléonore-Jeanne de (Le Poupet de La Boularderie), IV, 468
Beauharnais de Miramion, Marie de. *See* Bonneau de Rubelles
Beauharnois, Anne de (Phélypeaux de Pontchartrain), III, 51
Beauharnois, Claude-Charles de, III, 47
Beauharnois de Beaumont, Claude de, II, 52
Beauharnois de Beaumont et de Villechauve, Claude de, II, **52–53**; III, 42, 50
Beauharnois de Beaumont et de Villechauve, Renée de. *See* Hardouineau
Beauharnois de Beauville, Guillaume de, II, 52
Beauharnois de La Boische, Charles de, Marquis de Beauharnois, II, 35, 52, 66, 91, 126, 147, 156, 209, 210,

211, 239, 253, 269, 284, 301, 316, 317, 327, 333, 346, 358, 389, 390, 433, 457, 503, 520, 530, 531, 580, 632, 665; III, **41–51**, 7, 13, 14, 15, 16, 24, 26, 27, 38, 52, 56, 57, 74, 75, 81, 99, 107, 114, 115, 117, 118, 119, 135, 150, 153, 154, 161, 162, 168, 178, 179, 202, 203, 223, 234, 238, 239, 240, 242, 246, 249, 250, 251, 252, 253, 284, 312, 328, 339, 340, 341, 349, 351, 352, 353, 354, 355, 359, 374, 375, 384, 412, 422, 431, 434, 450, 451, 482, 486, 491, 492, 495, 550, 551, 563, 569, 570, 579, 584, 585, 603, 604, 612, 617, 621, 623, 631, 646, 647, 650, 675; IV, 11, 56, 76, 143, 153, 177, 220, 221, 236, 265, 284, 289, 305, 318, 319, 355, 356, 358, 360, 361, 362, 363, 364, 376, 424, 425, 440, 458, 463, 464, 465, 488, 601, 611, 612, 617, 633, 636, 651, 663, 666, 667, 728, 783

Beauharnois de La Boische, François de, II, 52; III, 41, 51

Beauharnois de La Boische, Jeanne-Élisabeth de (Bégon de La Picardière), II, 52; III, 51, 57, 61

Beauharnois de La Boische, Marguerite-Françoise de. *See* Pyvart de Chastullé

Beauharnois de La Boische, Renée de, Marquise de Beauharnois. *See* Pays

Beauharnois de La Boische et de La Chaussée, François de, III, 50

Beauharnois de La Boische et de La Chaussée, Marie-Anne de. *See* Pyvart de Chastullé

Beauharnois de La Chaussaye, Anne de, Baronne de Beauville. *See* Desgrez

Beauharnois de La Chaussaye, François de, Baron de Beauville, II, 39, 52, 70, 74, 147, 155, 190, 201, 226, 374, 387, 409, 410, 426, 448, 484, 488, 509, 521, 555, 557, 578, 604; III, **51–54**, 42, 57, 433, 512; IV, 355

Beauharnois de Villechauve, François de, II, 52

Beaujeu. *See* Le Gallois; Liénard

Beaujot, Jean, I, 311

Beaujour. *See* Delestre

Beaulac. *See* Hertel

Beaulieu. *See* Gourdeau; Le Gay

Beaumarchais, Sieur de. *See* Juchereau de Saint-Denys, Charles

Beaumont. *See* Beauharnois; Couillard

Beaumont, Marie-Barbe de. *See* Le Prince

Beaune (Bône), Marie-Anne (Cirier), IV, 151

Beaunier. *See* Beaugny

Beaupré. *See* Bonhomme

Beaupré, Baron de. *See* Choiseul

Beaupré, Vicomte de. *See* Des Granches

Beauregard. *See also* Boudier

Beauregard, Barthélemy de, I, 533; II, 182

Beaurivage. *See* Rageot

Beauséjour. *See* Godin

Beausoleil. *See* Brossard

Beaussier, Claire. *See* Portanier

Beaussier, Louis, III, 54

Beaussier de Lisle, Louise-Françoise. *See* Jouenne de Lorière

Beaussier de Lisle, Louis-Joseph, III, **54–55**, 293

Beauvais. *See also* Legardeur

Beauvais, Étiennette (Pottier), II, 528

Beauval. *See* Durand

Beauville, Baron de. *See* Beauharnois

Beauville, Baronne de. *See* Desgrez

Beauvillier, Paul de, Duc de Saint-Aignan, II, 104

Beauvoir Du Roure de Combalet, Marie-Madeleine de. *See* Vignerot

Beawando. *See* Atecouando

Bécancour. *See* Robinau

Bécart de Granville, Jean-Baptiste, II, 53

Bécart de Granville, Louis, II, 53

Bécart de Granville, Marie-Anne. *See* Macard

Bécart de Granville, Pierre (father), I, 387; II, 53, 213, 296, 410, 532, 533; III, 55

Bécart de Granville, Pierre, III, 55

Bécart de Granville et de Fonville, Charles, II, **53**, 410; III, 55

Bécart de Granville et de Fonville, Paul, III, **55–56**, 374

Bécasseau, Gabrielle (Gobin), II, 251, 522

Bechourat. *See* Begourat

Becquet, Anne. *See* Vasse

Becquet, Jean, III, 98

Becquet, Julien, I, 86

Becquet, Marie. *See* Pellerin

Becquet, Marie-Jeanne (Barsalou), IV, 46

Becquet, Romain, I, **86**, 85, 106; II, 242, 448

Becquet, Romaine. *See* Boudet

Bédard, Jacques, II, 88

Bédard, Jeanne-Françoise-Louise-Luce. *See* Lajus

Bédard, Marie-Angélique. *See* Fiset

Bédard, Pierre-Laurent, IV, 42, 638

Bédard*, Pierre-Stanislas (1762–1829), IV, 432

Bédard, Thomas, IV, 49

Bédard, Thomas-Laurent, IV, **49–50**, 477, 511

Beddé, Gilles de, I, 474

Bedford, Duke of. *See* Russell

Bedout*, Jacques (1751–1818), III, 26

Bedout, Jean-Antoine, III, 26, 300

Bedout, Marie-Françoise. *See* Barolet

Beevin. *See* Bevan

Bégon, Catherine (Barrin de La Galissonière), III, 26, 57

Bégon, Catherine (Lafon de La Duye), III, 62

Bégon, François, III, 60

Bégon, Jeanne-Élisabeth (Lorgeril), III, 62; IV, 517

Bégon, Marie-Madeleine, III, 62

Bégon, Marie-Rose, III, 62

Bégon, Marie-Thérèse, III, 62

Bégon, Michel (great-grandfather), II, 470

Bégon, Michel, III, 62

Bégon, Scipion-Jérôme, III, 57, 59, 60, 62

Bégon de La Cour, Claude-Michel, II, xxi; III, **56**, 43, 57, 62, 445, 563, 564, 579; IV, 661

Bégon de La Cour, Claude-Michel-Jérôme, III, 56, 564

Bégon de La Cour, Marie-Catherine-Élisabeth (Michel de Villebois de La Rouvillière), III, 56, 445, 563, 564

Bégon de La Cour, Marie-Élisabeth. *See* Rocbert de La Morandière

Bégon de La Picardière, Mlle (Meulles), II, 472

Bégon de La Picardière, Jeanne-Élisabeth. *See* Beauharnois de La Boische

Bégon de La Picardière, Jeanne-Élisabeth, II, 460

Bégon de La Picardière, Madeleine. *See* Druillon

Bégon de La Picardière, Michel (father), II, 188, 197, 422, 470, 589; III, 51, 53, 56, 57

Bégon de La Picardière, Michel, II, 11, 25, 42, 43, 52, 56, 57, 58, 60, 77, 81, 92, 125, 135, 147, 150, 156, 171, 188, 208, 235, 273, 292, 299, 337, 402, 413, 416, 417, 447, 460, 463, 492, 508, 516, 519, 528, 535, 541, 543, 559,

561, 571, 598, 604, 649; III, **57–63**, 4, 5, 23, 26, 29, 51, 56, 69, 74, 77, 112, 113, 138, 153, 159, 161, 217, 224, 225, 227, 299, 305, 313, 353, 360, 419, 420, 445, 512, 520, 553, 563, 564, 567, 632, 633, 637; IV, 41, 356, 449, 720

Begourat, I, **86**, 61

Bélair. *See* Plessy

Belamy, Pierre de, III, 389

Béland, Angélique (Bolvin), III, 68

Bélanger, Charles, II, 440

Bélanger, Marguerite (Couillard de Lespinay), II, 156

Bélanger, Marguerite (Levasseur), III, 396

Bélanger, Marthe (Souhet; Soupiran), II, 613; III, 595

Bélanger, Philippe, IV, 629

Belcher, Abigail. *See* Allen

Belcher, James, II, 267; III, 414

Belcher, Jonathan (father), II, 254, 669; III, 274, 437, 584, 635; IV, 50

Belcher, Jonathan, III, 130, 174, 363, 364, 365, 366, 418, 650, 651, 664; IV, **50–54**, xxvii, 56, 110, 240, 258, 267, 273, 274, 291, 292, 313, 414, 528, 561, 562, 695, 723, 764

Belcher, Mary. *See* Partridge

Belcher, Mary (Vaughan), II, 644

Belcour. *See* Lafontaine

Belestre. *See* Picoté

Belet. *See* Blet

Belile. *See* Gotteville

Belin, Madeleine (Le Febvre de La Barre), I, 442

Bélisle. *See* Lamarre

Bell*, Mathew (1769–1849), IV, 198

Bell, Thomas, III, 173, 668, 670, 672, 673

Bellair. *See* Gautier

Bellanger, Françoise (Gamelain), I, 321

Belleau, *dit* La Rose, Michel, III, 424

Belleborne. *See* Nicollet

Bellecour (Bellecourt). *See* Lafontaine

Bellecourt. *See* Pouteret

Bellefeuille. *See* Lefebvre

Bellefonds. *See* Genaple

Bellefonds, Marquis de. *See* Gigault

Bellefontaine. *See* Fortin; Godin

Belle-Humeur. *See* Bourg

Belle-Isle. *See* Le Borgne; Lefebvre

Belle-Isle, Duc de. *See* Fouquet

Bellejambe, Jeanne (Jacob), II, 294

Bellenden, Mary (Campbell, Duchess of Argyll), IV, 131

Bellenger, Étienne, I, **87–89**, 421

Bellerive. *See* Groston

Bellerose. *See* Jourdain

Belleville. *See* Boucher; Boucher-Belleville; Gauchet; Guernon; Martel

Bellevue. *See* Pinguet

Bellevue, Antoinette de. *See* Dolebeau

Bellin, Jacques-Nicolas, III, 105, 108

Bellinger. *See* Bellenger

Bellinzani, Francesco, II, 31

Belliveau, Marguerite (Bourgeois), II, 94

Bellois, Cornelis (Corneille) de, I, 291, 294

Bellomont, Earl of. *See* Coote

Bellot, Charlotte-Marguerite. *See* Ramezay

Bellot, *dit* Lafontaine, I, **89**

Belmont. *See* Vachon

Belrieux de Virazel, Marie-Anne de (Chateigner de Cramahé et Des Rochers), IV, 787

Belt of Wampum. *See* Kaghswaghtaniunt

Belugard. *See* Dupin

Belzunce, Armand de, Vicomte de Belzunce, IV, 307

Beman, Esther. *See* Sayre

Bémont. *See* Du Saussay

Bénard, Louis, III, 63

Bénard, Marie. *See* Guy

Bénard, Marie-Germaine-Eustache. *See* Lanoullier de Boisclerc

Bénard, Michel, III, **63–64**, 353

Bénard, *dit* Carignan, Catherine (Spagniolini), III, 598

Bénard, *dit* Carignan, Joseph, III, 598

Benbow, John, II, 260, 666

Benedict XIV, III, 192, 416

Benet, Marie-Anne (Lamaletie), IV, 433

Benne, Commissioner, I, 419

Bennet, Stephen, I, 450

Bennett, Anne. *See* Hopson

Bennett, John, IV, 690

Bennett, Joseph, II, 668; III, 436

Bennett, Samuel, IV, 139

Benoist, Antoine-Gabriel-François, III, 94, 408; IV, **54–55**, 192, 637

Benoist, Claude, IV, 204

Benoist, Françoise. *See* Trevet

Benoist, Gabriel, IV, 54

Benoist, Geneviève (Dupleix Silvain), IV, 245, 246

Benoist, Joseph, II, 60; III, 603; IV, 265

Benoist, Marie-Louise. *See* Le Ber de Senneville

Benoît, Jacques, II, 517

Benoît, Pierre, IV, **55**

Benoît, Ursule (McCarty), IV, 495

Bentinck. *See* Cavendish

Bentley, Thomas, IV, 369

Benyovszky, Móric, Count de Benyovszky, IV, 513

Berbudeau, M., IV, 56

Berbudeau, Jean, IV, 56

Berbudeau, Jean-Gabriel, IV, **55–56**

Berbudeau, Marie-Anne. *See* Duvivier

Berbudeau, Marie-Gervaise. *See* Paris

Berbudeau, Marie-Reine (Texier de La Touche), IV, 56

Berchenbos, Catherine (Lafitau), III, 334

Berchereau. *See* Chavigny

Berenhardt, Jeanne-Catherine de (La Salle), II, 349

Beresford, William, IV, 218

Berey Des Essarts, Félix (baptized Charles), IV, 43, 231

Berger, Le. *See* Honatteniate

Berger, Charles, IV, 532

Berger, Éléonore. *See* Montalan

Berger, Jean, II, **54**

Berger, Jean-Claude, II, 54

Berger, Marie-Françoise. *See* Storer, Rachel

Bergeron, Dominique, II, 235

Bergeron, Louise-Catherine. *See* Denys de Saint-Simon

Bergeron, Marie-Anne (Landron), III, 347

Bergeron, Pierre, I, 409

Bergeron d'Amboise, Marie-Anne (Godin, *dit* Belle-fontaine, *dit* Beauséjour), IV, 305

Bergeron d'Amboise, Michel, IV, 305

Berges. *See* Renaud d'Avène

Bergier, Clerbaud, I, **89–90**, 258, 260, 298, 542; II, 408, 410, 630

Bergier, Jean-Jacques, II, 55

Bergier, Marc, II, **54–56**, 110, 227, 468; III, 639, 640

Bergier Deshormeaux (Des Ormeaux), I, 90; II, 408

Berhouague. *See* Martel

Bériault, Élisabeth (Simonet), III, 592

Beridge (Berridge), Frances (Gladwin), IV, 297

Bérin, Marguerite (Daumont de Saint-Lusson?), I, 249, 250

Bering, Vitus Jonassen, IV, 165, 166

Berkeley, Frances (Byron, Baroness Byron; Hay), IV, 121

Berley, George, II, **56**, 319, 320, 644

Berley, George (son), II, 56

Berlise. *See* Faure

Bermen, Laurent, I, **90–91**; II, xv

Bermen de La Martinière, Anne de. *See* Després

Bermen de La Martinière, Claude de, I, 39, 56, 107, 329, 430, 529, 581, 611; II, **56–58**, 325, 607; III, 59, 60, 64, 113

Bermen de La Martinière, Claude-Antoine de, II, 57; III, **64–65**, 627

Bermen de La Martinière, Françoise de. *See* Juchereau

Bermen de La Martinière, Hannah (Cathcrine) de. *See* Parsons

Bermen de La Martinière, Jean-Baptiste de, II, 57

Bermen de La Martinière, Jeanne-Françoise de, *dite* de Sainte-Hélène, II, 57

Bermen de La Martinière, Louis de, II, 56

Bermen de La Martinière, Marie de. *See* Molin

Bermen de La Martinière, Marie-Anne de. *See* Cailleteau

Bernard, André, I, 383

Bernard, Sir Francis, IV, 292

Bernard, Hannah (Goffe), II, 254

Bernard, Jean-Frédéric, II, 297

Bernard, Marie (Landry), II, 625

Bernard, Marie-Joseph. *See* Daveine

Bernard, Philip, IV, **56–57**

Bernard, Pierre-Joseph, IV, 123

Bernard, Renée (Dargent), III, 164

Bernard de La Rivière, Gabrielle. *See* Anneville

Bernard de La Rivière, Hilaire, I, 76; II, **58–59**, xxiii, 338, 467

Bernard de La Rivière, Marguerite. *See* Gillet

Bernard de La Rivière, Marie-Madeleine. *See* Voyer

Berners, Bridget (Vancouver), IV, 744

Bernier, Benoît-François (Joseph-Pierre), III, 19, 188; IV, **57–58**

Bernier, François, IV, 57

Bernier, Jeanne. *See* Villain

Bernier, Marie. *See* Malen

Bernier, Mathurin, I, 663

Bernier, Philippe, III, 227

Bernières, Henri de, I, **91–92**, 291, 355; II, 19, 207, 303, 329; III, 683

Bernières, Jourdaine de, I, 91

Bernières, Madeleine de, Baronne d'Acqueville. *See* Le Breton

Bernières, Pierre de, Baron d'Acqueville, I, 91

Bernières de Louvigny, Jean de, I, 91, 208, 291, 587; II, 18, 360

Bernini, Giovanni Lorenzo, II, 71

Bernis, M. de, IV, 69

Bernon, Anne (Lavergne), II, 524

Bernou, Claude, I, 174, 175, 179; II, 538, 589

Berrichon. *See* Bottier

Berridge. *See* Beridge

Berrin, Marguerite (Bouin), I, 250

Berruyer, Élisabeth (Petit de Levilliers), II, 523

Berry. *See also* Morillonnet

Berry, Duc de. *See* France, Charles de

Berry, Ann (Clark), IV, 152

Berry, Sir John, I, **92–93**, 24, 278, 370

Berry, Marie. *See* Mars

Berry, Paul, III, 168

Berry, Walter, IV, 352

Berryer, Nicolas-René, Comte de La Ferrière, III, 257, 467; IV, 68, 69, 187, 312, 422, 616, 632, 670, 673

Bersalou. *See* Barsalou

Bersolles, Yves-Augustin, IV, 421

Berson, *dit* Chatillon, Antoine, II, 294

Bertaut, Anne-Catherine de. *See* Pastour de Costebelle

Bertaut, Jacques de, II, 512

Berteau, Catherine (Pascaud), II, 508

Berthé de La Joubardière, Gabriel de, II, 412

Berthelot. *See also* Dubois

Berthelot, Charles, III, 554

Berthelot, François, Comte de Jouy et de Saint-Laurent, I, 661; II, 235, 305, 639

Berthelot* d'Artigny, Michel-Amable (1738–1815), IV, 89, 185

Berthet, Marie-Philippe (Picquet), IV, 637

Berthiaume, Jean-Jacques, IV, 8, 43

Berthier, Alexandre, II, 59, 60, 69

Berthier, Isaac (Alexandre), I, 494, 556, 565, 602; II, **59–60**, 155, 295

Berthier, Marguerite. *See* Bariac

Berthier, Marie. *See* Legardeur de Tilly

Berthier, Marie-Françoise. *See* Viennay-Pachot

Berthier, Michel, III, 165

Berthier, Pierre, II, 59

Bertier, Antoine, II, 60

Bertier, Antoinette. *See* Cochon

Bertier, Marie-Anne. *See* Denys de Saint-Simon

Bertier, Michel, II, **60**, 151; III, 67, 518; IV, 203, 265

Bertin, Louis, IV, 56

Bertrand, François, II, 411

Bertrand, Jeanne. *See* Giraudin

Bertrand (Bertrend), Laurent, IV, 384

Bertrand, Marguerite (Angeac), IV, 27

Bertrand, Marie-Josephte (Rousseau de Villejouin; Ailleboust), III, 6, 368; IV, 688

Bertrand, Pierre, II, 282

Bertrand, Renée (Leneuf de La Vallière et de Beaubassin), II, 411; III, 454; IV, 689

Bertrand, Thomas, II, 57, 561

Bertrand de Latour, Louis. *See* Latour, Bertrand de

Bérulle, Pierre de, I, 115

Berwick, Duke of. *See* Fitz-James

Besaillion. *See* Bisaillon

Beschefer, Thierry, I, 50, 108, 345, 445; II, **61–62**, 343

Besnard. *See also* Bénard

Besnard, Jacques, II, 83

Besnard, Jeanne (Gadois), II, 234; III, 232

Besnard, *dit* Bourjoly, René, II, 234
Besnard, *dit* Carignant, Charlotte. *See* Brebion
Besnard, *dit* Carignant, Félicité. *See* Pillet
Besnard, *dit* Carignant, Jean-Baptiste, IV, 58
Besnard, *dit* Carignant, Jean-Louis, IV, **58–59**, 485, 547
Besnard, *dit* Carignant, Marie-Joseph. *See* Gervaise
Besnard, *dit* Saint-André, Jacques, II, 168
Besné. *See* Du Chaffault
Besouat. *See* Tessouat
Bessabes, I, 69, 529
Best, George, I, **93–94**, 5, 85, 153, 316, 317, 318, 670
Béthune, Chevalier de, II, 270
Béthune, Armand de, II, 399
Bethune*, John (1751–1815), IV, 757
Béthune, Louis de, Comte de Béthune, II, 399
Béthune, Marguerite-Louise-Suzanne de (Gramont, Comtesse de Guiche), II, 440
Béthune, Marie-Armande de, II, 399
Béthune, Marie-Thérèse de, Comtesse de Béthune. *See* Pollet de La Combe-Pocatière
Béthune, Maximilien I de, Baron de Rosny, Duc de Sully, I, 293
Bethune, Véronique. *See* Waddens
Bettez, Jacob, IV, 37
Beuvy, Anne de. *See* Bury
Bevan, William, II, **62**, 10, 492, 563
Beverly, Robert, II, 498
Bezellon. *See* Bisaillon
Biard, Jean, I, 94
Biard, Jeanne. *See* Cluzel
Biard, Pierre, I, **94–96**, 67, 68, 69, 97, 98, 100, 101, 165, 299, 307, 347, 441, 442, 456, 470, 498, 500, 560, 604
Bibaud*, François-Maximilien (1823–87), III, 80; IV, 208, 510
Bica, Philippe (Massé), I, 497
Bidal, Abbé, II, 443
Bidal, Claude-François, Marquis d'Asfeld, II, 648; III, 118, 644
Bidaut, Michelle (Brossard), II, 105
Bidoux de Lartigue, M., I, 423
Bielke, Sten Carl, Baron Bielke, IV, 406
Biencourt, Charles de, I, 96
Biencourt, Florimond de, I, 96
Biencourt, Jacques de (uncle), I, 96
Biencourt, Jacques de, I, 96, 99
Biencourt, Jeanne de. *See* Salazar
Biencourt, Jeanne de, I, 96
Biencourt, Louis de, I, 96
Biencourt de Poutrincourt, Claude de. *See* Pajot
Biencourt de Poutrincourt et de Saint-Just, Jean de, I, **96–99**, 28, 64, 67, 94, 95, 99, 100, 101, 110, 189, 292, 293, 294, 299, 300, 307, 347, 367, 441, 469, 470, 476, 495, 500, 501, 507, 526, 527, 564, 592, 596, 604; IV, xix, xx
Biencourt de Saint-Just, Charles de, I, **99–102**, 25, 51, 67, 69, 94, 95, 97, 98, 293, 299, 307, 347, 470, 471, 476, 501, 592; IV, xix
Bienvenu. *See* Fontaine
Bienville. *See* Le Moyne
Bier, Anne de (La Cetière), II, 325
Bierne (Byrne), Abbé, III, 566
Bigeau, Marie-Joseph. *See* Dumouchel
Big Mouth. *See* Otreouti

Bignon, Jean-Paul, II, 595, 599
Bigot, Bonaventure, IV, 59
Bigot, Catherine. *See* Baillargeon
Bigot, Étienne, IV, 59
Bigot, François (d. 1708), II, **62–63**
Bigot, François (d. 1778), II, xxi, 225, 226; III, 6, 8, 18, 19, 75, 76, 78, 98, 118, 124, 137, 138, 141, 154, 160, 161, 169, 182, 188, 193, 195, 196, 198, 199, 225, 228, 231, 236, 237, 243, 255, 256, 271, 272, 291, 292, 300, 305, 321, 354, 355, 385, 389, 392, 409, 416, 425, 433, 441, 456, 461, 466, 468, 487, 494, 510, 511, 524, 537, 540, 551, 557, 561, 563, 564, 576, 611, 612, 644, 676, 677, 680; IV, **59–71**, 36, 45, 56, 76, 88, 91, 92, 124, 125, 145, 148, 187, 192, 202, 205, 206, 214, 236, 237, 247, 248, 249, 250, 252, 253, 254, 256, 257, 263, 264, 271, 286, 306, 312, 335, 344, 353, 364, 420, 421, 432, 435, 449, 456, 459, 460, 466, 512, 514, 517, 558, 588, 614, 615, 616, 620, 621, 623, 624, 629, 632, 639, 643, 644, 645, 646, 659, 660, 668, 670, 672, 673, 678, 691, 692, 720, 729, 750, 755
Bigot, Jacques, II, **63–64**, 5, 542; III, 24, 168
Bigot, Joseph-Amable, IV, 60
Bigot, Louis, IV, 59, 60
Bigot, Louis-Amable, IV, 59, 60
Bigot, Louis-Joseph, IV, 60
Bigot, Marguerite. *See* Lombard
Bigot, Marie. *See* Bouchard d'Orval
Bigot, Marie. *See* Renard
Bigot, Marie, II, 62
Bigot, Marie-Louise (Brulart de Sillery), IV, 59
Bigot, Vincent, II, **64–65**, 63, 95, 664; III, 104, 329; IV, 764, 765
Bigot, *dit* Lamothe, François, II, 62
Bigot, *dit* Lamothe, Marguerite. *See* Drapeau
Billeron, *dit* Lafatigue, Jeanne. *See* Dalgueuil, *dit* Labrèche
Billings*, Joseph (1758–1806), IV, 744
Billopp*, Christopher (1737–1827), IV, 327
Billouart de Kerlérec, Louis, III, 36, 531; IV, 667
Billy, Godefroy de, I, 469
Billy, Guillaume, II, 499
Billy, Madeleine. *See* Normandin
Bilodeau, Jean, III, 518, 519
Bilodeau, Marie. *See* Turgeon
Bineteau (Binneteau), Julien, II, 55, 109, 110, 454
Binney*, Jonathan (1723/24–1807), IV, 110, 111, 116, 199, 273, 275, 291, 450, 451, 581
Binot, Marie-Louise (Coron), III, 141
Birch. *See* Burch
Bird, Henry, IV, 260, 410, 499
Bird, Thomas, II, **65**, 51, 658; III, 489
Birnie, Samuel, IV, 403
Biron, Pierre, II, 160
Bisaillon, Louise. *See* Dublay
Bisaillon, Martha. *See* Coombe
Bisaillon, Michel, III, 65
Bisaillon, Peter, III, **65–66**; IV, 173
Bisaillon, Richard, III, 65
Bishop*, Charles (d. *c.* 1810), IV, 420, 569
Bishop, Nathaniel, II, **65**, 51, 492; III, 489
Bissell, Abigail. *See* Allen
Bissett, Mary (Jackson), II, 293
Bisson. *See also* Buisson

Bisson, Julienne (Demosny), I, 256
Bissot. *See also* Byssot
Bissot, Charles-François, I, 146; II, 66, 256, 300
Bissot, Charlotte (Lafontaine de Belcour), III, 339; IV, 315
Bissot, Claire-Françoise (Jolliet), I, 146, 395, 396; II, 66, 68, 300
Bissot, François-Joseph, II, **65–66**, 256, 300; III, 339; IV, 315
Bissot, Geneviève (Maheut), I, 480; II, 168
Bissot, Jeanne (Clément Du Vuault de Valrennes), II, 148
Bissot, Louise (Margane de Lavaltrie), II, 455; III, 429
Bissot, Marie. *See* Lambert Dumont
Bissot, Marie (Porlier; Gourdeau de Beaulieu et de La Grossardière), II, 256
Bissot de Vincenne (Vinsenne), Marie-Louise (Boisseau), IV, 75
Bissot de Vinsenne, François-Marie, I, 146; II, **66–68**, xxviii, 216, 436, 563, 632; III, 258; IV, 315
Bissot de Vinsenne, Jean-Baptiste, I, 146; II, **68**, 66, 128, 569; IV, 75
Bissot de Vinsenne, Marguerite. *See* Forestier
Bissot de Vinsenne, Marie. *See* Longpré
Bizaillon. *See* Bisaillon
Bizard, David, I, 102
Bizard, Guillemette. *See* Robert
Bizard, Jacques, I, **102–3**, 231, 540, 600; II, 70, 401, 526, 527, 563
Bizard, Jeanne-Cécile. *See* Closse
Bizard, Louise (Renaud), II, 563
Bjarni Herjólfsson, I, **103–4**, 448
Black*, John (fl. 1784–1819), IV, 501, 502
Black, Lydia (Davis), III, 168
Black*, William (1760–1834), IV, 19, 258
Blackaller, Joanna (Yonge), II, 670
Blackaller, Nicholas, II, 670
Blackbird. *See* Siginakee
Blackburn, John, IV, 676
Black Cauldron. *See* Chaudière Noire
Blacklandt, Martin van, II, 279
Blacksnake. *See* Thaonawyuthe
Blackstone, Sir William, IV, 184, 186
Blainville. *See* Céloron
Blair, Robert, I, 54
Blais, Françoise. *See* Baudoin
Blais, Joseph, IV, 71
Blais, Louis, IV, 72
Blais, Marguerite, *dite* de Saint-Pierre, IV, 72
Blais, Marie-Françoise. *See* Lizot
Blais, Marie-Joseph, *dite* de Saint-Michel, IV, 72
Blais, Michel, IV, **71–72**
Blais, Michel (son), IV, 72
Blais, Pierre (father), IV, 71
Blais, Pierre, IV, 71
Blais de Surlaville. *See* Le Courtois
Blaise Des Bergères, Jean, II, 69
Blaise Des Bergères, Marie. *See* Boucher
Blaise Des Bergères de Rigauville, Anne. *See* Richard de Goigni
Blaise Des Bergères de Rigauville, Charles-Régis, II, 69; IV, 96
Blaise Des Bergères de Rigauville, Jean-Baptiste-Marie, II, 69; IV, xliii, 547

Blaise Des Bergères de Rigauville, Jeanne-Cécile. *See* Closse
Blaise Des Bergères de Rigauville, Marguerite. *See* Vauvril de Blason
Blaise Des Bergères de Rigauville, Marie-Françoise. *See* Viennay-Pachot
Blaise Des Bergères de Rigauville, Marie-Joseph (Denys de Vitré), II, 70; IV, 209
Blaise Des Bergères de Rigauville, Nicolas, II, **68–69**, 70; III, 80, 208, 394, 450
Blaise Des Bergères de Rigauville, Raymond, I, 103, 231; II, **69–71**, 68, 162, 186, 441; III, 372
Blake*, Charles (d. 1810), IV, 82
Blake, Sarah (Gridley), IV, 314
Blake, William, IV, 19
Blakeney, William, Lord Blakeney, III, 33; IV, 335
Blanchard, Guillaume, II, **71**, 105, 629, 654
Blanchard, Huguette. *See* Gougeon
Blanchard, Jean, II, 71
Blanchard, Joseph-Henri, IV, xxii
Blanchard, Madeleine (Richard), II, 105
Blanchard, Radegonde. *See* Lambert
Blanchet, Marie. *See* Sédilot
Blanchet, René, II, 11
Blancheteau, Jeanne-Catherine (Doreil), III, 187
Blanchon, Anne. *See* Convent
Blanchon, Marie-Charlotte (Carpentier), IV, 133
Blanzy. *See* Danré
Blarye, *dit* Titailt, M., I, 425
Blas, Hernando, I, 157
Blason. *See* Vauvril
Blathwayt, William, II, 279
Blawbek (Blewbeck). *See* Cagenquarichten
Blay. *See* Blais
Blet (Belet, Blette), Jeanne (Deguire, *dit* Desrosiers), IV, 201
Bleury. *See* Sabrevois
Bligh, William, I, 378
Blondeau*, Angélique (Cotté) (1755–1837), IV, 171
Blondeau, Catherine-Apolline (Godefroy de Linctot), IV, 302
Blondeau, Isabelle (Isabeau) (Phélypeaux de Villesavin), I, 484
Blondeau, Joseph-Barthélemy, IV, 366
Blondeau, Marie-Madeleine (Legardeur; Céloron de Blainville), III, 99
Blondeau*, Maurice-Régis (1734–1809), IV, 171, 277
Blondeau, Nicolas, IV, 592
Blondeau, Suzanne (Hertel de Saint-François), III, 289; IV, 347
Blondin, Joseph, IV, 331
Blowers*, Sampson Salter (1743–1842), IV, 737
Blundeville, Thomas, I, 678
Bobé, Jean, III, 248
Bocall, Stevan de, I, 306, 671, 672
Bochart. *See also* Du Plessis-Bochart
Bochart, Guillaume, II, 72
Bochart, Jean, II, 72
Bochart de Champigny, Jean (grandfather), II, 72
Bochart de Champigny, Jean (father), II, 71
Bochart de Champigny, Jean, Sieur de Noroy et de Verneuil, I, 56, 103, 114, 138, 141, 239, 299, 320, 338, 398, 488,

528, 577, 582, 664; II, **71–80**, 16, 17, 32, 53, 58, 70, 86,
100, 102, 110, 114, 115, 120, 129, 133, 137, 148, 149,
162, 185, 195, 213, 214, 228, 229, 230, 338, 340, 346,
353, 371, 383, 401, 404, 410, 413, 427, 432, 440, 450,
456, 458, 464, 466, 473, 483, 486, 488, 491, 513, 524,
539, 540, 561, 566, 568, 576, 580, 586, 594, 596, 598,
617, 618, 655; III, 7, 15, 22, 190, 233, 237, 309, 310,
311, 372, 396, 563
Bochart de Champigny, Marie. *See* Boivin
Bochart de Champigny, Marie (Prouville), I, 554
Bochart de Champigny, Marie-Madeleine. *See* Chaspoux
Bocquet, Marie-Jeanne (Lanoullier de Boisclerc), III, 352
Bocquet, Simple, II, 173, 174
Boddington, John, IV, 93
Bodeau, Mme, I, 610
Bodega, Francisca de Mollineda de la. *See* Mollineda
Bodega y de las Llanas, Tomás de la, IV, 72
Bodega y Quadra, Juan Francisco de la, IV, **72–74**, 568, 746
Bodquín. *See* Flórez
Boehme, Jacob, IV, 19
Boerhaave, Hermann, II, 595
Bœsson, Jacques-Ange, III, 612
Boeve, Jacobus, I, 369
Boganientim, II, 646
Boileau, Marguerite (Serreau de Saint-Aubin), II, 604
Boiret, Denis, IV, 75
Boiret, René, IV, 74
Boiret, Urbain, IV, **74–75**, 387, 643
Bois*, Louis-Édouard (1813–89), IV, 493, 801
Boisberthelot. *See* Dubois
Boisbriand. *See* Dugué
Boisbuisson. *See* Boucher
Boisclerc. *See* Lanoullier
Boisdon, Jacques, I, **104**
Boisguibert. *See* Le Verrier
Boishébert. *See* Deschamps
Bois-le-Duc. *See* Cnoyen
Boismenay, Marie (Simonnet), IV, 708
Boismorel. *See* Petit
Boispineau, Charles, I, 108; III, 67
Boispineau, Jean-Jard, I, 108; III, **66–67**, 35, 518
Boisseau, Josias, I, **104–6**, 290, 396, 397, 541; II, 29, 483
Boisseau, Marguerite. *See* Gérin
Boisseau, Marie. *See* Colombier
Boisseau, Marie-Anne. *See* Pagé, *dit* Carcy
Boisseau, Marie-Louise. *See* Bissot de Vincenne
Boisseau, Nicolas, IV, **75–76**, 263, 601, 692
Boisseau*, Nicolas-Gaspard (1726–1804), IV, 75, 692
Boisseau, Pierre, IV, 75
Boisseau, *dit* Cognac, Jacques, I, 267, 273
Boissel, Marguerite (Bouchard), I, 109
Boissemances. *See* Dufrost
Boissières, Catherine (Perrin), II, 516
Boissy, Madeleine (Pellegrin), IV, 620
Boisvert. *See* Rapine
Boit, John, IV, 420
Boivin, Anne (Lauson), I, 427
Boivin, Charles, I, 106
Boivin, François, I, **106**
Boivin, Guillaume, I, 106
Boivin, Marie (Bochart de Champigny), II, 71, 323
Boivin, Marie-Angélique (Paradis), III, 500
Boivin, Pierre, I, 106

Boivin, Thiennette. *See* Fafard
Bolduc, Marie-Françoise (Corriveau), III, 142
Bolingbroke, Viscount. *See* St John
Bollan, William, III, 108, 326
Bolman, Jane. *See* Brimner
Bolper, Marie-Louise (Quiniard, *dit* Duplessis), II, 534
Bolton. *See* Paulet
Bolton, Duchess of. *See* Lowther
Bolvin, Angélique. *See* Béland
Bolvin, Claire. *See* Jutras
Bolvin, Gilles, II, 200; III, **67–68**; IV, 40, 201, 649
Bolvin, Jean-Baptiste, III, 68
Bolvin, Jean-François, III, 67
Bolvin, Marguerite (Badeaux), IV, 40
Bolvin, Marie-Anne. *See* Isabeau
Bolvin, Marie-Marguerite. *See* Lamarque
Bomer, Louis, IV, 619
Bomoseen, II, 25, 452, 475, 476, 654, 664
Bonamour, Jean de, I, **106–7**
Bonaventure. *See also* Denys
Bonaventure, Brother, I, 386
Bonaventure, François, IV, 134
Bond, Captain, III, 380
Bond, Susan, I, 107
Bond, William, I, **107**, 361, 493, 529, 657; II, 265
Bondfield, Anna Marie (Allsopp), IV, 554
Bondfield, John Taylor, IV, 104, 654
Bondy. *See* Douaire
Bône. *See* Beaune
Boneval. *See* Benoît
Bonfils, Marguerite de (Galiffet d'Honon), III, 233
Bonfin, Richard-François, IV, 507
Bonfoy, Hugh, III, **68–69**, 189; IV, 226
Bonhomme, Anne (Minet; Bailly de Messein), IV, 41
Bonhomme, Jeanne (Thaumur de La Source), II, 628
Bonhomme, *dit* Beaupré, Agnès. *See* Morin
Bonhomme, *dit* Beaupré, Félicité. *See* Hamel
Bonhomme, *dit* Beaupré, Ignace, III, 69
Bonhomme, *dit* Beaupré, Noël, III, **69**, 617
Boniface, François, II, 61
Bonnaventure. *See* Denys
Bonne*, Pierre-Amable de (1758–1816), III, 70
Bonneau. *See* Preissac
Bonneau de La Varenne, Roger de, I, 573
Bonneau de Rubelles, Marie (Beauharnais de Miramion),
I, 117
Bonnécamps, Anne de. *See* Muerel
Bonnécamps, Joseph-Pierre de, III, 31, 100, 538, 540, 678;
IV, **76–77**, 298, 620
Bonnécamps, Nicolas de, IV, 76
Bonne de Missègle, Louis de, III, **69–70**
Bonne de Missègle, Louise de. *See* Prud'homme
Bonne de Missègle, Louis-Joseph de, III, 69
Bonne de Missègle, Marie de. *See* Villeneuve
Bonnefoy, Madeleine de (Sarrazin), II, 593
Bonnegrâce, Marie-Anne (Pellegrin), IV, 619
Bonnel, Marie (Turc de Castelveyre), III, 632
Bonnemere, Florent, I, **107–8**
Bonner, Jane, II, 81
Bonner, John, II, **80–81**, 287
Bonner, John (son), II, 81
Bonner, Mary. *See* Clark
Bonnerme (surgeon), I, 190, 300

Bonnes, Catherine de (Taffanel de La Jonquière), III, 609
Bonnet, Jeanne (Richard), I, 473
Bonrepaus. *See* Dusson
Bontemps, Sieur de, I, 348; II, 82
Bontemps, Jean, III, 422
Bonwah. *See* Benoît
Booth, Sir George, I, 369
Boquet, Charles, I, **108**, 315, 547, 635, 651; II, 61
Borda. *See* Laborde
Boré, Étienne, III, 36
Borland, John, II, 497
Borough, Stephen, I, 158
Borough, William, I, 333
Borry de Grandmaison, Laurent, II, 295
Borsalou. *See* Barsalou
Bory, Gabriel de, III, 31
Boscawen, Charlotte. *See* Godfrey
Boscawen, Edward, III, **70–71**, xxv, 72, 73, 92, 121, 131,
  209, 210, 268, 293, 362, 363, 606, 666, 667; IV, xxvi,
  21, 22, 327, 661, 668, 751
Boscawen, Frances. *See* Evelyn-Glanville
Boscawen, Hugh, 1st Viscount Falmouth, III, 70
Boschenry, Jean-Louis de, Baron de Drucourt, III, 71
Boschenry, Marie-Louise de, Baronne de Drucourt. *See*
  Godard
Boschenry de Drucour, Augustin de, III, **71–74**, xix, xxvii,
  6, 55, 230, 231, 268, 417, 440, 570, 667; IV, 22, 214,
  250, 644, 645, 646, 656, 673, 751
Boschenry de Drucour, Marie-Anne de. *See* Aubert de
  Courserac
Boschet de Saint-Martin, François, III, 156
Boschet de Saint-Martin, Marie-Charlotte (Morin de
  Fonfay), IV, 558
Boschette (Brusquet), Suzanne (Dupuy), II, 213
Bossac, Baron de. *See* Peschart
Bossac, Baronne de. *See* Dollier de Casson
Bossu, Jean-Bernard, III, 443
Bossuet, Jacques-Bénigne, I, 488; II, 259, 330; IV, 92
Bostwick, Henry, IV, 369
Bottier, *dit* Berrichon, Nicolas, IV, 252
Bouat, Abraham, I, 416; II, 81, 509
Bouat, Agathe. *See* Legardeur de Repentigny
Bouat, François-Marie, II, **81–82**, 381, 604; III, 159, 169,
  390, 539
Bouat, Jean-Marie, II, 160
Bouat, Louise-Jeanne (Daine), III, 159
Bouat, Madeleine. *See* Lambert Dumont
Bouat, Madeleine-Marguerite (Dazemard de Lusignan),
  III, 169
Bouat, Marguerite. *See* Névellet
Bouat, Marguerite (Pascaud), II, 81, 269, 509; III, 393
Bouat, Thérèse (Poulin de Courval; Gannes de Falaise;
  Jautard), III, 63, 539; IV, 391
Boucault, Françoise-Anne. *See* Devene
Boucault, Marguerite. *See* Buirette
Boucault, Nicolas-Gaspard (father), III, 74, 77
Boucault, Nicolas-Gaspard, II, xxiv, 151; III, **74–77**, 64,
  78, 135, 226, 291, 299; IV, 319, 360
Boucault de Godefus, Gilbert, III, **77–78**, 75, 500; IV, 271,
  386
Boucault de Godefus, Marie-Madeleine. *See* Lajoüe
Bouchard, Charles, III, 142
Bouchard, Étienne, I, **108–9**, 201

Bouchard, Marguerite. *See* Boissel
Bouchard, Marie-Josephte. *See* Corriveau
Bouchard, *dit* Dorval, Geneviève (Forestier; Barsalou),
  IV, 46
Bouchard d'Orval, Marie (Bigot), II, 63
Bouchard d'Orval, Marie-Antoinette. *See* Chouart Des
  Grosseilliers
Boucheau. *See* Pouchot
Boucher (merchant), I, 89
Boucher, Élisabeth (Guion), II, 271
Boucher, Florence. *See* Gareman
Boucher, François, II, 140
Boucher, Gaspard, I, 330; II, 82, 83
Boucher, Geneviève, *dite* de Saint-Pierre, III, **78–79**
Boucher, Jeanne. *See* Crevier
Boucher, Jeanne (Sabrevois), II, 86, 589; IV, 690
Boucher, Lucie-Angélique. *See* Cotté
Boucher, Madeleine (Baudry, *dit* La Marche), II, 48, 82, 83
Boucher, Madeleine (Legardeur de Tilly), II, 387
Boucher, Marguerite (Daneau de Muy), II, 168; III, 161, 162
Boucher, Marguerite (Toupin), II, 82
Boucher, Marguerite-Madeleine. *See* Goutin
Boucher, Marie (Blaise Des Bergères), II, 69
Boucher, Marie (Chaudillon), II, 140
Boucher, Marie (Gaultier de Varennes), I, 327; II, 85, 202,
  240; III, 245, 246, 247; IV, 234
Boucher, Marie (La Fond), II, 82, 83; III, 629
Boucher, Marie-Madeleine. *See* Ouebadinskoue
Boucher, Marin, I, 330
Boucher, Nicolas, II, 82
Boucher, Nicole. *See* Lemer
Boucher, Philippe, II, 523
Boucher, Pierre, I, 32, 45, 109, 123, 172, 200, 238, 283,
  327, 349, 354, 404, 468, 511, 512, 543, 579, 619; II,
  82–87, xvi, xvii, 16, 61, 62, 92, 168, 189, 202, 240, 387,
  433, 540, 589, 597, 599, 624; III, 78, 80, 81, 82, 83, 161,
  247, 629; IV, 234
Boucher, Pierre-François, IV, 69, 127
Boucher, Pierre-Jérôme, II, 154, 648; III, **79–80**, 229, 575,
  644
Boucher, Renée (Paris), III, 501
Boucher, *dit* Belleville, Jean-Baptiste, III, 220, 234; IV,
  203, 659
Boucher, *dit* Boisbuisson, Louis-Marin, I, 619
Boucher-Belleville*, Jean-Baptiste (1763–1839), IV, 639
Boucher de Boucherville, Charlotte. *See* Denys de La Trinité
Boucher de Boucherville, Charlotte (Perrault), IV, 623
Boucher de Boucherville, Claire-Françoise (Pommereau;
  Legardeur de Croisille et de Montesson), III, 339, 525;
  IV, 109, 447
Boucher de Boucherville, Marguerite. *See* Raimbault
Boucher de Boucherville, Marie-Marguerite (La Corne),
  IV, 427
Boucher de Boucherville, Pierre (father), II, 617; III, 80, 525
Boucher de Boucherville, Pierre, II, 542; III, **80–81**, 269;
  IV, 427, 623
Boucher* de Boucherville, René-Amable (1735–1812),
  IV, 346
Boucher de Boucherville et de Montarville, Charles, II, 296
Boucher de Boucherville et de Montarville, Françoise. *See*
  Bourot
Boucher de Grandpré, Geneviève (Hertel de Chambly;
  Simonet d'Abergemont), III, 592

Boucher de Grandpré, Lambert, I, **109**; II, 70; III, 592
Boucher de Grandpré, Marguerite. *See* Vauvril de Blason
Boucher de La Bruère (La Bruyère), Françoise (Le Mercier), IV, 458
Boucher de La Perrière, François-Clément, III, 81; IV, 142
Boucher de La Perrière, Françoise. *See* Malhiot
Boucher de La Perrière, Marie-Madeleine (Pécaudy de Contrecœur), III, 81; IV, 618
Boucher de La Perrière, René, II, 201; III, **81–82**, 44, 80, 103, 269; IV, 618
Boucher de Montbrun, François, III, 82
Boucher de Montbrun, Françoise. *See* Godefroy de Saint-Paul
Boucher de Montbrun, Françoise, *dite* Saint-Placide, III, 630
Boucher de Montbrun, Françoise-Claire. *See* Charest
Boucher de Montbrun, Jacques-Timothée, IV, 303
Boucher de Montbrun, Jean, III, **82**
Boucher de Montbrun, Jean-Baptiste, III, 82
Boucher de Montbrun, Madeleine. *See* Godefroy de Saint-Paul
Boucher de Montbrun, René, III, 82
Boucher de Montizambert, Jacques, II, 433
Boucher de Niverville, Françoise (Spagniolini), III, 598
Boucher de Niverville, Jean-Baptiste, III, **82–83**, 598; IV, 690
Boucher de Niverville, Jean-Baptiste (fils), IV, 150
Boucher* de Niverville, Joseph-Claude (1715–1804), III, 83, 375, 429; IV, 332, 634
Boucher de Niverville, Marguerite-Thérèse. *See* Hertel de La Fresnière
Boucher de Niverville, Marie-Josephte. *See* Chastelain
Boucher de Niverville de Montisambert, Louis, IV, 653
Boucher de Niverville (Nebourvele) Grandpré, François, IV, 214, 240
Boucherville. *See* Boucher
Bouchette*, Jean-Baptiste (1736–1804), IV, 547
Boudeau. *See* Baudeau
Boudet, Anne (Du Calvet), IV, 227
Boudet, Romaine (Becquet), I, 86
Boudier de Beauregard, Antoine, I, 344
Boudier de Beauregard, Éléonore. *See* Grandmaison
Boudon, Henri-Marie, II, 360
Boudor, Jean, II, 160, 453
Boudor, Marguerite. *See* Seigneuret
Boudrot, Abraham, I, 427
Boudrot, Élisabeth (Le Blanc), IV, 441
Boudrot, François, III, 97
Boudrot, Marguerite. *See* Bourgeois
Boudrot, Marguerite (Bourg), III, 83
Bouette, Jeanne (Roussel), I, 583
Bougainville, Jean-Pierre de, IV, 755
Bougainville*, Louis-Antoine de, Comte de Bougainville (1729–1811), III, 86, 293, 328, 408, 459, 464, 466, 535, 560, 671, 672; IV, 54, 68, 76, 207, 208, 214, 335, 479, 507, 588, 620, 646, 670, 671, 672, 691, 754, 755
Bouge, Ange, known as La Corruble, I, 203; II, 243
Bougret Dufort, Marguerite (Bourgy; Simonnet), IV, 709
Bouillet de Chevalet, Claude, II, 88
Bouillet de La Chassaigne, Anne. *See* Bartaud
Bouillet de La Chassaigne, Gaudefroy, II, 87
Bouillet de La Chassaigne, Jean, II, **87–88**, 125, 603; III, 60, 191; IV, 663

Bouillet de La Chassaigne, Marie-Anne. *See* Le Moyne de Longueuil
Bouillon, Duc de. *See* La Marck
Bouin, Julien, I, 250
Bouin, Marguerite. *See* Berrin
Boujonnier, Florent, II, 83
Boulanger. *See* Le Boulanger
Boulanger, Bernard-Joseph, IV, 539
Boulay. *See* Boullet; Talon
Boulay, Marquise de. *See* Molé
Boulduc, Élisabeth. *See* Hubert
Boulduc, Gilette. *See* Pijart
Boulduc, Louis, II, **88–89**, xxiv, 213
Boulduc, Louise, II, 89
Boulduc, Pierre, II, 88
Bouler, Robert, II, **89–90**, 295
Boulic, Marie-Renée, *dite* de la Nativité, II, 303
Boullard, Étienne, II, **90–91**, 211, 587; III, 15, 45, 114, 201, 202, 240, 330, 522, 553, 646
Boullé, Eustache, I, **109–10**, 193, 195, 200, 311, 495, 509
Boullé, Hélène, *dite* de Saint-Augustin (Champlain), I, **110**, 109, 161, 190
Boullé, Marguerite. *See* Alix
Boullé, Nicolas, I, 109, 110
Boullet (Boulay), Captain, I, 110
Boullongne, Eustache de. *See* Quéan
Boullongne, Florentin de, I, 43, 110
Boullongne, Marie-Barbe de (Ailleboust de Coulonge et d'Argentenay), I, **110–11**, 43, 44, 47, 113, 204, 206, 217, 230, 412, 612; II, 605, 639; III, 548
Boullongne, Philippine-Gertrude de, *dite* de Saint-Dominique, I, 43, 44, 111, 217, 230
Boullot, Pierre, IV, 678
Boumois. *See* Gaultier
Bound, John, IV, 565
Bouquet, Henry, III, xxvi, 219, 529, 530; IV, 24, 25, 38, 85, 86, 297, 347, 408, 409
Bouquin, Claude, I, 361; II, 189
Bourassa, *dit* La Ronde, Agnès. *See* Gagné
Bourassa, *dit* La Ronde, Charlotte-Ambroisine (Mouet de Langlade), IV, 78, 563
Bourassa, *dit* La Ronde, François, IV, 77
Bourassa, *dit* La Ronde, Ignace, IV, 78
Bourassa, *dit* La Ronde, Marie. *See* Le Ber
Bourassa, *dit* La Ronde, Marie-Catherine. *See* Leriger de La Plante
Bourassa, *dit* La Ronde, René, III, 205; IV, **77–78**, 563
Bourassa, *dit* La Ronde, René (son), IV, 78
Bourbon. *See also* Condé
Bourbon, César de, Duc de Vendôme, I, 129, 434, 436, 514
Bourbon, Charles de, Cardinal de Bourbon, I, 87, 88, 89, 421
Bourbon, Charles de, Comte de Soissons, I, 186, 191, 294
Bourbon, François de, Duc de Beaufort, II, 98
Bourbon, François de, Duc de Montpensier, I, 421
Bourbon, Louis-Alexandre de, Comte de Toulouse, II, 273, 417, 425, 648; III, 74, 105, 106, 108, 118, 345
Bourbon, Louis-François de, Prince de Conti, IV, 477, 558
Bourbon, Louis-Jean-Marie de, Duc de Penthièvre, III, 108, 118
Bourbon, Louis-Joseph de, Prince de Condé, IV, 344, 481
Bourbon, Marie-Anselme de. *See* Abbadie de Saint-Castin
Bourbonnière. *See* Gaudry

Bourcier, Françoise (Chartier), I, 202
Bourdages, Esther. *See* Leblanc
Bourdages*, Louis (1764–1835), IV, 79
Bourdages, Marie-Anne. *See* Chevalier
Bourdages, Pierre, IV, 78
Bourdages, Raymond, IV, **78–79**
Bourdon, Anne. *See* Gasnier
Bourdon, Anne, *dite* de Sainte-Agnès, I, 112, 113, 430; II, **91–92**
Bourdon, Geneviève. *See* Amaugère
Bourdon, Geneviève, *dite* Marie de Saint-Joseph, I, 113; II, 92
Bourdon, Jacqueline. *See* Potel
Bourdon, Jacques, II, **92**
Bourdon, Jean, II, 92
Bourdon, Jean (known as M. de Saint-Jean or Sieur de Saint-François), I, **111–13**, 45, 49, 106, 114, 202, 204, 227, 339, 340, 344, 353, 359, 371, 372, 373, 389, 396, 397, 404, 430, 472, 480, 523, 538, 580, 584, 585, 587, 588, 589; II, xvii, 82, 91, 92, 137
Bourdon, Marguerite. *See* Legris
Bourdon, Marguerite, *dite* de Saint-Jean-Baptiste, I, 113; II, **92–93**, 613
Bourdon, Marie. *See* Ménard
Bourdon, Marie (Gloria), I, 339
Bourdon, Marie, *dite* de Sainte-Thérèse-de-Jésus, I, 113; II, 92
Bourdon, Nicolas, I, 114
Bourdon d'Autray, Jacques, I, **113–14**, 111, 178; II, 672
Bourdon de Dombourg, Jean-François, I, **114**, 112, 113; II, 176, 205, 347
Bourdon de Dombourg, Jean-François, III, 417, 425; IV, **79–80**
Bourdon de Dombourg, Jeanne. *See* Jannière
Bourdon de Dombourg, Marguerite. *See* Gautier
Bourdon de Dombourg et de La Pinaudière, Jean-François, IV, 79
Bourdon de Dombourg et de La Pinaudière, Madeleine. *See* Poirel
Bourdon de Romainville, Catherine, I, 114
Bourdon de Romainville, Jean, I, **114–15**, 257
Bourdon de Romainville, Madeleine. *See* Daguerre
Bourduceau, Anne-Françoise (Sailly), I, 592
Bourduceau, Médéric, I, 592
Bourg, Abraham, II, **93–94**, 23
Bourg, Anne. *See* Hébert
Bourg, Antoine, II, 93
Bourg, Antoinette. *See* Landry
Bourg, François, III, 83
Bourg, Joseph-Mathurin, IV, **80–82**, 13, 136, 153, 423, 436, 444, 469, 470, 511, 736
Bourg, Madeleine (Maisonnat; Le Blanc), II, 449; III, 421, 665
Bourg, Marguerite. *See* Boudrot
Bourg, Marguerite (Allain), III, 254
Bourg, Marie. *See* Brun
Bourg, Michel, IV, 80
Bourg, *dit* Belle-Humeur, Alexandre, II, 23; III, **83–84**, 366, 421, 427; IV, 80, 441
Bourg, *dit* Belle-Humeur, Anne (Leblanc, *dit* Le Maigre), III, 366; IV, 441
Bourg, *dit* Belle-Humeur, Marguerite. *See* Melanson, *dit* La Verdure

Bourgchemin. *See* Hamelin
Bourgeois, Anne. *See* Dugas
Bourgeois, Anne (Caissy), III, 426
Bourgeois, Charles, II, 94
Bourgeois, Germain, II, 94
Bourgeois, Guillaume, I, 67; II, 93, 94
Bourgeois, Jacques (father), II, 94
Bourgeois, Jacques (Jacob), I, 67, 510; II, **94**, 410, 449; IV, xx
Bourgeois, Jeanne. *See* Trahan
Bourgeois, Jeanne (Robichaux), IV, 676
Bourgeois, Madeleine. *See* Dugas
Bourgeois, Marguerite. *See* Belliveau
Bourgeois, Marguerite (Boudrot; Mirande; Maisonnat), II, 449
Bourgeois, Marianne. *See* Aprendestiguy
Bourgeois, Marie (Leblanc), III, 366; IV, 441
Bourgeois de Boynes, Pierre-Étienne, IV, 70
Bourgeoys, Abraham, I, 115
Bourgeoys, Anne, I, 115
Bourgeoys, Guillemette. *See* Garnier
Bourgeoys, Marguerite, *dite* du Saint-Sacrement, I, **115–19**, 31, 213, 220, 231, 344, 453, 486, 487, 564, 598; II, 44, 47, 132, 222, 233, 249, 376, 377, 601; III, 332, 385, 386, 407, 580, 629, 630; IV, 638
Bourget, Claude, II, 159
Bourget, Élisabeth (Jacquet), IV, 386
Bourget, Marie. *See* Couture
Bourgina, Hélène (Gaschet), III, 237
Bourgine, Hilaire, II, 11
Bourgmond. *See* Véniard
Bourgogne, Duc de. *See* Louis de France
Bourgonnière de Hauteville, Barthélemy-François, II, 116, 483
Bourguignon. *See* Janot
Bourgy, Léger, IV, 709
Bourgy, Marguerite. *See* Bougret Dufort
Bourjoly. *See* Besnard
Bourlamaque, François-Charles de, III, **84–87**, 12, 19, 243, 259, 459, 467, 535, 565, 591; IV, 23, 211, 347, 382, 427, 479, 588, 729
Bourlamaque, Jean-François de, III, 84
Bourlet, Nicolas, II, 33, 273, 464, 465, 508
Bourloton, Charlotte (Spagniolini), III, 598
Bourne*, George (1780–1845), III, 305
Bournicat, Marie (Degeay), IV, 200
Bouron, Henri, IV, 270
Bourond, Marie-Louise (Landriaux), IV, 434
Bourot, Françoise (Chaviteau; Jérémie, *dit* Lamontagne; Boucher de Boucherville et de Montarville), II, 296, 298
Boursier, Joseph, I, 461
Bourville. *See* Le Coutre
Boussat, Jean, I, 108
Boutet de Saint-Martin, Catherine. *See* Soulage
Boutet de Saint-Martin, Catherine (Phélippeaux; Soullard), II, 612
Boutet de Saint-Martin, Marie, I, 119
Boutet de Saint-Martin, Martin, I, **119**, 359; II, 17, 227, 228, 508, 612
Bouteville, Geneviève (Peuvret de Gaudarville), II, 525
Bouthier, François, IV, 653
Bouthier, Françoise. *See* Denys de La Ronde
Bouthier, Guillaume, II, 14

Boutilier, M., I, 503
Boutillac, Jean de, I, 424
Boutin, Charles-Robert, IV, 632
Boutin, Renée (Taschereau de Sapaillé), III, 616
Boutineau, Susannah (Francklin), IV, 272
Boutroue, Mlle de (daughter of CLAUDE), I, 322
Boutroue d'Aubigny, Claude de, I, **119–20**, 322, 326, 534, 571, 624; II, xix, 166
Boutroue d'Aubigny, Marie de. *See* Lescot
Bouvart, Martin (baptized Samuel), II, **94–95**, 245, 331, 332
Bouvier (Boyer) (trader), I, 382
Bouvier, Michel, I, 78; II, 105
Bouvot de Chevilly, François, I, 213
Bouvot de Chevilly, Jacqueline. *See* Chomedey
Bove, M., IV, 160
Boves, Charles de, I, 386, 417
Bowler. *See* Bouler
Bowman, James, IV, **82–83**, 511
Bowman, Whitney, IV, 82
Boy, Michel-Philibert, II, 190
Boyat, Jeanne-Marie (Le Roy), II, 424
Boyer. *See also* Bouvier
Boyer, Charles, IV, 262, 585
Boyer, Daniel, I, 193, 194, 291
Boyer, Marie (Gervaise), III, 257
Boyle, Henry, Earl of Shannon, II, 461
Boyle, John, IV, 267
Boyle, Robert, I, 385
Boyles, Hannah, IV, 778
Boynes. *See* Bourgeois
Boyrie, Marie (Madeleine) de (Dauger), II, 35
Boysdale. *See* MacDonald
Boyvinet, Gilles de, I, 468, 582; II, 193, 380
Braco, Baron. *See* Duff
Bradbury, Judith (Moody), III, 470
Braddock, Edward, II, 660; III, xvii, xxiv, xxv, 89, 149, 161, 185, 186, 214, 218, 219, 306, 320, 362, 378, 401, 496, 508, 526, 600; IV, 84, 207, 257, 278, 281, 302, 395, 408, 500, 552, 563, 668, 733
Bradford, William, I, 392
Bradley, Mary (Moor), III, 471
Bradley, Thomas, I, **120**, 150, 164, 641
Bradbury, Agathe. *See* Saint-Étienne de La Tour
Bradstreet, Edward, II, 590; IV, 83
Bradstreet, John (Jean-Baptiste), II, 590; III, xxv, xxviii, xxxviii, 10, 102, 373, 409, 495, 507, 530, 641, 652; IV, **83–87**, xix, 4, 117, 297, 347, 552, 587, 612, 670, 734, 762
Bradstreet, Mary. *See* Aldridge
Bradstreet, Simon (brother of JOHN), II, 590; IV, 83
Bradstreet, Simon (governor), II, 410
Bradt, Catalyntje, known as Catharine Bratt (Butler), IV, 117, 120
Bragelonne, Claude, II, 440
Bragg, Sir James, I, 605
Brainerd, David, III, 607
Brandeau, David, II, 95
Brandeau, Esther, II, **95–96**
Branquais, Jeanne (Quiniard), II, 534
Bransac (Branssat). *See* Migeon
Branscombe, William, IV, 712
Brant, Catharine. *See* Adonwentishon

Brant, Charlotte (Smith), IV, 416
Brant, Joseph. *See* Thayendanegea
Brant, Joseph, IV, 416
Brant, Mary (Molly). *See* Koñwatsiʔtsiaiéñni
Brant, Nicholas, IV, 692
Bras-de-fer de Chateaufort, Marc-Antoine, I, **120–21**, 127, 372, 454
Brasen, Christoph, IV, 334
Brassard, Dorothée (Ménage), II, 467
Brassard, Jean-Baptiste, IV, 87
Brassard, Louis-Marie, IV, **87**
Brassard, Marie-Françoise. *See* Huppé, *dit* Lagroix
Brassard Deschenaux, Charles, IV, 88
Brassard* Deschenaux, Charles-Joseph (1752–1832), IV, 89
Brassard Deschenaux, Joseph, IV, **87–89**, 69, 125
Brassard Deschenaux, Madeleine. *See* Vallée
Brassard Deschenaux, Marie-Joseph. *See* Hébert
Brassard* Deschenaux, Pierre-Louis (1759–1802), IV, 89
Brassard Deschenaux, Suzanne-Élisabeth. *See* Filion
Brasseuse. *See* Des Friches
Brassier, Gabriel-Jean, IV, **89–90**, 272, 544
Brassier, Jacques, I, 267
Bratt, Catharine. *See* Bradt, Catalyntje
Brault. *See* Bro
Braun, Antoine-Théodore, IV, 318
Bray, Margery (Pepperrell), II, 516; III, 505
Bréanainn. *See* Brendan
Bréard, Jacques, IV, 91
Bréard, Jacques-Michel, III, 124; IV, **90–92**, 66, 67, 128, 263, 264, 435, 474, 517, 614, 615, 750
Bréard*, Jean-Jacques (1751–1840), IV, 92
Bréard, Marcellin-Nicolas, IV, 91
Bréard, Marie. *See* Chasseriau
Bréard, Marie-Anne. *See* Marcellin
Breault. *See* Bro
Breaux, Marie (Brun), II, 93
Brébeuf, Georges de, I, 121
Brébeuf, Jean de, I, **121–26**, 9, 31, 60, 64, 73, 130, 203, 205, 206, 219, 247, 253, 281, 369, 388, 390, 411, 413, 414, 420, 458, 459, 460, 461, 483, 521, 522, 527, 549, 561, 562, 609, 610, 639, 661; II, 82
Brébeuf, Nicolas de, I, 121
Brebion, Charlotte (Besnard, *dit* Carignant), IV, 58
Brebner*, John Bartlet (1895–1957), IV, xvii, xxii, xxvi, 30, 199, 273, 450, 528, 562, 696
Breçon, M. de, III, 229
Bréhant, Mathurin de, I, 126
Bréhant de Galinée, René de, I, **126–27**, 35, 173, 174, 248, 393, 572, 625, 647; II, 191, 192, 517
Bréhaut Delisle, Achille (Antoine-Louis?) de, I, **127–28**, 121, 372, 446; II, xv
Brehm, Dietrich, IV, 39
Brekenmacher, François (baptized Jean-Melchior), I, 312
Brendan, Saint, I, **675**
Brenton*, James (1736–1806), IV, 111, 112, 581, 604, 696
Brenton, Mary (Gerrish), IV, 292
Brereton, John, I, 364
Breslay, René-Charles de, II, **96–97**, 23, 24, 46, 195, 524; III, 181, 517, 584
Brésoles. *See* Moreau
Bressani, François-Joseph, I, **128–29**, 59, 71, 124, 389, 549
Brethous, Jeanne. *See* Picot

Brethous, Léon, III, 157; IV, 245
Brétigny. See Poncet de La Rivière
Bretonvilliers. See Le Rageois
Brewse, John, IV, **92–93**, 559, 737
Brewse, Mary (Kesterman), IV, 93
Brewse, Mary (wife of JOHN), IV, 92
Breynton, Elizabeth (wife of JOHN), IV, 94
Breynton, John (father), IV, 93
Breynton, John, III, 133, 635, 651; IV, **93–94**, 29, 258, 292, 451, 625, 764, 775, 776
Breynton, Mary. See Cradock
Briand, Mlle, IV, 95
Briand, Catherine-Anne-Marie, IV, 95, 98, 102
Briand, François, IV, 95
Briand, Jean-Joseph, IV, 95
Briand, Jeanne. See Burel
Briand, Jeanne. See Desbois
Briand, Jean-Olivier, II, 200; III, 36, 193, 197, 199, 547, 549; IV, **94–103**, xlii, 6, 7, 8, 9, 41, 42, 43, 49, 80, 81, 109, 134, 135, 141, 142, 188, 189, 201, 205, 270, 271, 286, 287, 296, 298, 299, 305, 370, 371, 372, 373, 388, 423, 425, 430, 469, 497, 509, 510, 511, 543, 544, 549, 571, 572, 639, 642, 686, 720, 752, 753, 779, 788, 789, 798
Briand, Yves, IV, 95
Briant, Marie (Normandin), II, 499
Briault, Antoine, IV, 265
Bricault de Valmur, Louis-Frédéric, II, **97**, 447, 530; III, 146, 153; IV, 284, 356
Brice, Mme de, I, **129**, 380, 434, 514
Brice de Sainte-Croix, M. de, I, 129, 434, 514
Brickwood, John, IV, 403
Briderie. See Romanet
Bridgar, John, I, **129–30**, 39, 56, 83, 227, 337, 338, 518, 528, 601, 696; II, 247, 391, 538
Bridge, Thomas, IV, 696
Bridges, Timothy, II, **97–98**, 293, 438, 486, 487
Bridgewater, Earl of. See Egerton
Bridou, Marie (Noyelles), III, 491
Brienne, Henri de, Comte de Conflans, III, 556
Briet, Louise (La Bazanière), II, 424
Brigeac, Claude de, I, **130**, 274, 662; II, 164
Briggs, Henry, I, 311, 312
Brijat. See Brigeac
Brimner, Jane (Knaut; Bolman), IV, 414
Brinon, Marie de (Chauvin de Tonnetuit), I, 209
Brisac. See Brigeac
Brisacier, Jacques de, II, 248
Brisay, François de, II, 98
Brisay, Marie de. See Hémard
Brisay de Denonville, Catherine de, Marquise de Denonville. See Courtin de Tangeux
Brisay de Denonville, Jacqueline de. See Orléans
Brisay de Denonville, Jacques de, II, 98
Brisay de Denonville, Jacques-René de, Marquis de Denonville, I, 56, 103, 109, 112, 114, 119, 137, 138, 204, 239, 295, 308, 320, 327, 397, 446, 463, 465, 488, 523, 526, 528, 537, 572, 582, 650, 653, 664; II, **98–105**, xxxi, 6, 13, 15, 32, 49, 57, 60, 62, 63, 69, 72, 73, 86, 88, 89, 113, 124, 137, 148, 162, 168, 169, 182, 185, 186, 195, 202, 213, 214, 218, 228, 229, 237, 252, 254, 261, 263, 269, 270, 282, 284, 295, 302, 303, 304, 321, 341, 343, 344, 345, 371, 380, 385, 386, 391, 401, 403, 406, 410, 440,

472, 473, 478, 488, 491, 518, 532, 533, 539, 566, 576, 583, 586, 592, 594, 620, 635, 636, 643; III, 65, 82, 109, 373, 548
Brisay de Denonville, Louise de. See Alès de Corbet
Brisay de Denonville, Pierre de, II, 98
Brisay de Denonville, Pierre de, Vicomte de Montbazillac, II, 98
Brisay d'Huillé, Charles de, II, 98
Brison. See Roquemont
Brisset, Gervais, III, 173
Bro*, Jean-Baptiste (1743–1824), IV, 80
Brochet, Le. See Kinongé
Brodhead, Daniel, IV, 410
Brompton, Richard, IV, 702
Brooke, Frances. See Moore
Brooke, John, III, 296; IV, **103–5**, 399, 553, 554, 555, 753
Brooke, Sir John, I, 311
Brooke, John Moore, IV, 555
Brookes, Elizabeth. See Lawrear
Brossard, Agnès. See Tibaudeau
Brossard, Alexandre, III, 87
Brossard, Catherine. See Richard
Brossard, Catherine (Sareau), II, 105
Brossard, Jean-François, II, **105**; III, 87
Brossard, Madeleine (Campot), II, 105
Brossard, Marguerite. See Tibaudeau
Brossard, Mathurin, II, 105
Brossard, Michelle. See Bidaut
Brossard, Pierre, II, 105
Brossard, Urbain, I, 78; II, **105–6**
Brossard, Urbaine. See Hodiau
Brossard, dit Beausoleil, Agnès. See Thibodeau
Brossard, dit Beausoleil, Alexandre, II, 105
Brossard, dit Beausoleil, Joseph, II, 105; III, **87–88**; IV, xxv, 541
Brosseau, Pierre, II, 521
Brouague. See Martel
Broudou, Louise-Éléonore (Galaup, Comtesse de Lapérouse), IV, 282
Brouet, Ambroise, I, 461
Brouilhet. See Drouilhet
Brouillan. See Monbeton
Brouillan, Isabeau de, II, 478
Browallius, Johan, IV, 406
Brower, Mary (Munro), IV, 566
Brown*, Andrew (d. 1833 or 1834), IV, xxx, 560
Brown, Arthur, IV, 570
Brown, Isabel (Neilson), IV, 580
Brown, John (father of WILLIAM), IV, 105
Brown, John (officer), IV, 675
Brown, Mary. See Clark
Brown, William, IV, **105–7**, 184, 186, 295, 392, 393, 423, 424, 533, 534, 557, 580, 689
Browne, Elizabeth (Rogers), IV, 679
Browne, Maurice, I, 229, 334, 531, 532
Browne (Brownel), Oliver. See Brunel
Browne, Richard, I, 380
Broyeux. See Desbrieux
Bruce. See also Brewse
Bruce, Mr (father of ROBERT GEORGE), IV, 107
Bruce, Elizabeth (Beatson), IV, 48
Bruce, Margaret. See Hay
Bruce, Robert George, IV, **107–8**

Bruce, William, III, 452
Brucy. *See* La Frenaye
Brulart de Sillery, Madeleine (Faure), I, 484
Brulart de Sillery, Marie-Louise. *See* Bigot
Brulart de Sillery, Nicolas, I, 484
Brulart de Sillery, Noël, I, 263, 470, 484, 516, 565
Brûlé, Étienne, I, **130–33**, 16, 59, 190, 191, 192, 196, 381, 493, 494, 516, 590, 603, 639; II, xl
Brun, Marie. *See* Breaux
Brun, Marie (Bourg), II, 93
Brun, Vincent, II, 93
Brunel (Brownel, Browne), Olivier (Oliver), I, 408
Brunet (Brunnet), Jean-Jacques, IV, 136
Brunet, Mathieu, II, 63
Brunet (Brunel), *dit* La Sablonnière, Jean (father), III, 88
Brunet, *dit* La Sablonnière, Jean, III, **88**
Brunet, *dit* La Sablonnière, Louise. *See* Maugue
Brunet, *dit* La Sablonnière, Marie-Madeleine. *See* Richaume
Brunswick, Duke of. *See* Charles William Ferdinand
Bruslart, Louis-Philogène, Marquis de Puysieux, IV, 401
Bruslé, Michel, II, **106**
Bruslon. *See* Gaultier
Bruyas, Jacques, I, 321, 635, 651; II, **106–8**, 20, 114, 126, 237, 341, 404, 410, 621, 631; III, 335, 337
Bruyères, Anne-Françoise (Pothier), IV, 109
Bruyères, Catherine-Élisabeth. *See* Pommereau
Bruyères, Janet. *See* Dunbar
Bruyères, Jeanne-Marie-Catherine (Kennelly; O'Sullivan), IV, 109
Bruyères, John, III, 525; IV, **108–9**, 316, 447
Bruyères, Marguerite (Burton), IV, 109
Bruyères*, Ralph Henry (d. 1814), IV, 109
Bry, Catherine (Pennisseaut), IV, 621
Brymer, Alexander, IV, 111
Brymer, William, III, 37, 38; IV, 194, 195, 599
Brymner*, Douglas (1823–1902), III, 695; IV, 232, 502
Bryzelius, Paulus, III, 474
Buache de La Neuville, Philippe, I, 676, 677
Buade, Anne de, Comtesse de Frontenac et de Palluau. *See* La Grange
Buade, Anne de, Comtesse de Frontenac et de Palluau. *See* Phélypeaux de Pontchartrain
Buade, Antoine de, I, 134
Buade, François-Louis de, I, 134, 142; II, 259
Buade, Henri de, Comte de Frontenac et de Palluau, I, 133, 134
Buade, Louis de, Comte de Frontenac et de Palluau, I, **133–42**, 32, 35, 40, 47, 49, 83, 84, 102, 104, 105, 106, 109, 174, 175, 177, 178, 185, 201, 204, 226, 238, 239, 245, 250, 286, 287, 288, 289, 290, 291, 295, 297, 309, 320, 323, 326, 327, 340, 361, 398, 399, 400, 402, 410, 417, 420, 439, 440, 443, 444, 448, 464, 466, 488, 489, 498, 499, 502, 528, 534, 535, 539, 540, 541, 544, 545, 565, 572, 573, 575, 576, 578, 581, 582, 583, 584, 585, 599, 600, 602, 613, 620, 622, 627, 632, 634, 650; II, xix, xxxi, 5, 6, 11, 12, 13, 15, 16, 17, 29, 31, 34, 36, 47, 48, 57, 59, 60, 61, 68, 70, 72, 73, 74, 75, 76, 77, 78, 80, 88, 89, 99, 103, 107, 113, 114, 118, 119, 120, 137, 142, 144, 148, 149, 153, 155, 162, 168, 169, 170, 172, 175, 178, 183, 184, 185, 186, 190, 193, 194, 202, 203, 205, 222, 224, 228, 229, 230, 242, 243, 248, 249, 253, 255, 258, 259, 262, 263, 264, 269, 276, 282, 283, 286, 295, 302, 303, 317, 320, 321, 322, 326, 327, 330, 335, 338, 343, 344, 345, 346, 350, 352, 353, 354, 369, 370, 375, 380, 383, 385, 386, 392, 393, 398, 401, 403, 404, 408, 409, 410, 412, 416, 418, 419, 420, 421, 425, 426, 427, 432, 441, 442, 446, 449, 450, 451, 456, 458, 459, 464, 470, 474, 483, 488, 491, 501, 504, 505, 507, 513, 514, 517, 518, 519, 523, 524, 525, 526, 532, 538, 540, 542, 545, 561, 566, 567, 573, 576, 578, 579, 580, 582, 585, 586, 588, 591, 592, 593, 594, 601, 602, 603, 618, 620, 621, 626, 631, 635, 654, 672; III, 7, 22, 44, 82, 83, 190, 233, 247, 308, 311, 344, 373, 446, 505, 578, 587; IV, xvii, 655
Bucareli y Ursúa, Antonio Maria, IV, 165, 622, 623
Buchanan, George, I, 50
Buchanan, Thomas, I, 50
Buck. *See also* Burch
Buck, Miss (Saunders, Lady Saunders), IV, 699
Buck, James, IV, 699
Buckingham, Duke of. *See* Villiers
Buckton, C., IV, 613
Budai Parmenius István. *See* Parmenius
Buday Fleury, Charlotte de (Loustelneau), II, 179
Budemon. *See* Derivon
Bueil, Honorat de, I, 421
Buffon, Comte de. *See* Leclerc
Bugaret, Catherine (La Tourasse), I, 427
Bugaret, Catherine (Petitpas), II, 524
Buhl, Anna Maria (Ermatinger), IV, 262
Buil, Friar, I, 150
Buirette, Marguerite (Boucault), III, 74
Buisset, Luc, I, 438, 501; II, 278, 421
Buisson, Gervais, II, 108
Buisson, Marie. *See* Lereau
Buisson, Paul, I, 352
Buisson, *dit* Saint-Cosme, Michel, II, 109
Buisson, *dit* Saint-Cosme, Suzanne. *See* Delicérasse
Buisson de Saint-Cosme, Jean-François (d. 1712), II, **108–9**, 240
Buisson de Saint-Cosme, Jean-François (1667–1706), II, **109–10**, 55, 108, 171; III, 469, 522
Buisson de Saint-Cosme, Marie-Françoise, *dite* de Saint-Pierre, II, 109
Buisson de Saint-Cosme, Michel, II, 55, 108, 109
Bujeau, Amand, III, 427
Bulkeley, Elizabeth, Lady Bulkeley. *See* Freke
Bulkeley, James Michael Freke, IV, 111, 112
Bulkeley, John, IV, 111
Bulkeley, Sir Lawrence, IV, 109
Bulkeley, Mary. *See* Burgess
Bulkeley, Mary. *See* Rous
Bulkeley, Richard, III, 91, 365, 573; IV, **109–13**, 258, 342, 703
Buller, Rebecca (Watson), III, 659
Bullingbrooke, Edward, IV, 50
Bullion, Angélique de. *See* Faure de Berlise
Bullion, Claude de, I, 484
Bulteau, Guillaume, II, **110–11**
Bunt. *See* Hotsinoñhyahta?
Bunyan, John, I, 378
Burbidge, Rebecca. *See* Dudley
Burch, John, IV, **113**
Burch, Martha (Ramsey; wife of JOHN), IV, 113
Burchett, Elizabeth (Hardy, Lady Hardy), IV, 326

Burchett, Josiah, II, 661
Burel, Gilbert, I, 121
Burel, Jacquette. *See* Quémar
Burel, Jeanne (Briand), IV, 95
Burel, Mathurin, IV, 95
Burgess, Mary (Bulkeley), IV, 110
Burghley, Baron. *See* Cecil
Burgoyne, Anna Maria. *See* Burnestone
Burgoyne, Lady Charlotte. *See* Stanley
Burgoyne, John (father), IV, 113
Burgoyne, John, IV, **113–15**, 3, 118, 121, 130, 155, 375, 395, 403, 427, 428, 442, 503, 549, 564, 603, 694, 771, 792
Burke, Edmund, IV, 90, 335, 413, 701
Burke*, Edmund (1753–1820), IV, 43, 445
Burke, John, IV, 415
Burnaby, Andrew, III, 587
Burnestone, Anna Maria (Burgoyne), IV, 113
Burnet, William, II, 87, 209, 572, 603, 625; III, 43
Burney, Frances (Arblay), IV, 555, 763
Burpee*, Lawrence Johnston (1873–1946), IV, 555
Burrow, James, IV, 389
Burt*, Alfred Leroy (1888–1970), IV, 279, 321, 336, 350
Burton. *See also* Christie
Burton, Clarence Monroe, III, 706; IV, 817
Burton, Margaret, III, 90
Burton, Marguerite. *See* Bruyères
Burton, Ralph, III, **88–90**, 525, 541, 669; IV, xxxiii, xxxv, 85, 108, 109, 188, 279, 290, 300, 316, 331, 369, 379, 491, 570, 572, 685, 787, 793, 794
Burton, Robert, III, 89
Burwash*, Nathanael (1839–1918), IV, 495
Bury (Burry), Anne de (Talon), I, 614
Busby, Thomas, IV, **115–16**
Busby*, Thomas (1768–1836), IV, 116
Bushel, John, III, 90
Bushel, Rebecca. *See* Parker
Bushell, Elizabeth. *See* Strowbridge
Bushell, John, III, **90–91**, 267, 404; IV, 342, 343
Bute, Earl of. *See* Stuart
Buteux, Jacques, I, **142–43**, 106, 214, 287, 341, 432, 453, 481, 549, 551, 558, 566, 640; II, 158
Buteux, Jean, I, 142
Butler, Andrew, IV, 119
Butler, Catalyntje. *See* Bradt
Butler, Lady Charlotte (Cornwallis, Baroness Cornwallis), IV, 168
Butler, Deborah. *See* Dennison
Butler, Jean, III, 58, 59, 60, 228
Butler, John (bishop), IV, 511
Butler, John (d. 1791), IV, **116–17**, 53, 111, 131, 199, 266, 273, 275, 450, 526, 527, 528, 529, 696
Butler, John (d. 1796), IV, **117–20**, 113, 121, 155, 394, 405, 417, 731, 735
Butler, John Butler. *See* Dight
Butler, Rachel (Wall; wife of JOHN, d. 1791), IV, 116
Butler, Richard, 1st Earl of Arran, IV, 168
Butler, Robert, II, 520
Butler, Thomas, IV, 117
Butler, Walter (grandfather), IV, 117
Butler, Walter, IV, **120–21**, 117, 118, 683
Buttar, William, IV, 384
Butterworth, Mary (Haven), IV, 333

Button, Barbara. *See* Merrick
Button, Margaret. *See* Lewis
Button, Mary. *See* Rice
Button, Miles (grandfather), I, 144
Button, Miles, I, 144
Button, Thomas, II, 123
Button, Sir Thomas, I, **144–45**, 20, 74, 312, 329, 362, 378, 515
Butts, Robert, III, 634
Butts, Thomas, I, 371
Bylot, Robert, I, **145**, 20, 74, 75, 144, 329, 374, 376, 377, 378
Byng, George, 1st Viscount Torrington, II, 316, 609; III, 91, 496
Byng, John, III, **91–92**, 31, 70, 209, 293, 496, 629; IV, 171
Byng, Margaret, Viscountess Torrington. *See* Masters
Byng, Sarah (Osborn), III, 496
Byrne. *See* Bierne
Byrne, William, IV, 763
Byron, Frances, Baroness Byron. *See* Berkeley
Byron, George Gordon, 6th Baron Byron, IV, 122
Byron, John, III, xxv, 132; IV, **121–23**, 28, 80, 155, 158, 176, 195, 282, 600, 707
Byron, John (son), IV, 122
Byron, Sophia. *See* Trevannion
Byron, William, 4th Baron Byron, IV, 121
Byrsarius, Torquatus, II, 98
Byssot. *See also* Bissot
Byssot de La Rivière, François, I, **145–46**, 395, 447, 480, 620, 622; II, 65, 68, 158, 159, 256; IV, 182
Byssot de La Rivière, Marie. *See* Couillard
Byssot Du Hommée, Jean, I, 145
Byssot Du Hommée, Marie. *See* Assour

CABANAC. *See* Desjordy
Cabarrus, Dominique, IV, 421
Cabart de Villermont, Esprit de, II, 62, 589, 633
Cabazié, Delphine. *See* Desbordes
Cabazié, Jeanne. *See* Guiberge
Cabazié, Pierre (father), II, 111
Cabazié, Pierre, II, **111**
Cabot, Catalina. *See* Medrano
Cabot, Elizabeth, I, 158
Cabot, John, I, **146–52**, 19, 21, 22, 41, 120, 153, 154, 164, 166, 171, 234, 240, 304, 316, 333, 386, 641, 643
Cabot, Juana (Joanna), I, 158
Cabot, Lewis (Ludovico), I, 147
Cabot, Sancio, I, 147
Cabot, Sebastian, I, **152–58**, 19, 21, 146, 147, 148, 149, 151, 316, 375, 378, 565, 643
Caboto, Giulio, I, 146
Caboto, Mattea, I, 146
Caboto, Piero, I, 146
Cabrara, Father, III, 204
Caché, Marguerite (Perrault), III, 509
Cachointioni. *See* Kakȣenthiony
Cachupín. *See* Vélez
Cadart, Nicolas, II, 244
Cadet, Angélique. *See* Fortier
Cadet, Angélique (Rossay), IV, 124
Cadet, Augustin, III, 571; IV, 123
Cadet, Françoise (Esprit de Vantelon), IV, 124
Cadet (Caddé), François-Joseph, IV, 123

Cadet, Joseph, III, 156
Cadet, Joseph-Michel, III, 19, 76, 124, 141, 321, 322, 435,
    441, 477, 510, 537; IV, **123–28**, 5, 64, 66, 67, 69, 88, 92,
    263, 312, 378, 433, 435, 461, 572, 612, 615, 621, 632,
    660
Cadet, Louise (Rouffio), III, 571, 572; IV, 123
Cadet, Marie-Anne (Amiot), III, 13; IV, 123
Cadet, Marie-Joseph. *See* Daveine
Cadet, Marie-Joseph (Vignau), IV, 123
Cadet, Michel, III, 569
Cadet, Michel-François, IV, 123
Cadet Deschamps, Joseph, IV, 124
Cadieu, Charles, I, 585
Cadieu de Courville, Charles, II, 30
Cadillac. *See* Laumet
Cadogan, Sir William, II, 513
Cadot*, Jean-Baptiste (b. 1723, d. in or after 1803), IV, 675
Cadsedan-hiunt. *See* Kaghswaghtaniunt
Caën, Emery de, I, **159**, 30, 58, 160, 161, 194, 195, 197,
    211, 266, 296, 297, 405, 407, 411, 419, 441, 473, 479,
    533, 546
Caën, Ézéchiel de, I, 159, 160
Caën, Guillaume de (father), I, 159, 419
Caën, Guillaume de, I, **159–62**, 30, 110, 194, 247, 266,
    346, 368, 411, 419, 433, 473, 521
Caën, Hélène de, I, 161
Caën, Marie de. *See* Langlois
Caën, Marie de. *See* Sores
Caën, Marie de, I, 161
Caën, Suzanne de. *See* Petit
Caesar, Julius, I, 89
Caffin. *See* Galiffet
Cagenquarichten, II, **111–12**, xxxix; III, xl
Caghswoughtiooni. *See* Kak8enthiony
Cahideuc, Emmanuel-Auguste de, Comte Dubois de La
    Motte, III, **92–93**, 55, 70, 72, 358; IV, 282, 327, 699
Cahideuc, Gilonne-Charlotte de, Comtesse Dubois de La
    Motte. *See* Langan
Cahideuc, Jean-François de, Comte Dubois de La Motte,
    III, 92
Cahideuc, Jeanne-Françoise de, Comtesse Dubois de La
    Motte. *See* Andigné de La Chaise
Cahouet, Marie-Anne. *See* Maisonnat, *dit* Baptiste
Cailhault de La Tesserie, Éléonore de. *See* Grandmaison
Cailhault de La Tesserie, Jacques de, I, 285, 344, 345, 537,
    589; II, 61
Cailhe (Caille), Michel, II, 129, 143, 196
Caillé, Jean, II, 467
Cailleteau, Françoise (Denys de Fronsac; Rey Gaillard),
    I, 260; II, 106
Cailleteau, Marie-Anne (Bermen de La Martinière), II, 57;
    III, 64
Cailleux, Françoise de (Dollier de Casson), II, 190
Cailly, Anne-Marie. *See* Volant
Cailly, François-Joseph, II, 424; III, **93–94**, 392
Cailly, Jean-Christophore, III, 93
Cailly, Marie-Salomé. *See* Duvallier
Cair, John, I, 150
Cairns, Catherine (Cuthbert), IV, 190
Caissy, Anne. *See* Bourgeois
Caissy (Keissis), Marguerite (Mangeant), III, 426
Caissy, *dit* Roger, Jean, III, 426

Calanne, M. de, IV, 669
Caldwell*, Henry (1738–1810), IV, 146, 150, 493, 538,
    548, 554, 753
Calignon, Jeanne de (Saint-Ours), II, 592
Callbeck, Ann. *See* Coffin
Callbeck, Phillips, IV, **128–29**, 353, 608, 609, 610, 708
Callendar, Alexander, III, 634
Callet, Donat-Nicolas, III, 94
Callet, Luc (baptized Léonard-Philibert), III, **94–95**
Callicum, IV, 568
Callière, Louis-Hector de, I, 103, 138, 139, 140, 204, 540,
    541, 581, 583, 634; II, **112–17**, xxi, xxx, xxxi, 15, 16,
    17, 20, 53, 70, 74, 77, 79, 80, 87, 102, 103, 108, 110,
    119, 130, 133, 140, 143, 144, 148, 155, 156, 162, 168,
    175, 180, 186, 218, 220, 237, 300, 322, 323, 330, 336,
    338, 346, 353, 354, 383, 386, 387, 402, 404, 410, 411,
    416, 423, 428, 433, 446, 450, 451, 456, 459, 466, 474,
    483, 499, 500, 502, 504, 505, 507, 519, 527, 532, 533,
    566, 567, 573, 580, 587, 593, 598, 603, 618, 621, 631,
    642, 665; III, xxxv, 53, 147, 310, 433, 611; IV, liii, 662
Callières, François de, II, 112, 114, 116, 567
Callières, Jacques de, II, 112
Callières, Jehan de, II, 112
Callières, Madeleine de. *See* Potier de Courcy
Callières, Perrette de. *See* Du Fort
Calmonotius. *See* Chaumonot
Calquieres, Marie (Dumas), IV, 243
Calvarin, Goulven, II, **117**, 628; III, 442, 443, 640
Calvert, Alice. *See* Crosland
Calvert, Anne, Baroness Baltimore. *See* Mynne
Calvert, Cecil, 2nd Baron Baltimore, I, 163, 369, 406;
    II, 580
Calvert, Frederick, 7th Baron Baltimore, IV, 84
Calvert, George, 1st Baron Baltimore, I, **162–63**, 23, 365,
    369, 405, 406, 419, 522, 567, 614, 653, 655, 672
Calvert, Jane, Baroness Baltimore (wife of GEORGE), I, 162
Calvert, Leonard (grandfather), I, 162
Calvert, Leonard, I, 163
Calvet, Pierre, IV, 227
Calvonotti. *See* Chaumonot
Camagne, Benoîte (Malepart de Beaucourt; Franchère),
    IV, 507
Camagne, Joseph-Gaëtan, IV, 507
Camanne, Charles-Étienne, III, 420
Camaret, Marie, I, 197
Cambridge, Earl of. *See* Hamilton
Cambridge*, John (1748–1831), IV, 152, 609
Camden, Earl of. *See* Pratt
Camelford. *See* Pitt
Camerlique, II, 7, 8, 9
Cameron, Duncan (?), IV, 727
Camoin, Élisabeth-Charlotte (Forestier), III, 220
Campagna, Charles, III, 292
Campagna, Marguerite. *See* Lareau
Campagna, Simon, III, 559
Campan, Gabriel, I, 213
Campau. *See* Campot
Campbell, Agathe. *See* Saint-Étienne de La Tour
Campbell, Alexander, III, 590
Campbell, Archibald, 7th Earl of Argyll, I, 50
Campbell, Colin (fl. 1699–1710), II, **117–18**, 165, 293,
    351, 583

Campbell*, Colin (d. before 1805), IV, 769
Campbell, Donald, III, **95–96**, 167, 258, 320, 526, 528; IV, 761
Campbell*, Duncan (d. 1886), III, 439
Campbell, Hugh, II, 590
Campbell, James, II, 117, 118, 316; III, 618
Campbell, Sir James, III, 218
Campbell, John (general), IV, 707
Campbell, John (governor), IV, 159, 260, 402
Campbell, John, IV, **129–31**, 117, 149, 150, 155, 294, 394, 427, 547, 612, 634, 759
Campbell, John, 2nd Duke of Argyll, II, 250
Campbell, John, 4th Duke of Argyll, IV, 131, 571
Campbell, John, 5th Duke of Argyll, IV, 130
Campbell, John, 4th Earl of Loudoun, III, xxv, xxvi, xxix, 72, 89, 218, 283, 295, 364, 460, 573, 586; IV, 3, 4, 21, 57, 84, 85, 115, 278, 282, 297, 308, 314, 326, 335, 396, 415, 478, 487, 552, 772, 775
Campbell*, John Douglas Sutherland, Marquess of Lorne, 9th Duke of Argyll (1845–1914), III, 722
Campbell, Marie-Anne. See La Corne
Campbell, Mary, Duchess of Argyll. See Bellenden
Campbell, Mary (Maclean), IV, 503
Campbell, Robert, IV, 607
Campbell, Sarah. See Izard
Campbell, William, IV, 626
Campbell, Lord William, IV, **131–32**, 41, 110, 116, 266, 274, 313, 450, 528, 561, 596, 737
Campion, Étienne-Charles, IV, **132–33**, 233
Campion, Madeleine. See Gautier
Campion, Marie-Josephte. See Maillet
Campion, dit Labonté, Charlotte. See Pepin
Campion, dit Labonté, Étienne, IV, 132
Campot, Catherine. See Paulo
Campot, Étienne, II, 105, 106; III, 96
Campot, François, II, 106
Campot, Jacques, III, **96**
Campot, Jeanne-Cécile. See Catin
Campot, Madeleine. See Brossard
Camus (Le Camus), Claude (Charron de La Barre), I, 200, 201; II, 132
Canaghquiesa (Kanaghgwasea), IV, 691
Canchy de Lerole, Louis de, I, 40, 308; II, 61
Cangé (Canger). See Conigan
Cannard. See Renaud
Cannehoot (Cannehouet). See Tekanoet
Cannon (Canon). See Kanon
Canot, Claude-Joseph-Marie, II, 531
Cantino, Alberto, I, 235
Capdeviolle, Marie de (Catalougne), II, 120
Capeau, Antoinette (Mesplet), IV, 532
Capel, Antoine, IV, 5
Capelli, Fiametta (da Verrazzano), I, 657
Capitanal, I, **163–64**
Capon, Peter, II, 123
Captain Jecob. See Winninnewaycappo
Captain John. See Deserontyon
Captain John. See Nagiscoig
Captain Joseph. See Wowurna
Captain Louis. See Wahawanulet
Captain Pipe. See Konieschguanokee
Captain Swan. See Swan

Caradec, Zacharie, IV, 466
Carbery, Earl of. See Vaughan
Carbonariis, Giovanni Antonio de, I, **164**, 150
Carbonnel, Jean, IV, 125
Carcy. See Pagé
Cardenat, M. de, I, 359
Cardeneau, Bernard, III, **96–97**
Cardeneau, Marie-Anne. See Guérin
Cardin, Marguerite (Chastelain), III, 8, 430
Cardin, Maurice, I, 553
Cardinal, Pierre, IV, 591
Carheil, Étienne de, I, 322, 331; II, **118–19**, 237, 353, 453, 501; III, 355, 446
Carignant. See Besnard
Carigouan, I, **164–65**, 6, 533
Carion. See also Dufresnoy
Carion, M. de, I, 600
Carle, Anne (Clinton), III, 126
Carleill, Christopher, I, 333, 336, 363, 364
Carlet de la Rozière, Marie-Claude (Potot de Montbeillard), IV, 641
Carleton*, Guy, 1st Baron Dorchester (1724–1808), II, 69; III, 102, 154, 172, 478, 541, 609, 669, 670; IV, xxxvii, xxxviii, xli, xlii, xliii, xliv, xlv, xlvi, xlvii, xlviii, 6, 12, 25, 37, 41, 42, 50, 58, 72, 80, 82, 86, 98, 101, 102, 104, 106, 107, 114, 117, 118, 120, 130, 131, 135, 138, 139, 144, 146, 147, 149, 150, 154, 155, 162, 171, 179, 183, 184, 185, 188, 190, 198, 201, 202, 215, 228, 229, 231, 233, 234, 269, 271, 276, 281, 282, 298, 299, 304, 320, 321, 324, 327, 328, 330, 344, 345, 346, 347, 349, 350, 367, 371, 372, 373, 374, 375, 379, 380, 388, 399, 400, 415, 427, 428, 432, 436, 442, 445, 477, 484, 485, 491, 492, 493, 503, 510, 513, 530, 538, 544, 546, 547, 548, 549, 550, 556, 564, 570, 573, 577, 579, 592, 602, 604, 618, 619, 634, 635, 643, 697, 698, 715, 716, 717, 725, 729, 738, 739, 752, 753, 759, 787, 788, 790, 791, 793, 794
Carleton*, Thomas (d. 1817), IV, 136, 150, 211, 229, 328, 436, 483, 603, 627
Carli, Bernardo, I, 658, 659
Carlié, Marie (Fézeret), II, 221
Carlier, Anne (Du Saussay de Bémont), I, 583
Carlton, Jane (Cochin), IV, 156
Caro, Gregorio, I, 156
Caron*, Alexis (1764–1827), IV, 502
Caron, Antoinette (Du Bos), I, 286
Caron, François (habitant), III, 227
Caron, François (surgeon's aid), I, 109
Caron, Marguerite (Maillou, dit Desmoulins), III, 346, 420
Caron, Marie. See Crevet
Caron, Nicolas, III, 429
Caron, Nicolas-François, known as Brother Pacifique, III, 292
Caron, Robert, I, 417
Caron, Vital, III, 429
Carpentier, Bonaventure (baptized Étienne), IV, **133–34**
Carpentier, Étienne, IV, 133
Carpentier, Jeanne. See Toussaint
Carpentier, Marie-Charlotte. See Blanchon
Carre, Jane (Knox), IV, 416
Carré de Luzançay, Nicolas-Philippe, II, 596
Carrel, Louis, II, 29

Carrerot, André (Andres), II, 119; III, **97–98**, 76, 173, 389; IV, 247, 249, 252, 305, 420, 558, 644, 645

Carrerot, Angélique (Allard de Sainte-Marie), IV, 14

Carrerot, Barbe-Blanche (Du Pont Duchambon Dumaine), IV, 249

Carrerot, Françoise-Ovide (Delort), II, 119; III, 173

Carrerot, Louise (Godefroy de Tonnancour), IV, 303, 305

Carrerot, Marguerite-Thérèse (Prevost de La Croix), IV, 644

Carrerot, Marie. *See* Picq

Carrerot, Marie-Anne (La Salle de Sertrouville), II, 119; III, 235

Carrerot, Marie-Josephte. *See* Chéron

Carrerot, Marie-Thérèse. *See* Gaultier

Carrerot, Philippe, II, 119; III, **98**, 76, 97, 172, 389; IV, 14, 60

Carrerot, Pierre, II, **119–20**; III, 97, 98, 173, 387

Carrignan. *See* Bénard

Carroll, Charles, IV, 270, 549, 759

Carroll, John, IV, 270, 371, 445

Carruthers, John, II, 319

Carter, Robert, IV, 784

Carteret, John, 2nd Baron Carteret, 1st Earl Granville, III, 283, 405

Cartier, Angélique. *See* Sarasin Depelteau

Cartier, Bonaventure, III, 134

Cartier, Catherine. *See* Des Granches

Cartier*, Sir George-Étienne (1814–73), IV, 403

Cartier, Jacques (1491–1557), I, **165–72**, 7, 11, 19, 21, 22, 27, 188, 191, 275, 276, 301, 371, 372, 384, 409, 423, 424, 426, 432, 469, 500, 520, 553, 557, 612, 659, 680; II, xxxi, 8; III, xxxv, 99, 248

Cartier*, Jacques (1750–1814), IV, 403

Cartier, Jeanne (Noël), I, 520

Cartier, Joseph, III, 250

Cartier, Marie-Régis (Levasseur, *dit* Delor), IV, 475

Cartier, René (navigator), IV, 475

Cartier, René (seigneur), IV, 326, 709

Cartier, Toussaint, known as 'the hermit of Saint-Barnabé,' III, **98–99**, 572

Cartland, Elizabeth. *See* Denson

Cartland, George, IV, 208

Cartwright*, George (1739–1819), III, 411; IV, 158, 159, 195, 600, 712

Cartwright, Sir George, I, 226, 337

Cartwright, John (clergyman), I, 667

Cartwright, John (reformer), IV, 413, 600

Cartwright, Richard, IV, 120

Cartwright*, Richard (1759–1815), IV, 494, 495, 777

Carundawana, III, 147

Carver, Jonathan, III, 452; IV, 681

Cary, Elizabeth (Amherst, Baroness Amherst), IV, 26

Cary, George, IV, 26

Cary, Henry, 1st Viscount Falkland, I, 365, 632, 655, 669

Cary*, Thomas (1751–1823), IV, 106, 107

Casgrain*, Henri-Raymond (1831–1904), III, 34, 166, 185, 256, 468, 553

Caslon, William (father), IV, 105, 295

Caslon, William, IV, 556

Casot, Jacques, IV, 134

Casot, Jean-Joseph, IV, **134–35**, 298, 299

Casot, Jeanne. *See* Dauvin

Cassaignolles, Blaise, III, 156; IV, 253

Casselle, Laurence (Vallée), III, 636

Cassera. *See* Castera

Cassiet*, Pierre (1727–1809), IV, 456

Casson. *See* Dollier

Casswettune. *See* Kakᴕenthiony

Castagnac de Pontarion, Jean-Marie, III, 677

Castaing, Antoine, IV, 135

Castaing, Charlotte-Isabelle. *See* Chevalier

Castaing, Isabau. *See* Sareillier

Castaing, Jean, IV, 135

Castaing, Pierre-Antoine, IV, **135–36**

Castaing, Rose (Rodrigue), IV, 135, 136

Castaing, Willobe (Olive). *See* King

Castanet, Jean-Baptiste-Marie, IV, **136–37**, 81

Casteel, Anthony, III, 34, 136, 137, 358

Castel, Françoise-Jeanne, Comtesse de Saint-Pierre, Marquise de Crèvecœur et de Kerfily. *See* Kerven

Castel, Louis-Hyacinthe, Comte de Saint-Pierre, Marquis de Crèvecœur et de Kerfily, II, 35, 96, 120, 219, 254, 255; III, 156, 175, 178, 532, 567

Castellane. *See* Lauris

Castelli, Joseph-Marie, IV, 97

Castelveyre. *See* Turc

Castera (de Cassera), Saubade (Imbert), IV, 378

Castille, Marie (Olivier), III, 494

Castille, Pierre de, I, 470

Castlemaine, Countess of. *See* Villiers

Castonguay, Émile, IV, 104

Castries, Marquis de. *See* La Croix

Castro, Isabel de (Corte-Real), I, 236

Catalogne, Élisabeth de (Gannes de Falaise), III, 235

Catalogne, Gédéon (de), II, **120–22**, 31, 63, 86, 154, 195, 196, 254, 327, 491, 592; III, 117, 191, 234, 235, 505, 649

Catalogne, Joseph de, II, **122**, 120

Catalogne, Louis-François-Gédéon de, II, 122

Catalogne, Marie-Anne de. *See* Lemire

Catalogne, Marie-Charlotte de. *See* Renaud Dubuisson

Catalon, Catherine (Foucault), III, 225

Catalougne, Gédéon (father), II, 120

Catalougne, Gédéon, II, 120

Catalougne, Marie. *See* Capdeviolle

Catchamisse. *See* Scatchamisse

Cathcart, Robert, IV, 352

Catherine. *See also* Gandeacteua

Catherine (daughter of Tᴏᴛɪʀɪ), I, 652

Catherine (Iroquois), II, 595

Catherine (wife of Aᴛɪʀᴏɴᴛᴀ (Jean-Baptiste)), I, 71

Catherine de Médicis, Queen of France, I, 367, 421, 680

Catignon, Charles, II, 133

Catin, Henri, II, 446

Catin, Jeanne-Cécile (Campot), III, 96

Cato (slave), IV, 764

Cats, Jacob, II, 279

Cauchois, Madeleine (Curot), IV, 189

Caulet, Isidore, II, 381

Caulfeild, Anne. *See* Margetson

Caulfeild, Thomas, II, **122–23**, 22, 198, 289, 498, 651, 667, 668; III, 208, 439, 516, 665; IV, xxi

Caulfeild, William, 2nd Viscount Charlemont, II, 122

Caulfield, Susan, IV, 115

Caulincourt, Marie de (Lespinay), I, 425

Caumont, Pierre de, I, **172**

Caupemartissue Winnekee, IV, 726

Cavagnial. *See* Rigaud

Cavelier. *See also* Rivet
Cavelier, Catherine. *See* Geest
Cavelier, Colette (Le Ber), II, 374
Cavelier, Jean (father), I, 172; II, 123
Cavelier, Jean, I, 79, 180, 183; II, **123–24**, 441, 443
Cavelier, Louise-Anne. *See* Du Souchet
Cavelier, Perrette (Godefroy), I, 340
Cavelier, Pierre, II, 124, 576
Cavelier de La Salle, René-Robert, I, **172–84**, 35, 79, 113,
    126, 136, 226, 248, 289, 290, 379, 415, 420, 438, 440,
    444, 446, 464, 501, 502, 557, 572, 573, 600, 625, 653;
    II, xxviii, xxxii, 29, 31, 48, 49, 76, 123, 124, 133, 169,
    170, 173, 190, 191, 197, 203, 228, 230, 262, 263, 264,
    270, 278, 280, 281, 328, 343, 348, 349, 374, 375, 380,
    396, 397, 441, 443, 483, 488, 517, 537, 538, 584, 585,
    589, 631, 633, 634, 635, 636, 672; III, xxxiv, xxxvi, xl,
    65, 106, 380, 469, 558; IV, lii, lvi
Cavendish, Thomas, I, 252
Cavendish Bentinck, William Henry, 3rd Duke of Portland,
    IV, 522, 767
Cavilhe, Louis, IV, 89
Cébet, Étienne, IV, 127
Cecil, Robert, 1st Earl of Salisbury, I, 162, 364, 365
Cecil, William, Baron Burghley, I, 306, 362, 363, 364, 391,
    409, 450, 671
Cécile, I, 523
Cécile de Sainte-Croix, I, 353
Cecilia. *See* Natoukwabekwe
Céleste. *See* Ogenheratarihiens
Cèllere, Giulio, Count of Cèllere, I, 187, 658
Celles Duclos, Barbe. *See* Poisson
Celles Duclos, Gabriel, II, 221
Céloron, Antoine, II, 125
Céloron, Catherine, II, 125
Céloron, Marie. *See* Rémy
Céloron de Blainville, Catherine. *See* Eury de La Pérelle
Céloron de Blainville, Geneviève. *See* Damours de Chauf-
    fours
Céloron de Blainville, Geneviève-Gertrude. *See* Legardeur
    de Tilly
Céloron de Blainville, Hélène. *See* Picoté de Belestre
Céloron de Blainville, Hélène (Saint-Ours), II, 125; III, 577
Céloron de Blainville, Jean-Baptiste, I, 410; II, **124–25**, 88,
    336, 527; III, 99
Céloron de Blainville, Marie-Madeleine. *See* Blondeau
Céloron de Blainville, Pierre-Joseph, II, 125; III, **99–101**,
    xlii, 12, 28, 31, 158, 162, 373, 383, 384, 526, 611, 623;
    IV, 76, 77, 145, 213, 241, 256, 463, 512, 563, 582, 617,
    633, 666
Céloron de Blainville, Pierre-Joseph (son), III, 100
Céloron de Blainville, Suzanne. *See* Piot de Langloiserie
Celsius, Anders, IV, 406
Cendre Chaude. *See* Ogenheratarihiens
Cerré*, Jean-Gabriel (1734–1805), IV, 303, 592
Cerry. *See* Ailleboust
Cerry d'Argenteuil. *See* Ailleboust de Cerry
Certain, André, I, 504
César (slave), II, 457
Césarée, Brother, III, 208
Chabanel, Noël, I, **184–85**, 412, 414
Chabert, Jeanne de, I, 213
Chabert, Joseph-Bernard, Marquis de Chabert, III, 31
Chabert de Joncaire, Antoine-Marie, II, 125

Chabert de Joncaire, Gabrielle. *See* Hardi
Chabert de Joncaire, Louis-Thomas, II, **125–27**, xxxix, 20,
    114, 323, 404, 553, 567, 572, 623, 631; III, xxxvi, xl, 43,
    101, 105, 320; IV, 137, 187
Chabert de Joncaire, Madeleine. *See* Renaud Dubuisson
Chabert de Joncaire, Madeleine-Thérèse (Cuny Dauterive),
    IV, 187
Chabert de Joncaire, Marie-Madeleine. *See* Le Gay de
    Beaulieu
Chabert de Joncaire, Philippe-Thomas, II, 127, 436;
    III, **101–2**, 401, 611, 613; IV, 137
Chabert de Joncaire de Clausonne, Daniel-Marie, II, 125,
    127; III, 101; IV, **137–38**, 187, 595
Chabert de Joncaire de Clausonne, Marguerite-Élisabeth-
    Ursule. *See* Rocbert de La Morandière
Chaboillez. *See also* Chaboulié
Chaboillez, Charles, II, 127; III, 122
Chaboillez*, Charles-Jean-Baptiste (d. 1808), II, 127; IV,
    58, 592
Chaboillez*, Louis (1766–1813), II, 127; IV, 188, 698
Chaboillez, Louis-Joseph, IV, 58
Chaboillez, Marie-Anne. *See* Chevalier
Chaboillez, Pierre-Louis, IV, 592
Chabot, François, IV, 548
Chabot, Philippe de, I, 660
Chaboulié, Angélique. *See* Dandonneau Du Sablé
Chaboulié, Charles, II, **127–28**, 430
Chaboulié, Jean, II, 127
Chaboulié, Marie. *See* Le Hour
Chabrand, David, IV, 138
Chabrand, Marguerite. *See* Roussel
Chabrand Delisle, David, III, 296; IV, **138–40**, 104, 753,
    754
Chabrand Delisle, Margaret. *See* Henry
Chabrat, Jeanne (Gougeon), II, 71
Chachagouesse (Chachagwessiou, Chachagouache,
    Chachagonache, Chachagonesse), II, **128**, 435
Chacornacle (Chacornac, Chacornade). *See* Joannès
Chagny, André, IV, 637
Chaigneau, Léonard, II, **128–29**
Chalain. *See* Fouquet
Chalet, François, IV, 360
Chalifour, Paul, I, 460
Chaline, Jean-Daniel, I, 311, 593, 597
Challe. *See* Delhalle
Challoner, Sir Thomas, I, 530
Chalmette. *See* Martin
Chalmette, Antoinette (Martin de Lino), II, 464
Chalmette, Jean-François, II, 276, 464
Chalus. *See* Lechtier; Raudot
Chambalon, Geneviève. *See* Roussel
Chambalon, Louis (father), II, 129
Chambalon, Louis, I, 583; II, **129–30**, 32, 116, 138, 201,
    235, 256, 382, 413, 447, 533; III, 26, 291, 647
Chambalon, Marie. *See* Prieur
Chambalon, Marie-Anne. *See* Pinguet
Chambellan, François, III, 144, 181
Chambellé, Perrine de (Dugué de La Boulardière), I, 295
Chamberland, Catherine (Chartier), III, 111, 112
Chamberlen, Elizabeth (Walker), II, 658
Chamberlen, Peter, II, 658
Chambers, Robert William, IV, 397
Chambly. *See also* Hertel

Chambly, Jacques de, I, **185**, 40, 63, 399, 556; II, 4, 5, 284, 629
Chambly, Louise de. *See* Laulne
Chambly, Philippe de, I, 185
Chambrois, Edmée (Imbert), III, 299
Champagne. *See* Foureur; Macard
Champaigne. *See* Champion
Champdoré. *See* Angibault
Champernowne, Katherine (Gilbert), I, 331
Champflour, Bertrand de, I, 186
Champflour, Étienne de, III, 633
Champflour, François de, I, **186**, 370, 403, 489, 548, 640; II, xv, 158
Champigny. *See* Bochart
Champion (Champaigne), Captain, I, 380
Champion, Marie (Muiron), III, 478
Champion, Pierre, I, 563
Champion de Cicé, Charles, II, 130
Champion de Cicé, Judith. *See* Thévin
Champion de Cicé, Louis-Armand, II, **130**
Champlain. *See also* Dupéré; Pézard de La Tousche
Champlain, Anthoine de, I, 186
Champlain, Hélène de. *See* Boullé
Champlain, Marguerite de. *See* Le Roy
Champlain, Samuel de, I, **186–99**, 7, 10, 11, 12, 13, 16, 27, 28, 29, 34, 35, 36, 53, 59, 61, 64, 70, 72, 76, 80, 86, 87, 96, 99, 100, 101, 109, 110, 120, 121, 122, 123, 125, 127, 130, 131, 132, 143, 159, 160, 161, 163, 164, 200, 208, 209, 211, 222, 236, 237, 238, 253, 262, 263, 265, 283, 292, 293, 294, 297, 300, 302, 303, 307, 311, 339, 340, 341, 342, 345, 346, 347, 366, 367, 368, 372, 373, 381, 382, 386, 405, 406, 407, 411, 424, 428, 432, 433, 436, 437, 452, 454, 470, 471, 473, 479, 482, 487, 488, 493, 494, 495, 500, 501, 507, 508, 509, 511, 516, 517, 526, 529, 557, 558, 564, 565, 567, 568, 569, 570, 578, 579, 591, 593, 602, 603, 604, 613, 615, 638, 639, 659, 662, 663, 680; II, xv, xxxv, 86, 363, 367, 429; III, 250
Champs. *See* Des Champs
Champvallon. *See* Harlay
Champy, Gélase, II, **130–31**
Champy Desclouzeaux, Hubert (de), II, 589
Chancellor, Richard, I, 158
Chandler*, Kenelm (1737–1803), IV, 738
Chandler, Thomas Bradbury, IV, 485
Changouessi (Changouessy, Changouossy). *See* Chingouessi
Chanmazart, Pierre, III, 165
Chantal. *See* Rabutin-Chantal
Chaouerindamaguetch. *See* Boullongne, Marie-Barbe de
Chapais*, Sir Thomas (1858–1946), IV, 183
Chapeau, Madeleine (Levasseur), III, 397
Chapelier, Marie (Drouin), I, 281
Chapman, William, III, 528
Chapoton, André, III, 102
Chapoton, Anne. *See* Lassaigne
Chapoton, Jean-Baptiste, III, **102–3**
Chapoton, Marguerite. *See* Estève
Chapouin. *See* Garnier
Chappell*, Benjamin (1740–1825), IV, 152
Chappuis. *See* Joram
Chaptes. *See* La Corne
Chaptes (Chap, Chapt) de La Corne. *See* La Corne, Luc de

Charbonner, Marie-Madeleine (Lenoir, *dit* Rolland), II, 413
Chardon, Jean-Baptiste, II, 455, 501; III, **103**, 81
Chardon de Tressonville, Jacques de, I, 87
Charest. *See also* Dufy
Charest, Anne-Thérèse. *See* Duroy
Charest, Catherine (Trottier Desauniers), III, 631; IV, 739
Charest, Étienne (grandfather), I, 620; III, 82, 433
Charest, Étienne (father), II, 131, 561; III, 631; IV, 140
Charest, Étienne, III, 631; IV, **140–41**, 298, 432, 739
Charest, Françoise-Claire (Boucher de Montbrun), III, 82
Charest, Joseph, III, 165
Charest, Marguerite. *See* Trottier Desauniers
Charest, Marie-Catherine. *See* Trottier Desauniers
Charest, Marie-Charlotte (Martel de Brouague; Le Gardeur de Courtemanche), II, 8, 9, 383, 384, 458, 459; III, 134, 429, 433, 434
Charest, Thérèse (Charly Saint-Ange), II, 131
Charité, I, **199–200**, 196, 237, 366, 452, 494
Charlemont, Viscount. *See* Caulfeild
Charles. *See also* Ondaaiondiont
Charles, Captain, I, 451
Charles I, King of England, Scotland, and Ireland, I, 50, 51, 52, 53, 54, 81, 163, 311, 369, 384, 405, 406, 407, 419, 605, 613, 655, 673; IV, xix
Charles II, King of France, II, 98
Charles II, King of England, Scotland, and Ireland, I, 62, 82, 226, 241, 242, 337, 369, 406, 407, 436, 481, 513, 604, 636, 637; II, 391, 537, 580, 650; III, 369, 596; IV, xvii
Charles II, King of Spain, II, 115
Charles III, King of Spain, IV, 568
Charles IV, King of Spain, IV, 73
Charles V, Holy Roman Emperor, I, 27, 155, 156, 157, 158, 168, 342, 423
Charles V, King of France, III, 703
Charles VI, Holy Roman Emperor, III, 609
Charles VI, King of France, I, 202
Charles VII, King of France, I, 107, 287
Charles IX, King of France, I, 96, 573
Charles Edward, the Young Pretender, III, 27, 91, 357, 497, 666; IV, 400, 503
Charles Emmanuel I, Duke of Savoy, I, 300, 301
Charles William Ferdinand, Duke of Brunswick, IV, 589
Charlevoix, Antoinette de. *See* Forestier
Charlevoix, François de, III, 104
Charlevoix, Pierre-François-Xavier de, I, 45, 76, 100, 112, 183, 239, 267, 355, 357, 424, 440, 455, 466, 471, 492, 522, 523, 545, 633, 635, 649, 650; II, 116, 118, 119, 168, 173, 182, 218, 255, 256, 267, 270, 283, 297, 387, 423, 436, 448, 453, 495, 504, 505, 536, 544, 554, 566, 577, 581, 596, 600, 606, 627; III, **103–10**, 81, 184, 248, 249, 308, 309, 310, 315, 330, 335, 337, 395, 443, 444, 627; IV, 500
Charlier, M., IV, 69
Charlot Kaské, III, 530
Charlotte de Sainte-Hélène. *See* Daneau de Muy
Charlotte de Saint-Ignace. *See* Barré
Charlton, Edward, IV, 133
Charly, Jacques, III, 220
Charly, Louis, III, 220
Charly, *dit* Saint-Ange, André, II, 131, 132
Charly, *dit* Saint-Ange, Marie. *See* Dumesnil
Charly Saint-Ange, Jacques, II, 131; III, 110, 111; IV, 141

Charly Saint-Ange, Jean-Baptiste, II, **131–32**; III, 110; IV, 612

Charly Saint-Ange, Jean-Baptiste-François, II, 131; III, 110

Charly Saint-Ange, Louis, II, 131; III, **110–11**, 178, 179, 631; IV, 356, 360

Charly Saint-Ange, Louise-Catherine. *See* Ailleboust de Manthet

Charly Saint-Ange, Marie-Catherine, *dite* du Saint-Sacrement, I, 117; II, **132**

Charly Saint-Ange, Marie-Charlotte. *See* Le Conte Dupré

Charly Saint-Ange, Thérèse. *See* Charest

Charly Saint-Ange, Ursule. *See* Godefroy de Tonnancour

Charnisay. *See* Menou

Charnock, John, IV, 595

Charny. *See* Lauson

Charon, Geneviève (Pijart), I, 549

Charon de La Barre, François, II, **132–35**, 48, 127, 195, 377, 378, 556; III, 292, 299, 314, 407, 493, 612, 632, 633; IV, 236, 237, 708, 720

Charpentier, Brother, III, 208

Charpentier, M., II, 119

Charpentier, Marie. *See* Picq

Charron, Jean-Jacques, Marquis de Ménars, II, 472

Charron, Marie (Colbert), III, 57

Charron de La Barre, Claude. *See* Camus

Charron de La Barre, Claude, I, **200–1**, 478, 588, 589; II, 27, 132, 133

Charron de La Barre, Élisabeth. *See* Damours de Chauffours

Charry, Jean-Antoine, Marquis Desgouttes, III, 55, 72, 268

Chartier, Alain, I, 202; II, 137

Chartier, Anne. *See* Destroismaisons

Chartier, Catherine. *See* Chamberland

Chartier, Charles, III, 112

Chartier, Françoise. *See* Bourcier

Chartier, Jean, IV, 654

Chartier, Jeanne. *See* Chartré; Grondin

Chartier, Joseph, I, 202

Chartier, Louis, I, **201**, 109

Chartier, Marguerite. *See* Amelotte

Chartier, Marie. *See* Lenoir

Chartier, Marie. *See* Magné

Chartier, Martin, III, 65, 66

Chartier, Michel (father), III, 111

Chartier, Michel, II, 146; III, **111–12**

Chartier, Peter, III, 66, 162

Chartier, Philippe, I, 202

Chartier, René, I, 452

Chartier, René (chaplain), I, 202, 662

Chartier de La Broquerie, Louis, I, 201

Chartier de Lotbinière, Angélique (Martin de Lino; Renaud d'Avène Des Méloizes), II, 463, 465; III, 112, 550; IV, 659

Chartier de Lotbinière, Clément, I, 202

Chartier de Lotbinière, Élisabeth. *See* Damours

Chartier de Lotbinière, Eustache, II, 90, 91, 211, 457, 463; III, **112–15**, 45, 240, 491, 648; IV, 141, 142, 143, 221, 440, 539

Chartier de Lotbinière, Eustache (son of EUSTACHE, 1688–1749), III, 115; IV, 142

Chartier de Lotbinière, Eustache (baptized François-Louis), III, 115; IV, **141–43**

Chartier de Lotbinière, Françoise. *See* Jachée

Chartier de Lotbinière, Louise, *dite* de Saint-Eustache, III, 115

Chartier de Lotbinière, Louise-Madeleine. *See* Chaussegros de Léry

Chartier de Lotbinière, Louise-Philippe (Mariauchau d'Esgly), II, 457; III, 112; IV, 510

Chartier de Lotbinière, Louis-Théandre, I, **201–3**, 112, 245, 399, 588, 589, 617, 629; II, xvi, xix, xxiii, 136, 243, 301; III, 112

Chartier de Lotbinière, Marie-Charlotte (De Bonne; MacKay), IV, 143

Chartier de Lotbinière, Marie-Françoise. *See* Renaud d'Avène de Desmeloizes

Chartier de Lotbinière, Marie-Françoise (Joybert de Soulanges et de Marson), I, 202, 203, 399, 400; II, 301

Chartier de Lotbinière, Marie-Françoise (Juchereau Duchesnay), III, 115

Chartier de Lotbinière, Marie-Louise (Denys de La Ronde), III, 110, 175, 176, 177, 179

Chartier de Lotbinière, Marie-Madeleine. *See* Lambert

Chartier de Lotbinière, Michel, Marquis de Lotbinière, II, 52; III, 31, 113, 115, 119; IV, **143–45**, 142, 364

Chartier* de Lotbinière, Michel-Eustache-Gaspard-Alain (1748–1822), IV, 143, 185, 591

Chartier de Lotbinière, Pierre-Alain, III, 112, 113

Chartier de Lotbinière, René-Louis, I, 202; II, **135–39**, xxi, xxii, xxiv, 213, 457, 463, 465, 520, 526, 561, 587; III, 112, 176, 420, 550

Chartier de Lotbinière, René-Pierre, I, 202; II, 136

Chartier de Lotbinière, Valentin (baptized Antoine), III, 112, 113

Charton, François, I, 121

Charton, Nicolas, I, 48

Chartrain, Noël, II, 303

Chartré, Jeanne (Chartier), III, 112

Chartroux, Madeleine (La Salle), II, 349

Chase, Elizabeth. *See* Lawrear

Chase, Samuel, IV, 270, 549, 759

Chasle, Catherine. *See* Fol

Chasle, Claude (father), I, 255

Chasle, Claude, III, 350

Chasle, Marie-Anne (Gouze; Perthius), IV, 624

Chasle, Marie-Marguerite. *See* Duroy

Chaspoux, Marie-Madeleine de, Dame de Verneuil et Du Plessis-Savari (Bochart de Champigny), II, 71; III, 22

Chasseriau, Marie (Bréard), IV, 92

Chassin, Charlotte de. *See* Thyerry

Chassin, Marie-Agnès (Tisserant de Moncharvaux), III, 626

Chassin, Nicolas de, III, 115

Chassin de Thierry, François-Nicolas de, III, **115–16**, 645

Chassin de Thierry, Marie-Josephte de. *See* Rousseau de Souvigny

Chaste, Aymar de, I, 27, 188, 209, 210, 346

Chasteigner, Charlotte de (Aloigny, Marquise de La Groye), II, 15

Chastelain, Marguerite. *See* Cardin

Chastelain, Marie-Josephte (Boucher de Niverville), III, 8, 430

Chastelard, Henri de, Marquis de Salières, I, 286, 555, 570, 602; II, 11, 412

Chastellain, Pierre, I, **203–4**, 125, 324; II, 613

Chastullé. *See* Pyvart

Chatchmaid, William, I, 350

Chateaubriand, François-René, Vicomte de Chateaubriand, II, 444; III, 24, 108

Chateaufort. *See* Bras-de-Fer

Châteauguay. *See* Le Moyne

Châteauneuf. *See* Meneux

Chateauverdun, Marie de (Rigaud de Vaudreuil, Baronne de Vaudreuil), II, 565

Châteauvieux. *See* Gamelin

Chateigner de Cramahé et Des Rochers, Hector-François, IV, 787

Chateigner de Cramahé et Des Rochers, Marie-Anne. *See* Belrieux de Virazel

Châtel, Edmée, I, 116

Châtellerault. *See* Roy

Chatham, Earl of. *See* Pitt

Chatillon. *See* Berson; Godin; Mignot

Châtillon, Maréchal de. *See* Coligny

Chaton de La Jannaye, Étienne, I, 520

Chauchetière, Claude, I, 651; II, **139–40**, 107

Chaudière Noire, I, **204–5**

Chaudillon, Antoine, II, **140–41**

Chaudillon, Antoinette. *See* Tin

Chaudillon, Claude, II, 140

Chaudillon, Marie. *See* Boucher

Chaudron. *See* Le Page

Chauffours. *See* Damours

Chaufour, Jean-Baptiste, IV, 376

Chaulnes, Duc de. *See* Albert

Chaumeaux. *See* Citoys

Chaumier, Catherine. *See* Nafrechoux

Chaumine. *See* Tessier

Chaumonot, Pierre-Joseph-Marie, I, **205–7**, 111, 121, 123, 124, 244, 269, 271, 273, 345, 415, 461, 523, 563, 612, 633, 665; II, 82, 94, 160, 536, 540, 643; III, 337

Chaumont. *See also* Guillet

Chaumont, Alexandre de (father), II, 141

Chaumont, Alexandre de, I, 554; II, **141**

Chaumont, Isabelle de. *See* Du Bois Des Cours

Chauniers. *See* Sabourin

Chaüosé. *See* Le Mercier, François-Joseph

Chaussegros, Anne. *See* Vidalle

Chaussegros, Gaspard, III, 116

Chaussegros de Léry, François-Joseph, Vicomte de Léry, III, xxii; IV, 435

Chaussegros de Léry, Gaspard-Joseph (father), I, 76; II, xxi, 202, 209, 431, 432, 434, 515, 593; III, **116–19**, 47, 79, 115, 191, 194, 229, 231, 241, 307, 420, 534, 610, 631; IV, 143, 145, 174, 203, 435, 448, 474

Chaussegros de Léry, Gaspard-Joseph (son), III, xxii, 28, 31, 116, 118, 162, 171, 222, 408, 434, 451, 459, 613; IV, **145–47**, xliii, 89, 150, 395, 464, 651, 733

Chaussegros de Léry, Josephte-Antoinette, *dite* de Sainte-Marie, IV, 203

Chaussegros de Léry, Louise. *See* Martel de Brouague

Chaussegros de Léry, Louise-Madeleine (Chartier de Lotbinière), III, 115, 119; IV, 143, 144

Chaussegros de Léry, Marie-Gilles (Landrière Des Bordes), IV, 435

Chaussegros de Léry, Marie-Madeleine-Régis (Legardeur de Repentigny), III, 119; IV, 448

Chaussegros de Léry, Marie-Renée. *See* Legardeur de Beauvais

Chausson, Marie-Élisabeth, III, 552

Chauveau, François, I, 214

Chauveton, Urbain, I, 154

Chauvigny, Jeanne. *See* Du Bouchet

Chauvigny, Marie-Madeleine de (Gruel de La Peltrie), I, **207–8**, 43, 205, 215, 217, 230, 352, 354, 373, 457, 483, 485, 552, 604, 640, 665; IV, 535

Chauvigny et de Vaubougon, Guillaume de, I, 207, 208

Chauvin, Anne. *See* Archambault

Chauvin, François, I, 209

Chauvin, Marie (Noyon), III, 493

Chauvin, Marie-Marthe (Lupien, *dit* Baron), III, 412

Chauvin, Michel, I, 557

Chauvin, Pierre, II, 105

Chauvin de La Pierre, Pierre, I, **208–9**, 80, 190

Chauvin de Tonnetuit, Jeanne de. *See* Mallemouche

Chauvin de Tonnetuit, Madeleine de, I, 210

Chauvin de Tonnetuit, Marie de. *See* Brinon

Chauvin de Tonnetuit, Pierre de, I, **209–10**, 27, 208, 291, 345, 422, 601

Chauvreulx, Claude-Jean-Baptiste, II, 513; III, **119–21**, 166, 256, 257; IV, xxv, 296

Chavagnac, Louis-Henri de, Comte de Chavagnac, II, 398

Chavenault, Marie-Françoise (Levasseur de Neré), II, 432

Chaverlange, Antoine de, I, 474

Chaverlange, Jeanne de (Levasseur, *dit* L'Espérance), I, 474

Chaverlange, Marthe de. *See* Guérin

Chavigny, Élisabeth de (Landron), III, 347

Chavigny de Berchereau, Éléonore de. *See* Grandmaison

Chavigny de Berchereau, François de, I, 56, 344, 345; II, 141, 223; III, 379

Chavigny de Berchereau, Geneviève de (Amiot; Couillard de Lespinay), I, 59; II, 17, 155

Chavigny de Berchereau, Madeleine de (Lemoine), II, 236; III, 379

Chavigny de Berchereau, Marguerite de (Douaire de Bondy; Fleury Deschambault), I, 309, 418; II, 223, 224, 433; III, 216

Chavigny Lachevrotière, Antoinette de. *See* Poussans

Chavigny Lachevrotière, François de, I, 345, 394; II, **141–42**

Chavigny Lachevrotière, François de (son), II, 142

Chavigny Lachevrotière, Geneviève de. *See* Guion Desprez

Chavigny Lachevrotière, Louise de, II, 142

Chavin. *See* Chauvin

Chaviteau, Françoise. *See* Bourot

Chaviteau, Jean, II, 298

Chavoy. *See* Payen

Chawchinahaw, IV, 339

Chazel, Guillaume, II, 208; III, 62

Chazy, M. de, I, 40, 308; II, 159

Chefdostel, Thomas, I, **210**, 421, 422

Chenard de La Giraudais, François, III, xxv, 606; IV, 28, 80, 207, 208

Chenery, Hannah (Peters), IV, 624

Chenet Dubreuil, Pierre, II, 182, 459, 521, 522

Chenughiyata. *See* Hotsinoñhyata?

Chéron, Charles, III, 75, 429, 602; IV, 11

Chéron, Marguerite (Trottier Desauniers), III, 631

Chéron, Marie-Josephte (Carrerot), III, 97

Chéron, Marie-Madeleine (Ailleboust de Cerry), IV, 10

Chéron, Marie-Ursule, *dite* des Anges, IV, 189

Chéron, Martin, II, 66; III, 631

Cherououny, I, **210–11**, 302, 303, 479
Cherrier, Benjamin-Hyacinthe-Martin, IV, 148
Cherrier*, Côme-Séraphin (1798–1885), IV, 148
Cherrier, François, IV, 147
Cherrier*, François (1745–1809), IV, 148, 592, 639
Cherrier, François-Pierre, IV, **147–49**, 270
Cherrier, Joseph-Marie, IV, 148
Cherrier, Joseph-Marie-Simon, IV, 148
Cherrier, Marie. *See* Dubuc
Cherrier, Marie-Charlotte (Lartigue), IV, 148
Cherrier, Périne-Charles (Viger), IV, 148
Cherrier, Rosalie (Papineau), IV, 148
Cherrier, Séraphin, IV, 148
Chesné (Chesnay), Élisabeth. *See* Auber
Chesne, *dit* Labutte, Pierre, III, 528
Chesneau, Anne. *See* Lalande
Chesneau, Guillaume, I, 287
Chesnel, Judith (Du Gua de Monts), I, 291
Cheval, Geneviève. *See* Leduc
Cheval, Gilette. *See* Nève
Cheval, Marie-Renée. *See* Cousineau
Cheval, Thomas, III, 121
Cheval, *dit* Saint-Jacques, and *dit* Chevalier, Jacques-Joseph, III, **121**
Chevalier. *See also* La Tourasse
Chevalier, M., I, 564
Chevalier, Catherine (Noyon), I, 250
Chevalier, Charlotte-Isabelle (Castaing), IV, 135
Chevalier, Françoise-Marthe. *See* Barton
Chevalier, Jacques, II, 142
Chevalier, Jean, II, 142
Chevalier, Jean-Baptiste (merchant), IV, 659
Chevalier, Jean-Baptiste, III, **121–22**; IV, 78
Chevalier, Jean-Charles (Jean-Baptiste), III, **122**
Chevalier, Jeanne. *See* Vilain
Chevalier, Joseph (armourer), III, 430
Chevalier, Joseph (father of JEAN-BAPTISTE), III, 121
Chevalier, Joseph (voyageur), IV, 331
Chevalier, Louis, III, 223
Chevalier, Louise (Roy), II, 584
Chevalier, Marie (L'Hermitte), II, 434
Chevalier, Marie-Anne (Bourdages), IV, 78
Chevalier, Marie-Anne (Chaboillez), III, 122
Chevalier, Marie-Anne (Dubreuil), II, 201
Chevalier, Marie-Françoise. *See* Alavoine
Chevalier, Paul, II, 142
Chevalier, Pierre, II, 133
Chevalier, *dit* Beauchêne, Robert, II, **142–43**
Chevallier, Louis-Thérèse, III, 122
Chevallier, Marie-Madeleine. *See* Réaume
Chevenaux. *See* Chauvreulx
Chevigny. *See* Choiseul
Chévigny. *See* Vallette
Chevilly. *See* Bouvot
Chevreau, Judith de (Aumasson de Courville), IV, 35
Chevremont. *See* Gaudron
Chevrier, Pierre, Baron de Fancamp, I, 214, 215; III, 395
Chevrières. *See* La Croix
Chevry. *See also* Duret
Chevry, Marquis de, IV, xxiv
Chew, John, IV, 149
Chew, Joseph, IV, **149**
Chew, William Johnson, IV, 149

Chèze, François, II, **143**; III, 603
Chicagou, II, 646
Chichikatelo (Chichicatato), II, **143–44**, xxxiii
Chicot, Jean, I, 463
Chicoyneau, Catherine (La Maisonfort Du Boisdecourt, Marquise de La Maisonfort), III, 345
Chihwatenha (Chiohoarehra), I, **211–12**, 344, 388, 523
Chinard, Gilbert, III, 337
Chingouessi, II, **144**, xxxvii
Chiniquy*, Charles (1809–99), IV, 43
Chinn, Edward, IV, 369, 592
Chinn, John, IV, 369
Chinoniata. *See* Hotsinoñhyahta?
Chipman, Thomas Handley, IV, 19
Chipman*, Ward (1754–1824), IV, 55, 329, 516, 723, 769
Chiquet (carpenter), III, 139
Chiquot (Cicotte), Zacharie, III, 529
Chkoudun. *See* Secoudon
Choiseul, Étienne-François, Duc de Choiseul, Comte de Stainville, II, 270; III, xvi, 86, 97, 142, 300, 442, 538, 601; IV, 31, 56, 68, 69, 207, 257, 457, 481, 602, 621, 634, 646, 660, 673, 734, 739, 752
Choiseul, François-Joseph de, Baron de Beaupré, known as Comte de Choiseul, III, 474, 475
Choiseul-Chevigny, César-Gabriel de, Duc de Praslin, IV, 646, 657
Choisser, Jean, IV, 748
Cholenec, Pierre, I, 635; II, **144–45**; III, 649
Cholmondeley, Robert, IV, 103
Chomedey, Hierosme de, I, 213
Chomedey, Jacqueline de (Bouvot de Chevilly), I, 213
Chomedey, Louis de, I, 212
Chomedey, Louise de, *dite* de Sainte-Marie, I, 115, 213, 220
Chomedey, Marie de. *See* Thomelin
Chomedey, Odard de, I, 213
Chomedey de Maisonneuve, Paul de, I, **212–22**, 32, 43, 44, 45, 46, 47, 109, 115, 130, 200, 208, 230, 231, 266, 273, 284, 297, 310, 319, 330, 344, 373, 412, 427, 430, 447, 453, 457, 464, 485, 486, 487, 540, 543, 547, 548, 557, 558, 598, 640, 648; II, xv, 131, 193, 234, 375, 376, 469, 490; III, 692
Chomel, Sieur, III, 676
Chomina, I, **222–23**, 80, 302, 509, 516, 578, 639
Chomonot. *See* Chaumonot
Chorel de Saint-Romain, Edmond, III, 311, 312
Chorel de Saint-Romain, *dit* d'Orvilliers, Élisabeth (Groston de Saint-Ange), II, 267
Chorel de Saint-Romain, *dit* d'Orvilliers, François, II, 267, 616; III, 311
Chorel de Saint-Romain, *dit* d'Orvilliers, Madeleine (Lefebvre Duplessis Faber), III, 372
Chorel de Saint-Romain, *dit* d'Orvilliers, Marie-Anne. *See* Aubuchon
Chorel de Saint-Romain, *dit* d'Orvilliers, Marie-Madeleine (Gadois, *dit* Mauger), III, 232
Chorel de Saint-Romain, *dit* d'Orvilliers, Marie-Marguerite (Lorimier de La Rivière), II, 445; III, 408
Chorel de Saint-Romain, *dit* d'Orvilliers, Marie-Renée (Le Picard Du Mesnil de Norrey), II, 416, 520
Chorest, Jean-Baptiste, III, 272
Chotard, Jean-Baptiste, II, 516
Chotard, Marie-Anne (Perrin), II, 516

Chotard, Marie-Catherine. *See* Fortin
Chou, Juan, I, 263
Chouart, Marie. *See* Poirer
Chouart, Médard, I, 223
Chouart Des Groseilliers, Hélène. *See* Martin
Chouart Des Groseilliers, Jean-Baptiste, I, 39, 223, 227;
 II, 538, 539, 647
Chouart Des Groseilliers, Marguerite. *See* Hayet
Chouart Des Groseilliers, Marguerite, I, 223, 228
Chouart Des Groseilliers, Marie-Anne, I, 223
Chouart Des Groseilliers, Marie-Antoinette (Jalot; Bouchard
 d'Orval), I, 223; II, 647
Chouart Des Groseilliers, Médard, I, **223–28**, 16, 20, 39,
 48, 49, 50, 56, 82, 83, 129, 250, 271, 282, 337, 338, 385,
 397, 429, 464, 495, 518, 528, 578, 602, 607, 625; II, 298,
 391, 501, 535, 536, 537, 538, 647
Chouart Des Groseilliers, Médard (son), I, 223
Choumin. *See* Chomina
Chrestien, Father. *See* Le Clercq
Chrestienne, Marie-Madeleine. *See* Ouebadinskoue
Chrétien, Brother. *See* Turc de Castelveyre, Louis
Chrétien, Jean, II, 179
Chrétien, Marie-Charlotte (Denys de Vitré), II, 179
Christian (Mohawk), II, 477
Christian (servant), II, 486, 487
Christian I, King of Denmark, Norway, and Sweden, I, 679
Christian IV, King of Denmark and Norway, I, 243, 360,
 514, 515
Christie. *See also* Plenderleath
Christie, Catherine. *See* Napier
Christie, Catherine, IV, 151
Christie, Gabriel, IV, **149–51**, 146, 269, 278, 464, 570,
 612, 691
Christie, Gabriel (son), IV, 151
Christie, George, IV, 151
Christie, James (grandfather), IV, 150
Christie, James, IV, 151
Christie, Sarah. *See* Stevenson
Christie, Sarah (Tunstall), IV, 151
Christie, William, IV, 151
Christie Burton, Napier, IV, 150, 151
Christmas, Anne (Vaughan), I, 656
Christmas, John, I, 656
Chubb, Pascoe, II, 394
Chudleigh, Sir John, I, 669
Church, Alice. *See* Southworth
Church, Benjamin, I, 26, 427, 577; II, **145–46**, 177, 287,
 382, 409, 410, 480, 481, 605, 638; III, 111, 112, 273, 596
Church, Elizabeth. *See* Warren
Church, Richard, II, 145
Church, Thomas, II, 146
Churchill, Arabella (Godfrey), III, 70
Churchill, John, 1st Duke of Marlborough, I, 493; II, 21,
 265, 286, 287, 351, 513, 659; III, xxvii, 70, 135; IV, 26
Churchill, Sarah, Duchess of Marlborough. *See* Jennings
Churchyard, Thomas, I, 335
Churiau, Catherine, II, 95
Cicé. *See* Champion
Cicotte. *See* Chiquot
Cinq-Mars, Marquis de. *See* Coiffier de Ruzé
Ciquard*, François (d. 1824), IV, 5
Cirier, Antoine, IV, **151–52**
Cirier, Marguerite. *See* Desroches

Cirier, Marie-Anne. *See* Beaune
Cirier, Marie-Joseph. *See* Lenoir
Cirier, Martin, IV, 151
Citoys de Chaumeaux, François, II, 143
Clairambault, Charles, II, 146
Clairambault, Claude, II, 146
Clairambault, Nicolas, II, 146
Clairambault, Pierre, II, 146
Clairambault d'Aigremont, François, II, **146–48**, xxii, xxiii,
 13, 135, 354, 355, 415, 475, 484, 505, 547, 559, 569,
 606, 618, 632, 645; III, 74, 220, 499
Claparède, Jacques, III, 123
Claparède, Jean, III, **123**
Claparède, Marie. *See* Guy
Claparède, Marie-Josephe. *See* Seigneur
Claparède, Renée. *See* Grosse
Claparède, Renée, III, 123
Clarendon, Earl of. *See* Hyde
Claret, Charles-Pierre, Comte de Fleurieu, I, 280
Clarina, Baron. *See* Massey
Clark. *See also* Clarke
Clark*, Andrew Hill (d. 1975), IV, xxiii, xxvi, xxxi, 559
Clark, Ann. *See* Berry
Clark, Elizabeth (wife of Robert CLARK), IV, 152
Clark, Elizabeth (wife of Robert Hale, father), III, 274
Clark, Elizabeth (wife of Robert HALE), III, 274
Clark, George, III, **123–24**
Clark, George Rogers, IV, 303, 322, 324, 337, 564
Clark*, James (d. 1807), IV, 505
Clark, John, IV, 608
Clark, Mary (mother of ROBERT), IV, 152
Clark, Mary (Bonner), II, 81
Clark, Mary (Brown), IV, 105
Clark, Rebecca (Alline), IV, 16
Clark, Robert, IV, **152–53**, 129, 606, 608, 609
Clark*, Robert (1744–1823), IV, 495
Clark, Wotherton, IV, 152
Clarke. *See also* Clerke
Clarke*, Sir Alured (d. 1832), IV, 43, 130
Clarke, Ann (Hicks), IV, 350
Clarke, Elizabeth. *See* Mitton
Clarke, Elizabeth (Tyng), I, 654; III, 635
Clarke, Job Bennet, IV, 627
Clarke (Clerke), John (Brownist), I, 390, 391, 392
Clarke, John (trader), IV, 33
Clarke, Peter, I, 407
Clarke, Richard, I, **228–30**, 334, 335, 363, 532
Clarke, Thaddeus, I, 654
Clarkson, John, IV, 111, 604, 627, 628
Clarkson, Thomas, IV, 627
Claude, Joseph, IV, **153–54**, 180
Claudius Clavus. *See* Swart
Claus, Adam Frederic, IV, 154
Claus, Ann. *See* Johnson
Claus, Anna Dorothea (mother of CHRISTIAN DANIEL),
 IV, 154
Claus, Christian Daniel, III, 409, 452; IV, **154–55**, 59, 105,
 117, 118, 119, 120, 130, 139, 149, 368, 393, 394, 396,
 397, 416, 417, 586, 587, 613, 692, 753
Claus*, William (1765–1826), IV, 155
Clausonne. *See* Chabert
Claverie, Jean, III, 124
Claverie, Jeanne. *See* La Barthe

Claverie, Marie-Anne. *See* Dupéré
Claverie, Pierre, III, **124–25**, 141, 142; IV, 66, 125, 264, 755
Cleaskina, IV, 325
Cleaveland. *See* Cleveland
Cleeves, William, III, 618, 619
Cleland, John, IV, 631
Clement X, Pope, III, 11, 546
Clement XI, Pope, II, 332
Clement XII, Pope, IV, 220
Clement XIII, Pope, IV, 99, 543
Clement XIV, Pope, IV, 510
Clément, Catherine (La Croix), III, 334
Clément (Vincent), Jacquette (Jeanneau), III, 313
Clément, Marie (Vézina), III, 648
Clément Du Vuault de Monceaux, Anne. *See* Gasnier
Clément Du Vuault de Monceaux, Claire-Françoise (Ruette d'Auteuil), I, 585; II, 585
Clément Du Vuault de Monceaux, Jean, I, 113, 585
Clément Du Vuault de Valrennes, Jeanne. *See* Bissot
Clément Du Vuault de Valrennes, Philippe, II, **148–49**, 13, 103, 168, 269, 386, 603
Clements, Eleanor (Parr), IV, 603
Clérin. *See* Estienne; Desvoges
Clerk, William, I, 386
Clerke, Charles, IV, **155–56**, 73, 165, 412
Clermont, Comte de. *See* Orléans
Cléron d'Haussonville, Joseph-Louis-Bernard de, Comte d'Haussonville, IV, 31, 32
Cleveland, Duchess of. *See* Villiers
Cleveland, Aaron (father), III, 125
Cleveland, Aaron, III, **125–26**; IV, 527
Cleveland, Abigail. *See* Waters
Cleveland, Grover, III, 126
Cleveland, Sarah. *See* Rudduck
Cleveland, Susannah. *See* Porter
Clevett (Cleverley), Ann, IV, 701
Clignancour. *See* Damours
Clinton, Anne. *See* Carle
Clinton, Francis Fiennes, 6th Earl of Lincoln, III, 126
Clinton, George, II, 251; III, **126–27**, 49, 101, 324, 327, 365, 588, 623; IV, 173, 595
Clinton, Sir Henry, III, 127; IV, 3, 504, 682
Clinton, James, IV, 121
Clinton, Lucy Mary (Roddam), III, 127
Clinton, Susan. *See* Penniston
Clive, Robert, 1st Baron Clive, III, 659; IV, 114
Clodoré (Closdoré), Jean de, I, 443
Closse, Cécile. *See* Delafosse
Closse, Élisabeth. *See* Moyen Des Granges
Closse, Élisabeth, I, 231, 266
Closse, Jean, I, 230
Closse, Jeanne-Cécile (Bizard; Blaise Des Bergères de Rigauville), I, 103, 231; II, 70
Closse, Raphaël-Lambert, I, **230–32**, 103, 219, 266, 271, 274, 297, 463; II, 70, 105; III, 580
Closson, Joseph, II, 285
Cloutier, Anne (Drouin), I, 232, 281, 330
Cloutier, Louise (Marguerie; Mignot, *dit* Chatillon; Mataut), I, 490
Cloutier, Madeleine. *See* Esmard
Cloutier, Xainte. *See* Dupont
Cloutier, Zacharie, I, **232**, 330, 359, 490; II, 158, 205

Cloutier, Zacharie (son), I, 473
Cluzel, Jeanne de (Biard), I, 94
Cnoyen, James, I, 678
Coates, John, IV, 524
Coats, Mary. *See* McCliesh
Coats, William, III, **127–28**, 123, 407, 415, 449, 454, 489
Cobb, Elisha, III, 128
Cobb, Elizabeth. *See* Rider
Cobb, Jabez, III, 129
Cobb, Lydia. *See* Rider
Cobb, Silvanus, III, **128–30**, 572; IV, 193, 219
Cobbie, Diana (Hall), I, 233
Cobbie, Eliza (mother of Walsall), I, 233
Cobbie, Walsall, I, **232–33**
Cobreth, William, I, 667
Cochin. *See also* Cocking
Cochin, Jane. *See* Carlton
Cochin, Richard, IV, 156
Cochon, Antoinette (Bertier), II, 60
Cochrane, John, IV, 185
Cochrane, Susannah, Countess of Dundonald. *See* Hamilton
Cockburn*, James Pattison (1778–1847), III, 305
Cockeye. *See* Questach
Cocking, Matthew, IV, **156–58**, 47, 277, 341, 384, 647, 760
Cocreaumont. *See* Dubois
Codde, Pierre, II, 279
Codman, Richard, IV, 273
Codner, John, IV, 159
Codrington, Christopher, II, 659
Coëtnempren de Kersaint, Guy-François de, III, 356
Coeuret, Claude-Audet, IV, 645
Coffin, Ann (Callbeck), IV, 128
Coffin*, John (1729–1808), IV, 548
Coffin*, John (1756–1838), IV, 301, 328
Coffre (soldier), III, 139, 140
Coghlan, Jeremiah, III, 411, 412; IV, **158–60**, 712, 713, 714
Coghlan, Joanna (wife of Jeremiah), IV, 158
Cognac. *See* Boisseau
Cohen*, Jacob Raphael (d. 1811), IV, 719
Coiffier de Ruzé, Henri, Marquis de Cinq-Mars, II, 656
Coigny, Duc de. *See* Franquetot
Coindat, Marguerite (La Colombière), II, 326
Colbert, Charles, Marquis de Croissy, I, 513
Colbert, Jean-Baptiste, I, 25, 33, 34, 49, 63, 74, 115, 116, 120, 127, 135, 136, 137, 185, 227, 283, 284, 285, 287, 315, 326, 327, 396, 410, 418, 442, 443, 499, 534, 541, 555, 556, 565, 571, 581, 587, 589, 600, 615, 616, 617, 618, 619, 620, 621, 622, 623, 624, 627, 628, 629, 630, 648; II, xviii, 28, 59, 76, 80, 85, 86, 100, 115, 184, 262, 295, 350, 366, 368, 369, 400, 470, 538, 585, 586, 628; III, xvii, 57, 701, 702; IV, 354, 355
Colbert, Jean-Baptiste, Marquis de Seignelay, I, 56, 119, 138, 179, 181, 250, 289, 290, 443, 446, 448, 526, 537, 586; II, 57, 63, 86, 99, 104, 124, 147, 184, 197, 253, 261, 262, 263, 344, 371, 401, 442, 470, 471, 472, 473, 533, 539, 577, 583
Colbert, Marie. *See* Charron
Colbert de Terron, Charles, I, 62, 418, 419, 443, 534, 621, 627
Colden, Cadwallader, II, 619, 622, 623; III, 126; IV, 427
Cole, John, IV, **160**, 366

Coleman, John, II, 288
Colen*, Joseph (d. 1818), IV, 726, 727
Coleridge, Samuel Taylor, I, 385
Coles, Edward, II, 265
Coligny, Gaspard I de, known as Maréchal de Châtillon, II, 98
Coligny, Gaspard II de, known as Amiral de Coligny, I, 27
Colin, Françoise (Gaultier), III, 675
Colin, Michel, I, **233**, 265
Collégien. *See* Saillant
Collet. *See also* Callet
Collet, Anne (Raisin), I, 564
Collet, Antoinette. *See* Thomé
Collet, Benoît, II, 149
Collet*, Charles-Ange (b. 1721, d. after 1800), III, 94, 553; IV, 430
Collet, Élisabeth. *See* Denys de Saint-Simon
Collet, Hippolyte, III, 94
Collet, Marie (Lemaître, *dit* Jugon; Frémont), III, 377
Collet, Mathieu, II, 151
Collet, Mathieu-Benoît, II, **149–52**, xxv, 449, 523; III, 74, 83, 299, 352, 576, 646, 647
Colletet, Guillaume, I, 469
Colleton, Sir Peter, I, 519
Collier (merchant), I, 293
Collier, Christiana, Lady Collier. *See* Gwyn
Collier, Cordelia (Murray), IV, 569
Collier, Elizabeth, Lady Collier. *See* Fryer
Collier, Elizabeth (Southworth), II, 145
Collier, George, IV, 160
Collier, Sir George, IV, **160–61**, 504, 693
Collier, John, III, **130–31**, 363; IV, 53, 527, 562, 724
Collier Pendu, Le. *See* Kaghswaghtaniunt
Collins, Edward, II, 152
Collins, Hallet, IV, 259
Collins, John, II, **152–53**, 163, 164, 534, 619
Collins, John, IV, **161–62**, 12, 153, 154, 477, 574, 613
Collins, Margaret (wife of JOHN), IV, 162
Collins, Mary (Rankin), IV, 162
Collins, Sophia Augusta. *See* Pernette
Colnett*, James (1752–1806), IV, 218, 244, 245, 411, 520, 568, 767
Coloma, Carlos, I, 187
Colombet, Antoinette de (Rigaud de Vaudreuil), II, 566, 571
Colombier. *See* Pouteret
Colombier, Marie (Boisseau), I, 104
Colson, Nicolas, I, 109
Colston, Elizabeth. *See* Gittens
Colston, William (father), I, 233
Colston, William, I, **233–34**, 350
Columbus, Christopher, I, 12, 21, 147, 148, 150, 155, 157, 234, 303, 657, 658, 677, 678
Colvill, Baroness. *See* Erskine; Johnston
Colvill, Alexander, 7th Baron Colvill, III, **131–33**, 209, 210, 606; IV, 31, 163, 223, 481, 701
Colvill, Charles, III, 133
Colvill, John, 6th Baron Colvill, III, 131
Colvill, Sophia, III, 133
Colville, James Alexander, III, 133
Colville, John Mark Alexander, 4th Viscount Colville, III, 133
Combalet. *See* Beauvoir
Combes (Combles). *See* Lombard

Côme de Mantes, I, **234**, 434
Comhommon. *See* Onedahauet
Comingo*, Bruin Romkes (1723–1820), IV, 490, 705
Commeau, Pierre, IV, xx
Compain*, Pierre-Joseph (1740–1806), IV, 265
Comporté. *See* Gaultier
Comte, Benjamin, IV, 591
Comtois. *See* Dextreme; Joram
Conception. *See* Roy
Condé, Prince de. *See* Bourbon
Condé, Princesse de. *See* Montmorency
Condé, Henri II, Prince de, I, 42, 98, 186, 187, 191, 192, 193, 194, 294, 386
Condé, Louis II, Prince de, known as Le Grand Condé, I, 225, 283, 561, 563; II, 85, 262, 545
Condé, Louis-Henri, Prince de, Duc de Bourbon, II, 646
Condren, Charles de, I, 115, 208
Coney, Mr, I, 93
Conflans, Comte de. *See* Brienne
Conflans, Hubert de, Comte de Conflans, IV, 282
Congreve, Sir William, IV, 773
Conigan de Cangé, Charles de, I, 257
Conneequese, IV, 339
Conner, John, III, 136, 137
Constantin, Denis, III, 134
Constantin, Guillaume, III, 134
Constantin, Jeanne. *See* Masse
Constantin, Justinien (baptized Louis-Alexandre), III, **133–34**
Constantin, Louise. *See* Bacon
Constantin, Marguerite-Suzanne. *See* Guyon Durouvray
Constantin, Nicolas-Bernardin, II, **153**, 173
Constantin (Lavallée Constantin), Pierre, II, 8, 276, 384; III, **134–35**, 75, 226; IV, 91
Contant, Élisabeth (Tranchant), III, 398, 399
Contant, *dit* Lafranchise, Nicolas, III, 398, 399
Contarini, Gasparo, I, 148, 153, 155, 157
Contarini, Marcantonio, I, 153
Conti, Prince de. *See* Bourbon
Contrecœur. *See* Pécaudy
Convent, Anne (Amiot; Maheu; Blanchon), I, 59, 60
Conway, Henry Seymour, IV, 759
Conyngham, Williams, IV, 399, 414, 570
Cook, Elizabeth. *See* Batts
Cook, Ephraim, III, 364, 457; IV, 526
Cook, Grace. *See* Pace
Cook, James (father), IV, 163
Cook, James, III, 133, 210; IV, **162–67**, lv, 28, 73, 156, 217, 218, 223, 283, 325, 340, 341, 411, 412, 413, 519, 567, 568, 569, 599, 600, 601, 622, 700, 744, 746, 758, 762, 763
Cooke, Elizabeth (Hoby, Lady Hoby; Russell, Lady Russell), I, 362
Coombe, Martha (Bisaillon), III, 65
Cooper, Anthony Ashley, 1st Earl of Shaftesbury, I, 519
Coote, Richard, 1st Earl of Bellomont, II, 46, 108, 114, 404, 410, 450, 591, 603, 622; III, 493
Cope, Henry, III, **135–36**, 665
Cope, Jane. *See* Patteshall
Cope, Jean-Baptiste, III, **136–37**, 34, 294, 298
Cope, Joseph, III, 136
Copley, Sir Godfrey, III, 449
Copley, John Singleton, IV, 292, 553

Coquart, Claude-Godefroy, II, 296, 608; III, **137–38**, 197, 252; IV, 241, 423
Corbarboineau, Anne de (Péan), III, 503
Corbet. *See also* Alès
Corbet, Elizabeth (Durell), III, 208
Corbin, André (father), IV, 167
Corbin, André, IV, **167–68**
Corbin, Charlotte. *See* Rainville
Corbin, David (father), III, 138
Corbin, David, III, **138–39**
Corbin, Étienne, III, 138, 139
Corbin, Geneviève. *See* Gariépy
Corbin, Joseph-Marie, III, 138, 139
Corbin, Louise. *See* Petit
Corbin, Marie. *See* Parent
Corbin, Marie-Jeanne. *See* Faveron
Corbin, Véronique. *See* Baby
Corcelles. *See* Motin
Cordé, Catherine de (Legardeur de Tilly), I, 446, 447
Coré, Catherine (Decoste), IV, 200
Cormier, Anne (Haché-Gallant), II, 272
Cormier, Jean, IV, 436
Cormier, Marie. *See* Terriot
Cornbury, Lord. *See* Hyde
Cornet, Marguerite de (Monic), II, 482
Cornplanter. *See* Kaiũtwahʔkũ
Cornuti, Jacques-Philippe, II, 596; III, 108, 678
Cornwallis, Charles, 4th Baron Cornwallis, IV, 168
Cornwallis, Charles, 1st Marquess and 2nd Earl Cornwallis, IV, 121, 694
Cornwallis, Charlotte, Baroness Cornwallis. *See* Butler
Cornwallis, Edward, III, 120, 125, 128, 130, 212, 261, 298, 343, 361, 362, 404, 405, 417, 439, 457, 473, 514, 517, 518, 573, 583, 585, 634, 666; IV, **168–71**, xxiv, xxv, 51, 92, 93, 110, 112, 249, 296, 312, 414, 455, 526, 559, 581, 703, 775
Cornwallis, Frederick, IV, 168
Cornwallis, Mary. *See* Townshend
Corolère, Christophe, III, 139
Corolère, Françoise. *See* Laurent
Corolère, Jean, III, **139–40**
Corolère, Marie. *See* Dorollaire
Coron, Angélique-Françoise. *See* Roland
Coron, Charles-François, III, **140–41**
Coron, François, III, 140
Coron, Marie. *See* Cyr
Coron, Marie-Louise. *See* Binot
Coron, Victoire (Jendon), III, 141
Corporon, Isabelle (Johnson), IV, 392
Corpron, Charles, III, 141
Corpron, Jean, III, **141–42**; IV, 66, 125, 127, 435, 517
Corpron, Marie. *See* Gabriel
Corpron, Marie. *See* Roy
Corrigal, Jacob, IV, 774
Corrivault, Marguerite (Maheut), I, 479
Corriveau, Joseph, III, 142
Corriveau, Joseph (father of MARIE-JOSEPHTE), III, 142, 143; IV, 299
Corriveau, Marie-Françoise. *See* Bolduc
Corriveau, Marie-Josephte, known as La Corriveau (Bouchard; Dodier), III, **142–43**; IV, 299, 692
Corruble, La. *See* Bouge
Corry (Curray, Currie), Thomas, IV, 47, 160, 277, 761

Cort, John, IV, 195, 196
Corte-Real, Gaspar, I, **234–36**, 19, 21, 151, 166, 171, 236, 304
Corte-Real, Isabel. *See* Castro
Corte-Real, João Vaz, I, 234, 236
Corte-Real, Miguel, I, **236**, 19, 21, 166, 171, 234, 235
Corte-Real, Vasco Añes, I, 236
Corvaisier, Charles, III, 613
Corwin, George, I, 242
Cosa, Juan de la, I, 148, 149, 150, 151, 304
Cosby, Alexander (father), III, 143
Cosby, Alexander, II, 23, 663; III, **143–44**, 4, 421, 426, 437, 517, 518, 665
Cosby, Anne. *See* Winniett
Cosby, Elizabeth. *See* L'Estrange
Cosby, Elizabeth (Philipps), III, 143, 518
Cosby, Philipps, III, 144
Cosby, William, III, 144
Cosineau de Mareuil, Jacques-Théodore. *See* Mareuil, Jacques de
Cosme, Father, IV, xxiii
Cosnier, Marie (Denys de La Thibaudière), I, 256, 261
Cossit*, Ranna (1744–1815), IV, 522, 523
Coste, Madeleine (Petitpas), III, 512
Coste (Costa), Mathieu de, I, 452
Costé, Michel, I, 87
Costebelle. *See* Pastour
Coster, Gerritje (Roseboom), III, 568
Cuswentannea. *See* Kaghswaghtaniunt
Côté. *See also* Cotté
Côté, Anne. *See* Martin
Côté, Jean, I, 495
Côté, Marie-Geneviève (Gabriel; Levasseur), IV, 471
Coté, Simone (Soumande), II, 275, 612, 613
Cotentin, *dit* Lavallée, Guillaume, II, 16
Cotesworth, Charles, II, 231, 266
Coton, Pierre, I, 97, 100, 121, 498
Cottard, Claude, III, 566
Cotté. *See also* Kotte
Cotté, Agathe. *See* Roy-Desjardins
Cotté, Angélique. *See* Blondeau
Cotté, Gabriel, IV, **171–72**, 403
Cotté (Côté), Lucie-Angélique (Boucher; Laframboise), IV, 172
Cotté, Marianne, IV, 171
Cotté, Marie-Catherine-Émilie (Larocque), IV, 172
Cotté, Marie-Claude. *See* Levasseur
Cotté, Marie-Josephte (Quesnel), IV, 172
Cotté, Nicolas, IV, 171
Cotté, Pierre-Gabriel, IV, 172
Cotterell, William, III, 137, 365; IV, 110
Cottnam, George, IV, 199
Cottnam, Henrietta Maria (Day), IV, 199
Cottnam, Margaret Ramsey (Scott), IV, 704
Cottnam, Martha Grace (Tonge), IV, 736
Cotton. *See also* Couton
Cotton, Barthélemy, II, 520; III, 550; IV, **172–73**, 376
Cotton, Françoise. *See* Gagnon
Cotton, Hester (Salusbury), III, 583
Cotton, Jean-François, IV, 173
Cotton, Marguerite, IV, 173
Cotton, Marie. *See* Willis
Cotton, Michel, III, **144–45**, 181, 346, 348; IV, 173

Cotton, Sir Robert, III, 583

Couagne, Anne de. *See* Mars

Couagne, Charles de (father), II, 153

Couagne, Charles de, II, **153–54**, 413, 526, 529; III, 145, 146, 379, 493

Couagne, Charles-René de, III, 145

Couagne, François-Marie de, III, 333; IV, 268

Couagne, Jean-Baptiste de (uncle), II, **154**, 121, 153, 285, 339, 648; III, 79, 229, 236, 644; IV, 174

Couagne, Jean-Baptiste de (nephew), III, 146, 652; IV, **173–74**

Couagne, Jean-François de, II, 154

Couagne, Jeanne de. *See* Loppinot

Couagne, Louise de. *See* Pothier

Couagne, Marguerite-Madeleine de. *See* Gannes de Falaise

Couagne, Marie de. *See* Gaudé

Couagne, Marie-Anne de. *See* Hubert de Lacroix

Couagne, Marie-Josephe de. *See* Mius d'Entremont

Couagne, Marie-Josephte de (Lemoine, *dit* Monière), III, 379

Couagne, Michel de, II, 154; III, 229; IV, **174–75**, 28

Couagne, René de, II, 153; III, **145–46**, 351; IV, 173

Couagne, René de (son), III, 145

Couagne, Renée de. *See* Greffière

Couagne, Thérèse de (Poulin de Francheville), II, 153, 529; III, **146–47**, 537

Couc, Elizabeth (?) (La Chenette, Techenet; Montour), II, 505, 645; III, **147–48**, 607

Couc, *dit* Lafleur, Marie. *See* Mite8ameg8k8e

Couc, *dit* Lafleur, Pierre, III, 147

Couc Montour, Jean (John), III, 147

Couc Montour, Louis, III, 147

Coughlan, Betsey, IV, 176

Coughlan, Laurence, IV, **175–77**, 402

Couillard, André, IV, 424

Couillard, Élisabeth. *See* Vesins

Couillard, Élisabeth-Simone. *See* Lajus

Couillard, Geneviève (Denys Du Tartre), II, 176

Couillard, Guillaume, I, 236

Couillard, Jean-Baptiste, IV, 71

Couillard, Joseph, III, 560

Couillard, Louise (Letardif), I, 473

Couillard, Marie (Byssot de La Rivière; Lalande de Gayon), I, 145, 146, 395, 661; II, 65, 68

Couillard, Marie-Geneviève. *See* Alliés

Couillard, Nicolas, I, 366, 367

Couillard de Beaumont, Charles, IV, 71

Couillard de Beaumont, Charles-Marie, III, 69

Couillard de Beaumont, Charles-Thomas, II, 159

Couillard de Beaumont, Louise. *See* Couture

Couillard de Lespinay, Catherine-Gertrude (Aubert de La Chesnaye), II, 33

Couillard de Lespinay, Élisabeth (Guyon Du Buisson), I, 359, 366

Couillard de Lespinay, Geneviève. *See* Chavigny de Berchereau

Couillard de Lespinay, Geneviève. *See* Desprès

Couillard de Lespinay, Guillaume, I, **236–37**, 109, 145, 200, 287, 359, 366, 452, 473, 517, 578; II, 33, 213, 448

Couillard de Lespinay, Guillaume (son), I, 366

Couillard de Lespinay, Guillemette. *See* Hébert

Couillard de Lespinay, Jacques, I, 161; II, 155

Couillard de Lespinay, Jean-Baptiste, II, **154–55**, xxiv, 17; III, 15, 74, 569

Couillard de Lespinay, Jeanne (Dupuy de Lisloye), II, 213

Couillard de Lespinay, Louis (father), I, **237–38**, 48, 420, 430; II, 155, 213

Couillard de Lespinay, Louis (son), II, **155–56**, 256

Couillard de Lespinay, Louise. *See* Nolin

Couillard de Lespinay, Marguerite. *See* Bélanger

Couillard de Lespinay, Marguerite (Nicollet de Belleborne; Macard), I, 84, 369, 517; II, 16, 181, 448

Couillard de Lespinay, Marie. *See* Fortin

Couillard de Lespinay. Marie. *See* Vandry

Couillard Des Islets, Catherine (Dambourgès; Oliva), IV, 589

Couillard Des Islets, Louis, IV, 589

Couillaud. *See* La Roque

Coulanges. *See* Petit de Levilliers

Coulaud (Couleau), Catherine (Courreaud de La Coste), IV, 178

Coulogne. *See* Robin

Coulon de Villiers, Angélique. *See* Jarret de Verchères

Coulon de Villiers, Élisabeth. *See* Groston de Saint-Ange

Coulon de Villiers, François, II, 267; IV, **177–78**

Coulon de Villiers, Jumonville, IV, 178

Coulon de Villiers, Louis, II, 156; III, **148–49**, 150, 151, 320, 502; IV, 33, 177, 257, 459, 617

Coulon de Villiers, Louise. *See* La Fosse

Coulon de Villiers, Madeleine-Marie-Anne. *See* Tarieu de La Pérade

Coulon de Villiers, Marie (Dagneau Douville), IV, 192

Coulon de Villiers, Marie-Amable. *See* Prud'homme

Coulon de Villiers, Marie-Anne (Aubert de Gaspé), IV, 33, 34

Coulon de Villiers, Marie-Geneviève. *See* Énault de Livaudais

Coulon de Villiers, Marie-Madeleine. *See* Marin

Coulon de Villiers, Marie-Madeleine (Regnard Duplessis; Marin de La Perrière; Damours Des Plaines), II, 156; III, 432

Coulon de Villiers, Nicolas-Antoine (father), II, **156**, 284, 316, 317; III, 46, 148, 149, 150, 432, 491; IV, 33, 177, 192

Coulon de Villiers, Nicolas-Antoine (son), III, **149–50**, 49, 87, 260, 331, 378, 432, 484, 676; IV, 177, 459, 512, 559, 651

Coulon de Villiers, Raoul-Guillaume, II, 156

Coulon de Villiers de Jumonville, Joseph, II, 156; III, **150–51**, 148, 376, 600, 614; IV, 33, 34, 177, 178, 227, 459, 647

Coulon de Villiers de Jumonville, Marie-Anne-Marguerite. *See* Soumande

Coulonge. *See* Ailleboust

Coundo. *See* Est

Courault, *dit* La Coste, Angélique (Lupien, *dit* Baron), III, 412

Courcelle. *See* Rémy

Courcelles. *See* Motin

Courcillon, Louis de, Abbé de Dangeau, II, 589

Courcy. *See* Potier

Courier, Joseph, III, 443

Cournoyer. *See also* Hertel

Cournoyer, Élisabeth de (Pascaud), IV, 605

Courpont, M. de, I, 297

Courreaud de La Coste, Catherine. *See* Coulaud
Courreaud de La Coste, Élie, IV, 178
Courreaud de La Coste, Marguerite. *See* Aubuchon, *dit*
    L'Espérance
Courreaud de La Coste, Marie-Anne. *See* Massé
Courreaud de La Coste, Marin, IV, 179
Courreaud de La Coste, Pierre, II, 614; IV, **178–79**, 732
Courserac. *See* Aubert
Courseron, Gilbert, I, **238**
Coursier, Catherine (Genaple), II, 241
Courtade, Suzanne (Masclé), III, 440
Court de La Bruyère, Claude-Élisée de, III, 27, 557, 609,
    610; IV, 256
Courtemanche. *See* Legardeur; Le Gardeur
Courtenay, Princesse de, Marquise de Bauffremont
    (Beauffremont), IV, 469
Courthiau, Marie-Anne (La Forest), II, 336
Courthiau, Pierre-Noël, III, 394
Courtin, Michel, II, 238
Courtin de Tangeux, Catherine (Brisay de Denonville, Mar-
    quise de Denonville), II, 98, 99
Courtin de Tangeux, Germain, II, 98
Courtois, Maurice, IV, 509
Courval. *See* Poulin
Courville. *See* Aumasson; Cadieu
Cousineau, Marie-Renée (Cheval), III, 121
Coussez, Captain, I, 422
Couteron, Louise-Élisabeth (Deschevery, *dit* Maisonbasse),
    III, 181, 182
Coutlée*, Thérèse-Geneviève (1742–1821), IV, 462
Couton. *See also* Cotton
Couton, Barthélemy, III, 144; IV, 172
Couton, Jeanne. *See* Le Rouge
Coutré, Marquis de, II, 77
Couttes. *See* Le Fascheux
Couture, Anne. *See* Esmard
Couture, Guillaume (father), II, 157
Couture, Guillaume, I, 42, 60, 124, 145, 227, 282, 298,
    344, 387, 388, 396, 403, 404, 523; II, **157–59**, 635
Couture, Jean, I, 79; II, 635
Couture, Louise (Couillard de Beaumont), II, 159
Couture, Madeleine. *See* Mallet
Couture, Marguerite (Marsolet), II, 159
Couture, Marie (Vézier; Bourget), II, 159
Couture, Peter, IV, 613
Couture de La Cressonnière, Joseph-Oger, II, 159
Couturier, Jean, II, 530; III, 119, 192, 256, 486; IV, 89,
    237, 542
Couturier, Marie. *See* Guillier
Couturier, Michel, II, 159
Couturier, *dit* Le Bourguignon, Charlotte (Janson, *dit*
    Lapalme), II, 160
Couturier, *dit* Le Bourguignon, Jeanne-Charlotte (Janson,
    dit Lapalme), III, 307
Couturier, *dit* Le Bourguignon, Marguerite. *See* Payet
Couturier, *dit* Le Bourguignon, Marie-Joseph (Janson, *dit*
    Lapalme), II, 160; III, 307
Couturier, *dit* Le Bourguignon, Michel-Étienne, IV, 204
Couturier, *dit* Le Bourguignon, Pierre, II, **159–60**, 546;
    III, 307; IV, 732
Couvert, Michel-Germain de, II, **160–61**, 337
Couvreur, Jeanne (Soullard), II, 612

Coux, Anne de. *See* Du Pont Duchambon de Mézillac
Coux, Louis de, IV, 248
Cox, Deborah (wife of NICHOLAS), IV, 179
Cox, John Henry, IV, 325
Cox, Nicholas, IV, **179–80**, 153
Cox, William, I, 334, 335, 363
Coxe, Daniel, III, 65
Coya (Coyour). *See* Koyah
Cozer, Françoise-Marie (Guichart), IV, 317
Cradock, Mary (Gerrish; Breynton), IV, 94, 292
Cragg, James, II, 288
Craigie*, John (d. 1813), IV, 493
Cramahé. *See also* Chateigner
Cramahé, Hector Theophilus, III, 111, 142; IV, **787–93**,
    xxxviii, xxxix, xlvi, xlvii, 100, 107, 109, 189, 229, 323,
    484, 503, 538, 547, 550, 570, 575, 618, 739
Cramahé, Margaret (wife of HECTOR THEOPHILUS), IV, 793
Cramer, Christy, IV, 703
Cramolet, M., I, 64
Crampporn, Jane (Yonge), II, 672
Crampporn, Thomas, II, 672
Crapanoz. *See* Vachon
Crapaut. *See* Chomina
Crasset, Jean, III, 104
Craston, William, I, 450, 451
Creighton*, John (1721–1807), IV, 780
Créquy. *See* Aide-Créquy
Crespel, Emmanuel (baptized Jacques-Philippe), II, 390;
    IV, **180–82**
Crespel, Louise-Thérèse. *See* Devienne
Crespel, Sébastien, IV, 180
Crespi, Juan, IV, 623
Crespieul, François de, I, 49, 396, 483; II, **161–62**, 61, 296,
    357, 501, 607
Crespieul, Jean de, II, 161
Crespieul, Marguerite de. *See* Théry
Crespin, Antoine, III, 203
Crespin, Jean, III, 182; IV, 263
Cressé. *See also* Poulin
Cressé, Louise (Poulin de Courval), II, 529; III, 539
Cressé, Marguerite. *See* Denys
Cressé, Michel, II, 529
Cressé*, Pierre-Michel (1758–1819), III, 540
Creste, Jeanne (Juchereau), I, 401, 402
Crevant, Louis de, Duc d'Humières, II, 401
Crèvecœur, Marquis de. *See* Castel
Crèvecœur, Marquise de. *See* Kerven
Crevel de Moranget, M., I, 182, 183; II, 197
Crevet, Marie (Caron; Langlois), I, 417
Crevier, Christophe, I, 475; II, 86
Crevier, Jeanne. *See* Énard
Crevier, Jeanne (Boucher), I, 109; II, 86; III, 78, 81, 82, 83
Crevier, Joseph, I, 239
Crevier, Louis, I, 239; II, 283
Crevier, Marguerite (Fournier; Gamelain de La Fontaine;
    Renou, *dit* La Chapelle; Groston de Saint-Ange), I, 321;
    II, 236, 267; IV, 315
Crevier, Marie (Gastineau Duplessis), III, 237
Crevier, *dit* La Meslée, Christophe, I, 238
Crevier de Saint-François, Jean, I, **238–39**, 321, 369
Crevier de Saint-François, Marguerite. *See* Hertel de La
    Fresnière

133

Crevier Duvernay, Jean-Baptiste, III, 493
Crey, Élisée, II, 130
Crignon, Pierre, I, 235, 532
Crisafy, Antoine de, Marquis de Crisafy, I, 239; II, **162–63**, 15, 70, 186, 203, 303, 485, 533
Crisafy, Françoise de. *See* Grimaldi
Crisafy, Marie-Claire de, Marquise de Crisafy. *See* Ruette d'Auteuil
Crisafy, Mathieu de, II, 162
Crisafy, Thomas, I, **239**; II, 70, 162, 523; III, 310
Crisp, Delivrance (Longley), III, 407
Crochet, Le. *See* Kiotseaeton
Croft, Thomas, I, **239–40**, 19, 21, 147, 386
Croft, William, I, 239
Croghan, George, III, 49, 323, 495, 502, 526, 530, 614; IV, 395, 408, 409, 499
Croisille (Croizille). *See* Legardeur
Croissy, Marquis de. *See* Colbert
Crokatt, Charles, IV, 330
Cromartie, John, III, 124
Cromberger. *See* Noremberguer
Cromwell, Oliver, I, 242, 406, 407, 474, 595, 604, 605, 636, 652; IV, xvii
Cromwell, Thomas, I, 566
Crosland, Alice (Calvert), I, 162
Crosland, John, I, 162
Cross, Sarah Mary (Hill), II, 287
Croston. *See* Groston
Crout, Henry, I, **240–41**, 233, 670, 671
Crow, Robert, II, 493
Crowe, Josias, II, **163–64**, 152, 534, 636
Crown. *See* Crowne
Crowne, Agnes. *See* Mackworth
Crowne, John, I, 241, 242
Crowne, William, I, **241–42**, 25, 434, 435, 595, 605, 636; IV, xxiv
Crozat, Antoine, II, 203, 355, 356, 425; III, 380
Cruickshank*, Robert (d. 1809), IV, 206, 629, 702, 748
Cruse, Thomas, I, **242–43**
Crusoe, Robinson, III, **151**
Crusson, *dit* Pilote, François, I, 267
Cruzat, Francisco, IV, 303
Cryn. *See* Togouiroui
Crynssen, Abraham, I, 443
Cuadra. *See* Bodega
Cugnet, Mme, IV, 127
Cugnet, Antoine, IV, 182
Cugnet, François-Étienne, II, 530; III, **151–55**, 16, 48, 146, 159, 224, 237, 340, 353, 490, 538, 592, 608, 617, 647; IV, 45, 64, 66, 167, 182, 264, 284, 344, 358, 359, 360, 361, 362, 590
Cugnet, François-Joseph, III, 154; IV, **182–87**, xlv, 105, 146, 315, 349, 388, 602
Cugnet, Gilles-Louis, III, 154; IV, 182, 185, 430
Cugnet, Jacques-François, IV, 182, 184, 185
Cugnet, Jean (Jean-Baptiste), III, 151; IV, 182
Cugnet, Jean-Baptiste (uncle), III, 152; IV, 182
Cugnet, Jean-Baptiste, III, 154
Cugnet, Louise-Charlotte (Liénard de Beaujeu), III, 16
Cugnet, Louise-Madeleine. *See* Dusautoy
Cugnet, Madeleine. *See* Baudin
Cugnet, Marie-Josephte. *See* Lafontaine de Belcour

Cugnet, Thomas-Marie, III, 154, 647; IV, 182, 185
Cuillerier, Angélique (Porlier), IV, 638
Cuillerier, Julien, II, 164
Cuillerier, Julienne. *See* Faifeu
Cuillerier, Marie. *See* Barbeau, *dit* Lucault
Cuillerier, Marie-Anne-Véronique, III, **155–56**, 238
Cuillerier, René, I, 130, 598, 662; II, **164–65**; III, 155
Cuillerier, *dit* Beaubien, Angélique (Sterling), IV, 722
Cuillerier, *dit* Beaubien, Antoine, III, 528
Cuillerier, *dit* Beaubien, Marie-Catherine. *See* Trottier Desruisseaux
Cull*, William (fl. 1803–23), IV, 714
Cumberland, Duke of. *See* William Augustus
Cumberlege, S. A., IV, 578
Cumings, Archibald, II, **165**, 118, 316, 583, 610, 611, 643
Cumshewa, IV, 420
Cunningham, John, I, **243**, 360, 408
Cuny, Élisabeth. *See* Dupont
Cuny, Philippe-Antoine, IV, 187
Cuny Dauterive, Madeleine-Thérèse de. *See* Chabert de Joncaire
Cuny Dauterive, Philippe-Antoine de, IV, **187**
Curatteau, Claude, IV, 188
Curatteau, Jean-Baptiste, IV, **187–89**, 90
Curatteau, Jeanne. *See* Fonteneau
Curatteau, Pierre (father), IV, 187
Curatteau, Pierre, IV, 188
Curatteau, René, IV, 188
Curaux. *See* Curot
Curchot, Jacques, IV, 303, 304
Cureux, *dit* Saint-Germain, Marie-Anne (Fortier), IV, 271
Curie, Henriette-Edwige, Baronne de L'Espérance (Sandersleben), II, 424
Curie, Richard, II, 424
Curie, Sébastienne, Baronne de L'Espérance (Sifert), II, 424
Curler, Arent van, I, 308
Curot, Madeleine. *See* Cauchois
Curot, Marie-Louis, *dite* de Saint-Martin, IV, **189–90**
Curot, Martin, IV, 189
Curray (Currie). *See* Corry
Curtis, Mary (Loring), IV, 486
Curtis*, Sir Roger (1746–1816), IV, 708
Curtius, Charles, IV, 384
Cushing, Lucy (Aylwin), IV, 37
Cusson, Catherine, IV, 235
Cusson, Jacqueline. *See* Pépin
Cusson, Jean (father), II, 166
Cusson, Jean, II, **165–66**, xix, 11; III, 4
Cusson, Marie. *See* Foubert
Cusson, Michelle (Adhémar de Saint-Martin), II, 11; III, 4
Cussy, Geneviève (Paradis), III, 500
Cuthbert, Alexander (grandfather), IV, 190
Cuthbert, Alexander, IV, 191
Cuthbert, Beatrix (Cuthbert), IV, 190
Cuthbert, Catherine. *See* Cairns
Cuthbert, James, IV, **190–91**, 379, 579
Cuthbert*, James (1769–1849), IV, 191
Cuthbert, Margaret. *See* Mackenzie
Cuthbert, Rebecca. *See* Stockton
Cuthbert*, Ross (1776–1861), IV, 191
Cutt, Margaret (Vaughan), II, 644
Cuvier, Frédéric, III, 679

Cuyler, Abraham, III, 528, 529
Cuyler*, Abraham Cornelius (1742–1810), IV, 293, 522
Cyr, Marie (Coron), III, 140, 141
Cyrier. *See* Cirier

DABLON, Claude, I, **244**, 48, 49, 58, 205, 206, 207, 282, 393, 394, 395, 396, 445, 461, 491, 492, 523; II, 61, 62, 158, 218, 347, 501, 517, 536; III, xxxix; IV, lvi
Daccarrette, Catherine. *See* Gonillon
Daccarrette, Catherine (Lagoanere), III, 156
Daccarrette, Jacques (father), III, 156
Daccarrette, Jacques, III, 156
Daccarrette, Jeanne. *See* Gonillon
Daccarrette, Joannis, III, 156
Daccarrette, Marguerite. *See* La Borde
Daccarrette, Marie. *See* Gastaignol
Daccarrette, Marie-Charlotte (Leneuf de Beaubassin), III, 157
Daccarrette, Michel (father), II, 220; III, **156–57**, 350, 452, 532; IV, 245, 253
Daccarrette, Michel (son), III, **157–58**; IV, 421, 422, 645
Dache, Jacques, II, 513
Dagneau de Quindre de La Picanier, Guillaume-François, III, 159
Dagneau Douville, Alexandre, IV, **191–92**, 54
Dagneau Douville, Alexandre-René, IV, 192
Dagneau Douville, Marie. *See* Coulon de Villiers
Dagneau Douville, Marie. *See* Lamy
Dagneau Douville, Michel, III, 158; IV, 191
Dagneau Douville de Lamothe, Guillaume, III, 159; IV, 192
Dagneau Douville de La Saussaye, Philippe, IV, 192
Dagneau Douville de Quindre, Archange (Maurin), III, 441
Dagneau Douville de Quindre, Françoise-Marie-Anne. *See* Picoté de Belestre
Dagneau Douville de Quindre, Louis-Césaire, III, **158–59**, 432, 441; IV, 192
Daguerre, Madeleine (Bourdon de Romainville), I, 114
Dagworthy, John, III, 261
Dahon, Laurens-Alexandre, IV, 124
Daigre, Jacques, II, 549
Daillon. *See* La Roche
Daine, Angélique. *See* Pagé
Daine, Antoinette. *See* Pelletier
Daine, François, III, **159–61**, 15, 64, 139, 203, 226, 272, 291, 340, 505, 608; IV, 66, 75, 264, 602, 614
Daine, Jacques (father), III, 159
Daine, Jacques, III, 159
Daine, Louise. *See* Pécaudy de Contrecœur
Daine, Louise-Jeanne. *See* Bouat
Daine, Marius-Basile, III, 159
Daine, Nicolas, III, 159
Dakeyne, Mary (Gladwin), IV, 297
Dalard. *See* Allard
Dalgueuil (Delguiel), *dit* Labrèche, Jeanne (Billeron, *dit* Lafatigue), IV, 34
Dalgueuil (Delguiel), *dit* Labrèche, Louise-Françoise (Augé), IV, 34
Dalison, Jane (Amherst, Lady Amherst), IV, 25
Dalling, Sir John, III, 12; IV, 779
Dalmas, Antoine, I, **244–45**; II, 161
Dalquier. *See* Alquier
Dalrymple, Alexander, IV, 218, 244, 245, 325, 340, 741

Dalyell (Dalzell), James, III, 528, 529; IV, 297, 308, 680
Damboise, Jeanne (Deschevery), III, 181
Dambourgès, Catherine. *See* Couillard Des Islets
Dambourgès, François, IV, 386, 548
Dame, George, IV, 304
Damestoye, Bernard, III, 157
Damienne (servant), I, 426
Damours, Charlotte (Raimbault), II, 542
Damours, Élisabeth. *See* Tessier
Damours, Élisabeth (Chartier de Lotbinière), I, 202, 245; II, 136
Damours, Jean, I, 245
Damours, Louis, I, 245
Damours de Chauffours, Élisabeth (Charron de La Barre), I, 201; II, 133
Damours de Chauffours, Geneviève (Céloron de Blainville), II, 125, 442
Damours de Chauffours, Louis, I, 245, 246; II, **166–67**, 3, 271, 626; III, 273, 474, 681
Damours de Chauffours, Marguerite. *See* Guyon
Damours de Chauffours, Marguerite (Testard de Montigny), II, 627
Damours de Chauffours, Marie. *See* Marsolet de Saint-Aignan
Damours de Chauffours, Marie (Villedonné), II, 653
Damours de Chauffours, Marie-Charlotte (Abbadie de Saint-Castin, Baronne de Saint-Castin), II, 3, 4
Damours de Chauffours, Marie-Joseph (Morpain), III, 474
Damours de Chauffours, Mathieu, I, **245**, 137, 201, 202, 289, 587, 588, 589; II, xvii, 125, 166, 167, 442, 588, 653; III, 681
Damours de Clignancour, Françoise-Charlotte. *See* Legardeur de Tilly
Damours de Clignancour, Louis-Mathieu, III, 178, 233
Damours de Clignancour, Mathieu-Benjamin, IV, 375
Damours de Clignancour, René, I, 245; II, **167–68**, 166, 626
Damours de Freneuse, Antoine, III, 681
Damours de Freneuse, Joseph, IV, 181
Damours de Freneuse, Louis, II, 7
Damours de Freneuse, Louise. *See* Guyon
Damours de Freneuse, Mathieu, I, **245–46**, 245, 577; II, 166, 271, 626; III, 111, 552, 681
Damours de Freneuse, Ursule. *See* Abbadie de Saint-Castin
Damours de Louvières, Louis, II, 633
Damours de Plaines, Bernard, I, 245
Damours Des Plaines, Joseph, III, 432
Damours Des Plaines, Marie-Madeleine. *See* Coulon de Villiers
Danao. *See* David
Dance, Nathaniel, IV, 601
Dandane Danseville de L'Étendard, Marie-Anne. *See* Dupéré
Dandane Danseville de L'Étendard, Nicolas-Antoine, III, 125
Dandin. *See* Daudin
Dandonneau, Isabelle. *See* Fain
Dandonneau, Jacques, II, 168
Dandonneau, Périnne (Lamarre, *dit* Bélisle), II, 340
Dandonneau, *dit* Lajeunesse, Françoise. *See* Jobin
Dandonneau, *dit* Lajeunesse, Jeanne (Babie), I, 74
Dandonneau, *dit* Lajeunesse, Pierre, I, 74; II, **168**
Dandonneau Du Sablé, Angélique (Chaboulié), II, 127

Dandonneau Du Sablé, Louis, II, 168; III, 247
Dandonneau Du Sablé, Marguerite. *See* Sabrevois de Bleury
Dandonneau Du Sablé, Marie-Anne (Gaultier de Varennes et de La Vérendrye), II, 168, 239; III, 241, 244, 247, 252; IV, 288
Dandonneau Du Sablé, Marie-Louise (Robinau de Portneuf), III, 560
Daneau, Catherine. *See* Driot
Daneau, Jacques, II, 168
Daneau de Muy, Catherine. *See* Ailleboust Des Muceaux
Daneau de Muy, Charlotte, *dite* de Sainte-Hélène, III, **161**
Daneau de Muy, Jacques-Pierre, II, 168; III, **161–63**, 601; IV, 634
Daneau de Muy, Louise-Geneviève. *See* Ruette d'Auteuil
Daneau de Muy, Marguerite. *See* Boucher
Daneau de Muy, Marguerite (Robinau de Portneuf), II, 580; III, 559, 560
Daneau de Muy, Nicolas, II, **168–69**, 395, 416, 504, 580, 588, 603, 617; III, 161, 162, 380, 505
Dangé, François, I, **246**
Dangeac (Danjaique). *See also* Angeac
Dangeac, Gabriel, II, 424
Dangeac, Marguerite (L'Espérance), II, 424; IV, 470
Dangeau. *See* Courcillon
Danguel Lamarche, Jacques, III, 165
Daniel. *See also* Garakontié
Daniel (miner), I, 334
Daniel (servant), III, 425
Daniel, André, I, 247
Daniel, Antoine (father), I, 247
Daniel, Antoine, I, **246–47**, 70, 122, 124, 125, 128, 206, 252, 253, 388, 414, 461, 633, 637, 638, 639
Daniel, Catherine. *See* Quevillon
Daniel, Charles, I, **247–48**, 25, 53, 252, 261, 305, 482, 521, 567, 613, 665
Daniel, François (author), IV, 344
Daniel, François (brother of CHARLES), I, 247
Daniel, Marguerite. *See* Martin
Daniélou, Jean-Pierre, III, **163**; IV, 289
Danio. *See* Noyon
Danks, Benoni, IV, **192–94**
Danks, Lucy (wife of BENONI), IV, 193
Danks, Mary. *See* Morris
Danks, Rebecca. *See* Rust
Danks, Robert, IV, 192
Danré de Blanzy, Charles, III, 163
Danré de Blanzy, Louis-Claude, II, 92; III, **163–64**, 121, 211; IV, 270, 621, 720
Danré de Blanzy, Suzanne. *See* Estienne Du Bourgué de Clérin; Morillon
Danseville. *See* Dandane
Danton. *See* Michel
Daprandestiguy. *See* Aprendestiguy
Daquin, Marie (Aigron), I, 42
D'Arblay. *See* Arblay
Darby, George, III, 189; IV, 226
Darby, Hatty. *See* Vanacott
Darby, Mary, known as Perdita (Robinson), IV, 195
Darby, Nicholas, III, 411; IV, **194–95**, 536, 712
D'Arcy, Robert, 4th Earl of Holderness, III, 364, 502; IV, 422
Dardaine, Françoise (Olivier), I, 524
Daret, Françoise (Pinaud), II, 526

Dargent, François, III, 164
Dargent, Joseph, III, **164–65**
Dargent, Renée. *See* Bernard
Darguinarat, Joannis, III, 157
Darles, Sieur, II, 134
Darles, François, III, 633; IV, 720
Darles de Lignières, M., IV, 187
Darmeville. *See* Olivier
Darnaud (Darnault). *See* Arnaud
Darontal. *See* Atironta (fl. 1615)
Darouet, Simon, IV, 331
Darrigrand. *See* Arrigrand
Dartmouth, Earl of. *See* Legge
Dasilva, Dominique, III, 165
Dasilva, Jeanne. *See* Greslon Laviolette
Dasilva, Pedro, III, 165
Dasilva, *dit* Portugais, Élisabeth. *See* Laisné
Dasilva, *dit* Portugais, Marie-Gabrielle. *See* La Roche
Dasilva, *dit* Portugais, Nicolas, III, **165**, 420; IV, 263
Dassemat. *See* Dazemard
Dassilva. *See* Dasilva
Datte, Nicolas, III, 613
Daudin, Henri, III, **165–66**, 120, 257
Dauger. *See also* Auger
Dauger, Jean (father), II, 35
Dauger, Jean, II, 35
Dauger, Jourdain, II, 35
Dauger, Marie (Madeleine). *See* Boyrie
Daulac (Daulat). *See* Dollard
Daulé*, Jean-Denis (1766–1852), IV, 136
Daulier Des Landes, André, II, 381; III, 390
Daumont de Saint-Lusson, Jean-Baptiste, I, 250
Daumont de Saint-Lusson, Magdeleine, I, 249
Daumont de Saint-Lusson, Marguerite. *See* Bérin; La Verge
Daumont de Saint-Lusson, Simon-François, I, **248–50**, 35, 57, 63, 127, 226, 345, 393, 394, 572, 625, 626; II, 141, 347, 517, 537
Daunet, Gertrude (Senet), II, 604
Dauphin de La Forest, Charlotte-Françoise. *See* Juchereau de Saint-Denis
Dauphin de La Forest, François, I, 178, 661; II, **169–70**, 76, 270, 305, 306, 355, 435, 562, 588, 634, 636
Dauphin de Montorgueuil, I, **250**, 299
Dauterive. *See* Cuny
Dauteuil, Marie (Barolet), III, 26
Dauvin, Jeanne (Casot), IV, 134
Dauzet, Marguerite (Taché), III, 608
Davaugour. *See* Dubois
Daveine, Gabriel, IV, 123
Daveine (Davenne, Davesne), Marie-Joseph (Cadet; Bernard), IV, 123
Davène de Fontaine, M., I, 424
Davenport, Addington, III, 200
Davenport, Elizabeth (Dudley), III, 200
Davers, Sir Charles, III, 167
Davers, Sir Jermyn, III, 166
Davers, Margaretta, Lady Davers. *See* Green
Davers, Sir Robert, III, **166–67**, 528, 559
David. *See* Karonghyontye
David (Danao) (privateer), III, 497
David, Albert, III, 34; IV, 458
David, Claude, I, **250–51**, 225
David, Jacques, II, **170–71**; III, 316

David, Lazarus, IV, 332, 385
David, Marie. *See* Montet
David, Marie-Louise. *See* Normandin, *dit* Le Sauvage
David, Paul, II, 170
David, Suzanne. *See* Noyon
Davidson. *See also* Davison
Davidson*, Arthur (d. 1807), IV, 295
Davidson, Hugh, III, 583; IV, 170
Davidson, James, IV, 82, 295
Davidson, Jane. *See* Fraser
Davidson, Sarah. *See* Nevers
Davidson*, Walter (1790–1825), IV, 276
Davidson, William (grandfather), IV, 195
Davidson, William, IV, **195–97**, 328
Davies*, Thomas (d. 1812), III, 592
Davion, Albert, II, **171**, 227, 331; III, 469, 639
Davis, Faith. *See* Fulford
Davis, George, IV, 175
Davis, Isaac, III, 168
Davis, John, I, **251–52**, 20, 75, 336, 360, 375, 377, 378, 397, 676
Davis, Joseph, II, **171–72**, 56, 232, 267, 319, 662
Davis, Lydia. *See* Black
Davis, Marie-Anne, *dite* de Saint-Benoît, III, **167–68**
Davis, Marie-Anne, *dite* de Sainte-Cécile, II, 65
Davis, Sarah. *See* Davis, Marie-Anne
Davis, Silvanus, II, **172**, 145, 579
Davison, Alexander, IV, 197
Davison*, Alexander (1750–1829), IV, 197, 198, 317, 320, 324
Davison, Dorothy. *See* Neal
Davison, George, IV, **197–99**, 324, 538
Davost, Ambroise, I, **252–53**, 122, 125, 388
Davys. *See also* Davis
Davys, Samuel, IV, 194, 195
Dawbeny, Oliver, I, 371
Dawson, Mary (Hamilton), IV, 321
Day, George, IV, 199
Day, Henrietta Maria. *See* Cottnam
Day, John (merchant), I, 21, 148, 149, 150, 240, 302, 643
Day, John, IV, **199**, 116, 451, 581, 704
Day, Sarah (Mercer; wife of JOHN), IV, 199
Dazé. *See* Daret
Dazemard de Lusignan, Jeanne. *See* Babie
Dazemard de Lusignan, Louis-Antoine, III, 169
Dazemard de Lusignan, Madeleine-Marguerite. *See* Bouat
Dazemard de Lusignan, Paul-Louis (father), III, 168
Dazemard de Lusignan, Paul-Louis, III, **168–69**, 31, 64
Deair. *See* Heer
Deanaghrison. *See* Tanaghrisson
Deane, Joseph, III, 132, 133, 606
Dease, John, IV, 119
Déat, Antoine (father), III, 169
Déat, Antoine, III, **169–70**; IV, 236
Déat, Catherine. *See* Metayer
D'Eath, Elizabeth (How), III, 297
Debelius, Domine, II, 108
Debin, Élisabeth (Deschamps), II, 181
De Bonne, Marie-Charlotte. *See* Chartier de Lotbinière
Debrier, Anne-Marie (Le Normant de Mézy), III, 386; IV, 465
Debuire, Marie-Marguerite (Hantraye), IV, 326
Decanesora. *See* Teganissorens

Decaraffe, Jean-Baptiste, IV, 206
D'echambault (Déchambault). *See* Fleury
Dechart (Duhart), Catherine (Laborde), IV, 420
Decheuraineville, Marie (Lamy), II, 458
Decheverry, Bernard, IV, 253, 421
Decoste, Catherine. *See* Coré
Decoste, Jean-Baptiste, IV, **200**
Decoste, Jean-Christophe, IV, 200
Decoste, Louis, IV, 200
Decoste, Marie-Joseph. *See* Dumouchel
Decoste, Marie-Renée. *See* Marchand
Decous (Decoust). *See* Descouts
Decwando. *See* Atecouando
Dee, John, I, 148, 302, 316, 332, 333, 336, 643, 677, 678
Deering, Ann (Monk), III, 457
Defoe, Daniel, IV, 711
Defosse, Anne (Le Conte), II, 381
Deganawidah. *See* Dekanahwideh
Degawehe. *See* Gawèhe
Degeay, Henri, IV, 200
Degeay, Jacques, IV, **200–1**
Degeay, Marie. *See* Bournicat
Degonnor, Nicolas, III, 81, 249, 269, 355; IV, 270
Degoutin. *See* Goutin
De Guerne. *See* Le Guerne
Deguire, Jean, IV, 732
Deguire, Marie-Josephte (Waddens), IV, 757
Deguire, *dit* Desrosiers, Angélique. *See* Pepin
Deguire, *dit* Desrosiers, Jeanne. *See* Blet
Deguire, *dit* Desrosiers, Joseph, IV, **201–2**
Deguire, *dit* Desrosiers, Marie (Leverrier), IV, 202
Deguire, *dit* Desrosiers, Pierre, IV, 201
Deguise, *dit* Flamand, Élisabeth. *See* Laisné, *dit* Laliberté
Deguise, *dit* Flamand, Élisabeth (Falardeau), IV, 203
Deguise, *dit* Flamand, François (son of GIRARD-GUILLAUME), III, 170
Desguise, *dit* Flamand, François (son of JACQUES), IV, 203
Deguise, *dit* Flamand, Girard-Guillaume, III, **170**, 420; IV, 202, 659
Deguise, *dit* Flamand, Guillaume, III, 170; IV, 202
Deguise, *dit* Flamand, Jacques, III, 170; IV, **202–4**, 659
Deguise, *dit* Flamand, Marie-Anne. *See* Morin
Deguise, *dit* Flamand, Marie-Anne. *See* Rouillard
Deguise, *dit* Flamand, Marie-Françoise. *See* Jourdain, *dit* Bellerose
Deguise, *dit* Flamand, Thérèse. *See* Rinfret, *dit* Malouin
Dehaire. *See* Heer
Dehorné. *See* Horné
Deiaquande. *See* Teyohaqueande
Dejean*, Philippe (b. 1736, d. in or after 1809), IV, 321, 702, 722
Dejordy. *See also* Desjordy
Dejordy de Villebon, Catherine. *See* Trottier Desrivières
Dejordy de Villebon, Charles-René, III, **170–71**, 243
Dekanahwideh, I, **253–55**, 7; II, xxix; III, xli; IV, lvii
Delaborde, Jean, III, **172**
Delafosse, Cécile (Closse), I, 230
Delagarde. *See* Lagarde
Delage, Maître, IV, 127
Delain, Marie (Papineau), II, 507
DeLancey, James, III, 126, 497, 655
DeLancey, Stephen (grandfather), III, 394, 655
De Lancey*, Stephen (1738–1809), IV, 675

DeLancey, Susannah (Warren), III, 655
Delannes, Pierre, IV, 124
Delaunay, Anne (Maillou, *dit* Desmoulins), III, 419
Delaunay, Charles, II, **173**, 264; III, 88, 523; IV, 46
Delaunay, Françoise. *See* Pinguet
Delaunay, Marie-Anne. *See* Legras
Delaunay, Marie-Joseph (Lenoir, *dit* Rolland), II, 173
Delaunay, Pierre, II, 173
DeLaune, Henry, III, 172
DeLaune, Lucy (mother of WILLIAM), III, 173
DeLaune, William, III, **172–73**, 669, 672
De La Warr, Baron. *See* West
Delesdernier*, Moses (d. 1811), IV, xxix
Delesderniers, John Mark Crank, IV, 516
Delesnerac, Marguerite (Monseignat), II, 483
Delestre, Alonié, I, 267
Delestre, *dit* Beaujour, Pierre, III, 165
Delezenne, Ignace-François, IV, **204–7**, 619, 629, 748
Delezenne*, Joseph-Christophe (d. 1820), IV, 205
Delezenne, Marie-Catherine. *See* Janson, *dit* Lapalme
Delezenne*, Marie-Catherine (Pélissier; Fabre, *dit* Laterrière) (1755–1831), IV, 205, 618, 619
Delezenne, Marie-Christine. *See* Jacquemart
Delezenne, Martin, IV, 204
Delezenne, Michel, IV, 205
Delguiel. *See* Dalgueuil
Delhalle, Constantin, II, **173–74**, 414, 475, 505, 645; III, 355
Delicérasse, Suzanne (Buisson, *dit* Saint-Cosme), II, 109
Deliette. *See* Liette; Tonty
Delique, Charles-François, IV, 748
Delisle. *See also* Bréhaut; Chabrand
Delisle, Claude, III, 248
Delisle, Françoise (Toupin, *dit* Dussault; Raby), IV, 650
Delisle, Guillaume, II, 428, 653; III, 248
De Lisle*, Jean-Guillaume (1757–1819), IV, 534
Delisle, Joseph-Nicolas, I, 677; IV, 76, 77,
De Lisle* de La Cailleterie, Jean (d. 1814), IV, 6, 7, 189, 543
Dellius, Godfrey, II, 474, 603; III, 622
Delongrais. *See* Deslongrais
Delor. *See* Levasseur
Delort, Barbe. *See* Leneuf de La Vallière et de Beaubassin
Delort, Françoise-Ovide. *See* Carrerot
Delort, Guillaume, II, 119; III, **173–74**, 97; IV, 433
Delort, Guillaume (son), III, 173, 174
Delort, Jacques, III, 173
Delort, Louis, II, 119; III, 173, 174
Delort, Marie-Charlotte. *See* Gaultier
Delort, Michel, III, 173
Delort, Philippe, III, 173
Delort, Suzanne. *See* Despenan
Demay, André, II, 273
Demay de Termont, Charles-Gilbert, IV, 99
Demers Dessermont, Marie-Catherine, IV, 235
Demers Monfort, Catherine. *See* Thunay, *dit* Dufresne
Demers Monfort, François, III, 295
Demesi. *See* Le Normant
Demesnu. *See* Peuvret
Demeule, Joseph-Étienne, IV, 42
Demeulle. *See* Meulles
Deming, Hannah (Gridley), IV, 313
Deminiac. *See* Miniac

Demoiselle, La. *See* Memeskia
Demontreau, M., II, 164
Demosny, Catherine. *See* Fol
Demosny, Catherine (Lamarre, *dit* Bélisle), II, 340
Demosny, Jean (Jean-Baptiste), I, **255–56**, 249, 550, 583; II, 340
Demosny, Jean (son), I, 256
Demosny, Julienne. *See* Bisson
Demosny, Marie. *See* Filleul
Demosny, Marie-Louise. *See* Albert
Demosny, Paul, I, 255
Denaut*, Pierre (1743–1806), IV, 135, 374, 436, 799
Denbigh, Earl of. *See* Feilding
Deneau, Anne. *See* Morin
Deneau, René, II, 447
Deniau-Destaillis, Joseph, II, 11
Denis. *See also* Denys
Denis, Françoise (Outlaw), I, 529
Denis, Jean, II, 582
Denis, Marie-Gabrielle, *dite* de l'Annonciation, II, 93, 613
Denis, Michel, III, 307
Denis, Pierre-François, known as Brother Denis, III, 292
Denis de Saint-Simon, Antoine-Charles, IV, **207–8**
Denison, Deborah. *See* Griswold
Denison, Joanna. *See* Stanton
Denison, Prudence. *See* Sherman
Denison, Robert (father), III, 174
Denison, Robert, III, **174–75**; IV, 217, 351
Denmark, Prince of. *See* George
Dennison, Deborah (Ely; Butler), IV, 117
Denny, Plato, IV, 597
Denonville. *See* Brisay; Hémard
Denson, Edith (wife of HENRY DENNY), IV, 208
Denson, Elizabeth (Cartland), IV, 208
Denson, Henry Denny, IV, **208–9**, 17, 29, 217, 451
Denton, Sarah (Toosey), IV, 738
Denys. *See also* Denis
Denys, Jean, I, **256**, 22
Denys, Joseph (baptized Jacques), I, 536; II, **174–76**, 110, 130, 131, 178, 222, 223, 245, 294, 419, 429, 506; III, 233
Denys, Louis-Jean, IV, 732
Denys, Marguerite. *See* Lafite
Denys, Marguerite (Cressé), II, 529
Denys, Marguerite (Forsayth), I, 258
Denys, Marie (Leneuf de La Vallière et de Beaubassin), I, 258; II, 236, 408, 409, 411, 654
Denys, Nicolas, I, **256–59**, 25, 32, 66, 89, 90, 114, 260, 261, 277, 383, 433, 434, 476, 503, 505, 514, 568, 595, 597, 621; II, 178, 217, 408, 409; III, 108
Denys de Bonaventure, Jeanne. *See* Jannière
Denys de Bonaventure, Simon-Pierre, I, 114, 246, 576, 654; II, **176–78**, 14, 37, 206, 257, 449, 450, 481; III, 175, 176, 499, 500, 552, 681, 682; IV, 10
Denys de Bonnaventure, Claude-Élisabeth, II, 17; III, **175–76**, 183, 236, 264, 268; IV, 56, 79, 239, 688
Denys de Bonnaventure, Louise. *See* Denys de La Ronde
Denys de Fronsac, Anne. *See* Parabego
Denys de Fronsac, Françoise. *See* Cailleteau
Denys de Fronsac, Louis, I, 261
Denys de Fronsac, Marie-Anne (Merçan), I, 260; II, 477
Denys de Fronsac, Nicolas, I, 260
Denys de Fronsac, Richard, I, **259–61**, 90, 258, 649; II, 106, 178, 217, 256, 409, 477; IV, 195

Denys de La Ronde, Anne-Ursule (Aubert de La Chesnaye), II, 34; III, 22

Denys de La Ronde, Catherine. *See* Leneuf de La Poterie

Denys de La Ronde, Françoise (Bouthier; Ailleboust de Manthet), II, 14

Denys de La Ronde, Louis, II, 17, 123, 154, 198, 203, 219, 254, 285, 339, 411, 452, 498, 511, 668; III, **176–80**, 22, 47, 110, 175, 208, 374, 436, 454, 475; IV, 358, 359

Denys de La Ronde, Louise (Denys de Bonnaventure), III, 175

Denys de La Ronde, Marguerite-Renée (Lanouguère; Fleury Deschambault), I, 418; II, 224; III, 311, 312

Denys de La Ronde, Marie-Angélique (Aubert de La Chesnaye), II, 33; III, 21, 22, 192, 233

Denys de La Ronde, Marie-Charlotte (Ramezay), II, 545, 548, 606; III, 543; IV, 41, 650, 653, 690

Denys de La Ronde, Marie-Louise. *See* Chartier de Lotbinière

Denys de La Ronde, Marie-Louise (Ailleboust d'Argenteuil), II, 12; III, 5; IV, 10

Denys de La Ronde, Philippe, III, 179

Denys de La Ronde, Pierre, I, 85, 260, 418; II, **178–79**, 12, 28, 33, 34, 131, 174, 176, 224, 545; III, 176

Denys de La Ronde, Pierre-François-Paul, III, 179

Denys de La Thibaudière, Jacques, I, 256, 261

Denys de La Thibaudière, Marie. *See* Cosnier

Denys de La Trinité, Barbe (Pécaudy de Contrecœur; Gannes de Falaise), I, 535; II, 236; III, 505

Denys de La Trinité, Charlotte (Dupas; Boucher de Boucherville), III, 80

Denys de La Trinité, Françoise. *See* Du Tartre

Denys de La Trinité, Françoise (Leneuf de La Vallière et de Beaubassin), II, 409

Denys de La Trinité, Jeanne. *See* Dubreuil

Denys de La Trinité, Simon, I, **261–62**, 257, 261, 514, 535, 589; II, 174, 176, 178, 179, 236, 409; III, 178

Denys de Saint-Pierre, Simon-Pierre, II, 176

Denys de Saint-Simon, Charles-Paul, II, 179; III, **180**, 549, 551; IV, 207

Denys de Saint-Simon, Élisabeth (Collet), II, 151

Denys de Saint-Simon, Louise-Catherine (Bergeron; Gaillard), II, 235

Denys de Saint-Simon, Marie-Anne (Bertier), II, 60, 151

Denys de Saint-Simon, Marie-Joseph. *See* Prat

Denys de Saint-Simon, Marie-Madeleine. *See* Peiras

Denys de Saint-Simon, Paul, I, 35, 49, 226, 396, 625; II, **179**, 60, 151, 514, 520, 537; III, 180; IV, 209

Denys de Vitré, Catherine. *See* Loustelneau

Denys de Vitré, Charles, II, **179–80**, 32, 78, 137, 276, 295, 448

Denys de Vitré, Guillaume-Emmanuel-Théodose, IV, 209

Denys de Vitré, John, IV, 210

Denys de Vitré, Marie-Charlotte. *See* Chrétien

Denys de Vitré, Marie-Gabrielle (Descayrac de L'Autheur), II, 179

Denys de Vitré, Marie-Joseph. *See* Blaise Des Bergères de Rigauville

Denys de Vitré, Théodose-Matthieu, IV, **209–10**, 650

Denys Du Tartre, Geneviève. *See* Couillard

Denys Du Tartre, Pierre, II, 176

Deowando. *See* Atecouando

Depelteau. *See* Sarasin

Depéret, Élie, III, **180–81**

Depéret, Jean, III, 180

Depéret, Valère. *See* Limousin

De Peyster, Abraham, IV, **210–11**

De Peyster*, Arent Schuyler (1736–1832), IV, 233, 302, 303, 337, 369, 496

De Peyster, Catherine. *See* Livingston

De Peyster, James (Jacobus), IV, 210

De Peyster, Sarah. *See* Reade

Depin, Joseph, IV, 202

Derby, Earl of. *See* Stanley

Dering, Sir Edward, II, 309

Derivon de Budemon, Marie. *See* Gaudé

Derivon de Budemon, Pierre, II, 153; III, 146

Dermer, Thomas, I, **262**, 650

Derome, Marie-Bénigne (Gaudron de Chevremont), III, 239

Derré de Gand, François, I, **262–63**, 297, 637; II, xv

De Ruyter. *See* Ruyter

Déry, Maurice, II, 111

Desandrouins, Benoît-Nicolas, IV, 211

Desandrouins, Jean-Nicolas, III, xix, 406, 534, 536, 606; IV, **211–12**

Desandrouins, Marie-Scholastique. *See* Hallot

Des Assises. *See* La Grive

Desauniers. *See also* Trottier

Desauniers, Marguerite, III, 47, 611, 627

Desauniers, Marie-Anne, III, 47, 611, 627

Desauniers, Marie-Madeleine, III, 47, 611, 627

Desautels, Joseph-Marie, IV, 533, 534

Desbarats*, Pierre-Édouard (1764–1828), IV, 107, 303

Desbarres, François. *See* Bigot, François

DesBarres*, Joseph Frederick Wallet (1721–1824), III, 133, 620; IV, 208, 292, 293, 522, 603, 613

Des Bergères. *See* Blaise

Desbois, Jeanne (Briand), IV, 95

Desbois, Olivier, IV, 95

Des Bordes. *See also* Landriève

Desbordes, Sieur, II, 491

Desbordes, Delphine (Cabazié), II, 111

Desbordes, Marie (Migeon), I, 508

Des Bordes Landriève, Gabriel-Alexis, IV, 435

Des Bordes Landriève, Marguerite. *See* Mercier

Desbrieux, François, II, 189

Desbrieux, Jean, II, 186, 189, 616

Desbrieux, Marguerite. *See* Dizy, *dit* Montplaisir

Desbrisay*, Thomas (d. 1819), IV, 129, 353, 608, 609, 610

Des Butes (Desbuttes). *See* Baudry

Descaris, Jean-Baptiste, IV, 732

Descaris, Jeanne. *See* Lefebvre

Des Cars. *See* Pérusse

Descary, Gabriel, IV, 178

Descary, Louise (Maugenest), IV, 524

Descayrac de L'Autheur, Marie-Gabrielle. *See* Denys de Vitré

Desceliers, Pierre, I, 170

Deschaillons. *See* Saint-Ours

Deschambault. *See* Fleury

Deschamps. *See also* Cadet

Deschamps, Anne (Mangeant), III, 426

Deschamps, Élisabeth. *See* Debin

Des Champs, Guillaume, I, 293

Deschamps*, Isaac (1722–1801), IV, 110, 111, 116, 526, 528, 604

Deschamps, Jean, II, 181

Deschamps de Boishébert, Claude-Louis, II, 181
Deschamps de Boishébert, Henri-Louis, II, **180–81**, 409;
    III, 65, 102; IV, 212, 654, 728
Deschamps de Boishébert, Louise-Geneviève. *See* Ramezay
Deschamps de Boishébert, Louise-Geneviève (Tarieu de La
    Naudière), IV, 728, 729
Deschamps de Boishébert et de Raffetot, Charles, II, 181;
    III, 28, 29, 87, 128, 183, 358, 417, 573, 610; IV, **212–15**,
    78, 79, 125, 169, 290, 305, 392, 447, 453, 614, 616, 688,
    729
Deschamps de Boishébert et de Raffetot, Charlotte-
    Élisabeth-Antoinette (Deschamps de Boishébert et
    de Raffetot), IV, 212
Deschamps de Fellière, Marie-Anne (Vallette de Chévigny),
    III, 637
Deschamps de La Bouteillerie, Catherine-Gertrude. *See*
    Macard
Deschamps de La Bouteillerie, Charles-Joseph, II, 181
Deschamps de La Bouteillerie, Jean-Baptiste-François, II,
    181, 180
Deschamps de La Bouteillerie, Jeanne-Marguerite. *See* Le
    Chevalier
Des Chatelets. *See* Juchereau
Deschenaux. *See* Brassard
Deschevery, Jean, III, 181
Deschevery, Jeanne. *See* Damboise
Deschevery, *dit* Maisonbasse, Jean-Baptiste, III, **181–82**,
    346, 499
Deschevery, *dit* Maisonbasse, Louise-Élisabeth. *See*
    Couteron
Deschevery, *dit* Maisonbasse, Marie-Françoise, III, 181
Desclaux, Pierre, IV, 124, 125, 126, 127
Desclouzeaux. *See* Champy
Descombes. *See* Lombard
Descouando. *See* Atecouando
Des Cours. *See* Du Bois
Descouts, Martin, III, **182**; IV, 56
Desdames, Thierry, I, **263–64**, 266, 579
Desdevens de Glandons, Gabrielle. *See* Avet Forel
Desdevens de Glandons, Joseph, IV, 215
Desdevens de Glandons, Marie-Thérèse. *See* Mathon
Desdevens de Glandons, Maurice, IV, **215–16**
Desenclaves. *See* Gay
Deserontyon* (d. 1811), IV, liv
Des Essarts. *See* Berey
Desferières Renaud, Sieur, III, 135
Des Fontaines. *See* Leduc
Des Forges. *See also* Robin
Desforges, Anne-Céleste (Foureur), IV, 272
Des Forges, Marie. *See* Viel
Des Friches de Brasseuse, Artus, II, 182
Des Friches de Meneval, Louis-Alexandre, I, 426, 436, 533,
    542, 544, 576, 578; II, **182–84**, 257, 352, 522, 578, 638
Desglis (Desgly). *See* Mariauchau
Desgoutins. *See* Goutin
Desgouttes, Marquis. *See* Charry
Des Granches, Alizon (Jalobert), I, 384
Des Granches, Antoine, I, 167
Des Granches, Catherine (Cartier), I, 167, 170
Des Granches, Guyon, Vicomte de Beaupré, I, 169
Des Granches, Jacques, I, 170
Des Granges. *See also* Lanoullier; Moyen
Des Granges de Mauprée, Alixe. *See* La Feuillée

Des Granges de Mauprée, Louis, I, 415
Desgrez, Anne. *See* Hugot
Desgrez, Anne (Beauharnois de La Chaussaye, Baronne de
    Beauville), III, 51
Desgrez, François, III, 51
Des Groseilliers. *See* Chouart
Deshaies-Gendron, Claude, I, 328, 550
Deshayes, Catherine, known as La Voisin (Monvoisin), III,
    143
Deshayes, Jean, I, 56; II, **184–85**, 230; III, 620
Desherbert de Lapointe, Joseph-Simon, IV, 252, 263, 433
Des Herbiers, Antoine-Auguste, Marquis de L'Étenduère,
    III, 183
Des Herbiers, Armand, III, 182
Des Herbiers, Henri-François, Marquis de L'Étenduère, III,
    27, 182, 183, 557; IV, 699
Des Herbiers, Marie-Olive (Des Herbiers de La Ralière), III,
    183
Des Herbiers de La Ralière, Charles, III, **182–84**, 30, 294,
    570; IV, 254, 454, 455, 655
Des Herbiers de La Ralière, Marie-Olive. *See* Des Herbiers
Deshormeaux. *See* Bergier
Des Islets. *See* Couillard
Desjardins. *See also* Augier; Roy-Desjardins
Desjardins*, Philippe-Jean-Louis (1753–1833), I, 314; IV,
    90, 136
Desjardins* (Desjardins de Lapérière), *dit* Desplantes,
    Louis-Joseph (1766–1848), IV, 81, 136, 137
Desjardins Du Val (agent), I, 383, 503, 504
Desjean de Pointis, Jean-Bernard-Louis, III, 488
Desjordy. *See also* Dejordy; Jordy
Desjordy de Cabanac, François, I, 361; II, 633
Desjordy de Cabanac, Joseph, II, **185–86**, 580
Desjordy de Cabanac, Madeleine. *See* Pézard de La Tousche
    Champlain
Desjordy de Cabanac, Melchior, II, 185, 186
Desjordy Moreau de Cabanac, Anne. *See* Nolan
Desjordy Moreau de Cabanac, François, I, 361; II, **186–87**,
    185, 189, 190; III, 171
Desjordy Moreau de Cabanac, Louise-Catherine. *See* Robi-
    nau de Bécancour
Des Landes. *See also* Daulier
Deslandes, Jean, II, 105, 159
Des Landes, Joseph, III, **184**, 108
Des Lauriers. *See* Basset
Deslauriers. *See* Le Cavelier; Normandeau
Desliettes. *See* Liette; Tonty
Desloges, Anne (Guenet), I, 347
Deslongrais, Nicolas, III, **184–85**
Desmaisons, Gabriel, III, 519
Des Maizerets. *See* Ango
Desmarais. *See also* Godet
Desmarais, Innocent, I, 264
Desmarais, Michel, III, 518
Desmarais, Paul, III, 519
Desmarest. *See* Le Roy; Pinet
Desmarets, M., III, 566
Desmarets (painter or engraver), I, 313
Desmarets, Jean-Baptiste-François, Marquis de Maillebois,
    IV, 181
Des Maretz (Desmarets). *See* Godet
Desmeloizes (Des Méloizes). *See* Renaud
Desmoulins. *See* Maillou

Des Muceaux. *See* Ailleboust

Des Ormeaux. *See* Bergier; Dollard; Hazeur

Despard*, John (1745–1829), IV, 523

Despeiroux (Desperoux). *See* Lestage

Despenan, Suzanne (Delort), III, 173

Despiaube, Catherine (Olabaratz), IV, 589

Despins. *See* Lemoine

Des Plaines. *See* Damours

Desplantes. *See* Desjardins

Desportes, Françoise. *See* Langlois

Desportes, Hélène (Hébert; Morin), I, **264**, 367, 495; II, 489

Desportes, Pierre, I, 233, 264, 495

Desportes de Lignères, Pierre, I, 248, 264

Després. *See also* Guyon; Le Loutre

Després, Anne (Lauson; Bermen de La Martinière), I, 428, 430; II, 56, 57

Després, Étiennette (Guillemot), I, 349

Després, Geneviève (Couillard de Lespinay), I, 237; II, 60, 155, 213

Desprez. *See* Guion; Guyon

Desquerac. *See* Escairac

Des Reaux, Marie (Léger), II, 387

Desrivières. *See also* Trottier

Desrivières, Hypolite, IV, 592

Desrivières-Beaubien. *See* Trottier

Des Rochers. *See* Chateigner

Desroches, Jean, II, 517

Desroches, Marguerite (Cirier), IV, 151

Des Roches Duplesy, Charlotte (Monbeton de Brouillan), III, 454

Desrosiers. *See also* Deguire; Jutras

Desrosiers, Anne. *See* Leneuf Du Hérisson

Desrosiers, Antoine, I, 468

Desrues, Jeanne (Baudouin), I, 80

Des Ruisseaux (Desruisseaux). *See* Trottier

Dessailliant, *dit* Richeterre, Michel, II, **187–88**, 613

Dessermont. *See* Demers

Destaillis. *See* Deniau

Destailly, Sieur, III, 83

Des Touches. *See* Peronne

Destroismaisons, Anne (Chartier), III, 112

Desvoges de Clérin, Françoise (Estienne Du Bourgué), II, 220

Détailleur, Joseph, IV, 82

Dethunes, Exupère, I, **264–65**, 438, 439; II, 174, 420, 429, 430

Deupet, Louisa (Mallet), III, 423

Devarenne. *See* Gaultier

Devau, Benoît, IV, 216

Devau, Marie. *See* Potier

Devau, *dit* Retor, Claude, IV, **216**

Devau, *dit* Retor, Marie-Madeleine. *See* Gendron

Devene, Françoise-Anne (Boucault), III, 74, 77

Devennes, Gilles, I, 109; II, 105

Device. *See* Davis

Devienne, Louise-Thérèse (Crespel), IV, 180

Devin, Sieur (engineer), II, 525

Devotion, Rachel (Kellogg), III, 325

Dewando. *See* Atecouando

Dextreme, *dit* Comtois, Pierre, IV, 336

Deyohninhohhakarawenh. *See* Theyanoguin

Dhiarse (Dihars, Hiarse), Jeanne (Lartigue), II, 381; III, 357

Diaquande. *See* Teyohaqueande

Díaz de Solís, Jean, I, 155

Dick, John, III, 212

Dickinson, Sarah (Lane; Kellogg), III, 324

Dickinson, Tertullus, IV, 327, 328

Diderot, Denis, II, 444

Didot. *See* Firmin

Diehl, John Justus, IV, 703

Dielle, Paul, IV, 40, 331

Dières, Guyon, II, 188

Dières, Jacques, II, 188

Dières, Jacques-Christophe, II, 188

Dières, Pierre, II, 188

Dièreville, I, 577, 649; II, **188–89**, 597; IV, xx

Dièreville, Jehan, II, 188

Diesbach, Comte de, IV, 70

Diescaret. *See* Pieskaret

Dieskau, Jean-Armand, Baron de Dieskau, III, **185–86**, xix, 18, 21, 174, 188, 214, 322, 376, 409, 458, 459, 623, 624; IV, 57, 67, 224, 307, 353, 395, 426, 459, 642, 668, 669

Digby, Sarah. *See* Moore

Digges, Sir Dudley, I, 374, 377

Dight* Butler, John Butler (d. 1834), IV, 529

Digoine Du Palais, Camille de, II, 479

Dihars. *See* Dhiarse

Dijean. *See* Dejean

Dillon, Peter, IV, 283

Dimock, Abigail. *See* Doane

Dimock, Daniel, IV, 217

Dimock, Eunice. *See* Marsh

Dimock*, Joseph (1768–1846), IV, 217

Dimock, Percilla. *See* Hovey

Dimock, Sarah. *See* Knowlton

Dimock, Shubael, IV, **216–17**

Dimock (Dimmick), Timothy, IV, 216

Dinan, *dit* Saint-Étienne, Pierre, III, 258

Dinwiddie, Robert, III, 375, 376, 600; IV, 227

Dion. *See also* Guyon

Dion, Claude, III, 142

Diron. *See* Artaguiette

Dirop, Saturnin, II, 382

Discombe, Reece, IV, 283

Disney, Daniel, IV, 759

Disy. *See* Dizy

Diverny, *dit* Saint-Germain, Charles, IV, 205, 629

Dix, Elizabeth (Kelsey), II, 313, 314

Dixon, George, IV, **217–19**, 166, 244, 245, 325, 419, 498, 499, 744

Dizet, Pierre, III, 621

Diziers, Marquise de. *See* Alavoine

Dizy, *dit* Montplaisir, Charles, II, 190

Dizy, *dit* Montplaisir, Élisabeth (Hamelin de Bourgchemin et de L'Hermitière), I, 360

Dizy, *dit* Montplaisir, Marguerite (Desbrieux), I, 361; II, **189–90**, 186

Dizy, *dit* Montplaisir, Marie. *See* Drouillet

Dizy, *dit* Montplaisir, Marie-Jeanne. *See* Baudouin

Dizy, *dit* Montplaisir, Michel-Ignace, II, **190**, 189; III, 187

Dizy, *dit* Montplaisir, Pierre, I, 360; II, 189, 190; III, 187

Dizy de Montplaisir, Marguerite, *dite* de Saint-Pierre, III, 187

Dizy de Montplaisir, Marie-Madeleine. *See* Baudouin

Dizy de Montplaisir, Pierre, II, 190; III, **187**

Doane, Abigail (Dimock), IV, 216

141

Doane, Edmund, IV, 593, 594
Doane, Elizabeth. *See* Osborn
Dobbs, Arthur, I, 677; II, xxviii, 314, 493, 604; III, xxxiii, 302, 303, 342, 447, 448, 449, 471, 472, 482, 483, 489, 544, 561, 562, 594, 624, 662, 663; IV, 680
Dobie*, Richard (d. 1805), IV, 58, 277, 311, 330, 485, 757
Dodd*, Archibald Charles (d. 1831), IV, 523
Dodier, Louis, III, 142
Dodier, Marie-Josephte. *See* Corriveau
Dodier, Sébastien, I, 468
Dodun, Charles-Gaspard, II, 646; III, 382
Doggett, Abigail. *See* House
Doggett, Ebenezer, IV, 219
Doggett, Elizabeth. *See* Rickard
Doggett, John, IV, **219–20**
Doggett, Samuel, IV, 219
Dolabaratz, Jean, IV, 588
Dolbeau. *See also* Dolebeau
Dolbeau, Jean, I, **265–66**, 233, 266, 385, 437, 590
Dolbec, Joseph-Romain, III, 227
Dolbec, Romain, IV, 124
Dolebeau, Antoinette (Bellevue), I, 484
Dolebeau, Charles, I, 484
Dolebeau, Jean, I, **266**, 477, 483
Dolebeau, Nicolas, I, 483
Dolebeau, Simon, I, 483
Dollard Des Ormeaux, Adam, I, **266–75**, 11, 32, 40, 65, 201, 225, 463, 547, 612, 633; II, 193, 469, 656
Dollier de Casson, Mlle (Peschart, Baronne de Bossac), II, 194, 272
Dollier de Casson, Charles, II, 190
Dollier de Casson, François, I, 35, 78, 126, 173, 174, 180, 213, 215, 217, 219, 220, 230, 231, 248, 266, 269, 270, 273, 274, 319, 393, 410, 416, 439, 483, 484, 485, 486, 540, 547, 556, 558, 572, 598, 599, 613, 625, 647; II, **190–97**, 11, 45, 96, 111, 124, 128, 133, 222, 223, 241, 245, 272, 326, 376, 594, 638, 642; III, 221, 469, 542
Dollier de Casson, Françoise. *See* Cailleux
Dollier de Casson, Julienne-Angélique, *dite* de Jésus Pâtissant, II, 191
Dolobarats. *See* Olobaratz
Dolphyn, William, I, 371
Dolu, Jean-Jacques, I, 160, 194, 433
Domagaya, I, 11, 166, 167, 168, 275, 276
Dombourg. *See* Bourdon
Domerque, Sieur, II, 603
Domingué Meyracq, Laurent de, IV, 644
Domitilde (Villeneuve; Mouet de Langlade), IV, 563
Donay, Armand, III, 221, 612
Donck, Adrien van der, I, 525
Dongan, Thomas, I, 444, 445, 526; II, 61, 69, 101, 184, 343, 344, 585, 643; III, 568
Donge, Comtesse de, III, 16
Don Jacque. *See* Angeac
Donnacona, I, **275–77**, 11, 166, 167, 168, 169
Dontaille, Anne-Madeleine (La Croix), III, 334
Dontigny. *See* Lucas
Dorchester, Baron. *See* Carleton
Doreil, André (Jean-Baptiste), III, **187–89**, 18, 19, 186, 300, 463, 464; IV, 57, 68, 307, 308, 353, 513, 514, 616, 669, 670
Doreil, Jeanne-Catherine. *See* Blancheteau
Doreil, Marguerite-Charlotte-Baptistine. *See* Pontevès

Doreil, Philippe, III, 187
Dorfeuille, Pierre, I, 361
Dormicourt. *See* Huart
Dornelos (Dorvelos), Juan de, I, 41
Dornon, Marianne. *See* Lafontaine
Dorollaire, Marie (Corolère), III, 139
Dorothy de Saint-Joseph. *See* Jeryan
Dorrill, Elizabeth (wife of RICHARD), III, 189
Dorrill, Richard, III, **189**; IV, 259
Dorset, Duke of. *See* Sackville
Dorval. *See* Bouchard
Dosque, Bernard-Sylvestre, IV, 497
Dosquet, Anne-Jeanne. *See* Goffar
Dosquet, Laurent, IV, 220
Dosquet, Pierre-Herman, II, 135, 530, 542; III, 40, 41, 47, 114, 115, 119, 122, 169, 193, 194, 196, 202, 223, 263, 284, 292, 319, 349, 361, 386, 390, 413, 426, 470, 480, 481, 487, 544, 545, 557, 574, 575, 630, 638; IV, **220–22**, 356, 387, 429, 440, 491, 509, 510, 535, 538, 539, 654
Dosta. *See* Hosta
Dostyne, Louis van der, II, 279
Doty*, John (1745–1841), IV, 139, 753
Douaire de Bondy, Cécile. *See* Gosselin
Douaire de Bondy, Charles-Dominique, IV, 265
Douaire de Bondy, Louise (Allemand; Pinaud), I, 56; II, 526
Douaire de Bondy, Marguerite. *See* Chavigny de Berchereau
Douaire de Bondy, Thomas, II, 223
Douay, Anastase, I, 180, 182, 183; II, **197**, 441
Doublet, François (father), I, 277
Doublet, François, I, **277**
Doublet, Jean-François, I, 277
Doublet, Madeleine. *See* Fontaine
Doublet, Marguerite. *See* Auber
Doucet, François, IV, 222, 441
Doucet, Jeanne (Marie) (Dubreuil; Loppinot), II, 445
Doucet, Marguerite. *See* Petitot, *dit* Saint-Sceine
Doucet, Marie-Madeleine (Aigron, *dit* Lamothe), I, 42
Doucet, Marie-Marguerite. *See* Le Blanc
Doucet, Olivier, IV, 222
Doucet, Pierre, IV, **222–23**, xxix, 441
Doucet de La Verdure, Germain, II, 94
Doucett, Honoria, II, 199
Doucett, Isabella, II, 199
Doucett, John, II, **198–99**, 22, 96, 668; III, 143, 208, 436, 512, 515, 516, 517, 518
Doughty*, Sir Arthur George (1860–1936), III, 257; IV, xlv, 416
Douglas, Charles, Comte de Douglas, IV, 224
Douglas, Sir Charles, III, 132; IV, **223–24**, 28, 549
Douglas, Charles-Luc, IV, 224
Douglas, Charlotte. *See* La Corne
Douglas, François-Prosper, Chevalier de Douglas, IV, **224–25**, 242
Douglas*, Sir Howard (1776–1861), IV, 223
Douglas, James (ship's captain), III, 210
Douglas, James, 4th Earl of Morton, IV, 224
Douglas*, James (d. 1803), IV, 551
Douglas, Jane, Lady Douglas. *See* Baillie
Douglas, Lady Jane (Stewart), IV, 401
Douglas, John, IV, 167, 341, 412
Douglas, Louis-Archambaud, Comte de Douglas, IV, 224
Douglas, Lydia. *See* Schimmelpinck
Douglas, Marie-Anne, Comtesse de Douglas. *See* Lilia

Douglas, Sarah, Lady Douglas. *See* Wood

Douglas*, Thomas, 5th Earl of Selkirk (1771–1820), IV, 551

Douglass, William, III, 200

Douhet de Larivière, *dit* de L'Étang, Marie-Jeanne. *See* Jarret de Verchères

Dourado. *See* Vaz

Doussin, René, I, 267, 273

Doussineau, Gillette (Gendron), I, 328

Douville. *See also* Dagneau; Jérémie

Douville, Joseph-Antoine-Irénée, IV, 87

Dovan (Devon), Earl of. *See* Alexander, William, Earl of Stirling

Dover, Baron. *See* Yorke

Downing, John (father), I, 278

Downing, John, I, **277–78**, 24, 93

Downing, William, I, **277–78**, 370

Dowse, Relief (Gill), II, 246

Dowse, Thomas, I, 417

Dowset. *See* Doucet

Doyon, Marie-Louise (Baudry, *dit* Saint-Martin), III, 37

Doyon, Nicolas, III, 37

Drachart, Christian Larsen, IV, **225**, liii, 334, 536, 537, 599

Drage, Theodorus Swaine, I, 677

Drake, Sir Bernard, I, **278–80**, 23, 364, 668

Drake, Sir Francis, I, **280**, 278, 318, 336, 362, 364, 378; IV, 226

Drake, Sir Francis Henry, IV, 226

Drake, Francis William, IV, **226**

Drake, George, I, 306, 672

Drake, Gertrude. *See* Fortescue

Drake, Hugh, I, 278

Drake, John, I, 280

Drake, Samuel, III, 497

Drapeau, Marguerite (Bigot, *dit* Lamothe), II, 62

Draper, John, III, 267

Draper, Lyman Copeland, IV, 416

Draper, Thomas, I, **280–81**, 324; II, 264

Draper, Sir William, IV, 577

Dreuillettes. *See* Druillettes

Drew, Gruzzel (Tutty), III, 634

Drew, John, I, 667

Driot, Catherine (Daneau), II, 168

Drouard, Robert, II, 520, 597

Drouet de Richerville, Jean, IV, 332

Drouet de Richerville, Joseph, II, 67

Drouilhet (Brouilhet), Gratien, III, 124, 441; IV, 66, 125, 621

Drouillet (Drouillard), Marie (Dizy, *dit* Montplaisir), II, 189, 190; III, 187

Drouillettes. *See* Druillettes

Drouin, Anne. *See* Cloutier

Drouin, Marie. *See* Chapelier

Drouin, Marie. *See* Dubois

Drouin, Robert (father), I, 281

Drouin, Robert, I, **281**, 232, 330

Drucour (Drucourt). *See* Boschenry

Drucourt, Baronne de. *See* Godard

Drué, Juconde, I, 312; II, **199–200**, 451; IV, 649

Druillettes, Gabriel, I, **281–82**, 49, 59, 244, 340, 379, 396, 402, 491, 498, 516, 558; II, 18, 158, 517

Druillon, Madeleine (Bégon de La Picardière), III, 56, 57

Druillon, Marie. *See* Bachaddelebat

Druillon, Pierre-Jacques, IV, 226

Druillon de Macé, Marie-Anne. *See* Petit de Thoizy

Druillon de Macé, Pierre-Jacques, IV, **226–27**

Drummond, Colin, IV, 402, 403, 618

Drummond*, Sir Gordon (1772–1854), IV, 487

Drummond, John, IV, 403

Drummond, William (of Hawthornden), I, 51

Duaime. *See* Le Maître

Du Bellineau, Catherine (Petit), II, 521

Du Boccage, Joseph, III, 566

Dubocq, Laurent, I, 286

Dubocq, Marie-Félix. *See* Marie-Felix

Dubocq, Michelle. *See* Mars

Duboct. *See* Dubok

Du Bog, Jacques, I, 167

Dubois. *See also* Filiau

Dubois, M., III, 464

Dubois, Anne (Lemort; Pécaudy de Contrecœur), I, 535

Dubois, Donatien, II, 374

Dubois, Guillaume, Cardinal Dubois, II, 288, 588

Dubois, Jacques, I, 550

Dubois, Jeanne (Hertel de Rouville), II, 286

Dubois, Marie (Drouin), I, 281

Dubois Berthelot, Jacques-Hyacinthe, III, 189

Dubois Berthelot, Péronelle. *See* Magnan

Dubois Berthelot de Beaucours, Gabrielle-Françoise. *See* Aubert de la Chesnaye

Dubois Berthelot de Beaucours, Georges-François, III, 192

Dubois Berthelot de Beaucours, Josué (Jean-Maurice-Josué), II, 36, 58, 121, 160, 180, 186, 255, 269, 337, 338, 432, 545, 649; III, **189–92**, 24, 331, 384, 445, 575, 630, 650; IV, 41, 663

Duboiscuvier, Louise (La Brosse), IV, 423

Dubois Davaugour, Pierre, I, **282–85**, 32, 146, 200, 202, 305, 325, 387, 402, 494, 537, 538, 563, 587, 647; II, 85, 86, 136, 158, 178, 365, 367

Dubois de Cocreaumont et de Saint-Maurice, Jean-Baptiste, I, **285–86**

Du Boisdecourt. *See* La Maisonfort

Dubois de La Milletière, Honoré, III, 102

Dubois de La Motte, Comte. *See* Cahideuc

Dubois de La Motte, Comtesse. *See* Andigné de La Chaise; Langan

Du Bois Des Cours, Adrien, II, 141

Du Bois Des Cours, Isabelle (Chaumont), II, 141

Dubois d'Esgriseilles, Jean-Baptiste, I, 285

Du Bois Duclos, Jean-Baptiste, II, 355

Dubok, I, **286**

Du Bos, Antoinette. *See* Caron

Du Bos, Nicolas (father), I, 286

Du Bos, Nicolas, I, **286**

Du Bouchet, Jeanne (Chauvigny), I, 207

Du Bouëxic, Luc-Urbain, Comte de Guichen, III, 55

Du Bourg. *See* Morillon

Du Bourget, Marie-Anne (Auger de Subercase), II, 39

Du Bourgué. *See* Estienne

Dubreil, Angélique-Sylvie, Comtesse de Pontbriand. *See* Marot de La Garaye

Dubreil, Joseph-Yves, Comte de Pontbriand, III, 192

Dubreil de Pontbriand, Henri-Marie, III, **192–99**, 10, 11, 36, 50, 103, 120, 122, 134, 137, 223, 246, 256, 259, 263, 279, 285, 296, 314, 416, 435, 486, 487, 538, 546, 547, 559, 580, 617, 625, 628, 638, 643; IV, 64, 87, 95, 96, 97,

141, 142, 151, 201, 220, 236, 237, 256, 287, 289, 295, 304, 319, 370, 387, 429, 430, 452, 453, 457, 458, 509, 521, 536, 539, 542, 572, 645, 752, 779
Dubreuil. *See also* Chenet; La Corne
Du Breuil. *See* Le Creux
Dubreuil, M., II, 445
Dubreuil, Catherine. *See* Lemarinier
Dubreuil, Jean, II, 201
Dubreuil, Jean-Étienne, II, **201**, 129; III, 77, 144
Dubreuil, Jeanne (Marie). *See* Doucet
Dubreuil, Jeanne (Denys de La Trinité), I, 261; II, 178
Dubreuil, Marguerite. *See* Legardeur
Dubreuil, Marie-Anne. *See* Chevalier
Dubreuil, Marie-Jeanne. *See* Routier
Dubuc, Marie (Cherrier), IV, 148
Dubuc, Marie-Angélique (Pillard), III, 521
Dubuc, Michel (churchwarden), IV, 148
Dubuc, Michel (mason), II, 105
Dubuc, Pierre, II, 526
Du Buisson. *See* Guyon; Poitiers
Dubuisson. *See* Potier; Renaud
Duburon. *See also* Feré
Duburon, Joseph, IV, 203
Du Calvet, Anne. *See* Boudet
Du Calvet, Guy, IV, 231
Du Calvet, Marie-Louise. *See* Jussaume, *dit* Saint-Pierre
Du Calvet, Pierre, IV, **227–32**, xliv, 7, 336, 344, 436, 492, 493, 534, 687, 759, 791
Du Calvet, Pierre (nephew), IV, 230
Du Calvet, Pierre (baptized John), IV, 231
Ducas, Catherine (Martinet), II, 465
Ducasse, Jean-Baptiste, II, 260, 666
Ducasse, Marthe (La Rochefoucauld, Marquise de Roye), III, 356
Du Chaffault, Louis-Charles, Comte Du Chaffault de Besné, IV, 282
Du Chaigneau. *See* Chaigneau
Duchambon. *See* Du Pont
Ducharme, Catherine (Roy), III, 574
Ducharme*, Dominique (baptized François) (1765–1853), IV, 592
Ducharme*, Jean-Marie (1723–1807), IV, 58, 592
Ducharme, Julien, III, 144
Ducharme, Laurent, IV, **233**
Ducharme, Louis, IV, 233, 268
Ducharme, Marguerite. *See* Métivier
Ducharme, Marie. *See* Picard
Ducharme, Pierre, I, 452
Du Chartran. *See* Gaudais
Duchatelet, Marie (Potier), IV, 640
Duché, Jean-Baptiste, II, 425
Duchesnay. *See* Juchereau
Duchesne. *See also* Du Quesne
Du Chesne. *See also* Le Ber
Du Chesne, Adrien, I, **287**, 463, 495
Du Chesne, Judith (Le Moyne), I, 287, 463
Duchesne, Léonard, I, 264; II, 278
Duchesneau de La Doussinière et d'Ambault, M., I, 105, 137
Duchesneau de La Doussinière et d'Ambault, Jacques, I, **287–90**, 103, 104, 105, 136, 177, 179, 203, 238, 245, 340, 345, 396, 397, 399, 438, 445, 448, 464, 537, 553, 565, 575, 581, 582; II, 29, 72, 88, 137, 194, 252, 253,

262, 263, 335, 369, 370, 409, 412, 470, 532, 533, 574, 575, 576, 585, 586, 616, 647
Duchouquet. *See* Lefebvre
Duclos. *See* Celles; Dubois
Duclos, *dit* Saint-Front, Jean-Baptiste, III, 140
Duclos de Beaumanoir, M., II, 185
Du Cloux, Catherine (Dutisné), II, 215
Du Coigne. *See* Couagne
Du Cosnier. *See* Michelet
Du Coudray. *See* Le Borgne
Ducourday Feuillet, M., III, 172
Du Creux, François, I, 523; II, 429
Du Daugnon, Comte. *See* Foucault
Dudevant, Arnauld-Germain (baptized Arnaud), IV, **233–34**
Dudevant, Jacques, IV, 234
Dudevant, Jeanne. *See* Barbequière
Dudevoir, Claude, II, 105
Dudley, Ambrose, Earl of Warwick, I, 316
Dudley, Ann (Hilton), II, 287
Dudley, Anne, Countess of Warwick. *See* Russell
Dudley, Elizabeth. *See* Davenport
Dudley, Joseph, I, 654; II, 38, 145, 285, 289, 437, 452, 480, 495, 511, 543, 606, 651, 664, 667; III, 178, 200; IV, 764
Dudley, Paul, III, 325
Dudley, Rebecca. *See* Tyng
Dudley, Rebecca (Gerrish; Burbidge), IV, 290
Dudley, Thomas, II, 287
Dudley, William, III, **200–1**, 587
Dudouyt, Jean, I, **290–91**, 89, 92, 105, 249, 359, 506; II, 19, 29, 244, 369, 638; III, 683
Du Faradon. *See* Legrand; Normant
Du Fau, Abbé, III, 417
Dufaux, François, II, 640
Du Fay, Polycarpe, I, 590
Dufebvre, Bernard. *See* Castonguay, Émile
Duff, Mary (Abercromby), IV, 4
Duff, Robert, IV, 437, 708
Duff, William, 1st Earl Fife, Baron Braco, IV, 4
Dufloc, Catherine (Petit), II, 521
Duforillon. *See* Aubert
Dufort. *See* Bougret
Du Fort, Perrette (Callières), II, 112
Dufournel, Guillaume, III, 201
Dufournel, Louis-Gaspard, II, 90, 200, 367, 587; III, **201–3**
Dufresne. *See also* Thunay
Dufresne, M., I, 130, 662
Dufresne, Jacques, II, 164
Dufresne, Jean-Baptiste, III, 140
Dufresne, Nicolas, IV, 268
Dufresnoy Carion, Jeanne (Le Moyne de Sainte-Hélène; Monic), I, 466; II, 482
Dufresnoy Carion, Philippe, II, 105
Dufrost, Charles. *See* Youville, Charles-Marie-Madeleine d'
Dufrost de Boissemances, Christophe, II, 202
Dufrost de Boissemances, Marguerite. *See* La Forest
Dufrost de La Gemerais, Charles, IV, 234
Dufrost de La Gemerais, François-Christophe, I, 204; II, 201, 202; III, 234, 247, 603; IV, 234
Dufrost de La Gemerais, Joseph, IV, 234, 509
Dufrost de La Gemerais, Marie-Clémence (Gamelin Maugras), III, 234; IV, 235
Dufrost de La Gemerais, Marie-Louise (Gamelin), IV, 235, 283

Dufrost de La Gemerais, Marie-Renée. *See* Gaultier de Varennes

Dufrost de La Jemerais, Christophe, II, **201–2**, 239; III, 241, 244, 245, 247, 249, 250, 251, 444; IV, 234

Dufrost de Lajemmerais, Marie-Marguerite (Youville), II, 110, 135, 202, 378, 414, 673; III, 195, 314, 385, 486, 604, 643, 691; IV, **234–39**, 265, 283, 434, 462, 508, 779, 780, 799

Dufy. *See* Trottier

Dufy Charest, Joseph, III, 631, 632; IV, 141

Dugard, Robert, III, 281, 282

Dugardin, L., I, 487

Dugas, Abraham, IV, xx

Dugas, Agnès (Thibodeau), III, 87

Dugas, Anne (Bourgeois), II, 94

Dugas, Joseph (father), III, 97; IV, 239

Dugas, Joseph, IV, **239–40**, 252

Dugas, Louise. *See* Arseneau

Dugas, Madeleine (Bourgeois), II, 94

Dugas, Marguerite. *See* Leblanc

Dugas, Marguerite. *See* Richard

Dugas, Marie (Melanson), I, 500

Dugast, Jean-Baptiste, II, 294, 523

Dugay, Anne. *See* Baillargeon

Dugay, Catherine. *See* Laubret

Dugay, Jacques, II, **202–3**

Dugay, Jeanne. *See* Baudry, *dit* La Marche

Dugay, Michel, II, 202

Dugey Rozoy de Mannereuil, Charles, II, 380

Duglas, Bishop, I, 469

Du Gousset, Jeanne (Provost), II, 532

Du Gua, Claire. *See* Goumard

Du Gua, Guy, I, 291

Du Gua de Monts, Judith. *See* Chesnel

Du Gua de Monts, Pierre, I, **291–95**, 23, 28, 69, 72, 95, 96, 98, 99, 186, 188, 189, 190, 191, 197, 209, 300, 346, 367, 422, 452, 469, 470, 495, 500, 526, 527, 529, 564, 565, 601, 603, 604; IV, xvii, xix, xx

Du Guay. *See* Le Guet

Duguay-Trouin, René, III, 42, 92, 609

Dugué, Louis-Rémy, II, 521

Dugué de Boisbriand, Charlotte (Petit), II, 521

Dugué de Boisbriand, Jean-Sidrac, II, 527

Dugué de Boisbriand, Marie. *See* Moyen Des Granges

Dugué de Boisbriand, Marie-Thérèse (Piot de Langloiserie), II, 527; IV, 638

Dugué de Boisbriand, Michel-Sidrac, I, **295**, 308; II, 203, 521, 527; IV, 638

Dugué de Boisbriand, Pierre, I, 308; II, **203–4**, 215, 216

Dugué de La Boulardière, Perrine. *See* Chambellé

Dugué de La Boulardière, Pierre, I, 295

Du Guesclin. *See* Lefebvre

Duhaget. *See* Tarride

Duhamel Du Monceau, Henri-Louis, III, 30, 77, 675, 677, 678, 679, 680

Duhart. *See* Dechart

Duhaut, Dominique, I, 182, 183

Duhaut, Pierre, I, 182, 183; II, 197

Du Hérisson. *See* Leneuf

Du Hommée. *See* Byssot

Du Houssaye, Alliette (Morel de La Durantaye), II, 488

Du Jardin (merchant), I, 100

Du Jardin, Marie (Le Mercier), I, 458

Du Jaunay, Pierre, III, 12, 306, 347; IV, **240–42**

Du Laurent, Christophe-Hilarion, III, **203–4**, 160, 194, 647; IV, 88

Du Lescöat. *See* Le Pape

Dulhut (Duluth). *See* Greysolon

Dumaine. *See* Du Pont Duchambon

Dumanoir. *See* Faucon

Du Marché, Charles, I, 214, 453

Dumas*, Alexandre, (d. 1802), III, 555; IV, 205, 243, 618, 619

Dumas, Anne. *See* Martin

Dumas*, Antoine-Libéral (d. 1816), IV, 244, 752

Dumas, François, II, 42

Dumas, Jean-Daniel, III, xxiv, 378, 402, 465, 496, 526, 578; IV, **242–43**, 224, 302, 408, 476, 531, 563, 633, 672

Dumas, Marie. *See* Calquieres

Dumas, Marie. *See* Montmainier

Dumas, Michel, IV, 244

Dumas, Pierre, IV, 243

Dumas, Samuel, IV, 242

Dumas Saint-Martin, Jean, III, 555; IV, **243–44**, 228, 232, 403, 618

Dumas Saint-Martin, Madeleine. *See* Morisseau

Du Mazel. *See* Agrain

Dumergue, François, IV, 200

Du Mesnil. *See* Le Picard

Dumesnil. *See also* Peronne

Dumesnil, Marie (Charly, *dit* Saint-Ange), II, 131, 132

Dummer, Shubael, III, 476

Dummer, William, II, 665; III, 43, 200, 265, 506, 584, 587

Dummier, Mr, II, 601

Du Monceau. *See* Duhamel

Dumons. *See* Monts

Dumont. *See* Lambert

Dumont d'Urville, Jules-Sébastien-César, IV, 283

Dumontet, *dit* Lagrandeur, Jean-Baptiste, III, 210

Dumontier, François, II, 304

Dumontier, François (Barolet), III, 26

Du Mortier, Madeleine (Roussel), I, 583

Dumouchel, Marie-Joseph (Bigeau; Decoste), IV, 200

Dumoulin, M., I, 302, 509

Dumoulin (apprentice), III, 144

Dunbar, David, II, 669; III, 453

Dunbar, Janet (Bruyères), IV, 109

Dunbar, Thérèse-Josèphe. *See* Fleury Deschambault

Dunbar, Thomas, IV, 281

Dunbar, William, IV, 269

Duncan, Charles, IV, **244–45**, 218, 419

Duncan*, Henry (d. 1814), IV, 223

Duncan, John, IV, 261, 722

Dundas, Henry, 1st Viscount Melville, IV, 626, 717

Dundonald, Countess of. *See* Hamilton

Dunière, Louis (father), III, 509

Dunière*, Louis (1723–1806), IV, 48, 49

Dunk, George Montagu, 2nd Earl of Halifax, III, 90, 129, 340, 361, 362, 363, 365, 366, 496, 497, 583, 663, 664; IV, xxxv, xxxvi, xxxviii, xl, xli, xliii, 168, 228, 559, 571, 686, 787

Dunlop (Dunlap), William, IV, 105, 294, 392

Dunmore, Earl of. *See* Murray

Dunn*, Thomas (1729–1818), III, 541; IV, 37, 197, 243, 324, 538, 570, 602, 618, 716, 788, 790, 791

Du Palais. *See* Digoine

Du Parc. *See* Godet
Duparc, Jean-Baptiste, II, 448; III, **204–5**, 24, 330, 361, 427
Duparc, Jeanne. *See* Meur
Duparc de Tenanguer, Claude, III, 204
Dupas, Charlotte. *See* Denys de La Trinité
Du Paty (Patés), Jean, II, 449
Dupaul, Pierre, IV, 320
Dupeer, Susannah, IV, 583
Dupéré, Jean-Baptiste, III, 125
Dupéré, Marie-Anne (Claverie; Dandane Danseville de L'Étendard), III, 125
Dupéré, *dit* Champlain, Jean-Baptiste-François-Xavier, IV, 206
Duperié (Duperier), Anne. *See* Le Borgne de Belle-Isle
Duperié (Duperier), Jean, II, 582
Du Peron, François, I, **295–96**, 48, 205, 206, 217, 461, 602
Du Peron, Joseph-Imbert, I, 295, 296, 523
Dupéront (Dupéron, Duperron). *See* Baby
Du Perron, Thalour, I, **296**, 25, 89, 323
Dupin de Belugard, Jean-Baptiste, IV, 458
Duplaix, Catherine. *See* Gonillon
Duplaix (Duplex Silvain), Claude, IV, 245
Dupleix, Joseph-François, IV, 126
Duplex Silvain, Geneviève. *See* Benoist
Duplex Silvain, Jean-Baptiste, IV, **245–46**, 28, 678
Duplessis. *See also* Gastineau; Lefebvre; Quiniard; Radisson; Regnard; Robereau; Robreau
Du Plessis. *See also* Schomberg; Vignerot
Du Plessis, Armand-Jean, Cardinal de Richelieu, I, 29, 53, 115, 121, 124, 129, 159, 160, 161, 186, 195, 196, 203, 248, 261, 297, 372, 427, 428, 471, 482, 484, 504, 521, 567, 568, 579, 593, 615, 642; II, xv, 72, 228, 656
Du Plessis, Charles, Duc de Liancourt, I, 98
Duplessis, Madeleine, IV, 591
Duplessis (Gastineau Duplessis; Radisson, *dit* Duplessis), Marguerite, III, **205**
Du Plessis, Marie (Pastour de Costebelle), II, 509
Duplessis, Pacifique, I, **296**, 108, 368, 379, 385, 552, 590
Du Plessis-Bochart, Charles, I, **296–97**, 159, 349, 527, 633; II, 82
Du Plessis de Liancourt, Antoinette. *See* Pons
Duplessis de Mornay, Louis-François, II, 333; III, 40, 41, 114, 193, 284, 319, 545, 638, 640; IV, 220, 221
Du Plessis-Kerbodot. *See* Guillemot
Du Plessis-Savari. *See* Chaspoux
Duplesy. *See* Des Roches
Duplex. *See* Duplaix
Du Ponceau. *See* Favry
Dupont. *See also* Gaudais-Dupont
Du Pont. *See also* Gravé
Dupont, M. *See* Poulet
Dupont, Élisabeth (Cuny), IV, 187
Dupont, Étienne-Claude, IV, 69
Dupont, Guillaume, III, 165
Dupont, Jean, II, 204
Dupont, Jeanne. *See* Gaudais
Dupont, Marie. *See* Gauchet
Dupont, Siméon, II, **204**
Dupont, Xainte (Cloutier), I, 232
Dupont, *dit* Printemps, Jean, III, 422
Du Pont de Gourville, Michel, IV, 61, 252, 253, 255, 466, 783

Dupont de Neuville, Françoise-Thérèse (Renaud d'Avène de Desmeloizes), I, 572; II, 205; III, 112, 550
Dupont de Neuville, Marie-Madeleine (Le Moyne de Maricourt), II, 205, 404; III, 407
Dupont de Neuville, Nicolas, I, 114, 232, 325, 572; II, **204–5**, 369, 387, 404, 463; III, 112, 550
Du Pont de Renon, Anne. *See* Goutin
Du Pont de Renon, Anne-Claire (L-Espérance), IV, 470
Du Pont de Renon, Michel, II, **205**; IV, 246, 251, 470
Du Pont de Renon, Philippe-Michel, IV, 247
Du Pont Duchambon, Charles-François-Ferdinand, IV, 249
Du Pont Duchambon, François, IV, 247, 248
Du Pont Duchambon, Jean-Baptiste-Ange, IV, 248
Du Pont Duchambon, Jeanne. *See* Mius d'Entremont de Pobomcoup
Du Pont Duchambon, Louis, II, 205, 220; III, 116, 236, 368, 393, 475, 508, 533, 615, 644, 645, 656; IV, **246–49**, 15, 29, 60, 62, 239, 251, 252, 254, 688, 783
Du Pont Duchambon, Marguerite-Josephe. *See* Rodrigue
Du Pont Duchambon, Marie-Anne. *See* Roma
Du Pont Duchambon de Mézillac, Anne (Coux), IV, 248
Du Pont Duchambon de Vergor, Joseph, IV, 251
Du Pont Duchambon de Vergor, Louis, III, 72, 547, 570, 588, 672; IV, **249–51**, xxv, 29, 36, 60, 247, 248, 452, 457, 541, 631
Du Pont Duchambon de Vergor, Marie-Joseph. *See* Riverin
Du Pont Duchambon Dumaine, Barbe-Blanche. *See* Carrerot
Du Pont Duchambon Dumaine, Mathieu, IV, 248, 249
Du Pont Duvivier, Anne-Marie, II, 206
Du Pont Duvivier, François (father), II, **205–6**; III, 499, 552; IV, 246, 251, 783
Du Pont Duvivier, François (son), II, 206; III, 84, 175, 176, 236, 255, 260, 277, 287, 297, 366, 392, 438, 456, 475, 507; IV, **251–55**, xxiv, 29, 60, 61, 62, 239, 247, 249, 454, 466, 588, 676, 783
Du Pont Duvivier, Hugues, II, 205; IV, 246
Du Pont Duvivier, Joseph, II, 206; III, 567; IV, **783–84**, 247, 251, 255
Du Pont Duvivier, Joseph-Michel, II, 206
Du Pont Duvivier, Louis, II, 206
Du Pont Duvivier, Marie. *See* Hérauld de Gourville
Du Pont Duvivier, Marie. *See* Mius d'Entremont de Pobomcoup
Du Pont Duvivier, Marie-Joseph, II, 206
Du Pont Duvivier, Marie-Josephe. *See* Gautier, *dit* Bellair
Du Pont Duvivier, Marie-Josephe. *See* Le Borgne de Belle-Isle
Du Pont Duvivier de Gourville, Michel, II, 206; III, 570
Duport, Frances (Suckling), IV, 724
Duport, John, IV, 128, 267
Du Poyet. *See* Girault
Duprac, Françoise. *See* Lamoureux
Duprac, Jacques, II, 206
Duprac, Jean-Robert, II, **206**, 639
Duprac, Marguerite. *See* Vachon
Duprac, Noël, II, 206
Du Pratz (Duprat). *See* Le Page
Dupré. *See also* Le Comte; Le Conte
Dupré, M., IV, 148
Dupré, Anne de (Preissac), IV, 642
Dupré, François, I, 488; II, **206–7**; III, 546
Dupré, Philippe, II, 207
Dupré de Saint-Maur, Nicolas, IV, 55

146

Du Prévert. *See* Sarcel

Dupuis, Jean, II, 517

Dupuy, Claude, II, 207, 208

Dupuy, Claude-Thomas, II, **207–13**, 90, 91, 147, 151, 235, 277, 334, 433, 449, 520, 535, 548, 577, 597, 606; III, 15, 26, 44, 45, 46, 48, 62, 114, 118, 153, 178, 182, 204, 225, 226, 227, 240, 291, 299, 330, 352, 353, 410, 420, 499, 553, 569, 603, 616, 620, 621; IV, 355, 356, 359, 488

Dupuy, Élisabeth. *See* Aubry

Dupuy, Étienne, II, 207, 208

Dupuy, Jacques, II, 207

Dupuy, Jeanne. *See* Fauvenel

Dupuy, Jeanne. *See* Groisard

Dupuy, Jean-Patrice, IV, 69

Dupuy, Louise (Milly; Laborde), IV, 420

Dupuy, Marie (Orillat), IV, 591

Dupuy, Marie-Madeleine. *See* Lefouyn

Dupuy, Simon, II, 285, 437, 606

Dupuy, Suzanne. *See* Boschette

Dupuy, Suzanne (Petit), II, 521

Dupuy, Zacharie, I, **297–98**, 102, 416

Dupuy de La Grandrive, Thomas, II, 208

Dupuy de Lisloye, Jeanne. *See* Couillard de Lespinay

Dupuy de Lisloye, Paul, II, **213–14**, xxiv, 303

Dupuy de Lisloye, Simon, II, 213

Duquerny, Jeanne (Lomeron), I, 476

Du Quesne, M., III, 164

Du Quesne (Duchesne) (merchant), I, 100

Duquesne, Abraham, I, 257

Duquesne, Abraham (father of ANGE), IV, 255

Duquesne, Jacob, I, 257

Duquesne, Ursule-Thérèse. *See* Possel

Duquesne de Menneville, Ange, Marquis Duquesne, III, xxiv, 72, 76, 100, 118, 119, 148, 149, 162, 243, 385, 431, 432, 435, 628; IV, **255–58**, 213, 426, 447, 457, 459, 514, 563, 595, 605, 614, 617, 621, 636, 656, 667, 691, 733

Duquesnel. *See* Le Prévost

Du Quesnoy. *See* Talon

Duquet, Catherine. *See* Gauthier

Duquet, Denis, I, 298

Duquet, Françoise (Madry; Morel de La Durantaye), I, 479; II, 235, 488; III, 60

Duquet de La Chesnaye, Anne. *See* Lamarre

Duquet de La Chesnaye, Pierre, I, **298**, 73, 305, 474, 479, 537; II, 88, 136, 158, 418

Durand, Jean, I, 91

Durand, Jeanne (Féré Duburon), IV, 306

Durand, Justinien, II, 45, 238; III, **207–8**, 240, 516, 552

Durand, Laurent, IV, 533

Durand, Marie-Anne (Marchand), IV, 509

Durand, Pierre, II, 63

Durand de Beauval, M., II, 215

Durand de La Garenne, II, **214–15**, 336, 482

Durand de Villegaignon, Nicolas, I, 469, 679

Durang, John, IV, 557

Durantal. *See* Atironta (fl. 1615)

Duras, Duc de. *See* Durfort

Durell, Elizabeth. *See* Corbet

Durell, John, III, 208

Durell, Madeline. *See* Saumarez

Durell, Mrs. *See* Skey

Durell, Mrs (Taylor; wife of PHILIP), III, 208

Durell, Philip, III, **208–10**, 71, 132, 133, 507, 573, 669; IV, 163, 209, 210, 650, 699, 700

Durell, Thomas, II, 199; III, 208; IV, 169

Duret, Louise (Rageot), I, 560

Duret de Chevry, Charles-François, Marquis de Villeneuve, I, 89, 298, 436; II, 182, 183, 257

Duret de Chevry de La Boulaye, Charles, I, **298–99**, 90

Du Revest. *See* Nobel

Durfort, Jacques-Henri de, Duc de Duras, III, 14

Durham, Earl of. *See* Lambton

Durocher*, Jean-Baptiste-Amable (1754–1811), IV, 534

Durocher, Joseph (father), III, 210

Durocher, Joseph, III, **210–11**

Durocher, Marguerite. *See* Gaudé

Durocher, Marguerite. *See* Le Roy

Durocher, Marie-Louise-Catherine. *See* Juillet

Durosoy, Geneviève, I, 117

Du Roure. *See* Beauvoir

Durouvray. *See* Guyon

Duroy, Anne-Thérèse (Charest), IV, 140

Duroy, Charlotte (Bazil), III, 38, 224

Duroy, Marie-Marguerite (Chasle; Lanoullier de Boisclerc), III, 350

Du Sablé. *See* Dandonneau

Du Saussay de Bémont, Anne. *See* Carlier

Du Saussay de Bémont, Jacques, I, 583

Du Saussay de Bémont, Marie-Anne (Rouer de Villeray), I, 583

Dusautoy (Dusaultoir), Charles, III, 152

Dusautoy, Henri, III, 35

Dusautoy (Dusaultoir), Louise-Madeleine (Cugnet), III, 152; IV, 182

Dusautoy, Marie-Anne. *See* Roussel

Du Sicquet d'Esmainville, Françoise (Le Roy de La Potherie de Bacqueville), II, 421

Du Sillar, Marguerite (Le Marchand de Lignery), II, 389

Du Souchet, Louise-Anne (Cavelier), II, 576

Dusourdy. *See* Landriaux

Dussault. *See* Toupin

Dusson de Bonrepaus, François, II, 280, 443, 444

Dussy, Chevalier, II, 555, 560

Du Tartre. *See also* Basset; Denys

Du Tartre, Françoise (Denys de La Trinité), I, 261; II, 176, 179, 236

Du Tartre (de Tard), *dit* La Verdure, Jean, II, 47

Dutast, Captain, II, 440

Dutch Bastard. *See* Flemish Bastard

Duteau, *dit* Tourville, Charles, II, 190

Du Thet, Gilbert, I, **299**, 68, 95, 98, 100, 101, 441, 470, 560

Du Tillet. *See* Hélie

Du Tilly. *See also* Testu

Du Tilly, Sieur, II, 511

Dutisné, Catherine. *See* Du Cloux

Dutisné, Charles, II, 216

Dutisné, Claude-Charles (father), II, 215

Dutisné, Claude-Charles, II, **215–16**, xxix, xxxvii, 646; III, xxxiii, xxxix

Dutisné, Louis-Marie-Charles, II, 67, 216

Dutisné, Louis-Marie-Joseph, II, 216

Dutisné, Marguerite. *See* Margane de Lavaltrie

Dutisné, Marie-Anne. *See* Gaultier de Comporté

Du Tremblay. *See also* Gaultier

Du Tremblay, François-Joseph, known as Father Joseph, I, 428
Du Val. *See* Desjardins
Duval. *See also* Thuot
Duval, Catherine (Horné), II, 292
Duval*, Charles (fl. 1767–1828), IV, 206
Duval, Jean, I, **299–300**, 190, 346
Duval, Nicolas, I', 271
Duvallier, Marie-Salomé (Cailly), III, 93
Duvergé, Bertrand, IV, 378
Duverger. *See also* Forget
Duverger, Élisabeth (Rocbert de La Morandière), III, 563
Du Verger d'Aubusson, Marie-Jeanne. *See* Jarret de Verchères
Du Vergier. *See* Véniard
Duvernay. *See* Crevier
Du Vignau, Captain, II, 590
Duvivier. *See also* Du Pont
Duvivier, Adrienne (Hébert; Le Cavelier), II, 226
Duvivier, Marie-Anne (Berbudeau), IV, 56
Du Vuault (Vault). *See* Clement
Dyaderowane. *See* Ottrowana
Dyce, William, IV, 569
Dyckhuyse, Swantie (Schuyler), III, 587
Dyer, Edward, I, 531
Dymond, Joseph, IV, 758
Dysan. *See* Dejean
Dyson, Anne (Philipps), III, 514

EAGLESON, John, IV, **258–59**
Eagleson, Sophia Augusta. *See* Pernette
Eastburn, Robert, III, 588
Easton, Peter, I, **300–1**, 24, 240, 350, 481, 668
Eau. *See* Aux
Echevete, Matias de, I, **301**
Échon. *See* Brébeuf, Jean de
Échon (Héchon). *See* Chaumonot, Pierre-Joseph-Marie
Eddy*, Jonathan (1726/27–1804), IV, 13, 29, 161, 193, 258, 309, 451, 562, 693, 723, 736
Eden, Richard, I, 153, 154, 155
Eder de La Fontanelle, Guy, I, 186
Edewancho. *See* Atecouando
Edgcombe, Leonard, I, **301–2**; II, 42, 265, 266
Édouin, Charles, II, 187
Edward III, King of England, I, 678
Edward IV, King of England, I, 239
Edward VI, King of England and Ireland, I, 157, 158
Edward Augustus*, Duke of Kent and Strathearn (1767–1820), IV, 43, 147, 190, 523, 718
Edwards, Charity (Goldthwait), III, 259
Edwards*, Edward (d. 1813), IV, 689
Edwards, George, III, 302
Edwards, Henry, II, 534
Edwards, Richard, IV, **259–60**, 159, 402, 437, 648
Edwards, Thomas, II, 117
Effingham. *See* Howard
Egede, Hans, I, 252
Egerton, John, 2nd Earl of Bridgewater, II, 496
Eghohund, IV, 27
Egmont, Earl of. *See* Perceval
Egremon, John, II, 265
Egremont, Earl of. *See* Wyndham

Egushwa, IV, **260**, lvi
Ehrhard. *See* Erad
Eirikr Thorvaldsson, I, **676**, 17, 103, 448, 612, 642, 643
Eirikr upsi Gnupsson, I, **675–76**
Eiriksson. *See* Leifr
Elibank, Baron. *See* Murray
Éliçagaray. *See* Renau
Élie. *See also* Hélie
Élie, Jacques, II, **216–17**, 549
Élie, Madeleine. *See* Hélie
Élie, Marie-Joseph. *See* Maréchal
Eliot, Hugh, I, **302**, 21, 148, 343, 386, 643
Eliot, Sir John, I, 522
Élisabeth (You de La Découverte), I, 573; II, 673
Eliza* y Reventa, Francisco de (1759–1825), IV, 520, 568
Elizabeth I, Queen of England and Ireland, I, 93, 229, 279, 331, 333, 365, 566, 667, 678
Elizabeth Charlotte, Princess Palatine, II, 401
Ellice*, Alexander (1743–1805), IV, 39, 144, 261, 403
Elice, James, IV, 261
Ellice, Mary. *See* Simpson
Ellice, Robert, IV, **261–62**
Ellice, William, IV, 261
Elliot, Elizabeth (Vaughan), II, 644; III, 641
Elliot, John, IV, 784
Elliot, Robert, III, **211–12**; IV, 28, 80
Elliott*, Matthew (d. 1814), IV, 302, 499, 777
Elliott, Thomas, I, 242, 636, 637
Ellis, Edward, III, 326
Ellis, Henry, I, 677; III, 303, 472, 562, 664; IV, 51
Ellis, Sarah (Kilby), III, 326
Ellis, Thomas, I, 318
Ellis, Welbore, IV, 336, 571
Elmsley*, John (1762–1805), IV, 12
Ely, Deborah. *See* Dennison
Elyot. *See also* Eliot
Elyot, Richard, I, 371
Embito. *See* Ruis-Embito
Emerson, Ralph Waldo, III, 471
Émery. *See also* Particelli
Émery, Jacques-André, IV, 90, 544
Emmanuel, Father. *See* Veyssière, Leger-Jean-Baptiste-Noël
Émonnot, Catherine (Mance), I, 483
Énard, Jeanne (Crevier), I, 238; II, 86
Énault de Barbaucannes, Philippe, I, 260; II, **217**
Énault de Livaudais, Marie-Geneviève (Fontenelle; Coulon de Villiers), IV, 177
Endemare, Georges d', I, 388
Endicot, John, I, 241
Enjalran, Jean, II, **217–18**, 61, 383
Entheaume, Samuel, II, 223
Entremont. *See* Mius
Épernon, Duc d'. *See* Nogaret
Erad, Johann Burghard, III, **212**, 405
Éraque, M. d', II, 428
Erasmus, IV, 175
Erhardt, John Christian, III, **212–13**
Eric, Bishop. *See* Eirikr upsi Gnupsson
Eric the Red. *See* Eirikr Thorvaldsson
Ermatinger, Anna Maria. *See* Buhl
Ermatinger*, Charles Oakes (d. 1833), IV, 263

Ermatinger*, Frederick William (d. 1827), IV, 263
Ermatinger, Jemima. *See* Oakes
Ermatinger, Laurenz, IV, 262
Ermatinger, Lawrence, IV, **262–63**, 330, 585
Ermatinger, Lawrence Edward, IV, 263
Ermon. *See* Ormond
Erouachy (Eroachy), I, **302–3**, 211, 222, 479, 509
Erskine. *See also* Askin
Erskine, Alexander, 5th Earl of Kellie, III, 131
Erskine, Janet (Alexander, Countess of Stirling), I, 50
Erskine, Lady Elizabeth (Macfarlane; Colvill, Baroness Col-
    vill), III, 131
Erskine, John, 3rd Earl of Mar, I, 50
Erskine, Sir William, I, 50
Escairac, Pierre d', II, 410, 603
Eschaux, Bertrand d', I, 352
Escourre, Pierre, IV, 124
Esgly (Esglis). *See* Mariauchau
Esgriseilles. *See* Dubois
Esmainville. *See* Du Sicquet
Esmanville, Father d', I, 180
Esmard, Anne (Couture), II, 158, 159
Esmard (Esmart), Barbe (Michel; Letardif), I, 473; II, 158
Esmard, Madeleine (Cloutier), II, 158
Esmond, Marie-Anne, II, 141
Esnault. *See also* Énault
Esnault, Marie (Pichon), IV, 630
Espagnoli. *See* Spagniolini
Espérance, I, **199–200**, 196, 237, 366, 452, 494
Espiet, Jean-Georges d', II, 220
Espiet de La Plagne, Pierre-Paul d', II, 220; IV, 783
Espiet de Pensens, Jacques d', II, **218–20**, 123, 339, 412,
    498, 668; III, 20, 173, 178, 436, 532, 533, 566, 615; IV,
    15, 247
Espiet de Pensens, Jean d', II, 220
Espinay de Saint-Luc, François d', Marquis de Saint-Luc,
    I, 133
Espinay de Saint-Luc, Timoléon d', Marquis de Saint-Luc,
    I, 133
Esprit, Marie-Louise (Guillet de Chaumont), III, 269
Esprit de Vantelon, François, IV, 124
Esprit de Vantelon, Françoise. *See* Cadet
Esquairac. *See* Escairac
Esrouachit. *See* Erouachy
Est*, *dit* Coundo, François (d. 1838), IV, 154
Estaing, Jean-Baptiste-Charles d' (baptized Charles-Henri),
    Comte d'Estaing, IV, 122, 153, 282
Este, Rinaldo d', Prince of Este, II, 144
Estèbe, Arnaud (Armand), IV, 263
Estèbe, Élisabeth. *See* Garde
Estèbe, Élisabeth-Cécile. *See* Thibierge
Estèbe, Guillaume, III, 124, 125, 160, 165, 300, 433, 524,
    593; IV, **263–64**, 66, 67, 91, 209, 271, 361, 433, 447,
    615, 750, 755
Estève, Marguerite (Chapoton), III, 102
Estienne Du Bourgué, Denis d', II, 220
Estienne Du Bourgué, Françoise d'. *See* Desvoges de Clérin
Estienne Du Bourgué de Clérin, Denis d', II, **220–21**, 673;
    III, 164; IV, 720
Estienne Du Bourgué de Clérin, Jeanne d'. *See* Le Selle
Estienne Du Bourgué de Clérin, Marie-Louise d' (Souste),
    IV, 720

Estienne Du Bourgué de Clérin, Suzanne d' (Danré de
    Blanzy), III, 164
Estourmel, Constantin-Louis d', III, **213–14**, 356, 610;
    IV, 454
Estourmel, Louis d', Marquis d'Estourmel, III, 213
Estourmel, Marie-Aimée d', Marquise d'Estourmel. *See*
    Hautefort de Montignac
Estrades, Godefroi-Louis, Comte d'Estrades, I, 185, 284,
    554, 587
Estrées, Jean d', I, 443; II, 538
Estrées, Lucie-Félicité d', Duchesse d'Estrées. *See* Noailles
Etherington, George, III, 13, 262, 306; IV, 233, 241, 564
Étienne. *See also* Annaotaha; Pigarouich; Totiri
Étienne, Claude, I, 223, 495
Étienne, Hélène. *See* Martin
Étioles. *See* Le Normant
Étouat, I, 516
Eudes, Jean, II, 303
Eury de La Pérelle, Catherine (Céloron de Blainville), III, 99
Eury de La Perelle, Jean-François, II, 339
Eustache. *See* Ahatsistari
Evans, John, IV, 161, 471
Evans, Lewis, III, 607
Evans, Simon, IV, 759
Evans, William, IV, 634
Eveleth, Sarah (Glasier), IV, 299
Evelin, Robert, I, 673
Evelyn-Glanville, Frances (Boscawen), III, 70
Everill, Elizabeth. *See* Phillips
Evertsen, Cornelis, I, 196
Evison, Robert, III, **214**, 520
Exmouth, Viscount. *See* Pellew
Eymard, Jean, III, 272
Eyquem de Montaigne, Michel, III, 334
Eyre, William, III, **214–15**; IV, 299

Faber (Fabert). *See also* Lefebvre
Faber, John, III, 624
Fabre, *dit* Laterrière, Dorothée (Lehoulier), IV, 619
Fabre, *dit* Laterrière, Marie-Catherine. *See* Delezenne
Fabre*, *dit* Laterrière, Pierre (d. 1815), IV, 205, 206, 288,
    336, 589, 618, 619
Fabry de La Bruyère, André, III, 424
Fabus, Michel-Henri, IV, 422
Fabvre, Bonaventure, II, 161
Fafard, Jean, II, 488
Fafard, Thiennette (Boivin), I, 106
Fafard de La Framboise, Jean-Baptiste, III, 541
Fagot, Marie-Madeleine (Jourdain, *dit* Labrosse), III, 316
Fagundes, João Alvares, I, **303–4**, 21, 166, 171, 422
Faifeu, Julienne (Cuillerier), II, 164
Faillon*, Étienne-Michel (1799–1870), III, 629, 692
Fain, Isabelle (Dandonneau), II, 168
Fairbanks, Joseph, IV, 704
Fairborne, Sir Stafford, II, 290, 373, 564
Fairly, Marion (Veitch), II, 650
Falaise. *See* Gannes
Falardeau, Élisabeth. *See* Deguise, *dit* Flamand
Falardeau, Joseph, IV, 203
Falcon, Mary. *See* Grant
Falcon*, Pierre (1793–1876), IV, 310
Falconer, Thomas, IV, 300

Falcoz, Mathieu, III, 422
Falkingham, Edward, II, 25, 316; III, **215–16**, 126
Falkingham, Edward (son), III, 216
Falkland, Viscount. *See* Cary
Falmouth, Viscount. *See* Boscawen
Fancamp, Baron de. *See* Chevrier
Faneuil (father or uncle of Peter), II, 482
Faneuil, Peter, II, 482; III, 326; IV, 253, 273
Fanning*, Edmund (1739–1818), IV, 129, 551, 610
Faradon. *See* Normant
Farmer, Ferdinand. *See* Steinmeyer, Ferdinand
Farr, Walter, I, 578; II, 318
Farrar. *See* Ferrar
Faucher, Geneviève-Françoise (Lefebvre Angers), III, 371
Fauchois, Michel, II, 378
Faucon, Antoine, IV, 521
Faucon Dumanoir, Marie (Payen de Noyan), III, 502
Faucrolle, Françoise (La Porte), II, 345
Faure, Madeleine. *See* Brulart
Faure de Berlise, Angélique (Bullion), I, 484, 485, 486; II, 491
Faure de Berlise, Guichard, I, 484
Faustin, Élisabeth (Le Coutre de Bourville), III, 367
Fauteux*, Ægidius (1876–1941), III, 603; IV, 34, 36, 107, 698, 755
Fauteux, Joseph-Noël, IV, 376
Fautoux, Sieur, III, 124
Fautoux, Georges, III, 216
Fautoux, Léon, III, **216**, 281, 357, 501
Fautoux, Marie. *See* Meyracq
Fautoux, Marie-Madeleine. *See* Lartigue
Fauvault, Jeanne (Le Prévost), III, 391
Fauvel, Louise (Léger), II, 387
Fauvenel, Jeanne (Dupuy), I, 297
Faveron, Marie-Jeanne (Corbin), III, 138
Favery, Marie (Legardeur de Repentigny), I, 447, 637; II, 385
Favre, René, I, 105
Favry Du Ponceau, Anne-Marie (Martel de Bouague), III, 434
Faye, Anne de (Mars), II, 301
Faye, Claude de (Gallard), II, 235
Fear-a-Ghlinne. *See* MacDonald of Glenaladale, John
Féderbe, Louis-Laurent de, Comte de Maudave, IV, 752
Feild*, Edward (1801–76), IV, 438
Feilding, Basil, 2nd Earl of Denbigh, I, 241
Félix, Jeanne (Léger), II, 387
Fellière. *See* Deschamps
Fels. *See* Feltz
Felt, Joseph Barlow, III, 707
Feltz, Cécile. *See* Gosselin
Feltz, Charles-Elemy-Joseph-Alexandre-Ferdinand, IV, **264–65**, 434
Feltz, Elemy-Victor, IV, 264
Feltz, Marie-Ursule. *See* Aubert de La Chesnaye
Feltz, Marie-Ursule. *See* Mouthe
Fénelon, Abbé de. *See* Salignac
Fenton, Edward, I, 317
Fenwick, Benedict Joseph, II, 544
Ferchaud, Laurent, I, 593
Ferchault de Réaumur, René-Antoine, II, 595, 599; III, 675, 678, 679, 680
Fercourt. *See* Perrot

Ferdinand II, King of Aragon and Sicily, I, 41, 147, 154, 155, 241
Feré Duburon, Jean-Joseph, II, 274; IV, 123, 306
Feré Duburon, Jeanne. *See* Durand
Feré Duburon, Louise-Élisabeth (Goguet), IV, 123, 306
Ferguson, Israel, IV, 710
Ferguson (?), Nancy (Singleton), IV, 710
Ferguson, Patrick, IV, 211
Fernandes, Francisco, I, 228, 229, 302, 304, 343
Fernandes, João, I, **304–5**, 19, 21, 153, 234, 343
Fernández. *See* Martínez
Fernandez, Simon, I, 332, 333
Férolles, Marquis de. *See* La Ville
Ferrand, Élizabeth-Françoise. *See* Levasseur
Ferrand, Laurent-René, IV, 354
Ferrant, Marguerite (Verrier), III, 643
Ferrar, Constance, I, **305**, 248, 613
Ferrer Maldonado, Lorenzo, I, **676–77**
Ferrière, La. *See* Erouachy
Feuille, La. *See* Wahpasha
Feuillet. *See* Ducourday
Feuillon, Michel, I, 305
Feuquières, Marquis de. *See* Pas
Fevret de Fontette, Charles-Marie, II, 422
Fézeret, Claude, II, 221
Fézeret, Marie. *See* Carlié
Fézeret, Marie. *See* Philippe
Fézeret, Marie-Joseph (baptized Marie-Rose) (Thiersant), II, 221
Fézeret, René, I, 663; II, **221**
Fézeret, Suzanne. *See* Guillebaut
fforbes. *See* Forbes
Fidler, James, II, 233
Fidler*, Peter (1769–1822), IV, 160, 310, 684, 741
Fiedmont. *See* Jacau
Fiennes, Marquis de. *See* Fontanieu
Fiennes, William, 1st Viscount Saye and Sele, I, 435, 636
Fife, Earl. *See* Duff
Filiastre, Luc, II, **221–23**, 110, 130, 204, 421
Filiau, *dit* Dubois, François, IV, 272
Filiau, *dit* Dubois, Jean-Baptiste, IV, 272
Filiau, *dit* Dubois, Marie-Amable (Orillat), IV, 591
Filion, Suzanne-Élisabeth (Brassard Deschenaux), IV, 89
Filleul, Marie (Demosny), I, 255
Fillion, André, I, 305
Fillion, Antoine, I, 305
Fillion, Antoinette, I, 305
Fillion, Gabrielle. *See* Senler
Fillion, Jean, I, 305
Fillion, Joseph, IV, 659
Fillion, Marguerite. *See* Auber
Fillion, Michel, I, **305–6**, 589; II, xvi
Fillis, Elizabeth. *See* Stoddard
Fillis, John (father), IV, 266
Fillis, John, IV, **266–67**, 116, 131, 526, 527, 528, 696
Fillis, John (son), IV, 267
Fillis, Sarah. *See* Rudduck
Fillon, François, I, 536
Fillon, Michel, I, 305
Fin, Louis, I, 221
Finch, Daniel, 8th Earl of Winchelsea, III, 131
Finlay*, Hugh (1732–1801), IV, 323, 324, 570, 716, 794
Finucane, Bryan, IV, 328, 562

Fiott, Nicholas, IV, 176
Firmin-Didot, Ambroise, II, 422
Fiset, Marie-Angélique (Bédard), IV, 49
Fisher, Anne (Leverett), I, 474
Fisher, Cuthbert, IV, 93
Fisher*, James (fl. 1776–1816), IV, 107, 493, 589
Fisher, Richard, I, **306–7**, 364, 409, 450, 671, 672
Fisher, Robert, I, 306
Fitzgerald, Lord Edward, IV, 159
Fitzgerald, Gerald, 11th Earl of Kildare, I, 168
Fitzgerald, James Fitzmaurice, I, 421
Fitzgerald, Pamela. *See* Simms
Fitz-James, James Stuart, Duke of Berwick, III, 458
Fitzroy, Lady Charlotte (Lee, Countess of Lichfield), III, 369
Flamand (Flamant). *See* Deguise
Flame (Flemme). *See* Phlem
Flat Button, IV, 260
Fléché, Jessé, I, **307**, 95, 97, 99, 500, 501
Flemish Bastard, I, **307–8**, 7, 40, 41, 325, 555, 556, 602
Flesche. *See* Fléché
Fletcher, Alexander, IV, 129
Fletcher, Benjamin, I, 634
Fletcher, John, I, **308–9**, 611; II, 266
Fletcher, Mary (wife of JOHN), I, 308
Fletcher, Pendleton, II, 54
Fletcher, Robert, IV, **267–68**, 51, 342, 343
Fleuche (Fleuchy). *See* Fléché
Fleuriau, Charles-Jean-Baptiste de, Comte de Morville, III, 106; IV, 60
Fleurieu, Comte de. *See* Claret
Fleurimont. *See* Noyelles
Fleury. *See also* Buday; Guyart
Fleury, André-Hercule de, Cardinal de Fleury, II, 530, 551; III, 40, 192, 196; IV, 355, 358
Fleury, Charles, I, 68, 299, 441
Fleury, Jacques, II, 223
Fleury, Jean, II, 424
Fleury, Perrine. *See* Gabar
Fleury de La Gorgendière, Charlotte de (Marin de La Malgue), IV, 512
Fleury de La Gorgendière, Claire de. *See* Jolliet
Fleury de La Gorgendière, Joseph de, II, 66, 224; III, **216–18**, 62, 300, 333, 339, 616, 617, 621; IV, 268, 512, 661, 739
Fleury de La Gorgendière, Louise de (Rigaud de Vaudreuil), IV, 661
Fleury de La Gorgendière, Marie-Claire de (Taschereau), III, 616, 617
Fleury de La Gorgendière, Marie-Thomas de (Trottier Dufy Desauniers), IV, 739
Fleury de La Janière, Simon-Thomas de, II, 224; III, 217
Fleury Deschambault, Catherine. *See* Véron de Grandmesnil
Fleury Deschambault, Charles de, II, 224, 654; III, 217
Fleury Deschambault, Jacques de, I, **309**; II, 224
Fleury Deschambault, Jacques-Alexis de, I, 309, 344, 418; II, **223–24**, 81, 433; III, 216, 311; IV, 268
Fleury Deschambault, Jeanne-Charlotte de (Le Verrier de Rousson; Rigaud de Vaudreuil de Cavagnial, Marquise de Vaudreuil), I, 345; II, 224, 433; IV, 286, 476, 663
Fleury Deschambault, Joseph, III, 217, 243; IV, **268–70**
Fleury Deschambault, Marguerite de. *See* Chavigny de Berchereau

Fleury Deschambault, Marguerite-Renée de. *See* Denys de La Ronde
Fleury Deschambault, Marie-Anne-Catherine (Le Moyne de Longueuil, Baronne de Longueuil; Grant), IV, 268
Fleury Deschambault, Thérèse-Josèphe (Dunbar), IV, 269
Fleutelot, François, Marquis de Rompré (Rompray), II, 162, 499
Flibot, Jean, II, 273
Floquet, Pierre-René, IV, **270–71**, 544
Florence, Chevalier de, II, 4
Flórez Maldonado Martínez de Angulo y Bodquín, Manuel Antonio, IV, 519, 520
Florin (Florentin), Jean, I, 658
Flowerdew, Edward, Baron of the Exchequer, I, 280
Foi, I, **199–200**
Foissey, Marie (Simonet d'Abergemont), III, 592
Foix, Comte de. *See* Gaston III
Fol, Catherine (Demosny; Chasle), I, 249, 255
Follin, Nicolas, I, 621
Fonblanche. *See* Martinet; Quesnel
Fond, Anne de. *See* Manet
Fond, Jean de, II, 581
Fonds (Fond), Jean de. *See* Rodrigue, Jean-Baptiste
Fondville. *See* Rouillard
Fonfay. *See* Morin
Fontaine. *See also* Davène
Fontaine, Jacques, I, 277
Fontaine, Madeleine (Doublet), I, 277
Fontaine, *dit* Bienvenu, Pierre, III, 311
Fontanieu, Gaspard-Moïse-Augustin de, Marquis de Fiennes, IV, 353
Fontanille, M. de, IV, 622
Fontanille, Marie-Marguerite de. *See* Lemoine, *dit* Monière
Fontarabie, Pierre, I, 143
Fonte, Bartholomew de, I, **677**, 676; IV, 165, 746
Fontenay. *See* Prévost
Fonteneau, Jean, known as Jean Alfonse, I, **309**, 423, 680
Fonteneau, Jeanne (Curatteau), IV, 187
Fonteneau, Jérémie, I, 78
Fonteneau, Marie (Bailly), I, 78
Fonteneau, Valentine. *See* Alfonse
Fontenelle. *See* Le Bovier
Fontenelle, Marie-Geneviève. *See* Énault de Livaudais
Fontette. *See* Fevret
Fonville. *See* Bécart
Forant, Isaac-Louis de, II, **224–26**; III, 17, 18, 256, 368, 392, 456, 557, 630; IV, 15, 60, 253
Forant, Job de, II, 224
Forant, Marguerite de, II, 225; III, 630
Forbes, Elizabeth. *See* Graham
Forbes, John (father), III, 218
Forbes, John, III, **218–19**, 261, 283, 378, 526, 558; IV, 4, 177, 408, 670
Forbin, Claude de, Comte de Forbin, III, 42, 609
Forcade, Pierre de, II, 270; IV, 358
Ford, John, I, 301; II, 265
Ford, Thomas, III, 323
Fordyce, John, III, **219–20**, 504
Forel. *See* Avet
Forestier. *See also* Fortier
Forestier, Antoine, II, **226**, 68, 465; III, 220
Forestier, Antoine-Bertrand, II, 226; III, **220–21**
Forestier, Antoinette (Charlevoix), III, 104

Forestier, Élisabeth (Istre), III, 220
Forestier, Élisabeth-Charlotte. *See* Camoin
Forestier, Françoise. *See* Ricard
Forestier, Geneviève. *See* Bouchard, *dit* Dorval
Forestier, Jean, II, 226
Forestier, Jean-Baptiste, III, 220
Forestier, Marguerite (Bissot de Vinsenne), II, 66, 68; III, 69
Forestier, Marie, *dite* de Saint-Bonaventure-de-Jésus, I, **310**, 347, 353, 609, 611
Forestier, Marie-Madeleine. *See* Le Cavelier
Forestier, Marie-Madeleine (Poulin de Courval), II, 529
Forestier, Pierre, IV, 46
Foretier*, Pierre (1738–1815), IV, 58, 140, 592
Forget, Antoine, III, **221**, 612
Forget Duverger, Jacques-François, III, **221–22**, 442
Forière, La. *See* Erouachy
Fork. *See* Nissowaquet
Fornel, Anne-Thérèse. *See* Levasseur
Fornel, Jean, III, 222, 224
Fornel, Joachim, II, 328, 381; III, **222–24**, 284, 285, 553; IV, 44
Fornel, Louis, III, **224–25**, 38, 154, 205, 222, 226, 280, 281, 282; IV, 44, 45, 66
Fornel, Marie-Anne. *See* Barbel
Forrester, Andrew, I, **310–11**, 568, 593
Forsayth, James, I, 258
Forsayth, Marguerite. *See* Denys
Forster, Christopher Henry, III, 179
Forster, John Adam, III, 179
Forster, William, III, 87
Forsyth*, John (1762–1837), IV, 261
Forsyth*, Joseph (1764–1813), IV, 494
Forsyth, William, IV, 506
Forsyth*, William (d. 1814), IV, 197
Fort, Claude, IV, 124
Fortel. *See* Robert
Fortelle. *See* Robinau
Fortescue, Gertrude (Drake), I, 278
Fortescue, Sir John William, I, 546; IV, 26
Fortier. *See also* Forestier
Fortier, Angélique. *See* Manseau
Fortier, Angélique (Cadet), IV, 123
Fortier (Forestier), Étienne, III, 472
Fortier (Forestier), Françoise (Moreau), III, 472
Fortier, Marie-Anne. *See* Cureux, *dit* Saint-Germain
Fortier, Michel (father), IV, 123, 271
Fortier, Michel, IV, **271–72**
Fortier, Pierre-Michel, IV, 271
Fortin (settler), I, 116
Fortin, Louise. *See* Sommillard
Fortin, Marie (Couillard de Lespinay), II, 156
Fortin, Marie-Catherine (Chotard), II, 516
Fortin, *dit* Bellefontaine, Julien, I, 432
Forton*, Michel (1754–1817), IV, 702
Fossambault. *See* Nau de La Boissière
Foster, Thomas, IV, 219
Fotherby, Charles, II, **226–27**, 637
Fothersall, Ann (Williams), IV, 771
Foubert, Marie (Cusson), II, 166
Foucault, Catherine. *See* Catalon; Nafrechoux; Sabourin, *dit* Chauniers
Foucault, Eusèbe, III, 225

Foucault, François (father of Simon), III, 227
Foucault, François, III, **225–27**, 75, 135, 300, 400, 491, 525, 539, 647; IV, 318, 359, 360, 361, 433
Foucault, Françoise (Poulin de Courval), III, 538, 539
Foucault, Louise-Catherine (Nouchet), III, 226, 491
Foucault, Marie-Claude-Geneviève (Guillimin), III, 226; IV, 318
Foucault, Marie-Thérèse (Lamaletie), III, 226; IV, 433
Foucault, Michelle-Élisabeth (Liénard de Beaujeu), III, 400
Foucault, Nicolas, I, 361; II, **227**, 186, 189, 190; III, 380
Foucault, Nicolas-Denis, III, 226
Foucault, Simon (baptized Pierre), III, **227**
Foucault de Saint-Germain-Beaupré, Louis de, Comte Du Daugnon, I, 324
Foucher, I, **311**
Foucher*, Antoine (1717–1801), III, 141; IV, 534
Foucher, Charlotte-Élisabeth. *See* Goubert
Foucher, François, III, **227–28**, 279; IV, 11, 356
Foucher, François (son), III, 228
Foucher, Jacques, III, 227
Foucher*, Louis-Charles (1760–1829), IV, 345, 346
Foucher, Marie-Bernadette. *See* Lebé
Foucher, Marie-Joseph. *See* Le Gardeur de Courtemanche
Foucher, Marie-Madeleine-Françoise (Panet), IV, 601
Foucher de Labrador, Charles, III, 228
Foucrelle. *See* Faucrolle
Fougeray, M., I, 293
Fouilleuse, Louise de (Prouville, Marquise de Tracy), I, 557
Fount, William de la, I, 239, 240
Fouquet, Charles-Louis-Auguste, Duc de Belle-Isle, III, 458; IV, 307, 670,
Fouquet (Foucquet), Nicolas, I, 296, 323
Fouquet de Chalain, Christophe, I, 257
Fourche, La. *See* Nissowaquet
Foureur, Anne-Céleste. *See* Desforges
Foureur, Pierre, IV, 272
Foureur, *dit* Champagne, Catherine. *See* Guertin
Foureur, *dit* Champagne, Charlotte (Rousseau), IV, 272
Foureur*, *dit* Champagne, Jean-Louis (1745–1822), IV, 151, 272
Foureur, *dit* Champagne, Louis, IV, **272**
Foureur, *dit* Champagne, Pierre, IV, 272
Fourier, Louis, IV, 200
Fourier, Pierre, I, 115, 118
Fourière, La. *See* Erouachy
Fournel. *See also* Fornel
Fournel, Jean, III, 569
Fournier, Catherine (Roussel), I, 583
Fournier, Françoise. *See* Hébert
Fournier, Guillaume, I, 264
Fournier, Marguerite. *See* Crevier
Fournier, Pierre, IV, 386
Fowle, Daniel, III, 91
Fowler, Sarah (Batt), IV, 46, 47
Fox, Anne. *See* Barnard
Fox, Charles James, IV, 350
Fox, George, I, 81, 82, 84
Fox, Henry, 1st Baron Holland, IV, 57, 606
Fox, Luke, I, **311–12**, 20, 144, 329, 362, 375, 384, 668
Fox, Richard, I, 311
Foxcroft, Samuel, I, 499
Foy, Elizabeth (Southack), III, 596

Foyrière, La. *See* Erouachy
France, Charles de, Duc de Berry, II, 98, 104, 301, 618; IV, 663
Franceway. *See* Jérôme, *dit* Latour, François
Franchère, Benoîte. *See* Camagne
Franchère, Gabriel (father), IV, 508
Franchère*, Gabriel, (1786–1863), IV, 508
Francheville. *See also* Poulin; Terrier
Francheville, Pierre, I, 393; II, **227–28**, 460
Francis, Mr, I, 370
Francis, Samuel, II, 293
Francklin, Edith. *See* Nicholson
Francklin, George Germaine Sackville, IV, 502
Francklin, James Boutineau, IV, 781
Francklin, Michael (father), IV, 272
Francklin, Michael, IV, **272–76**, 13, 29, 80, 111, 116, 131, 132, 258, 291, 292, 300, 308, 313, 352, 450, 502, 504, 528, 561, 696, 723, 736, 781
Francklin, Susannah. *See* Boutineau
François, Father, II, 8
François, Father, III, 369
François, Mlle (Havy), III, 282
François (son of Oumasasikweie), I, 527
François I, King of France, I, 27, 126, 165, 166, 168, 309, 384, 423, 424, 658, 659, 660; III, 703
François, Claude, known as Brother Luc, I, **312–15**, 55, 359, 420; II, 199, 200, 344
François, Jeanne (Le Borgne), I, 435
François, Mathieu, I, 312
François, Perrette. *See* Prieur
François, *dit* Saint-François, Joseph, IV, 386
François-Marie de Paris (Sieur Marie), I, 505
François-Xavier. *See also* Arosen; Tonsahoten
François-Xavier, II, 665
Franklin, Benjamin, I, 255; III, 125; IV, 105, 230, 270, 407, 532, 549, 759
Franklin*, Sir John (1786–1847), I, 20, 375, 378
Franklyn (Franklin), Mary (Montgomery), IV, 545
Franks, Abraham, IV, 332
Franks, David Salisbury, IV, 332
Franks, John, IV, 332
Franks, Rebecca (Solomons), IV, 718
Franquelin, Élisabeth. *See* Auber
Franquelin, Élisabeth (Lemieux), II, 230
Franquelin, Jean-Baptiste-Louis, I, 119, 537, 664; II, **228–31**, 352, 427, 594, 599
Franquelin, Marie-Anne (Quesnel), II, 230
Franquet, Jean-Baptiste, III, 228
Franquet, Louis, III, **228–32**, 24, 79, 80, 117, 118, 183, 255, 267, 268, 440, 699, 700; IV, 64, 68, 174, 304, 344, 645, 656, 657
Franquet, Marie-Marguerite. *See* Romby
Franquetot, François de, Duc de Coigny, IV, 477
Fraser, Alexander (commander), IV, 130, 146, 418
Fraser, Alexander (lieutenant), III, 525, 530
Fraser, Alexander, IV, **276**
Fraser*, Alexander (1763–1837), IV, 685
Fraser, Jane. *See* McCord
Fraser, Jane (Davidson), IV, 276
Fraser, John, IV, 229, 269, 345, 346, 492, 570, 574, 602, 634, 759
Fraser*, Malcolm (d. 1815), IV, 107, 150, 548, 574

Fraser, Margaret, IV, 276
Fraser, Simon, IV, 190
Fraysse, Françoise (Veyssières), IV, 752
Fréchette*, Louis-Honoré (1839–1908), III, 148
Frederick II, King of Prussia, IV, 67
Frederick Augustus, Duke of York, IV, 25
Frederick Louis, Prince of Wales, III, 658
Fredin, Claude. *See* Robin
Fredin, Claude (André de Leigne), III, 14
Fredin, Gabriel, III, 14
Fredin, Jean, II, 133, 377; III, 15, 407
Freeman, Elisha, IV, 219
Frégault*, Guy (1918–77), IV, xxv, 61, 68, 71, 355, 634, 660, 674
Freke, Elizabeth (Bulkeley, Lady Bulkeley), IV, 109
Frémin, Jacques, I, **315**, 48, 108, 445, 461, 547, 635, 650; II, 61, 341, 540; III, 335
Frémont, Jean-Louis, III, 377; IV, 303
Frémont, Marie. *See* Collet
Frémont, Reine (Godefroy de Tonnancour), IV, 303
French, John, I, **315**, 605
French, Lawrence, I, 315
French, Margaret, III, 147
Frenel, Joseph-Antoine de, II, 632
Frenel, Marie-Anne de. *See* La Marque
Freneuse. *See* Damours
Fresnay. *See* Guyon
Fresnoy, Marquis de, IV, 622
Fresnoy, Marie-Marguerite de. *See* Lemoine, *dit* Monière
Fressel, Jeanne (Jacob), II, 294
Freydis, I, 449, 643
Frichet, Charles, IV, 502
Friday, III, 151
Friedrich I, Duke of Württemberg, I, 632
Frin. *See* Fin
Frisius, Gemma, I, 154, 679
Frobisher, Benjamin, IV, **276–78**, 262, 532
Frobisher, Bernard, I, 316
Frobisher, Dorothy (Widmerpole; wife of Sir MARTIN), I, 318
Frobisher, Isabel (wife of Sir MARTIN), I, 318
Frobisher, Joseph, IV, 276
Frobisher*, Joseph (1740–1810), IV, 47, 133, 139, 276, 277, 278, 647
Frobisher, Sir Martin, I, **316–19**, 19, 85, 86, 93, 94, 153, 332, 375, 385, 607, 669, 670, 677, 679, 680; IV, liii
Frobisher, Peter, I, 318
Frobisher, Rachel. *See* Hargrave
Frobisher, Thomas, IV, 276
Fromont, *dit* La Bouille, Thomas, I, 167, 169
Fronsac. *See* Denys
Frontenac, Comte de. *See* Buade
Frontenac, Comtesse de. *See* La Grange; Phélypeaux de Pontchartrain
Frontigny, Catherine (Mourongeau), III, 78
Frontigny, Marie-Madeleine. *See* Lajoüe
Frontigny, Pierre, III, 77
Frost, John, IV, 565
Frotté, M., I, 423
Froyer de La Baronnière, Jeanne (La Roche Daillon), I, 420
Frye, Joseph, III, 87, 129
Fryer, Elizabeth (Collier, Lady Collier), IV, 160

Fuca, Juan de, I, **677**, 676; IV, 165, 244, 746
Fulford, Andrew, I, 278
Fulford, Faith (Davis), I, 251
Fulford, Sir John, I, 251
Fullartine, John, II, **231–33**, 49, 50, 51, 266, 311, 312, 319, 492; III, 414
Fuller, Amos, IV, 351
Fustel, Charles, II, 451

GABAR, Perrine (Fleury), II, 223
Gaboto, Antonio, I, 304
Gabriel, Gilles, IV, 471
Gabriel, Jacques, III, 235
Gabriel, Marie (Corpron), III, 141
Gabriel, Marie-Geneviève. *See* Côté
Gabrielle, Suzanne de (Robutel de La Noue), II, 581
Gadois. *See also* Gadoys
Gadois, Jeanne. *See* Besnard
Gadois, Jeanne-Françoise (Hattanville), II, 234
Gadois, Marie. *See* Pontonnier
Gadois, Pierre, I, 319; II, **233–34**; III, 232
Gadois, *dit* Mauger, Jacques, II, 234; III, **232–33**, 181; IV, 204, 748
Gadois, *dit* Mauger, Marie-Madeleine. *See* Chorel de Saint-Romain, *dit* d'Orvilliers
Gadoys, Françoise (Godé), I, 319
Gadoys, Jean-Baptiste, I, 319; II, 234
Gadoys, Louise. *See* Mauger
Gadoys, Pierre, I, **319**, 218, 464, 557; II, 233; III, 232
Gadoys, Roberte (Prud'homme; Verrier), I, 319, 557; II, 466
Gage, Benedicta Maria Theresa, Viscountess Gage. *See* Hall
Gage, Margaret. *See* Kemble
Gage, Thomas, III, xxvii, 89, 141, 145, 292, 333, 367, 410, 495; IV, **278–82**, xxxiii, xxxv, xxxvii, xxxix, 3, 17, 36, 85, 86, 114, 138, 148, 188, 266, 297, 300, 331, 337, 369, 375, 393, 396, 435, 451, 503, 506, 546, 570, 572, 575, 582, 587, 606, 675, 680, 681, 709, 720, 734, 768, 787, 793, 794
Gage, Thomas, 1st Viscount Gage, IV, 278
Gaghswaghtaniunt. *See* Kaghswaghtaniunt
Gagné, Agnès (Bourassa, *dit* La Ronde), IV, 77
Gagnier, Geneviève (Touchet), II, 90
Gagnon, Charles-Octave, III, 712
Gagnon, Françoise. *See* Goudeau
Gagnon, Françoise (Cotton), III, 144
Gagnon, Jacques (Joseph), IV, 153, 154
Gagnon, Jean, I, 319
Gagnon, Joseph, III, 222, 443
Gagnon, Madeleine-Renée. *See* Roger
Gagnon, Marie-Madeleine (Lepage de Sainte-Claire), III, 390
Gagnon, Mathurin, I, **319–20**
Gagnon*, Philéas (1854–1915), IV, 424
Gagnon, Pierre (father), I, 319
Gagnon, Pierre, I, 319
Gahickdodon, III, 614
Gaiachoton. *See* Kayahsota?
Gaignard, Philippe, I, 277
Gaignier, Marguerite (Pinard), I, 550
Gaignon. *See* Gagnon
Gaillard. *See also* Rey
Gaillard, Catherine. *See* Leduc

Gaillard, Guillaume, II, **234–35**, 43, 409, 448, 487; III, 45, 153
Gaillard, Hilaire, II, 234
Gaillard, Jean-Baptiste, III, 647
Gaillard, Joseph-Ambroise, IV, 430
Gaillard, Louise-Catherine. *See* Denys de Saint-Simon
Gaillard, Marie-Catherine. *See* Neveu
Gaillard, Marie-Louise, *dite* de la Sainte-Vierge, IV, 535
Gaillard, Mathieu, I, **320**; II, 618
Gailliard, Françoise (Moreau de Brésoles), I, 512
Gaingnon. *See* Gagnon
Gainsborough, Thomas, IV, 26
Galan (Galand, Gallant). *See* Haché-Gallant
Galard. *See* Gallard
Galaup, Jean-François de, Comte de Lapérouse, IV, **282–83**, 157, 244, 341, 366, 383, 518, 519, 584, 684, 741, 743
Galaup, Louise-Éléonore de, Comtesse de Lapérouse. *See* Broudou
Galaup, Marguerite de. *See* Rességuier
Galaup, Victor-Joseph de, IV, 282
Galhet (soldier), III, 310
Galiano. *See* Alcalá-Galiano
Galiffet de Caffin, Catherine de. *See* Aubert de La Chesnaye
Galiffet de Caffin, François de, I, 524; II, 402, 523, 527; III, **233**
Galiffet d'Honon, Joseph de, III, 233
Galiffet d'Honon, Marguerite de. *See* Bonfils
Galiffet d'Honon, Pierre de, III, 233
Galinée. *See also* Bréhant
Galinée, Seigneur de, I, 126
Galinier, Dominique, I, 220, 612, 644
Gallard, Charlotte, II, **235–36**, 466, 606; III, 220, 238, 369
Gallard, Claude. *See* Faye
Gallard, René, II, 235
Galleran, Guillaume, I, **320**, 417
Galliot, Jacques, I, 313
Galochau, Jean, III, 621
Galvão, António, I, 154, 235
Gálvez, José de, IV, 622
Galway, Viscount. *See* Monckton
Galway, Viscountess. *See* Manners
Gamache, Nicolas, II, 155
Gamard (ship's pilot), I, 256
Gambier, James, IV, 161
Gamelain, Françoise. *See* Bellanger
Gamelain, Françoise (Pinard), I, 321
Gamelain, Michel, I, 321
Gamelain de La Fontaine, Marguerite. *See* Crevier
Gamelain de La Fontaine, Michel, I, **320–21**, 418, 468, 550; II, 236, 584, 616; III, 311
Gamelin, Angélique. *See* Giasson
Gamelin, Angélique (Hervieux), III, 290
Gamelin, Charlotte (Malhiot), III, 422
Gamelin, Ignace, II, **236**, 457; III, 234, 422; IV, 283, 287
Gamelin, Ignace, II, 236, 530; III, 146, 153, 234, 249, 485, 503, 592, 617; IV, **283–85**, 11, 46, 235, 287, 362, 590
Gamelin, Jacques-Alexis, II, 236
Gamelin, Joseph, IV, 285
Gamelin, Joseph-Jacques, III, 290
Gamelin, Marguerite. *See* Lemoine
Gamelin, Marie-Anne. *See* Lemaître-Lamorille
Gamelin, Marie-Élisabeth. *See* Spagniolini

154

Gamelin, Marie-Jeanne. *See* Maugras
Gamelin, Marie-Louise. *See* Dufrost de La Gemerais
Gamelin, Marie-Louise. *See* Lorimier
Gamelin, Michel-Joseph, III, 598
Gamelin, Pierre, II, 236; III, 233
Gamelin, Pierre-Joseph, IV, **285–87**
Gamelin, *dit* Châteauvieux, Antoine, IV, 294
Gamelin, *dit* Châteauvieux, Laurent-Eustache, II, 239; III, 249; IV, 77
Gamelin, *dit* Châteauvieux, Suzanne (Gill), IV, 294
Gamelin Maugras, Marie-Clémence. *See* Dufrost de La Gemerais
Gamelin Maugras, Pierre, III, **233–34**, 242; IV, 235, 287
Gancleau, Jean, II, 441
Gand. *See* Derré
Gandeacteua (Gandeaktena, Gandiaktua), I, **321–22**, 651; II, 107
Ganet, François, II, 220, 292, 649, 650; III, **234–35**, 20, 456, 478, 479, 636, 644
Gangnon. *See* Gagnon
Ganiodaio (Handsome Lake), IV, lvi
Gannassatiron, II, 255
Ganneaktena. *See* Gandeacteua
Gannenrontié. *See* Lauzon, Pierre de
Gannensagouas (Marie-Thérèse), I, 118
Gannenstenhawi. *See* Williams, Eunice
Gannes de Falaise, Anne de (Rousseau de Villejouin), IV, 688, 689
Gannes de Falaise, Barbe de. *See* Denys de La Trinité
Gannes de Falaise, Bernardin de (baptized Louis-Joseph), IV, 81
Gannes de Falaise, Élisabeth de. *See* Catalogne
Gannes de Falaise, François de, II, 236; III, 384
Gannes de Falaise, Françoise de. *See* Le Bloy
Gannes de Falaise, Jean-Baptiste de, IV, 391
Gannes de Falaise, Louis de (father), II, 236
Gannes de Falaise, Louis de, II, **236**, 579; III, 235; IV, 688
Gannes de Falaise, Louise de. *See* Legardeur de Tilly
Gannes de Falaise, Louis-François de, III, 236
Gannes de Falaise, Marguerite de. *See* Leneuf de La Vallière et de Beaubassin
Gannes de Falaise, Marguerite-Madeleine de (Couagne), II, 154; IV, 174
Gannes de Falaise, Michel de, III, **235–36**, 6, 175; IV, 15, 254, 443, 678, 688, 783
Gannes de Falaise, Pierre de, III, 223
Gannes de Falaise, Thérèse de. *See* Bouat
Gannett, Caleb, IV, 258
Ganong*, William Francis (1864–1941), III, 416
Gantès, Jean-François de, III, 188
Garakontié, I, 445
Garakontié, I, **322–23**, 462, 464, 525, 555; II, 194, 237, 342
Garat, Pierre, I, 476
Garaud, M., IV, 66
Garault, Anne de (Garnier), I, 324
Garaut. *See* Garreau
Garcia, Diego, I, 156
Garde (Gardes), Élisabeth (Estèbe), IV, 263
Gardner, Alan, 1st Baron Gardner, IV, 744, 745
Gareman, Florence (Boucher), II, 140
Gargas, Sieur de, I, 577; II, 182, 184
Gargot. *See also* Lorit

Gargot, Anne. *See* Lardeau
Gargot, Hilaire, I, 323
Gargot, Jean, I, 323
Gargot de La Rochette, Nicolas, I, **323–24**, 296, 594
Garhio (Garhi, Marie), I, 522
Gariépy, Geneviève (Corbin), III, 138
Gariépy, Marie (Renaud, *dit* Cannard), IV, 659
Garland, Katherine (wife of THOMAS), I, 324
Garland, Thomas, I, **324**
Garneau*, François-Xavier (1809–66), I, 112; III, 254; IV, xxxiii, 232, 320
Garnett, Mr, IV, 437
Garnier, Anne. *See* Garault
Garnier, Charles, I, **324–25**, 41, 125, 203, 388, 461, 562, 652
Garnier, Françoise. *See* Grenier
Garnier, Guillemette (Bourgeoys), I, 115
Garnier, Jean, I, 324
Garnier, Jean-Baptiste, III, 621
Garnier, Julien, I, 322; II, **237–38**, 107, 473, 540, 643; III, 330, 335, 336, 337, 360
Garnier, *dit* Nadeau, Jean, II, 16
Garnier de Chapouin, Jacques, I, 590
Garohiaé (Garonhiagué). *See* Ogenheratarihiens
Garreau. *See also* Maugue-Garreau
Garreau, Élisabeth (Lalande; Guy), III, 271
Garreau, François, III, 598
Garreau, Léonard, I, **325**, 282, 307, 308, 651
Garreau, Marguerite (Payne), II, 513
Garreau, Pierre, II, 513
Garreau, *dit* Saint-Onge, Marie-Anne. *See* Maugue
Garreau, *dit* Saint-Onge, Pierre (father), IV, 287, 529
Garreau, *dit* Saint-Onge, Pierre, IV, **287–88**, 510
Garrick, David, IV, 114
Garrish, Sarah, II, 303
Gasche, Cécile (Adhémar), II, 11
Gaschet, Françoise. *See* Phélypeaux
Gaschet, Hélène. *See* Bourgina
Gaschet, Pierre, III, 237
Gaschet, René, I, 81, 583; III, **236–37**
Gascoing, Marguerite (Guillouet d'Orvilliers), II, 270
Gasnier, Anne (Clément Du Vuault de Monceaux; Bourdon), I, 113, 585; II, 585
Gaspar, Marguerite (Schindler), IV, 702
Gaspar Soiaga. *See* Kondiaronk
Gaspé. *See* Aubert
Gastaignol, Marie (Daccarrette), III, 156
Gastaldo, Giacomo, I, 659
Gastineau de Sainte-Marie, Louis, IV, 11
Gastineau Duplessis, Charlotte. *See* Le Boulanger
Gastineau Duplessis, Jean-Baptiste, III, **237–38**; IV, 360, 591
Gastineau Duplessis, Louis, III, 237
Gastineau Duplessis, Marguerite. *See* Duplessis
Gastineau Duplessis, Marie. *See* Crevier
Gastineau Duplessis, Marie-Joseph (Olivier de Vézin), III, 237; IV, 591
Gastineau Duplessis, Nicolas (father), I, 231; III, 237
Gastineau Duplessis, Nicolas, II, 283
Gaston III, *dit* Phébus, Comte de Foix, II, 4
Gatchell, Dorothy (Pote), III, 531
Gates, Horatio, IV, 110, 114

Gatin, Élisabeth (Martel de Belleville), III, 433
Gatin, Geneviève (Nouchet), III, 490, 491
Gatin, Jean, III, 490
Gatrowani. *See* Ottrowana
Gaubert, Mathurin, IV, 95
Gaubil, Antoine, III, 336
Gauchet, Marie (Dupont), II, 204
Gauchet de Belleville, Catherine (Migeon de Branssat), I, 508; III, 450; IV, 535
Gaudais, Jeanne (Dupont), II, 205, 365
Gaudais Du Chartran, Nicolas, I, 326
Gaudais-Dupont, Louis, I, **325–26**, 79, 248, 323, 428, 512, 538, 629; II, xvii, 205, 365
Gaudar, Marie (Lauson), I, 428, 429, 431
Gaudarville. *See* Peuvret
Gaudé, Dominique, III, 145
Gaudé, Françoise, III, **238–39**, 369
Gaudé, Françoise (Jourdain, *dit* Labrosse), III, 316
Gaudé, Marguerite. *See* Picard
Gaudé, Marguerite (Jarry; Durocher), III, 210
Gaudé, Marie (Couagne; Derivon de Budemon), II, 153, 154, 529; III, 145, 146
Gaudé, Nicolas, III, 238
Gaudet*, Placide (1850–1930), IV, 470
Gaudin. *See* Godin
Gaudion, Pierre-Nicolas, III, 61, 549, 567
Gaudreau, Catherine (Basset), I, 79
Gaudron, Marie. *See* Gohel
Gaudron, Nicolas, III, 239
Gaudron de Chevremont, Charles-René, III, **239–40**
Gaudron de Chevremont, Marie-Bénigne. *See* Derome
Gaudry, *dit* Bourbonnière, Nicolas, I, 45
Gaufin, Jean-Philippe, III, 240
Gaufin, Marie-Joseph. *See* Moreau
Gaufin, Valérien (baptized Jean-Philippe), III, **240–41**, 295
Gaulin, Antoine, II, **238**, 22, 106, 187, 199
Gaulin, François, II, 238
Gaulin, Marie. *See* Rocheron
Gaultier, Françoise. *See* Colin
Gaultier, Jean-Baptiste, III, 98, 173
Gaultier, Jean-François, II, 596, 597; III, **675–81**, 29, 30, 31, 154, 180, 315, 334, 648; IV, 45, 91, 407, 729
Gaultier, Madeleine-Marie-Anne. *See* Tarieu de La Pérade
Gaultier, Marie. *See* Guyon Desprez
Gaultier, Marie (Quintal), IV, 649
Gaultier, Marie-Anne (Soupiran), III, 596
Gaultier, Marie-Charlotte (Delort), III, 173
Gaultier (Gauthier), Marie-Thérèse (Carrerot; Hertel de Rouville), III, 98; IV, 14
Gaultier, René, III, 675
Gaultier de Bruslon, Jean, II, 429, 515
Gaultier de Comporté, Angélique (Riverin), I, 326; II, 187, 576
Gaultier de Comporté, Marie. *See* Bazire
Gaultier de Comporté, Marie-Anne (Peuvret de Gaudarville; Dutisné), I, 326; II, 42, 215, 525
Gaultier de Comporté, Philippe, I, **326**, 84, 105, 106; II, xxiv, 29, 251, 275, 375, 525, 576
Gaultier de La Vérenderie, Adam-Pierre, I, 327
Gaultier de La Vérenderie, Bertrande. *See* Gourdeau
Gaultier de La Vérendrye, Jean-Baptiste, II, **238–40**, 40, 202; III, 46, 241, 244, 245, 249, 250, 251; IV, 77, 288, 289

Gaultier de La Vérendrye, Louis, III, 245, 247
Gaultier de La Vérendrye, Louise-Antoinette. *See* Mézières de Lépervanche
Gaultier de La Vérendrye, Louis-Joseph, III, **241–44**, 171, 234, 245, 251, 252, 375; IV, 288, 289, 425, 427, 513
Gaultier de La Vérendrye, Marie-Amable. *See* Testard de Montigny
Gaultier de La Vérendrye de Boumois, Pierre, III, **244–45**, 241, 249, 252, 375; IV, 284, 288, 289
Gaultier de Rinault, Gillette. *See* Vernon
Gaultier de Rinault, Philippe, I, 326
Gaultier de Varennes, Charlotte-Louise-Angélique. *See* Sarrazin
Gaultier de Varennes, Jacques-René, II, 578; III, **245–46**, 247, 604
Gaultier de Varennes, Jean-Baptiste, II, **240–41**, 19, 109; IV, 439
Gaultier de Varennes, Jean-Hippolyte, II, 598; III, 246
Gaultier de Varennes, Marie. *See* Boucher
Gaultier de Varennes, Marie-Jeanne. *See* Le Moyne de Sainte-Hélène
Gaultier de Varennes, Marie-Renée (Dufrost de La Gemerais; Sullivan), II, 201, 202; III, 234, 246, 247, 603, 604; IV, 234, 235
Gaultier de Varennes, René, I, **326–28**, 468; II, 32, 85, 202, 240, 523, 545; III, 245, 246, 247, 603; IV, 234
Gaultier de Varennes, René (grandson), III, 246, 603
Gaultier de Varennes et de La Vérendrye, Marie-Anne. *See* Dandonneau Du Sablé
Gaultier de Varennes et de La Vérendrye, Pierre, I, 11, 37; II, xxix, xxxii, xxxv, 10, 35, 40, 168, 201, 202, 239, 240; III, **246–54**, xxxiv, xxxvii, 46, 47, 82, 107, 121, 137, 158, 234, 241, 242, 244, 285, 301, 331, 341, 375, 376, 432, 444, 485, 492, 580, 595, 603, 604; IV, 77, 178, 234, 283, 284, 288, 289, 359
Gaultier Du Tremblay, François, III, 241, 243, 249, 252; IV, **288–89**
Gaultier Du Tremblay, Madeleine (Petit de Levilliers), II, 523
Gauron, Marguerite (Lozeau), III, 410
Gaustrax, III, 452; IV, 138
Gauthier, Augustin, III, 316
Gauthier, Catherine (Duquet), I, 298
Gauthier, Guillaume, I, 479
Gauthier de La Chenaye, Marie. *See* Pichon
Gauthier de La Chenaye, Philippe, I, 606
Gautier, Antoine, IV, 320
Gautier, Catherine (Lozeau), III, 410
Gautier, Gabriel, I, 89, 90, 258
Gautier, Jean-Jacques, IV, 124
Gautier, Joseph, III, 254
Gautier, Joseph-Nicolas, III, 255
Gautier, Madeleine (Campion), IV, 132
Gautier, Marie-Renée (Varin, *dit* La Pistole), IV, 748
Gautier, Nicolas-Gabriel, III, 254
Gautier, Pierre, III, 254, 255
Gautier, *dit* Bellair, Joseph-Nicolas, III, **254–55**, 366; IV, xxv, 79, 252
Gautier, *dit* Bellair, Marguerite (Bourdon de Dombourg), IV, 79
Gautier, *dit* Bellair, Marie. *See* Allain
Gautier, *dit* Bellair, Marie-Josephe (Du Pont Duvivier), IV, 252

Gautier de Verville, Charles, IV, 302, 564
Gauvin, François, III, 569
Gauvreau, Marie (Martel de Saint-Antoine), IV, 148
Gauvreau, Marie-Geneviève (Rageot de Saint-Luc), II, 540
Gauvreau, Pierre, II, 430; III, 498
Gaverocke, Alice (Hayman), I, 365
Gawèhe (Gawickie), III, **255–56**, xxxviii
Gay, Robert-Michel, II, **241**; III, 268, 542, 543
Gayahgwaahdoh. *See* Kaieñ?kwaahtoñ
Gay Desenclaves, Jean-Baptiste de, III, **256–57**, 120, 166, 343, 438; IV, xxv, 254
Gayon. *See* Lalande
Gayot, Jean-Baptiste, II, 575; III, 352
Gayot (Goy), Nicolas, II, 33, 464, 465, 508, 509
Gazan, François, IV, 125
Geanneau. *See* Jeanneau
Geddes, David, IV, 399
Gédouin, Madeleine de (Le Picard de Norrey), II, 415
Geest, Catherine (Cavelier), I, 172; II, 123
Gellée, Pierre, I, 277
Genaple, Catherine. *See* Coursier
Genaple, Claude, II, 241
Genaple de Bellefonds, François, I, 203, 561, 565, 664; II, **241–43**, xxii, xxiii, xxiv, 286, 418, 451, 514, 576
Genaple de Bellefonds, Jean-François, II, 243
Genaple de Bellefonds, Joseph, II, 243
Genaple de Bellefonds, Marie-Anne. *See* La Porte
Gendron. *See also* Deshaies
Gendron, Éloi, I, 328
Gendron, François, I, **328**, 550
Gendron, Gillette. *See* Doussineau
Gendron, Marie-Madeleine (Devau, *dit* Retor), IV, 216
Gendron, Pierre, II, 582
Genest, André, IV, 376
Geneviève de l'Enfant-Jésus. *See* Regnard Duplessis
Geneviève de Saint-Augustin. *See* Juchereau Duchesnay
Geneviève de Sainte-Madeleine. *See* Gosselin
Geneviève de Saint-Pierre. *See* Boucher
Geneviève-Agnès de Tous-Les-Saints. *See* Skanudharoua
Genlis, Comte de, IV, 448
Genner, Samuel, II, 378
Gensanne, M. de, II, 212
Geoffroy, Catherine (Paillard), II, 506
Geoffroy, Louis, II, **243–44**, 522
George I, King of Great Britain and Ireland, II, 123, 198, 287, 443, 498, 652, 661, 668; III, 295, 405; IV, xxi
George II, King of Great Britain and Ireland, II, 93, 670; III, 283, 363, 405, 447, 508, 586, 623, 642, 654, 663, 669, 673; IV, xxii, 21, 109, 455, 503, 676
George III, King of Great Britain and Ireland, III, 108, 143, 213, 367, 704; IV, xxvii, xl, xlvi, xlviii, 25, 38, 41, 97, 106, 146, 161, 179, 280, 304, 323, 434, 452, 543, 686, 763
George IV, King of Great Britain and Ireland, III, 650; IV, 195, 230
George, Prince of Denmark, II, 286
George*, David (d. 1810), IV, 515, 627
Georgemé, Séraphin, II, **244–45**
Georges, Pierre, I, 476
Georges, Samuel, I, 98, 101, 293, 476, 565
Georges, Suzanne (Lomeron), I, 476
Gérard, Louis-Bertrand, III, 204
Gergy. *See* Languet

Gérin, Abbé, IV, 75
Gérin (Guérin), Marguerite (Boisseau), IV, 75
Germain. *See also* Langlois
Germain, Antoine, III, 478
Germain, Charles, IV, **289–90**, 79, 214, 423, 633, 783
Germain, François, III, 478
Germain (Sackville), George, 1st Viscount Sackville, IV, 5, 22, 23, 281, 350, 428, 452, 571, 726, 792
Germain*, Joseph-Charles (1707–79), III, 163, 417, 425
Germain, Joseph-Louis, II, **245–46**, 40, 41, 161, 341, 474, 608; III, 359
Germain, Marguerite (Moreau), III, 472
Germon, Barthélemi, II, 455
Gerrard*, Samuel (1767–1857), IV, 311
Gerrard, Sir Thomas, I, 333
Gerrish, Benjamin, III, 174; IV, **290–91**, 52, 116, 266, 273, 274, 292, 414, 528, 704
Gerrish, Elizabeth (Green), IV, 312
Gerrish, John, IV, 290, 291
Gerrish, Joseph, III, 174, 365; IV, **291–92**, 52, 94, 273, 290, 414
Gerrish, Mary. *See* Brenton
Gerrish, Mary. *See* Cradock
Gerrish, Rebecca. *See* Dudley
Gerrish, Sarah. *See* Hobbes
Gervais, Charles, III, 257
Gervais, Jean, I, 508
Gervaise, Louis, III, **257–58**
Gervaise, Marie. *See* Boyer
Gervaise, Marie-Joseph (Besnard, *dit* Carignant), IV, 58
Gervaise, Marie-Madeleine. *See* Langlois
Geyer, George, I, **328–29**, 39, 301, 509, 606, 657; II, 50, 265, 266, 309, 310
Geyesutha. *See* Kayahsota?
Giard, Antoine, III, **258**, 443
Giard, Antoine (son), III, 258
Giard, Claude. *See* Prat
Giard, Gabriel, III, 258
Giard, Marianne. *See* Lafontaine
Giard, Nicolas, III, 258
Giasson, Angélique (Gamelin), IV, 285
Giasson, Jacques, IV, 268
Gibault*, Pierre (d. 1802), IV, 171, 303
Gibbon, Edward, IV, xlvi
Gibbons, Edward, I, 223, 241, 594, 636
Gibbons, Margaret (wife of Edward), I, 241
Gibbons, Richard (father), IV, 292
Gibbons, Richard, IV, **292–93**, 266, 274, 522, 562
Gibbons, Richard Collier Bernard Des Barres Marshall, IV, 293
Gibbons, Suzanna. *See* Sheperd
Gibbons, Susannah (mother of RICHARD), IV, 292
Gibbons, William, I, **329**, 20, 74, 144, 145
Gibson, Edmund, II, 663
Gibsone, Sir John, II, **246**, 274, 293, 395, 564, 580, 666; III, 488
Gié, Sire de. *See* Rohan
Gien, Comte de. *See* Séguier
Giengwahtoh. *See* Kaieñ?kwaahtoñ
Giffard, Denise. *See* Peiras
Giffard, Jeanne. *See* Poignant
Giffard, Joseph, I, 326, 331, 428; II, 30, 307, 514, 639
Giffard, Louise (Lauson de Charny), I, 331, 428, 431

Giffard, Marc, I, 330

Giffard, Marie. *See* Regnouard

Giffard, Marie (Juchereau de La Ferté), I, 331, 400; II, 33, 302, 303, 304

Giffard, Marie-Françoise, *dite* Marie de Saint-Ignace, I, **329–30**, 348; II, 303

Giffard, Marie-Thérèse (Juchereau de Saint-Denis), I, 331, 402, 550; II, 305, 307, 427; III, 317

Giffard, Michèle-Thérèse. *See* Nau de La Boissière et de Fossambault

Giffard de Moncel, Robert, I, **330–31**, 30, 218, 232, 281, 297, 319, 326, 329, 344, 359, 401, 417, 428, 431, 447, 584; II, xvi, 82, 514

Gigault, Bernardin, Marquis de Bellefonds, II, 343

Gigou, Anne (Guyart), III, 272

Gilbert, Adrian, I, 251, 336

Gilbert, Anne. *See* Aucher

Gilbert, Sir Humphrey, I, **331–36**, 19, 23, 154, 228, 229, 251, 278, 362, 363, 364, 380, 531, 532, 668, 677

Gilbert, Sir John, I, 279, 333, 335, 336

Gilbert, Katherine. *See* Champernowne

Gilbert, Otho, I, 331

Gill, Antoine, IV, 294

Gill*, Ignace (1808–65), IV, 294

Gill, Joseph-Louis, known as Magouaouidombaouit, IV, **293–94**, 290

Gill, Marie-Jeanne. *See* Nanamaghemet

Gill, Michael, II, **246–47**, 388

Gill, Michael (son), II, 246; III, 68, 324

Gill, Moses, II, 246

Gill, Nicholas, II, 246

Gill, Relief. *See* Dowse

Gill, Rosalie. *See* James

Gill, Samuel, IV, 293

Gill, Suzanne. *See* Gamelin, *dit* Châteauvieux

Gill, Xavier, IV, 294

Gillam. *See also* Kelly

Gillam, Abigail (wife of BENJAMIN), II, 247

Gillam, Abigail (daughter of BENJAMIN), II, 247

Gillam, Ann, II, 247

Gillam, Benjamin (grandfather), I, 337

Gillam, Benjamin (uncle), I, 337; II, 537

Gillam, Benjamin, I, 39, 129, 130, 227, 338, 528, 601; II, **247**, 538

Gillam, Hannah (mother of ZACHARIAH), I, 337

Gillam, Hannah (Sharpe), I, 338

Gillam, Martha, I, 338

Gillam, Phoebe. *See* Phillips

Gillam (Williams), Thomas, II, 478

Gillam, Zachariah, I, **336–38**, 82, 83, 129, 226, 227, 385, 519, 601, 607; II, 247, 537

Gillam, Zachariah (son), I, 338

Gillet (valet), II, 116

Gillet, Marguerite (Bernard de La Rivière), II, 58

Gilliland, Susan (Macaulay), IV, 494

Gilliland, William, IV, 494

Gillray, James, IV, 578

Gilman, Elizabeth (Hale), III, 274

Gilmore, Mary. *See* Lillicoe

Gilmore, Thomas, IV, **294–95**, 105, 106, 392, 393, 423, 424, 533

Gimbal, Madeleine. *See* Morisseau

Ginkel, Godert, 1st Earl of Athlone, II, 279

Gioux, Françoise (Raudot), II, 555

Giovio, Giulio, I, 660

Giovio, Paolo, I, 660

Gipson, Lawrence Henry, III, 149

Girard. *See also* Giard

Girard, Jacques, III, 257, 343, 425, 426; IV, **295–97**, 453, 457

Girard, Jean, III, 612, 613

Girard, Jeanne-Élisabeth (Legardeur de La Mothe-Tilly), III, 376

Girard, Madeleine (Tantouin de La Touche), II, 618

Girard de La Place, Simon. *See* La Place, Simon-Gérard de

Girardin, Jeanne (Barbe), II, 276

Giraud, Jeanne de (Saurel), I, 602

Giraudin, Jeanne (Bertrand), II, 411

Girault Du Poyet, Marguerite (Le Prévost Duquesnel), III, 392

Girot, Jehan, I, 421

Girouard*, Antoine (1762–1832), IV, 81

Giroux, Louis, IV, 484

Giroux, Louise (Jacquet), IV, 386

Giroux, Thomas, II, 82

Girty, James (brother of Simon*), IV, 777, 778, 779

Girty, James (slave), IV, 778

Girty*, Simon (1741–1818), IV, 410, 499, 777, 778

Giscaro, Marquis de. *See* Rivière

Giscaro, Marquise de. *See* Pastour de Costebelle

Gittens, Elizabeth (Colston), I, 233

Gittens, William, I, 233

Gitton, Jean, II, 28, 275, 464, 465

Gladwin, Frances. *See* Beridge

Gladwin, Henry (father), IV, 297

Gladwin, Henry, III, 95, 306, 527, 528, 529, 558, 652; IV, **297**, 241, 337, 552, 587, 722, 762, 768

Gladwin, Mary. *See* Dakeyne

Glandelet, Charles de, I, 117, 506; II, **247–49**, 19, 44, 45, 90, 132, 259, 329, 332, 372, 629; III, 168, 545, 684

Glandons. *See* Desdevens

Glanville. *See* Evelyn-Glanville

Glapion, Augustin-Louis de, III, 142, 580; IV, **297–99**, 134, 135, 372

Glasier, Ann (Stevens; wife of BEAMSLEY PERKINS), IV, 299

Glasier, Beamsley Perkins, IV, **299–301**

Glasier, Benjamin, IV, 300

Glasier, Sarah. *See* Eveleth

Glasier, Stephen, IV, 299

Glaude. *See* Claude

Gledhill, Bathsheba Placentia, II, 250

Gledhill, Grace America, II, 250

Gledhill, Isabella. *See* Atkinson

Gledhill, Isabella. *See* Richmond

Gledhill, Joseph, II, 250, 251

Gledhill, Margaret Carolina, II, 250

Gledhill, Robert, II, 249

Gledhill, Samuel, II, **249–51**; III, 324, 516, 517

Glemet, Pierre, IV, 125, 271, 565, 566, 754

Glen, John Sanders, III, 587

Glenaladale. *See* MacDonald

Glenie*, James (1750–1817), IV, 329

Glikhikan (Glickhican), IV, **301–2**

Gloria, Jean, I, **339**; II, xvi

Gloria, Marie. *See* Bourdon

Gloria, Perrette. *See* Vaulthier

Gloria, Pierre, I, 339
Glory, Laurent, II, 302
Gloucester, Duke of. *See* William
Gnupsson. *See* Eirikr
Gobeil, Jeanne-Angélique (Prat), II, 531
Gobert, Catherine (Liénard de Beaujeu), III, 402
Gobin, Gabrielle. *See* Bécasseau
Gobin, Jean, II, **251–52**, 32, 217, 273, 276, 522
Gobin, Jeanne (Petit), II, 522
Godard (Godart), Marie-Louise (Boschenry, Baronne de Drucourt), III, 71
Godbout, Archange, III, 94, 690, 722
Godé. *See also* Gaudé
Godé, Françoise. *See* Gadoys
Godé, Mathurine (Saint-Père; Le Moyne de Sainte-Marie), I, 598; II, 386, 405; III, 385, 580
Godé, Nicolas, I, 319, 598; III, 580
Godeau, Antoine, I, 644
Godefroy, Barbe, I, 340
Godefroy, Charlotte, I, 340
Godefroy, Jean-Amador, II, 190
Godefroy, Jean-Paul, I, **339–40**, 45, 112, 145, 341, 344, 447, 623; II, xvi, 83
Godefroy, Marie. *See* Marteau
Godefroy, Marie-Madeleine. *See* Legardeur de Repentigny
Godefroy, Perrette. *See* Cavelier
Godefroy, Pierre, I, 340
Godefroy, Robert, I, 339
Godefroy, Thérèse (Renaud Dubuisson), III, 551
Godefroy de Linctot, Catherine-Apolline. *See* Blondeau
Godefroy de Linctot, Daniel-Maurice, IV, **302–3**, 564
Godefroy de Linctot, Hyacinthe, IV, 302
Godefroy de Linctot, Louis-René, IV, 302
Godefroy de Linctot, Marie-Charlotte (Ailleboust de La Madeleine), IV, 11
Godefroy de Linctot, Maurice-Régis, IV, 302
Godefroy de Linctot, René, III, 269
Godefroy de Lintot, Jean, I, **340–41**, 121, 223, 369, 467; II, 168, 252, 253
Godefroy de Lintot, Marie. *See* Leneuf
Godefroy de Lintot, Marie-Charlotte (Hertel de La Fresnière), III, 288
Godefroy de Lintot, Michel, II, **252**, 70; III, 288
Godefroy de Lintot, Perrinne. *See* Picoté de Belestre
Godefroy de Lintot, René, II, 252
Godefroy de Normanville, Louis, II, 252
Godefroy de Normanville, Marguerite. *See* Seigneuret
Godefroy de Normanville, Thomas, I, **341**, 340, 489, 490
Godefroy de Saint-Paul, Françoise. *See* Lepellé
Godefroy de Saint-Paul, Françoise (Boucher de Montbrun), III, 82
Godefroy de Saint-Paul, Jean-Amador, II, **252**; III, 82, 224
Godefroy de Saint-Paul, Madeleine (Boucher de Montbrun), III, 82
Godefroy de Saint-Paul, Marguerite. *See* Jutrat
Godefroy de Tonnancour, Charles-Antoine, II, 253; III, **258–59**
Godefroy de Tonnancour, Charles-Antoine, IV, **303–4**, 332
Godefroy de Tonnancour, Louise. *See* Carrerot
Godefroy de Tonnancour, Louise (Ramezay), IV, 650
Godefroy de Tonnancour, Louis-Joseph, II, 253; III, 430, 539; IV, **304–5**, 185, 303, 316, 547
Godefroy de Tonnancour, Marguerite. *See* Ameau

Godefroy de Tonnancour, Marguerite-Renée, *dite* de la Croix, IV, 319
Godefroy de Tonnancour, Marie-Geneviève, *dite* de Sainte-Hélène, IV, 319
Godefroy de Tonnancour, Mary. *See* Scamen
Godefroy de Tonnancour, Reine. *See* Frémont
Godefroy de Tonnancour, René, II, **252–53**, 204, 529; III, 110, 258, 539, 551; IV, 304, 319, 650
Godefroy de Tonnancour, Ursule (Charly Saint-Ange), III, 110
Godefroy de Vieuxpont, Catherine. *See* Poulin de La Fontaine
Godefroy de Vieuxpont, Jacques, I, **341**, 274
Godefroy de Vieuxpont, Joseph, I, 553; II, **253–54**
Godefus. *See* Boucault
Godet, Gédéon, II, 538, 539
Godet, Margaret Charlotte (Radisson), II, 539
Godet, Rolland, I, **341–42**, 245; II, xvi
Godet Des Maretz, Christine de, I, 342
Godet Des Maretz, Claude de, I, **342**, 190, 346
Godet Des Maretz, Cléophas de, I, 342
Godet Des Maretz, François de, I, 342
Godet Des Maretz, Jeanne de. *See* Gravé Du Pont
Godet Des Maretz, Marie de. *See* La Marck
Godet Des Maretz, Paul de, I, 342
Godet Du Parc, Jean de, I, 190, 342
Godfrey, Arabella. *See* Churchill
Godfrey, Charlotte (Boscawen), III, 70
Godfroy, Jacques, III, 528, 529
Godin (Gaudin), Louise (Vézina), III, 648
Godin, *dit* Bellefontaine, *dit* Beauséjour, Joseph, IV, **305–6**
Godin, *dit* Bellefontaine, *dit* Beauséjour, Marie-Anne. *See* Bergeron d'Amboise
Godin, *dit* Chatillon, *dit* Bellefontaine, Gabriel, IV, 305
Godin, *dit* Chatillon, *dit* Bellefontaine, Marie-Angélique. *See* Robert Jasne
Godsman, John. *See* Davidson, William
Godsman, William, IV, 195
Godson. *See* Gotson
Goes, Damien de, I, 234, 235
Goffar, Anne-Jeanne (Dosquet), IV, 220
Goffe, Edmund, II, **254**
Goffe, Elijah, III, 213
Goffe, Hannah. *See* Bernard
Goffe, Hannah. *See* Lynde
Goffe, Mary. *See* Norden
Goffe, Samuel, II, 254
Goforth, William, IV, 320
Gofton, Ingram, II, 493, 663
Goguet, Denis (father), IV, 306
Goguet, Denis, III, 145, 485, 608, 643; IV, **306–7**, 35, 66, 69, 123, 126, 128, 182, 362, 422, 624, 632
Goguet, Louise-Élisabeth. *See* Feré Duburon
Goguet, Marguerite-Thérèse-Sibylle (mother of DENIS), IV, 306
Gohel, Marie (Gaudron), III, 239
Gohin, Pierre-André, Comte de Montreuil, III, 186; IV, **307–8**, 651, 672
Gohin de Montreuil, Monique-Françoise. *See* Petit
Gohin de Montreuil, Nicolas, IV, 307
Goigni. *See* Richard
Golard, Françoise (Petit de Levilliers de Coulanges), II, 523
Goldfrap, James, IV, 570

Goldsmith, Eliza (Small), IV, 766, 767
Goldthwait, Benjamin, III, **259–60**, 484; IV, 651
Goldthwait, Charity. *See* Edwards
Goldthwait, John, III, 259
Goldthwait, Sarah. *See* Hopkins
Golkowsky, George, III, 212
Gómara, López de, I, 154
Gombert, Sieur, II, 418
Gomes, Estevão, I, **342–43**, 21
Gonʔaongote. *See* Williams, Eunice
Góngora. *See* Lújan
Gonillon, Catherine de (Duplaix; Daccarrette), III, 157; IV, 245
Gonillon, Jeanne (Daccarrette), III, 156
Gonsales, João, I, **343**, 153, 302, 304
Gonwatsijayenni. *See* Koñwatsiʔtsiaiéñni
González, Gertrudis (Martínez), IV, 519
Gooch, Elizabeth (Austin), II, 287
Goodall, Lydia, III, 295
Goossens, Pierre-François, IV, 565
Gordan, Antoine, IV, 375
Gordon, William, IV, 398
Goreham, Anne. *See* Spry
Goreham, Elizabeth (Hunter; wife of JOSEPH), IV, 308
Goreham, Joseph, III, xxix, 129, 257, 664; IV, **308–10**, 111, 161, 193
Gorel, Hélène (Marin), II, 458
Gorges, Sir Ferdinando, I, 51, 262, 497
Gorham, Elizabeth. *See* Allyn
Gorham, John, III, **260–61**, 438, 483, 532, 583, 653; IV, 169, 308, 679
Gorham, Mary. *See* Thacter
Gorham, Shobal (Shubael), III, 260; IV, 308
Gorrell, James, III, **261–62**, 410, 528
Gorribon, Pierre de, I, 400
Gorry, Jean, I, 216
Gorst, Thomas, I, **343**, 47, 49, 50, 83, 226, 337, 477; II, 537
Gosnold, Bartholomew, I, 189, 364
Gosselin*, Amédée-Edmond (1863–1941), III, 691; IV, 755, 801
Gosselin*, Auguste-Honoré (1843–1918), III, 11, 553, 560; IV, 637
Gosselin, Cécile (Douaire de Bondy; Feltz), IV, 265
Gosselin, Gabriel, II, 273
Gosselin, Geneviève, *dite* de Sainte-Madeleine, II, 93
Gosselin, Jean-Baptiste, III, **262–64**, 193, 223, 315
Gosselin, Louis (coureur de bois), III, 493
Gosselin, Louis (son of Gabriel), II, 273
Gosselin, Louise. *See* Guillot
Gotson (Godson), Christiana. *See* Veyssière
Gotteville de Belile, Robert-David, II, **254–55**; III, 178, 191
Gouault, Gaspard, I, 108
Goubert, Charlotte-Élisabeth (Foucher), III, 227
Goudeau, Françoise (Gagnon), I, 320
Gouentagrandi, I, 634; II, **255–56**, xxxvi
Gougeon, Antoine, II, 71
Gougeon, Huguette (Blanchard), II, 71
Gougeon, Jeanne. *See* Chabrat
Gough, Françoise-Renée. *See* Pommereau
Gough, John, III, 525
Goulaine de Laudonnière, René de, I, 469
Gould, Sir Charles, IV, 83, 84, 85
Gould, King, II, 591; III, 9; IV, 83

Goulet, Thomas, III, 396
Goumard, Claire (Du Gua), I, 291
Goupil, René, I, **343–44**, 42, 124, 388, 389, 523; II, 157
Goupy (Goupil), Marie (Aubert), II, 26
Gourdan, Claude-Madeleine (Le Normant), III, 386
Gourdeau, Bertrande (Gaultier de La Vérendrie), I, 327
Gourdeau de Beaulieu, Antoine, I, 345; II, 256
Gourdeau de Beaulieu, Éléonore. *See* Grandmaison
Gourdeau de Beaulieu, Jacques, I, 344, 345; II, 256, 449
Gourdeau de Beaulieu, Jeanne-Renée (Macard), I, 345; II, 449
Gourdeau de Beaulieu et de La Grossardière, Jacques, I, 345; II, **256–57**, 296
Gourdeau de Beaulieu et de La Grossardière, Marie. *See* Bissot
Gourdeau de Beaulieu et de La Grossardière, Pierre-Jacques, II, 256
Gourdon, M., II, 146
Gourges, Dominique de, I, 381, 469
Gournay, Marie de (Rousseau), I, 484
Gourville. *See* Du Pont; Hérauld
Goussé, M., II, 149, 151
Goussé, Charles-Gaspard de, Chevalier de La Rochalar, III, 633
Goutin, Abraham (Alexandre) de, II, 257
Goutin, Anne de (Du Pont de Renon; Hertel de Cournoyer), II, 205, 257
Goutin, Antoine de, II, 257
Goutin, François-Marie de, II, 219, 257, 258; III, **264–65**, 79, 184, 389, 533, 567; IV, 41, 56, 455
Goutin, Jacques de, II, 257
Goutin, Jeanne de. *See* Tibaudeau
Goutin, Jeanne de, II, 257
Goutin, Joseph de, II, 257
Goutin, Louise de, II, 257
Goutin, Magdelaine de, II, 257
Goutin, Marguerite de, II, 257
Goutin, Marguerite-Madeleine de (Boucher), III, 79
Goutin, Marie-Angélique de. *See* Aubert de La Chesnaye; Puyperoux de La Fosse
Goutin, Marie-Anne de (Bailly de Messein), IV, 41
Goutin, Marie-Joseph de, II, 257
Goutin, Mathieu de, I, 577; II, **257–58**, 37, 45, 182, 183, 205, 352, 462, 480, 481, 579, 625, 630, 654; III, 79, 264, 681, 682
Goutin, Mathieu de (son), II, 257
Gouyé, Thomas, II, 270
Gouze, Guillaume, IV, 624
Gouze, Marie-Anne. *See* Chasle
Governor Blacksnake. *See* Thaonawyuthe
Gowding (Goudon), Elizabeth (Kirke), I, 404
Goweaaey (Goweah). *See* Gawèhe
Goy. *See* Gayot
Goyer, Olivier, II, **258–59**, 106, 176, 249, 268
Gozon, Marthe de (Montcalm), III, 458
Grace, James, III, 136, 137
Gradis, Abraham, IV, 67, 69, 92, 209, 632
Gradis, David, IV, 66, 657
Graham*, Andrew (d. 1815), II, 310; III, 285, 287, 304; IV, 156, 157, 160, 340, 377, 378, 518, 524, 647, 742, 743, 758, 761
Graham, Elizabeth (Forbes), III, 218
Graham, Richard, Viscount Preston, II, 538

Grais. *See* Le Gouès
Gramont, Antoine-Charles, Duc de Gramont, II, 434
Gramont, Armand de, Comte de Guiche, II, 440
Gramont, Marguerite-Louise-Suzanne de, Comtesse de Guiche. *See* Béthune
Granby, Marquess of. *See* Manners
Grand Agnier, Le. *See* Togouiroui
Grandchamp. *See* Allenou
Grand Condé, Le. *See* Condé, Louis II, Prince de
Grande Armée, La. *See* La Grande Armée
Grande Gueule, La. *See* Otreouti
Grandet, Joseph, II, 196
Grande Terre, La. *See* Ohonsiowanne
Grandfontaine. *See* Andigné
Grandison, Viscount. *See* St John
Grandmaison. *See also* Borry
Grand Maison. *See* Malepart
Grandmaison, Éléonore de (Boudier de Beauregard; Chavigny de Berchereau; Gourdeau de Beaulieu; Cailhault de La Tesserie), I, **344–45**, 56, 418, 537; II, 141, 223, 256, 449
Grandmesnil. *See* Véron
Grandmont, Sieur de, I, 507
Grandpré. *See* Boucher; La Court
Grand Sauteux, Le. *See* Minweweh
Grandval. *See* Morthon
Grandville. *See* Bécart
Grange, Captain, II, 266
Grange, Geneviève (Levasseur), I, 473, 474
Grangula (Grangular). *See* Otreouti
Granpré. *See* La Court
Grant, Alexander, IV, 52, 291
Grant*, Alexander (1734–1813), IV, 777
Grant, Charles, IV, 385
Grant, Cuthbert (Quebec merchant), IV, 310
Grant, Cuthbert (Trois-Rivières merchant), IV, 310
Grant, Cuthbert, IV, **310**
Grant*, Cuthbert (1793–1854), IV, 310
Grant, David, IV, 310
Grant, David Alexander, IV, 269
Grant, James (fur-trader), IV, **311**, 133
Grant, James (officer), III, 219, 378
Grant, James (son of CUTHBERT), IV, 310
Grant, John, IV, 171
Grant, Margaret (Grant), IV, 310
Grant, Marie-Anne-Catherine. *See* Fleury Deschambault
Grant, Marie-Charles-Joseph. *See* Le Moyne de Longueuil
Grant, Mary (Falcon), IV, 310
Grant, Robert (fur-trader), IV, 365, 366
Grant, Robert (merchant), III, 130, 365
Grant*, William (d. 1805), III, 111; IV, 127, 197, 315, 324, 477, 492, 538, 571, 686, 716, 725, 755, 794
Grant*, William (1743–1810), IV, 133, 304, 311, 754
Grantham, Baron. *See* Robinson
Grantley, Baron. *See* Norton
Granville. *See* Bécart
Granville, Earl. *See* Carteret
Grape, The. *See* Chomina
Grass, Michael, IV, 683
Grasse, Marie-Reine (Lanoullier), III, 350
Grasset de Saint-Sauveur, André, III, 611; IV, **311–12**
Grasset de Saint-Sauveur, André (son), IV, 312
Grasset de Saint-Sauveur, Jacques, IV, 312

Grasset de Saint-Sauveur, Jean, IV, 311
Grasset de Saint-Sauveur, Louise. *See* Roussel
Grasset de Saint-Sauveur, Marie-Anne. *See* Nolan Lamarque
Grasset de Saint-Sauveur, Marie-Joseph. *See* Quesnel Fonblanche
Gravé* de La Rive, Henri-François (1730–1802), IV, 7, 42, 43, 49, 50, 74, 100, 370, 371, 373, 424, 510, 511, 642
Gravé Du Pont, Christine. *See* Martin
Gravé Du Pont, François, I, **345–46**, 28, 61, 64, 86, 98, 160, 188, 189, 190, 191, 194, 208, 209, 210, 265, 292, 293, 300, 342, 347, 386, 422, 432, 433, 470, 473, 601, 602, 638
Gravé Du Pont, Jeanne (Godet Des Maretz), I, 342, 346
Gravé Du Pont, Robert, I, **346–47**, 95, 98, 346
Graveline, M., III, 83
Gravelle, Marguerite. *See* Prieur
Gravelle, Pierre, II, 648
Gravenor, Elizabeth (Stourton), I, 614
Graves, Booty, IV, 160, 365
Graves, Samuel, IV, 790
Graves*, Thomas, 1st Baron Graves (1725–1802), III, 132; IV, 163, 598, 599
Gravier, Charles, Comte de Vergennes, IV, 144, 312
Gravier, Jacques, II, **259–60**, 110, 197, 347, 454, 455, 468, 469, 543, 653; III, 380
Gravois, Joseph, IV, 222
Gray, Alexander, IV, 37, 492, 716
Gray, Ann (wife of Alexander), IV, 37
Gray*, Benjamin Gerrish (1768–1854), IV, 291
Gray*, Edward William (1742–1810), IV, 59, 263, 385, 386, 442, 533, 549, 703
Gray, John (deacon), III, 471
Gray, John (printer), IV, 532, 534
Gray*, John (d. 1829), IV, 37
Gray, Joseph, IV, 290
Gray*, Robert (1755–1806), IV, 73, 218, 411, 412, 419, 519
Gray*, Robert (d. 1828), IV, 551
Gray, Robert Don Quadra, IV, 73
Gray, Thomas, IV, 273
Graydon, John, II, **260–61**, 36, 274, 348, 373, 486, 565, 583, 659, 666
Gray Lock, II, 665; III, **265–67**
Great Mohawk. *See* Togouiroui
Great Sun, II, 110
Great World. *See* Ohonsiowanne
Green, Bartholomew (father), III, 267
Green, Bartholomew, III, **267**, 90
Green, Benjamin, III, 130; IV, **312–13**, 51, 169, 199, 274, 560
Green, Benjamin (son), IV, 193, 313, 764
Green, Elizabeth. *See* Gerrish
Green, Hannah. *See* Hammond
Green, John, IV, 312
Green, Joseph (father), IV, 312
Green, Joseph, IV, 312
Green, Margaret. *See* Pierce
Green, Margaretta (Lady Davers), III, 166
Green, Maria (Mary?). *See* Mather
Green, Susanna. *See* Wenman
Greene, Anne (Mason), I, 496
Greene, Edward, I, 496

Greene, Elizabeth, III, 133

Greene, Henry, I, 145, 374, 375, 376, 377, 378

Greenway, Richard, I, 476, 666

Greese, Margaret. *See* Miller

Greffière, Renée (Couagne), II, 153

Gregory*, John (d. 1817), IV, 366, 506

Gregory, William, IV, 350, 570, 724, 725

Grelleau, Sieur, III, 477

Grenet, Simon, I, 267

Grenier (Garnier), Françoise (Langlois), I, 417

Grenolle, M., I, 132

Grenouille, La. *See* Oumasasikweie

Grenville, Anne, Baroness Grenville. *See* Pitt

Grenville, George, IV, xxxiv, 571, 788

Grenville (Greynvile), Sir Richard, I, 278; IV, 744

Grenville, William Wyndham, 1st Baron Grenville, IV, 346, 698, 717

Greslon Laviolette, Jeanne (Dasilva), III, 165

Grey, William de, 1st Baron Walsingham, IV, xxxiii, xli, xlvii

Greysac, Gabriel, III, 642

Greysolon de La Tourette, Claude, II, **261**, 31, 263, 264, 633

Greysolon Dulhut, Daniel, I, 132, 227, 228, 289, 290, 400; II, **261–64**, xxxiii, 13, 31, 105, 279, 302, 317, 440, 471, 488, 633, 635; III, 237, 373, 493

Gribond, Jeanne (Trotain), II, 637

Gridley, Hannah. *See* Deming

Gridley, Rebecca (mother of RICHARD), IV, 313

Gridley, Richard (father), IV, 313

Gridley, Richard, IV, **313–14**

Gridley, Samuel, IV, 314

Gridley, Sarah. *See* Blake

Griffith, Sir John, I, 477

Griffith, Richard, III, 296

Griffyn, Owen, I, 316, 317

Grignon, Jean, II, 28, 275

Grignon, Pierre, IV, 171

Grillot de Poilly, Claude-Victor, III, 267

Grillot de Poilly, François-Claude-Victor, III, **267–68**, 229, 230, 440, 700

Grimaldi, Françoise de (Crisafy), II, 162

Grimère, Richarde (Lory), II, 446

Grimes, John, IV, 158, 159, 713

Grimington, Anne (wife of MICHAEL, father), II, 267

Grimington, Michael (father), I, 308; II, **264–67**, 42, 50, 171, 231, 232, 311, 319, 395, 644

Grimington, Michael (son), II, **267**

Gripière de Moncroc, Joseph de, Marquis de Laval, IV, 208

Grisé, Antoine (father), IV, 315

Grisé, Antoine, IV, **315**, 270

Grisé, Catherine. *See* Lévesque

Grisé, Françoise. *See* Marcoux

Grisé, Françoise. *See* Poyer

Grisé, Jean-Baptiste, IV, 315

Griswold, Deborah (Denison), III, 174

Grob, Anna (Knaut), IV, 414

Gröen, Élisabeth (Mariauchau d'Esgly), II, 456

Groisard, Jeanne (Dupuy), I, 297

Grondin. *See also* Pardaillan

Grondin, Jeanne (Chartier), III, 112

Groot, Hugo de, known as Grotius, IV, 230

Groseilliers. *See* Chouart

Grosse, Renée (Claparède), III, 123

Grossin, Élisabeth-Marguerite. *See* Veau, *dit* Sylvain

Groston, Jean, II, 267

Groston, Marie. *See* Rebourceau

Groston de Saint-Ange, Élisabeth. *See* Chorel de Saint-Romain, *dit* d'Orvilliers

Groston de Saint-Ange, Élisabeth (Coulon de Villiers), II, 267; IV, 177

Groston de Saint-Ange, Louis, IV, 316

Groston de Saint-Ange, Louis-Daniel, IV, 316

Groston de Saint-Ange, Marguerite. *See* Crevier

Groston de Saint-Ange, Marie-Rose, II, 267

Groston de Saint-Ange, Pierre (father), II, 67, 216, 267

Groston de Saint-Ange, Pierre, II, 267

Groston de Saint-Ange, Robert, II, **267–68**, 156; III, 105, 491; IV, 315

Groston de Saint-Ange et de Bellerive, Louis, II, 267; III, 530; IV, **315–16**, 683

Grotius. *See* Groot

Grotton. *See* Groston

Groulx*, Lionel (1878–1967), III, 722; IV, 232, 376

Grouvel, Marguerite. *See* Auber

Grouvel, Martin, I, 305

Grove*, Frederick Philip (1872–1948), IV, 555

Grove, Hannah (Moulton), IV, 564

Grover, William, III, 287, 304

Gruel de La Peltrie, Chevalier de, I, 207

Gruel de La Peltrie, Marie-Madeleine de. *See* Chauvigny

Guay. *See also* Gay

Guay, Marguerite (Levasseur), II, 430

Gudridr, I, 612, 642

Guémenée, Prince de. *See* Rohan

Güemes Pacheco Horcasitas Padilla, Juan Vicente de, 2nd Count of Revilla Gigedo, IV, 520

Guen, Hamon, III, **268–69**, 542; IV, 507, 636

Guénet. *See also* Quenet

Guenet, Anne. *See* Desloges

Guenet, Marie, *dite* de Saint-Ignace, I, **347–49**, 310, 353

Guénet, Marie-Clémence, III, 369

Guenet, Roger, I, 347

Guénet, Toussaint, I, 575; II, 27

Guénin, Hilarion, I, 55, 420, 438; II, 344, 345

Guer. *See* Kirke

Guercheville, Marquise de. *See* Pons

Guérin, Jean, I, 282

Guérin, Jeanne (Lom d'Arce), II, 440

Guérin, Louis, III, 304

Guérin, Madeleine (La Joue), II, 337

Guérin, Marie-Anne (Jacquin, *dit* Philibert; Cardeneau), III, 96, 304; IV, 66

Guérin, Marthe (Chaverlange), I, 474

Guerne. *See* Le Guerne

Guernon, Jeanne (Saint-Georges), II, 381

Guernon*, *dit* Belleville, François (d. 1817), IV, 151, 201, 507

Guérout, Pierre-Guillaume, IV, 477

Guerry, Lewis, IV, 738

Guertin, Catherine (Foureur, *dit* Champagne), IV, 272

Guesdron, Julien, II, **268**

Gueslis. *See* Vaillant

Guettard, Jean-Étienne, III, 675, 676, 679, 680

Gueudeville, Nicolas, II, 443

Gugi, Hans George, IV, 316

Gugi, Thérèse. *See* Reis
Gugy, Barthélemy, IV, 317
Gugy, Conard, IV, **316–17**, 320
Gugy*, Louis (1770–1840), IV, 317
Guiberge, Jeanne (Cabazié), II, 111
Guibert, Jacques-Antoine-Hippolyte de, III, 468
Guibert, Michel-Claude, II, 181
Guichard, Charlotte (Sabrevois de Bleury), IV, 690
Guichard, Jean, IV, 690
Guichart, Françoise-Marie. *See* Cozer
Guichart, Sylvestre, IV, 317
Guichart (Guichart de Kersident), Vincent-Fleuri, IV, **317–18**
Guiche, Comte de. *See* Gramont
Guichen, Comte de. *See* Du Bouëxic
Guignard, Gilles, I, 505
Guignas, Michel, III, **269**, 44, 81
Guignecourt (Guignicourt), M., I, 423, 425
Guilbaut, Jeanne (Lorimier), II, 445
Guilhermy, Hélène (Martin), III, 435
Guillebaut, Suzanne (Fézeret), II, 221
Guillebert, *dit* Laframboise, Jean, II, 507
Guillemin, Étienne, III, 613
Guillemot, Anne, I, 349
Guillemot, Étiennette. *See* Després
Guillemot, François, I, 349
Guillemot, *dit* Du Plessis-Kerbodot, Guillaume, I, **349**, 297, 428, 430, 431, 574; II, 83, 84
Guillemote, Catherine (Jacquiés, *dit* Leblond), II, 294
Guillet, Marie-Élisabeth, *dite* Sainte-Barbe, III, 630
Guillet, Paul, III, 217
Guillet de Chaumont, Antoine, III, 269
Guillet de Chaumont, Félicité. *See* Ailleboust Des Muceaux
Guillet de Chaumont, Marie-Catherine. *See* Legras
Guillet de Chaumont, Marie-Louise. *See* Esprit
Guillet de Chaumont, Nicolas-Auguste, III, **269–70**, 88, 210; IV, 46
Guillier(?), Marie (Couturier), II, 159
Guillimin, Angélique-Jeanne (Latouche MacCarthy), III, 357
Guillimin, Charles, II, **268–69**, 447; III, 153, 357, 376, 549, 558; IV, 318, 319
Guillimin, Charles (son), II, 269
Guillimin, Françoise. *See* Lemaître-Lamorille
Guillimin, Geneviève-Élisabeth (Regnard Duplessis de Morampont), III, 549
Guillimin, Guillaume (grandfather), II, 268
Guillimin, Guillaume, II, 269; III, 75, 226, 596, 647; IV, **318–19**
Guillimin, Marie-Charlotte (Riverin; Badelart), III, 558
Guillimin, Marie-Claude-Geneviève. *See* Foucault
Guillimin, Marie-Françoise, *dite* de Saint-Antoine, IV, **319–20**
Guillimin, Marie-Geneviève. *See* Foucault
Guillimin, Marie-Joseph (Legardeur de Saint-Pierre; La Corne), III, 376; IV, 426
Guillon, Jean, I, 296, 323
Guillon (Guyon), Jean-Baptiste, IV, 461
Guillon (Guyon), Marguerite (Lemoine Despins), IV, 461
Guillory, Simon, III, 178, 179
Guillot, Gefroy, I, 392, 554
Guillot, Jacques, IV, 320
Guillot, Louise (Gosselin; Haimard), II, 273

Guillot, Marguerite. *See* Loiseleur
Guillot, Marie. *See* Abancourt
Guillot, *dit* Larose, François, IV, **320–21**, 316
Guillot, *dit* Larose, Marie. *See* Rateau
Guillot de La Forest, M., II, 450
Guillouet d'Orvilliers, Anne-Marie. *See* Le Febvre de La Barre
Guillouet d'Orvilliers, Claude, II, **269–70**, 186, 603; III, 190
Guillouet d'Orvilliers, Claude (son), II, 270
Guillouet d'Orvilliers, Gilbert, II, 270
Guillouet d'Orvilliers, Jean, II, 270
Guillouet d'Orvilliers, Louis, II, 270
Guillouet d'Orvilliers, Marguerite. *See* Gascoing
Guillouet d'Orvilliers, Marie-Claude. *See* Vicq
Guillouet d'Orvilliers, Paul, II, 270
Guillouet d'Orvilliers, Rémy, I, 664; II, **270–71**, 269
Guinet, Sieur de, I, 538
Guion, Denis, II, 271, 352
Guion, Élisabeth. *See* Boucher
Guion, François, II, **271**, 352
Guion, Joseph, II, 271
Guion, Marie-Anne. *See* Roberge
Guion, Marie-Thérèse (Laumet, *dit* de Lamothe Cadillac), I, 416; II, 271, 352
Guion Desprez, Geneviève (Chavigny Lachevrotière), II, 142
Guisc, Duc de. *See* Lorraine
Guiton de Monrepos, Jacques-Joseph, III, **270–71**, 140, 228, 246, 279, 340, 445, 450, 604
Guittel. *See* Quittel
Guitton, Madeleine (Hamelin de Bourgchemin), I, 360
Guiyahgwaahdoh. *See* Kaieñʔkwaahtoñ
Gunn, Alexander, IV, 534
Gunn, George, II, 62
Gunn, William, IV, 534
Gunnbjörn Ulfsson, I, 676
Gutiérrez, Diego, I, 157
Guy, Anne (wife of JOHN), I, 351
Guy, Élisabeth. *See* Garreau
Guy, Élisabeth. *See* Leduc
Guy, Jeanne. *See* Truillier, *dit* Lacombe
Guy, John, I, **349–51**, 23, 233, 240, 241, 243, 300, 365, 496, 534, 584, 655, 656, 668, 670
Guy, Marie (Bénard), III, 63
Guy, Marie (Claparède), III, 123
Guy, Nicholas, I, **351**, 656
Guy, Nicolas, III, 271
Guy, Philip, I, 233, 350
Guy, Pierre, III, **271–72**, 290; IV, 204
Guy*, Pierre (1738–1812), III, 271; IV, 34, 35, 59
Guyar (Guyer). *See* Geyer
Guyart, Anne. *See* Gigou
Guyart, Florent, I, 351
Guyart, Jean-Baptiste, III, 272
Guyart, Jeanne. *See* Michelet
Guyart, Marie, *dite* de l'Incarnation (Martin), I, **351–59**, 8, 30, 31, 32, 41, 55, 65, 108, 113, 198, 205, 208, 223, 225, 226, 231, 268, 269, 274, 325, 414, 430, 446, 455, 457, 511, 512, 516, 523, 536, 551, 552, 555, 556, 603, 604, 610, 618, 624, 632, 647, 665; II, 84, 91, 361, 365, 536, 537, 657; III, 106
Guyart de Fleury, Élisabeth. *See* Jobin

Guyart de Fleury, Jean-Baptiste, III, **272**
Guyasuta. *See* Kayahsota?
Guyon. *See also* Guillon; Guion
Guyon, Barbe (Paradis), II, 508
Guyon, Denis, I, 396; II, 158, 161, 347
Guyon, Françoise-Charlotte, Marquise de Diziers. *See* Alavoine
Guyon, Jacques, I, 359
Guyon, Jean, I, **359**
Guyon, Louise. *See* Racine
Guyon, Louise (Thibault; Damours de Freneuse), I, 246; II, 166, 177, 257, 481; III, **681–82**, 207, 499, 552
Guyon, Marguerite (Damours de Chauffours), II, 166; III, 474, 681
Guyon, Marie (wife of Jacques), I, 359
Guyon, Simon, I, 359; II, 166; III, 681
Guyon Després, Angélique (Margane de Lavaltrie), II, 456; III, 429
Guyon Després, Joseph, III, 473, 523
Guyon Desprez, Marie (Gaultier), III, 98, 173
Guyon Desprez, Marie-Joseph (Marin de La Malgue), III, 431; IV, 512
Guyon Du Buisson, Élisabeth. *See* Couillard de Lespinay
Guyon Du Buisson, Jean (father), I, **359**, 232, 281, 330
Guyon Du Buisson, Jean (son), I, **359–60**, 238
Guyon Du Buisson, Mathurine. *See* Robin
Guyon Durouvray, Jean, III, 134
Guyon Durouvray, Marguerite-Suzanne (Constantin), III, 134
Guyon Durouvray, Marie-Élisabeth (Le Moyne de Martigny et de La Trinité), II, 405
Guyon Fresnay, Marie-Thérèse (Baudoin), III, 35
Guyot de Lamirande, Marie-Claire-Françoise (Rigaud de Vaudreuil), III, 556
Guyotte, Étienne, I, 78; II, **271–72**, 412, 594
Guytard, Jean, II, 517
Gwillim*, Elizabeth Posthuma (Simcoe) (1766–1850), IV, 418
Gwyn, Christiana (Collier, Lady Collier), IV, 160
Gyard. *See* Girard
Gyart. *See* Giard
Gylberte. *See* Gilbert
Gyles, Hannah. *See* Heath
Gyles, John, II, 26, 167, 476, 665, 669; III, **272–73**, 265
Gyles, Ruth. *See* True
Gyles, Thomas, III, 273

HACHÉ-GALLANT, Anne. *See* Cormier
Haché-Gallant, Michel, II, **272**
Hackenwelder (Heckewelder), John Gottlieb Ernestus, IV, 301, 302
Haguenier, Marguerite (Malepart de Grand Maison, *dit* Beaucour; Lasselin), III, 422; IV, 507
Haguenier, Paul, II, 14
Haies. *See* Hayes
Haimard, Étienne, II, 273
Haimard, Louise. *See* Guillot
Haimard, Martine. *See* Hurault
Haimard, Pierre, II, **272–73**, 43
Hains. *See* Ainsse
Hair. *See* Heer
Haitor (Hayter), Martha (Slade), IV, 711
Hake, Samuel, IV, 327

Hakluyt, Richard (father), I, 332, 333, 530, 531
Hakluyt, Richard, I, 88, 89, 151, 158, 170, 333, 336, 363, 364, 371, 380, 409, 531, 532, 586, 659, 660, 672, 678
Haldimand, François-Louis, IV, 793
Haldimand, Sir Frederick, III, 89, 274, 332, 409, 620; IV, **793–94**, xlviii, liv, lvii, 3, 5, 6, 7, 8, 39, 40, 49, 109, 118, 119, 120, 121, 130, 147, 155, 162, 179, 181, 185, 190, 197, 205, 229, 230, 231, 232, 276, 277, 279, 280, 281, 289, 290, 294, 299, 303, 305, 316, 317, 321, 322, 323, 324, 330, 331, 336, 337, 347, 352, 367, 369, 370, 371, 385, 391, 394, 398, 418, 428, 442, 446, 476, 485, 492, 493, 506, 532, 537, 538, 543, 544, 549, 566, 613, 623, 635, 658, 682, 683, 687, 694, 723, 735, 757, 778, 787, 791, 792
Haldimand, Jean-Abraham, III, 273
Haldimand, Marie-Madeleine. *See* Treytorrens
Haldimand, Peter Frederick, III, **273–74**
Hale, Elizabeth. *See* Clark
Hale, Elizabeth. *See* Gilman
Hale, John, IV, 527
Hale, Robert (father), III, 274
Hale, Robert, III, **274–75**
Halevear. *See* Olivier
Half King. *See* Pomoacan; Tanaghrisson
Halhead, Edward, III, **275–76**, 635
Halifax, Earl of. *See* Dunk; Montagu
Hall, Benedicta Maria Theresa (Gage, Viscountess Gage), IV, 278
Hall*, Charles Francis (1821–71), I, 94, 318
Hall, Christopher, I, 316, 317, 318, 375
Hall, Diana. *See* Cobbie
Hall, James, I, **360**, 5, 20, 74, 243, 408
Hall, Prince, IV, 515
Hallam, Lewis, IV, 556
Hallé, Marie-Joseph, *dite* de Saint-François d'Assise, IV, 472
Hallot, Marie-Scholastique (Desandrouins), IV, 211
Halstead, John, IV, 403
Hamare, Gratiane. *See* Moreau
Hamare, Julien, II, 273
Hamare de La Borde, Geneviève. *See* Lambert
Hamare de La Borde, Geneviève-Louise, II, 273
Hamare de La Borde, Jean-Baptiste-Julien, II, **273–74**; III, 74, 291
Hamel, Anne-Félicité. *See* Levasseur
Hamel, Félicité (Bonhomme, *dit* Beaupré), III, 69
Hamel, Jean, I, 473
Hamel, Pierre, III, 135
Hamel*, Théophile (baptized François-Xavier) (1817–70), I, 170
Hamel*, Thomas-Étienne (1830–1913), III, 691; IV, 801
Hamelin, Angélique (Pollet), III, 524
Hamelin, Louis, III, 249, 250, 432
Hamelin, Nicolas, IV, 678
Hamelin de Bourgchemin, François, I, 360
Hamelin de Bourgchemin, Madeleine. *See* Guitton
Hamelin de Bourgchemin et de L'Hermitière, Anne-Marie, I, 361
Hamelin de Bourgchemin et de L'Hermitière, Élisabeth. *See* Dizy, *dit* Montplaisir
Hamelin de Bourgchemin et de L'Hermitière, François, I, 361
Hamelin de Bourgchemin et de L'Hermitière, Jacques-François, I, **360–61**; II, 190

Hamelin de Bourgchemin et de L'Hermitière, Marguerite, I, 361

Hamilton, Andrew, I, **361**, 107, 493, 657

Hamilton, Elizabeth. *See* Lee

Hamilton, George, Earl of Orkney, II, 104

Hamilton, Grizel (wife of Thomas), III, 276

Hamilton, Grizel (daughter of OTHO), III, 276

Hamilton, Henry (father), IV, 321

Hamilton, Henry, IV, **321–25**, 37, 49, 82, 197, 198, 260, 337, 367, 371, 399, 493, 496, 499, 506, 564, 702, 722, 792

Hamilton, Isaac, IV, 768

Hamilton, James, III, 502

Hamilton, James, 1st Duke of Hamilton, 2nd Earl of Cambridge, I, 369, 405, 613

Hamilton, John (office-holder), III, 587

Hamilton, John (officer), IV, 791

Hamilton, John (son of OTHO), III, 276, 277

Hamilton, Mary. *See* Dawson

Hamilton, Mary. *See* Handfield

Hamilton, Mary. *See* Herkimer

Hamilton, Otho, II, 670; III, **276–77**, 10, 514

Hamilton, Otho (son), III, 276

Hamilton*, Robert (1749–1809), IV, 494, 505, 777

Hamilton, Lady Susannah (Cochrane, Countess of Dundonald; Hay, Marchioness of Tweeddale), III, 283

Hamilton, Thomas, III, 276

Hammond, Hannah (Green), III, 267

Hamond, Sir Andrew Snape, IV, 111

Hamond, Marie (Hantraye), IV, 326

Hampshire, Sir Thomas, I, 229

Hampson, John, I, 611

Hancock, John (HBC employee), II, 313, 315

Hancock, John (politician), IV, 144

Hancock, Thomas, III, 33, 403; IV, 560

Handasyde, Roger, II, 274

Handasyde, Thomas, II, **274**, 246, 564

Handfield, Elizabeth. *See* Winniett

Handfield, John, III, **277–78**, 421, 665; IV, xxvi, 676

Handfield, John (son), III, 277

Handfield, Mary (Hamilton) III, 277

Handfield, Thomas, III, 277

Hands*, William (1755–1836), IV, 778

Handsome Lake. *See* Ganiodaio

Hangard, Catherine de. *See* La Roque

Hangard, Robert de, I, 425

Hanna, James, IV, **325–26**, 411, 498, 568

Hannah (slave, fl. 1800), IV, 777, 778

Hannah (slave, fl. 1804), IV, 779

Hannam, John, I, 584

Hannam, William, I, 584

Hannay*, James (1842–1910), III, 439; IV, xxi

Hanover, Elector of. *See* George I

Hans, III, 322

Hantraye, Claude, IV, **326**

Hantraye, Marie. *See* Hamond

Hantraye, Marie-Françoise. *See* Viger

Hantraye, Marie-Marguerite. *See* Debuire

Hantraye, Noël, IV, 326

Haouilamek. *See* Ouenemek

Harakontie. *See* Garakontié

Harboard, William, IV, 55

Harborne, William, I, 85

Harcourt, Comte d'. *See* Lorraine

Harcourt, Margaret Irene. *See* Sarney

Harcourt, Robert, I, 366

Hardi, Gabrielle (Chabert de Joncaire), II, 125

Hardouineau, Renée (Beauharnois de Beaumont et de Villechauve), II, 52

Hardouineau de Landianière, Pierre, III, 42

Hardouineau de Landianière, Renée. *See* Pays

Hardwicke, Earl of. *See* Yorke

Hardy, Catherine, Lady Hardy. *See* Stanyan

Hardy, Sir Charles (father), IV, 326

Hardy, Sir Charles, III, 132, 668; IV, **326–27**, 84

Hardy, Elias, IV, **327–29**, 196

Hardy, Elizabeth, Lady Hardy. *See* Burchett

Hardy, Emma. *See* Huggeford

Hardy (Ardie), Jeanne (Trotain, *dit* Saint-Seürin), II, 637

Hardy, Marguerite (Macard), II, 448

Hardy, Mary, Lady Hardy. *See* Tate

Hargon, Jeanne de (Martel de Berhouague), II, 458

Hargrave, Rachel (Frobisher), IV, 276

Harismendy, Jean, IV, 66

Harlay de Champvallon, François de, I, 646, 647; II, 361, 362, 363, 368

Harley, Robert, 1st Earl of Oxford, II, 659, 660

Harman, John, I, 443

Harmon, Johnson, II, 544; III, 476, 477

Harot, Marie (La Salle), II, 348

Harries*, John (1763–1810), IV, 402

Harris, Elizabeth, I, 81

Harris, John, III, 614

Harris, Jonathan, IV, 351

Harrison, Edward, IV, **329–31**, 477, 571

Harrison, John, II, **274–75**; III, 421

Harry, Marguerite (Pollet), III, 523

Hart, Aaron, IV, **331–33**, 40, 384, 754

Hart, Alexander, IV, 332

Hart*, Benjamin (d. 1855), IV, 332, 754

Hart, Catherine, IV, 332

Hart, Charlotte, IV, 332

Hart, Dorothy. *See* Judah

Hart, Elizabeth, IV, 332

Hart*, Ezekiel (d. 1843), IV, 332, 333, 754

Hart, Henry, IV, 331

Hart, Lemon, IV, 331

Hart, Moses, IV, 331, 332

Hart*, Moses (1768–1852), IV, 332

Hart, Sarah, IV, 332

Hartley, Thomas, IV, 405

Harvey, Thomas, I, 574

Harwick, Abraham van, I, 450

Harwick, Stephen van, I, 391, 450

Hastings, Susanna. *See* Willard

Hastings, Warren, IV, 115

Haswell, Mary (Montresor), IV, 552

Haswell*, Robert (1768–1801), IV, 419

Hateouati. *See* Otreouti

Hathorne, John, I, 26, 246; II, 145, 167, 450, 579, 654

Hattanville, Antoine, II, 234

Hattanville, Jeanne-Françoise. *See* Gadois

Hatton, Sir Christopher, I, 93, 94

Haubichon, Jean, I, 270

Haudebourg. *See* Volant

Haussonville, Comte d'. *See* Cléron

Hautefort de Montignac, Marie-Aimée de (Estourmel, Marquise d'Estourmel), III, 213
Hauteville. *See* Bourgonnière; Le Vieux
Hautmesnil (Hautmesnyl). *See* Philippe
Hautraye. *See* Hantraye
Havard de Beaufort, François-Charles, known as L'Avocat, III, **278–79**, 625
Haven, Jens, III, 213, 411; IV, **333–34**, liii, 225, 536, 537, 599
Haven, Mary. *See* Butterworth
Haviland, Caroline. *See* Lee
Haviland, Peter, IV, 334
Haviland, Salusbury. *See* Aston
Haviland, William, III, 86; IV, **334–36**, 23, 24, 143, 481, 495, 545, 569, 679, 680, 769
Havy, Mme. *See* François
Havy, François, III, **280–83**, 38, 210, 216, 224, 271, 305, 370, 371, 501; IV, 45, 126, 357, 476
Hawke, Edward, 1st Baron Hawke, III, 71, 209, 557, 657; IV, 126, 282, 327, 699
Hawkeridge, William, I, **362**, 144
Hawkins*, Alfred (d. 1854), III, 305
Hawkins, Sir John, I, 228, 316, 331, 380, 381, 530
Hawkins, William, I, 228
Hawkridge. *See* Hawkeridge
Hawley, Henry, III, 666
Hawthorne. *See* Hathorne
Hay, Charles, IV, **336**
Hay, Charles, 3rd Marquis of Tweeddale, III, 283
Hay, Lord Charles, III, **283–84**, 218, 662; IV, 3
Hay, Frances. *See* Berkeley
Hay, George, IV, 496
Hay, Jehu (John), IV, **336–37**, 322, 762
Hay, Julie-Marie. *See* Réaume
Hay, Margaret (Bruce), IV, 107
Hay, Mary (wife of CHARLES), IV, 336
Hay, Susannah, Marchioness of Tweeddale. *See* Hamilton
Hay, Udney, IV, 336
Hayenwatha. *See* Hiawatha
Hayes, Edward, I, **362–65**, 334, 335, 336, 531, 532
Hayes, Thomas, I, 365
Hayet, Madeleine. *See* Hénaut
Hayet, Marguerite (Véron de Grandmesnil; Chouart Des Groseilliers), I, 223, 228; II, 535, 647
Hayet, Sébastien, I, 223; II, 535
Hayman, Alice. *See* Gaverocke
Hayman, Grace. *See* Spicer
Hayman, Henry, II, 291
Hayman, Nicholas, I, 365
Hayman, Robert, I, **365–66**, 584, 656, 669
Hayne, Thomas, II, 610
Hayot, Angélique, *dite* de Saint-Joseph, III, 318
Hayot, Louise (Normandin), II, 499
Hays (Hayes), Andrew, IV, 332
Hayter. *See also* Haitor
Hayter, John, IV, 711
Hayward, Nicholas, I, 226
Hazen*, Moses (1733–1803), IV, 150, 230, 269, 271, 305, 320, 548, 691
Hazen*, William (1738–1814), IV, 196, 389
Hazeur, Anne. *See* Soumande
Hazeur, Catherine. *See* Martin de Lino
Hazeur, Élisabeth. *See* Barbe

Hazeur, François (father), II, 275
Hazeur, François, II, **275–77**, 180, 300, 484, 526, 575, 576, 598; III, 134, 284; IV, 337
Hazeur, François (grandson), IV, 339, 357
Hazeur, François-Marie-Joseph, II, 277
Hazeur, Jean-François (uncle), II, 234, 275
Hazeur, Jean-François, II, **277**, 276, 465, 598
Hazeur, Jeanne-Louise, II, 275
Hazeur, Joseph-Thierry, II, 276, 277, 598; III, **284–85**, 114, 223, 354, 616; IV, 142, 286, 337, 338, 339
Hazeur, Louis-Ignace, II, 277
Hazeur, Madeleine, II, 275
Hazeur, Marie. *See* Proust
Hazeur, Marie-Anne (Sébille), II, 275
Hazeur, Marie-Anne-Ursule (Sarrazin), II, 276, 597, 598; III, 675
Hazeur de L'Orme, Pierre, II, 60, 249, 276, 277, 598, 640; III, 50, 62, 63, 108, 115, 192, 193, 223, 239, 284, 285, 344, 354, 390, 481, 616, 675; IV, **337–39**, 142, 220, 429, 430, 440, 539, 661
Hazeur Des Ormeaux, Charles, II, 129
Hazeur Des Ormeaux, Léonard, II, 129, 275
Hazeur Des Ormeaux, Marie-Anne. *See* Pinguet
Hearne, Diana (mother of SAMUEL), IV, 339
Hearne, Samuel (father), IV, 339
Hearne, Samuel, I, 378; II, xxviii, 232, 320, 615; III, xxxiii, 303; IV, **339–42**, 47, 157, 165, 166, 245, 283, 384, 518, 519, 523, 524, 583, 584, 647, 684, 727, 741, 742, 743, 758, 760
Heath, Hannah (Gyles), III, 273
Heavy. *See* Le Pesant
Hébécourt. *See* Le Dossu
Hébert, Adrienne. *See* Duvivier
Hébert, Anne (Bourg), IV, 80
Hébert, Anne (Jonquet), I, 264, 368, 437, 578
Hébert, Françoise (Fournier), I, 264
Hébert, Guillaume, I, 264, 367, 368, 578; II, 489
Hébert, Guillemette (Couillard de Lespinay), I, **366–67**, 109, 145, 236, 237, 264, 368, 386, 517, 578; II, 33
Hébert, Hélène. *See* Desportes
Hébert, Jacques, I, 367
Hébert, Joseph, I, **367**, 264
Hébert, Joseph (son), I, 367
Hébert, Louis, I, **367–68**, 29, 96, 101, 108, 189, 195, 236, 237, 238, 264, 347, 366, 437, 578; II, 33, 148, 213; III, 678, 680
Hébert, Louis (apothecary), I, 367
Hébert*, Louis-Philippe (1850–1917), I, 221, 232
Hébert, Marie. *See* Rollet
Hébert, Marie-Charlotte. *See* Poytiers
Hébert, Marie-Joseph (Brassard Deschenaux), IV, 88
Hébert, Nicolas, I, 367
Hébert, *dit* Larivière, Roland, I, 267
Héchon. *See* Échon
Heckewelder. *See* Hackenwelder
Hecquet de La Cloche, Marie-Catherine. *See* Homasset
Hedouin, Madeleine-Ursule. *See* Rancin
Heer*, Louis-Chrétien de (b. 1760, d. before 1808), IV, 442
Hegan, Sampson, II, 25
Heine, William, III, 624
Heineman, Pines (Phineas), IV, 332
Heinrich (Henrich), Anton. *See* Henry, Anthony
Heire. *See* Heer

Hélène, III, 266
Hélène de Saint-Augustin. *See* Boullé
Hélie (Élie) Du Tillet, Madeleine (Mius d'Entremont, Baronne de Pobomcoup), I, 510
Hémard de Denonville, Charles de, II, 98
Hémard de Denonville, Marie de (Brisay), II, 98
Hénault, Gabriel, IV, 463
Hénault, Pierre, IV, 463
Hénaut. *See also* Énault
Hénaut, Madeleine (Hayet; Radisson), I, 223; II, 535
Henday, Anthony, II, 309; III, **285–87**, xxxii, 171, 303, 304, 332, 342, 595; IV, 740, 761
Hendrick. *See* Theyanoguin
Hendry. *See* Henday
Henley, Robert, 1st Earl of Northington, IV, xli, 571
Hennepin, Gaspard, II, 277
Hennepin, Jeanne, II, 278
Hennepin, Louis (baptized Antoine), I, 175, 176, 226, 379, 415, 420, 438, 439, 440; II, **277–81**, xxxiii, 197, 262, 419, 443; III, 325
Hennepin, Norbertine. *See* Leleu
Henri. *See also* Membertou
Henri (servant), I, 302, 366, 509
Henri II, King of France, I, 372, 421, 424; II, 328
Henri III, King of France, I, 261, 324, 421, 520
Henri IV, King of France, I, 23, 42, 96, 97, 99, 100, 134, 187, 188, 190, 209, 210, 214, 291, 299, 307, 323, 421, 422, 453, 471, 498, 501, 521, 601; III, 41; IV, xvii
Henrietta Maria (Queen Consort of Great Britain), I, 81, 534, 596
Henry VII, King of England, I, 120, 148, 149, 153, 164, 239, 302, 304, 343, 641
Henry VIII, King of England and Ireland, I, 155, 157, 565, 566, 585, 586, 643, 660
Henry*, Alexander (1739–1824), I, 225; III, 167, 452, 659, 660; IV, 132, 277, 365, 366, 389, 403, 496, 564, 675
Henry, Anthony, III, 91; IV, **342–43**, 19, 112, 267
Henry, Barbara (Spring; wife of ANTHONY), IV, 343
Henry, Margaret. *See* Miller
Henry, Margaret (Chabrand Delisle), IV, 138
Henry Frederick, Prince of Wales, I, 144
Heracouansit. *See* Mog
Hérauld de Gourville, Marie (Du Pont Duvivier), II, 205; IV, 246
Hérault, Mme. *See* Moreau de Séchelles
Herbault. *See* Phélipeaux
Herbert, Philip, 4th Earl of Pembroke, I, 369, 405
Herbert, Sir Thomas, I, 678
Herbin, Frédéric-Louis, III, 450
Herbin, Louis, IV, 733
Herincx, Guillaume, II, 278
Herjólfr Bárdarson, I, 103
Herjólfsson. *See* Bjarni
Herkimer, Mary (McLean; Hamilton), IV, 505
Herkimer, Nicholas, IV, 405, 694
Herlin, Claude, II, 84
Hernández. *See* Pérez
Héron, Antoine, I, 90
Héron, Marie-Élisabeth (Le Moyne de Serigny et de Loire), II, 406; III, 557
Heron, Patrick, III, **287–88**, 9, 392; IV, 62, 253
Herovin. *See* Irwin
Herrera y Tordesillas, Antonio de, I, 342

Herries, Elizabeth (Marrant), IV, 515
Herse*, Jacques-Clément (fl. 1740–1816), IV, 532, 534
Hertel, Jeanne. *See* Miriot
Hertel, Nicolas, I, 368
Hertel de Beaubassin, Catherine. *See* Jarret de Verchères
Hertel de Beaubassin, Pierre-Joseph, IV, 347
Hertel de Beaulac, Claude, II, 284
Hertel de Chambly, Charles, III, 551, 592
Hertel de Chambly, Geneviève. *See* Boucher de Grandpré
Hertel de Chambly, Michel, II, 284
Hertel de Chambly, René, II, 284, 285
Hertel de Cournoyer, Anne. *See* Goutin
Hertel de Cournoyer, Jacques, II, 284; III, 105, 233
Hertel de Cournoyer, Lambert, II, 284
Hertel de Cournoyer, Marie-Josephte (Lefebvre de Bellefeuille), IV, 445
Hertel de Cournoyer, Michel, II, 205
Hertel de Cournoyer, Thérèse (Saint-Ours), III, 577
Hertel de La Fresnière, Jacques, I, **368–69**, 238, 550; II, 282, 648
Hertel de La Fresnière, Joseph-François, I, 185, 239, 368, 369; II, **282–84**, 603, 628; III, 7, 83, 288, 289, 642; IV, 343
Hertel de La Fresnière, Madeleine (Véron de Grandmesnil), III, 642
Hertel de La Fresnière, Marguerite. *See* Thavenet
Hertel de La Fresnière, Marguerite (Crevier de Saint-François), I, 238, 369
Hertel de La Fresnière, Marguerite-Thérèse (Boucher de Niverville), III, 83
Hertel de La Fresnière, Marie. *See* Marguerie
Hertel de La Fresnière, Marie-Charlotte. *See* Godefroy de Lintot
Hertel de La Fresnière, Marie-Madeleine (Pinard), I, 369, 550
Hertel de La Fresnière, Zacharie-François, II, 54, 283, 284, 632; III, **288–89**, 83
Hertel de Moncours, Pierre, II, **284**; III, 7
Hertel de Moncours, Pierre (son), II, 284
Hertel de Moncours, Thérèse. *See* Ailleboust de Périgny
Hertel de Rouville, Charlotte-Gabrielle. *See* Jarret de Verchères
Hertel de Rouville, Jean-Baptiste, II, **284–86**, 38, 54, 154, 296, 411, 437, 456, 495, 579, 606, 667; III, 35, 81, 104, 247, 324, 450, 493, 579; IV, 343, 770
Hertel de Rouville, Jean-Baptiste-François, II, 286; IV, 343, 653, 654
Hertel* de Rouville, Jean-Baptiste-Melchior (1748–1817), III, 14; IV, 344
Hertel de Rouville, Jeanne. *See* Dubois
Hertel de Rouville, Louis-Antoine, IV, 98
Hertel de Rouville, Louise-Catherine. *See* André de Leigne
Hertel de Rouville, Marie-Anne. *See* Baudouin
Hertel de Rouville, Marie-Anne. *See* Legras
Hertel de Rouville, Marie-Thérèse. *See* Gaultier
Hertel de Rouville, René-Ovide, II, 286; III, 14, 15, 285, 430, 433, 648; IV, **343–47**, 168, 229, 304, 316, 391, 492, 493, 532, 549, 602
Hertel de Saint-François, Étienne, III, **289–90**
Hertel de Saint-François, Joseph (father), II, 284; III, 289; IV, 347
Hertel de Saint-François, Joseph, III, 289
Hertel de Saint-François, Joseph-Hippolyte, IV, **347–48**

Hertel de Saint-François, Louis-Hippolyte, IV, 347
Hertel de Saint-François, Marie-Anne. *See* Le Comte Dupré
Hertel de Saint-François, Pierre-Antoine, IV, 348
Hertel de Saint-François, Suzanne. *See* Blondeau
Hertel de Saint-Louis, Louis, II, 284
Hertford, Earl of. *See* Seymour
Hervé, Marie. *See* Le Ber
Hervé (Hervet), Renée (Tibierge), III, 625
Hervieux, Angélique. *See* Gamelin
Hervieux, Catherine. *See* Magnan
Hervieux, Jacques, III, 290; IV, 268
Hervieux, Léonard-Jean-Baptiste, III, 290
Hervieux, Louise. *See* Quesnel
Hervieux, Louis-François, III, **290**, 367; IV, 268
Hervieux, Marie-Anne (La Corne), IV, 426
Hervieux, Marie-Anne (Le Comte Dupré), III, 367; IV, 347, 442
Hervieux, Marie-Geneviève, *dite* Sainte-Gertrude, III, 630
Hervieux, Marie-Jeanne (Sanguinet), IV, 698
Hervieux, Michelle (La Corne Dubreuil), III, 333
Het, Mary (Smith), IV, 714
Heu, *dit* Millet, Joseph, III, 541
Hey, Elizabeth (Markham; Palmer; mother of WILLIAM), IV, 348
Hey, Thomas, IV, 348
Hey, Mrs William. *See* Paplay
Hey, William, IV, **348–50**, xlii, xliv, xlv, 104, 183, 229, 321, 725, 749, 790
Heylyn, Peter, I, 678
Hezeta, Bruno de, IV, 72, 623
Hianveu, Mathieu, III, 580
Hiarse. *See* Dhiarse
Hiawatha, I, 7, 253, 254; II, xxix; III, xli; IV, lvii
Hiché, Bernard, III, 290
Hiché, Charlotte. *See* Soupiran
Hiché, François-Gaspard, III, 292
Hiché, Henry, II, 234; III, **290–92**, 44, 78, 398, 434, 511, 596
Hiché, Marguerite. *See* Legardeur de Saint-Pierre
Hiché, Marguerite-Françoise, *dite* de Saint-Henri, III, 292
Hiché, Marie-Catherine. *See* Masson
Hiché, Marie-Josephte-Madeleine (Perthuis), III, 291, 292, 511
Hicks, Ann. *See* Clarke
Hicks, Elizabeth. *See* Russell
Hicks, John, IV, **350–51**
Hicks, Thomas, IV, 350
Hickson, Thomas, IV, 537
Higgins, David, IV, **352–53**, 551
Higgins, Elizabeth. *See* Prince
Highmore, Joseph, III, 674
Hilaire, Antoinette (Lombard), III, 406
Hildsley, Francis, II, 265
Hill, Aaron. *See* Kanonraron
Hill, Abigail (Masham), II, 286, 659
Hill, Alice, II, 286
Hill, Christian (Leake), II, 372
Hill, David. *See* Karonghyontye
Hill, Elizabeth. *See* Austin
Hill, John (brother of SAMUEL), II, 287
Hill, John (Moravian), IV, 225
Hill, John, II, **286–87**, 122, 437, 643, 651, 659, 661, 667
Hill, Peter (father of Roger), II, 287

Hill, Peter (merchant), I, 306, 450
Hill, Ralph, I, 450, 451
Hill, Richard, II, 372
Hill, Roger, II, 287
Hill, Samuel, II, **287**
Hill, Sarah Mary. *See* Cross
Hill, William, I, **369**, 163, 405
Hill, Wills, 1st Earl of Hillsborough, III, 411; IV, xxxv, xxxvii, xxxviii, xlii, xliii, xliv, xlv, xlvi, 104, 202, 228, 309, 352, 428, 606, 607, 618, 634, 676, 725, 739, 788, 789
Hillaire de La Rochette, Alexandre-Robert (d'), III, 97, 300; IV, **353–54**, 57, 91
Hillaire de La Rochette, Barbe-Madeleine (Martin), IV, 354
Hillaire de La Rochette, Marie-Anne. *See* Levasseur
Hillaire de Moissacq et de La Rochette, Charles-Robert, IV, 353
Hillaire de Moissacq et de La Rochette, Élisabeth. *See* Martin
Hillsborough, Earl of. *See* Hill
Hilton, Ann. *See* Dudley
Hilton, Ann. *See* Wilson
Hilton, Edward, II, 287
Hilton, Winthrop, II, **287–88**, 452, 543
Hilton, Winthrop (son), II, 288
Hinchelwood, Archibald, IV, 631
Hingue de Puygibault, Marguerite-Barbe (Rocbert de La Morandière; Pécaudy de Contrecœur), IV, 618
Hinton, Sir Thomas, I, 369
Hinton, William (father), I, 369, 370
Hinton, William, I, **369–70**, 93
Hiou, Anne, I, 116
Hiriart, Jean, IV, 69
Hiriberry, Joannis de, II, **288**, 610
Hirouin. *See* Irwin
Hirst, Mary (Lady Pepperrell), III, 505
Hispanioli. *See* Spagniolini
Hiyoua. *See* Wikinanish
Hobbé, Françoise (Roy, *dit* Châtellerault), II, 584
Hobbes (Hobbs), Sarah (Gerrish), IV, 290, 291
Hobby, Ann (wife of William), II, 288
Hobby, Sir Charles, II, **288–90**, 122, 238, 651; III, 3, 682
Hobby, John, II, 289
Hobby, Sir William, II, 288
Hoby, Elizabeth, Lady Hoby. *See* Cooke
Hochstetter, J. G., IV, 580
Hocquart, Anne-Catherine. *See* La Lande
Hocquart, Gilles, II, 60, 66, 71, 95, 96, 97, 210, 235, 253, 269, 317, 373, 374, 380, 413, 447, 530, 531, 541, 542, 606, 617; III, 7, 14, 15, 26, 27, 38, 48, 50, 55, 56, 63, 64, 67, 74, 75, 76, 77, 78, 83, 99, 107, 115, 118, 135, 137, 139, 140, 145, 146, 153, 154, 159, 161, 164, 168, 178, 179, 180, 194, 202, 203, 205, 224, 225, 226, 227, 228, 237, 238, 239, 246, 249, 263, 270, 281, 284, 291, 299, 307, 315, 334, 339, 340, 344, 349, 350, 351, 352, 353, 354, 359, 377, 390, 399, 412, 433, 434, 444, 445, 456, 473, 482, 486, 490, 519, 520, 524, 525, 539, 540, 541, 550, 555, 557, 579, 580, 592, 593, 602, 603, 604, 608, 612, 617, 621, 631, 632, 637, 643, 647, 679; IV, **354–65**, 45, 61, 63, 64, 75, 76, 88, 95, 124, 167, 200, 209, 221, 236, 253, 264, 265, 284, 289, 318, 319, 344, 376, 432, 463, 464, 465, 473, 474, 488, 517, 539, 590, 601, 624, 636, 651, 690, 709, 720, 749, 750

Hocquart, Jean-Hyacinthe (father), IV, 354
Hocquart, Jean-Hyacinthe, IV, 354, 355
Hocquart, Jean-Hyacinthe-Louis-Emmanuel, IV, 354
Hocquart, Marie-Françoise. *See* Michelet Du Cosnier
Hodges, Charles Howard, IV, 30
Hodiau, Urbaine (Brossard), II, 105
Hodiau, *dit* Lafosse, Sébastien, II, 105
Hodiesne, Gervais, III, **292**; IV, 200
Hodiesne, Julien, III, 292
Hodiesne, Marguerite. *See* Lareau
Hodiesne, Renée. *See* Hubert
Hoffman, John William, III, 513; IV, 780
Holburne, Francis, III, xxv, 72, 93, 132, 209, 293; IV, 326, 327, 597
Holden, Martha (Lyon), IV, 490
Holderness, Earl of. *See* D'Arcy
Holdsworth, Arthur (father), II, 290
Holdsworth, Arthur, II, **290–91**, 348, 439, 564
Holdsworth, Arthur (3rd), II, 291
Holdsworth, Elizabeth. *See* Lane
Holdsworth, Robert, II, 290, 291
Holland, Baron. *See* Fox
Holland, Earl of. *See* Rich
Holland*, Anthony Henry (1785–1830), IV, 343
Holland*, Samuel Jan (1728–1801), III, 274; IV, 79, 161, 162, 163, 552, 561, 570, 613, 716
Holles. *See* Pelham-Holles
Hollows, Catherine. *See* Tutty
Holman, William, II, 590
Holmes, Charles, III, **293–94**, 55, 209, 669; IV, 699, 701
Holmes, George, IV, 695
Holmes, Henry, III, 293
Holmes, Mary (Holmes), III, 293
Holmes, Nathaniel, IV, 695
Holmes, Robert, III, 527
Holmes, Sarah (Salter), IV, 695
Holmes, William, IV, **365–66**
Holt, John, IV, 483
Holyoke, Mary (Arnold), II, 25
Homasset, Marie-Catherine (Hecquet de La Cloche), III, 548
Home, Sir George, I, 54, 311
Homem, Lopo, I, 304
Homer, John, IV, 593
Honarreennha (Louis), I, 185
Honatteniate, I, **370–71**, 404, 548
Honeyman, James, II, 663
Honneur, Anne (Le Sueur), II, 427
Honon. *See* Galiffet
Hood, Samuel, 1st Viscount Hood, IV, 339
Hooper, William, IV, 714
Hoore. *See* Hore
Hoosiens, III, 355
Hope, Charles, 1st Earl of Hopetoun, IV, 366
Hope, Henry, IV, **366–68**, 323, 324, 330, 694, 716
Hope, Sarah. *See* Jones
Hope Weir, Anne. *See* Vane
Hope Weir, Charles, IV, 366
Hopetoun, Earl of. *See* Hope
Hopkins, Samuel, II, **291–92**
Hopkins, Sarah (Goldthwait), III, 259
Hopson, Anne (Bennett), III, 295
Hopson, Grace, III, 295
Hopson, Peregrine Thomas, III, **294–95**, 136, 166, 183,

212, 283, 362, 363, 364, 405, 417, 513, 583, 586, 604; IV, xxv, 50, 110, 169, 170, 313, 512, 526, 560, 562, 581, 780
Hopsonn, Sir Thomas, III, 294
Hopton, Ralph, Lord Hopton, I, 653
Horcasitas. *See* Güemes
Hore, Richard, I, **371–72**, 5, 19, 565, 566
Horehouasse. *See* Ourehouare
Horné, Catherine de. *See* Duval
Horné, Jacques de, II, 292
Horné, *dit* Laneuville, Jacques de, II, **292**
Horné, *dit* Laneuville, Marie de. *See* Sivadier
Horner, Samuel, IV, 483
Hoskins, John Box, IV, 568
Hosta (Dosta), M. d', II, 603
Hot Ash (Hot Powder). *See* Ogenheratarihiens
Hotchig, III, 406
Hoteouate (Hotrehouati, Houtreouati). *See* Otreouti
Hotham, William, 1st Baron Hotham, IV, 160
Hotman, François, I, 42, 43
Hotman, Suzanne (Manthet d'Argentenay; Ailleboust), I, 42, 43
Ḥotsinoñḥyahtaʔ, IV, **368**, 596, 735
Houdin, Antoine-Pierre, IV, 127
Houdin, Catherine. *See* Thunay, *dit* Dufresne
Houdin, Elizabeth, III, 296
Houdin, Jean-Michel, known as Father Potentien, III, **295–97**, 240; IV, 103
Houdin, John, III, 296
Houdin, Kitty, III, 296
Houdon, Madeleine (Le Verrier), II, 433
Houel, Louis, I, 192, 386, 590
House, Abigail (Doggett), IV, 219
Houssart, Hubert, II, 371, 372
Hovey, Percilla (Dimock), IV, 217
How, David, III, 297
How, Edward, III, **297–98**, 8, 34, 136, 326, 416, 417, 421, 514, 583, 665; IV, 455
How, Elizabeth. *See* D'Eath
How, Marie-Madeleine. *See* Winniett
Howard, Charles, 2nd Baron Howard of Effingham, 1st Earl of Nottingham, I, 668
Howard, John, IV, 369, 403
Howard, Joseph, IV, **369–70**, 348, 403, 759
Howard, Marguerite. *See* Réaume
Howard, Thomas, 2nd Earl of Arundel, I, 241
Howard, Thomas, Earl of Surrey, 3rd Duke of Norfolk, I, 566
Howard, William, IV, 78
Howe*, Alexander (1749–1813), IV, 627
Howe, Elizabeth (Sedgwick), I, 604
Howe, George Augustus, 3rd Viscount Howe, III, 462; IV, 4, 5, 85, 278
Howe*, John (1754–1835), IV, 343
Howe, Richard, 4th Viscount Howe, IV, 708
Howe, William, 5th Viscount Howe, III, xxvii, 172, 173, 672; IV, 3, 94, 114, 115, 160, 394, 706, 708, 790
Howell, John, IV, 411, 412
Howell, Thomas Bayley, IV, 502
Howland, Elizabeth (Little), III, 403
Howting, John, I, 565
Hoyt, Munson, IV, 329
Hsüen-yeh. *See* K'ang-hsi

Huard, Thérèse (Lambert), III, 346
Huart Dormicourt, Marc-Antoine, III, 205
Huault, Jacques, I, 372
Huault de Montmagny, Charles, I, **372–74**, 43, 44, 45, 111, 121, 124, 127, 128, 186, 197, 203, 205, 215, 216, 217, 218, 237, 250, 324, 344, 348, 354, 370, 389, 401, 403, 404, 414, 446, 454, 472, 481, 482, 485, 523, 548, 567, 574, 595, 596, 602, 663, 665; II, xv, 82, 83, 158, 253, 307, 540
Hubbud (Hubbald), James, II, 314
Hubert, Angélique-Jeanne (Lajus), IV, 432
Hubert, Élisabeth (Boulduc), II, 88, 89
Hubert, Jacques-François, IV, 370
Hubert, Jean-François, IV, **370–75**, 7, 42, 43, 72, 82, 90, 102, 136, 190, 234, 288, 318, 367, 432, 436, 445, 453, 469, 470, 511, 534, 698, 779, 799
Hubert, Marc-Antoine, II, 425; III, 381
Hubert, Marie (Thirement), II, 514
Hubert, Marie-Anne. *See* La Porte
Hubert, Marie-Louise. *See* Maranda
Hubert, René, II, xxiv, 201, 243, 485; III, 372
Hubert, Renée (Hodiesne), III, 292
Hubert de Lacroix, Marie-Anne (Couagne; La Corne), III, 331
Hubou (Huboust, Hubout), Guillaume, I, 554, 578
Hubou, Marie. *See* Rollet
Huck-Saunders, Jane. *See* Kinsey
Hudson, Mr, IV, 420
Hudson, Hannah (Leverett), I, 475
Hudson, Henry, I, **374–79**, 20, 74, 83, 144, 145, 190, 252, 312, 318, 329, 384, 385, 668, 679
Hudson, John, I, **379**, 377
Huet, M. *See* Le Loutre, Jean-Louis
Huet, Catherine (Le Loutre Després), IV, 453
Huet, Paul, I, **379**, 296, 552; II, 278
Huet* de La Valinière, Pierre (1732–1806), IV, 511, 544
Huggeford, Martha (Hardy), IV, 327, 329
Huggeford, Peter, IV, 329
Hughes*, James (d. 1825), IV, 115
Hughes, Mary (Osborn), IV, 594
Hughes*, Sir Richard (d. 1812), IV, 30, 111, 196
Hugo of Ireland, I, 678
Hugot, Anne (Desgrez), III, 51
Huguet, Jean, IV, 375
Huguet, Joseph, IV, **375–76**, 544
Huguet, Scholastique-Geneviève. *See* Verhoune
Huguet, *dit* Latour, Louis-Alexandre, IV, 702
Huguet*, *dit* Latour, Pierre (1749–1817), III, 346; IV, 629, 702
Huillé. *See* Brisay
Huiquinanichi. *See* Wikinanish
Hull, Mary. *See* Spencer
Hulot, Philippe, II, 338
Hume, David, III, 601; IV, 4
Hume, Edward, I, 611
Humfrey, Laurence, I, 531
Humières, Duc d'. *See* Crevant
Hunt, Thomas, I, 262, 650
Hunter, Elizabeth. *See* Goreham
Hunter, James, IV, 613
Hunter*, Peter (d. 1805), IV, 778, 779
Hunter, Robert. *See* Carundawana
Hunter, Robert, II, 112, 498, 547

Huppé, *dit* Lagroix, Antoine, IV, 142
Huppé, *dit* Lagroix, Charlotte. *See* Jérémie, *dit* Lamontagne, *dit* Douville
Huppé, *dit* Lagroix, Jacques, IV, 376
Huppé, *dit* Lagroix, Joseph, IV, **376–77**, 172
Huppé, *dit* Lagroix, Marie-Françoise (Brassard), IV, 87
Huppé, *dit* Lagroix, Michel, IV, 376
Huppé, *dit* Lagroix, Suzanne. *See* Le Normand
Hurault, Henri-Emmanuel, Marquis de Vibraye, III, 116
Hurault, Marie (Rousselot; Testu de La Richardière), III, 620
Hurault, Martine (Haimard), II, 273
Huret, Grégoire, I, 551
Hurtebise (Hurtubise), Marin, IV, 178
Huss, John (Jan Hus), II, 9
Hussey, John, III, 358; IV, 630
Hussey, Thomas, IV, 6, 511
Hutchins, Margaret (wife of THOMAS), IV, 377
Hutchins, Thomas, IV, **377–78**, 390, 524, 525, 726, 741, 758
Hutchinson, Anne, I, 601
Hutchinson, Bridget (Sanford; Phillips), I, 337, 601
Hutchinson, Faith (Savage), II, 601
Hutchinson, Thomas, II, 496, 544; III, 200, 477; IV, 300, 769
Hyde, Edward, 3rd Earl of Clarendon, II, 546

Iberville. *See* Le Moyne
Idotliazee, IV, 339, 584
Ignace, IV, 375
Ignace de Paris, I, **379–80**
Ignon Ouaconisen, II, 646
Ilanos, Matheo, III, 157
Imbault, Maurice (baptized Jean-Jacques), III, **298–99**, 94
Imbert, Agathe. *See* Trefflé, *dit* Rottot
Imbert, Anne-Louise. *See* Lagrange
Imbert, Bertrand, III, 350; IV, **378–79**
Imbert, Catherine-Agathe, IV, 128
Imbert, Edmée. *See* Chambrois
Imbert, Jacques, III, **299–300**, 491, 648; IV, 67, 88, 91, 127, 128, 187, 205, 353, 629
Imbert, Jean, III, 299
Imbert, Jean-Simon, IV, 187
Imbert, Marie-Anne. *See* Maisonnat, *dit* Baptiste
Imbert, Pierre, IV, 378
Imbert, Saubade. *See* Castera
Imbert, Simon, I, 95, 98, 100, 299, 470
Inglis*, Charles (1734–1816), IV, 94, 139, 244, 259, 327, 604, 626, 738, 753, 769
Ingraham, Joseph, IV, 420
Ingram, David, I, **380–81**, 333
Inkster, James, III, 124
Innes, Alexander, IV, 744
Innocent XI, II, 329
Ironside*, George (d. 1831), IV, 778
Iroquet, I, **381–82**, 70, 131, 190, 603
Irumberry* de Salaberry, Édouard-Alphonse d' (1792–1812), IV, 43
Irumberry* de Salaberry, Ignace-Michel-Louis-Antoine d' (1752–1828), IV, 43
Irving, Judith. *See* Westfield
Irving, Paulus Æmilius, III, 542; IV, **379–80**, 491, 538, 570, 579
Irving, Sir Paulus Æmilius, IV, 380

Irving, William, IV, 379
Irwin, Marie, *dite* de la Conception, I, **382**
Isaac. *See* Glikhikan
Isabeau, Antoinette (Planton), II, 292; III, 234, 235
Isabeau, Arnoud, II, 292; III, 234
Isabeau, Marie-Anne (Bolvin), III, 67
Isabeau, Michel-Philippe, II, **292**, 120, 648, 649, 650; III, 234, 235, 636, 644
Isabel, Guillaume, I, 468
Isambart, Joseph, II, 153; IV, 147, 148
Isambart, Périnne, IV, 147
Isbister, Adam, IV, 380
Isbister, George, IV, 32
Isbister, Helen. *See* MacKinlay
Isbister, Joseph, II, 232; III, 127, 301, 341, 654; IV, **380–81**, 33, 383
Isbister, Judith. *See* Middleton
Isbister, William, III, **300–1**; IV, 380
Isbister, William (labourer), III, 300
Isham, Ann. *See* Skrimshire
Isham, Catherine. *See* Mindham
Isham*, Charles Thomas (d. 1814), III, 304; IV, 33, 47, 157
Isham, James, II, 310; III, **301–4**, 285, 286, 287, 448, 472, 482, 483, 490, 520, 593, 594, 595, 661, 662; IV, 46, 47, 383, 517, 518, 523
Isham, Whitby, III, 301
Ishquaketa, III, 13
Isnard, Danty d', II, 595, 596
Istre, Élisabeth. *See* Forestier
Istre, Joseph, III, 220
Itarey, I, 451
Itouralde. *See* Artaguiette
Ivar Bárdarson, I, 679
Izard, Sarah (Campbell), IV, 131

JACAU, Anne. *See* Melanson, *dit* La Verdure
Jacau, Jeanne (Allard de Sainte-Marie), IV, 14
Jacau, Jeanne-Françoise (Rodrigue), IV, 678
Jacau (Jacault, Jacob), Thomas, IV, 382
Jacau de Fiedmont, Louis-Thomas, III, xxii, 87; IV, **382–83**, 14, 36, 250, 459, 631, 641, 652, 678
Jachée, Françoise (Chartier de Lotbinière), II, 138
Jack (slave), IV, 779
Jackman, Charles, I, 317
Jackson, Hannah (Loring), IV, 486
Jackson, John, II, **293–94**, 350, 351, 438, 486, 487, 564, 583
Jackson, Margaret, II, 486
Jackson, Mary. *See* Bissett
Jacob. *See also* Jacau
Jacob, Étienne (father), II, 294
Jacob, Étienne, II, **294**, 648
Jacob, Jeanne. *See* Bellejambe
Jacob, Jeanne. *See* Fressel
Jacobs, Abraham, IV, 386
Jacobs, Angélique, IV, 385
Jacobs, Baptist Samuel, IV, 385
Jacobs, Ferdinand, III, 595; IV, **383–84**, 47, 157, 377, 518, 523, 583, 647
Jacobs, John Baptist, IV, 385
Jacobs, John Levy, IV, 385
Jacobs, Marie-Josette. *See* Audette, *dit* Lapointe

Jacobs, Mary Geneviève, IV, 385
Jacobs, Mary Marianne, IV, 385
Jacobs, Samuel, IV, **384–86**, 37, 330, 331, 332
Jacobs, Samuel (son), IV, 385
Jacobs, Samuel (son of FERDINAND), IV, 384
Jacobs, Thomas, IV, 385
Jacquelin, Françoise-Marie (Saint-Étienne de La Tour), I, **383–84**, 505, 594, 595; IV, xxiii
Jacquelin, Jean-François, III, 282
Jacquemart, Marie-Christine (Delezenne), IV, 204
Jacquerault (Jacquero). *See* Jacrau
Jacquereau, Anne (Mercier), III, 442, 443
Jacques (slave), II, 375
Jacquet, Élisabeth. *See* Bourget
Jacquet, François, II, 467
Jacquet, François, IV, **386–87**, 45
Jacquet, Joseph, IV, 386
Jacquet, Louise. *See* Giroux
Jacquier, Anne (Lestringant), II, 426
Jacquiés, Barbe. *See* Segris
Jacquiés, Luc, II, 294
Jacquiés, *dit* Leblond, Catherine. *See* Guillemote
Jacquiés, *dit* Leblond, Jean, II, **294–95**
Jacquin, Anne. *See* Perrot
Jacquin, Jean-Claude, III, 304
Jacquin, *dit* Philibert, Marie-Anne. *See* Guérin
Jacquin, *dit* Philibert, Nicolas, III, **304–5**, 96; IV, 66, 449
Jacquin, *dit* Philibert, Pierre-Nicolas, III, 304
Jacquinot, Barthélemy, I, 455, 539
Jacrau, Joseph-André-Mathurin, III, 194, 399; IV, **387–88**, 74, 100, 183, 642, 643, 719
Jadis, Charles Newland Godfrey, IV, **388–89**
Jadis, Elizabeth. *See* Newland
Jadis, John Godfrey Maximilian, Count d'Adié, IV, 388
Jadis, Margaret (wife of CHARLES NEWLAND GODFREY), IV, 388
Jager, Claude, I, 205
Jago, George, II, 295
Jago, John, II, **295**
Jallais, Marie (Leclerc), II, 380
Jallot (Jalleau), Jeanne (Terrier de Francheville et de Repentigny; Poulin de La Fontaine), I, 553; II, 227, 254, 529
Jalobert, Alizon. *See* Des Granches
Jalobert, Bertrand, I, 384
Jalobert, Jehanne. *See* Maingard
Jalobert, Macé, I, **384**, 167, 169, 520
Jalot, Marie-Antoinette. *See* Chouart Des Groseilliers
Jamay. *See* Jamet
Jambe de Bois. *See* Gargot
James I, King of Great Britain and Ireland (James VI of Scotland), I, 23, 50, 51, 52, 67, 69, 144, 243, 369, 481, 496, 597, 667, 668; IV, xvii, xix
James II, King of Great Britain and Ireland, I, 92, 227, 329, 544, 605, 631; II, 100, 101, 496, 497, 539, 636, 643; III, 176, 428, 602
James (slave, fl. 1800), IV, 778
James (slave, fl. 1804), IV, 779
James, the Old Pretender, III, 116
James, Richard, I, 229
James(?), Rosalie (Gill), IV, 293
James, Thomas (mayor), I, 349, 384
James, Thomas, I, **384–85**, 20, 83, 144, 311, 329, 349, 362, 376, 377, 408

James, William, I, 306
Jamet, Denis, I, **385**, 192, 265, 296, 437, 590
Jamet, John, III, **305–6**, 452
Jamin, Gilles, I, 265
Jamin, Pierre, I, 503, 504
Jandet, Marguerite, III, 94
Janes, John, I, 375
Jangouessy. *See* Chingouessi
Jannière, Jeanne (Bourdon de Dombourg; Denys de
　Bonaventure), I, 114; II, 176; III, 175, 552, 682
Janot. *See also* Jeanneau
Janot, *dit* Bourguignon, Henri, III, 171
Janson, Paul, I, 213
Janson, *dit* Lapalme, Charles, III, 306, 307
Janson, *dit* Lapalme, Charlotte. *See* Couturier, *dit* Le Bour-
　guignon
Janson, *dit* Lapalme, Christophe, II, 530; III, 306
Janson, *dit* Lapalme, Dominique, II, 160; III, **306–8**, 165;
　IV, 204, 732
Janson, *dit* Lapalme, Jeanne-Charlotte. *See* Couturier, *dit*
　Le Bourguignon
Janson, *dit* Lapalme, Louis, II, 160; III, 306, 307
Janson, *dit* Lapalme, Madeleine. *See* Trefflé, *dit* Rottot
Janson, *dit* Lapalme, Madeleine-Ursule. *See* Rancin
Janson, *dit* Lapalme, Marie-Catherine (Delezenne), IV, 204
Janson, *dit* Lapalme, Marie-Geneviève. *See* Pelletier
Janson, *dit* Lapalme, Marie-Joseph. *See* Couturier, *dit* Le
　Bourguignon
Janson, *dit* Lapalme, Philippe, III, 306, 307
Janson, *dit* Lapalme, Pierre, II, 111, 200, 338, 418; III, 304,
　306, 307
Jantot. *See* Jeantot
Jaques, Richard, III, 477
Jarret, Claudine. *See* Pécaudy
Jarret, Jean, II, 295
Jarret de Verchères, Alexandre, II, 295; III, 310
Jarret de Verchères, Angélique (Coulon de Villiers), II, 156;
　III, 148, 150; IV, 177
Jarret de Verchères, Antoine, III, 308
Jarret de Verchères, Catherine (Hertel de Beaubassin), IV,
　347
Jarret de Verchères, Charlotte-Gabrielle (Raimbault de
　Saint-Blaint; Hertel de Rouville), IV, 344
Jarret de Verchères, François, II, 295; III, 308
Jarret de Verchères, François-Michel, III, 308
Jarret de Verchères, Jean, III, 399
Jarret de Verchères, Jean-Baptiste, II, 367
Jarret de Verchères, Louis, II, 285
Jarret de Verchères, Madeleine. *See* Ailleboust de Manthet
Jarret de Verchères, Marguerite-Gabrielle (Levrault de
　Langis), III, 399
Jarret de Verchères, Marie. *See* Perrot
Jarret de Verchères, Marie-Jeanne (Douhet de Larivière, *dit*
　de L'Étáng; Du Verger d'Aubusson), III, 308
Jarret de Verchères, Marie-Madeleine (Tarieu de La Pérade),
　I, 239, 418; II, 156, 224, 295; III, **308–13**, 676; IV, 728
Jarret de Verchères, Pierre, II, **295–96**, 285; III, 310
Jarry, Émery, II, 163
Jarry, Jean-Baptiste, III, 210
Jarry, Marguerite. *See* Gaudé
Jartoux, Pierre, III, 336
Jarvis, Edward, IV, **389–90**, 32, 743
Jasne. *See* Robert Jasne

Jautard, Thérèse. *See* Bouat
Jautard, Valentin, IV, **390–92**, 36, 229, 336, 532, 533, 534,
　547, 697
Jay, John (merchant), I, 386
Jay, John (tucker), I, 386
Jay, John, I, **386–87**, 19, 21, 147, 239, 240
Jean, Jacqueline (Véniard de Bourgmond), II, 645
Jean-Armand. *See* Andehoua
Jean-Baptiste, III, 266
Jeanneau, Catherine. *See* Perrot
Jeanneau, Étienne (father), III, 313
Jeanneau, Étienne, III, **313–14**, 299; IV, 71
Jeanneau, Jacquette. *See* Clément
Jeanne de Sainte-Marie, I, 348
Jeanne-Françoise de Sainte-Hélène. *See* Bermen de La Mar-
　tinière
Jeanne-Françoise de Saint-Ignace. *See* Juchereau de la Ferté
Jeannin, Pierre, known as Président Jeannin, I, 470
Jeanson. *See also* Janson
Jeanson, Guillaume, IV, **392**, xxix
Jeanson, Jean-Baptiste, IV, 392
Jeanson, Marie-Josette. *See* Aucoin
Jeantot, Jean, III, **314**
Jefferson, Thomas, IV, 303, 322, 337, 412
Jefferys*, Charles William (1869–1951), IV, 120
Jefferys, Thomas, III, 108
Jemison, Mary, IV, 405
Jendon, Pierre, III, 141
Jendon, Victoire. *See* Coron
Jenkins, Ann, II, 664
Jenkinson, Anthony, I, 331
Jenkinson, Charles, 1st Earl of Liverpool, IV, 571
Jennings, Sarah (Churchill, Duchess of Marlborough), II,
　286, 659
Jennison, John, III, 620
Jensen, Stephen, IV, 334
Jérémie, Claude, I, 387
Jérémie, Hélène. *See* Macart
Jérémie, *dit* Lamontagne, Catherine (Aubuchon; Lepallieur
　de Laferté), II, 296, 413; III, **314–15**, 408
Jérémie, *dit* Lamontagne, Françoise. *See* Bourot
Jérémie, *dit* Lamontagne, Françoise, II, 296
Jérémie, *dit* Lamontagne, Jeanne. *See* Pelletier
Jérémie, *dit* Lamontagne, Marie-Madeleine. *See*
　Tetesigaguoy
Jérémie, *dit* Lamontagne, Marie-Madeleine (Mallet), II, 451
Jérémie, *dit* Lamontagne, Nicolas, II, **296–300**, 256, 319,
　406, 614; III, 489
Jérémie, *dit* Lamontagne, Noël, I, **387**, 60; II, 159, 256,
　296, 451; III, 314
Jérémie, *dit* Lamontagne, *dit* Douville, Charlotte (Huppé,
　dit Lagroix), IV, 376
Jérôme. *See* Atecouando
Jérôme, *dit* Latour, François (Franceway), IV, 365
Jervis, John, 1st Earl of St Vincent, III, 132
Jeryan, Dorothy, *dite* de Saint-Joseph, III, 24
Jeskakake, III, 320, 614
Jessup*, Edward (1735–1816), IV, 710
Jewer, John, II, 10, 62, 563
Jilbert. *See* Gilbert
Joannès, Armand de, IV, 652
Joannès, François-Augustin de, Baron de Chacornacle, II,
　300

Joannès de Chacornacle, II, **300**, 220
Joannès de Chacornacle, Balthazar de, II, 300
Joannès de Chacornacle, Catherine de. *See* Mortier
Jobert, Jean-Baptiste, IV, 82
Jobin, Élisabeth (Guyart de Fleury), III, 272
Jobin, François, II, 516
Jobin, Françoise (Dandonneau, *dit* Lajeunesse), II, 168
Joe, IV, **392–93**, 295
Jogues, Isaac, I, **387–90**, 11, 41, 42, 112, 124, 125, 203, 344, 370, 371, 373, 403, 404, 410, 411, 414, 454, 457, 459, 461, 462, 523, 524, 566; II, 157, 158
Johannes, Bishop. *See* Watteville
Johnson, Ann (Nancy) (Claus), IV, 155
Johnson, Anne. *See* Warren
Johnson, Bethiah. *See* Barker
Johnson, Catherine. *See* Weissenberg
Johnson, Christopher, IV, 394
Johnson, Francis, I, 390, 391, 392, 450, 451
Johnson, George (son of Sir WILLIAM), IV, 418
Johnson, George, I, **390–92**, 450, 451
Johnson, Guy, IV, **393–94**, 117, 118, 119, 120, 130, 149, 155, 308, 368, 397, 405, 409, 410, 730, 731, 735
Johnson, Isabelle. *See* Corporon
Johnson*, Sir John (1742–1830), IV, 119, 130, 149, 330, 393, 394, 397, 406, 417, 494, 566, 710, 735
Johnson, Martin, II, 265
Johnson, Mary (Polly) (Johnson), IV, 393
Johnson, Mathew, IV, 321
Johnson, Peter Warren, IV, 417, 418
Johnson, Samuel, III, 583; IV, 554, 555
Johnson, Susanna. *See* Willard
Johnson*, Urbain (1824–1918), IV, 392
Johnson, William. *See also* Jeanson, Guillaume; Tekawironte
Johnson, William (father of Guillaume JEANSON) IV, 392
Johnson, William (soldier), IV, 731
Johnson, Sir William, III, xxxvii, xxxviii, xli, 49, 95, 101, 126, 158, 159, 174, 185, 186, 214, 255, 256, 262, 320, 321, 322, 409, 410, 452, 495, 526, 527, 530, 536, 561, 588, 607, 614, 623, 624, 651, 652, 655; IV, **394–98**, xxxvi, xxxvii, xxxviii, lvii, 23, 24, 26, 27, 57, 84, 86, 117, 119, 130, 137, 138, 149, 154, 155, 173, 174, 241, 279, 280, 282, 297, 299, 307, 309, 314, 337, 347, 368, 375, 393, 404, 408, 409, 417, 418, 489, 506, 582, 586, 587, 595, 596, 668, 669, 675, 676, 679, 681, 691, 692, 730, 731, 733, 734, 735, 762
Johnston, Mr (councillor), IV, 398
Johnston, Alexander (captain), IV, 398
Johnston, Alexander, IV, **398–99**
Johnston, Ann, IV, 400
Johnston, Elizabeth (Colvill, Baroness Colvill), III, 131
Johnston, James, IV, **399–400**, 37, 295, 571, 618, 645, 646
Johnston, John, IV, 399
Johnston, John Purss, IV, 400
Johnston, Margaret. *See* Macnider
Johnston, Richard, IV, 482
Johnstone, James, IV, 400
Johnstone, James, known as Chevalier de Johnstone, III, 136, 137; IV, **400–1**, 455
Johonerissa. *See* Tanaghrisson
Joibert. *See* Joybert
Joinville, Gabriel de, I, 434
Jolicœur (soldier), II, 645

Jolliet. *See also* Aux
Jolliet, Adrien, I, 173, 225, 227, 248, 393, 536, 626; II, 192, 347
Jolliet, Charles, II, 66
Jolliet, Claire (Fleury de La Gorgendière), II, 224; III, 216; IV, 268, 661
Jolliet, Claire-Françoise. *See* Bissot
Jolliet, Jean-Pierre, known as Chevalier d'Au, III, 7
Jolliet, Louis, I, **392–98**, 11, 15, 35, 76, 84, 104, 105, 146, 173, 174, 175, 178, 225, 226, 227, 289, 345, 400, 452, 480, 491, 492, 565, 572, 625, 657, 665; II, xxxi, xxxviii, 8, 66, 68, 141, 148, 192, 227, 228, 230, 256, 273, 296, 300, 302, 347, 413, 422, 489, 607, 634; III, xxxv, 216, 339, 380, 609, 616, 620; IV, 268
Jolliet, Marie. *See* Viel
Jolliet, Zacharie, I, 394, 396, 606, 657; II, 231
Jolliet d'Abancourt, François, II, 300
Jolliet d'Anticosti, Charles, II, 301; III, 281
Jolliet de Mingan, Jean-Baptiste, II, **300–1**; III, 609
Jolliet de Mingan, Jean-Joseph, II, 301
Jolliet de Mingan, Marie. *See* Mars
Jolliet de Mingan, Marie-Anne (L'Archevêque; Taché), III, 608, 609
Jollivet, Louis, III, 199; IV, 109, 286
Jollyet, Jean, I, 392, 554
Jollyet, Marie. *See* Abancourt
Joly, Jean, II, 32
Joly, Julien, III, 622
Joly-Cœur. *See* Perrot
Joncaire. *See* Chabert
Jones*, Augustus (d. 1836), IV, 12, 756
Jones, Henry, III, **315–16**, 327, 504
Jones*, James (d. 1805), IV, 81, 511
Jones, John, IV, **401–2**, 437
Jones, Rice, I, 671
Jones*, Robert (d. 1805), IV, 82
Jones, Sarah (Hope), IV, 366
Jones, Stephen, IV, 490
Jonquet, Anne. *See* Hébert
Jonquet, Étienne, I, 437, 578
Jonquières, Catherine de (Latour), IV, 439
Joram Chappuis, *dit* Comtois, Jean, IV, 748
Joram Chappuis, *dit* Comtois, Marie-Louise. *See* Varin, *dit* La Pistole
Jordan, Ann. *See* Livingston
Jordan, Jacob, IV, **402–4**, 58, 59, 243, 286, 399
Jordan, Marie-Anne. *See* Raby
Jordy, Élisabeth de. *See* Pradines
Jordy, Louise de. *See* Rathery
Jordy, Pierre de, II, 185
Jordy, Pierre-François de, II, 185, 186
Joseph. *See* Chihwatenha; Manitougatche; Teouatiron; Togouiroui
Joseph, Bishop. *See* Spangenberg
Joseph, Father. *See* Du Tremblay, François-Joseph
Joseph (potter), IV, 386
Joseph, Benjamin, I, 74
Joseph-Claude. *See* Claude
Josephte-Antoinette de Sainte-Marie. *See* Chaussegros de Léry
Jossard, Élisabeth (Poitiers Du Buisson), III, 532
Josselin, Nicolas, I, 267
Joubert, Captain, I, 263

Jouenne de Lorière, Louise-Françoise (Beaussier de Lisle), III, 54

Jouet, Louis, IV, 252

Jouin, Bernardine (Lafontaine), III, 339

Joulin, Étienne, II, 28

Jourdain, Anne (Perrot de Rizy), II, 520

Jourdain, Michel, III, 170

Jourdain, *dit* Bellerose, Marie-Françoise (Deguise, *dit* Flamand), IV, 203

Jourdain, *dit* Bellerose, Pierre, IV, 203

Jourdain, *dit* Labrosse, Denis (father), III, 316

Jourdain, *dit* Labrosse, Denis, III, 316

Jourdain, *dit* Labrosse, Dominique, III, 316

Jourdain, *dit* Labrosse, Françoise. *See* Gaudé

Jourdain, *dit* Labrosse, Marie-Madeleine. *See* Fagot

Jourdain, *dit* Labrosse, Paul, III, 316

Jourdain, *dit* Labrosse, Paul-Raymond, III, **316–17**; IV, 472

Jourdan. *See also* Launé-Jourdan

Jourdan, M., II, 587

Jourdan, Françoise (Simon de Longpré), I, 607

Jousserand, Nicole de (Menou), I, 502

Jousset, Louise (Maugue; La Sague), I, 498

Joutel, Henri, I, 79, 180, 182; II, 124, 197, 441; III, 106

Jouve, Odoric-Marie, III, 690; IV, 142

Jouvency, Joseph, III, 23

Jouy, Comte de. *See* Berthelot; Rouillé

Jovenazo, Duke of, II, 443

Joybert, Jacques, I, 399

Joybert, Pierre-Jacques, I, 399

Joybert de Soulanges, Marie-Geneviève (Le Moyne de Longueuil), IV, 463

Joybert de Soulanges et de Marson, Louise-Élisabeth de (Rigaud de Vaudreuil, Marquise de Vaudreuil), I, 399; II, **301–2**, 202, 547, 558, 567, 570, 580; III, 7, 118, 176, 247, 372, 555, 556, 603; IV, 660, 662

Joybert de Soulanges et de Marson, Marie-Françoise de. *See* Chartier de Lotbinière

Joybert de Soulanges et de Marson, Pierre de, I, **398–400**, 25, 40, 62, 63, 185, 203, 667; II, 5, 166, 301, 409, 477

Joyer, René-Pierre, IV, 137

Joyeuse, Anne, Duc de Joyeuse, I, 87, 88, 89, 421

Joyeuse, François de, Cardinal de Joyeuse, I, 386

Juan Chou, I, 263

Juana (the Mad), Queen of Castile, I, 41

Jubé, Jacques, III, 639

Juchereau, Françoise (Berman de La Martinière), II, 56

Juchereau, Jean, I, 401, 402

Juchereau, Jeanne. *See* Creste

Juchereau de La Ferté, Charlotte, I, 400

Juchereau de La Ferté, Denis-Joseph, I, 400; II, **302–3**, 304, 388, 441

Juchereau de La Ferté, Jean, I, **400**, 108, 202, 331, 401, 402, 580, 584, 587, 588, 589; II, 33, 228, 302, 303, 304

Juchereau de La Ferté, Jeanne-Françoise, *dite* de Saint-Ignace, I, 111, 231, 310, 329, 359, 400, 487, 631; II, **303–4**, 44, 80, 93, 116, 130, 132, 161, 528; III, 369, 547, 711; IV, 440

Juchereau de La Ferté, Marie. *See* Giffard

Juchereau de La Ferté, Marie, *dite* de Sainte-Thérèse, I, 400

Juchereau de La Ferté, Marie-Louise (Aubert de La Chesnaye), I, 400; II, 33, 34; III, 22

Juchereau de La Ferté, Noël, I, 108, 400; II, 304

Juchereau de Maur, Geneviève (Legardeur de Tilly), I, 448, 602; II, 236, 387; III, 373

Juchereau de Maur, Jean, I, **401**, 60, 330, 400, 402, 448; II, 35

Juchereau de Maur, Marie. *See* Langlois

Juchereau de Maur, Paul-Augustin, I, 400; II, **304–5**, 35; III, 22

Juchereau de Saint-Denis, Charlotte-Françoise, known as Comtesse de Saint-Laurent (Viennay-Pachot; Dauphin de La Forest), I, 661; II, **305**, 69, 170, 256, 306, 557, 587

Juchereau de Saint-Denis, Emanuela. *See* Ramón de Navarro

Juchereau de Saint-Denis, Joseph, I, 402

Juchereau de Saint-Denis, Louis, II, 306, 307, 355; III, **317–18**, 383, 423

Juchereau de Saint-Denis, Louise-Madeleine (Lestringant de Saint-Martin), II, 426

Juchereau de Saint-Denis, Marie-Anne (Pollet de La Combe-Pocatière; Ruette d'Auteuil), I, 550, 551; II, 391, 586

Juchereau de Saint-Denis, Marie-Catherine (Legardeur de Repentigny), IV, 447, 448

Juchereau de Saint-Denis, Marie-Thérèse. *See* Giffard

Juchereau de Saint-Denis, Nicolas, I, **401–2**, 48, 146, 331, 448, 550, 661; II, 56, 305, 307, 426; III, 317

Juchereau de Saint-Denys, Charles, I, 508; II, **305–7**, 180, 224, 468, 508, 525, 645; III, 317, 402

Juchereau de Saint-Denys, Joseph-Charles, II, 307

Juchereau de Saint-Denys, Thérèse-Denise. *See* Migeon de Branssat

Juchereau Des Chatelets, Noël, I, **402–3**, 319, 401, 447, 448; II, xv

Juchereau de Vaulezar, François, II, 525

Juchereau Duchesnay, Antoine (father), III, 115, 549

Juchereau* Duchesnay, Antoine (1740–1806), IV, 344, 702

Juchereau Duchesnay, Geneviève, *dite* de Saint-Augustin, II, 91; III, 318, 349, 543

Juchereau Duchesnay, Ignace, I, 402, 543; II, **307**, 42, 448, 540; III, 318

Juchereau Duchesnay, Marie-Catherine. *See* Peuvret Demesnu

Juchereau Duchesnay, Marie-Françoise. *See* Chartier de Lotbinière

Juchereau Duchesnay, Marie-Joseph, *dite* de l'Enfant-Jésus, III, **318–19**, 349, 543, 544

Juchereau Duchesnay de Saint-Denis, Madeleine-Louise (Sallaberry), III, 582

Judah, Dorothy (Hart), IV, 331

Judah, Isaac, IV, 332

Judah, Joseph, IV, 332

Judah, Samuel, IV, 331, 332, 385

Judah, Uriah, IV, 331, 332

Juet, Robert, I, 374, 375, 376, 377, 378

Jugier, Jérôme, IV, 286

Jugon. *See* Lemaître

Juillet, Blaise, I, 271

Juillet, Marie-Louise-Catherine (Durocher), III, 210

Julian, Étiennette (Saint-Père), I, 598

Julienne-Angélique de Jésus Pâtissant. *See* Dollier de Casson

Jullien, Louis, IV, 566

Jumeau, Emmanuel, I, 438

Jumonville. *See* Coulon

Jung, Jean, III, 501
Jurie, Robert, I, 267
Jussaume, *dit* Saint-Pierre, Marie-Louise (Du Calvet), IV, 231
Jussaume, *dit* Saint-Pierre, Pierre, IV, 228, 231
Jussieu, Antoine de, II, 595, 596, 597, 600; III, 675
Jussieu, Antoine-Laurent de, II, 596
Jussieu, Bernard de, III, 30, 675, 678
Just, Madeleine (Le Gay de Beaulieu; You de La Découverte), II, 127, 673; IV, 235
Juste, Angélique (Levasseur), IV, 473
Jutra, Marie (Poulin), II, 529; III, 537
Jutras, Claire (Bolvin), III, 68
Jutras, *dit* Desrosiers, Jean-Baptiste, III, 24
Jutrat, Marguerite (Godefroy de Saint-Paul), II, 252

KAGHSWAGHTANIUNT (Kachshwuchdanionty), III, **319–20**, 614
Kaghswoughdioony, III, 321
Kahikohan, I, 48
Kaieñ?kwaahtoñ, IV, **404–6**, lvi, 118, 396, 417, 730
Kaigwiaidosa. *See* Madjeckewiss
Kaiūtwah?kū (Cornplanter), IV, lvi, 118, 405, 410
Kajnquiratiton. *See* Cagenquarichten
Kak8enthiony (Kaghswoughtioony, Kaghswughtioni), III, **320–21**, 451, 494
Kalm, Anna Magaretha. *See* Sjöman
Kalm, Catherine. *See* Ross
Kalm, Gabriel, IV, 406
Kalm, Pehr, II, 595, 596, 597; III, 145, 169, 315, 675, 676, 679, 680; IV, **406–8**
Kalogg. *See* Kellogg
Kamehameha, IV, 746
Kanaghgwasea. *See* Canaghquiesa
Kanaghkwase. *See* Karaghtadie
Kanaharighton (Kanakarighton). *See* Cagenquarichten
K'ang-hsi (Hsüen-yeh), III, 470
Kanon, Jacques, III, **321–22**; IV, 125, 601, 616, 729
Kanonraron (Aaron Hill), IV, 692, 730
Kan tuck ee gun, III, 525
Karaghiagigo, IV, 735
Karaghtadie (Karaghiagdatie), III, **322–23**, 331, 623
Karekowa (Karikohe). *See* Tarbell, John
Karonghyontye (David Hill), IV, 692
Karpik, IV, 225, 536
Karrer, Louis-Ignaz, III, 93, 94
Kaské. *See* Charlot
Katalouibois. *See* Koutaoiliboe
Kateri. *See* Tekakwitha
Kayahsota? (Kayashoton), III, 95, 652; IV, **408–10**
Kayenquaraghton. *See* Kaieñ?kwaahtoñ
Kaylus. *See* Thubières
Keen, William, II, 152, 153, 609; III, **323–24**, 10, 68, 506
Keen, William (son), III, 91, 324
Keissis. *See* Caissy
Keith, Sir William, III, 66
Kelley, Arthur Reading, IV, 811
Kellie, Earl of. *See* Erskine
Kellogg, Joanna, III, 324, 325
Kellogg, Jonathan, III, 324
Kellogg, Joseph, III, **324–26**; IV, 770
Kellogg, Louise Phelps, III, 106

Kellogg, Martin (father), III, 324
Kellogg, Martin, III, 324, 325
Kellogg, Rachel. *See* Devotion
Kellogg, Rebecca, III, 324
Kellogg, Sarah. *See* Dickinson
Kelly, James (alias Gillam; Sampson Marshall), I, 301
Kelsey, Elizabeth. *See* Dix
Kelsey, Elizabeth, II, 313
Kelsey, Henry, I, 227, 329, 529, 611; II, **307–15**, xxviii, 10, 42, 50, 51, 267, 298, 319, 320, 394, 395, 454, 616, 617; III, xxxiii, 285, 414, 415, 489, 599
Kelsey, John (father), II, 308
Kelsey, John, II, 308
Kelsey, John (son of HENRY), II, 314
Kelsey, Mary, II, 313
Kelsey, Thomas (army officer), II, 308
Kelsey, Thomas (goldsmith), II, 308
Kélus. *See* Thubières
Kelynge, Martha (Osborn, Lady Osborn), IV, 594
Kemble, Gertrude. *See* Bayard
Kemble, Margaret (Gage), IV, 279
Kemble, Peter, IV, 279
Kempthorne, Sir John, II, 315
Kempthorne, Thomas, III, **315–16**, 25, 226, 580, 637
Kendrick, Huldah. *See* Pease
Kendrick, John, IV, **410–12**, 419, 420, 519
Kendrick, John (son), IV, 411
Kennelly, David Thomas, IV, 109
Kennelly, Jeanne-Marie-Catherine. *See* Bruyères
Kenougé. *See* Kinongé
Kensey (MacKenzie), William, III, 129
Kent and Strathearn, Duke of. *See* Edward Augustus
Kenwick (Kenwrick). *See* Kendrick
Kenwrick, Elizabeth. *See* Atkins
Kenwrick, Solomon, IV, 410
Kepitanal (Kepitenat). *See* Capitanal
Keppel, Augustus, 1st Viscount Keppel, IV, 259, 327, 600, 701
Keppel, George, 3rd Earl of Albermarle, IV, 501
Keppel, William Anne, 2nd Earl of Albemarle, IV, 278
Kerbodot. *See* Guillemot
Kerdement, Captain, I, 421
Kerdisien. *See* Pichot
Kerfily, Marquis de. *See* Castel
Kerfily, Marquise de. *See* Kerven
Kerlérec. *See* Billouart
Kerr, Charles, IV, 37
Kerr, John, I, 544
Kerrill, Elizabeth (Amherst), IV, 20
Kerrivan, Peter, IV, **784–85**
Kersaint. *See* Coëtnempren
Kersident. *See* Guichart
Kertk. *See* Kirke
Kervan, Thomas, IV, 784
Kerven, Françoise-Jeanne de (Castel, Comtesse de Saint-Pierre, Marquise de Crèveœur et de Kerfily), II, 306
Kesterman, Mary. *See* Brewse
Kesterman, William, IV, 93
Ketelby, Thomas, I, 522
Khisipikiwam (Agatha), I, 481
Kiala, II, **316–17**, xxx, 503; III, xxxiv, 46; IV, lii
Kiashuta. *See* Kayahsota?

Kilby, Christopher (father of THOMAS), III, 326
Kilby, Christopher, III, 10, 326, 586
Kilby, Sarah. *See* Ellis
Kilby, Sarah. *See* Sempkins
Kilby, Thomas, III, **326–27**; IV, 312
Kildare, Earl of. *See* Fitzgerald
Kilpatrick, Robert, III, **327**, 315
King, Boston, IV, 515
King, James, IV, **412–13**, 156
King, John, I, 376, 377
King, William, IV, 48
King, Willobe, known as Olive Le Roy (Castaing), IV, 136
King Hendrick. *See* Theyanoguin
Kingminguse, IV, **413**
King Newcomer. *See* Netwatwees
King of Kanadesaga. *See* Kaieñ?kwaahtoñ
King Philip. *See* Pometacom
Kingsford*, William (1819–98), IV, xlviii, 502
Kinloch, Anne (Maclean), IV, 504
Kinonchamek, III, 529
Kinongé, II, **317–18**, xxxvii, 415, 505
Kinousaki, III, **328**, xxxix, 451
Kinsey, Jane (Huck-Saunders), IV, 701
Kiotseaeton, I, **403–4**, 7, 65, 112, 186, 371, 373, 389, 548, 665; II, 82, 158
Kiouet, I, 204
Kipling, John, IV, 727, 743, 744
Kirby*, Ann (Macaulay) (1770–1850), IV, 494
Kirby*, John (1772–1846), IV, 494
Kirby*, William (1817–1906), III, 143, 304, 677; IV, 449, 660
Kirkby, Richard, II, 666
Kirke, Lady (wife of Sir DAVID), I, 406
Kirke, David, I, 406
Kirke, Sir David, I, **404–7**, 24, 25, 29, 53, 54, 59, 76, 110, 122, 133, 159, 160, 161, 162, 163, 196, 199, 200, 237, 243, 278, 287, 303, 311, 313, 330, 340, 342, 366, 368, 369, 411, 428, 452, 453, 489, 494, 495, 498, 511, 521, 533, 561, 567, 579, 613, 652, 653, 665
Kirke, Elizabeth. *See* Gowding
Kirke, George, I, 406, 567
Kirke, Gervase (Jarvis), I, 404; II, 538
Kirke, James (Jarvis), I, 405, 406, 407, 652
Kirke, Sir John, I, 405, 406, 407; II, 538
Kirke, Sir Lewis, I, **407**, 199, 242, 405, 406, 408, 473, 487, 495, 636
Kirke, Mary, II, 538
Kirke, Philip, I, 406
Kirke, Thomas (consul), I, 408
Kirke, Thomas, I, **407–8**, 405, 487
Kirkland, Samuel, III, xxxviii; IV, 117, 368, 731
Kirwin. *See* Irwin
Kisensik, III, **328**, xxxvii
Kitchin, Eusebius Bacchus, IV, 32, 726
Kittier, William, IV, 711
Kiyasuta. *See* Kayahsota?
Klingancourt. *See* Damours de Clignancour, Mathieu-Benjamin
Klock, George, IV, 692
Kluck, William, IV, 602
Knaut, Anna. *See* Grob
Knaut, Benjamin, IV, 414
Knaut, Catherine (Newton), IV, 414

Knaut, Jane. *See* Brimner
Knaut, Philip Augustus, IV, **414**, 52, 291
Kneeland, John, IV, 695
Kneller, Henry, IV, **414–15**, 398, 726
Knight, Elizabeth (Livingston), II, 436
Knight, Elizabeth (wife of JAMES), II, 320
Knight, Gabriel, I, 408
Knight, Gilpin, II, 320
Knight, James, I, 385; II, **318–20**, 20, 42, 50, 51, 56, 171, 231, 232, 266, 267, 291, 311, 312, 313, 314, 394, 406, 407, 604, 614, 615, 616, 617, 627, 628, 644, 658, 663; III, 414, 446, 489, 599; IV, 339
Knight, John, I, **408**, 5, 20, 243, 360, 375, 397
Knight, Richard, II, 318
Knollys, Henry, I, 332
Knorr, Hannah (Sower), IV, 721
Knowles, Sir Charles, III, 276, 293, 294, 572, 628, 656; IV, 83, 93, 169, 737
Knowles, Mary (Moore), IV, 553
Knowlton, Sarah (Masters; Dimock), IV, 217
Knox, Andrew, I, 496
Knox, Jane. *See* Carre
Knox, John (father), IV, 415
Knox, John, III, 89, 305, 360, 421; IV, **415–16**, 487, 773
Knox, William, IV, xl, xlvi, xlviii
Koé (Kouée, Koweahe). *See* Gawèhe
Kointaguettez. *See* Ohquandageghte
Kolno. *See* Scolvus
Kondiaronk, II, **320–23**, xxx, 20, 102, 103, 108, 119, 344, 423, 441, 444, 593, 643; III, xxxv; IV, liii
Konieschguanokee (Captain Pipe), IV, 302
Koñwatsi?tsiaiéñni, IV, **416–19**, 119, 397, 405, 410
Kotsinoghyâtà. *See* Hotsinoñhyahta?
Kotte (Koth, Cotté), Lewis, IV, 613
Kouategeté. *See* Ohquandageghte
Koutaoiliboe (Koutaaouileone), II, **323–24**, xxxvii, 317, 415, 453, 503; III, 576
Koyah, IV, **419–20**, 218, 411
Krainguille, M., I, 593
Krum, John Christian, III, 212
Kryn. *See* Togouiroui
Kunz, Matthew, III, 212
Kuriahtaaty. *See* Karaghtadie

LABAIG, Jean de, II, 4, 7
Labaig, Marie de. *See* Abbadie de Saint-Castin
La Balluë. *See* Magon
La Barbotière, Captain, I, 499
La Baronnière. *See* Froyer
La Barre. *See also* Charon; Charron; Le Febvre
La Barre, Anne de. *See* Adhémar de Lantagnac
La Barre, Augustin-Antoine de, III, 5
La Barthe, Jeanne (Claverie), III, 124; IV, 125
La Barthe, Jean-Pierre, IV, 66, 126
Labat, M., II, 480
Labatut, Baron de. *See* Navailles
Labatut, Baronne de. *See* Mius d'Entremont de Pobomcoup
La Bazanière, Louise de. *See* Briet
La Bazanière, Marie-Suzanne de (Lorant; Le Roy Desmarest), II, 424; III, 396
La Bazanière, Pierre de, II, 424
L'Abbé, Captain, I, 100, 101
La Beaume. *See* Tailhandier

Laberge, François, III, 346
Laberge, Marie-Françoise (Lambert, *dit* Saint-Paul), III, 346
La Blanchetière. *See* Renardin
La Boische. *See* Beauharnois
La Boissière. *See* Nau
Labonté. *See also* Campion
Labonté (soldier), III, 310
La Borde. *See also* Delaborde; Hamare; Mullois
Laborde, Catherine. *See* Dechart
Laborde, Catherine (Soupiran), II, 613
La Borde, Jean, III, 157, 158, 172, 452, 567; IV, **420–23**, 126, 558, 644, 645, 646, 678
La Borde, Jean de (notary), III, 172
Laborde, Louise. *See* Dupuy
La Borde, Marguerite (Daccarrette), III, 157
Laborde, Sébastien-Charles, IV, 422
Laborde (Borda) d'Aloperca, Martin, IV, 420
La Bouille. *See* Fromont
La Boularderie. *See* Le Poupet
La Boulardière. *See* Dugué
La Boulasserie. *See* Ailleboust
La Boulaye. *See* Duret
La Bouteiller de La Bouteillerie, Suzanne, II, 181
La Bouteillerie. *See* Deschamps
Labrador. *See* Foucher
Labrador, The. *See* Fernandes, João
Labrèche. *See* Dalgueuil
La Brèche, Sieur, II, 530
La Brède, Baron de. *See* Secondat
La Bretonnière. *See also* Neveu
La Bretonnière, Jacques-Quintin de, III, **329**, 480
La Broquerie. *See* Chartier
Labrosse. *See* Jourdain
La Brosse, M., I, 423
La Brosse, Jean de, IV, 423
La Brosse, Jean-Baptiste de, II, 296; IV, **423–25**, 106, 294, 295
La Brosse, Louise de. *See* Duboiscuvier
La Bruère. *See* Boucher
La Bruyère. *See* Boucher; Court; Fabry
Labutte. *See* Chesne
La Caille, Nicolas-Louis de, III, 31
La Cailleterie. *See* De Lisle
La Cardonnière. *See* Rouer
La Cetière, Anne de. *See* Bier
La Cetière, Florent de, II, **325**, 43, 170, 273, 576, 577; III, 398, 647
La Cetière, Jean de, II, 325
La Chaise. *See also* Aix; Andigné
La Chaise, Jacques de, II, 204; III, 40
La Chapelle. *See also* Chabrand; Renou
La Chapelle, Sieur, II, 95
La Chassaigne (La Chassagne). *See* Bouillet
La Chasse, Edmée. *See also* Roussol
La Chasse, Joseph de, III, 329
La Chasse, Pierre de, II, xxxvii, 333, 475, 543, 544, 664, 665, 669; III, **329–31**, xxxix, 23, 24, 359, 477, 580
La Chaussaye. *See* Beauharnois
La Chauvignerie. *See* Maray
La Chenaye. *See* Gauthier
La Chenette, M., II, 645
La Chenette, Mme. *See* Couc, Elizabeth
La Chesnardière. *See* Ruis-Embito

La Chesnaye. *See* Aubert; Duquet
Lachevrotière. *See* Chavigny
Laciseraye. *See* Lefebvre
La Citière. *See* Lauson
La Cloche. *See* Hecquet
La Colle, III, **331**
La Colombière. *See also* La Corne
La Colombière, Bertrand de, II, 326
La Colombière, Claude de, II, 326
La Colombière, Joseph de, I, 78, 506; II, **325–27**, 134, 240, 360, 376, 528, 594, 597; IV, 535
La Colombière, Marguerite de. *See* Coindat
Lacombe. *See also* Truillier
Lacombe, Catherine. *See* Quevillon
Lacombe, Jacques-Joseph, IV, 216
La Combe-Pocatière. *See* Pollet
La Corne, Antoinette de. *See* Allemagne
La Corne, Charlotte de (Douglas), IV, 224
La Corne, Élisabeth de. *See* Ramezay
La Corne, Jean-Marie de, II, 249
La Corne, Louis (Jean-Louis, Louis-François, Louis-Luc, Pierre) de, known as Chevalier de La Corne, III, **331–32**, 183, 285, 322, 333, 361, 375, 623; IV, 54, 169, 425, 426, 427, 434, 461, 633, 637, 651, 793
La Corne, Louis de, known as La Corne *l'aîné*, III, 390; IV, 224
La Corne, Luc de, II, 327
La Corne, Luc de, known as Chaptes de La Corne or La Corne Saint-Luc, III, 48, 243, 332, 333, 376, 600, 652; IV, **425–29**, xliii, 41, 59, 129, 149, 155, 289, 442, 513, 543, 564, 633, 634, 759, 794
La Corne, Marie-Anne de. *See* Hervieux
La Corne, Marie-Anne de. *See* Hubert de La Croix
La Corne, Marie-Anne de (Campbell), IV, 129, 427
La Corne, Marie-Joseph de. *See* Guillimin
La Corne, Marie-Louise-Charlotte de (Le Comte Dupré), IV, 427, 442
La Corne, Marie-Marguerite de. *See* Boucher de Boucher-ville
La Corne, Marie-Marguerite de (Lennox; Viger), IV, 427
La Corne, Maurice de (baptized Jean-Louis), IV, 454
La Corne de Chaptes, Jean-Louis de, II, **327–28**, 456; III, 331, 332, 333; IV, 425, 429
La Corne de Chaptes, Joseph-Marie (Jean-Marie) de, IV, **429–31**, 96, 338, 571
La Corne de Chaptes, Marie de. *See* Pécaudy de Contrecœur
La Corne de Chaptes, Marie-Madeleine de, *dite* du Saint-Sacrement, III, **332–33**
La Corne de La Colombière, Pierre-Antoine de, III, 76
La Corne Dubreuil, François-Josué de, III, **333**; IV, 425, 633
La Corne Dubreuil, François-Michel de, III, 333
La Corne Dubreuil, Michelle de. *See* Hervieux
La Corne Saint-Luc. *See* La Corne, Luc de
La Corriveau. *See* Corriveau, Marie-Josephte
La Corruble. *See* Bouge, Ange
La Coste (La Côte). *See* Courault; Courreaud
La Couèche. *See* Le Blanc, Madeleine
La Cour. *See* Bégon
La Court de Pré-Ravillon et de Granpré, I, **408–9**, 306, 450, 671
La Cressonière. *See* Couture
Lacroix. *See also* Hubert
La Croix. *See also* Milly; Prevost; Réaume

Lacroix, M., III, 493
La Croix, Anne-Madeleine de. *See* Dontaille
La Croix, Catherine de. *See* Clément
La Croix, Charles-Eugène-Gabriel de, Marquis de Castries, IV, 471, 646
La Croix, Dominique de, III, 334
Lacroix, Hubert-Joseph, III, 334
La Croix, Hubert-Joseph de, III, **334**, 315, 675
La Croix, Jean, II, 507; III, 113
La Croix, Jean de, II, 328
La Croix de Chevrières de Saint-Vallier, Jean de, II, 328
La Croix de Chevrières de Saint-Vallier, Jean-Baptiste de, I, 56, 76, 77, 80, 92, 117, 141, 175, 286, 291, 338, 361, 439, 506, 507, 536, 540, 635, 649; II, **328–34**, 14, 19, 40, 44, 55, 58, 60, 76, 90, 92, 93, 95, 99, 109, 110, 117, 124, 128, 132, 133, 134, 135, 137, 140, 151, 160, 171, 174, 175, 176, 186, 189, 194, 199, 200, 207, 210, 222, 227, 235, 240, 244, 245, 247, 248, 258, 259, 272, 304, 326, 336, 337, 341, 346, 350, 357, 366, 371, 372, 377, 379, 381, 429, 431, 449, 456, 462, 466, 478, 491, 492, 506, 522, 528, 533, 545, 571, 586, 594, 597, 608, 613, 628, 629, 638, 640, 641; III, 5, 23, 40, 44, 51, 62, 63, 78, 113, 114, 168, 180, 193, 194, 195, 199, 201, 202, 204, 222, 223, 227, 233, 240, 259, 284, 306, 318, 319, 330, 333, 348, 349, 352, 369, 386, 390, 413, 419, 443, 469, 487, 512, 522, 523, 564, 574, 575, 616, 629, 632, 633, 640, 681, 683, 684; IV, 180, 220, 222, 338, 387, 509, 535, 649, 708, 765
La Croix de Chevrières de Saint-Vallier, Marie de. *See* Sayve
Ladan, Adrien, II, **334–35**, 370, 419, 421
La Dauversière. *See* Le Royer
La Découverte. *See* You
La Demoiselle. *See* Memeskia
La Doussinière. *See* Duchesneau
La Durantaye. *See* Morel
La Duye. *See* Lafon
La Fare, Marquis de, III, 458
La Fargue, Jacques. *See* Brandeau, Esther
Lafatigue. *See* Billeron
La Faye, Louis-François de, II, **335–36**
La Fayette, Marie-Joseph de, Marquis de La Fayette, IV, 229, 230
La Ferre, Marie de, I, 478, 512
La Ferrière. *See* Erouachy
La Ferrière, Comte de. *See* Berryer
La Ferté. *See* Juchereau
Laferté. *See* Lepallieur
La Ferté de La Madeleine, Abbé de, I, 494
La Feuille. *See* Wahpasha
La Feuillée, Alixe de (Des Granges de Mauprée; La Motte de Lucière), I, 415
Lafitau, Catherine. *See* Berchenbos
Lafitau, Jean, III, 334
Lafitau, Joseph-François, II, 237, 596; III, **334–38**, 106, 184, 315
Lafitau, Pierre-François, III, 334, 336
Lafite, Marguerite (Denys), I, 258, 259
Laflèche (coureur de bois), I, 225
Lafleur. *See* Bailly; Couc; Petitpas; Pinsonneau; Richard
Lafleur, *dit* Plamondon, Ignace, IV, 141
Lafond. *See* Richard
La Fond, Étienne de, II, 83; III, 629

La Fond, Geneviève de (Trottier), III, 629
La Fond, Marie de. *See* Boucher
Lafon de La Duye, Catherine de. *See* Bégon
Lafontaine. *See also* Bellot
La Fontaine. *See* Gamelain; Marion; Poulin
Lafontaine, Bernardine de. *See* Jouin
Lafontaine, Catherine (Mercier), III, 442
Lafontaine, Jean-Baptiste de, III, 339
Lafontaine, Marianne (Martin; Giard; Dornon), III, 258, 443
Lafontaine de Belcour, Antoine de, IV, 315
Lafontaine de Belcour, Charlotte de. *See* Bissot
Lafontaine de Belcour, Geneviève de. *See* Lambert
Lafontaine de Belcour, Gilles de, III, 602
Lafontaine de Belcour, Jacques de, II, 66; III, **338–41**, 47, 48, 75, 154, 217, 270, 422, 509, 602, 608, 647; IV, 183, 381, 571, 602
Lafontaine de Belcour, Marie-Josephte de (Cugnet), IV, 182, 315
La Fontanelle. *See* Eder
Laforce. *See* Pépin
La Forest. *See also* Dauphin; Guillot; Tavernier; Testard
La Forest, Gabriel de, II, 169
La Forest, Jeanne de. *See* Noreau
La Forest, Marc-Antoine de, II, **336**; III, 98
La Forest, Marie-Anne de. *See* Courthiau
La Forest, Pierre de, III, 158
La Forest de La Gemerais, Marguerite de (Dufrost de Boissemances), II, 202
Laforey, John, III, 71
Laforge. *See* Sageot
La Forière. *See* Erouachy
Laforme (innkeeper), III, 139
Lafosse. *See* Hodiau
La Fosse. *See also* Puyperoux
La Fosse, Antoine de, II, 156
La Fosse, Louise de (Coulon de Villiers), II, 156
La Fourche. *See* Nissowaquet
La Fourière (La Foyrière). *See* Erouachy
La Framboise. *See* Fafard
Laframboise, Lucie-Angélique. *See* Cotté
Laframboise*, Maurice (1821–82), IV, 172
La France, Joseph, III, **341–42**
Lafranchise. *See* Contant
La Frenaye, François de (baptized Pierre-Antoine), II, **336–37**, 125
La Frenaye, Geneviève de. *See* Lepage
La Frenaye, Martin de, I, 409
La Frenaye de Brucy, Antoine de, I, **409–10**, 547, 600; II, 336
La Frenaye de Brucy, Hélène de. *See* Picoté de Belestre
La Frésillière. *See* Loppinot
La Fresnière. *See* Hertel
La Galissonière. *See* Barrin
La Garaye. *See also* Marot
La Garaye, Comte de, III, 192
La Garde, Pierre de, II, 637
Lagarde, Pierre-Paul-François de, IV, **431–32**, 318, 521, 636
La Garenne. *See also* Durand
La Garenne, Marie (Peuvret), I, 542
La Gauchetière. *See* Migeon
La Gemerais. *See* Dufrost; La Forest
La Gesse. *See* Ramezay

La Giraudais. *See* Chenard
La Giraudière (La Girodière). *See* Baye
Lagny, Jean-Baptiste de, II, 74, 76, 182
Lagoanere, Blaise, IV, 245
Lagoanere, Catherine. *See* Daccarrette
La Gondalie. *See* La Goudalie
La Gorgendière. *See* Fleury
La Goudalie, Charles de, III, **342–43**, 120, 438
La Grande Armée, II, 469
La Grande Gueule. *See* Otreouti
La Grande Terre. *See* Ohonsiowanne
Lagrandeur. *See* Dumontet
La Grandrive. *See* Dupuy
La Grange. *See also* Léger
La Grange, Sieur de. *See* Varlet
La Grange, Anne de (Buade, Comtesse de Frontenac et de Palluau), I, 134, 135, 142; II, 483
Lagrange, Anne-Louise (Imbert), IV, 378
Lagrange, Gabrielle. *See* Anneville
Lagrange, Jean-Baptiste, III, 222; IV, 390
Lagrange, Jean-Baptiste-Martin, IV, 378
Lagrange, Mathieu, II, 59
Lagrené, Pierre dc, II, **337**
La Grenouille. *See* Oumasasikweie
La Grive Des Assises, M., IV, 645
Lagroix (Lagrouais, La Groy, Lagroye). *See* Huppé
La Grossardière. *See* Gourdeau
La Groye, Marquis de. *See* Aloigny
La Groye, Marquise de. *See* Chasteigner; Macard
Laguer de Morville, Claude-Dorothée, II, 337; III, 191
Laguer de Morville, Marie-Thérèse. *See* Lajoüe
Laguide Meynier, Madeleine (Perrot), I, 117, 540
Lahaille*, Jean-Baptiste (1750–1809), IV, 234
La Halle. *See* Delhalle
La Haye. *See also* Marguerie
La Haye, Father de, I, 356
La Héronnière, Sieur de, I, 582
Lahontan, Baron de. *See* Lom
La Houlière. *See* Marchant
Laigne, Julien, II, 58
Laigu, *dit* Lanoue, René-Charles, III, 278, 279
Laing, Mrs (wife of William), IV, 432
Laing, William, IV, 105, 432
Lair, M., II, 8, 9
Laisné, Élisabeth (Dasilva, *dit* Portugais), III, 165
Laisné, *dit* Laliberté, Marie-Élisabeth (Deguise, *dit* Flamand), IV, 203
La Janière. *See* Fleury
La Jannaye. *See* Chaton
La Jemerais (Lajemmerais). *See* Dufrost
Lajeunesse. *See* Dandonneau
La Jonquière. *See* Taffanel
La Jonquière, Marquise de. *See* La Valette
La Joubardière. *See* Berthé
Lajoüe, François de, II, **337–39**, 58, 451, 467; III, 398
La Joue, Jacques de, II, 337
La Joue, Madeleine de. *See* Guérin
Lajoüe, Marie-Agnès de (Lavasseur), II, 337; III, 398
Lajoüe, Marie-Anne de. *See* Ménage
Lajoüe, Marie-Madeleine de (Frontigny; Boucault de Godefus), III, 77, 78
Lajoüe, Marie-Thérèse de (Laguer de Morville), II, 337
Lajus, Angélique-Jeanne. *See* Hubert

Lajus, Anne. *See* Vigneau
Lajus, Élisabeth-Simone (Almain; Couillard), III, 345
Lajus, François, III, 345; IV, **432**
Lajus, François-Marie-Olivier-Hubert, IV, 432
Lajus, François-Michel, III, 345
Lajus, Jean, III, 344
Lajus, Jean-Baptiste (baptized Jean-François), III, 345
Lajus, Jean-Baptiste-Isidore-Hospice, IV, 432
Lajus, Jeanne-Françoise-Louise-Luce (Bédard), IV, 432
Lajus, Jordain, III, **344–45**, 519; IV, 432
Lajus, Louise-Élisabeth. *See* Moreau, *dit* Lataupine
Lajus, Marguerite. *See* Audet de Piercotte de Bailleul
Lajus, Marguerite-Ursule (Vaillant; Noël), III, 345
Lajus, Marie-Louise. *See* Roger
Lajus, René-Flavien, IV, 432
Lake, Sir Bibye, III, 302, 447
Lalancette. *See* Landriaux
Lalande. *See also* Lefrançois
Lalande, Anne de (Chesneau), I, 287
La Lande, Anne-Catherine de (Hocquart), IV, 354
Lalande, Élisabeth. *See* Garreau
Lalande, Étienne, III, 258
Lalande, Jean, III, 271
La Lande, Jean de, I, **410–11**, 390, 414; II, 158
La Lande, Robert de, I, 288
Lalande de Gayon, Jacques de, I, 104, 105, 146, 289, 395, 396, 397; III, 339
Lalande de Gayon, Marie de. *See* Couillard
La Lande Gayon, Marie-Thérèse de (Aubert de La Chesnaye), II, 34
Lalane, Christophe de, III, 194; IV, 387, 642, 719
Lalanne. *See also* Laporte
Lalanne, Pierre, IV, 270
Lalemand. *See* Allemand
Lalemant, Charles, I, **411–12**, 43, 111, 121, 125, 160, 197, 213, 214, 217, 246, 329, 413, 428, 447, 453, 456, 484, 493, 494, 498, 521, 561
Lalemant, Gabriel, I, **412–13**, 9, 31, 64, 124, 126, 219, 414, 459, 483, 561, 562
Lalemant, Jérôme, I, **413–15**, 91, 123, 246, 268, 284, 354, 355, 357, 374, 388, 389, 404, 410, 411, 412, 428, 430, 431, 456, 459, 461, 473, 477, 498, 561, 562, 640, 662, 665; II, xvi, 84, 158, 237, 460
Laliberté. *See also* Laisné; Senet
Laliberté*, Alfred (1878–1953), III, 143; IV, 424
Lalime. *See* Lépine
Lallemant, Louis, I, 126, 387, 563
Lally, Thomas-Arthur, Baron de Tollendal, Comte de Lally, IV, 126
La Lochetière. *See* Tavernier
La Londe, Marc, II, 524
Lalonde, *dit* L'Espérance, Jean, II, 350
La Londette (Lalonde), Louis, III, 242
La Madeleine. *See* Ailleboust; La Ferté
La Maisonfort Du Boisdecourt, Alexandre de, Marquis de La Maisonfort, III, **345–46**, 209, 636
La Maisonfort Du Boisdecourt, Catherine de, Marquise de La Maisonfort. *See* Chicoyneau
La Majour, Sieur de. *See* Arrigrand
Lamaletie, Jean-André, III, 226; IV, **433–34**, 67, 126, 615, 750
Lamaletie, Louis, IV, 433
Lamaletie, Marie-Anne. *See* Benet

Lamaletie, Marie-Thérèse. *See* Foucault
La Malgue. *See* Marin
La Malotière. *See* Ruette
La Marche. *See also* Baudry
Lamarche. *See* Danguel; Périnneau
La Marche, Dominique de (baptized François), II, **339**; IV, xxi
La Marche, Jacques de, I, 477
La Marche, Jean-François de, IV, 136, 374
La Marck, Marie de (Godet Des Maretz), I, 342
La Marck, Robert IV de, Duc de Bouillon, I, 424
La Marque. *See also* Marin
Lamarque. *See also* Nolan
La Marque, M., I, 246
La Marque, Jacques de, II, 421, 626
La Marque, Marie de. *See* Pournin
La Marque, Marie-Anne de (Nolan; Frenel; Tonty), II, 632; III, 485
Lamarque, Marie-Marguerite (Bolvin), III, 68
La Marre. *See* Varin
La Marre, Sieur de, I, 473
Lamarre, Anne (Duquet de La Chesnaye), I, 298
Lamarre, Antoine, II, 339
Lamarre, Marguerite. *See* Levasseur
Lamarre, *dit* Bélisle, Catherine. *See* Demosny
Lamarre, *dit* Bélisle, Henri, II, **339–40**
Lamarre, *dit* Bélisle, Jeanne. *See* Archambault
Lamarre, *dit* Bélisle, Marie-Catherine (Sicard), II, 340
Lamarre, *dit* Bélisle, Périnne. *See* Dandonneau
Lamars. *See* Lamarre
La Martinière. *See* Bermen; Lomeron
Lamb, William, III, 654; IV, 381
Lambert, Eustache, I, **415**, 146, 396
Lambert, Gabriel, II, 274
Lambert, Geneviève (Hamare de La Borde), II, 273
Lambert, Geneviève (Lafontaine de Belcour), III, 339
Lambert*, John (fl. 1775–1816), IV, 753
Lambert, Louis, II, 273
Lambert, Marie. *See* Laurence
Lambert, Marie-Madeleine (Chartier de Lotbinière), II, 138, 457; III, 112
Lambert, Marie-Renée. *See* Roussel
Lambert, Paul, III, 346
Lambert, Radegonde (Blanchard), II, 71
Lambert, Thérèse. *See* Huard
Lambert, Thérèse, *dite* Sainte-Marie-Médiatrice, III, 719
Lambert, *dit* Saint-Paul, Marguerite. *See* Maillou, *dit* Desmoulins
Lambert, *dit* Saint-Paul, Marie-Françoise. *See* Laberge
Lambert, *dit* Saint-Paul, Paul, III, **346–47**; IV, 535
Lambert de Baussy, Marie-Catherine (Philippe de Hautmesnil de Marigny), II, 525
Lambert Dumont, Charlotte-Louise (Poulin de Courval Cressé), III, 540
Lambert Dumont, Eustache, II, 82
Lambert Dumont, Eustache (son), III, 374, 540
Lambert Dumont, Madeleine (Bouat), II, 82
Lambert Dumont, Marie (Bissot), II, 66
Lambert Dumont, Sophie. *See* Vanneck
Lamberville, Jacques de, I, 635; II, **340–42**, xx, xxxiv, xxxvi, 343, 473, 643; III, 428
Lamberville, Jean de, I, 322, 323, 443, 445, 465, 525, 526, 633; II, **342–44**, xx, xxxvi, 62, 101, 340, 341, 474, 585; III, 335

Lambton*, John George, 1st Earl of Durham (1792–1840), IV, 655, 656
La Meilleraye, Sieur de, I, 434
Lamer, Marie de (Nicollet), I, 516
La Mer Monte. *See* Chomina
La Meslée. *See* Crevier
La Milletière. *See* Dubois
La Minotière. *See* Niort
Lamirande. *See* Guyot
Lamoignon, Guillaume de, I, 220; II, 656, 657
La Mollerie. *See* Maleray
La Monnerie, M. de, III, 310
Lamontagne. *See* Jérémie
La Morandière. *See* Rocbert
Lamorel Le Pippre de Nœufville, Simon, II, 566
Lamorille. *See* Lemaître
Lamorinie, Jean-Baptiste de, III, **347**; IV, 241
Lamothe. *See* Aigron; Bigot; Dagneau
La Mothe. *See also* Ango
La Mothe, Nicolas de, I, 441
Lamothe Cadillac. *See* Laumet
La Mothe-Fénelon. *See* Salignac
La Mothe-Tilly. *See* Legardeur
La Motte. *See also* Cahideuc; La Rue
La Motte (La Motte-Picquet). *See* Picquet
La Motte, Clémence. *See* Badon
La Motte, Jean de, I, 415
Lamotte, Marie de (Lepallieur), II, 413
La Motte de Lucière, Alixe de. *See* La Feuillée
La Motte de Lucière, Dominique, I, **415–16**, 175; II, 278
Lamotte de Saint-Paul, Pierre, I, **416**, 415
La Motte-le-Vilin, M., I, 68
Lamouline. *See* Landrière
Lamouraux-Rochefort, Madeleine (Morin), IV, 558
Lamoureux, Françoise (Duprac), II, 206
Lamoureux, *dit* Saint-Germain, Joseph, IV, 585
Lamy, Joseph, II, 458
Lamy, Louise (Marin de La Malgue; Legardeur de Beauvais), II, 458; III, 374, 432
Lamy, Marie. *See* Decheuraineville
Lamy, Marie (Dagneau Douville), III, 158; IV, 191
Lamyma, II, 562
La Nasse. *See* Manitougatche
Lanaudière (La Naudière). *See* Lanouguère; Tarieu
La Nauraye. *See* Niort
Lancaster, Sir James, I, 499
Lanctot*, Gustave (1883–1975), IV, 232
Landeau, Marie-Noëlle (Tétro), II, 627
Landianière. *See* Hardouineau
Landon, Simple, I, 55, 420; II, **344–45**
Landriaux, Louis, IV, 434
Landriaux, Louis-Nicolas, IV, **434–35**, 265
Landriaux, Marie-Anne. *See* Prud'homme
Landrieux, Marie-Louise. *See* Bourond
Landrière. *See also* Des Bordes
Landrière Des Bordes, Antoine-Gilles, IV, 435
Landrière Des Bordes, Jean-Marie, IV, **435–36**, 148, 580
Landrière Des Bordes, Marie-Gilles. *See* Chaussegros de Léry
Landrière Des Bordes, Pierre-Paul, IV, 436
Landrière Lamouline, Pierre, III, 401, 441, 442; IV, 125
Landrio. *See* Landriaux
Landron, M., IV, 320
Landron, Élisabeth. *See* Chavigny

Landron, Étienne, I, 56, 664; II, 32; III, 347
Landron, François-Xavier, III, 348
Landron, Jean-François, III, **347–48**, 181, 182, 346
Landron, Marie-Anne. *See* Bergeron
Landry, Alexis, IV, **436–37**, xxviii, 78, 240
Landry, Antoinette (Bourg), II, 93
Landry, Cécile (Terriot), II, 625
Landry, Charles, II, 93
Landry, Claire. *See* Le Blanc
Landry, Jean, IV, 436
Landry, Marie. *See* Bernard
Landry, Marie. *See* Terriot
Landry, René, II, 625
Lane, Daniel, I, **416–17**
Lane, Elizabeth (Vavasor; Holdsworth), II, 291
Lane, Henry, II, 291
Lane, John, II, 476
Lane, Sarah. *See* Dickinson
La Neuville. *See* Buache
Laneuville. *See* Horné
Langan, Gilonne-Charlotte de (Cahideuc, Comtesse Dubois de La Motte), III, 92
Lange, André de, IV, 125
Langevin*, Edmond (1824–89), IV, 75
Langhorn*, John (d. 1817), IV, 710
Langis. *See* Levrault
Langlade. *See* Mouet
Langlais, Guillaume, III, 398
Langlois, Adrienne (Larché), II, 272
Langlois, Françoise. *See* Grenier
Langlois, Françoise (Desportes), I, 264, 495
Langlois, Guillaume, I, 417
Langlois, Jacques, III, 348
Langlois, Jean, II, 158
Langlois, Jeanne. *See* Millet
Langlois, Marguerite (Martin), I, 495; II, 460
Langlois, Marguerite (Vachon), II, 639, 640
Langlois, Marie. *See* Crevet
Langlois, Marie (Caën), I, 159
Langlois, Marie (Juchereau de Maur), I, 400, 401
Langlois, Marie-Madeleine (Gervaise), III, 257
Langlois, Marie-Thérèse. *See* Lessard
Langlois, Marie-Thérèse, *dite* de Saint-Jean-Baptiste, III, **348–49**, 318, 319, 543
Langlois, Noël, I, **417**, 330
Langlois, Noël (son), II, 32
Langlois, *dit* Germain, Louis, IV, 44, 295
Langloiserie (L'Angloiserie). *See* Piot
Langman, Edward, IV, **437–38**, 194, 402, 771
Langman, John, IV, 437
Langoissieux, Charles (baptized Pierre), I, **417**, 320
Langon. *See* Trégu
Langristain. *See* L'Estobec
Languet de Gergy, Jean-Joseph, IV, 295
Langy. *See* Levrault
Lanne, Jean, IV, 421
Lannelongue, Anne. *See* Richard
Lannelongue, Armand, III, 349
Lannelongue, Jean-Baptiste, III, **349–50**; IV, 253, 378, 379
Lannelongue, Marie. *See* Barrière
Lannelongue, Pierre, III, 350
Lanogenu, M., IV, 126
La Noraye. *See* Niort
Lanoue. *See* Laigu

La Noue. *See* Legu; Robutel
Lanouette. *See* Rivard
Lanouguère, Jean de, I, 417
Lanouguère, Jeanne de. *See* Samalins
Lanouguère, Louis de, III, 311
Lanouguère, Louise-Rose de, *dite* de Sainte-Catherine, III, 311
Lanouguère, Marguerite-Renée de. *See* Denys de La Ronde
Lanouguère, Thomas de, I, **417–18**, 321, 600; II, 224, 616; III, 311
Lanoullier, Jean, III, 350, 352
Lanoullier, Marie. *See* Tollet
Lanoullier, Marie-Reine. *See* Grasse
Lanoullier de Boisclerc, Jean-Eustache, III, **350–52**, 74, 145, 159, 353, 374; IV, 203, 304, 359, 360, 590, 658, 749
Lanoullier de Boisclerc, Jeanne. *See* André de Leigne
Lanoullier de Boisclerc, Marie-Germaine-Eustache (Bénard), III, 63, 352
Lanoullier de Boisclerc, Marie-Jeanne. *See* Bocquet
Lanoullier de Boisclerc, Marie-Marguerite. *See* Duroy
Lanoullier de Boisclerc, Nicolas, II, 152; III, **352–54**, 14, 15, 48, 61, 62, 64, 77, 153, 170, 350, 616; IV, 88, 356
Lanoullier Des Granges, Paul-Antoine-François, III, 172, 353
Lansing, Gysbertje (Roseboom), III, 568
Lantagnac. *See* Adhémar
La Oja. *See* Wahpasha
Lapalice, Ovide-Michel-Hengard, IV, 655
Lapalme. *See* Janson
La Palme (de Palme), M., I, 89, 418
La Pause, Chevalier de. *See* Plantavit
Lapeire, Joseph-Guillaume, IV, 135
La Peltrie. *See* Gruel
La Pérade. *See* Tarieu
Lapérade, Marie-Louise (Roy), IV, 689
La Pérelle. *See* Eury
Lapérière. *See* Desjardins
La Périne. *See* Maleray
Lapérouse, Comte de. *See* Galaup
Lapérouse, Comtesse de. *See* Broudou
La Perrière. *See* Boucher; Marin
Lapeyre, Jean-Pierre, III, 608
La Picanier. *See* Dagneau
La Picardière. *See* Bégon
La Pierre. *See* Chauvin
La Pinaudière. *See* Bourdon
La Pistole. *See* Varin
La Place, Eustache de, II, 345
La Place, Jacques de, I, 215, 485
La Place, Louis-Hyacinthe de (baptized Jean-Claude), I, 339; II, **345**
La Place, Marie de. *See* Le Couteux
La Place, Pierre de, I, 338; II, 345
La Place, Simon-Gérard de (baptized Jean), I, **338–39**; II, 345, 579; III, 163, 273
La Plagne. *See* Espiet
La Plante. *See* Leriger
La Pocatière. *See* Pollet
Lapointe. *See* Audette; Desherbert
La Poippe, Sieur de, I, **418–19**, 530
La Pommeraye, Charles de, I, 167
Laporte, Arnaud de, III, 355
La Porte, Françoise de. *See* Faucrolle
La Porte, Jean de, II, 345

La Porte, Marie-Anne de (Genaple de Bellefonds; Hubert), II, 241

Laporte, Pierre-Arnaud de, III, 354, 355; IV, 358, 517, 644, 645, 655, 656, 668

Laporte de Lalanne, Jean (Armand) de, III, 226, **354–55**

La Porte de Louvigny, Louis de, II, **345–47**, xxi, 15, 70, 115, 218, 220, 223, 300, 316, 318, 386, 389, 433, 475, 488, 502, 515, 518, 547, 567, 571, 588; III, 81

La Porte de Louvigny, Marie de. *See* Nolan

La Porte de Louvigny, Marie-Anne de (Testard de Montigny), II, 627; III, 278; IV, 733

La Potardière, Sieur de, I, 626

La Poterie. *See* Leneuf

La Potherie. *See* Le Roy

La Prade. *See* Pelletier

La Ralde, Raymonde de, I, **419**, 162, 411, 521, 579

La Ralière (La Ratière). *See* Des Herbiers

La Ramée, Sieur de. *See* Melanson, Charles

Larché, Adrienne. *See* Langlois

Larche, Charles, IV, 58

Larché, Pierre, II, 272

Larcher, Henri-Michel, IV, 438

Larcher, Marie-Anne. *See* Marinier

Larcher, Nicolas, IV, **438–39**, 421, 558, 644, 678

L'Archevêque, Jean, III, 523

L'Archevêque, Marie-Anne. *See* Jolliet de Mingan

L'Archevêque, Marie-Thérèse (Tisserant de Moncharvaux), III, 626

Larchevesque, Marie-Madeleine. *See* Réaume

Larcum, Elizabeth (Townsend), III, 628

Lardeau, Anne (Gargot), I, 323

Lardeau, Jacques, I, 323

Lareau, Marguerite (Campagna; Hodiesne), III, 292

La Renaudière, M., II, 646

Largillier, Jacques, known as Le Castor, I, 394, 491; II, **347**, 144

La Ribourde, Gabriel de, I, **420**, 55, 176, 177, 265, 438, 499, 501; II, 278, 280, 344, 345

La Richardie, Armand de, III, **355–56**, 47, 102, 650; IV, 612, 640

La Richardière. *See* Testu

La Rigaudière. *See* Martaud

La Rive. *See* Gravé

Larivée, Charles, IV, 748

Larivée, Eustache, IV, 748

La Rivière. *See also* Bernard; Byssot; Le Mercier; Lorimier; Poncet

Larivière. *See* Douhet; Hébert

La Rivière, M., II, 414

Larkin, George, II, **348**, 260, 290

La Rochalar, Chevalier de. *See* Goussé

La Roche, M., II, 264

La Roche, Marie-Gabrielle (Dasilva, *dit* Portugais), III, 165

La Roche Daillon, Jacques de, I, 420

La Roche Daillon, Jeanne de. *See* Froyer de La Baronnière

La Roche Daillon, Joseph de, I, **420–21**, 132, 533

La Roche de Mesgouez, Troilus de, Marquis de La Roche-Mesgouez, I, **421–22**, 23, 27, 88, 209, 210, 345

La Rochefoucauld, Louis de, Marquise de Roye, III, 356

La Rochefoucauld, Marie-Louise-Nicole de (La Rochefoucauld de Roye, Marquise de Roucy, Duchesse d'Anville), III, 356

La Rochefoucauld, Marthe de, Marquise de Roye. *See* Ducasse

La Rochefoucauld de Roye, Jean-Baptiste-Louis-Frédéric de, Marquis de Roucy, Duc d'Anville, III, **356**, 27, 49, 50, 54, 98, 213, 214, 357, 367, 417, 438, 498, 610, 657; IV, 33, 62, 79, 421, 454, 459, 558, 588, 644, 651

La Rochefoucauld de Roye, Marie-Louise-Nicole de, Marquise de Roucy, Duchesse d'Anville. *See* La Rochefoucauld

La Rochefoucauld-Roye, Éléonore-Christine (Phélypeaux, Comtesse de Pontchartrain et de Maurepas), II, 296; III, 309, 310

La Roche-Guyon, Duchesse de. *See* Schomberg

La Rochette. *See* Gargot; Hillaire

Larocque*, François-Antoine (1784–1869), IV, 172

Larocque, Marie-Catherine-Émilie. *See* Cotté

La Rocque de Roberval, Jean-François de, I, **422–25**, 27, 159, 169, 301, 309, 384, 469; III, 109

La Rodde. *See* Senezergues

Laron. *See* Sauguaaram

La Ronde. *See* Bourassa; Denys

La Roque, Catherine de (Hangard), I, 425

La Roque, Charlotte de (Madaillan), I, 424

La Roque, Jean (Pierre) de, I, 424

La Roque, Marguerite de, I, **425–26**, 423, 424

La Roque, *dit* Couillaud, Bernard de, I, 422

La Roque, *dit* Couillaud, Isabeau de. *See* Poitiers

La Roque* de Roquebrune, Robert (1889–1978), IV, 269

La Rose. *See* Belleau

Larose. *See* Guillot; Pichon; Rousseau

La Rouvillière. *See* Michel

La Rozière. *See* Carlet

Larrante (Rende), Marie (Sagean), II, 589

Larsher, M., III, 676

Lartigue. *See also* Bidoux; La Salle

Lartigue, François, II, 381

Lartigue, Jean-Jacques, IV, 148

Lartigue*, Jean-Jacques (1777–1840), IV, 148

Lartigue, Jeanne. *See* Dhiarse

Lartigue, Joseph, II, 220, 381; III, **356–57**, 216, 387, 454

Lartigue, Marie-Charlotte. *See* Cherrier

Lartigue, Marie-Madeleine (Fautoux), III, 216

Lartigue, Pierre-Jérôme, IV, 558, 644, 645

Larue, Étienne de, II, 348

Larue*, François-Xavier (d. 1855), IV, 42, 43

Larue, Guillaume de (father), II, 348

Larue, Guillaume de, II, **348**, 282, 517

Larue, Marie de. *See* Pepin

Larue, Marie de. *See* Pouilliot

La Rue, Pierre de, Abbé de L'Isle-Dieu, III, 17, 18, 120, 121, 165, 166, 192, 194, 196, 198, 199, 223, 257, 343, 415, 416, 425, 426, 575; IV, 80, 95, 96, 97, 235, 237, 238, 289, 296, 452, 453, 454, 456, 529, 645

La Rue de La Motte, Louis de, I, 416

La Sablonnière. *See* Brunet; Varin

La Sague, Jean de, I, 498

La Sague, Louise de. *See* Jousset

La Salle. *See also* Cavelier; Perthuis

La Salle, Charles de, II, 348

La Salle, François de, II, 349

La Salle, Jean de, I, 425

La Salle, Jean-Baptiste de, II, 335; III, 221, 613

La Salle, Jeanne-Catherine de. *See* Berenhardt

La Salle, Madeleine de. *See* Chartroux

La Salle, Marie de. *See* Harot

La Salle, Nicolas de (father), II, 348

La Salle, Nicolas de, II, **348–49**, 260, 399; III, 380, 381
La Salle, Nicolas de (3rd), II, 349
La Salle, Rose de (Marquette), I, 490
La Salle, Simon de, II, 349
La Salle de Sertrouville, Marie-Anne de. *See* Carrerot
La Salle de Sertrouville, Quentin de, II, 119
La Saudrais, Girard de, IV, 247
La Saussaye. *See* Dagneau; Le Coq
Lascaris. *See also* Savoie
Lascaris, Charles-Emmanuel, Marquis d'Urfé et de Baugé, II, 349
Lascaris, Joseph-Marie, Marquis d'Urfé et de Baugé, Comte de Sommerive, II, 12
Lascaris, Marguerite, Marquise d'Urfé et de Baugé. *See* Allègre
Lascaris d'Urfé, François-Saturnin, I, 599, 600, 647; II, **349–50**
Lascoret, Anne. *See* Richard
Lascore, Jean-Baptiste, III, 350; IV, 253
La Source. *See* Thaumur
Lassaigne, Anne (Chapoton), III, 102
Lassay, Marquis de. *See* Madaillan
Lasselin, Marguerite. *See* Haguenier
Lasselin, Romain, IV, 507
Lasson, Georges de, III, 455
Lataupine (La Taupine). *See* Moreau
Laterrière. *See* Fabre
La Tesserie. *See* Cailhault
La Tête Blanche. *See* Gray Lock
Latham, John, IV, 377
Latham, Robert, II, **350–51**, 37, 118, 274, 293, 487, 583, 643
La Thibaudière. *See* Denys
La Tortue. *See* Mikinak
La Touche. *See* Aulneau; Tantouin; Texier
Latouche MacCarthy, Angélique-Jeanne. *See* Guillimin
Latouche MacCarthy, Charles, III, **357–58**; IV, 10
Latouche MacCarthy, Hélène. *See* Shee
Latouche MacCarthy, Timothée, III, 357
Latour. *See also* Huguet; Jérôme; Leblond
La Tour. *See* Saint-Étienne
Latour, Bertrand de, I, 291, 551, 630; II, 259, 365, 420, 628, 629; III, 115, 223, 318, 349, 543, 549, 638, 711; IV, **439–41**, 338, 539
Latour, Catherine de. *See* Jonquières
Latour, Jean de, II, 627; IV, 141, 601
Latour, Jean-Baptiste, IV, 178
Latour, Marguerite. *See* Prud'homme
Latour, Pierre, IV, 178
Latour, Pierre de, IV, 439
La Tour d'Auvergne, Henri de, Vicomte de Turenne, I, 283, 615; II, 182, 191, 433
La Tourasse, Catherine. *See* Bugaret
La Tourasse, Charles, known as Chevalier, I, **426–27**, 361, 544, 576; II, 183
La Tourette. *See* Greysolon
La Tousche. *See also* Pézard
La Tousche, Jacques de, II, 347
La Trinité. *See* Denys; Le Moyne
La Troche. *See* Savonnières
Latuilière, Jean, IV, 433
La Tuillerie. *See* Moufle
Laubara. *See* Olabaratz
Lauberivière. *See* Pourroy

Laubia. *See* Loubias
Laubret, Catherine (Dugay), II, 202
Laubrière. *See* Lefebvre
Laud, William, I, 406
Laudonnière. *See* Goulaine
Laughton, Sir John Knox, IV, 123
Laulne, Louise de (Chambly), I, 185
Laumet, Jean, II, 351
Laumet, Jeanne. *See* Péchagut
Laumet, *dit* de Lamothe Cadillac, Antoine, I, 141, 201, 582; II, **351–57**, xxxvii, 12, 41, 48, 77, 115, 116, 119, 134, 142, 144, 163, 170, 173, 181, 183, 187, 215, 218, 229, 271, 300, 317, 318, 324, 327, 339, 386, 414, 415, 425, 453, 468, 475, 501, 505, 508, 515, 546, 547, 558, 562, 568, 569, 571, 618, 631, 635, 643, 645, 646, 647, 655; III, xxxix, 51, 66, 80, 96, 147, 258, 317, 355, 379, 381, 446, 451, 640, 643; IV, lvi
Laumet, *dit* de Lamothe Cadillac, Marie-Thérèse. *See* Guion
Laumet de Lamothe Cadillac, Antoine, II, 356
Laumet de Lamothe Cadillac, Marie-Madeleine, II, 355
Laumet de Lamothe Cadillac, Marie-Thérèse, II, 173
Launay, Alain de, III, 444, 580
Launay-Rasilly, Claude de, I, 503, 504, 567, 569, 593, 594
Launé-Jourdan, M. de, I, 607
Laure, Pierre-Michel, II, **357–58**, xxxiv, 296; III, 330; IV, 424
Laurence, Marie (Lambert), I, 396, 415
Laurent, Anne (Saillant), IV, 692
Laurent, Françoise (Corolère), III, 140
Laurent, Guillaume-Antoine, III, 140
Laurent, Nicolas, III, 222, 443
Laurent, Paul, III, **358–59**
Lauris de Castellane, Marie-Thérèse-Charlotte de (Montcalm), III, 458
Lauson, Anne. *See* Boivin
Lauson, Anne de. *See* Després
Lauson, Charles-Joseph de, II, 57
Lauson, François de, I, 427, 428
Lauson, Gilles, I, **427**
Lauson, Jean de (father), I, **427–29**, 45, 112, 145, 146, 200, 202, 203, 214, 232, 237, 245, 340, 349, 372, 401, 412, 431, 473, 475, 542, 574, 579, 580, 606; II, xvi, 84, 85, 136, 158, 639; III, 26
Lauson, Jean de (son), I, **429–31**, 274, 428, 432, 574, 665; II, xvi, 56, 92
Lauson, Marie. *See* Archambault
Lauson, Marie de. *See* Gaudar
Lauson, Marie-Catherine-Antoinette (Barrin de La Galissonière, Marquise de La Galissonière), III, 26
Lauson, Pierre, I, 427
Lauson de Charny, Charles de, I, **431–32**, 46, 91, 92, 146, 331, 400, 428, 429, 537, 579, 580, 589; II, 639
Lauson de Charny, Louise de. *See* Giffard
Lauson de La Citière, Catherine de. *See* Nau de La Boissière et de Fossambault
Lauson de La Citière, Louis de, I, 428, 542
Lauson de Lirec, François de, I, 427
Lauson de Lirec, Isabelle de. *See* Lottin
L'Autheur. *See* Descayrac
Lauverjat, Étienne, III, **359–60**, 584
Lauvrière, Émile, IV, xxi, xxvi, xxxi
Lauzières, Pons de, Marquis de Thémines, I, 193
Lauzon, Marguerite de. *See* Riot
Lauzon, Pierre de (father), III, 360

Lauzon, Pierre de, III, **360–61**, 47, 269, 329, 480, 481, 580; IV, 488

La Vaivre, Jacques de, IV, 137

Laval, Marquis de. *See* Gripière

Laval, Anne-Charlotte de, II, 359

Laval, Emme de (Montmorency, Duchesse de Montmorency), II, 359

Laval, François de (brother), II, 359

Laval, François de, I, 31, 32, 33, 42, 46, 55, 57, 72, 76, 77, 78, 80, 85, 86, 91, 92, 111, 112, 116, 117, 120, 137, 198, 202, 203, 237, 245, 249, 264, 265, 283, 284, 286, 289, 290, 291, 310, 313, 315, 321, 322, 323, 325, 326, 331, 354, 355, 356, 359, 366, 393, 414, 431, 432, 438, 466, 472, 479, 507, 534, 536, 539, 542, 554, 555, 556, 563, 580, 587, 588, 589, 590, 599, 606, 609, 610, 629, 630, 644, 646, 647, 648, 649, 651, 665; II, **358–72**, xvii, xix, 5, 18, 19, 27, 29, 30, 31, 55, 72, 79, 91, 106, 108, 134, 194, 207, 227, 234, 237, 240, 244, 248, 271, 278, 294, 303, 304, 305, 326, 328, 329, 330, 332, 335, 337, 378, 379, 383, 390, 419, 420, 421, 426, 429, 448, 460, 471, 489, 501, 521, 522, 531, 541, 561, 586, 612, 627, 637, 638, 639, 640, 642, 643, 648, 655, 657; III, 11, 47, 104, 193, 199, 201, 202, 284, 522, 546, 648, 683, 684; IV, 338, 440, 649

Laval, Gabriel de, II, 359

Laval, Guy de, II, 359

Laval, Henri de, II, 359

Laval, Hugues de (father), II, 358, 359

Laval, Hugues de, II, 360

Laval, Isabelle de, II, 359

Laval, Jean-Louis de, II, 360

Laval, Michelle de. *See* Péricard

La Valette. *See also* Nogaret

La Valette, Marie-Angélique de (Taffanel de La Jonquière, Marquise de La Jonquière), III, 609

La Valinière. *See* Huet

Lavallée. *See* Cotentin; Pâquet

Lavallée, M., IV, 425

Lavallée, Louis, III, 541

Lavallée Constantin. *See* Constantin

La Vallière. *See* Leneuf

Lavaltrie. *See* Margane

La Varenne. *See* Bonneau

La Vau, Catherine de (Barbier), II, 44

Lavaud, Jean, III, 184

La Vente. *See* Roulleaux

La Verdure. *See* Doucet; Du Tartre; Melanson

Laverdure, Mary (Basset), II, 46

La Vérenderie (La Vérendrye). *See* Gaultier

La Verge, Marguerite (Daumont de Saint-Lusson), I, 249

Lavergne, Anne. *See* Bernon

Lavergne, Françoise (Petitpas), II, 524

Lavergne, Pierre, II, 524

La Vernède de Saint-Poncy, Claude de, III, 120, 438; IV, 453

La Viazère. *See* Senau

La Vieuville, Charles, Duc de La Vieuville, I, 521

Lavigne. *See* Levasseur; Tessier

Lavillangevin. *See* Allenou

La Ville. *See* Rocquant

La Ville, Pierre-Éléonor, Marquis de Férolles, II, 270

Laviolette. *See also* Greslon

La Violette (trafficker in spirits), I, 666

Laviolette (servant), III, 310

Laviolette, M., I, **432**, 121, 127, 143

L'Avocat. *See* Havard

La Voisin. *See* Deshayes

La Vrillière, Marquis de. *See* Phélypeaux

Law, Henry, IV, 328

Law, John, II, 425; III, 20, 152, 381; IV, 665

Law, William, IV, 19

Lawrear, Elizabeth (Chase; Brookes; Veyssière), IV, 752

Lawrence, Charles, III, **361–66**, 70, 71, 87, 120, 129, 130, 174, 212, 277, 293, 295, 298, 332, 418, 457, 479, 514, 573, 583, 586, 604, 662, 663, 666, 667; IV, xxv, xxvi, xxvii, 16, 21, 51, 52, 53, 93, 94, 110, 169, 170, 216, 217, 219, 290, 291, 292, 351, 414, 527, 540, 560, 581, 631, 695, 703, 704, 724, 764, 774, 776

Lawrence, Herbert, III, 361

Lawson*, David (fl. 1769–1803), IV, 353, 551

Layssard. *See* Marafret

Lazarus, David, IV, 332

Lead, William, III, 37

Leake, Andrew, II, 373

Leake, Christian. *See* Hill

Leake, Sir John, II, **372–73**, 226, 315, 637, 659

Leake, Richard (father of JOHN), II, 372

Leake, Richard, II, 373

Lean, Alexander, IV, 525

Leau. *See* Le Moyne

Leavis, Mr, II, 564

Le Baillif, Georges, I, **433**, 160, 194, 320, 437

Le Baillif, Olivier, I, 366, 452

Le Barbier, Marie (Marsolet de Saint-Aignan; Le Maistre), I, 494

Le Baron. *See also* Auger

Le Baron, II, 321; III, 446

Le Barroys, Claude, I, 400, 617, 628, 629

Le Baudy, Catherine (Tour; Le Gouès de Sourdeval), II, 389

Lebé, Françoise. *See* Lemaître-Lamorille

Lcbé, Marie-Bernadine (Foucher), III, 227

Lebeau, Sieur, III, 676

Lebeau, Claude, II, **373–74**

Lebel, Guillaume, I, 66

Le Ber (Leber). *See also* Le Bret

Le Ber, Colette. *See* Cavelier

Le Ber, François, II, 374

Le Ber, Jacques, I, 105, 178, 284, 289, 295, 410, 416, 444, 464, 508; II, **374–76**, 29, 178, 272, 275, 377; III, 407

Le Ber, Jeanne. *See* Le Moyne

Le Ber, Jeanne, I, 117; II, **376–77**, 375; III, 407; IV, 530

Le Ber, Marie (Bourassa, *dit* La Ronde; Hervé), IV, 77

Le Ber, Marie, *dite* de l'Annonciation, II, 374, 376

Le Ber, Pierre, I, 416; II, **377–78**, 127, 133, 134, 375; III, 407

Le Ber, Robert, II, 374

Le Ber de Saint-Paul, Louis, II, 375

Le Ber de Senneville, Jacques, II, 375, 377; III, 579; IV, 54

Le Ber de Senneville, Jean, IV, 265

Le Ber de Senneville, Marie-Louise (Benoist), IV, 54

Le Ber Du Chesne, Jean-Vincent, II, 133, 375, 376, 603

Le Berger. *See* Honatteniate

Le Berre, Charles-Joseph, IV, 387

Lebert, Michelle (Pépin, *dit* Laforce), III, 571

Le Bey, Jean, II, 366

Le Blais, Charlotte (Le Courtois), IV, 443

Leblanc, Anne (Ménage), II, 467
Leblanc, Antoine, III, 366; IV, 441
Leblanc, Benjamin, IV, 78
Le Blanc, Claire (Landry), IV, 436
Leblanc, Daniel, IV, xx
Le Blanc, Élisabeth. *See* Boudrot
Le Blanc, Esther (Bourdages), IV, 78, 79
Le Blanc, Jacques, IV, 441
Le Blanc (Le Bland), Jean. *See* Outoutagan
Leblanc, Jean-Baptiste, IV, 78
Le Blanc, Joseph, IV, 441
Le Blanc, Madeleine. *See* Bourg
Le Blanc, Madeleine, *dite* La Couèche, IV, 441
Leblanc, Marguerite (Dugas), IV, 239
Le Blanc, Marie. *See* Bourgeois
Le Blanc, Marie-Anne (Paris), III, 501
Le Blanc, Marie-Madeleine. *See* Babin
Le Blanc, Marie-Marguerite (Doucet), IV, 222
Le Blanc, Noël, II, 608
Le Blanc, Pierre, III, 421
Le Blanc, Pierre, IV, **441**, xxix, 222
Leblanc, René, IV, xx, 78
Leblanc, *dit* Le Maigre, Anne. *See* Bourg, *dit* Belle-Humeur
Leblanc, *dit* Le Maigre, Joseph, III, **366–67**, 84, 255; IV, **441**, xxv, 239, 240
Le Bland, Jean. *See* Outoutagan
Leblond. *See* Jacquiés
Leblond de Latour, Antoine, II, 378
Leblond de Latour, Jacques, II, **378–80**, 338, 451; III, 648
Leblond de Latour, Marc-Antoine, II, 378
Leblond de Latour, Pierre, II, 378
Le Bloy, Françoise (Gannes de Falaise), II, 236
Lebœuf, M., II, 338
Lebon, Pierre, I, 114
Le Borgne, Chevalier, III, 232
Le Borgne, Emmanuel, I, **433–35**, 62, 90, 129, 234, 257, 258, 259, 379, 380, 468, 469, 504, 505, 514, 595, 604
Le Borgne, Jeanne. *See* François
Le Borgne, Jeanne (Bazire), I, 84
Le Borgne de Belle-Isle, Alexandre, I, **435–36**, 62, 426, 433, 434, 513, 514, 636; II, 581
Le Borgne de Belle-Isle, Alexandre (son), II, 3, 7; III, 567
Le Borgne de Belle-Isle, Anne (Rodrigue; Duperié), II, 581, 582; IV, 678
Le Borgne de Belle-Isle, Marie. *See* Saint-Étienne de La Tour
Le Borgne de Belle-Isle, Marie-Josephe (Anastasie?). *See* Abbadie de Saint-Castin
Le Borgne de Belle-Isle, Marie-Josephe (Rondeau; Du Pont Duvivier), III, 567; IV, 783
Le Borgne de l'Île. *See* Tessouat
Le Borgne Du Coudray, André, I, 436
Le Borgne Du Coudray, Emmanuel, I, 434, 435
Le Boucher, Marie (Auber), I, 72
Le Boulanger, Charlotte (Gastineau Duplessis), III, 237
Le Boulanger, Madeleine-Louise (Poulin), III, 537
Le Boulanger, Marie-Anne, III, 233
Le Boulanger, Marie-Renée (Lemoine, *dit* Despins), IV, 461, 462
Le Boulanger (Boulanger), Pierre, II, 16
Le Boullenger, Jean-Antoine, II, 455, 469
Le Bourguignon. *See* Couturier; Verreau
Leboux, Guillaume, II, 419

Le Bovier de Fontenelle, Bernard, II, 422, 595
Le Bret (Leber, Le Ber), Élisabeth (Moyen Des Granges), I, 231, 295
Le Breton, Guillaume, I, 167
Lebreton, Jeanne (Villieu), II, 653
Le Breton, Madeleine (Bernières, Baronne d'Acqueville), I, 91
Le Breton-Bastille, Guillaume, I, 167
Le Brochet. *See* Kinongé
Le Brun, M., II, 417, 418
Le Brun, François, III, 360
Le Brun, Jean, III, 550
Le Cadet. *See* Chomina
Le Cain (Le Quesne), Alicia Maria (Ritchie), IV, 675
Le Cain (Le Quesne), Francis Barclay, IV, 675
Le Camus. *See also* Camus
Le Camus, Étienne, Cardinal Le Camus, II, 328
Le Caron, Joseph, I, **436–38**, 58, 193, 222, 223, 265, 385, 386, 433, 511, 546, 590, 591, 612, 661
Lecarulier. *See* Sareillier
Le Castor. *See* Largillier
Le Cavelier, Adrienne. *See* Duvivier
Le Cavelier, Marie-Madeleine (Forestier), II, 68, 226, III, 220
Lecavelier, Toussaint, IV, 58
Le Cavelier, *dit* Deslauriers, Robert, II, 226
Lechasseur, Jean, I, 286; II, **380**, 252, 518, 529
Le Chasseur, Roger-Chrétien, III, 553; IV, 539
Lechassier, François, II, 96, 567; III, 221, 342, 486
Le Chauvreulx. *See* Chauvreulx
Le Chevalier, Jeanne-Marguerite (Lévesque; Deschamps de La Bouteillerie), II, 181
Le Chevalier Roome, John, IV, 329
Lechtier (Lechter) de Chalus, M., II, 304
Le Clair, Jean-Baptiste, II, 380
Leclair, Pierre, II, 528
Leclaire, R., I, 77
Leclerc, Alix, I, 115
Leclerc, Georges-Louis, Comte de Buffon, III, 263, 334, 679
Leclerc, Hilaire, I, 447
Leclerc, Ignace, IV, 90
Le Clerc, Jacques, II, 509; III, 352
Leclerc, Jean-Baptiste, II, **380–81**
Leclerc, Marguerite. *See* Pepin
Leclerc, Marie. *See* Jallais
Leclerc*, Michel (1762–1813), IV, 318
Leclerc, Robert, II, 380
Le Clercq, Chrestien, I, **438–41**, 14, 211, 222, 223, 265, 411, 433, 437, 509, 552, 661; II, xxxiii, 174, 197, 217, 230, 278, 396, 419, 477; III, xxxvi, 416
Le Clercq, Maxime, I, 438; II, 421
Le Cocq. *See* Le Coq
Le Cointre, Anne, *dite* de Saint-Bernard, I, 310, 347, 353
Le Collier Pendu. *See* Kaghswaghtaniunt
Lecompte, Jean, I, 267
Le Comte. *See* Lenoir
Le Comte Dupré, Georges-Hippolyte, known as Saint-Georges Dupré, III, 367; IV, **441–43**, 427, 549
Le Comte Dupré, Jean-Baptiste, III, **367**; IV, 347, 442
Le Comte* Dupré, Jean-Baptiste (1731–1820), III, 367; IV, 442
Le Comte Dupré, Marie-Anne. *See* Hervieux

Le Comte Dupré, Marie-Anne (Hertel de Saint-François), IV, 347, 348
Le Comte Dupré, Marie-Charlotte. *See* Liénard de Beaujeu
Le Comte Dupré, Marie-Louise-Charlotte. *See* La Corne
Le Comte Dupré, Pierre-Hippolyte, IV, 442
Le Comte Dupré, Thérèse (Baby), IV, 38
Le Conte, Anne. *See* Defosse
Le Conte, Charles, II, 381
Le Conte Dupré, Louis, II, **381**, 81, 131; III, 367, 390
Le Conte Dupré, Marie-Catherine. *See* Saint-Georges
Le Conte Dupré, Marie-Charlotte (Charly Saint-Ange), II, 131; III, 110
Le Coq, Robert, I, **441**
Le Coq de La Saussaye, René, I, **441–42**, 67, 68, 69, 95, 98, 101, 299, 367
L'Écossais. *See* Martin, Abraham
Lecourt, Charles, III, 524
Le Courtois, Charlotte. *See* Le Blais
Le Courtois*, François-Gabriel (d. 1828), IV, 136
Le Courtois, Thomas, IV, 443
Le Courtois de Surlaville, Michel, III, 498; IV, **443–44**, 644, 645, 655, 656, 657, 688
Lecoustre, Claude, I, 91
Le Couteur, Sarah (Mauger), IV, 525
Le Couteux, Marie (La Place), I, 338; II, 345
Le Coutre de Bourville, Élisabeth. *See* Faustin
Le Coutre de Bourville, François (father), III, 367
Le Coutre de Bourville, François, II, 226, 412; III, **367–69**, 98; IV, 15, 247, 466
Le Coutre de Bourville, Marie-Anne. *See* Rousseau de Ville-jouin
Le Creux Du Breuil, Anne. *See* Motin
Le Creux Du Breuil, Nicolas, I, **442**, 503, 514, 568, 642
Le Crochet. *See* Kiotseaeton
Ledesma, Jacques, I, 125
Lediard, Thomas, II, 662
Le Dorz, Bénin, II, **381–82**
Le Dossu d'Hébécourt, Louis-Philippe, III, 85
Ledru, Jean-Antoine, IV, **444–45**
Leduc, Anne-Françoise, *dite* Saint-Joseph, III, **369**, 238
Leduc, Catherine (Gaillard), II, 234
Leduc, Élisabeth (Guy), III, 271
Leduc, Geneviève (Cheval; Migneron), III, 121
Leduc, Jean, III, 369
Leduc, Marie. *See* Soulignié
Leduc, Marie, III, 369
Leduc, Philippe, III, 234
Leduc Des Fontaines, Jessé, II, 149, 151, 448
Le Duff, Michel-Ange, II, 382
Lee, Caroline (Haviland), IV, 334
Lee, Charles, IV, 606
Lee, Charlotte, Countess of Lichfield. *See* Fitzroy
Lee, Dorothy (Temple), I, 636
Lee, Edmund, I, 636
Lee, Edward, I, 643
Lee, Edward Henry, 1st Earl of Lichfield, III, 369
Lee, Elizabeth (Hamilton), IV, 321
Lee, Fitzroy Henry, III, **369–70**, 324
Lee, Thomas, III, 477; IV, 187
Leeds, Duke of. *See* Osborne
Lees*, John (d. 1807), IV, 317, 320
Le Fascheux de Couttes, Françoise (Lom d'Arce), II, 440
Le Faucher, M., I, 161

Lefebvre, Anne. *See* Anjoult
Lefebvre, François, III, 346
Lefebvre, Geneviève. *See* Pelletier
Lefebvre, Gervais, III, 312
Lefebvre, Hyacinthe, II, 278
Lefebvre, Jacques, II, 382, 529
Lefebvre, Jean, III, **370–71**, 38, 210, 224, 271, 280, 281, 282, 305; IV, 45, 476
Lefebvre, Jeanne. *See* Aunois
Lefebvre, Jeanne (Descaris; Tessier, *dit* Lavigne), IV, 732
Lefebvre, Marie-Anne (Poulin de Courval Cressé), III, 539
Lefebvre, Marie-Hélène (Aide-Créquy), IV, 8
Lefebvre, Marie-Madeleine (Minet; Simon; Olivier), III, 494
Lefebvre, Pierre, II, 382
Lefebvre, Thomas, II, **382**; III, 371
Lefebvre, Thomas (son), II, 382
Lefebvre, Timothée, II, 382
Lefebvre, *dit* Duchouquet, Angélique (Sanguinet), IV, 697
Lefebvre, *dit* Laciseraye, Catherine. *See* Trottier
Lefebvre, *dit* Laciseraye, Marie-Anne (Alavoine), III, 7
Lefebvre, *dit* Laciseraye, Michel, II, **382–83**
Lefebvre Angers, Geneviève-Françoise. *See* Faucher
Lefebvre Angers, Jean-Baptiste, III, 371
Lefebvre Angers, Marie-Angélique, *dite* Saint-Simon, III, **371**; IV, 638
Lefebvre Angers, Simon, III, 371
Lefebvre Belle-Isle, Marie-Josephte, *dite* Saint-Benoît, III, 630
Lefebvre de Bellefeuille, Anne. *See* Baudry
Lefebvre de Bellefeuille, Antoine, IV, 446
Lefebvre de Bellefeuille, François, III, 372; IV, **445–46**, 29
Lefebvre de Bellefeuille, Geneviève (Angeac), IV, 29
Lefebvre de Bellefeuille, Georges, III, 372; IV, 445, 446
Lefebvre de Bellefeuille, Jean-François, III, **371–72**; IV, 445
Lefebvre de Bellefeuille, Marie-Josephte. *See* Hertel de Cournoyer
Lefebvre de Bellefeuille, Pierre (uncle), III, 372
Lefebvre de Bellefeuille, Pierre, IV, 445, 446
Le Febvre de La Barre, M., known as Chevalier de La Barre, I, 446
Le Febvre de La Barre, Anne-Marie (Guillouet d'Orvilliers), II, 269, 270
Le Febvre de La Barre, Antoine, I, 442
Le Febvre de La Barre, Joseph-Antoine, I, **442–46**, 103, 105, 114, 130, 137, 178, 179, 180, 227, 295, 338, 464, 465, 488, 523, 525, 526, 541, 554, 576, 650; II, 31, 32, 48, 49, 60, 61, 63, 98, 99, 101, 112, 120, 137, 162, 169, 194, 195, 205, 214, 217, 222, 223, 228, 237, 247, 252, 253, 261, 263, 270, 282, 302, 307, 341, 343, 375, 380, 390, 401, 440, 470, 471, 472, 473, 488, 517, 518, 532, 538, 575, 576, 586, 617, 620, 624, 634, 635, 641; III, 82, 373
Le Febvre de La Barre, Madeleine. *See* Belin
Le Febvre de La Barre, Marie. *See* Mandat
Lefebvre de Laubrière, Louise (Arsac, Marquise de Ternay), IV, 31
Lefebvre-Duchouquet, Charles, IV, 639
Lefebvre Du Guesclin, Dominique, I, 409
Lefebvre Duplessis Faber, Catherine-Geneviève. *See* Pelletier

Lefebvre Duplessis Faber, François (father), II, 69, 70, 578; III, 372
Lefebvre Duplessis Faber, François, III, **372–73**, 205, 375, 505, 611, 637; IV, 77
Lefebvre Duplessis Faber, François-Hippolyte, III, 373
Lefebvre Duplessis Faber, Joseph-Alphonse, III, 373
Lefebvre Duplessis Faber, Madeleine. *See* Chorel de Saint-Romain, *dit* d'Orvilliers
Lefebvre Duplessis Faber, Pierre, III, 372
Le Fène. *See* Phlem
Le Fevre, François, II, **383**, 271
Lefèvre d'Albon, Paul, II, 270
Le Flot, Michelle (Perrot, *dit* Vildaigre), II, 520
Le Fourreur. *See* Foureur
Lefouyn, Marie-Madeleine (Dupuy), II, 207
Le Franc, Marin-Louis (Marie-Louis), IV, 241
Lefrançois, Alexis, II, 520
Lefrançois, Nicolas, II, 520
Lefrançois, Pierre, II, 520
Lefrançois de Lalande, Joseph-Jérôme, IV, 636, 637
Le Gagneur, Captain, II, 61
Le Gall, Jacques, I, 425
Le Gallois de Beaujeu, Taneguy, I, 180, 181, 182
Legardeur, Marguerite (Dubreuil), II, 201
Legardeur, Marie-Madeleine. *See* Blondeau
Legardeur de Beauvais, Louise. *See* Lamy
Legardeur de Beauvais, Madeleine. *See* Marchand
Legardeur de Beauvais, Marie-Barbe. *See* Saint-Ours
Legardeur de Beauvais, Marie-Renée (Chaussegros de Léry), III, 116; IV, 145
Legardeur de Beauvais, René, I, 650; III, **373–74**, 116, 119; IV, 463
Legardeur de Beauvais, René (son), III, 357
Le Gardeur de Courtemanche, Augustin, II, **383–84**, 7, 8, 9, 13, 17, 114, 172, 185, 218, 287, 437, 458, 459, 523, 533, 567, 575, 603, 651; III, 134, 135, 228, 429, 433
Legardeur de Courtemanche, Jacques-François, IV, 192
Legardeur de Courtemanche, Marie, IV, 192
Le Gardeur de Courtemanche, Marie-Charlotte. *See* Charest
Le Gardeur de Courtemanche, Marie-Joseph (Foucher), III, 228
Legardeur de Croisille, Charles, II, 669; III, **374**, 367; IV, 446
Legardeur de Croisille, Marie-Anne-Geneviève. *See* Robinau de Bécancour
Legardeur de Croisille et de Montesson, Claire-Françoise. *See* Boucher de Boucherville
Legardeur de Croisille et de Montesson, Joseph-Michel, III, 525; IV, **446–47**, 109, 213, 512, 651
Legardeur de La Mothe-Tilly, Jean-Baptiste, III, 376
Legardeur de La Mothe-Tilly, Jeanne-Élisabeth. *See* Girard
Legardeur de Moncarville et de Tilly. *See* Legardeur de Tilly
Legardeur de Repentigny, Agathe. *See* Saint-Père
Legardeur de Repentigny, Agathe (Bouat), II, 82
Legardeur de Repentigny, Catherine (Ailleboust Des Muceaux), I, 47, 447, II, 12, 13, 14, 421; III, 7
Legardeur de Repentigny, Catherine-Angélique. *See* Payen de Noyan et de Chavoy
Le Gardeur de Repentigny, Ignace, II, 386
Legardeur de Repentigny, Jean-Baptiste, I, 517; II, **384–85**, 27, 383, 386; III, 374
Legardeur de Repentigny, Jean-Baptiste-René, II, 156, 385; IV, 447, 448

Legardeur de Repentigny, Louis, III, 69, 119; IV, **447–48**, 449, 733
Legardeur de Repentigny, Louis-Gaspard, IV, 448
Legardeur de Repentigny, Marguerite. *See* Nicollet de Belleborne
Legardeur de Repentigny, Marguerite (Leneuf de La Poterie), I, 446, 467, 468, 575; II, 409
Legardeur de Repentigny, Marguerite (Saint-Ours Deschaillons), III, 578
Legardeur de Repentigny, Marguerite-Jeanne. *See* Mignon
Legardeur de Repentigny, Marie. *See* Favery
Legardeur de Repentigny, Marie-Catherine. *See* Juchereau de Saint-Denis
Legardeur de Repentigny, Marie-Jeanne-Madeleine, *dite* de Sainte-Agathe, II, **385**; III, 581
Legardeur de Repentigny, Marie-Joseph, *dite* de la Visitation, III, 319, 544, 581
Legardeur de Repentigny, Marie-Madeleine (Godefroy), I, 340, 447
Legardeur de Repentigny, Marie-Madeleine-Régis. *See* Chaussegros de Léry
Legardeur de Repentigny, Pierre (grandfather), I, **446–47**, 216, 287, 330, 339, 353, 402, 467, 495; II, 105, 385
Legardeur de Repentigny, Pierre, II, **385–86**, 306, 459, 655; III, 579, 581
Legardeur de Repentigny, Pierre-Jean-Baptiste-François-Xavier, III, 289, 304; IV, **448–49**, 576, 612
Legardeur de Saint-Pierre, Jacques, II, 387; III, **374–76**, 46, 48, 151, 158, 162, 178, 243, 245, 322, 331, 332, 347, 611, 623; IV, 66, 256, 363, 426, 512, 514, 617, 618
Legardeur de Saint-Pierre, Jean-Paul, II, **386–87**, 12, 317, 324, 415; III, 105, 291, 324
Legardeur de Saint-Pierre, Marguerite (Hiché), III, 291, 292
Legardeur de Saint-Pierre, Marie-Anne (Nolan Lamarque), III, 485
Legardeur de Saint-Pierre, Marie-Joseph. *See* Guillimin
Legardeur de Saint-Pierre, Marie-Josette. *See* Leneuf de La Vallière
Legardeur de Tilly, Chevalier, III, 377
Legardeur de Tilly, Anne-Geneviève. *See* Rocbert de La Morandière
Legardeur de Tilly, Armand, III, 377
Legardeur de Tilly, Catherine. *See* Cordé
Legardeur de Tilly, Catherine (Saurel), I, 602; II, 59, 593
Legardeur de Tilly, Charles, I, **447–48**, 145, 288, 402, 446, 467, 468, 581, 582, 587, 588, 602; II, 32, 125, 167, 236, 387, 584, 593; III, 373; IV, 33
Legardeur de Tilly, Françoise-Charlotte (Damours de Clignancour), II, 167
Legardeur de Tilly, Geneviève. *See* Juchereau de Maur
Legardeur de Tilly, Geneviève-Gertrude (Céloron de Blainville), II, 125
Legardeur de Tilly, Jean-Baptiste, III, **376–77**, 582
Legardeur de Tilly, Louise (Gannes de Falaise), II, 236
Legardeur de Tilly, Madeleine. *See* Boucher
Legardeur de Tilly, Madeleine-Angélique (Aubert de Gaspé), IV, 33
Legardeur de Tilly, Marguerite. *See* Volant
Legardeur de Tilly, Marguerite (Le Gouès de Grais; Saint-Ours; Le Moyne de Longueuil, Baronne de Longueuil), II, 403, 593; III, 385
Legardeur de Tilly, Marie (Berthier), II, 59
Legardeur de Tilly, Marie-Anne, III, 377

Legardeur de Tilly, Marie-Louise (Rouer de Villeray et de La Cardonnière), II, 584; III, 570
Legardeur de Tilly, Pierre-Noël, I, 448; II, **387**, 32
Legardeur de Tilly, René, I, 446, 447
Legardeur de Villiers, Charles-Pierre, II, 517
Legardeur de Villiers, Marie-Charlotte (Robinau de Bécancour, Baronne de Portneuf), II, 577; III, 374
Le Gaudier, Antoine, I, 411
Le Gauffre, Thomas, II, 361
Le Gay de Beaulieu, Jean-Jérôme, II, 127, 673
Le Gay de Beaulieu, Madeleine. *See* Just
Le Gay de Beaulieu, Marie (Migeon de La Gauchetière), III, 450
Le Gay de Beaulieu, Marie-Madeleine (Chabert de Joncaire), II, 126; III, 101; IV, 137
Legendre, Lucas, I, 293
Léger, César, I, 557
Léger, Élie, II, 387
Léger, Jeanne. *See* Félix
Léger, Louise. *See* Fauvel
Léger, Marie. *See* Des Reaux
Léger, Marie-Jeanne (Picard), IV, 628
Léger de La Grange, Jean, II, **387–88**, 17, 138, 205, 246, 531
Legge, Francis, IV, **449–52**, 29, 53, 111, 116, 132, 209, 266, 267, 274, 275, 292, 309, 389, 529, 562, 581, 603, 705, 706, 737, 764
Legge, George, 1st Baron Dartmouth, I, 92
Legge, William, 1st Earl of Darmouth, II, 583, 637
Legge, William, 2nd Earl of Dartmouth, III, 111; IV, xxxviii, xxxix, xlv, xlvi, xlvii, 175, 275, 281, 309, 321, 349, 449, 450, 451, 452, 484, 571, 607, 676, 686, 726, 737, 759, 789, 790
Le Gouès de Grais, Catherine-Charlotte (Le Moyne de Longueuil, Baronne de Longueuil), III, 385
Le Gouès de Grais, Louis-Joseph, II, 403; III, 385
Le Gouès de Grais, Marguerite. *See* Legardeur de Tilly
Le Gouès de Merville, Claude-Charles, I, 465; II, 125
Le Gouès de Sourdeval, Catherine. *See* Le Baudy
Le Gouès de Sourdeval, Sébastien, II, **388–89**, 511
Legrand, François, II, 374
Legrand, Marie, Dame Du Faradon (Normant), III, 486
Le Grand Agnier. *See* Togouiroui
Legrand de Sintré, Gabriel-Christophe, III, 102
Le Grand Sauteux. *See* Minweweh
Legras, Françoise-Élisabeth (Neveu), III, 482; IV, 709
Legras, Jean, II, 221; IV, 46
Legras, Jean-Baptiste, III, 251, 485
Legras, Marie. *See* Philippe
Legras, Marie-Anne (Delaunay), II, 173
Legras, Marie-Anne (Hertel de Rouville), IV, 653
Legras, Marie-Catherine (Barsalou; Guillet de Chaumont), III, 270; IV, 46
Legris, Marguerite (Bourdon), II, 92
Le Gros, Marie-Thérèse (Lorit, *dit* Gargot), II, 447
Legu, *dit* La Noue, Jean-Baptiste, IV, 748
Leguay, François, IV, 534
Le Guerne, François, III, 425; IV, **452–53**
Le Guerne, Yves, IV, 452
Le Guet (Du Guay), Abbé, IV, 452
Le Guettier, Jean-Charles, III, 410
Le Héricy, Guillaume, I, 89
Lehoulier, Dorothée. *See* Fabre, *dit* Laterrière

Le Hour, Marie (Chaboulié), II, 127
Lehoux, Anne (Robidoux), III, 279
Leibniz, Gottfried Wilhelm, II, 443, 444
Leifr *heppni* Eiriksson (Leif the Lucky), I, **448–49**, 17, 104, 612, 642, 643, 676
Leigh, Charles, I, **449–52**, 391, 392, 409
Leigh, Joan. *See* Oliph
Leigh, John, I, 449
Leigh, Olyph, I, 452
Leigne. *See* André
Leisler, Jacob, I, 586
Le Jardinier. *See* Voyer
Le Jeune, Olivier, I, **452**, 366
Le Jeune, Paul, I, **453–58**, 70, 120, 122, 123, 124, 126, 143, 159, 164, 186, 197, 203, 205, 207, 214, 215, 287, 310, 341, 348, 404, 412, 432, 452, 473, 481, 482, 487, 494, 516, 517, 518, 527, 533, 549, 563, 633, 637, 661, 665, 673; II, 85
Le Jumeau, Renée, II, 490
Leleu, Norbertine (Hennepin), II, 277
Le Loutre, Jean-Louis, III, 29, 34, 120, 128, 136, 165, 183, 196, 295, 298, 332, 358, 362, 363, 415, 417, 425, 438; IV, **453–58**, xxiv, 36, 62, 93, 169, 170, 253, 256, 257, 289, 290, 452, 630, 636, 637
Le Loutre Després, Catherine. *See* Huet
Le Loutre Després, Jean-Maurice, IV, 453
Le Maigre. *See* Leblanc
Lemaire, Abbé, III, 120, 166
Le Maire, François, III, 639
Le Maire, Madeleine (Philippe(s) de Hautmesnil de Mandeville), II, 525
Lemaire, *dit* Saint-Germain, Venance, IV, 277
Le Maistre, Denis, I, 495
Le Maistre*, Francis (d. 1805), IV, 180
Le Maistre, Jacques, I, **458**, 525, 612, 662
Le Maistre, Marie. *See* Le Barbier
Lemaître, Bertrane. *See* Michelle
Lemaître, François, III, 263
Lemaître, François (father of François LEMAÎTRE, *dit* Jugon), III, 377
Lemaître, *dit* Jugon, François, III, **377–78**
Lemaître, *dit* Jugon, Jean, III, 377
Lemaître, *dit* Jugon, Marie. *See* Collet
Le Maître Duaime, François, IV, 317
Lemaître-Lamorille, François, I, 553
Lemaître-Lamorille, Françoise (Lebé; Guillimin), II, 268; IV, 318, 319
Lemaître-Lamorille, Marguerite. *See* Poulin de La Fontaine
Lemaître-Lamorille, Marie-Anne (Gamelin), IV, 286
Le Marchand de Lignery, Anne. *See* Robutel de La Noue
Le Marchand de Lignery, Constant, II, 316, 316, 386, 475, 503, 529, 547, 563, 569; III, 43, 80, 81, 103, 245, 329, 378, 402; IV, 180, 463, 651, 663, 732
Le Marchand de Lignery, François-Marie, II, 39; III, **378–79**, 158, 219, 535, 536; IV, 396, 513, 670, 733
Le Marchand de Lignery, Joseph, II, 389
Le Marchand de Lignery, Marguerite. *See* Du Sillar
Le Marchand de Lignery, Marie-Thérèse. *See* Migeon de La Gauchetière
Le Marchand de Lignery, Marie-Ursule. *See* Aubert de La Chesnaye
Le Marchant, Jeanne (Leneuf), I, 340, 467
Le Marié, Guillaume, I, 167

Lemarinier, Catherine (Dubreuil), II, 201
Le Meilleur, Jacques, II, 241
Lemelin, Jeanne (Moore), II, 487
Lemer (Lemaire), Nicole (Boucher), II, 82, 83
Le Mercier, Andrew, III, 135
Le Mercier, Charlotte. *See* Le Rebours
Le Mercier, Françoise. *See* Boucher de La Bruère
Le Mercier, François-Joseph, I, **458–60**, 108, 125, 212, 244, 255, 461, 552, 562, 563; II, 139
Le Mercier, François-Marc-Antoine, III, xix, 537; IV, **458–61**, 211, 227, 382, 616, 641
Le Mercier, Marie. *See* Du Jardin
Le Mercier, Nicolas-François, IV, 458
Le Mercier, Paul, I, 458
Le Mercier de La Rivière de Saint-Médard, Pierre-Paul, IV, 65
Lemieux, Élisabeth. *See* Franquelin
Lemieux, Joseph, II, 230
Le Minime. *See* Barbier
Lemire, Jean, I, **460**, 589; II, 120, 506
Lemire, Louise. *See* Marsolet
Lemire, Marie-Anne (Catalogne), II, 120, 122
Lemire-Marsolais, Darie-Aurélie, *dite* Sainte-Henriette, III, 719, IV, 830
Lemire Marsolet, Jean, IV, 732
Le Moine*, Sir James MacPherson (1825–1912), III, 143, 305
Lemoine, Jean, II, 236; III, 379
Lemoine, Madeleine. *See* Chavigny de Berchereau
Lemoine, Marguerite (Gamelin), II, 236; IV, 283
Lemoine, Marie-Louise. *See* Zemballe
Lemoine, *dit* Despins, Marie-Renée. *See* Le Boulanger
Lemoine, *dit* Despins, René-Alexandre, III, 379; IV, 5, 461, 462
Lemoine, *dit* Monière, Alexis, III, **379**, 233, 477; IV, 11, 461, 621
Lemoine, *dit* Monière, Marie-Josephte. *See* Couagne
Lemoine, *dit* Monière, Marie-Marguerite (Pennisseaut; Fresnoy; Fontanille), IV, 621, 622
Lemoine, *dit* Monière, Pierre-Alexis, III, 379, 477
Lemoine Despins, Jacques-Alexis, IV, 461
Lemoine Despins, Jacques-Joseph, IV, **461–62**, 5, 67, 125, 148, 435, 592, 750
Lemoine Despins, Jean-Baptiste (uncle), IV, 7, 125
Lemoine Despins, Jean-Baptiste, IV, 461
Lemoine Despins, Marguerite. *See* Guillon
Lemoine Despins, Marguerite (Adhémar), IV, 5
Lemoine Despins, Marguerite-Charlotte. *See* Rocbert de La Morandière
Lemoine Despins, Marguerite-Thérèse, **462–63**, 238, 508
Lemoisin, Louis, III, 65
Lemonnier, Louis-Guillaume, III, 30
Lemonnier, Pierre-Charles, III, 30
Lemort, Anne. *See* Dubois
Lemort, Jacques, I, 535
Le Moyne, Anne (Messier), II, 469
Le Moyne, Élisabeth (Rémy), II, 561
Le Moyne, Jeanne (Le Ber), II, 375, 376, 377
Le Moyne, Judith. *See* Du Chesne
Le Moyne, Pierre, I, 463
Le Moyne, Simon, I, **460–62**, 10, 66, 70, 130, 206, 244, 295, 307, 315, 322, 414, 429, 458, 502, 523, 525, 563; II, xxxiv, 282, 624, 625

Le Moyne d'Assigny, Nicolas, IV, 765
Le Moyne de Bienville, François, I, **463**; II, 392; III, 379
Le Moyne de Bienville, Jean-Baptiste, I, 463; II, xxviii, 67, 203, 204, 215, 259, 260, 267, 306, 349, 355, 396, 408, 425, 428, 455, 457, 513, 525, 636, 646, 653; III, **379–84**, xxxiii, 36, 40, 99, 148, 150, 317, 423, 424, 503, 626; IV, li, 54, 137, 315, 633, 663, 664
Le Moyne de Châteauguay, Antoine, II, 408
Le Moyne de Châteauguay, Louis, I, **463**; II, 394, 407, 513
Le Moyne de Leau, Nicolas, III, 581
Le Moyne de Longueuil, Catherine-Charlotte, Baronne de Longueuil. *See* Le Gouès de Grais
Le Moyne de Longueuil, Charles, Baron de Longueuil (father), I, 464; II, **401–3**, xxxvi, 87, 112, 126, 389, 404, 503, 567, 573, 598; III, 42, 43, 76, 159, 217, 245, 328, 384, 385, 568, 649; IV, 41, 235, 463
Le Moyne de Longueuil, Charles, Baron de Longueuil, (son), II, 403; III, **384–85**, 5, 21, 47, 378, 383, 612; IV, 148, 237, 256, 265, 268, 296, 407, 476, 633, 662, 692, 729
Le Moyne de Longueuil, Charles-Jacques, Baron de Longueuil, IV, 268, 269
Le Moyne de Longueuil, Claude-Élisabeth, Baronne de Longueuil. *See* Souart d'Adoucourt
Le Moyne de Longueuil, Joseph, II, 403
Le Moyne* de Longueuil, Joseph-Dominique-Emmanuel (1738–1807), IV, 346, 347, 464, 634
Le Moyne de Longueuil, Louise. *See* Prud'homme
Le Moyne de Longueuil, Marguerite, Baronne de Longueuil. *See* Legardeur de Tilly
Le Moyne de Longueuil, Marie-Anne (Bouillet de La Chassaigne), II, 87
Le Moyne de Longueuil, Marie-Anne-Catherine, Baronne de Longueuil. *See* Fleury Deschambault
Le Moyne de Longueuil, Marie-Catherine (Tarieu de La Naudière), IV, 729
Le Moyne* de Longueuil, Marie-Charles-Joseph, Baronne de Longueuil (Grant) (1756–1846), IV, 269
Le Moyne de Longueuil, Marie-Geneviève. *See* Joybert de Soulanges
Le Moyne de Longueuil, Paul-Joseph, known as Chevalier de Longueuil, III, 49, 451, 495, 496, 600; IV, **463–65**, 146, 150, 368, 582, 651
Le Moyne de Longueuil et de Châteauguay, Catherine. *See* Thierry
Le Moyne de Longueuil et de Châteauguay, Catherine-Jeanne (Payen de Noyan), II, 513; III, 502; IV, 611
Le Moyne de Longueuil et de Châteauguay, Charles, I, **463–65**, 103, 105, 225, 231, 271, 287, 289, 295, 319, 322, 444, 445, 507, 508, 555; II, xvii, 29, 253, 375, 390, 397, 401, 403, 405, 406, 469, 508, 536, 581, 624; III, 379, 580
Le Moyne de Maricourt, Gabrielle-Françoise. *See* Aubert de La Chesnaye
Le Moyne de Maricourt, Marie-Madeleine. *See* Dupont de Neuville
Le Moyne de Maricourt, Paul, I, 465, 653; II, **403–5**, xxxvi, 20, 34, 107, 114, 126, 160, 205, 391, 394, 401, 402, 621, 622, 631; III, 192, 407
Le Moyne de Martigny, Félicité-Élisabeth. *See* Bailly de Messein
Le Moyne de Martigny, Jacques, IV, 43
Le Moyne de Martigny et de La Trinité, Jacques, II, 405, 406

Le Moyne de Martigny et de La Trinité, Jean-Baptiste, II, **405–6**, 298, 302
Le Moyne de Martigny et de La Trinité, Marie-Élisabeth. *See* Guyon Durouvray
Le Moyne de Sainte-Hélène, Catherine (Robutel de La Noue), II, 581
Le Moyne de Sainte-Hélène, Jacques, I, **465–67**, 463, 545, 653; II, 13, 391, 392, 401, 403, 482, 581, 608; III, 245, 586
Le Moyne de Sainte-Hélène, Jacques (son), I, 466
Le Moyne de Sainte-Hélène, Jeanne. *See* Dufresnoy Carion
Le Moyne de Sainte-Hélène, Marie-Jeanne (Gaultier de Varennes), III, 245
Le Moyne de Sainte-Marie, Catherine (Robutel de La Noue), III, 581
Le Moyne de Sainte-Marie, Françoise, III, 385
Le Moyne de Sainte-Marie, Jacques, II, 405, 470; III, 385, 580
Le Moyne de Sainte-Marie, Marguerite, *dite* du Saint-Esprit, III, **385–86**
Le Moyne de Sainte-Marie, Mathurine. *See* Godé
Le Moyne de Serigny, M., Chevalier de Loire, II, 408
Le Moyne de Serigny et de Loire, Élisabeth-Catherine (Rigaud de Vaudreuil, Marquise de Vaudreuil), III, 557
Le Moyne de Serigny et de Loire, Joseph, I, 463; II, **406–8**, 203, 298, 394, 395, 398, 403, 513; III, 557
Le Moyne de Serigny et de Loire, Marie-Élisabeth. *See* Héron
Le Moyne d'Iberville, François-Jean, II, 399
Le Moyne d'Iberville, Jean-Baptiste, II, 399
Le Moyne d'Iberville, Jean-Charles, II, 399
Le Moyne d'Iberville, Marie-Thérèse, II, 399
Le Moyne d'Iberville, Pierre-Joseph-Louis, II, 399
Le Moyne d'Iberville et d'Ardillières, Marie-Thérèse. *See* Pollet de La Combe-Pocatière
Le Moyne d'Iberville et d'Ardillières, Pierre, I, 26, 61, 80, 179, 227, 308, 339, 361, 400, 463, 465, 493, 529, 547, 551, 577, 582, 611, 641, 649, 653; II, **390–401**, 6, 36, 42, 50, 62, 65, 116, 140, 145, 167, 169, 177, 197, 203, 227, 228, 231, 232, 246, 257, 265, 266, 271, 298, 302, 303, 305, 306, 307, 311, 319, 349, 354, 355, 387, 403, 405, 406, 407, 408, 417, 421, 427, 428, 446, 449, 450, 454, 458, 479, 487, 495, 510, 513, 534, 581, 589, 590, 605, 608, 626, 635, 636, 654, 666; III, 42, 81, 176, 317, 380, 414, 450, 454, 469, 470, 488, 599
Leneuf, Jeanne. *See* Le Marchant
Leneuf, Marie (Godefroy de Lintot), I, 340, 467; II, 252, 253
Leneuf, Mathieu, I, 340, 467
Leneuf de Beaubassin, M., IV, 588
Leneuf de Beaubassin, Marguerite (Poulin de Courval), III, 539
Leneuf de Beaubassin, Marie-Charlotte. *See* Daccarrette
Leneuf de Beaubassin, Philippe, II, 412; III, 157; IV, 28, 245, 246, 588
Leneuf de La Poterie, Catherine (Denys de La Ronde), I, 418; II, 33, 174, 176, 178, 224, 545; III, 176
Leneuf de La Poterie, Jacques, I, **467**, 60, 186, 446, 467, 468, 575, 589; II, 16, 83, 84, 168, 174, 178, 272, 409
Leneuf de La Poterie, Marguerite. *See* Legardeur de Repentigny
Leneuf de La Poterie, Marie-Anne (Robinau de Bécancour, Baronne de Portneuf), I, 467, 575, 576; II, 577, 579

Leneuf de La Vallière, Jacques, II, 410
Leneuf de La Vallière, Judith (Villieu), II, 654
Leneuf de La Vallière, Louis, II, 412; III, 34; IV, 455
Leneuf de La Vallière, Marie-Josette (Legardeur de Saint-Pierre), II, 387; III, 374
Leneuf de La Vallière, Michel, IV, 252
Leneuf de La Vallière et de Beaubassin, Alexandre, I, 90; II, **408–9**, 180, 235, 287, 388, 410, 452, 495, 543; III, 596; IV, 764
Leneuf de La Vallière et de Beaubassin, Barbe (Aubert Duforillon), III, 22, 291
Leneuf de La Vallière et de Beaubassin, Barbe (Delort; Rousseau de Villejouin), IV, 689
Leneuf de La Vallière et de Beaubassin, Françoise. *See* Denys de La Trinité
Leneuf de La Vallière et de Beaubassin, Marguerite (Gannes de Falaise), II, 236; III, 235; IV, 688
Leneuf de La Vallière et de Beaubassin, Marie. *See* Denys
Leneuf de La Vallière et de Beaubassin, Michel (father), I, 90, 258, 260, 396, 399, 467; II, **409–11**, 32, 71, 94, 236, 272, 387, 408, 477, 629, 630, 654; III, 22
Leneuf de La Vallière et de Beaubassin, Michel (son), II, **411–12**; III, 454; IV, 689
Leneuf de La Vallière et de Beaubassin, Renée. *See* Bertrand
Leneuf Du Hérisson, Anne, *dite* Du Hérisson (Desrosiers), I, 468
Leneuf Du Hérisson, Michel, I, **467–68**, 340, 550; II, xvi, 85, 86, 252, 253
Lennox, Charles, 2nd Duke of Richmond, Lennox, and Aubigny, III, 405
Lennox, John, IV, 427
Lennox, Marie-Marguerite. *See* La Corne
Le Nobletz, M., II, 414
Lenoir, Claudine (wife of ROLLAND), II, 412
Lenoir, Marie (Chartier), I, 202
Lenoir, Marie-Joseph (Cirier), IV, 151
Lenoir, Rolland, II, 412
Lenoir, Vincent, III, 316; IV, 151
Lenoir, *dit* Le Comte, Gilles, III, 398
Lenoir, *dit* Rolland, François, I, 47; II, **412–13**, 271
Lenoir, *dit* Rolland, Gabriel, II, 173
Lenoir, *dit* Rolland, Marie-Joseph. *See* Delaunay
Lenoir, *dit* Rolland, Marie-Madeleine. *See* Charbonner
Lenoir de Rouvray, Laurent-François, IV, 187
Le Normand, Suzanne (Huppé, *dit* Lagroix), IV, 376
Le Normant, Ange, III, 386
Le Normant, Claude-Madeleine. *See* Gourdan
Le Normant de Mézy, Anne-Marie. *See* Debrier
Le Normant de Mézy, Élisabeth. *See* Lescoffier
Le Normant de Mézy, Jacques-Ange, II, 255, 292, 582, 612, 649; III, **386–89**, 98, 264, 396, 455, 456, 512, 532, 567, 574, 575, 576, 644; IV, 465
Le Normant de Mézy, Marie-Louise-Augustine. *See* Salignac
Le Normant de Mézy, Sébastien-François-Ange, III, 98, 264, 357, 387, 389, 455, 567, 576, 644; IV, **465–68**, 60, 61, 67, 252, 253, 254, 255, 420, 665, 668
Le Normant d'Étioles, Jeanne-Antoinette. *See* Poisson
Lens, Bernard, III, 624
Lent, Catherine (McCarty; McDougall), IV, 494
Leonard*, George (1742–1826), IV, 328
Léonard d'Auxerre, Father, I, 129
Léonard de Chartres, I, **468–69**, 434

Leopold Eberhard, Prince of Montbéliard, II, 424
Lepage, Geneviève (La Frenaye), I, 409
Lepage, Marie-Rogère (Peuvret Demesnu), I, 543
Lepage, René, II, 305, 584
Le Page, *dit* Chaudron, M., I, 425
Lepage de Saint-Barnabé, Pierre, III, 99
Lepage de Sainte-Claire, Louis, II, 81, 153; III, **390–91**, 122, 285, 522, 593; IV, 11, 356, 358, 359, 361, 690, 779
Lepage de Sainte-Claire, Marie-Madeleine. *See* Gagnon
Lepage de Sainte-Claire, René, III, 390
Le Page Du Pratz, Antoine-Simon, II, 598, 653
Lepallieur, Jean, II, 413
Lepallieur, Marie. *See* Lamotte
Lepallieur de Laferté, Catherine. *See* Jérémie, *dit* Lamontagne
Lepallieur de Laferté, Catherine (Adhémar), III, 4
Lepallieur de Laferté, François-Michel, II, 413; III, 500
Lepallieur de Laferté, Marie-Louise (Lorimier de La Rivière), III, 408
Lepallieur de Laferté, Michel, II, **413–14**, xxiv, 164, 297; III, 4, 314, 315, 347, 408, 473
Le Pape Du Lescöat, Jean-Gabriel-Marie, II, **414**; III, 169; IV, 235
Lepellé, Antoine, II, 252
Lepellé, Françoise (Vauvril; Godefroy de Saint-Paul), II, 252
Le Pers, Jean-Baptiste, III, 107
Lépervanche. *See* Mézières
Le Pesant, II, **414–15**, xxxiii, xxxvii, 12, 173, 317, 318, 324, 354, 386, 475, 505, 506; III, 576
Le Piat. *See* Piat
Le Picard. *See also* Olivier
Le Picard, Anne (Oriol; Ailleboust Des Muceaux), II, 14; IV, 11
Le Picard, Jean, II, 276; III, 642
Le Picard, Joseph, III, 642, 643
Le Picard, Marie-Anne (Barbel), II, 42; III, 642; IV, 44
Le Picard, Marie-Catherine (Véron de Grandmesnil), III, 642
Le Picard de Letéland Du Mesnil, Louis, II, 417
Le Picard de Norrey, Auguste-Philippe, II, 415
Le Picard de Norrey, Louis, II, 416
Le Picard de Norrey, Madeleine. *See* Gédouin
Le Picard Du Mesnil de Norrey, Jacques, II, **415–17**, 520
Le Picard Du Mesnil de Norrey, Marie-Renée. *See* Chorel de Saint-Romain, *dit* d'Orvilliers
Le Picart, Pierre, IV, 338
Lépine, *dit* Lalime, Joseph, III, 142
Lépine, *dit* Lalime, Marie. *See* Roy
Le Pippre. *See* Lamorel
Le Poitevin. *See* Paillard
Le Pont. *See* Gravé Du Pont
Le Porc-épic. *See* Noro
Le Poupet de La Boularderie, Antoine, II, 417; III, 475; IV, **468–69**, 644, 645
Le Poupet de La Boularderie, Éléonore-Jeanne. *See* Beaugny
Le Poupet de La Boularderie, Louis-Simon, II, **417–18**, 38; III, 177; IV, 252, 468
Le Poupet de La Boularderie, Madeleine. *See* Melançon
Le Poupet de La Boularderie, Marie-Madeleine (Mazière), II, 417
Le Poupet de Saint-Aubin, Antoine, II, 417
Le Poupet de Saint-Aubin, Jacqueline. *See* Arnoulet

Le Prestre de Vauban, Sébastien, I, 664; II, 230, 337, 649; III, 117, 190, 645
Le Prévost, Jacques, III, 391
Le Prévost, Jeanne. *See* Fauvault
Le Prévost, Pierre-Gabriel, II, 379; III, **391–92**
Le Prévost Duquesnel, Jean-Baptiste-Louis, III, **392–93**, 93, 94, 175, 182, 236, 288, 368, 416, 609, 645; IV, 56, 60, 61, 62, 83, 247, 253, 254, 588, 643
Le Prévost Duquesnel, Marguerite. *See* Girault Du Poyet
Le Prince, Marie-Barbe (Beaumont), IV, 631
Le Proust, Jean, III, 430
Le Quesne. *See* Le Cain
Le Rageois de Bretonvilliers, Alexandre, I, 540, 600
Le Raisin. *See* Chomina
Le Rat. *See* Kondiaronk
Lereau, Marie (Buisson), II, 108
Le Rebours, Charlotte (Le Mercier), IV, 458
Leriger de La Plante, Marie-Catherine (Bourassa, *dit* La Ronde), IV, 77
Lerole. *See* Canchy
Le Rouge, Jean, I, 619, 664; II, **418–19**, 338; III, 306
Le Rouge, Jeanne. *See* Poitevin
Le Rouge, Jeanne (Couton), III, 144; IV, 172
Leroux*, Laurent (d. 1855), IV, 310
Le Roux, Louise (Olivier), IV, 590
Le Roux, Thomas-François, IV, **469–70**, 81, 444
Leroux, Valentin, I, 439, 440; II, **419**, 174, 222, 335, 420, 421
Lcroux-Duplessis. *See* Robreau
Le Roy, Catherin, II, 424
Le Roy, Henri, I, 265; II, **419–21**
Le Roy, Jacques, IV, 252
Le Roy, Jeanne-Marie. *See* Boyat
Le Roy, Marguerite (Champlain), I, 186
Le Roy, Marguerite (Durocher), III, 210
Le Roy, Marie (Paumart), I, 534
Le Roy, Marie (Regnard Duplessis), II, 561; III, 547, 549
Le Roy, Olive. *See* King, Willobe
Le Roy de La Potherie, Charles-Auguste, II, 422
Le Roy de La Potherie, Élisabeth. *See* Saint-Ours
Le Roy de La Potherie, Marc-René-Augustin, II, 422
Le Roy de La Potherie, Pierre-Denis, II, 422
Le Roy de La Potherie, *dit* Bacqueville de La Potherie, Claude-Charles, I, 40, 77, 112, 249, 522, 611; II, **421–23**, xxviii, 64, 87, 114, 127, 143, 162, 297, 322, 323, 379, 483, 486, 494, 499, 504, 517, 519, 533, 546, 593, 618, 624; III, xxxiii, 308, 309, 310, 311
Le Roy de La Potherie de Bacqueville, Charles-Auguste, II, 421
Le Roy de La Potherie de Bacqueville, Françoise. *See* Du Sicquet d'Esmainville
Le Roy Desmarest, Claude-Joseph, II, **424**; III, 172, 396, 397; IV, 420
Le Roy Desmarest, Marie-Suzanne. *See* La Bazanière
Le Royer de La Dauversière, Jeanne. *See* Baugé
Le Royer de La Dauversière, Jérôme (father), I, 214
Le Royer de La Dauversière, Jérôme, I, 31, 109, 213, 214, 216, 218, 219, 220, 221, 412, 454, 457, 478, 480, 485, 487, 512, 648; II, 489, 490, 491; III, 395
Le Royer de La Dauversière, Joseph, I, 214
Le Royer de La Dauversière, Renée (Marie). *See* Oudin
Léry. *See also* Chaussegros
Léry, Jean de, I, 469

Lesage, Alain-René, II, 142

Le Saulniers*, Candide (1756–1830), IV, 90

Le Sauvage. *See* Normandin

Lescarbot, Claude, I, 471

Lescarbot, Françoise. *See* Valpergue

Lescarbot, Marc, I, **469–72**, 12, 28, 64, 67, 69, 72, 95, 96, 97, 98, 99, 170, 188, 189, 197, 198, 292, 293, 294, 300, 307, 346, 367, 500, 501, 526, 527, 564, 568, 591, 604; II, 429; III, 337

Lescarbot, Marc (probably nephew), I, 471

Lescöat (Lescouat). *See* Le Pape

Lescoffier, Élisabeth (Letellier; Le Normant de Mézy), IV, 467

Lescot (Lescault), Marie (Boutroue d'Aubigny). I, 120

Lesdiguières, Duchesse de. *See* Rochechouart

Le Selle, Jeanne (Estienne Du Bourgué Du Clérin), II, 221

Leslye, William, IV, 564

Lesparre. *See* Madaillan

L'Espérance. *See also* Aubuchon; Lalonde; Levasseur; Magnan

L'Espérance, Baronne de. *See* Curie

L'Espérance, M., III, 308

Lespérance, M. (merchant), II, 492

L'Espérance, Anne-Claire de. *See* Du Pont de Renon

L'Espérance, Charles-Gabriel-Sébastien de, Baron de L'Espérance, II, 424; IV, **470–71**, 29, 679

L'Espérance, Charles-Léopold-Ébérard de, II, **424–25**; IV, 470

L'Espérance, Jeanne-Françoise de. *See* Rodrigue

L'Espérance, Marguerite de. *See* Dangeac

Lespinay. *See also* Couillard

Lespinay, Hutin de, I, 425

Lespinay, Jean-Michel de, II, **425–26**; III, 381

Lespinay, Marie de. *See* Caulincourt

Lespinay, Nicolas de, I, 423, 425

Lessard, Étienne de, II, **426**

Lessard, Marguerite de. *See* Sevestre

Lessard, Marie-Thérèse de (Langlois), III, 348

Lesseps, Jean-Baptiste-Barthélemy de, Baron de Lesseps, IV, 283

Lestage, Esther de. *See* Sayward

Lestage, Jean de (father), III, 393

Lestage, Jean de, III, 393, 394

Lestage, Joseph-Alphonse, III, 426

Lestage, Marie de, III, 394

Lestage, Marie-Madeleine de. *See* Rivet

Lestage, Pierre de (farmer), III, 394

Lestage (Lestage Desperoux), Pierre de, II, 69, 463, 509, 602; III, **393–94**, 253, 307, 353, 491; IV, 356, 357, 360

Lestage, Saubade de. *See* Noliboise

L'Estang. *See* Petit

Lester*, Benjamin (1724–1802), IV, 159, 712

Lester, Isaac, IV, 159, 712, 713

L'Estobec de Langristain, Marie-Gabrielle-Élisabeth (Prevost), IV, 643

L'Estrange, Elizabeth (Cosby), III, 143

Lestringant, Anne de. *See* Jacquier

Lestringant, Nicolas de, II, 426

Lestringant de Saint-Martin, Alexandre-Joseph, II, **426–27**; III, 22

Lestringant de Saint-Martin, Louise-Madeleine. *See* Juchereau de Saint-Denis

Lestringant de Saint-Martin, Madeleine-Thérèse, II, 427

Lestringant de Saint-Martin, Marie-Anne-Josette (Montéléon; Aubert de La Chesnaye), II, 90, 427; III, 22

Le Sueur, Anne. *See* Honneur

Le Sueur, Jacques-François, III, **394–95**

Le Sueur, Jean, known as Abbé de Saint-Sauveur, I, **472**, 111, 112, 310, 339; II, 82, 158, 366

Le Sueur, Jean-Paul, II, 428

Le Sueur, Marguerite. *See* Messier

Le Sueur, Pierre (priest), III, **395–96**, 369; IV, 201

Le Sueur, Pierre (trader), II, **427–29**, 180, 230, 508, 589; III, 493

Le Sueur, Victor, II, 427

Le Suisse. *See* Miville

Leszczyńska, Marie. *See* Marie Leszczyńska, Queen of France

Le Tac, Xiste, II, **429–30**, 175, 244

Le Talon, II, 504

Letancour, Sieur de. *See* Decoste, Jean-Baptiste

L'Étang. *See* Douhet

Letardif, Barbe. *See* Esmard

Letardif, Louise. *See* Couillard

Letardif, Olivier, I, **473**, 72, 163, 344, 452, 517, 518, 554; II, 27, 158

Letartre, Élisabeth (Pagé, *dit* Carcy), III, 498

Letéland Du Mesnil. *See* Le Picard

Letellier, Élisabeth. *See* Lescoffier

Le Tellier, François-Michel, Marquis de Louvois, I, 535

L'Étendard. *See* Dandane

Letendre, Geneviève (Pelletier; Volant de Radisson), II, 655

L'Étenduère, Marquis de. *See* Des Herbiers

Le Tort, Jacques, III, 65

Le Tort, James, III, 65

Letourneau. *See* Siginakee

Létourneau, Jean, IV, 172

Létourneau, Marie. *See* Rateau

Létourneau, Michel, IV, 629

Leuduger, Jean, III, 10; IV, 95

Le Valois, Father, II, 328

Le Vasseur, M., I, 423, 425

Levasseur, Angélique. *See* Juste

Levasseur, Anne. See Ménage

Levasseur, Anne-Félicité (Hamel), I, 474

Levasseur, Anne-Thérèse (Fornel), III, 222, 224

Levasseur, Charles, III, 397, 398

Levasseur, Élisabeth-Françoise (Ferrand), IV, 354

Levasseur, François-Noël, II, 431; III, 397; IV, **471–73**, 475

Levasseur, G. (cartographer), I, 188

Levasseur, Geneviève. *See* Grange

Levasseur, Geneviève, III, 238

Levasseur, Guillaume, IV, xvii

Levasseur, Jeanne (Rouillard), III, 572

Levasseur, Louis (son of Jean LEVASSEUR, *dit* Lavigne), I, 473

Levasseur, Louis (father of LOUIS), III, 396

Levasseur, Louis, III, **396–97**, 172, 389, 575

Levasseur, Louis-Armand, IV, 354, 473

Levasseur, Madeleine. *See* Chapeau

Levasseur, Madeleine. *See* Vilers

Levasseur, Marguerite. *See* Bélanger

Levasseur, Marguerite. *See* Guay

Levasseur, Marguerite (Lamarre), II, 339

Levasseur, Marie-Agnès. *See* Lajoüe

Levasseur, Marie-Anne. *See* Lorent

Levasseur, Marie-Anne (Hillaire de La Rochette), IV, 353
Levasseur, Marie-Claude (Cotté), IV, 171
Levasseur, Marie-Françoise-Renée (Martin), III, 435
Levasseur, Marie-Geneviève. *See* Côté
Levasseur, Marie-Madeleine. *See* Turpin
Levasseur, Michel, II, **430**; III, 498, 499
Levasseur, Noël (father), I, 473; II, 430
Levasseur, Noël, I, 473, 474; II, **430–32**, 127; III, 397, 648;
IV, 471, 475, 535, 649
Levasseur, Pierre (father of Pierre-Noël), II, 467; III, 397
Levasseur, Pierre (son of René-Nicolas), IV, 474, 475
Levasseur, Pierre-Noël, I, 474; II, 200, 337, 431; III,
397–98; IV, 471, 472
Levasseur, Pierre-Noël (son), III, 398
Levasseur, René-Nicolas, III, 139, 435, 539, 540, 612; IV,
473–75, 354, 361, 620
Levasseur, Stanislas, III, 398
Levasseur, Thérèse, III, 172
Levasseur, Ursule (Roger), II, 582
Levasseur, *dit* Delor, Jean-Baptiste-Antoine, II, 431; III,
397; IV, **475–76**, 471, 472
Levasseur, *dit* Delor, Marie-Régis. *See* Cartier
Levasseur, *dit* Lavigne, Jean, I, **473–74**, 645; II, xvi, 430;
III, 397; IV, 471
Levasseur, *dit* Lavigne, Marguerite. *See* Richard
Levasseur, *dit* L'Éspérance, Jeanne. *See* Chaverlange
Levasseur, *dit* L'Espérance, Pierre, I, **474**, 225; III, 397; IV,
471
Levasseur de Neré, Jacques, II, **432–33**, 121, 229, 337, 553,
559, 569, 578; III, 190
Levasseur de Neré, Marie-Françoise. *See* Chavenault
Léveillé, M., IV, 592
Léveillé, Mathieu, III, **398–99**, 279
Le Veneur, Jean, I, 165
Leverett, Anne. *See* Fisher
Leverett, Hannah. *See* Hudson
Leverett, John, I, **474–75**, 573, 595, 605, 636
Leverett, Sarah. *See* Sedgwick
Leverett, Thomas, I, 474
Le Verrier, Madeleine. *See* Houdon
Leverrier, Marie. *See* Deguire, *dit* Desrosiers
Leverrier, Pierre, IV, 202
Le Verrier de Boisguibert, Nicolas, II, 433
Le Verrier de Rousson, François, II, **433**, xxi, 224, 589; III,
579; IV, 476, 663
Le Verrier de Rousson, Jeanne-Charlotte. *See* Fleury Des-
chambault
Le Verrier de Rousson, Louis II, 433; IV, **476**
Lévesque, Catherine. *See* Trottier Desauniers Beaubien
Lévesque, Catherine (Grisé), IV, 477
Lévesque, François (father), IV, 476
Lévesque, François, III, 282, 370; IV, **476–77**, 229
Lévesque, Jeanne-Marguerite. *See* Le Chevalier
Lévesque, Marie. *See* Pouchet
Lévesque, Robert, II, 181
Le Vieux, Pierre, III, 433
Le Vieux de Hauteville, Marguerite. *See* Lyonne
Le Vieux de Hauteville, Marie. *See* Renardin de La Blanche-
tière
Le Vieux de Hauteville, Nicolas (father), I, 475
Le Vieux de Hauteville, Nicolas, I, **475**, 431; II, xvi
Levilliers. *See* Petit
Levingston. *See* Livingston

Lévis (Lévy), Henri de, Duc de Ventadour, I, 58, 186, 195,
521
Lévis, François de, Duc de Lévis, III, xxi, xxii, xxv, xxvii,
12, 84, 85, 86, 89, 132, 211, 332, 400, 441, 459, 461,
462, 463, 467, 468, 469, 510, 535, 552, 555, 578, 591;
IV, **477–82**, 14, 24, 34, 58, 64, 137, 144, 183, 214, 307,
401, 448, 449, 460, 476, 517, 531, 563, 621, 637, 641,
642, 652, 670, 671, 672, 673, 674, 701, 739, 751
Lévis, Gabrielle-Augustine de, Duchesse de Lévis. *See*
Michel de Danton
Lévis, Jean de, Baron d'Ajac, IV, 477
Lévis, Jeanne-Marie de, Baronne d'Ajac. *See* Maguelonne
Lévis, Pierre-Marc-Gaston de, Duc de Lévis, IV, 482
Lévis-Mirepoix, Gaston-Charles-Pierre de, Duc de Lévis-
Mirepoix, IV, 477, 482
Levrard, Charles, IV, 729
Levrault de Langis, Alexis, III, 399, 400
Levrault de Langis, Léon-Joseph, III, 399
Levrault de Langis, Marguerite-Gabrielle. *See* Jarret de
Verchères
Levrault de Langis Montegron, Jean-Baptiste, III, **399–400**
Levrault de Langis Montegron, Madeleine. *See* Aillcboust
de Manthet
Levreau, Charles, III, 509
Levreau (L'Heureux), Marie (Phlem, *dit* Yvon), III, 518
Levret, Suzanne (Arnoux), III, 18
Lévy. *See* Lévis
Lcvy. *See also* Thubières
Levy, Mr, IV, 556
Levy, Eleazar, IV, 331, 332, 384, 571
Levy, Gershom, IV, 332, 385, 718, 719
Levy, Hayman, IV, 718
Levy, Isaac, IV, 332, 385
Levy, Simon, IV, 332
Lewis, Edward, I, 144
Lewis, Elizabeth (wife of William), IV, 482
Lewis, Margaret (Button), I, 144
Lewis, William, IV, **482–84**, 721
Lexington, Baroness. *See* St Leger
Lhalle. *See* Delhalle
L'Hermitière. *See* Hamelin
L'Hermitte, Jacques (father), II, 435
L'Hermitte, Jacques, II, **433–35**, 36, 154, 339, 479, 482
L'Hermitte, Marie. *See* Chevalier
L'Hermitte, Marie. *See* Preaux
L'Heureux. *See also* Levreau
L'Heureux, Jacques, II, 578
L'Huillier, Alexandre, II, 428
L'Huissier, Christophe, IV, 202
Liancourt, Duc de. *See* Du Plessis
Liancourt, Marquise de. *See* Schomberg
Liard, Suzanne (Mounier), IV, 565
Libert, Nicolas, I, 248
Lichfield, Countess of. *See* Fitzroy
Lichfield, Earl of. *See* Lee
Liddall. *See* Lydall
Lidius. *See* Lÿdius
Liébert*, Philippe-Pierre (1733–1804), IV, 151, 201
Liebrich, Anna Justina. *See* Schwartz
Liégeois, Jean, I, **475–76**
Liénard, Bonaventure, II, 173, 174
Liénard, Geneviève (Mallet), II, 451
Liénard de Beaujeu, Catherine. *See* Gobert

Liénard de Beaujeu, Charlotte (Varin de La Marre), III, 402; IV, 749

Liénard de Beaujeu, Daniel-Hyacinthe-Marie, III, **400–2**, 31, 403, 524; IV, 207, 242, 442, 447, 617, 733

Liénard de Beaujeu, Louis, II, 390, 529; III, **402–3**, 384, 400, 422; IV, 749

Liénard de Beaujeu, Louise-Charlotte. *See* Cugnet

Liénard de Beaujeu, Louis-Joseph, III, 403

Liénard de Beaujeu, Marie-Charlotte (Le Comte Dupré), IV, 442

Liénard de Beaujeu, Michelle-Élisabeth. *See* Foucault

Liénard de Beaujeu, Philippe, III, 402

Liénard de Beaujeu, Thérèse-Denise. *See* Migeon de Branssat

Liénard* de Beaujeu de Villemomble, Louis (1716–1802), III, 403, 529; IV, 41, 72, 639

Liette. *See also* Tonty

Liette, Isabelle de (Tonty), II, 631, 633

Liette, Pierre-Charles de, II, **435–36**, 128, 569, 631, 636; III, 627

Light, Alexander, II, 493; III, 302

Lignères. *See* Desportes

Lignery. *See* Le Marchand

Lignières. *See* Darles

Ligondès (Ligondez) de Linars, Jean de, III, 368

Ligonier, John (Jean-Louis), 1st Earl Ligonier, III, 218, 668, 669; IV, 3, 20, 21, 22, 84, 773

Lilburne, William, II, 290, 564

Lilia, Marie-Anne (Douglas, Comtesse de Douglas), IV, 224

Lillicoe, Mary (Gilmore), IV, 295

Lily of the Mohawks. *See* Tekakwitha

Limoges, Joseph de, II, 55

Limousin, Valère (Depéret), III, 180

Linars. *See* Ligondès

Lincoln, Earl of. *See* Clinton

Lincourt. *See* Amiot

Linctot. *See* Godefroy

Lindenow, Godske, I, 243

Linnaeus (Linné, von Linné), Carl (Carolus), II, 596; III, 108, 676, 678; IV, 406, 407

Lino. *See* Martin

Lintot. *See* Godefroy

Lionne. *See* Lyonne

Lirec. *See* Lauson

Lisle. *See* Beaussier

L'Isle-Dieu, Abbé de. *See* La Rue

Lisloye. *See* Dupuy

Listenois, Prince de. *See* Bauffremont

Lister, Sarah (Robinson), IV, 677

Little, Elizabeth. *See* Howland

Little, Isaac, III, 403

Little, Mary. *See* Otis

Little, Mary (Winslow), IV, 774

Little, Otis, III, **403–5**, 90; IV, 581

Little Abraham. *See* Teiorhéñhsere?

Little Beard. *See* Sequidonquee

Littlefield, Hannah (?) (Moulton), III, 476

Littlefield, Josiah, II, 664

Livaudais. *See* Énault

Livaudière. *See* Péan

Livernois, Gilles, II, 379

Liverpool, Earl of. *See* Jenkinson

Livingston, Alida. *See* Schuyler

Livingston, Ann (Jordan), IV, 402

Livingston, Catherine (De Peyster), IV, 210

Livingston, Elizabeth. *See* Knight

Livingston*, James (1747–1832), IV, 142, 546

Livingston, Janet (Montgomery), IV, 545

Livingston, Janet (Smith), IV, 714, 718

Livingston, John (fur-trader), IV, 402

Livingston, John, II, **436–38**, 4, 650; III, 8

Livingston, Margaret (Vetch), II, 650, 652

Livingston, Mary. *See* Winthrop

Livingston, Philip John, IV, 300

Livingston, Robert, II, 112, 436, 650

Livingston, William, IV, 714, 715

Livingstone, Mary (Stewart), I, 613

Livius, Anna Elizabeth. *See* Tufton Mason

Livius, Peter (father), IV, 484

Livius, Peter, IV, **484–86**, 58, 230, 232, 350, 398, 492, 791

Lizeiras. *See* Delicérasse

Lizot, Joseph, IV, 71

Lizot, Marie-Françoise (Blais), IV, 71

Llanas. *See* Bodega

Lloyd. *See also* Loyd

Lloyd (explorer), I, 239

Lloyd, David (brother of Thomas), II, 439

Lloyd, David (lawyer), IV, 526

Lloyd, James, I, 545

Lloyd, John, I, 19, 386

Lloyd, Thomas, II, **438–39**, 97, 98, 118, 152, 218, 261, 291, 293, 350, 351, 486, 487, 565, 582, 583, 610, 619, 643; III, 177, 454, 618

Llwyd, Humphrey, I, 677

Locke, John, I, 519; IV, 230

Lockman, Carolina, III, 405

Lockman, John, III, 405

Lockman, Leonard, III, **405**, 212

Lockman, Tanalia (wife of Leonard), III, 405

Løvendal (Loewendahl). *See* Lowendahl

Logan, James, III, 66

Loire. *See* Le Moyne de Serigny

Loiseau. *See also* Lozeau

Loiseau, Antoine, IV, 148

Loiseau, Jean, III, 410

Loiseleur, Marguerite (Guillot), IV, 320

Loisy, Catherine (Badeaux), IV, 40

Lok, Michael, I, 316, 317, 318, 332, 659, 676, 677

L'Ollivier de Tronjoly, François-Jean-Baptiste, IV, 77, 598

Lombard, Antoinette de. *See* Hilaire

Lombard, Jean-Adrian de, III, 406

Lombard, Marguerite (Bigot), IV, 59, 60

Lombard de Combles, Jean-Claude-Henri de, III, **405–6**; IV, 211

Lombard de Combles, Marie-Rose de. *See* Périn

Lom d'Arce, Françoise de. *See* Le Fascheux

Lom d'Arce, Isaac de, Baron de Lahontan, II, 440

Lom d'Arce, Jeanne de. *See* Guérin

Lom d'Arce, Louis-Armand de, Baron de Lahontan, I, 526; II, **439–45**, 72, 142, 322, 328, 478, 510; III, 456

Lomeron, David, I, **476**, 101, 248, 592

Lomeron, Jeanne. *See* Duquerny

Lomeron, Suzanne. *See* Georges

Lomeron de La Martinière, Daniel, I, 476

Long, John, IV, **486**

Long Coat. *See* Anandamoakin

Longfellow, Henry Wadsworth, IV, xx, xxiii
Longland, John, III, **406–7**, 127, 453, 454
Longley, Betty, III, 407
Longley, Delivrance. *See* Crisp
Longley, John, III, 407
Longley, Lydia (rebaptized Lydia-Madeleine), *dite* Sainte-Madeleine, III, **407–8**
Longley, William (father), III, 407
Longley, William (son), III, 407
Longmoor*, Robert (fl. 1771–1812), IV, 157, 366, 518, 684, 760
Longmore, George, IV, 589
Longpré. *See also* Simon
Longpré, Marie (Bissot de Vinsenne), II, 67
Longueuil. *See* Le Moyne
Longueiul, Baronne de. *See* Fleury Deschambault; Legardeur de Tilly; Le Goués de Grais; Souart d'Adoucourt
Longueval, Robert de, I, 423, 425
Longueville, Duc de. *See* Orléans
Longueville, Henri, Duc de Longueville, I, 58
Loosley, Charles, IV, 483
Loppinot, Jean-Chrysostome, II, **445**, 654
Loppinot, Jean-Chrysostome (son), II, 445
Loppinot, Jeanne (Marie). *See* Doucet
Loppinot, Jeanne (Couagne), IV, 174
Loppinot, Louis, II, 445
Loppinot de La Frésillière, Marie-Josephe. *See* Seigneur
Loranger. *See* Rivard
Lorans, Angélique (Pressart), IV, 642
Lorant, Jean-François, II, 424; III, 396
Lorant, Marie-Anne (Levasseur), III, 396
Lorant, Marie-Suzanne. *See* La Bazanière
Lord. *See also* Delort
Lord, Jeanne (Marié), II, 534
Lord, Mary. *See* Moulton
Loreau, Angélique (Saint-Étienne de La Tour), II, 592
Lorgeril, Jeanne-Élisabeth de. *See* Bégon
Lorière. *See* Jouenne
Lorimier*, Claude-Nicolas-Guillaume de (1744–1825), IV, 375
Lorimier, Guillaume de, II, 445
Lorimier, Jeanne de. *See* Guilbaut
Lorimier, Marie-Louise de (Gamelin), IV, 285
Lorimier de La Rivière, Claude-Nicolas de, II, 446; III, **408–9**; IV, 54, 636, 637
Lorimier de La Rivière, Guillaume de, I, 109; II, **445–46**, 513; III, 408
Lorimier de La Rivière, Marie-Louise de. *See* Lepallieur de Laferté
Lorimier de La Rivière, Marie-Marguerite de. *See* Chorel de Saint-Romain, *dit* d'Orvilliers
Lorimier de Verneuil, Marguerite. *See* Sabrevois de Bleury
Lorin, Françoise (Nau), III, 480
Lorin, Henri, I, 142
Loring (Loron). *See also* Sauguaaram
Loring, Hannah. *See* Jackson
Loring, Joshua (father), IV, 486
Loring, Joshua, III, xxv; IV, **486–88**, 3, 23, 24, 588
Loring, Mary. *See* Curtis
Loring*, Robert Roberts (d. 1848), IV, 487
Loring, Thomas L., IV, 486
Lorit, *dit* Gargot, François, II, **446–47**
Lorit, *dit* Gargot, Marie-Thérèse. *See* Le Gros

Lorit, *dit* Gargot, Perrette. *See* Parement
L'Orme. *See* Hazeur
Lormel, Captain, II, 82
Lorne, Marquess of. *See* Campbell
Loron. *See* Saguaarum
Lorraine, Charles de, Duc d'Aumale, I, 96
Lorraine, Charles de, Duc de Guise, I, 214
Lorraine, Henri de, Comte d'Harcourt, I, 248
Lorris (Lory). *See* Lorit
Lorson, Catherine (Marcol), III, 427
Lort. *See* Delort
Lory, César, II, 446
Lory, Richarde. *See* Grimère
Losada. *See* Mollineda
Losee*, William (d. 1832), IV, 495
Lotbinière. *See* Chartier
Lothman de Barrois, Marie (Navarre), IV, 579
Lottin, Isabelle (Lauson de Lirec), I, 427
Lottridge, John, III, **409–10**
Lottridge, Richard, III, 409
Lottridge, Thomas, III, 409
Loubias (Laubia), Arnoult de, I, 327
Loubier, Louise, III, 620
Loubinois de Tourneuve, Jean, II, 125
Loudoun, Earl of. *See* Campbell
Louet, Anne. *See* Morin
Louet, Catherine. *See* Thierry
Louet, Claude, II, 447; III, 421, 620
Louet, Jean, II, 447
Louet, Jean-Claude, II, **447**, xxiv, 151
Loughborough, Baron. *See* Wedderburn
Louis. *See also* Ogenheratarihiens; Taondechoren
Louis (French youth), I, 603
Louis (Montagnais), I, 511
Louis (son of MEMBERTOU), I, 500, 501
Louis, Captain. *See* Wahawanulet
Louis IX (St Louis), King of France, I, 121, 126; III, 169
Louis XIII, King of France, I, 100, 102, 133, 134, 160, 191, 194, 196, 217, 405, 433, 437, 501, 502, 584, 592, 593, 594; II, 87, 98, 136; IV, xix
Louis XIV, King of France, I, 32, 35, 40, 55, 60, 62, 74, 76, 92, 104, 108, 109, 117, 119, 134, 135, 136, 137, 138, 139, 141, 174, 180, 202, 216, 220, 227, 238, 249, 261, 284, 288, 290, 330, 429, 443, 446, 467, 487, 510, 511, 513, 528, 535, 541, 542, 556, 561, 570, 571, 572, 576, 585, 587, 615, 616, 624, 631, 636, 646, 647, 648, 664; II, xvii, xviii, xix, 4, 26, 29, 32, 71, 72, 73, 76, 77, 85, 87, 88, 89, 90, 95, 98, 99, 100, 101, 103, 104, 112, 113, 114, 115, 129, 133, 134, 137, 141, 146, 155, 162, 175, 186, 205, 213, 229, 235, 262, 278, 280, 295, 302, 307, 325, 327, 328, 329, 330, 332, 333, 335, 353, 361, 363, 364, 365, 366, 367, 368, 369, 370, 375, 396, 397, 401, 420, 424, 431, 444, 448, 470, 471, 472, 483, 495, 496, 511, 518, 527, 538, 547, 554, 567, 570, 577, 578, 591, 595, 605, 620, 628, 633, 635, 641, 649; III, xvi, xvii, xx, 42, 57, 59, 60, 67, 248, 328, 356, 381, 552, 554, 557; IV, xx, 355, 465
Louis XV, King of France, II, xx, 52, 87, 476, 530, 570, 605; III, xvi, 8, 19, 140, 192, 240, 242, 248, 270, 291, 338, 350, 353, 384, 467, 486, 491, 566; IV, 65, 227, 355, 401, 439, 469, 472, 636, 637, 664, 673, 750
Louis XVI, King of France, III, 115; IV, 750
Louis, Jean, III, 382

Louis de France, Dauphin, II, 98, 104
Louis de Sainte-Foi. *See* Amantacha
Louise de Saint-Augustin. *See* Soumande
Louise de Sainte-Marie. *See* Chomedey
Louise de Saint-Eustache. *See* Chartier de Lotbinière
Louise-Olive de Saint-Paul. *See* Roy
Louise-Rose de Sainte-Catherine. *See* Lanouguère
L'Ours. *See* Le Pesant
Loustelneau, Catherine de (Denys de Vitré), II, 179
Loustelneau, Charles de, II, 179
Loustelneau, Charlotte de. *See* Buday Fleury
Louvigny. *See also* Bernières; La Porte
Louvigny d'Orgemont, Paul, II, 147
Louvois, Marquis de. *See* Le Tellier
Lovaine, Baron. *See* Percy
Lovelace, Francis, II, 107
Lowendahl (Løvendal, Loewendahl), Ulrich-Frédéric-
    Valdemar (Ulrik Frederick Woldemar), Comte de Lowen-
    dahl, IV, 504
Lowther, Katherine (Powlett, Duchess of Bolton), III, 669
Lowther, Robert, III, 669
Loyard, Jean-Baptiste, II, **447–48**, 198; III, 23, 163
Loyd, Captain, I, 308; II, 266
Loyseau, Charles, II, 211
Lozeau, Catherine. *See* Gautier
Lozeau, François, III, 410
Lozeau, Jean-Baptiste, III, **410–11**
Lozeau, Marguerite. *See* Gauron; Mercier
Lozeau, Pierre-Louis, III, 410
Luc, Brother. *See* François, Claude
Lucas, Francis, III, **411–12**; IV, 158, 334, 536, 537
Lucas, Jacqueline (Auber), I, 72
Lucas, Joseph, IV, 702
Lucas, Richard, I, **476–77**, 315, 417, 606, 666; II, 318
Lucas Dontigny, François, III, 187
Lucas Dontigny, Marie-Madeleine. *See* Baudouin
Lucault (Lucau). *See* Barbeau
Lucciniani, Carlo. *See* Lusignan, Charles
Lucière. *See* La Motte
Ludlow*, Gabriel George (1736–1808), IV, 329
Ludlow, George Duncan, IV, 55
Luján Silva y Góngora, Pedro Francisco, Duke of Almo-
    dóvar del Río, I, 676; IV, 687
Luna, Pedro de, I, 342
Lunette, Françoise (Ménage), II, 467
Lupien, *dit* Baron, Angélique. *See* Courault, *dit* La Coste
Lupien, *dit* Baron, Antoine, III, 412
Lupien, *dit* Baron, Jean-Marie, III, 412
Lupien, *dit* Baron, Marie-Marthe. *See* Chauvin
Lupien, *dit* Baron, Nicolas, III, 412
Lupien, *dit* Baron, Pierre, III, **412–13**, 139; IV, 362, 690
Lusignan. *See* Dazemard
Lusignan*, Charles (1718–1825), IV, 7, 8, 534
Lussigny, M., II, 262, 345
Luteau, Apollinaire, II, 130, 223
Luxembourg. *See* Raphaël
Luzançay. *See* Carré
Lydall, Sir Richard, I, 477
Lydall, William, I, **477**, 83, 343
Lÿdius, Geneviève. *See* Massé
Lÿdius, Isabella (mother of JOHN HENDRICKS; Staats), IV,
    488
Lÿdius, Johannes, IV, 488

Lÿdius, John Hendricks, III, 322, 623; IV, **488–90**, 173
Lymburner*, Adam (d. 1836), IV, 58, 399, 557
Lynch, Isidore, IV, 35
Lynde, Hannah (Goffe), II, 254
Lynde, Samuel, II, 254
Lynne, Marrianne (White), IV, 766
Lyon (Lyons), Benjamin, IV, 332, 718, 719
Lyon, James, IV, **490**
Lyon, Martha. *See* Holden
Lyon, Mary (mother of JAMES), IV, 490
Lyon, Sarah. *See* Skillen
Lyon, Zopher, IV, 490
Lyon de Saint-Ferréol, Jean, II, 577; III, **413–14**, 223, 522
Lyonne, Marguerite (Le Vieux de Hauteville), I, 475
Lyonne, Martin de, I, **477–78**, 558
Lyons, Mr, IV, 495
Lyons, Barnett, IV, 332
Lyschander, Claus C., I, 675
Lyttleton, Sir Richard, IV, 84, 85

MABANE, Mrs. *See* Wedel
Mabane, Adam, III, 541, 542; IV, **491–94**, 6, 104, 278,
    323, 324, 345, 367, 379, 380, 547, 554, 574, 579, 602,
    658, 716, 791, 794
Mabane, Isabell, IV, 493
Macain, Jean, I, 98, 101, 293, 476, 565
Macard, Catherine-Gertrude (Deschamps de La Bouteille-
    rie), II, 180, 181
Macard, Charles, I, 345; II, **448–49**, 149, 276; III, 493
Macard, Geneviève (Bazire; Provost; Aloigny, Marquise de
    La Groye), I, 84, 85; II, 16, 533
Macard, Jeanne-Renée. *See* Gourdeau de Beaulieu
Macard, Marguerite. *See* Couillard de Lespinay
Macard, Marguerite. *See* Hardy
Macard, Marie-Anne (Bécart de Granville), II, 53, 213; III,
    55
Macard, Marie-Thérèse (Alavoine), III, 7
Macard, Thomas, II, 448
Macard, *dit* Champagne, Nicolas, I, 84; II, 16, 181, 448
Macarmick*, William (1742–1815), IV, 293, 522
Macart, Hélène (Jérémie), I, 387
Macarty Mactigue, Barthélemy de, II, 523
Macátepilesis. *See* Mécatépilésis
Macaulay, Ann. *See* Kirby
Macaulay*, John (1792–1857), IV, 494
Macaulay, Robert, IV, **494**
Macaulay, Susan. *See* Gilliland
Macaulay, William, IV, 494
Macaulay*, William (1794–1874), IV, 494
Macaulay*, Zachary (1739–1821), IV, 759
McBeath*, George (d. 1812), IV, 311
MacCarthy. *See also* Latouche
MacCarthy, Mary Elizabeth (Sullivan), III, 602
MacCarthy, Robert, Viscount Muskerry, II, 251; III, 619
McCarty, Catherine. *See* Lent
Maccarty, Charles, IV, 247
McCarty, Charles Justin (James), IV, **494–95**
McCarty, John, IV, 495
McCarty, Richard, IV, **495–96**
McCarty, Ursule. *See* Benoît
McCarty, Ursule (Perrault), IV, 496
McCauley. *See* Macaulay
McCliesh, Elizabeth (Norton), III, 489; IV, 583

McCliesh, Mary (Coats), III, 127
McCliesh, Mary (wife of THOMAS), III, 415
McCliesh, Thomas (uncle), III, 414
McCliesh, Thomas, II, 10, 51, 56, 65, 291, 313, 492; III, **414–15**, 127, 489, 599, 662
McCord, Jane (Fraser), IV, 276
McCormick, Cæsar, IV, 228
McCuen, Charles, IV, 756
MacDhomñaill, Seumas. *See* MacDonald, James
MacDonald, Donald (cousin of JAMES), IV, 496, 607
Macdonald, Donald (servant), IV, 43
MacDonald, James, IV, **496–97**, 444
MacDonald, John, IV, 496, 497
McDonald*, John (d. 1866), IV, 310
MacDonald of Boisdale, Colin, IV, 497
MacDonald* of Glenaladale, John, known as Fear-a-Ghlinne (1742–1810), IV, 129, 152, 496, 497, 607, 608, 610
McDonnell*, Archibald (d. 1830), IV, 495
McDonell* (Aberchalder), John (d. 1809), IV, 683
Macdonell*, John (1768–1850), IV, 310
McDougall, Catherine. *See* Lent
McDougall, George, III, 95, 528
McDougall, John, IV, 495
Macdowall, Margaret (Stewart), I, 613
Macdowall, Uchtred, I, 613
Macé. *See also* Druillon; Massé
Macé, Catherine, I, **478**, 220, 458, 480, 487, 512
Macé, Guillé, I, 478
Macé, Philippe. *See* Martineau
Macé, René, I, 478
MacEachern*, Angus Bernard (d. 1835), IV, 497
Macfarlane, Elizabeth. *See* Erskine
Macfarlane, Walter, III, 131
McGill*, James (1744–1813), IV, 5, 59, 277, 278, 319, 547, 698, 703, 757
McGill, John, IV, 48
McGillivray*, Duncan (d. 1808), IV, 310
McGovock (McGovack), George, IV, 759
McGregor, Gregor, IV, 506
Machault d'Arnouville, Jean-Baptiste de, III, 18, 55, 72, 171, 230, 300, 461; IV, 88, 242, 250, 257, 258, 307, 467, 615, 617, 750
Machikeweece (Machiquawish). *See* Madjeckewiss
McIlworth, Thomas, IV, 397
McIlwraith, Jean Newton, IV, 401
McKay, Agnes (Moore), IV, 556
McKay*, Alexander (d. 1811), IV, 757
MacKay, Donald, IV, 310
McKay, Hugh, IV, 557
Mackay, John, IV, **498–99**
McKay, Marguerite. *See* Waddens
MacKay, Marie-Charlotte. *See* Chartier de Lotbinière
McKay, Samuel, III, 542
McKee, Alexander, IV, **499–500**, 119, 260, 337, 777, 778
McKee, Thomas (grandfather), IV, 499
McKee*, Thomas (d. 1815), IV, 499, 778, 779
Mackellar, Elizabeth. *See* Basaline
Mackellar, John, IV, 501
Mackellar, Patrick, III, 33, 89, 667; IV, **500–1**, 93
McKenna, John, IV, 271
MacKenzie. *See also* Kensey
Mackenzie, Alexander (brewer), IV, 384

Mackenzie, Alexander (merchant), IV, 571
Mackenzie*, Sir Alexander (1764–1820), I, 378; II, xxviii; III, xxxiii; IV, 310, 506, 741, 746, 757
McKenzie, James, IV, 304
McKenzie*, James (d. 1849), IV, 424
Mackenzie, Margaret (Cuthbert), IV, 190
MacKenzie, Roderick, IV, 153, 240, 436
Mackenzie, William, IV, 571
McKindlay, John, IV, 757
MacKinlay, Helen (Isbister), IV, 380
McKinnon*, William (d. 1811), IV, 523
Macklin (?), Sarah (Noble), III, 483
Macklish. *See* McCliesh
McKown, John, IV, 769
McKown, Mary. *See* Willard
Mackworth, Agnes (Watts; Crowne), I, 241, 242
Mackworth, Humphrey, I, 241
McLane, David, IV, **501–3**
Maclean, Allan, IV, **503–4**, 229, 309, 336, 548, 606, 791
MacLean*, Allan (1752–1847), IV, 505
Maclean, Anne. *See* Kinloch
McLean*, Archibald (1791–1865), IV, 505
Maclean, Donald, IV, 503
McLean, Francis, IV, **504–5**, 161, 503, 606
McLean, Harriet (McLean; Walker), IV, 505
Maclean, Janet (Maclean), IV, 503
Maclean, Mary. *See* Campbell
McLean, Mary. *See* Herkimer
McLean, Neil, IV, **505**, 495, 683
Maclean, William, IV, 504
McLennan*, John Stewart (1853–1939), III, 73, 229
McLennan, William, IV, 401
MacLeod, Cécile. *See* Robert
MacLeod, Normand, IV, **505–6**
McLoughlin*, John (1784–1857), IV, 757
McLoughlin, Marguerite. *See* Waddens
MacMechan*, Archibald McKellar (1862–1933), IV, 169, 170
Macnamara, John, IV, 506
Macnider*, John (1760–1829), IV, 400
Macnider, Margaret (Johnston), IV, 400
Macnider, Mathew, IV, 400
McNutt*, Alexander (b. 1725, d. *c.* 1811), III, 664; IV, 527, 529, 781
Macquin. *See* Macain
McTavish*, Simon (1750–1804), IV, 48, 262, 277, 311
Mactigue. *See* Macarty
Macuina. *See* Muquinna
Madaillan, Charlotte de. *See* La Roque
Madaillan, Louis de, I, 424
Madaillan de Lesparre, Armand de, Marquis de Lassay, II, 262
Madeleine (slave), IV, 233
Madeleine (wife of TOTIRI), I, 651
Madeleine de la Résurrection. *See* Bâcon
Madgshon, John, III, 213
Madjeckewiss* (d. *c.* 1805), III, 660; IV, 241, 486, 564
Madoc (Madog ab Owain Gwynedd), I, **677–78**
Madokawando, II, 5, 6
Madry, Françoise. *See* Duquet
Madry, Jean, I, **478–79**, 47, 80, 109, 255; II, 488
Magdelaine, I, 640
Magellan, Ferdinand, I, 155, 342, 658

Magesse. *See* Martel

Maggiolo (Maiollo), Viscount of, I, 304, 659

Magnan, Catherine (Hervieux), III, 290

Magnan, Jean-Baptiste, IV, 658

Magnan, Péronelle de (Dubois Berthelot), III, 189

Magnan, Pierre, I, **479**, 211, 303, 509

Magnan, *dit* L'Espérance, Marie-Anne (Picoté de Belestre), IV, 634

Magné (Magnié, Manié), Marie (Chartier), III, 111

Magnien, François, II, 642

Magnus, Olaus, I, 680

Magon de La Balluë, Luc, IV, 506

Magon de La Balluë, Pélagie. *See* Porrée

Magon de Terlaye, François-Auguste, IV, **506–7**, 431, 521

Magos. *See* Martel

Magouaouidombaouit. *See* Gill, Joseph-Louis

Magregory, Patrick, III, 568

Maguelonne, Jeanne-Marie de (Lévis, Baronne d'Ajac), IV, 477

Mahan, Alfred Thayer, IV, 123

Maheu, M., I, 645

Maheu, Anne. *See* Convent

Maheu, René, I, 494

Maheut, Geneviève. *See* Bissot

Maheut, Jean, I, 480

Maheut, Louis, I, **479–80**; II, 168

Maheut, Louis (brother), I, 479, 480

Maheut, Marguerite. *See* Corrivault

Maheut, René, I, 479

Mahiet, Michel, IV, 124

Mahigan Aticq Ouche. *See* Miristou

Mahyet, Madeleine (Riverin), II, 574

Mailhiot. *See* Malhiot

Maillard, Pierre, II, 412; III, **415–19**, 34, 183, 358, 425, 497, 498; IV, 41, 74, 79, 214, 290, 296, 453, 454, 455, 644, 676, 776

Maillebois, Marquis de. *See* Desmarest

Maillet (Mailhet). *See also* Mallet

Maillet, Gilbert, II, 159

Maillet, Jean, I, 480

Maillet, Marie. *See* Rivard

Maillet, Marie, I, **480**, 220, 458, 478, 487, 512

Maillet, Marie-Josephte (Campion), IV, 132

Maillou, Amable, IV, 205, 629

Maillou*, Benjamin-Nicolas (1753–1810), IV, 288

Maillou, *dit* Desmoulins, Anne. *See* Delaunay

Maillou, *dit* Desmoulins, Jean-Baptiste, II, 120; III, **419–21**, 165, 170, 234, 307, 637; IV, 202, 659

Maillou, *dit* Desmoulins, Joseph (uncle), III, 419, 420

Maillou, *dit* Desmoulins, Joseph, III, 346, 420

Maillou, *dit* Desmoulins, Louise. *See* Phélippeaux

Maillou, *dit* Desmoulins, Louis-Marie, III, 420

Maillou, *dit* Desmoulins, Marguerite. *See* Caron

Maillou, *dit* Desmoulins, Marguerite (Lambert, *dit* Saint-Paul), III, 346

Maillou, *dit* Desmoulins, Marguerite (Vallette de Chévigny), III, 637

Maillou, *dit* Desmoulins, Marie-Catherine. *See* Amiot, *dit* Villeneuve

Maillou, *dit* Desmoulins, Marie-Joseph, *dite* de Saint-André, III, 420

Maillou, *dit* Desmoulins, Pierre (father), III, 419

Maillou, *dit* Desmoulins, Pierre, III, 346, 420

Maillou, *dit* Desmoulins, Vital, III, 420

Mailloux, Élie, IV, 9

Maingard, Jehanne (Jalobert), I, 384

Maingart, Jacques, I, 167

Maintenon, Marquise de. *See* Aubigné

Mainwaring, Sir George, I, 481

Mainwaring, Sir Henry, I, **481**, 24, 668

Maiollo. *See* Maggiolo

Maisonbasse. *See* Deschevery

Maisonnat, Hélie, II, 449

Maisonnat, Jeanne. *See* Ségure

Maisonnat, Judith. *See* Soubiron

Maisonnat, Madeleine. *See* Bourg

Maisonnat, Marguerite. *See* Bourgeois

Maisonnat, Marie-Madeleine (Winniett), III, **421–22**, 277, 297, 665

Maisonnat, *dit* Baptiste, Marie-Anne (Cahouet; Imbert), IV, 378

Maisonnat, *dit* Baptiste, Pierre, I, 577; II, **449–50**, 3, 46, 167, 271, 394, 459, 667; III, 421, 596, 665; IV, 378

Maisonneuve. *See* Chomedey; Puybarau

Maitland, Alexander, IV, 610

Maître Abraham. *See* Martin

Maizerets. *See* Ango

Major Cope. *See* Cope

Makatachinga, III, 530

Makheabichtichiou, I, **481–82**, 527

Makisabi, II, 128, 515; III, 576

Maladre. *See* Sarrebource

Malalamet, III, 266

Malapart, André, I, **482**, 613

Malartic. *See* Maurès

Malaspina*, Alejandro (1754–1810), I, 676; IV, 568

Malbeque, Étiennette-Louise (Petit de Levilliers), II, 523

Maldonado. *See* Ferrer; Flórez

Malen (Mallen), Marie (Bernier), IV, 57

Malepart de Beaucourt, Benoîte. *See* Camagne

Malepart de Beaucour, François, III, 422; IV, **507–8**

Malepart de Grand Maison, *dit* Beaucour, Marguerite. *See* Haguenier

Malepart de Grand Maison, *dit* Beaucour, Paul, III, **422–23**; IV, 507

Maleray de La Mollerie, Jacques, II, 451

Maleray de La Mollerie, Louis-Hector, II, 451

Maleray de La Périne, Isaac, II, 450

Maleray de La Périne, Marie. *See* Tessier

Maleray de Noiré de La Mollerie, Françoise. *See* Picoté de Belestre

Maleray de Noiré de La Mollerie, Jacques, II, **450–51**

Malet. *See* Mallet

Malherbe, Father, I, 607

Malherbe, François, I, **483**

Malherbe, François de, I, 470

Malhiot, Charlotte. *See* Gamelin

Malhiot, Françoise (Boucher de La Perrière), III, 81

Malhiot, Guillaume, IV, 178

Malhiot, Jean, III, 374, 422

Malhiot, Jean-François, III, **422**, 81, 270; IV, 284

Malhiot, Madeleine. *See* Marchand

Malhiot, Marguerite-Alexis (Trottier Desrivières-Beaubien), IV, 508

Malhiot, Marie-Anne. *See* Massé

Mallemouche, Jeanne de (Chauvin de Tonnetuit), I, 209

Mallen. *See* Malen

Mallepart. *See* Malepart

Mallet, Denis, II, **451–52**, 200, 338, 379

Mallet, Geneviève. *See* Liénard

Mallet, Louisa. *See* Deupet

Mallet, Louis-Denis, II, 451

Mallet, Madeleine. *See* Thunay, *dit* Dufresne

Mallet, Madeleine (Couture), II, 157

Mallet, Marie-Madeleine. *See* Jérémie, *dit* Lamontagne

Mallet, Paul, III, 423, 424

Mallet, Pierre, III, 423

Mallet, Pierre-Antoine, III, **423–24**

Mallet, Renée. *See* Padouillet

Malouin. *See* Rinfret

Malqueneck, Baron de, II, 279

Maltot, Sieur de, II, 203

Man, Thomas, II, 319

Manach, Jean (Jacques), III, **424–26**, 358, 417; IV, 79, 214, 239, 296, 456, 457

Manby, Thomas, IV, 747

Mance, Catherine. *See* Émonnot

Mance, Charles, I, 483

Mance, Jeanne, I, **483–87**, 31, 43, 78, 208, 215, 216, 217, 219, 220, 230, 231, 310, 344, 412, 453, 457, 478, 480, 512, 547, 640, 648; II, 194, 376, 489, 490

Mancelin, Élisabeth de (Thavenet), II, 628

Manchot, II, 255

Mandat, Galiot, I, 446

Mandat, Marie (Le Febvre de La Barre), I, 446

Mandet, Marie (Allemand), I, 56

Mandeville. *See* Philippe

Manet, Anne (Fond), II, 581

Mangeant, Anne. *See* Deschamps

Mangeant, Louis, III, 426

Mangeant, Marguerite. *See* Caissy

Mangeant, *dit* Saint-Germain, François, II, 23; III, **426–27**, 84

Manié. *See* Magné

Manitou, III, 530

Manitouabeouich (Marie-Olivier-Sylvestre) (Prévost), I, 554

Manitougatche, I, **487–88**, 533

Mann, Edward Isaac, IV, 153

Mann*, Gother (1747–1830), IV, 108

Mannereuil. *See* Dugey Rozoy

Manners, Lady Elizabeth (Monckton, Viscountess Galway), IV, 540

Manners, John, Marquess of Granby, IV, 773

Manning, Joseph, III, 274

Manoel (Manuel) I, King of Portugal, I, 234, 236, 303, 304, 305

Manseau, Angélique (Fortier), IV, 271

Mansel, Lady. *See* Bayly

Mansel, Sir Edward, IV, 694

Mansel, Sir Robert, I, 144

Mansfield, Earl of. *See* Murray

Mantes. *See also* Côme

Mantes, M. de, I, 89

Manthet. *See* Ailleboust

Manthet d'Argentenay, Dorothée de (Ailleboust), I, 45, 47

Manthet d'Argentenay, Jean de, I, 42

Manthet d'Argentenay, Suzanne de. *See* Hotman

Manuel. *See also* Manoel

Manuel, Emmanuel, IV, 332

Manwaring. *See* Mainwaring

Maquet, Alexis, IV, 134, 298

Maquilla (Maquinna). *See* Muquinna

Mar, Earl of. *See* Erskine

Marafret Layssard, Pierre-Étienne, III, 222

Marais. *See* Marest

Maranda, Geneviève (Schindler), IV, 702

Maranda, Marie-Louise (Hubert), IV, 370

Maray de La Chauvignerie, Michel, II, 126, 625; III, 101, 320, 401, 614

Marcel (aide-de-camp), III, 467

Marcellin, Marie-Anne (Bréard), IV, 91

March. *See also* Marsh

March, Hugh, II, 452

March, Jemina. *See* True

March, John, II, **452–53**, 17, 37, 38, 177, 206, 238, 288, 409, 417, 495; III, 22, 25, 177, 200, 273, 470, 474, 552, 596

March, Judith (wife of Hugh), II, 452

Marchand, Étienne (father of ÉTIENNE), IV, 509

Marchand, Étienne (silversmith), IV, 205

Marchand, Étienne, III, 193; IV, **509–10**, 99, 101, 543, 574

Marchand, Jean, I, 77

Marchand*, Jean-Baptiste (1760–1825), IV, 90, 188

Marchand, Louis, III, 493

Marchand, Madeleine (Malhiot; Legardeur de Beauvais), III, 374, 422

Marchand, Marie-Anne. *See* Durand

Marchand, Marie-Renée (Decoste), IV, 200

Marchand, Nicolas, IV, 200

Marchant de La Houlière, Mathieu-Henri, III, 230, 440

Marchin, I, 507

Marcol, Catherine. *See* Lorson

Marcol, Gabriel, III, **427–28**, 580, 628

Marcol, Pascal, III, 427

Marconnay, Angélique-Renée-Françoise. *See* Péan

Marconnay, Louis-Michel de, known as Marquis de Marconnay, IV, 616, 660

Marcoux, Françoise (Grisé), IV, 315

Marcoux, Marthe (Baudoin), III, 35

Maréchal, Marie-Joseph (Élie), II, 216

Mareschal, Georges, III, 344

Marest, Joseph-Jacques, II, **453–54**, 317, 318, 324, 353, 415, 455, 503, 505; III, 103, 105, 269, 451, 577, 580

Marest, Pierre-Gabriel, I, 61; II, **454–55**, 55, 140, 306, 347, 453, 468, 469, 645; III, 103

Maret, Guillaume, II, 526

Mareuil, Jacques de, I, **488–89**, 139; II, 130, 586

Mareuil, Pierre de, III, **428–29**

Margane de Batilly, François-Marie, II, **455–56**; III, 429

Margane de Lavaltrie, Angélique. *See* Guyon Després

Margane de Lavaltrie, François, II, 384, 456; III, **429–30**, 524; IV, 91

Margane de Lavaltrie, Louise. *See* Bissot

Margane de Lavaltrie, Louis-François, III, 429

Margane de Lavaltrie, Madeleine-Louise (Ailleboust de Périgny), III, 7

Margane de Lavaltrie, Marguerite (Dutisné), II, 215

Margane de Lavaltrie, Pierre-Paul, IV, 476

Margane* de Lavaltrie, Pierre-Paul (1743–1810), IV, 191, 403

Margane de Lavaltrie, Séraphin, II, 455; III, 7, 429

Margetson, Anne (Caulfeild), II, 122
Margetson, James, II, 122
Margon. *See* Plantavit
Margry, Pierre, III, 254
Marguerie, François, I, 489
Marguerie, Jean, IV, 421
Marguerie, Louise. *See* Cloutier
Marguerie, Marie (Hertel de La Fresnière; Moral de Saint-
Quentin), I, 238, 369, 550; II, 282, 648
Marguerie, Marthe. *See* Romain
Marguerie de La Haye, François, I, **489–90**, 60, 186, 341,
369, 639; II, 282
Marguerie, IV, 35
Marguerite d'Angoulême, Queen of Navarre, I, 424, 425,
426
Marguerite de Saint-Jean-Baptiste. *See* Bourdon
Marguerite de Saint-Pierre. *See* Blais; Dizy de Montplaisir
Marguerite de Valois, known as La Reine Margot, Queen of
Navarre, I, 549
Marguerite-Françoise de Saint-Henri. *See* Hiché
Marguerite-Renée de la Croix. *See* Godefroy de Tonnancour
Mariauchau d'Esgly, Élisabeth. *See* Gröen
Mariauchau d'Esgly, François, II, **456–57**, 186, 558; III,
112, 434; IV, 299, 510
Mariauchau d'Esgly, François-Louis, II, **457**
Mariauchau d'Esgly, Louise (Martel de Brouague), III, 434
Mariauchau d'Esgly, Louise-Philippe. *See* Chartier de
Lotbinière
Mariauchau d'Esgly, Louis-Philippe, III, 112, 434; IV,
510–12, 42, 81, 87, 101, 102, 142, 371, 372, 430, 444,
543, 789, 799
Mariauchau d'Esgly, Pierre, II, 456
Maricourt. *See* Le Moyne
Marie. *See also* Aonetta
Marie, Sieur. *See* François-Marie de Paris
Marie (slave), III, 482
Marie (wife of MEMBERTOU), I, 501
Marie (wife of NEGABAMAT), I, 516
Marie, III, **430–31**, 8
Marié, Denise (Quesneville), II, 534
Marié, Jeanne. *See* Lord
Marié, Pierre, II, 534
Marie de la Conception. *See* Irwin
Marie de l'Annonciation. *See* Le Ber
Marie de l'Assomption. *See* Barbier
Marie de l'Incarnation. *See* Guyart
Marie de Médicis, Queen of France, I, 98, 99, 100
Marie de Saint-Bernard. *See* Savonnières
Marie de Saint-Bonaventure-de-Jésus. *See* Forestier
Marie de Sainte-Thérèse. *See* Juchereau de La Ferté
Marie de Sainte-Thérèse-de-Jésus. *See* Bourdon
Marie de Saint-Ignace. *See* Giffard; Guenet
Marie de Saint-Joseph. *See* Bourdon; Savonnières
Marie des Anges. *See* Sayward
Marie-Andrée de Sainte-Hélène. *See* Regnard Duplessis
Marie-Anne de la Nativité. *See* Migeon de Branssat
Marie-Anne de Saint-Benoît. *See* Davis
Marie-Anne de Sainte-Cécile. *See* Davis
Marie-Anne-Louise de Saint-François-Xavier. *See*
Taschereau
Marie-Catherine de Saint-Augustin. *See* Simon de Longpré
Marie-Catherine de Saint-Joachim. *See* Tibierge

Marie-Catherine du Saint-Sacrement. *See* Charly Saint-
Ange
Marie-Charlotte de Saint-Claude de la Croix. *See* Ramezay
Marie-Charlotte de Saint-Michel. *See* Aubert de La
Chesnaye
Marie-Félix (Dubocq), I, 286
Marie-Françoise de Saint-Antoine. *See* Guillimin
Marie-Françoise de Saint-Pierre. *See* Buisson de Saint-
Cosme
Marie-Gabrielle de l'Annonciation. *See* Denis
Marie-Geneviève de Sainte-Hélène. *See* Godefroy de Ton-
nancour
Marie-Jeanne-Madeleine de Sainte-Agathe. *See* Legardeur
de Repentigny
Marie-Joseph-Angélique, II, **457–58**
Marie-Joseph de la Visitation. *See* Legardeur de Repentigny
Marie-Joseph de l'Enfant-Jésus. *See* Juchereau Duchesnay;
Wheelwright
Marie-Joseph de Saint-André. *See* Maillou, *dit* Desmoulins
Marie-Joseph de Saint-François d'Assise. *See* Hallé
Marie-Joseph de Saint-Michel. *See* Blais
Marie-Josephte de la Nativité. *See* Paquet
Marie Leszczyńska, Queen of France, III, 24
Marie-Louise de la Sainte-Vierge. *See* Gaillard
Marie-Louise de Saint-Martin. *See* Curot
Marie-Madeleine de Saint-Louis. *See* Maufils
Marie-Olivier-Sylvestre. *See* Manitouabeouich
Marie-Renée de la Nativité. *See* Boulic
Mariet, Joseph, II, 130, 241
Marie-Thérèse. *See* Gannensagouas
Marie-Thérèse de Saint-Jean-Baptiste. *See* Langlois
Marie-Thérèse of Austria, Infanta of Spain, Queen of
France, I, 499
Marie-Ursule des Anges. *See* Chéron
Marigny. *See also* Philippe
Marigny, Sieur de, II, 558, 559
Marillac. *See also* Auger
Marillac, Louise de, I, 484
Marin, Hélène. *See* Gorel
Marin, Jacques, II, 458
Marin, Lancelot, I, 121
Marin, Louis, III, 491
Marin, Marie-Madeleine (Coulon de Villiers), IV, 177
Marin de La Malgue, Catherine. *See* Niquet
Marin de La Malgue, Charles-Paul, II, **458**; III, 374, 431,
432
Marin de La Malgue, Charlotte. *See* Fleury de La Gorgen-
dière
Marin de La Malgue, Joseph, II, 458; III, 171, 243, 244,
400, 431; IV, **512–14**, 449, 680, 733
Marin de La Malgue, Louise. *See* Lamy
Marin de La Malgue, Marie-Joseph. *See* Guyon Desprez
Marin de La Malgue, Paul, II, 581; III, **431–32**, xl, 46, 47,
48, 49, 101, 162, 255, 319, 367, 375, 378, 438, 532, 578,
611, 614; IV, lvi, 54, 63, 213, 239, 248, 256, 268, 432,
458, 489, 512, 513, 617, 618, 733
Marin de La Perrière, Claude, II, 458; III, **432**, 158
Marin de La Perrière, Marie-Madeleine. *See* Coulon de
Villiers
Marinier, Marie-Anne (Larcher), IV, 438
Marion, Denise (Peiras), II, 514
Marion, Nicolas, III, 519

Marion, *dit* La Fontaine, Abel, II, 440; III, 568
Mark. *See* March
Markham, Elizabeth. *See* Hey
Markland*, Thomas (1757–1840), IV, 494
Marlborough, Duchess of. *See* Jennings
Marlborough, Duke of. *See* Churchill
Maroist, Guillaume, II, 648
Marot, Bernard, I, **490**, 442, 505, 593, 642
Marot, Clément, I, 423, 424
Marot de La Garaye, Angélique-Sylvie (Dubreil, Comtesse de Pontbriand), III, 161, 192
Marquette, Jacques, I, **490–93**, 15, 35, 58, 174, 175, 178, 244, 248, 282, 394, 395, 453, 460; II, xxxi, xxxvi, xxxvii, xxxviii, 128, 144, 259, 347, 501, 634; III, xxxv, 380
Marquette, Rose. *See* La Salle
Marquette de Tombelles, Nicolas, I, 490
Marr, John, IV, 108
Marrant, Elizabeth. *See* Herries
Marrant, John, IV, **514–16**
Mars, Anne. *See* Faye
Mars, Anne (Couagne), II, 153
Mars, Jean, II, 105
Mars, Marie (Jolliet de Mingan; Volant d'Haudebourg), II, 301
Mars, Marie (Rivière; Berry), III, 168
Mars, Michelle (Dubocq; Riverin), III, 557
Mars, Simon, II, 301; III, 557
Marsain, Anne (Bailly de Messein), IV, 41
Marseille. *See* Sicard
Marsh. *See also* March
Marsh, Elizabeth, I, 493
Marsh, Eunice (Dimock), IV, 217
Marsh, John, I, **493**, 39, 107, 361, 529, 657, 672; II, 50, 231, 265
Marshall, Sampson. *See* Kelly, James
Marshe, Witham, III, 147
Marsolais. *See* Lemire-Marsolais
Marsolet. *See also* Lemire
Marsolet, François. *See* Sasousmat
Marsolet, Jean, II, 159
Marsolet, Louise (Lemire), I, 460; II, 120
Marsolet, Marguerite. *See* Couture
Marsolet de Saint-Aignan, Marie. *See* Le Barbier
Marsolet de Saint-Aignan, Marie (Damours de Chauffours), I, 201, 245; II, 166, 167, 653
Marsolet de Saint-Aignan, Nicolas, I, **493–95**, 133, 196, 199, 200, 245, 452, 516, 574; II, 16, 121, 159
Marsollet, Nicolas, I, 473
Marson. *See* Joybert
Marsters. *See* Masters
Marston, Benjamin (father), IV, 516
Marston, Benjamin, IV, **516–17**, 197
Marston, Elizabeth. *See* Winslow
Marston, Margaret (Philipse; Ogilvie), IV, 586
Marston, Sarah. *See* Swett
Martaud La Rigaudière, Agathe (Pélissier), IV, 618
Martch. *See* March
Marteau, Marie (Godefroy), I, 339
Marteau, Renée (Robinau de Bécancour), I, 574
Marteilhe, John, III, 478; IV, 602

Martel, François, II, 460
Martel, Isaac, I, 209
Martel, Joseph-Nicolas, II, 460; IV, 517
Martel, Louise-Catherine, II, 459
Martel, Marie-Agathe. *See* Baudoin
Martel, Marie-Anne. *See* Trottier Des Ruisseaux
Martel, Nicolas, II, 459
Martel, Pierre (brother hospitaller), III, 314
Martel, Pierre (son of RAYMOND), II, 459
Martel, Pierre-Michel (Philippe-Michel), II, 460; IV, **517**, 632
Martel, Raymond, II, **458–59**, 383, 533; III, 433
Martel de Belleville, Élisabeth. *See* Gatin
Martel de Belleville, Jean-Urbain, II, 460; III, **432–33**; IV, 344, 517
Martel de Berhouague, Jeanne. *See* Hargon
Martel de Berhouague, Pierre, II, 458
Martel de Brouague, Anne-Marie. *See* Favry Du Ponceau
Martel de Brouague, François, II, 7, 8, 9, 384; III, **433–35**, 75, 228, 354, 429, 631, 632; IV, 145, 271, 650, 754
Martel de Brouague, Louise. *See* Mariauchau d'Esgly
Martel de Brouague, Louise (Chaussegros de Léry), III, 434; IV, 145
Martel de Brouague, Marie-Charlotte. *See* Charest
Martel de Brouague, Pierre-Gratien, II, 383, 458; III, 433
Martel de Magos, Jean, I, 577; II, **459–60**, 450; III, 433; IV, 517
Martel de Magos, Marie-Anne. *See* Robinau
Martel de Saint-Antoine, Jean-Baptiste-Grégoire, II, 460; IV, 148, 461, 517, 750
Martel de Saint-Antoine, Marie. *See* Gauvreau
Marten, Humphrey, III, 304; IV, **517–19**, 33, 47, 157, 390, 684, 740, 742, 743, 760, 761
Marten, John America, IV, 518
Martignon. *See* Aprendestiguy
Martigny. *See* Le Moyne
Martin. *See also* Mécabou
Martin, Abraham, known as L'Écossais or Maître Abraham, I, **495–96**, 223, 233, 263, 264, 287, 379, 417; II, 460
Martin, Anne (Côté), I, 495
Martin, Anne (Dumas), IV, 242
Martin, Barbe-Madeleine. *See* Hillaire de La Rochette
Martin, Barthélemy, III, **435**; IV, 124, 126, 353, 354
Martin, Catherine. *See* Vigneau
Martin, Charles-Amador, I, 495; II, **460–61**, 227
Martin, Charles-Bruno, IV, 353
Martin, Christine (Gravé Du Pont), I, 346, 347
Martin, Christopher, I, **496**
Martin, Claude (father), I, 351
Martin, Claude, I, 351, 352, 355, 356, 357, 358, 552; III, 106
Martin, Élizabeth (Hillaire de Moissacq et de La Rochette), IV, 353
Martin, Énarde (Pécody), I, 535
Martin, Eustache, I, 109, 264, 386, 495
Martin*, Félix (1804–86), II, 237; III, 689; IV, 797
Martin, Gabrielle (Sabrevois de Sermonville), II, 588
Martin, George, II, **461**, 274, 497
Martin, Hélène. *See* Guilhermy
Martin, Hélène (Étienne; Chouart Des Groseilliers), I, 223, 495
Martin, Jean-Baptiste-Tropez, III, 435; IV, 124, 126, 127, 353, 354

Martin, Louis, I, 267
Martin, Marguerite. *See* Langlois
Martin, Marguerite (Daniel), I, 247
Martin, Marguerite (Racine), I, 263, 379, 495
Martin, Marianne. *See* Lafontaine
Martin, Marie. *See* Guyart
Martin, Marie-Françoise-Renée. *See* Levasseur
Martin, Mathieu, II, **462**
Martin, Nicolas, IV, 69
Martin, Pierre, II, 462
Martin, Thomas, I, 496
Martin, Vincent, III, 435; IV, 353
Martin de Lino, Angélique. *See* Chartier de Lotbinière
Martin de Lino, Antoine (baptized Guillaume), II, **462**, 204, 465
Martin de Lino, Antoinette. *See* Chalmette
Martin de Lino, Catherine. *See* Nolan
Martin de Lino, Catherine (Hazeur), II, 277, 465
Martin de Lino, Charles, II, 462, 465
Martin de Lino, Claude, II, 464
Martin de Lino, Geneviève-Françoise (Adhémar de Lantagnac), II, 465; III, 5
Martin de Lino, Ignace-François-Pierre (b. 1717, d. 1785 or 1786), II, 464; III, 134
Martin de Lino, Jean-François, II, **462–64**, 46; III, 352, 393, 550
Martin de Lino, Jean-Marie, II, 462, 465
Martin de Lino, Marie-Anne. *See* Peyrant
Martin de Lino, Marie-Anne, II, 465
Martin de Lino, Mathieu-François, I, 56; II, **464–65**, 33, 150, 161, 462, 463, 514, 526, 575; III, 5
Martin de Lino de Chalmette, Louis-Xavier, III, 424
Martineau, Philippe (Macé), I, 478
Martinet, Catherine. *See* Ducas
Martinet, Paul, II, 465
Martinet de Fonblanche, Jean, I, 109; II, **465–66**, 226
Martinet de Fonblanche, Marguerite. *See* Prud'homme
Martínez. *See also* Flórez
Martínez, Gertrudis González de. *See* González
Martínez Fernández y Martínez de la Sierra, Esteban José, IV, **519–21**, 73, 283, 325, 411, 568, 622, 623, 744
Martins, João, I, 234
Martire d'Anghiera, Pietro (Peter Martyr), I, 151, 152, 153, 154, 155
Martissans, Pierre, IV, 253
Maruffo, Raphael, I, 586
Mary I, Queen of England and Ireland, I, 157
Mary II, Queen of Great Britain and Ireland, I, 329, 426, 544, 545, 611; II, 50, 103, 231; IV, xxiv
Mary Stuart, Queen of Scots, I, 96, 382
Mascarene, Elizabeth. *See* Perry
Mascarene, Jean, III, 435
Mascarene, Margaret. *See* Salavy
Mascarene, Paul, II, 24; III, **435–40**, 4, 9, 84, 120, 128, 143, 144, 236, 256, 260, 261, 276, 277, 421, 427, 483, 517, 518, 583, 597, 665, 682; IV, xxii, xxv, 169, 239, 254, 295, 539, 559, 676, 783
Mascle, Jean, III, 440
Mascle, Suzanne. *See* Courtade
Mascle de Saint-Julhien, Jean, III, **440–41**, 72, 230, 231, 268, 667
Maseres*, Francis (1731–1824), xlii, xliv, xlv, xlviii, 7, 37,

104, 139, 150, 183, 184, 229, 230, 232, 295, 348, 349, 388, 398, 415, 554, 618, 642, 725, 753, 788, 789
Masham, Lady Abigail. *See* Hill
Masham, Samuel, 2nd Baron Masham, II, 287
Mash-i-pi-nash-i-wish. *See* Madjeckewiss
Mason. *See also* Tufton
Mason, Anne. *See* Greene
Mason, Hannah (Waldo), III, 652
Mason, Isabella. *See* Steed
Mason, John (father), I, 496
Mason, John, I, **496–97**, 51, 243, 262, 350, 650, 655
Massard, Leopold, I, 170
Massasoit, II, xxxv
Masse, Denis, II, 517
Massé, Énemond, I, **497–98**, 67, 68, 94, 95, 97, 98, 100, 101, 121, 142, 214, 299, 307, 338, 387, 411, 441, 442, 453, 470, 501, 560
Massé, François, I, 497
Massé, Geneviève (Lÿdius), IV, 488
Masse, Jeanne (Constantin), III, 134
Massé (Macé), Marie-Anne (Malhiot; Courreaud de La Coste), IV, 178
Massé, Philippe. *See* Bica
Massey, Eyre, 1st Baron Clarina, IV, 504, 706, 707
Massiac, Claude-Louis de, known as Marquis de Massiac, III, 18, 73; IV, 467, 616
Massicotte*, Édouard-Zotique (1867–1947), III, 232; IV, 269, 655
Massillon, Jean-Baptiste, I, 488
Masso, Imbert de, I, 498
Masson, François, I, 439
Masson (Musson), Lucresse (Arnoux), III, 18
Masson, Marie (Pézard de La Tousche), I, 543
Masson, Marie-Catherine (Hiché), III, 290
Masson de Montbrac, Jacques-Joseph, IV, 521
Massot, Joseph, IV, 125
Massot, Nicolas, IV, 124
Masters (Marsters), Abraham, IV, 217
Masters, John, III, 618
Masters, Margaret (Byng, Viscountess Torrington), III, 91
Masters, Ruth (Storer), II, 54
Masters, Sarah. *See* Knowlton
Matahachitoux (Soulier Rouge), IV, 664, 665
Mataut, Jean-Pierre, I, 490
Mataut, Louise. *See* Cloutier
Matchekewis. *See* Madjeckewiss
Mathé, Hugues, II, 29
Mather, Cotton, I, 544, 545; III, 25
Mather, Eleazar, II, 667
Mather, Eunice (Williams), II, 667; IV, 770
Mather, Increase, I, 544, 545
Mather, Maria (Mary) (Green), III, 267
Mathevet, Blanche. *See* Ranc
Mathevet, Claude, IV, 521
Mathevet, Jean-Claude, IV, **521–22**, 431, 507
Mathews, Catalina. *See* Abeel
Mathews, David, IV, **522–23**, 293
Mathews, David (son), IV, 523
Mathews, Edmond, III, 409
Mathews, Sarah. *See* Seymour
Mathews, Thomas, III, 131, 557, 610
Mathews, Vincent, IV, 522

Mathews, William Tryon, IV, 523
Mathieu, I, 71
Mathon, Marie-Thérèse (Desdevens de Glandons), IV, 215
Mathusson, Françoise (Plessy, *dit* Bélair), III, 523
Matonabbee, IV, **523–24**, 47, 339, 340, 341, 383, 584
Matthews, John, I, 567
Matthieu, Guillaume, II, 95
Maudave, Comte de. *See* Féderbe
Maudoux, Abel, I, 578; II, 45, 223, 445, 480; III, 207, 499
Maufils, Françoise (Picard) IV, 629
Maufils, Madeleine. *See* Poulain
Maufils, Marie-Madeleine, *dite* de Saint-Louis, II, **466**
Maufils, Pierre, II, 466
Maugean. *See* Mangeant
Maugenest, François, IV, 524
Maugenest (Maugenest, *dit* Saint-Horan), Germain, IV, **524–25**, 726
Maugenest, Louise. *See* Descary
Maugenest, Marie-Anne. *See* Saint-Horan
Maugenest, Rosalie. *See* Barrère
Mauger. *See also* Gadois
Mauger, Elizabeth (Mauger), IV, 525
Mauger, J., IV, 529
Mauger, Joshua, III, 364, 457, 583; IV, **525–29**, 52, 53, 116, 131, 266, 273, 274, 275, 291, 450, 452, 561, 695, 696, 780
Mauger, Josué, IV, 525
Mauger, Louise (Gadoys), I, 319, 557; III, 232
Mauger, Sarah. *See* Le Couteur
Mauger, Sarah, IV, 525
Maugis, Charlotte (Miville), I, 511
Maugras. *See also* Gamelin
Maugras, Jacques, II, 283
Maugras, Marguerite (Véronneau), III, 643
Maugras, Marie-Jeanne (Gamelin), III, 233
Maugue, Antoine, I, 498
Maugue, Claude, I, **498**; II, 226, 421, 440; IV, 529
Maugue, Françoise. *See* Rigaud
Maugue, Louise. *See* Jousset
Maugue, Louise (Brunet, *dit* La Sablonnière), III, 88
Maugue, Marie-Anne (Garreau, *dit* Saint-Onge), IV, 287, 529
Maugue-Garreau, Marie-Josèphe, *dite* de l'Assomption, IV, **529–30**, 638
Maumousseau, Françoise, II, **466–67**, 235
Maumousseau, Jean, II, 466
Maumousseau, Renée. *See* Verron
Maupas. *See* Pouchot
Maupassant, Eustache, I, **498–99**
Maupeou, Guillaume de, II, 442
Mauprée. *See* Des Granges
Maur. *See* Juchereau
Maurault*, Joseph-Pierre-Anselme (1819–70), IV, 294
Maurepas. *See* Phélypeaux
Maurepas, Comtesse de. *See* La Rochefoucauld-Roye
Maurès de Malartic, Anne-Joseph-Hippolyte de, Comte de Malartic, IV, **530–31**
Maurès de Malartic, Antoinette-Charlotte de, Comtesse de Montricoux. *See* Savignac
Maurès de Malartic, Pierre-Hippolyte-Joseph de, Comte de Montricoux, IV, 530
Maurice, Mrs, I, 605, 657

Maurice (Vignau), Jacques, III, 358
Maurice, Jean-Baptiste, III, 103, 137
Maurin, Archange. *See* Dagneau Douville de Quindre
Maurin, François, III, **441–42**; IV, 125, 127, 435, 461, 517, 565, 621
Maurin, Jean, IV, 559
Maurin, Marguerite-Geneviève. *See* Mounier
Maurin, Philippe, III, 441
Maury, Jean-Louis, IV, 529
Mauvide, Jean, III, 518
Mavit, Aymare, IV, 286
Maximilian II Emmanuel, Elector of Bavaria, II, 279, 643
May, Henry, I, **499**
Mayar (Mayard). *See* Maillard
Mayer, André, I, 88
Maynwaringe. *See* Mainwaring
Mayrac. *See* Meyracq
Mayrand, Sister, I, 117
Mayrand, Anne, II, 44
Mazarin, Jules, Cardinal Mazarin, I, 44, 389, 442, 615; II, 48, 362, 363, 631, 656
Mazas, Alexandre, II, 52
Mazé. *See* Peronne
Mazière, Marie-Madeleine. *See* Le Poupet de La Boularderie
Méan, Jean-Ferdinand, Baron de Méan, II, 332
Meares*, John (d. 1809), IV, 218, 244, 325, 520, 568, 746, 768
Mécabou (Martin), I, 199
Mécatépilésis, III, 527; IV, 408
Mechin, Jeanne (Baudry), III, 451
Meckinac. *See* Mikinak
Médicis. *See* Catherine de Médicis; Marie de Médicis
Medoux, Jean, IV, 252
Medoux, Louis, IV, 252
Medrano, Catalina de (Cabot), I, 158
Meesinkeeshick, III, 595
Megapolensis, Jan, I, 462
Meilleur*, Jean-Baptiste (1796–1878), IV, 801
Mekaoua, II, 474
Melançon, Madeleine (Le Poupet de La Boularderie), II, 417; IV, 468
Melanson, Anne (Saint-Étienne de La Tour), I, 514; II, 590; IV, xix
Melanson, Charles, I, **499–500**; II, 625; IV, xix
Melanson, Marie. *See* Dugas
Melanson, *dit* La Verdure, Anne (Jacau), IV, 382
Melanson, *dit* La Verdure, Marguerite. *See* Mius d'Entremont
Melanson, *dit* La Verdure, Marguerite (Bourg, *dit* Belle-Humeur), III, 83, 366; IV, 441
Melanson, *dit* La Verdure, Pierre, I, 436, 499, 500, 510; II, 46, 625; III, 83
Meldrum, Helen (Abercromby), IV, 4
Mellanson, Peter, II, 198
Melville, Viscount. *See* Dundas
Membertou, I, **500–1**, 69, 97, 100, 307, 367, 526, 529, 604
Membré, Zénobe, I, **501–2**, 176, 178, 179, 180, 420, 438, 440; II, 278, 419, 634
Memeskia (La Demoiselle, Old Britain), III, xlii, 100, 525; IV, liv, 563, 633, 666
Ménage, Anne. *See* Leblanc
Ménage, Anne (Levasseur), II, 467

Ménage, Dorothée. *See* Brassard
Ménage, François (grandfather), II, 467
Ménage, François, II, 467
Ménage, Françoise. *See* Lunette
Ménage, Jean-Baptiste, II, 467
Ménage, Marie-Anne (Lajoüe), II, 337, 467
Ménage, Pierre, I, 572; II, **467**, 337, 338
Ménard, Marie (Bourdon), II, 92
Ménard, Maurice, III, 147
Ménard, René, I, **502**, 65, 206, 225, 251, 461, 566; II, 157, 317
Ménars, Marquis de. *See* Charron
Méndez, Martin, I, 156
Mendoza, Pedro de, I, 342
Menehwehna. *See* Minweweh
Menendez (seaman), I, 310
Menescardi, Giustino, I, 152
Meneux, *dit* Châteauneuf, Jacques, I, 550
Meneval (Menneval). *See* Des Friches
Mennander, Carl Fredrik, IV, 406
Menneville. *See* Duquesne
Menou, Nicole de. *See* Jousserand
Menou d'Aulnay, Charles de, I, **502–6**, 25, 32, 62, 63, 66, 90, 129, 234, 256, 257, 258, 259, 261, 323, 379, 380, 383, 433, 435, 442, 468, 469, 490, 514, 569, 593, 595, 596, 604; II, 94, 625
Menou d'Aulnay, Jeanne de. *See* Motin
Menou d'Aulnay, Marie de, I, 436
Menou de Charnisay, René de, I, 433, 502, 505
Menspéré, II, 646
Mentor, Dominique-François, IV, 204, 205
Mény, Marie-Madeleine. *See* Péan
Menzies*, Archibald (1754–1842), IV, 747
Mepomoit. *See* Nepomoit
Mequinac. *See* Mikinak
Mérand. *See* Mayrand
Merçan, Jean, I, 260
Merçan, Marie-Anne. *See* Denys de Fronsac
Mercator, Gerard, I, 678, 680
Mercer, James, III, 588
Mercer, Sarah. *See* Day
Mercereau, Pierre, II, 506
Mercier. *See also* Le Mercier
Mercier, Mme, III, 350, 353
Mercier, Anne. *See* Jacquereau
Mercier, Catherine. *See* Lafontaine
Mercier, Jean-Auguste, III, 443
Mercier, Jean-François, III, **442–43**, 258
Mercier, Jean-Pierre, II, 117, 628; III, **443–44**, 105, 442, 640
Mercier, John Dyer, IV, 791
Mercier, Joseph-Marie, III, 443
Mercier, Louis (father), III, 410, 442, 443
Mercier, Louis, III, 443
Mercier, Marguerite (Des Bordes Landriève), IV, 435
Mercier, Marguerite (Lozeau), III, 410
Mercœur, Duc de. *See* Vandémont
Mercure, M., IV, 148
Meredudd ap Rhys, I, 677
Meriel (Meriel de Meulan), Henri-Antoine, II, **467–68**, 606; IV, 765
Mérieu. *See* Pastour
Mérieux. *See* Saint-Germain

Merlac, André-Louis de, I, **506–7**; II, 249, 304, 326, 330
Mermande. *See* Sagean
Mermet, Jean, II, **468–69**, 306, 455, 501, 653
Merrick, Barbara (Button), I, 144
Merrick, Rhys, I, 144
Merveille, Captain, I, 347
Merveilleux, Louis-François de, II, 424
Merven, Tanguay, IV, 678
Merville. *See* Le Goüès
Mésaiger, Charles-Michel, III, **444**, 108, 249, 251, 580; IV, 289
Meschin, Jérémie de, III, 392
Mesgouez. *See* La Roche
Mesnu. *See* Peuvret
Meson Basse. *See* Deschevery
Mesplet, Antoinette. *See* Capeau
Mesplet, Fleury, IV, **532–34**, 107, 229, 336, 346, 373, 391, 689, 697, 698
Mesplet, Jean-Baptiste, IV, 532
Mesplet, Marie. *See* Mirabeau
Mesplet, Marie-Anne. *See* Tison
Messamouet, I, **507**, 96, 604
Messayé, Gabriel, IV, 386
Messein. *See* Bailly
Messier, Anne. *See* Le Moyne
Messier, David, II, 469
Messier, Élisabeth (Thierry), II, 469
Messier, Jacques, II, 469
Messier, Marguerite. *See* Bar
Messier, Marguerite (Le Sueur), II, 427
Messier, Martine (Primot), I, **507–8**, 465; II, 193, 469
Messier, *dit* Saint-Michel, Michel, II, **469–70**, 164, 427
Mestigoït, I, 164, 533
Mésy. *See* Saffray
Metacomet. *See* Pometacom
Metaminens. *See* Perrot, Nicolas
Metawiss, IV, 774
Metayer, Catherine (Déat), III, 169
Métivier, Marc-Anselme de, III, 612
Métivier, Marguerite (Ducharme), IV, 233
Métivier, Marie-Anselme de, II, 96
Metiwemig (Metigonèque, Mitewemeg), I, 65; II, 625
Métru, Nicolas, II, 159
Meulan. *See* Meriel
Meulles, Mme de. *See* Bégon de La Picardière
Meulles, Jacques de, I, 90, 178, 238, 265, 298, 327, 340, 443, 444, 445, 446, 508, 526, 578, 664; II, **470–73**, xxii, 31, 32, 63, 72, 75, 89, 99, 100, 177, 205, 228, 242, 263, 380, 409, 421, 524, 533, 576, 578, 583; III, 57, 648; IV, xvii
Meulles, Pierre de, II, 470
Meur, Jeanne de (Duparc), III, 204
Meurin, Sébastien-Louis, III, 36, 442; IV, 271, 390
Meusnier, Anne (Richard), I, 573
Meyer, Jeann(?) George, IV, 702
Meynier, Madeleine. *See* Laguide
Meyracq. *See also* Domingué
Meyracq (Mayrac), Marie (Fautoux), III, 216
Mézière*, Henry-Antoine (fl. 1771–1819), IV, 534
Mézière, Pierre-François, IV, 5, 270, 534
Mézières de Lépervanche, Louise-Antoinette de (Gaultier de La Vérendrye), III, 243; IV, 289
Mézillac. *See* Du Pont Duchambon
Mézy. *See* Le Normant; Saffray

Miatt. *See* Myatt
Miçel (Witzel), Gabriel, I, 157
Michaud, Louis, IV, 124
Michel, Barbe. *See* Esmard
Michel, Gilles, I, 473
Michel, Jacques, I, 405
Michelance, Marie de (Sallaberry), III, 582
Michelborne, Sir Edward, I, 252
Michel de Danton, Gabriel, IV, 481
Michel de Danton, Gabrielle-Augustine (Lévis, Duchesse de Lévis), IV, 481
Michel de Villebois, Anne. *See* Rostan
Michel de Villebois, Jean-Baptiste, III, 444
Michel de Villebois de La Rouvillière, Honoré, III, **444–46**, 30, 56, 240, 270, 295, 563, 564, 626; IV, 359, 665, 668, 709, 749, 750
Michel de Villebois de La Rouvillière, Honoré-Henri-Michel-Étienne, III, 445
Michel de Villebois de La Rouvillière, Marie-Catherine-Élisabeth. *See* Bégon de La Cour
Michel de Villebois de La Rouvillière, Marie-Catherine-Élisabeth, III, 240, 445
Michelet, Jeanne (Guyart), I, 351
Michelet Du Cosnier, Marie-Françoise (Hocquart), IV, 354
Michelle, Bertrane (Lemaître), III, 377
Michipichy, II, 505; III, **446**, xxxv, 495; IV, liii
Michon, Abel, II, 156; III, 237
Micoc. *See* Mikak
Middleton, Christopher, II, 10, 314, 493, 604; III, **446–50**, 302, 303, 415, 471, 472, 490, 520, 544, 599, 624, 625, 662, 663; IV, 218, 339, 377, 380
Middleton, Jane, III, 449
Middleton, Judith (Isbister), III, 449; IV, 380
Middleton, Roger, I, 300
Migeon, Jean, I, 508
Migeon, Marie. *See* Desbordes
Migeon de Branssat, Catherine. *See* Gauchet de Belleville
Migeon de Branssat, Jean-Baptiste, I, **508**, 47, 79, 105, 541; II, 193, 205, 223, 305; III, 402, 450; IV, 535
Migeon de Branssat, Marie-Anne, *dite* de la Nativité, IV, **535–36**
Migeon de Branssat, Thérèse-Denise (Juchereau de Saint-Denys; Liénard de Beaujeu), II, 305; III, 400, 402
Migeon de La Gauchetière, Daniel, II, 224; III, **450**, 378, 520
Migeon de La Gauchetière, Marie. *See* Le Gay de Beaulieu
Migeon de La Gauchetière, Marie-Thérèse (Le Marchand de Lignery), III, 378; IV, 178
Mignac (Mignaque). *See* Miniac
Migneau, Louis, IV, 629
Migneron, Geneviève. *See* Leduc
Mignon, Marguerite-Jeanne (Legardeur de Repentigny), IV, 449
Mignon, Philippe-Jean-Baptiste, IV, 449
Mignot, Marie-Cécile (Raymond), III, 617
Mignot, *dit* Chatillon, Jean, I, 490
Mignot, *dit* Chatillon, Louise. *See* Cloutier
Mikak, III, 411; IV, **536–37**, 740
Mikinak, III, **450–51**, xxxix, 328, 496; IV, 464
Milan, Duke of. *See* Sforza
Mildmay, William, III, 30
Miles, Samuel, II, 663
Miller, Henry, IV, 714

Miller(?), Margaret (Greese; Henry), IV, 343
Miller, Michael, IV, 194
Miller, Thomas, I, 519
Millet. *See also* Heu
Millet, Jeanne (Langlois), I, 417
Millet, Pierre, I, 322, 634; II, **473–74**, xxxvi, 107, 237, 255; III, 104
Millidge*, Thomas (d. 1816), IV, 626
Mills, Edward, I, 672
Mills, Sir Thomas, IV, **537–38**, 198, 579, 792
Milly, Catherine. *See* Baudry
Milly, François, III, **451–52**; IV, 253
Milly, François (nephew), III, 452; IV, 645
Milly, Gaspard, III, 451
Milly, Jean, III, 451
Milly, Louise. *See* Dupuy
Milly, Marie. *See* Aubert
Milly, Thomas (brother of FRANÇOIS), III, 451
Milly, Thomas (nephew of FRANÇOIS), IV, 422
Milly, *dit* La Croix, Jean, III, 451; IV, 239
Milnes*, Sir Robert Shore (1746–1837), IV, 135
Milot, Jean, II, 105
Minavavana. *See* Minweweh
Minchilay, II, 503
Mindham, Catherine (Isham), III, 301
Mine, Jean de, II, 593
Mine, Marie-Anne de. *See* Saint-Ours
Minet (engineer), I, 180
Minet, Anne. *See* Bonhomme
Minet, Anne (Perthuis), II, 520
Minet, Marie-Madeleine. *See* Lefebvre
Minet, Marie-Madeleine, III, 494
Mingan. *See* Jolliet
Miniac, Jean-Pierre de , III, 120, 196, 203, 285, 343; IV, **538–40**, 295, 387, 430
Minweweh, III, **452–53**, xxxviii, 262, 530, 660; IV, lv, 78, 233, 241, 582
Mirabeau, Marie (Mesplet), IV, 532, 533, 534
Miramion. *See* Beauharnais
Miramont, M. de, II, 182, 184
Mirande, Marguerite. *See* Bourgeois
Miriot, Jeanne (Hertel), I, 368
Miristou, I, **508–9**, 61, 195, 479
Miscomote (Miscamote), II, **474**
Miscouaky (Misconky, Miscoualzy, Miskouaky), II, **474–75**, xxxvii, 414, 453, 505; III, 446
Misèle (Missègle). *See* Bonne
Miskouensa, II, 499
Missenden, Samuel, I, **509–10**
Mitchell, Miss, IV, 686
Mitchell, George, III, **453**
Mitchell, John, II, 439
Mitchell, Sarah. *See* Taylor
Mitchell, Thomas, III, **453–54**, 123, 127, 406, 533
Mitchikiweese. *See* Madjeckewiss
Mitewemeg. *See* Metiwemig
Miteȣamegȣkyȣ (Marie Couc, *dit* Lafleur), III, 147
Mitford, James, III, 287
Mitigoukwe (Jeanne), I, 640
Mitton, Elizabeth (Clarke), I, 654
Mius, Francis, III, 358, 359, 418
Mius d'Entremont, Anne, Baronne de Pobomcoup. *See* Saint-Étienne de La Tour

Mius d'Entremont, Jacques, Baron de Pobomcoup, I, 510, 514; II, 205, 512

Mius d'Entremont, Madeleine, Baronne de Popomcoup. *See* Hélie Du Tillet

Mius d'Entremont, Madeleine, I, 510

Mius d'Entremont, Marguerite (Melanson, *dit* La Verdure), I, 500, 510; III, 83

Mius d'Entremont, Marie-Josephe (Couagne), II, 154

Mius d'Entremont, Philippe, Baron de Pobomcoup, I, **510**, 595; IV, 247

Mius d'Entremont, Philippe (son), I, 510; II, 3, 7

Mius d'Entremont, Thérèse. *See* Abbadie de Saint-Castin

Mius d'Entremont de Pobomcoup, Anne (Saillans; Pastour de Costebelle; Navailles, Baronne de Labatut), II, 512

Mius d'Entremont de Pobomcoup, Jeanne (Du Pont Duchambon), IV, 247, 249

Mius d'Entremont de Pobomcoup, Marie (Du Pont Duvivier), II, 205; III, 499, 552; IV, 250, 783

Mius de Plemazais, Abraham, I, 510, 514

Mius de Plemazais, Marguerite. *See* Saint-Étienne de La Tour

Miville, Charlotte. *See* Maugis

Miville, François, I, 511

Miville, Jacques, I, 511

Miville, Marie (Amiot, *dit* Villeneuve), I, 60

Miville, Pierre, known as Le Suisse, I, **511**

Moffatt. *See* Johnstone

Mog (father), II, 475

Mog, II, **475–77**, xxxvi, 645; III, xxxvii, 477, 584

Mogé. *See* Gadois

Mohier, Gervais, I, **511**

Moireau, Claude, I, 264; II, **477–78**

Moissacq. *See* Hillaire

Molé, Marie-Louise (Talon, Marquise de Boulay). III, 458

Molière. *See* Poquelin, Jean-Baptiste

Molin, Laurent, I, 63

Molin, Marie (Bermen de La Martinière), II, 57

Mollineda y Losada, Francisca de (Bodega), IV, 72

Molyneux, Elizabeth (Shuldham), IV, 707

Molyneux, Émery, I, 252

Monbeton de Brouillan, Charlotte de. *See* Des Roches Duplesy

Monbeton de Brouillan, Georgette de. *See* Pouy

Monbeton de Brouillan, Jacques de, II, 478

Monbeton de Brouillan, Jacques-François de, I, 246, 530; II, **478–82**, 3, 6, 36, 37, 45, 64, 167, 169, 177, 246, 257, 258, 382, 395, 411, 434, 442, 445, 510, 579, 590, 605, 626, 654, 666; III, 177, 207, 454, 681, 682

Monbeton de Brouillan, *dit* Saint-Ovide, Joseph de, II, 12, 22, 23, 122, 152, 198, 218, 219, 220, 225, 255, 336, 339, 411, 412, 417, 439, 479, 482, 510, 511, 512, 524, 610, 611, 619, 643, 649; III, **454–57**, 6, 20, 22, 79, 93, 116, 120, 157, 173, 177, 178, 191, 208, 222, 264, 357, 368, 386, 387, 388, 389, 396, 475, 500, 512, 532, 566, 567, 574, 575, 576, 597, 630, 644; IV, 15, 247, 252, 360, 466

Moncarville. *See* Legardeur

Monceaux. *See* Clément; Ruette

Moncel. *See* Giffard

Moncharvaux. *See* Tisserant

Monchy. *See* Mouchy

Monckton, Elizabeth, Viscountess Galway. *See* Manners

Monckton, John, 1st Viscount Galway, IV, 540

Monckton, Robert, III, xxvi, 87, 129, 362, 363, 364, 365, 425, 479, 513, 570, 589, 590, 601, 605, 667, 668, 669, 670, 672; IV, **540–42**, xxv, xxviii, 22, 36, 93, 141, 193, 213, 250, 289, 335, 382, 436, 452, 453, 501, 570, 631, 668, 680, 700, 714, 769, 773, 774, 780

Moncours. *See* Hertel

Moncrieff, James, IV, 501

Moncroc. *See* Gripière

Monfort. *See* Demers

Monforton, M., IV, 702

Monic, Jean de, II, 482

Monic, Jeanne de. *See* Dufresnoy Carion

Monic, Joseph de, II, **482–83**, 36, 45, 214, 434, 479, 510; III, 454, 499

Monic, Marguerite de. *See* Cornet

Monière. *See* Lemoine

Monk, Ann. *See* Deering

Monk (Monck), Christopher, 2nd Duke of Albemarle, I, 544

Monk*, George Henry (1748–1823), III, 457

Monk, James, III, **457–58**; IV, 526, 560

Monk*, Sir James (1745–1826), III, 457; IV, 185, 229, 274, 313, 345, 400, 451, 581, 716

Monnoir. *See* Ramezay

Monplaisir. *See* Dizy

Monrepos. *See* Guiton

Monro*, David (1765–1835), IV, 198

Monro, George, III, 460; IV, 426

Mons. *See* Monts

Monseignat, Charles de, II, **483–86**, 276, 283, 352, 448, 576; III, 58, 60

Monseignat, Claude de. *See* Sainte

Monseignat, Hélène de. *See* Perchot

Monseignat, Jean de, II, 483

Monseignat, Louis-Denis de, II, 485

Monseignat, Marguerite de. *See* Delesnerac

Monson, Lewis, 1st Baron Sondes, IV, 348

Montagu, Anne (Wilmot), III, 663

Montagu, Edward, III, 663

Montagu, George, 1st Earl of Halifax, III, 663

Montagu, John, IV, 159, 259, 402, 437, 470

Montagu, John, 4th Earl of Sandwich, IV, 164, 600, 763

Montagu, Mary (Osborn), III, 496

Montaigne. *See also* Eyquem

Montaigne, Michel de, I, 471

Montalan, Éléonore (Berger), II, 54

Montarville. *See* Boucher

Montbazillac, Vicomte de. *See* Brisay

Montbeillard. *See* Potot

Montbéliard, Prince of. *See* Leopold Eberhard

Montbrac. *See* Masson

Montbrun. *See* Boucher

Montcalm, Angélique-Louise de, Marquise de Montcalm. *See* Talon de Boulay

Montcalm, Louis de, III, 458

Montcalm, Louis-Daniel de, III, 458

Montcalm, Louis-Joseph de, Marquis de Montcalm, II, 43; III, **458–69**, xviii, xix, xx, xxi, xxvi, 12, 19, 55, 84, 85, 86, 99, 102, 161, 171, 188, 198, 289, 293, 328, 400, 406, 408, 441, 510, 526, 534, 535, 537, 554, 555, 570, 588, 669, 670, 671, 672, 673, 676; IV, 5, 14, 23, 34, 54, 63, 68, 84, 88, 96, 143, 146, 183, 211, 214, 224, 242, 257, 307, 308, 312, 347, 353, 382, 395, 401, 426, 449, 459, 460, 478, 479, 480, 481, 482, 487, 495, 500, 503, 514, 521, 530, 531, 563, 582, 589, 612, 616, 620, 633, 636,

637, 641, 642, 651, 660, 662, 669, 670, 671, 672, 673, 674, 687, 729, 733, 739, 773
Montcalm, Marie-Thérèse-Charlotte de. *See* Lauris de Castellane
Montcalm, Marthe de. *See* Gozon
Montchervaux. *See* Tisserant
Monteagle, Baron. *See* Parker
Montecalunya. *See* Cabot, John
Montegron. *See* Levrault
Montéléon, Louis de, II, 90, 427
Montéléon, Marie-Anne-Josette de. *See* Lestringant de Saint-Martin
Montespan, Marquise de. *See* Rochechouart de Mortemart
Montesquieu, Baron de. *See* Secondat
Montesson. *See* Legardeur
Montet, Marie (David), II, 170
Montfort, François, III, 220
Montgolfier, Étienne, II, 414; III, 199, 296, 487; IV, **542–45**, 6, 89, 90, 98, 188, 201, 236, 238, 270, 286, 318, 371, 391, 430, 463, 509, 510, 532, 572, 639
Montgolfier, Jacques-Étienne, IV, 542
Montgolfier, Joseph-Michel, IV, 542
Montgolfier, Raymond, IV, 542
Montgomery, Earl of. *See* Herbert
Montgomery, Sir James, IV, 551
Montgomery, Sir James William, IV, 352, 353, 497, 550, 551, 607, 608
Montgomery, Janet. *See* Livingston
Montgomery, Margaret, Lady Montgomery. *See* Scott
Montgomery, Mary. *See* Franklyn
Montgomery, Richard, IV, **545–50**, 40, 215, 230, 262, 271, 336, 345, 347, 390, 427, 503, 532, 629, 791
Montgomery, Thomas, IV, 545
Montgomery, William, IV, **550–52**
Montignac. *See* Hautefort
Montigny. *See also* Testard
Montigny, François de, II, 110, 134, 171, 331; III, **469–70**, 263, 640, 684, 685
Montisambert; Montizambert. *See* Boucher
Montmagny. *See* Huault
Montmainier, Marie (Dumas), II, 42
Montmollin*, David-François de (d. 1803), IV, 104, 139, 140, 657, 698, 738, 753, 754
Montmorency, M. de, II, 520
Montmorency, Charlotte-Marguerite de (Princesse de Condé), I, 484
Montmorency, Emme de, Duchesse de Montmorency. *See* Laval
Montmorency, Henri II, Duc de Montmorency, I, 159, 186, 187, 194, 195, 427, 433
Montmorency, Mathieu II de, Duc de Montmorency, known as Le Grand, II, 359
Montorgueuil. *See* Dauphin
Montortier, M. de, I, 327
Montoson, Sieur de, II, 532
Montour (agent), II, 126
Montour, Mme. *See* Couc, Elizabeth
Montour, Andrew (Henry), III, 147, 502
Montour, Catherine, III, 147
Montour, Louis, III, 147
Montpensier, Duc de. *See* Bourbon
Montpensier, Duchesse de. *See* Orléans
Montplaisir. *See* Dizy

Montresor, Frances. *See* Tucker
Montrésor, Frank Montrésor, IV, 553
Montresor, James Gabriel, IV, 552
Montresor, John, IV, **552–53**
Montresor, Mary. *See* Haswell
Montreuil. *See* Gohin
Montricoux, Comte de. *See* Maurès
Montricoux, Comtesse de. *See* Savignac
Monts. *See also* Du Gua
Monts, Sieur de, I, **511–12**, 325, 615
Montsaulnin, Adrienne de (Renaud d'Avène de Des Méloizes et de Berges), I, 572
Monvoisin, Catherine. *See* Deshayes
Moodey, Samuel, II, 664
Moody, Ann (wife of JOHN), II, 487
Moody, Caleb, III, 470
Moody, Hannah. *See* Sewall
Moody*, James (d. 1809), IV, 222
Moody, John, II, **486–87**, 37, 97, 98, 117, 118, 165, 250, 293, 350, 351, 438, 439, 583, 619, 643; III, 618, 619
Moody, Joseph, III, 471
Moody, Judith. *See* Bradbury
Moody, Mary, III, 471
Moody, Ruth. *See* Plummer
Moody, Samuel, III, **470–71**
Moody, William, III, 470
Mooney, Edward L., IV, 397
Moor, Mary. *See* Bradley
Moor, William, III, **471–72**, 39, 303, 448, 449, 594, 625, 663
Moore, Agnes. *See* McKay
Moore, Cécile (Cecilia). *See* Richardson
Moore, Edward, II, 487
Moore, Frances (Brooke), IV, **553–56**, 103, 104
Moore, Jeanne. *See* Lemelin
Moore, Sir John, IV, 504
Moore, Mary. *See* Knowles
Moore, Pierre, II, 487
Moore, Sarah (Digby), IV, 553, 554
Moore, Thomas (father of FRANCES), IV, 553
Moore, Thomas (ship's captain), IV, 32
Moore, Thomas, II, **487–88**, 235, 409
Moore, William, IV, **556–58**, 107, 580
Moquet, Denis, II, 278
Mora. *See* Mouet
Moral de Saint-Quentin, Marie. *See* Marguerie
Moral de Saint-Quentin, Marie-Thérèse (Véron de Grandmesnil), II, 648; III, 642
Moral de Saint-Quentin, Quentin, I, 369; II, 16, 63, 648
Morampont. *See* Regnard
Moranget. *See* Crevel
Moras. *See* Peirenc
Moray, Elizabeth (Rollo, Baroness Rollo), III, 565
Mordaunt, Charles, 3rd Earl of Peterborough, II, 274
Mordaunt, Sir John, III, 666; IV, 171
More, Elizabeth (Rastell), I, 565
More, Sir Thomas, I, 565, 566
Moreau. *See also* Desjordy; Moireau
Moreau, M., IV, 755
Moreau, Catherine (Adhémar), III, 4; IV, 5
Moreau, Edme, III, **472–73**
Moreau, François, III, 300
Moreau, Françoise. *See* Fortier

Moreau, François-Urbain, III, 473

Moreau, Georges, III, 473

Moreau, Gratiane (Hamare), II, 273

Moreau, Jacques, III, 472

Moreau, Jean-Baptiste, III, **473–74**, 635, 650; IV, 775

Moreau, Marguerite. *See* Germain

Moreau, Marie-Joseph (Gaufin), III, 240

Moreau, Marie-Madeleine (Bazil), III, 38

Moreau, Marie-Madeleine (Roma), III, 566

Moreau, *dit* Lataupine, Louise-Élisabeth (Lajus), III, 344; IV, 432

Moreau, *dit* La Taupine, Pierre, I, 394; II, 532

Moreau de Brésoles, François, I, 512

Moreau de Brésoles, Françoise. *See* Gailliard

Moreau de Brésoles, Judith, I, **512–13**, 220, 458, 478, 480, 487; II, 164

Moreau de Saint-Méry, Médéric-Louis-Élie, III, 556, 634

Moreau de Séchelles, Mlle (Hérault), IV, 76, 755

Morel (merchant), III, 396

Morel, Captain, I, 292

Morel, Claude, I, 469

Morel, Fréderic, I, 469

Morel, Thomas, I, **513**, 108; II, 19

Morel de La Durantaye, Alliette. *See* Du Houssaye

Morel de La Durantaye, Françoise. *See* Duquet

Morel de La Durantaye, Joseph-François, II, 489

Morel de La Durantaye, Louis-Joseph, III, 291

Morel de La Durantaye, Olivier, I, 444, 479; II, **488–89**, 43, 48, 49, 217, 218, 235, 263, 303, 346, 388, 518, 635; III, 237, 373, 568

Morel de La Durantaye, Thomas, II, 488

Moreri, Louis, II, 208

Morgan, Lewis Henry, III, 335, 337

Morgann*, Maurice (1726–1802), IV, xlv, 348, 349

Morhouse, Abraham, IV, 37

Morillon, Suzanne (Danré de Blanzy), III, 163

Morillon Du Bourg, I, **513–14**, 435, 436, 636

Morillonnet, *dit* Berry, Claude, III, 633

Morimé. *See* Lamorinie

Morin. *See also* Roberol

Morin, Agnès (Bonhomme, *dit* Beaupré), III, 69

Morin, Anne (Louet; Deneau), II, 447

Morin, Antoine (brother of Jean-Baptiste MORIN de Fonfay), IV, 28, 421, 558, 559

Morin, Antoine (fisherman), IV, 124

Morin, Claude, IV, 558

Morin, Claude-Marie-François, IV, 205

Morin, Germain, I, 264, 392; II, **489**

Morin, Hélène. *See* Desportes

Morin, Jean-Baptiste, I, 264

Morin, Joseph, IV, 203

Morin, Madeleine. *See* Lamouraux-Rochefort

Morin, Marie, I, 78, 216, 221, 230, 231, 478, 480, 512; II, **489–92**, 133, 466; III, 155, 369

Morin, Marie-Anne (Deguise, *dit* Flamand), III, 170; IV, 202

Morin, Marie-Anne (Pinguet de Vaucour), III, 521

Morin, Marie-Françoise (Poireaux; Raby), IV, 650

Morin, Marie-Madeleine (Rageot), I, 561; II, 540, 541

Morin, Noël, I, 264; II, 489

Morin de Fonfay, Jean-Baptiste, IV, **558–59**, 421, 644, 645

Morin de Fonfay, Marie-Charlotte. *See* Boschet de Saint-Martin

Morisseau, Madeleine (Gimbal; Dumas Saint-Martin), IV, 243, 244

Morisseau, Marie-Josephte (Strouds), III, 602

Morisseaux, Jean-Baptiste-Laurent, IV, 571

Morisset*, Gérard (1898–1970), III, 67, 68, 346, 422, 645, 648, 695; IV, 206, 805, 806

Morley, Baron. *See* Parker

Mornay. *See* Duplessis

Morosini, Francesco, I, 135

Morpain, Jacques, III, 474

Morpain, Marguerite. *See* Audoire

Morpain, Marie-Joseph. *See* Damours de Chauffours

Morpain, Pierre, II, 3, 38, 142; III, **474–76**, 6, 507; IV, 248, 253, 588, 589

Morris, Charles (father of CHARLES), IV, 559

Morris, Charles, III, 128, 130, 174, 364, 365, 457, 583; IV, **559–63**, 53, 92, 110, 273, 300, 313, 351, 451, 581

Morris*, Charles (1731/32–1802), IV, 300, 562, 603, 626

Morris, Esther. *See* Rainsthorpe

Morris, Lewis, III, 587, 658

Morris, Mary. *See* Read

Morris, Mary (Danks), IV, 193

Morris, Robert, I, 601

Morris, Roger, III, 142

Morris*, Thomas (d. 1818), IV, 762

Morris, William, IV, 40

Morrison, James, IV, 330

Morse, Joseph, III, 588

Mortemart. *See* Rochechouart

Morthon de Grandval, Pierre de, II, 270

Mortier, Catherine (Joannès de Chacornacle), II, 300

Morton, Arthur Silver, III, 254

Morville. *See* Laguer

Morville, Comte de. *See* Fleuriau

Moses, Katy, IV, 416

Mossion, Robert, I, 474

Mostyn, John, IV, 577

Mostyn, Savage, III, 70, 363; IV, xxvi

Motin, Anne (Le Creux Du Breuil), I, 442

Motin, Jeanne (Menou d'Aulnay; Saint-Étienne de La Tour), I, **514**, 114, 129, 257, 261, 433, 434, 436, 442, 469, 503, 505, 510, 595; II, 591

Motin de Corcelles (Courcelles), Louis, I, 442, 503, 514

Mottin. *See* Motin

Mouchy, Nicolas de, I, **514**; II, 514

Mouet de Langlade, Augustin, IV, 563

Mouet de Langlade, Charles, IV, 563

Mouet de Langlade, Charles-Michel, III, xlii, 496, 526; IV, **563–64**, liv, 78, 303, 486, 582, 666, 718

Mouet de Langlade, Charlotte-Ambroisine. *See* Bourassa, *dit* La Ronde

Mouet de Langlade, Domitilde. *See* Domitilde

Mouet de Mora, Catherine (Amiot), III, 13

Moufle de La Tuillerie, Barthélemy, III, 398

Mouisset, David, IV, 387

Mouïsset, François, III, 398, 399

Moulton, Ebenezer, IV, **564–65**

Moulton, Hannah. *See* Ballard; Grove

Moulton, Hannah (?). *See* Littlefield

Moulton, Jeremiah, II, 477, 544; III, **476–77**

Moulton, Joseph, III, 476

Moulton, Mary (Lord; wife of JEREMIAH), III, 477

Moulton, Robert, IV, 564

Mounier, Adam, IV, 565
Mounier, François, III, **477–78**, 541; IV, 125, 187, 379, 565, 574, 579, 788
Mounier, Henry, III, 477; IV, 565
Mounier, Jean (uncle), IV, 566
Mounier, Jean, IV, 565, 625
Mounier, Jean-Mathieu, IV, **565–66**, 125, 128
Mounier, Marguerite-Geneviève (Maurin), III, 441
Mounier, Michel, IV, 566
Mounier, Suzanne. *See* Liard
Mountain*, Jacob (1749–1825), IV, 102, 372, 738, 753
Mountain*, Jehosaphat (1745–1817), IV, 753
Mourongeau, Catherine. *See* Frontigny
Mourongeau, Jacques, III, 78
Mouroy, Mlle de, I, 470
Mousseaux, Louise de (Pélerin de Saint-Amant), I, 256; II, 515
Mouthe, Marie-Ursule (Feltz), IV, 264, 265
Moxus, II, 475, 543, 666
Moyen Des Granges, Élisabeth. *See* Le Bret
Moyen Des Granges, Élisabeth (Closse), I, 231
Moyen Des Granges, Jean-Baptiste, I, 231, 295
Moyen Des Granges, Marie (Dugué de Boisbriand), I, 231, 295; II, 203
Moyer. *See* Mohier
Moyne, Alayne, I, 371
Mudjekewiss. *See* Madjeckewiss
Muerel, Anne (Bonnécamps), IV, 76
Muiron, Claudine. *See* Seroin
Muiron, David-Bernard, III, **478–79**, 20, 235, 644
Muiron, François, III, 478
Muiron, Marie. *See* Champion
Muis. *See* Mius
Mulberry, Susanna (Salter), IV, 695
Mullens, Priscilla (Alden), II, 14
Mullois, Marie (Saint-Ours), II, 592, 593; III, 505, 578
Mullois, Thomas, II, 592
Mullois de La Borde, Madeleine (Pézard de La Tousche Champlain), I, 543
Munck. *See* Munk
Munk, Erik Nielsen, I, 514
Munk, Jens Eriksen, I, **514–15**, 20; II, 265, 297
Munk, Katherine. *See* Adriansdatter
Munn*, Alexander (d. 1812), IV, 49
Munro. *See also* Monro
Munro, Henry, IV, 351
Munro, Hugh, IV, 566
Munro, John, IV, **566–67**
Munro, Mary. *See* Brower
Münster, Bishop of. *See* Von Galen
Muquinna, IV, **567–69**, lv, 73, 325, 411, 498, 519, 520, 767, 768
Murcé (Mursay), Marquis de. *See* Valois-Villette
Murderer. *See* Cherououny
Murdoch*, Beamish (1800–76), III, 34, 439, 498, 573
Murdoch, James, IV, 490
Mure, Hutcheson, IV, 352
Murphy, Arthur, IV, 556
Murray, Alexander (father), III, 479
Murray, Alexander, III, **479–80**, 363; IV, xxv
Murray, Alexander, 4th Baron Elibank, IV, 569
Murray, Anne. *See* Witham
Murray, Catharine (Rollo, Baroness Rollo), III, 565

Murray, Cordelia. *See* Collier
Murray, Elizabeth, Baroness Murray. *See* Stirling
Murray, Lord George, IV, 400
Murray, James, III, xxi, 26, 37, 64, 85, 86, 89, 90, 132, 138, 143, 197, 198, 199, 212, 272, 274, 289, 290, 293, 296, 340, 341, 365, 418, 477, 478, 541, 549, 606, 608, 668, 669, 670, 671; IV, **569–78**, xxxiii, xxxv, xxxvii, xl, xli, xliii, xlix, 23, 24, 37, 71, 74, 97, 98, 103, 104, 105, 106, 109, 129, 134, 137, 138, 139, 141, 146, 150, 162, 182, 183, 189, 190, 211, 228, 243, 265, 276, 279, 280, 290, 298, 299, 319, 324, 335, 344, 347, 348, 370, 379, 380, 381, 384, 399, 415, 430, 447, 464, 480, 481, 482, 491, 492, 493, 500, 509, 531, 535, 536, 537, 538, 541, 543, 552, 554, 579, 602, 618, 623, 641, 642, 643, 650, 672, 686, 692, 694, 700, 719, 725, 729, 752, 758, 759, 779, 787, 788
Murray, James Wolfe, III, 479
Murray*, John (d. 1824 or 1825), IV, 523
Murray, John, 4th Earl of Dunmore, IV, xxxviii, 626, 790
Murray, Marianne (wife of ALEXANDER), III, 479
Murray, Patrick, 5th Baron Elibank, IV, 577
Murray, Richard, IV, 579
Murray, Walter, IV, **579**, 379
Murray, William, 1st Earl of Mansfield, IV, xli, 537, 571
Muskerry, Viscount. *See* MacCarthy
Musson. *See* Masson
Mutigny de Vassan, Jean-Baptiste, III, 535; IV, 540
Muy. *See* Daneau
Myatt, Joseph, II, **492–93**, 10, 291, 292, 602; III, 599, 661
Mychell, William, I, 158
Myer, Joseph, IV, 228
Myers, Hyam, IV, 332, 384
Myers, Mary (Wood), IV, 775, 776
Mykok. *See* Mikak
Mynne, Anne (Calvert, Baroness Baltimore), I, 162
Mynne, George, I, 162
Myres, Sir John, III, 338
Myrick, Elizabeth. *See* Osborn
Myrick, William, IV, 593

NADEAU. *See* Garnier
Nafrechoux, Catherine (Chaumier; Foucault), III, 227
Nafrechoux, Françoise (Pommereau), III, 524
Nafrechoux, Isaac, II, 517
Nafrechoux, Louise (Raimbault), II, 542
Nagiscoig (Captain John), II, 476, 668
Nairne*, John (1731–1802), IV, 276, 548, 570, 574
Nameur, Louis de, I, 313
Namier, Sir Lewis Bernstein, IV, 528
Nanamaghemet, Marie-Jeanne (Gill), IV, 293
Nancy, III, 614
Naneogauchit, I, 222, 578
Napagabiscou, I, 511
Napier, Catherine (Christie), IV, 150
Napier*, Duncan Campbell (d. 1865), IV, 154
Naples, Queen of, I, 120
Napoleon I, Emperor of the French, III, xvi, xxii
Napper, James, II, **493**; III, 302
Narcis, Joseph-Philippe, III, 566
Natel, Antoine, I, 300
Nathan, Simon, IV, 385
Nathaniel, II, 668
Natoukwabekwe (Cecilia), I, 527

Nau, François, II, 40
Nau, Françoise. *See* Lorin
Nau, Lucas, III, 480
Nau, Luc-François, III, **480–81**, 361, 627
Nau de La Boissière et de Fossambault, Catherine (Lauson de La Citière; Peuvret Demesnu), I, 428, 542, 543; II, 524
Nau de La Boissière et de Fossambault, Jacques, I, 542; II, 525
Nau de La Boissière et de Fossambault, Michèle-Thérèse (Giffard), I, 326
Navailles, Anne de, Baronne de Labatut. *See* Mius d'Entremont de Pobomcoup
Navailles, Laurent de, Baron de Labatut, II, 512
Navarre, Queen of. *See* Marguerite d'Angoulême; Marguerite de Valois
Navarre, Antoine-Marie-François de, IV, 579
Navarre, Jeanne de. *See* Plugette
Navarre, Marie. *See* Lothman de Barrois
Navarre, Pierre, IV, 260
Navarre, Robert, III, 525; IV, **579–80**, 435
Navarro. *See also* Ramón
Navarro, Don Juan de, III, 610
Navières, Jean, III, 481
Navières, Joseph, III, **481–82**
Navières, Madeleine. *See* Sicot
Neal, Dorothy (Davison), IV, 197
Neatby*, Hilda (1904–75), IV, 59, 279, 350
Nebourvele. *See* Boucher
Necushin, IV, 33
Neele, J. S., IV, 578
Negabamat, I, **516**, 222, 282, 640
Negaskoumat, I, 516
Nègre, Marquèze (Rouffio), III, 571
Negushwa. *See* Egushwa
Neilson, Isabel. *See* Brown
Neilson*, John (1776–1848), IV, 43, 502, 581, 689, 690
Neilson, Samuel, IV, **580–81**, 43, 107, 393, 689
Neilson, William, IV, 580
Nelson, David, IV, 55
Nelson, Elizabeth. *See* Tailer
Nelson, Horatio, 1st Viscount Nelson, IV, 49
Nelson, John, I, 576, 637, 654; II, **493–94**, 14, 94, 177, 184, 442, 459, 464; III, 653
Nelson, Mary. *See* Temple
Nelson, Robert, I, 144; II, 494
Nenangoussikou, II, 495
Neogaouachit. *See* Naneogauchit
Neolin, III, 527
Nepean, Sir Evan, IV, 197, 218, 231, 324, 604, 687, 753, 766
Nepomoit (Joseph), II, 199, 670
Nepveu. *See* Neveu
Neré. *See* Levasseur
Néret, Jean-Baptiste, II, 465, 509, 575; III, 352
Nerkingoak, IV, 536
Nesbitt, Rebecca (Phelan; wife of WILLIAM), IV, 581
Nesbitt, William, III, 418; IV, **581–82**, 209, 451, 724
Nescambiouit, II, **494–96**, xxxviii, 25, 626, 627; III, 505
Nesle, Sieur de, II, 82
Nesmond, André de, Marquis de Nesmond, I, 309; II, 246, 452; III, 454
Nessegombewit. *See* Nescambiouit
Nestichio, IV, 48

Netawatwees, III, xxxiv; IV, lii
Neuman, Gottlob, III, 651
Neuville. *See also* Dupont
Neuville, Jean-Baptiste de, IV, 375
Neuvillette. *See* Robinau
Nève, Gilette (Cheval), III, 121
Névellet, Marguerite de (Bouat), II, 81, 509
Nevers, Duchesse de, I, 425
Nevers, Phineas, IV, 195
Nevers, Sarah (Davidson), IV, 195
Nevet, Comte de, III, 192, 199; IV, 319
Neveu, Françoise-Élisabeth. *See* Legras
Neveu, Jacques, III, 482
Neveu (Neveu de La Bretonnière), Jean-Baptiste, III, **482**; IV, 46, 709
Neveu, Marguerite (Simonnet), IV, 709
Neveu, Marie-Catherine (Gaillard), II, 234
Neveu, Marie-Denise. *See* Sevestre
Neveu, Marie-Jeanne. *See* Passard
Neveu, Philippe, III, 482
Newaukeshickwab, IV, 774
Newberry, William, IV, 778
Newcastle-upon-Tyne, Duke of. *See* Pelham-Holles
Newland, Elizabeth (Jadis), IV, 388
Newland, Robert, I, 82, 666; II, 537
Newman, Henry, II, 348
Newman, Ruth. *See* Plummer
Newton, Ensign, III, 343; IV, 539
Newton, Catherine. *See* Knaut
Newton, Henry, IV, 561
Newton, Sir Isaac, II, 595
Newton, John (office-holder), IV, 199, 414, 450, 451, 581, 695
Newton, John, III, **482–83**, 303, 593
Newton, John (son), III, 482, 483
Newton, Thomasina (wife of JOHN), III, 482
Neyon de Villiers, Pierre-Joseph, III, 528, 529
Nicanapé. *See* Chachagouesse
Nicholas (Nickus). *See* Karaghtadie
Nicholas of Lynne, I, **678–79**
Nicholson, Edith (Francklin), IV, 272
Nicholson, Francis, II, **496–99**, 3, 38, 39, 122, 123, 152, 165, 167, 177, 186, 198, 205, 206, 254, 258, 272, 274, 289, 437, 445, 461, 487, 547, 582, 588, 591, 603, 627, 644, 651, 652, 661, 668; III, 6, 177, 200, 207, 208, 264, 276, 421, 436, 500, 516, 579, 596, 622, 623, 665; IV, xxi, 251
Nicholson, Thomas, II, 496
Nick'a'thu'tin. *See* Primeau, Louis
Nicol, George, IV, 763
Nicolas. *See also* Orontony
Nicolas (clerk), I, 90, 238
Nicolas (Pawnee), II, 216
Nicolas (sailor), II, 9
Nicolas, Louis, II, 53
Nicollet, Marie. *See* Lamer
Nicollet, Thomas, I, 516
Nicollet de Belleborne, Jean, I, **516–18**, 35, 186, 197, 367, 369, 410, 473, 489, 639; II, xli, 383, 385, 448; III, 374
Nicollet de Belleborne, Marguerite. *See* Couillard de Lespinay
Nicollet de Belleborne, Marguerite (Legardeur de Repentigny), I, 517; II, 383, 385, 386; III, 374

Nicolls, Richard, I, 308
Nika, I, 183; II, 197
Nimimitt (Nimquid). *See* Wenemouet
Ninākon. *See* Minweweh
Ningausim, IV, 756
Ninivois, III, 527
Ninstints, IV, 420
Niort de La Minotière, Pierre de, III, 569
Niort de La Noraye, Louis de, I, 63; II, 426
Nipimoit. *See* Nepomoit
Niquet, Catherine (Marin de La Malgue), II, 458; III, 431
Nisbett, William, IV, 608
Nissowaquet, IV, **582–83**, 300, 563
Nitachinon. *See* Chabert de Joncaire, Philippe-Thomas
Nivard Saint-Dizier, Marie-Anne (Picoté de Belestre), IV, 633
Niverville. *See* Boucher
Nixon, Ann, I, 520
Nixon, Em, I, 520
Nixon, John, I, **518–20**, 39, 84, 232, 281, 324, 328, 416, 477, 543, 553, 605, 666; II, 49, 231, 318
Noah, II, 474
Noailles, Adrien-Maurice de, Comte d'Ayen, Duc de Noailles, III, 231, 556; IV, 750
Noailles, Anne-Jules de, Duc de Noailles, II, 567
Noailles, Louis de, Duc d'Ayen, III, 556
Noailles, Louis-Antoine de, II, 567
Noailles, Lucie-Félicité de (Estrées, Duchesse d'Estrées), III, 15
Noble, Arthur, III, **483–84**, 128, 150, 260, 261, 331, 514, 653; IV, 213, 291, 459, 559, 651
Noble, Francis, III, 483, 484
Noble, James, III, 483
Noble, John, IV, 712
Noble, Sarah. *See* Macklin
Noble Du Revest, Joseph-François de, III, 93; IV, 699
Nodogawerrimet, III, **484–85**, xxxviii, 585
Nodowance, IV, 260
Noegabinat. *See* Ouagabemat
Noël, Étienne, I, 167, 169, 384, 520
Noel, Frances (Philipps), III, 515
Noël, Jacques (servant), I, 598
Noël, Jacques, I, **520**, 23, 170, 384, 409
Noël, Jean (father of Étienne), I, 520
Noël, Jean (son of JACQUES), I, 520
Noël, Jean-Baptiste, IV, 134, 298
Noël, Jeanne. *See* Cartier
Noël, Marguerite-Ursule. *See* Lajus
Noël, Michel, I, 520
Nœufville. *See* Lamorel
Nogaret de La Valette, Jean-Louis, Duc d'Épernon, I, 427
Noinville, Noël-Alexandre de, III, 342
Noiré. *See* Maleray
Noirefontaine, M., I, 423, 425
Noiseux*, François-Xavier (1748–1834), III, 122; IV, 142, 754
Nolan, Anne (Desjordy Moreau de Cabanac), II, 186
Nolan, Catherine (Martin de Lino), II, 462, 463, 464, 465
Nolan, Jean-Baptiste, III, 485
Nolan, Jean-Marie, III, 251, 485
Nolan, Marie (La Porte de Louvigny), II, 346
Nolan, Marie-Anne. *See* La Marque
Nolan, Pierre, II, 186, 464

Nolan Lamarque, Charles, III, **485–86**, 251, 450, 520; IV, 46, 283, 284, 311
Nolan Lamarque, Jacques-Marie, III, 243
Nolan Lamarque, Marie-Anne. *See* Legardeur de Saint-Pierre
Nolan Lamarque, Marie-Anne (Grasset de Saint-Sauveur), IV, 311
Noliboise, Saubade de (Lestage), III, 393
Nolin, Louise (Couillard de Lespinay), II, 156
Noodogawirramet. *See* Nodogawerrimet
Nooth*, John Mervin (d. 1828), IV, 589
Norden, Mary (Goffe), II, 254
Norden, Nathaniel, II, 254
Noreau, Jeanne (La Forest), II, 169
Noremberguer, Lazaro (Lazaro Aleman or Cromberger), I, 157
Norfolk, Duke of. *See* Howard
Normand, Charles, IV, 203
Normandeau, Joseph, IV, 703
Normandeau, *dit* Deslauriers, Marie-Madeleine. *See* Sasseville
Normandin, Daniel, II, **499**, 170
Normandin, Jacob, II, 499
Normandin, Louise. *See* Hayot
Normandin, Madeleine (Billy), II, 499
Normandin, Marie. *See* Briant
Normandin, Pierre, II, 276
Normandin, *dit* Le Sauvage, Laurent, II, 170
Normandin, *dit* Le Sauvage, Marie-Louise (David), II, 170
Normant, Charles, III, 486
Normant, Marie. *See* Legrand
Normant Du Faradon, Louis, II, 143, 492; III, **486–88**, 164, 165, 193, 195; IV, 201, 235, 236, 237, 542
Normanville. *See* Godefroy
Noro, II, **499–500**, xxx, 504
Noroy, Sieur de. *See* Bochart
Norrey. *See* Le Picard
Norris, Elizabeth. *See* Aylmer
Norris, Sir John, II, 246, 293, 395, 564, 666; III, **488–89**, 655
North, Frederick, Lord North, IV, xlii, xliii, xlvi, xlvii, 6, 25, 129, 230, 260, 280, 349, 538, 571, 609, 726, 792
Northington, Earl of. *See* Henley
Northumberland, Duke of. *See* Percy
Norton, Elizabeth. *See* McCliesh
Norton, Fletcher, 1st Baron Grantley, IV, xli
Norton, John (clergyman), III, 162
Norton*, John (d. 1831), IV, 416
Norton, Mary (Polly), IV, 584
Norton, Moses, III, 490, 534; IV, **583–85**, 33, 339, 340, 523, 727
Norton, Richard, II, xxvii, 51, 65, 308, 310, 313, 493, 604, 616; III, **489–90**, xxxiii, 415, 447, 520, 599, 661; IV, 383, 523, 583
Norton, Sarah (mother of RICHARD), III, 489
Norton, Sarah (wife of MOSES), IV, 584
Nosawaguet. *See* Nissowaquet
Nottingham, Earl of. *See* Howard
Nouchet, Barbe. *See* Barrat
Nouchet, Geneviève. *See* Gatin
Nouchet, Joseph, III, **490–91**, 226
Nouchet, Joseph-Étienne, III, **491**, 226, 490; IV, 624
Nouchet, Julien, III, 490

Nouchet, Louise-Catherine. *See* Foucault
Nouë, Anne de, I, **52**, 121, 410, 453, 527; II, 83
Nouel. *See* Noël
Nouette, Jacques, III, 205
Nouvel, Henri, I, 50, 59, 282; II, **500–2**, 159, 347; III, 103
Nov dogg aw wer imet. *See* Nodogawerrimet
Noyan. *See* Payen
Noyelles, Marie de. *See* Bridou
Noyelles, Pierre-Philippe de, Baron de Fleurimont, III, 491
Noyelles de Fleurimont, Charles-Joseph de, III, 242, 245, 492
Noyelles de Fleurimont, Marie-Charlotte de. *See* Petit de Levilliers
Noyelles de Fleurimont, Nicolas-Joseph de, II, 156; III, **491–93**, 16, 46, 47, 242, 245, 253, 378, 430; IV, 34, 288
Noyelles de Fleurimont, Pierre-Philippe de, III, 492
Noyes, Sieur de, II, 578
Noyon, Abigail de. *See* Stebbins
Noyon, Catherine de. *See* Chevalier
Noyon, Dorothée de, IV, 765
Noyon, Édouard de, I, 250
Noyon, Jacques de, III, **493–94**, 248; IV, 173
Noyon (Danio), Jacques-René de, III, 493
Noyon, Jean de, III, 493
Noyon, Marie de. *See* Chauvin
Noyon, Marie de (Renaud), III, 494
Noyon, Suzanne de (David), I, 250
Noyrot, Philibert, I, **521–22**, 160, 411, 412, 579, 596, 665
Nutimus, IV, 27
Nutt, John, I, **522**
Nutt, Robert, I, 522

OAGIMONT. *See* Ouagimou
Oakes, Forrest, IV, **585–86**, 262, 263
Oakes, Jemima (Ermatinger), IV, 263
Oakes*, John (d. 1832), IV, 205, 206, 585
Oakes, John Meticamish, IV, 585
Oakley, Elizabeth (Southack), III, 596
Obiniguaro. *See* Oubignaro
Obwandiyag. *See* Pontiac
Ochagach (Ochakah). *See* Auchagah
Ochiltree, Lord. *See* Stewart
Ochterloney, David, III, 544
Odatsighta, II, 474, 502
Ogenheratarihiens (Ogeratarihen), I, **522–23**
Ogilvie, Captain, I, 305
Ogilvie*, James (d. 1813), IV, 523
Ogilvie, John, IV, **586–87**, liv, 139, 691
Ogilvie, Margaret. *See* Marston
Ogilvie, Susanna Catharine. *See* Symes
Ogilvie, William, IV, 586
Ohonsiowanne (Ohoengewaene), II, **502**, xxxvi, 20, 631
Ohquandageghte, IV, **587–88**
Oionhaton, I, **523–24**, 42, 212, 344
Oja, La. *See* Wahpasha
Ojeda, Alonso de, I, 151
Olabaratz, Catherine d'. *See* Despiaube
Olabaratz, Jean d', IV, 589
Olabaratz, Joannis-Galand d', III, 635; IV, **588–89**, 23, 61, 247, 253, 487, 657
Olaf I Tryggvesson, King of Norway, I, 448
Old Abraham, IV, 730
Old Belt. *See* Kaghswaghtaniunt

Old Britain. *See* Memeskia
Oldham, William, IV, 369, 403
Old King; Old Smoke. *See* Kaieñ?kwaahtoñ
Oldmixon, John, I, 50
Olier, Jean-Jacques, I, 45, 57, 111, 115, 213, 214, 215, 219, 220, 480, 486, 612, 644, 648; II, 414
Oliph, Joan (Leigh), I, 450
Oliva, Catherine. *See* Couillard Des Islets
Oliva, Frédéric-Godlip, IV, 589
Oliva, Frédéric-Guillaume, IV, **589–90**
Oliva, Jean-Paul (Giovanni Paolo), I, 460; II, 161
Olive, Gregory, IV, 592
Olivier. *See also* Le Jeune
Olivier, Abel, III, **494**, 281; IV, 203
Olivier, Antoine, III, 639
Olivier, François, III, 494
Olivier, Françoise. *See* Dardaine
Olivier, Hugues, IV, 590
Olivier, Louise. *See* Le Roux
Olivier, Marie. *See* Castille
Olivier, Marie-Anne. *See* Varlet
Olivier, Marie-Madeleine. *See* Lefebvre
Olivier, Nicolas-Joseph-Godefroy, IV, 591
Olivier, Simon, I, 524
Olivier, *dit* Le Picard, Marc-Antoine, I, **524**
Olivier Darmeville, M., IV, 590
Olivier de Saint-Maurice, Charles-Honoré, IV, 591
Olivier de Vézin, Marie-Joseph. *See* Gastineau Duplessis
Olivier de Vézin, Pierre-Darmeville, IV, 591
Olivier de Vézin, Pierre-François, III, 153, 154, 237, 351, 592, 593, 617; IV, **590–91**, 167, 284, 362
Ollivier, Jacques-David, IV, 69
Olmechin. *See* Onemechin
Onanguicé (Onanguisset). *See* Ounanguissé
Onaské, II, 324
Oñate, Juan de, II, xxxii
Ondaaiondiont, I, **524–25**, 65, 66, 71
Ondakion (Pierre), I, 610
Ondessonk. *See* Jogues, Isaac; Le Moyne, Simon
Onedahauet, II, 665; III, 266
Onemechin, I, 69, 507, 529
Onkiswathetami. *See* Swatana
Onondamokin. *See* Anandamoakin
Onontio. *See* Huault de Montmagny, Charles
Ononwarogo, III, **494–95**, 320
Onorotandi, I, 73
Onslow, George, IV, 226
Ontaniendo. *See* Atecouando
Onughranorum, IV, 734
Oonchiarey, I, 590
Orbigny, Claude d' (Potot de Montbeillard), IV, 641
Ord, John, III, 608
Orehaoue. *See* Ourehouare
Oreil. *See* Doreil
Orford, Earl of. *See* Walpole
Orgemont. *See* Louvigny
Orgeville. *See* Pannier
Orillat, Jean (father), IV, 591
Orillat, Jean, IV, **591–93**, 58, 403
Orillat, Marie. *See* Dupuy
Orillat, Marie-Amable. *See* Filiau, *dit* Dubois
Orillat, Marie-Luce-Amable (Réaume), IV, 593
Orillat, Thérèse-Amable. *See* Viger

Oriol, Anne. *See* Le Picard
Oriol, Vital, II, 14
Orkney, Earl of. *See* Hamilton; Sinclair
Orléans, Duc d' (1607–1611), I, 436
Orléans, Anne-Marie-Louise d', Duchesse de Montpensier, I, 134, 135
Orléans, Charles, Duc d', Comte de Clermont, I, 425
Orléans, Charles-Paris d', Comte de Saint-Pol, Duc de Longueville, II, 112
Orléans, Claude d', II, 98
Orléans, Jacqueline d' (Brisay de Denonville), II, 98
Orléans, Jean-Baptiste-Gaston d', I, 134
Orléans, Louise-Élisabeth d', Queen of Spain, III, 106
Orléans, Philippe, Duc d', Regent of France, I, 328; II, 338, 570; III, 104, 118, 248, 330, 336, 566; IV, 124, 468
Orme (Ormeaux). *See also* Hazeur
Orme, Robert, IV, 281
Ormond (Ermon), Marie-Bernardine (Vuadens), IV, 757
Orontony, II, xxx; III, **495–96**, xxxv, xxxvi, xxxix, xli, 46, 158, 328, 355, 451, 525, 607, 613; IV, liii, liv, 464, 640, 728
Orpheus Junior. *See* Vaughan, Sir William
Ortelius, Abraham, I, 280, 680
Orval. *See* Bouchard
Orville, Sieur d', I, 189, 293
Orvilliers. *See* Chorel; Guillouet
Osborn, Sir Danvers, III, **496–97**, 126
Osborn, Elizabeth (Myrick; Paine; Doane), IV, **593–94**
Osborn, Henry, II, 251; III, 126, 219, 315, 324, 517; IV, **594–95**, 257, 699
Osborn, Jedidah. *See* Smith
Osborn, John, III, 496
Osborn, Sir John, III, 496; IV, 594
Osborn, Martha, Lady Osborn. *See* Kelynge
Osborn, Mary. *See* Hughes; Montagu
Osborn, Samuel, IV, 593
Osborn, Sarah. *See* Byng
Osborne, Thomas, 1st Duke of Leeds, II, 152
Osgoode*, William (1754–1824), IV, 502, 766
Ostryge, Henry, I, 157, 158
O'Sullivan, Jeanne-Marie-Catherine. *See* Bruyères
O'Sullivan*, Michael (1784–1839), IV, 109
Otis, James, III, 403
Otis, Joseph, IV, 351
Otis, Mary (Little), III, 403
Otkwande (Otqueandageghte). *See* Ohquandageghte
O'Toole, Lawrence, I, 560
Otoutagon (Ottoutagan). *See* Outoutagan
Otreouti, I, **525–26**, 7, 322, 445, 458; II, 344, 440, 518, 620, 624
Otsinnonannhont (Barnabé), I, 652
Otsinughyada. *See* Hotsinoñhyahta?
Ottrowana, IV, **595–96**
Ouabache (Oubachas). *See* Wahpasha
Ouabangué, II, 500
Ouachala (Ouachalard), II, **502–3**, xxx, 316, 504
Ouaconisen. *See* Ignon
Ouagabemat (Noegabinat), I, 222
Ouagimou, I, **526–27**, 69, 529
Ouane. *See* Le Moyne, Simon
Ouangote. *See* Williams, Eunice
Ouaouënouroué, Nicolas, III, 266
Ouaourené. *See* Wowurna

Ouary, Françoise (Renardin de La Blanchetière), I, 475
Ouashala (Ouashalas). *See* Ouachala
Ouasson (Ousson, Owasser). *See* Wasson
Oudiette, Jean, II, 29, 30, 574, 575
Oudin, Renée (Marie) (Le Royer de La Dauversière), I, 214
Ouebadinskoue (Marie-Madeleine Chrestienne) (Boucher), I, 200, 354; II, 86
Ouechala. *See* Ouachala
Ouenanguenet. *See* Wenemouet
Ouenemek, II, **503–4**, xxxviii, 324, 502
Oughtred, Henry, I, 228, 229
Ouhensiouan. *See* Ohonsiowanne
Ouibignaro, II, 7, 8, 9
Ouikouiroumenit, II, 476
Ouilameg (Ouilamek). *See* Ouenemek
Oumasasikweie, I, **527–28**, 10
Oumasasikweie (Joseph), I, 548, 640
Ounanguissé, II, **504**, xxxviii, 503
Ouracha, I, 324
Ourehouare, I, **528**, 537
Oureouhat. *See* Otreouti
Ours, L'. *See* Le Pesant
Oussaye, Élisabeth (Roger), II, 582
Outaouliboy. *See* Koutaoiliboe
Outchetaguin, I, 381, 603
Outchiouanish (Marie) (Pelletier), II, 357
Outetoucos, I, 603
Outlan. *See* Outlaw
Outlaw, Françoise. *See* Denis
Outlaw, John, I, **528–29**, 39, 107, 130; II, 308
Outlaw, Mary. *See* Saille
Outoutagan, II, **504–6**, xxxvii, 173, 317, 414, 475; III, 147
Outreouhati. *See* Otreouti
Outsitsony, I, 574
Ouwoorana. *See* Wowurna
Owain Gwynedd, King of Gwynedd, I, 677
Owen, David, IV, 596
Owen, Sir Edward Campbell Rich, IV, 597
Owen, John (trader), III, 614
Owen, John (writer), I, 365
Owen, William, IV, **596–97**
Owen*, William Fitz William (1774–1857), IV, 597
Oxford, Earl of. *See* Harley
Oxford, Thomas, I, 24, 278, 370
Ozon, Potentien, II, **506**, 174, 419

Pace, Grace (Cook), IV, 163
Pacheco. *See* Güemes
Pachirini, I, 485
Pachot. *See* Viennay-Pachot
Pacifique, Brother. *See* Caron
Pacifique, Brother. *See* Duplessis
Pacifique de Provins, I, 129
Packnake, IV, 301
Padanuques, Jacques, III, **497–98**
Padilla. *See* Güemes
Padouillet, Renée (Mallet), II, 451
Page, Mr, I, 93
Pagé, Angélique (Daine), III, 159
Page, Mrs Susanna, IV, 767
Pagé, *dit* Carcy, Élisabeth. *See* Letartre
Pagé, *dit* Carcy, Guillaume, II, 347; III, 498
Pagé, *dit* Carcy, Jacques, II, 430; III, **498–99**, 182, 348, 509

Pagé, *dit* Carcy, Marie-Anne (Boisseau), IV, 75
Pagé, *dit* Carcy, Marie-Louise. *See* Roussel
Pagé, *dit* Carcy, Raymond, I, 473, 495; II, 347
Pagé, *dit* Carcy, Suzanne (Perrault), III, 509; IV, 623
Pagès, M., II, 654
Paillard, André, II, 506
Paillard, Catherine. *See* Geoffroy
Paillard, Charles, II, 507
Paillard, Gabriel, II, 507
Paillard, Léonard, known as Le Poitevin, II, **506–7**
Paillard, Louise-Marie. *See* Vachon
Pain, Félix, II, 198, 206, 219, 238, 512; III, **499–500**, 522, 681; IV, xxi
Paine, Elizabeth. *See* Osborn
Paine, Thomas, IV, 327
Paine, William (father), IV, 593
Paine, William, IV, 593
Paizs (Paizsos), István. *See* Parmenius, Stephanus
Pajet. *See* Pagé
Pajot, Claude (Biencourt de Poutrincourt), I, 96, 98, 99
Pajot, Isaac, I, 96
Pako, III, 248
Palatine, Princess. *See* Elizabeth Charlotte
Palliser. *See also* Tootac
Palliser, Hugh, IV, 597
Palliser, Sir Hugh, III, 37, 38, 411, 412; IV, **597–601**, 28, 29, 122, 158, 159, 163, 194, 225, 333, 334, 412, 437, 536, 701, 712,
Palliser, Mary. *See* Robinson
Palliser Walters, Sir Hugh, IV, 600
Pallu, François, II, 360
Palluau, Comte de. *See* Buade
Palluau, Comtesse de. *See* La Grange; Phélypeaux de Pont-chartrain
Palme. *See* La Palme
Palmer, Barbara. *See* Villiers.
Palmer, Edward, I, 306
Palmer, Elizabeth. *See* Hey
Palmer, John, II, 6
Paludy, Baron de. *See* Tonty
Panet*, Bernard-Claude (1753–1833), IV, 602
Panet*, Jacques (1754–1834), IV, 602
Panet*, Jean-Antoine (1751–1815), IV, 89, 603
Panet, Jean-Baptiste, IV, 603
Panet, Jean-Claude, III, 26, 555, 608; IV, **601–3**, 75, 124, 127, 243, 344, 492
Panet, Jean-Nicolas, IV, 601
Panet, Marie-Louise. *See* Barolet
Panet, Marie-Madeleine-Françoise. *See* Foucher
Panet, Nicolas-Gabriel, IV, 601
Panet*, Pierre-Méru (1731–1804), III, 146, 367, 441; IV, 185, 547, 601, 602, 716
Pangman*, Peter (d. 1819), IV, 160, 366, 585
Panneton, Théodore (father), III, 430
Panneton, Théodore, IV, 331
Pannier d'Orgeville, Jacques, III, 398
Panounias (Panoniac), I, **529–30**, 69, 293, 500, 526
Papin, Gilles, III, 493
Papin, Hélène (Verrier), III, 643
Papineau*, Joseph (1752–1841), IV, 148
Papineau*, Louis-Joseph (1786–1871), II, 193; IV, 148
Papineau, Marie. *See* Delain
Papineau, Rosalie. *See* Cherrier

Papineau, Samuel, II, 507
Papineau, *dit* Montigny, Catherine. *See* Quevillon
Papineau, *dit* Montigny, Samuel, II, **507**
Paplay, Miss (Hey), IV, 348
Paquet, Joséphine, I, 487
Paquet, Marie-Josephte, *dite* de la Nativité, IV, 319, 320
Paquet, René, III, 165
Paquet*, *dit* Lavallée, André (1799–1860), I, 77
Paquin, Marie-Madeleine (Perrault), III, 510
Paquine. *See* Pasquine
Parabego (Partarabego), Anne (Denys de Fronsac), I, 260; II, 477
Paradis, Barbe. *See* Guyon
Paradis, Catherine. *See* Batailler
Paradis, Claude, III, 500
Paradis, Geneviève. *See* Cussy
Paradis, Jean, II, **508**, 660
Paradis, Jean (son), II, 508
Paradis, Marie-Angélique. *See* Boivin
Paradis, Pierre, II, 508
Paradis, Roland, III, **500–1**; IV, 204, 748
Parant, Gilbert, I, 573
Parant, Suzanne. *See* Richard
Parat, Antoine, I, **530**, 26, 419; II, 46, 429
Pardaillan de Grondin, Antoine-François, Marquis d'Antin, III, 610
Paré, Ambroise, IV, 434
Paré, Catherine, *dite* Saint-Louis-des-Anges, III, 630
Parement, Perrette (Lorit, *dit* Gargot), II, 447
Parent, Étienne, III, 617
Parent, Jean-Louis-Laurent, III, 560
Parent, Marie (Corbin), III, 138
Parent, Marie-Madeleine. *See* Sasseville
Pargellis, Stanley McCrory, III, xxix
Paris, Antoine, III, 501
Paris, Bernard, III, **501**
Paris, Ferdinando John, IV, 695
Paris, Marie-Anne. *See* Le Blanc
Paris, Marie-Gervaise (Berbudeau), IV, 56
Paris, Renée. *See* Boucher
Parisel, Jean-François, I, 108
Parisette, Anne (Pillard), III, 521
Park, Theoda (Williams), II, 667
Park, William, IV, 722
Parker, Henry, 5th Baron Monteagle, 12th Baron Morley, I, 407
Parker, Rebecca (Bushel), III, 90
Parkhurst, Anthony, I, **530–31**, 332, 334, 363
Parkhurst, John, I, 530
Parkman, Francis, I, 142; III, 34, 149, 256, 707; IV, xxi, 24, 580, 681
Parmenius, Stephanus, I, **531–32**, 5, 333, 334, 335, 363
Parmentier, Charles, II, 27
Parmentier, Jean, I, **532–33**
Parmentier, Raoul, I, 532
Parnel, Elizabeth. *See* Southack
Parr, Eleanor. *See* Clements
Parr, John (father), IV, 603
Parr, John, IV, **603–5**, 57, 111, 112, 223, 292, 293, 328, 389, 444, 452, 516, 522, 556, 625, 626, 627, 723
Parr, Sara. *See* Walmesley
Parry*, Sir William Edward (1790–1855), I, 75, 312, 375, 378; III, 128, 449

Pars, Marie (Picoté de Belestre), I, 547
Parsons, Hannah (rebaptized Catherine) (Bermen de La Martinière), III, 64
Parsons, Philip, II, 454
Partarabego. See Parabego
Particelli d'Émery, Michel, I, 198
Partridge, Mary (Belcher), IV, 50
Pas, Isaac de, Marquis de Feuquières, I, 296
Pascal, Blaise, IV, 92
Pascal d'Auxerre, Father, I, 129
Pascal de Troyes, Father, I, 468, 504
Pascaud, Anne. See Puyperouse
Pascaud, Antoine (d. 1717), I, 400; II, **508–9**, 81, 269, 304, 387, 463, 464; III, 52, 352, 393; IV, 357, 605
Pascaud, Antoine (son of ANTOINE, d. 1717), II, 509; III, 290, 485, 486
Pascaud, Antoine (1729–86), IV, **605**, 306, 750
Pascaud, Catherine. See Berteau
Pascaud, Élisabeth. See Cournoyer
Pascaud, Guillaume (father of ANTOINE, d. 1717), II, 508
Pascaud, Guillaume (father of ANTOINE, d. 1786), IV, 605
Pascaud, Jean (grandfather), IV, 605
Pascaud, Jean (uncle), IV, 605
Pascaud, Jean, IV, 605
Pascaud, Joseph-Marie, II, 509; III, 290
Pascaud, Marguerite. See Bouat
Pascaud, Marie-Anne. See Baulos
Pascaud, Pierre, IV, 605
Pasqualigo, Lorenzo, I, 148, 149, 150
Pasqualigo, Pietro, I, 235
Pasquier, Jean, II, 33, 464, 465, 508
Pasquine, M., I, **533**, 586; II, 182
Passard, Marie-Jeanne (Neveu), III, 482
Passenger, William, II, 152, 487
Pastedechouan, I, **533–34**, 164, 265, 488
Pastour de Costebelle, Anne. See Mius d'Entremont de Pobomcoup
Pastour de Costebelle, Anne. See Tour
Pastour de Costebelle, Anne-Catherine de (Bertaut), II, 512
Pastour de Costebelle, Barthélemy, II, 509, 510
Pastour de Costebelle, François-Barthélemy, II, 509
Pastour de Costebelle, Françoise, II, 509
Pastour de Costebelle, Louis, II, 478, 509, 510
Pastour de Costebelle, Marie. See Du Plessis
Pastour de Costebelle, Marie-Josèphe (Rivière, Marquise de Giscaro), II, 512
Pastour de Costebelle, Philippe, I, 530; II, **509–13**, 15, 36, 152, 205, 214, 254, 285, 339, 388, 389, 411, 417, 442, 479, 482, 487, 611, 637; III, 177, 357, 455, 499, 618; IV, xxi
Pastour de Mérieu, Joseph, II, 509, 510
Patenotre, Marie (Plante), III, 522
Paterson, Charles, IV, 277, 365
Patin, Guy, I, 80
Patiner, Henry, I, 156
Patoulet, Jean-Baptiste, I, **534**, 63, 120, 581, 621, 627; II, 146, 147
Patriarch. See Fléché
Patron, Jean-Jacques, II, 262
Patterson, Elizabeth. See Todd
Patterson, George, I, 335
Patterson, Hester. See Warren
Patterson, John, IV, 606, 609

Patterson, Walter, IV, **605–11**, 128, 129, 152, 352, 551
Patterson, William, IV, 606
Patteshall, Jane (Cope), III, 136
Pattin, John, III, **501–2**, 496
Pauger, Adrien de, III, 105
Paugus, II, 26
Paul, I, 652
Paul V, Pope, I, 97
Paulet (Powlett), Charles, Lord St John of Basing, Marquis of Winchester, Duke of Bolton, II, 496, 497
Paulmy d'Argenson, Marquis de. See Voyer
Paulo, Catherine (Campot), III, 96
Paulus. See also Sahonwagy
Paulus, IV, 692
Paulus Petrus, IV, 691
Paumart, Guillaume, I, 534
Paumart, Jean, I, **534**
Paumart, Marie. See Le Roy
Paumereau. See Pommereau
Pauperet, Claude, II, 17, 388
Pawpitch, IV, 518
Paxinosa, IV, 27
Payen de Chavoy, Pierre, II, 513
Payen de Noyan, Catherine-Jeanne. See Le Moyne de Longueuil et de Châteauguay
Payen de Noyan, Gilles-Augustin, III, 382, 503
Payen de Noyan, Louise-Catherine. See Ailleboust de Manthet
Payen de Noyan, Marie. See Faucon Dumanoir
Payen de Noyan, Pierre, II, **513**, 131, 446; III, 502; IV, 611
Payen de Noyan, Pierre-Benoît, III, **502–3**
Payen de Noyan et de Chavoy, Catherine-Angélique (Legardeur de Repentigny), IV, 449, 612
Payen de Noyan et de Chavoy, Louise-Catherine. See Ailleboust de Manthet
Payen de Noyan et de Chavoy, Pierre-Jacques, II, 131, 180; III, 110, 373, 450, 492, 503, 588; IV, **611–12**, 85, 449
Payet, Marguerite (Couturier, dit Le Bourguignon), II, 160
Payet, dit Saint-Amour, Pierre, I, 633; II, 141
Payne, Benjamin Charnock, IV, 758
Payne, François-Amable, II, 513
Payne, Humphrey, II, 513
Payne, John, II, 513
Payne, John Howard, IV, 594
Payne, Lawrence, II, 513
Payne, Marguerite. See Garreau
Payne, Mary. See Rivers
Payne, Samuel, II, **513–14**; III, 346
Pays, Renée (Hardouineau de Landianière; Beauharnois de La Boische, Marquise de Beauharnois), III, 42
Payzant*, John (1749–1834), IV, 19
Peachey, James, IV, **612–14**
Péan, Angélique. See Renaud d'Avène Des Méloizes
Péan, Angélique-Renée-Françoise (Marconnay), IV, 616, 660
Péan, Anne. See Corbarboineau
Péan, Jean-Pierre, III, 503
Péan, Marie-Madeleine (Mény), V, 99
Péan, Michel-Jean-Hugues, III, 19, 124, 160, 300, 441, 464, 504, 525, 537, 551; IV, **614–17**, 65, 66, 67, 69, 70, 88, 91, 124, 125, 459, 517, 621, 642, 659, 670, 680, 750
Péan, René-Pierre, IV, 615
Péan de Livaudière, Jacques-Hugues, II, 339; III, **503–4**, 69, 102, 340, 505; IV, 315, 614, 654

Péan de Livaudière, Marie-Françoise. *See* Pécaudy de Contrecœur
Pearson, Bartholomew, I, **534–35**, 350
Pearson, Elizabeth. *See* Baguleughe
Pease, Captain, I, 567
Pease, Huldah (Kendrick), IV, 410
Peaseley, William, III, **504**; IV, 437
Pécaudy, Charles, I, 535
Pécaudy, Claudine (Jarret), II, 295
Pécaudy de Contrecœur, Anne. *See* Dubois
Pécaudy de Contrecœur, Antoine, I, **535–36**; II, 295, 592; III, 308, 505
Pécaudy de Contrecœur, Antoine (grandson), III, 505
Pécaudy de Contrecœur, Barbe. *See* Denys de La Trinité
Pécaudy de Contrecœur, Claude-François, IV, 617
Pécaudy de Contrecœur, Claude-Pierre, I, 536; III, 81, 94, 148, 149, 150, 373, 401, 505, 526, 600, 614; IV, **617–18**, xliii, 257, 459, 464, 634
Pécaudy de Contrecœur, François, III, 525
Pécaudy de Contrecœur, François-Antoine, I, 535; II, 495, 593; III, **505**, 55, 159, 160, 503, 637; IV, 614, 617
Pécaudy de Contrecœur, Jeanne. *See* Saint-Ours
Pécaudy de Contrecœur, Louise (Daine), III, 159, 505; IV, 66, 614
Pécaudy de Contrecœur, Marguerite-Barbe. *See* Hingue de Puygibault
Pécaudy de Contrecœur, Marie (La Corne de Chaptes), II, 327; III, 331, 332, 333; IV, 425, 429
Pécaudy de Contrecœur, Marie-Françoise (Péan de Livaudière), III, 503, 405; IV, 614
Pécaudy de Contrecœur, Marie-Madeleine. *See* Boucher de La Perrière
Péchagut, Jeanne (Laumet), II, 351
Peck, Kendrick, IV, 295
Peckham, Sir George, I, 333, 334, 336, 363, 380, 531, 677
Pécody, Benoît de, I, 535
Pécody, Énarde de. *See* Martin
Pedley*, Charles (1820–72), IV, 785
Peiras, Anne de. *See* Thirement
Peiras, Catherine de, II, 514
Peiras, Denise de. *See* Marion
Peiras, Denise de (Giffard), II, 514
Peiras, Élisabeth de (Pinguet de Targis), II, 514
Peiras, Jean de, II, 514
Peiras, Jean-Baptiste de, I, 581; II, **514**, 179, 369
Peiras, Louis de, II, 514
Peiras, Marie-Madeleine de (Denys de Saint-Simon), II, 60, 178, 514; III, 180
Peire, Philippe, I, 180
Peire (Peré), Pierre, II, 180, 214, 276, 526
Peirenc de Moras, François-Marie de, IV, 467
Peirese, Nicolas de, I, 294
Pelegrin. *See* Pellegrin
Pélerin, Ambroise (baptized Pierre), II, **514–15**, 244
Pélerin, Ignace, I, 256
Pélerin, Philippe, I, 91
Pélerin de Saint-Amant, Louise. *See* Mousseaux
Pélerin de Saint-Amant, Pierre, I, 256; II, 474, 515
Pelham, Henry, III, 658
Pelham-Holles, Thomas, 4th Duke of Newcastle-upon-Tyne, II, 22, 251; III, 9, 10, 33, 126, 127, 183, 261, 276, 293, 294, 362, 426, 517, 585, 587, 642, 653, 658; IV, 21, 57, 395, 571

Pélissier, Agathe. *See* Martaud La Rigaudière
Pélissier, Christophe, IV, **618–19**, 205, 243, 288, 399, 629
Pélissier, François-Christophe, IV, 618
Pélissier, Marie-Catherine. *See* Delezenne
Pélissier, Marthe. *See* Baudoin
Pellegrin, François, IV, 619
Pellegrin, Gabriel, III, 464, 621, 622; IV, **619–21**, 10, 271
Pellegrin, Madeleine. *See* Boissy
Pellegrin, Marie-Anne. *See* Bonnegrâce
Pellerin, Marie (Becquet), I, 86
Pellet. *See* Plet
Pelletier, Antoinette (Daine), III, 159
Pelletier, Catherine. *See* Vannier
Pelletier, Catherine, I, 439
Pelletier, Catherine-Geneviève (Lefebvre Duplessis Faber), III, 372, 373
Pelletier, Didace (baptized Claude), I, **536**, 439; II, 174, 176, 203, 248, 258, 268, 419, 506, 515, 528; III, 259, 344
Pelletier, François, I, 387; II, 158
Pelletier, Geneviève. *See* Letendre
Pelletier (Peltier), Geneviève (Lefebvre), II, 382; III, 371
Pelletier, Georges, I, 536
Pelletier, Jean-François-Xavier, II, 655; III, 372
Pelletier, Jeanne (Jérémie, *dit* Lamontagne), I, 387; II, 296; III, 314
Pelletier, Madeleine. *See* Thunay, *dit* Dufresne
Pelletier (Peltier), Marie. *See* Outchiouanish
Pelletier (Peltier), Marie-Geneviève (Janson, *dit* Lapalme), III, 304
Pelletier (Peltier), Nicolas, II, 357
Pelletier, René, II, 382
Pelletier (Peltier) de La Prade, Michel, I, 251, 494; II, 637
Pellew, Edward, 1st Viscount Exmount, IV, 784
Pelling, Mr, I, 578
Pellissier. *See* Pélissier
Peltier. *See* Pelletier
Pembroke, Earl of. *See* Herbert
Pemoussa, II, **515–16**, 502, 562; III, 577
Peñalossa, Diego, Count of Peñalossa, I, 179
Peña Saravia, Tomás de la, IV, 623
Penhallow, Samuel, II, 452, 495, 544
Pénigaut (Pénicaut), André-Joseph, II, 428, 455
Pénissault (Penisseau). *See* Pennisseaut
Penn, Sir William, I, 605; II, 667
Penn, William, III, 65
Pennant, Thomas, IV, 341, 377, 378
Pennasca (Sébastien), I, 396
Pennefather, Lavina (St Leger, Lady St Leger), IV, 694
Pennisseaut, Catherine. *See* Bry
Pennisseaut, Charles, IV, 621
Pennisseaut, Louis, III, 441, 442; IV, **621–22**, 66, 125, 127, 461, 517, 615, 616
Pennisseaut, Marie-Marguerite. *See* Lemoine, *dit* Monière
Penniston, Susan (Clinton), III, 126
Pensens. *See* Espiet
Penthièvre, Duc de. *See* Bourbon
Pepin, Angélique (Deguire, *dit* Desrosiers), IV, 201, 202
Pepin, Charlotte (Campion, *dit* Labonté), IV, 132
Pépin, Jacqueline (Cusson), II, 166
Pepin, Marguerite (Leclerc), II, 380
Pepin, Marie (Larue), II, 348
Pépin, Marie-Ursule (Pinard), I, 550
Pépin, *dit* Laforce, Marie-Joseph (Rouer de Villeray), III, 571

Pépin, *dit* Laforce, Michelle. *See* Lebert
Pépin, *dit* Laforce, Pierre, III, 239, 571; IV, 692
Pépin*, *dit* Laforce, René-Hippolyte (1728–1802), IV, 613
Pépin, *dit* Laforce, Véronique (Saillant), IV, 692
Pepperrell, Andrew, II, 516
Pepperrell, Andrew (great-grandson), III, 508
Pepperrell, Joan (wife of Andrew), II, 516
Pepperrell, Margery. *See* Bray
Pepperrell, Mary, Lady Pepperrell. *See* Hirst
Pepperrell, William, II, **516**; III, 505
Pepperrell, Sir William, II, 516; III, **505–9**, xxiv, 6, 10, 33, 49, 98, 116, 175, 209, 260, 264, 267, 274, 294, 345, 350, 356, 396, 452, 457, 470, 471, 475, 566, 615, 641, 642, 644, 653, 655, 656, 657; IV, 15, 62, 83, 84, 168, 213, 239, 248, 254, 299, 312, 314, 363, 420, 454, 688, 783
Pepys, Samuel, I, 226; II, 308, 659
Perceval, John, 2nd Earl of Egmont, III, 658; IV, 606
Perchot, Hélène (Monseignat), II, 483
Percy, Algernon, 2nd Baron Lovaine, IV, 197
Percy, Francis, II, 153
Percy, Hugh Smithson, 1st Duke of Northumberland, IV, 197, 198
Perdita. *See* Darby, Mary
Perdrigean, Françoise (Vienne), IV, 754
Péré. *See* Peire
Péré, Arnaud, I, 226, 537
Peré, Jean, I, **536–37**, 226, 393, 528, 572, 626, 627; II, 347
Père Joseph, I, 222
Pérez Hernández, Juan Josef, IV, **622–23**, lv, 72, 165, 519, 567
Péricard, François de, II, 359
Péricard, Michelle de (Laval), II, 358, 359
Perichon, Noël-Mathurin-Étienne, IV, 353
Périer, Étienne de, III, 40, 382
Perier de Salvert, Antoine-Alexis, IV, 247, 254, 588
Périgny. *See* Ailleboust
Périn, Marie-Rose (Lombard de Combles), III, 406
Périnault*, Joseph (1732–1814), IV, 140
Périnault, Marie-Josette (Varin, *dit* La Pistole), IV, 748
Périnneau, *dit* Lamarche, François, IV, 272
Perkins*, Simeon (1734/35–1812), IV, 116, 219, 222
Perkins, Thomas, III, 411; IV, 158
Pernette, Joseph, III, 212
Pernette, Sophia Augusta (Eagleson; Collins), IV, 258
Perny, Nicolas, IV, 124
Péroine, Marguerite (Phlem), III, 518
Peronne de Mazé, Louis, I, **537**, 468, 589
Peronne Des Touches, Michel, I, 537, 538; II, 385
Peronne Dumesnil, Jean, I, **537–39**, 112, 326, 401, 580, 606; II, 385
Perosse, Valeron, I, 88
Pérot, Gilles, I, **539**
Perras, M., IV, 619
Perrault. *See also* Perrot
Perrault, M., IV, 148
Perrault, Charles, IV, 624
Perrault, Charles-François, IV, 624
Perrault, Charlotte. *See* Boucher de Boucherville
Perrault, François, III, **509–10**, 501; IV, 623
Perrault, Guillaume-Michel, IV, 623
Perrault, Jacques (brother of FRANÇOIS), III, 509
Perrault, Jacques (father of FRANÇOIS), III, 509
Perrault, Jacques (father of PAUL), III, 510

Perrault, Jacques, known as Perrault, *l'aîné*, III, 13, 509, 510; IV, **623–24**, 148, 306, 461, 462, 591, 692
Perrault*, Jacques-Nicolas (1750–1812), III, 13; IV, 624
Perrault, Jean-Baptiste, IV, 304, 316, 623
Perrault*, Jean-Olivier (1773–1827), IV, 624
Perrault, Joseph-François, III, 510; IV, 287, 509, 574, 623
Perrault*, Joseph-François (1753–1844), III, 510; IV, 496, 698
Perrault, Julien, I, **539**
Perrault, Louis-François, IV, 623
Perrault, Marguerite. *See* Caché
Perrault, Marie-Anne. *See* Amiot
Perrault, Marie-Joseph. *See* Rivard, *dit* Lanouette
Perrault, Marie-Madeleine. *See* Paquin
Perrault, Pacôme, II, 419
Perrault, Paul, III, **510–11**
Perrault, Suzanne. *See* Pagé, *dit* Carcy
Perrault, Ursule. *See* McCarty
Perrault *l'aîné*. *See* Perrault, Jacques
Perreault, Hyacinthe, I, **539–40**; II, 222
Perrier, Philippe, I, 43
Perrin, Antoine, II, **516**
Perrin, Catherine. *See* Boissières
Perrin, Jacques, II, 516
Perrot. *See also* Perrault
Perrot, Anne (Jacquin), III, 304
Perrot, Bertrand, II, 43
Perrot, Cathcrine (Jeanneau), III, 313
Perrot, François, II, 517
Perrot, François-Marie, I, **540–42**, 66, 84, 102, 105, 117, 136, 175, 204, 287, 288, 295, 409, 410, 418 436, 464, 465, 508, 576, 581, 584, 600, 631; II, 6, 56, 112, 182, 184, 193, 194, 410, 412, 514, 522, 532, 616; IV, xviii
Perrot, John, I, 81
Perrot, Sir John, I, 228
Perrot, Joseph, II, 43
Perrot, Madeleine. *See* Laguide Meynier
Perrot, Madeleine. *See* Raclot
Perrot, Marie. *See* Sivot
Perrot, Marie (Jarret de Verchères), II, 295; III, 308, 311
Perrot, Nicolas, I, 40, 132, 174, 248, 249, 308, 547, 548, 625, 640; II, **516–20**, 129, 263, 380, 422, 423, 427, 453, 484, 488, 500, 504; III, 493
Perrot, *dit* Joly-Cœur, Nicolas, II, 517
Perrot, *dit* Vildaigre, Jacques, II, 518
Perrot, *dit* Vildaigre, Michelle. *See* Le Flot
Perrot de Fercourt, M., I, 541
Perrot de Rizy, Anne. *See* Jourdain
Perrot de Rizy, Marie. *See* Willis
Perrot de Rizy, Pierre, II, **520**; III, 631
Perry, Elizabeth (Mascarene), III, 435
Perthuis, Anne. *See* Minet
Perthuis, Charles (father), II, 520
Perthuis, Charles, II, **520–21**, 526; III, 511, 558; IV, 624
Perthuis, Charles-Régis, IV, 625
Perthuis, Jean-Baptiste-Ignace, III, **511–12**, 291; IV, 602, 625
Perthuis, Joseph, II, 520; III, 140, 478, 491; IV, **624–25**
Perthuis, Joseph (son), IV, 625
Perthuis, Marie (Rouer de Villeray), I, 579
Perthuis, Marie-Anne. *See* Chasle
Perthuis, Marie-Joseph (Riverin), III, 588
Perthuis, Marie-Josephte-Madeleine. *See* Hiché

Perthuis, Marie-Madeleine. *See* Roberge
Pérusse Des Cars, Marquis de, IV, 56, 457
Pesant, Le. *See* Le Pesant
Peschart, Mme, Baronne de Bossac. *See* Dollier de Casson
Peschart, Gabriel, Baron de Bossac, II, 191
Pétau, Denis, I, 203
Peter. *See* Kingminguse
Peterborough, Earl of. *See* Mordaunt
Peters, Abigail. *See* Thompson
Peters, Hannah. *See* Chenery
Peters, Hendrick. *See* Theyanoguin
Peters, John, IV, 393
Peters, Joseph, IV, **625–26**, 705
Peters, Pauly. *See* Sahonwagy
Peters, Sally (wife of THOMAS), IV, 626
Peters, Samuel Andrew, IV, 625, 626
Peters, Thomas, IV, **626–28**, 604
Peters, William, IV, 625
Petersen, Paulus. *See* Sahonwagy
Petit, Sieur, II, 630
Petit, Adrien, II, 521
Petit, Anne (Piot de Langloiserie), II, 526
Petit, Catherine. *See* Du Bellineau
Petit, Catherine. *See* Dufloc
Petit, Charlotte. *See* Dugué de Boisbriand
Petit, Émilion, IV, 67
Petit, François, II, 522
Petit, Gédéon, III, 65
Petit, Jean, I, 295; II, **521**, 527; III, 352
Petit, Jeanne. *See* Gobin
Petit, Louis, I, 544, 649; II, **521–22**, 183, 184, 477, 638
Petit, Louise (Corbin), IV, 167
Petit, Marguerite. *See* Véron de Grandmesnil
Petit, Monique-Françoise (Gohin de Montreuil), IV, 307
Petit, Pierre, (father of JEAN), II, 521
Petit, Pierre, II, **522–23**; III, 67, 540; IV, 167
Petit, Suzanne. *See* Dupuy
Petit, Suzanne (Caën), I, 161
Petit Boismorel, Jean, II, 521
Petit Boismorel, Marie-Anne (Plessy, *dit* Bélair), III, 523
Petitchouan. *See* Chomina
Petit de L'Estang, Marie (Troyes), I, 653
Petit de Levilliers, Charles, II, **523–24**; III, 491
Petit de Levilliers, Charles (son), II, 523
Petit de Levilliers, Élisabeth. *See* Berruyer
Petit de Levilliers, Étiennette-Louise. *See* Malbeque
Petit de Levilliers, Madeleine. *See* Gaultier Du Tremblay
Petit de Levilliers, Marie-Charlotte (Noyelles de Fleurimont), III, 491, 492
Petit de Levilliers, Robert, II, 523
Petit de Levilliers de Coulanges, Françoise. *See* Golard
Petit de Levilliers de Coulanges, Pierre-Louis, II, 523
Petit de Thoizy, Marie-Anne (Druillon de Macé), IV, 226
Petit de Verneuil, Jacques, II, 521
Petit de Verneuil, Marie. *See* Viel
Petitot, *dit* Saint-Sceine (Sincennes), Marguerite (Doucet), IV, 222
Petitpas, Barthélemy, III, **512–13**, 34
Petitpas, Catherine. *See* Bugaret
Petitpas, Claude, II, **524**; III, 512
Petitpas, Françoise. *See* Lavergne
Petitpas, Henriette (Robichaux), IV, 676
Petitpas, Jacques, II, 6, 605

Petitpas, Louis, III, 418
Petitpas, Madeleine. *See* Coste
Petitpas, Marguerite (Sevestre), I, 606
Petitpas, Marie-Thérèse (wife of CLAUDE), II, 524; III, 512
Petitpas de Lafleur, Claude, II, 524
Petiver, James, I, 677
Petrimoulx, Médard, IV, 653
Petrimoulx, Michel, III, 420, 429
Pett, Phineas, I, 144, 362
Petters. *See* Peters
Pettrequin, Jean, III, **513**; IV, 780
Petty, William, 2nd Earl of Shelburne, III, 296, 478; IV, xxxv, xl, xlii, 183, 298, 336, 399, 430, 571, 577, 603, 686, 753, 788, 792
Peuvret, Jacques, I, 542
Peuvret, Marie. *See* La Garenne
Peuvret de Gaudarville, Alexandre, I, 326, 543; II, **524–25**, 42, 215, 485
Peuvret de Gaudarville, Alexandre-Joseph, II, 525
Peuvret de Gaudarville, Geneviève. *See* Bouteville
Peuvret de Gaudarville, Marie-Anne. *See* Gaultier de Comporté
Peuvret de Gaudarville, Marie-Anne, II, 525
Peuvret Demesnu, Catherine. *See* Nau de La Boissière et de Fossambault
Peuvret Demesnu, François, I, 542
Peuvret Demesnu, Jean-Baptiste, I, **542–43**, 587; II, xvii, xix, 307, 524, 582
Peuvret Demesnu, Marie-Catherine (Juchereau Duchesnay), I, 543; II, 307; III, 318
Peuvret Demesnu, Marie-Rogère. *See* Lepage
Peyrant, Antoine, II, 465
Peyrant, Marie-Anne (Martin de Lino), II, 465
Peyton*, John (1749–1829), IV, 714
Pézard de La Tousche, Claude, I, 543
Pézard de La Tousche, Étienne, II, 186, 528
Pézard de La Tousche, Madeleine (Desjordy de Cabanac), II, 185
Pézard de La Tousche, Marie. *See* Masson
Pézard de La Tousche Champlain, Étienne, I, **543**; II, 168, 185
Pézard de La Tousche Champlain, Madeleine. *See* Mullois de La Borde
Phébus. *See* Gaston III
Phelan, Rebecca. *See* Nesbitt
Phelan, William, IV, 470
Phélipeaux d'Herbault, Georges-Louis, IV, 55
Phélippeaux, Catherine. *See* Boutet
Phélippeaux (Philipeaux, Philippeau), Charles, I, 201; II, 612
Phélippeaux, Louise (Maillou, *dit* Desmoulins), III, 420
Phelps, Benajah, IV, 490
Phélypeaux, Éléonore-Christine, Comtesse de Pontchartrain et de Maurepas. *See* La Rochefoucauld-Roye
Phélypeaux, Françoise (Senat; Gaschet), III, 237
Phélypeaux, Jean-Frédéric, Comte de Maurepas, II, 53, 66, 210, 225, 226, 239, 269, 284, 302, 374, 390, 457, 520, 530, 571, 573, 650; III, 13, 16, 17, 27, 29, 38, 40, 41, 42, 44, 45, 48, 49, 55, 61, 74, 75, 76, 78, 79, 80, 93, 107, 110, 117, 118, 119, 120, 135, 145, 153, 154, 175, 178, 179, 180, 182, 200, 203, 223, 224, 226, 228, 234, 239, 240, 246, 249, 250, 251, 252, 253, 255, 256, 259, 263, 264, 270, 284, 291, 292, 312, 319, 334, 339, 340, 343,

344, 353, 354, 361, 368, 382, 383, 389, 390, 398, 399, 416, 433, 434, 445, 455, 456, 492, 532, 539, 541, 545, 550, 558, 566, 575, 592, 593, 604, 627, 630, 631, 637, 644, 645, 646, 647, 675; IV, 56, 60, 62, 63, 76, 123, 167, 239, 284, 318, 339, 355, 358, 359, 361, 363, 364, 376, 435, 440, 465, 466, 467, 473, 539, 590, 611, 612, 624, 636, 663, 665, 666, 667, 749, 750

Phélypeaux, Jérôme, Comte de Pontchartrain et de Maurepas, II, 7, 39, 64, 68, 114, 115, 116, 121, 132, 134, 147, 230, 238, 270, 299, 301, 302, 304, 326, 349, 353, 354, 355, 384, 388, 422, 428, 453, 456, 457, 465, 466, 482, 495, 511, 531, 532, 543, 546, 547, 550, 551, 552, 554, 556, 557, 558, 559, 567, 568, 569, 570, 587, 589, 632, 672; III, 51, 53, 58, 59, 60, 61, 83, 96, 177, 200, 233, 368, 372, 380, 381, 429, 474, 498, 552, 557, 681; IV, xxi, 661

Phélypeaux, Louis, Comte de Pontchartrain, I, 138, 510, 534; II, 57, 73, 74, 79, 93, 167, 184, 197, 280, 305, 353, 421, 442, 443, 449, 483, 532, 549, 555, 575, 586; III, 41, 42

Phélypeaux, Louis, Comte de Saint-Florentin et Marquis de La Vrillière, II, 426

Phélypeaux, Marie-Suzanne. See Talon

Phélypeaux de Pontchartrain, Anne. See Beauharnois

Phélypeaux de Pontchartrain, Anne (Buade, Comtesse de Frontenac et de Palluau), I, 133

Phélypeaux de Pontchartrain, Paul, III, 51

Phélypeaux de Villesavin, Isabelle. See Blondeau

Phélypeaux de Villesavin, Jean, I, 484

Philibert. See Jacquin

Philip II, King of Spain, I, 187, 316

Philip III, King of Spain, I, 676

Philip V, King of Spain, II, 98, 104, 115, 397; III, 609

Philipeaux. See Phélippeaux

Philipot, Michel, I, 167

Philippe VI, King of France, III, 554

Philippe, Marie (Legras; Fézeret), II, 221

Philippe (Philippes) de Hautmesnil de Mandeville, Antoine, II, 525

Philippe (Philippes) de Hautmesnil de Mandeville, François, II, 525–26, 306

Philippe (Philippes) de Hautmesnil de Mandeville, Madeleine. See La Maire

Philippe de Hautmesnil (Hautmesnyl) de Marigny, Jean-Vincent, I, 508; II, 17, 105, 133, 525

Philippe de Hautmesnil (Hautmesnyl) de Marigny, Marie-Catherine. See Lambert de Baussy

Philippe de Hautmesnil de Marigny, Marie-Gabrielle (Amiot de Vincelotte), II, 17

Philippe de Saint-Lambert, Gabriel, II, 525

Philippeau. See Phélippeaux

Philippine-Gertrude de Sainte-Dominique. See Boullongne

Philipps, Ann. See Dyson

Philipps, Catherina. See Stratham

Philipps, Elizabeth. See Cosby

Philipps, Erasmus, III, 514

Philipps, Erasmus James, III, 514–15, 276, 298, 453, 665

Philipps, Frances. See Noel

Philipps*, John (d. 1801), IV, 776

Philipps, Richard (father), III, 515

Philipps, Richard, II, 22, 23, 24, 93, 96, 97, 152, 198, 199, 250, 274, 590, 591, 601, 652, 663, 664, 668, 670; III, 515–18, 9, 83, 135, 136, 143, 208, 276, 277, 287, 326,

342, 363, 426, 427, 436, 437, 439, 514, 597; IV, xxii, xxv, 83, 170, 539, 774

Philipse, Margaret. See Marston

Philipse, Philip, IV, 586

Phillips, Bridget. See Hutchinson

Phillips, Elizabeth (Everill; Alden), II, 15

Phillips, John, III, 212, 405

Phillips, Mary (wife of William, major), I, 337

Phillips, Phoebe (Gillam), I, 337, 338, 601; II, 247

Phillips, Thomas, II, 439

Phillips, William (British army officer), IV, 442

Phillips, William (major), I, 337, 601; II, 15

Phipps, Thomas (father), I, 543

Phipps, Thomas, I, 543–44, 39; II, 265

Phips, James, I, 544

Phips, Mary. See Spencer

Phips, Mary (mother of Sir WILLIAM), I, 544

Phips, Spencer, III, 128, 508

Phips, Sir William, I, 544–46, 26, 76, 90, 139, 146, 250, 260, 397, 402, 426, 436, 466, 542, 576, 577, 586, 649; II, 6, 14, 19, 36, 46, 80, 94, 109, 120, 137, 159, 160, 168, 172, 177, 183, 184, 185, 186, 222, 227, 229, 244, 257, 268, 283, 284, 326, 338, 352, 383, 401, 404, 410, 441, 452, 482, 483, 494, 522, 532, 591, 593, 601, 605, 638, 660, 662; III, 109, 155, 245, 586, 596, 669; IV, xix

Phlem, Guillaume, III, 518

Phlem, Marguerite. See Péroine

Phlem, dit Yvon, Marie. See Levreau

Phlem, dit Yvon, Yves, III, 518–20

Phokus Valerianos (Valerianatos). See Fuca, Juan de

Phyn, James, IV, 261

Piat, Irénée, I, 546–47

Picard, Françoise. See Maufils

Picard, Louis-Alexandre, III, 620; IV, 628–30, 205, 206, 548

Picard, Marguerite (Gaudé), III, 238

Picard, Marie (Ducharme), IV, 233

Picard, Marie-Jeanne. See Léger

Picard, Pierre, IV, 629

Picard, Pierre-François, IV, 628

Piccolomini, Monsignor, II, 362, 363

Pichery, Anne de, I, 265

Pichon. See also Pichot

Pichon, Jean, IV, 630

Pichon, Marie. See Esnault

Pichon, Marie (Gauthier de La Chenaye; Sevestre), I, 583, 606

Pichon, Thomas, III, 73, 166, 498, 589; IV, 630–32, 249, 250, 443, 645, 656, 657, 661

Pichon, dit Larose, M., II, 645

Pichot de Querdisien Trémais, Charles-François, IV, 632–33, 68, 517, 616

Pickersgill, Richard, IV, 165

Picot, Jeanne de (Brethous), IV, 245

Picoté de Belestre, François, I, 547; II, 411, 626

Picoté de Belestre, Françoise (Maleray de Noiré de La Mollerie), II, 450, 451

Picoté de Belestre, Françoise-Marie-Anne (Dagneau Douville de Quindre), III, 158

Picoté de Belestre, François-Louis, IV, 634

Picoté de Belestre, François-Marie (father), IV, 633

Picoté de Belestre, François-Marie, III, 527, 611; IV, 633–36, xliii, 346, 347, 442, 546, 680

Picoté de Belestre, Hélène (La Frenaye de Brucy; Céloron de Blainville), I, 410, 547; II, 125, 336; III, 99
Picoté de Belestre, Jeanne-Geneviève, I, 547; II, 390, 391, 447, 450
Picoté de Belestre, Marie. *See* Pars
Picoté de Belestre, Marie-Anne. *See* Magnan, *dit* L'Espérance
Picoté de Belestre, Marie-Anne. *See* Nivard Saint-Dizier
Picoté de Belestre, Marie-Anne (Tonty), I, 547; II, 631; III, 627
Picoté de Belestre, Marie-Catherine. *See* Trottier Desruisseaux
Picoté de Belestre, Perrinne (Godefroy de Lintot), I, 547; II, 252
Picoté de Belestre, Pierre, I, **547**, 266, 271, 273, 410, 508; II, 631
Picq, Marie (Charpentier; Carrerot), II, 119; III, 97, 98, 173
Picq, Thomas, II, 119
Picques, Bernard, II, 360
Picquet, André, IV, 636
Picquet, François, III, xxxvii, xxxviii, 28, 30, 47, 181, 256, 268, 269, 408, 494; IV, **636–38**, 36, 431, 506, 507, 521, 587
Picquet, Marie-Philippe. *See* Berthet
Picquet de La Motte, Toussaint-Guillaume, Comte Picquet de La Motte, known as La Motte-Picquet, IV, 282
Pidianske (Pidiwamiska) (Marie-Mathilde) (Abbadie de Saint-Castin, Baronne de Saint-Castin), II, 3, 5; III, 3
Pidou de Saint-Olon, Louis-Marie, III, 640
Piedmont. *See* Raimbault
Pier. *See* Saint-Aubin
Pierce, Margaret (Green), IV, 312
Piercotte. *See* Audet
Piernas, Pedro Josef, IV, 316
Pierre. *See also* Gawèhe
Pierre (Iroquois), IV, 375
Pierre (servant), II, 639
Pierre, III, **520**, xxxiv, 205, 450
Pierre-Antoine. *See* Pastedechouan
Pierre-Benoit. *See* Benoit
Pierre-Jean, *dit* La Tête Blanche. *See* Gray Lock
Pierron, Jean, I, **547**, 108, 315, 635; II, 61, 140
Pierson, Philippe, I, 321
Pieskaret, I, **547–48**, 71, 370, 403
Piet. *See* Picq
Pigarouich, I, **548–49**, 6, 640
Pigot, Hugh, IV, 223
Pijart, Claude (father), I, 549
Pijart, Claude, I, **549**, 231, 459, 566, 645; II, 234
Pijart, Geneviève. *See* Charon
Pijart, Gilette (Boulduc), II, 88
Pijart, Pierre, I, **549–50**, 125, 203, 328, 459
Pike. *See* Kinongé
Pilate (slave), II, 646
Piles, Roger de, I, 313
Pilgrim, Robert, III, **520–21**, 123, 214, 561, 562, 661, 662; IV, 33, 381, 383
Pillard, Anne. *See* Parisette
Pillard, Louis, III, **521**, 67
Pillard, Louis (son), III, 521; IV, 331
Pillard, Marguerite. *See* Beaudry
Pillard, Marie-Angélique. *See* Dubuc
Pillard, Pierre, III, 521

Pillet, Antoine, IV, 59
Pillet, Charles, I, 211
Pillet, Félicité (Besnard, *dit* Carignant), IV, 58
Pillet, Ignace, IV, 58
Pillet, Pascal, IV, 58, 592
Pillon, Boyer, IV, 229
Pilon, Jean, II, 166
Pilote. *See* Crusson
Pinard. *See also* Pyvart
Pinard, Claude, I, 321, 550
Pinard, Françoise. *See* Gamelain
Pinard, Jean, I, 550
Pinard, Louis, I, **550**, 321, 328, 369
Pinard, Marguerite. *See* Gaignier
Pinard, Marguerite (Resche), III, 553
Pinard, Marie. *See* Rivard
Pinard, Marie-Madeleine. *See* Hertel de La Fresnière
Pinard, Marie-Ursule. *See* Pépin
Pinaud, Françoise. *See* Daret
Pinaud, Jean, II, 526
Pinaud, Louise. *See* Douaire de Bondy
Pinaud, Nicolas, I, 56; II, **526**, 520; III, 569
Pinet (Desmarest), Gabrielle (Renaud Dubuisson), II, 563; III, 551
Pinet, Pierre-François, II, 55, 468, 501
Pinguet, Charles, II, 66; III, 522
Pinguet, Françoise (Delaunay), II, 173
Pinguet, Jean, III, 284, 522
Pinguet, Joseph-Régis, III, 522
Pinguet, Marie-Anne (Chambalon; Hazeur Des Ormeaux), II, 129
Pinguet de Bellevue, Nicolas-Charles, III, 522
Pinguet de Targis, Élisabeth. *See* Peiras
Pinguet de Vaucour, Jacques, III, 521
Pinguet de Vaucour, Jacques-Nicolas, III, **521–22**, 35, 499
Pinguet de Vaucour, Marie-Anne. *See* Morin
Pining (explorer), I, 679
Pinn. *See* Pynne
Pinolt. *See* Pinaud
Pinson*, Andrew (1728–1810), IV, 599, 712
Pinsonneau, *dit* Lafleur, Ignace, IV, 585
Pinteado, Captain, I, 316
Piot de Langloiserie, Anne. *See* Petit
Piot de Langloiserie, Charles-Gaspard, I, 295; II, **526–27**, 521; IV, 638
Piot de Langloiserie, Charlotte-Angélique, *dite* Sainte-Rosalie, IV, 638
Piot de Langloiserie, Louis, II, 527
Piot de Langloiserie, Marie-Charlotte (Ruette d'Auteuil de La Malotière), II, 527
Piot de Langloiserie, Marie-Marguerite, *dite* Saint-Hippolyte, IV, **638**, 529
Piot de Langloiserie, Marie-Thérèse. *See* Dugué de Boisbriand
Piot de Langloiserie, Martin, II, 526
Piot de Langloiserie, Suzanne (Céloron de Blainville), II, 527
Piozzi, Hester Lynch. *See* Salusbury
Piraube, Martial, I, 372, 374, 554
Piron, Pierre, I, 109
Piscot, Étienne, III, 240
Pitantouin. *See* Tantouin
Pitchy. *See* Peachey

Pithou, Pierre, I, 629
Pitt. *See also* Picq
Pitt, Anne (Grenville, Baroness Grenville), IV, 747
Pitt, John, 2nd Earl of Chatham, IV, 747
Pitt, Thomas, 1st Baron Camelford, IV, 747
Pitt, Thomas, 2nd Baron Camelford, IV, 747
Pitt, William, IV, 73, 115, 485, 715
Pitt, William, 1st Earl of Chatham, III, xxviii, xxix, 33, 71, 209, 588, 601, 654, 668; IV, xxxiii, 3, 21, 22, 23, 25, 84, 85, 106, 481, 571, 699, 700, 701
Pitton de Tournefort, Joseph, II, 188, 594, 595, 596, 600; III, 675
Pius VI, Pope, IV, 637
Pius IX, Pope, I, 354
Pius XI, Pope, I, 121, 184, 246, 324, 343, 410, 412
Pius XII, Pope, I, 121
Pivert, Nicolas, I, 233, 311
Plaines. *See* Damours
Plamondon. *See also* Lafleur
Plamondon*, Antoine (1804–95), IV, 9
Plantavit* de Margon, Jean-Guillaume-Charles de, Chevalier de La Pause (1721–1804), III, 510; IV, 308, 460, 531
Plante, Charles, III, **522–23**, 194, 263, 390, 546, 553; IV, 387
Plante, Claude, III, 522
Plante, Jean-Baptiste, IV, 748
Plante, Marie. *See* Patenotre
Planton, Antoinette. *See* Isabeau
Plattier, Jean, I, 394
Plemazais (Plemarch). *See* Mius
Plenderleath, Rachel, IV, 151
Plenderleath* Christie, William (1780–1845), IV, 151
Plessis*, Joseph-Octave (1763–1825), III, 524; IV, 42, 97, 98, 100, 101, 102, 137, 147, 445, 799
Plessy, *dit* Bélair, Charles, III, 524; IV, 654
Plessy, *dit* Bélair, Françoise. *See* Mathusson
Plessy, *dit* Bélair, Jean, III, 523
Plessy, *dit* Bélair, Jean-Louis, III, **523–24**; IV, 654
Plessy, *dit* Bélair, Joseph-Amable, III, 524
Plessy, *dit* Bélair, Marie-Anne. *See* Petit Boismorel
Plet, François, I, 177; II, 169
Plichon, *dit* Saint-Louis, Louis, III, 258
Ploumelle, Jeanne (Poulin), I, 553
Pluche, Noël-Antoine, IV, 640
Plugette (Pluiette), Jeanne (Navarre), IV, 579
Plumier, M., II, 188
Plummer, Ruth (Newman; Moody), III, 471
Plunket, Lady Catherine. *See* Aylmer
Pobomcoup. *See* Mius d'Entremont
Pobomcoup, Baronne de. *See* Hélie Du Tillet; Saint-Étienne de La Tour
Pocahontas, I, 67
Pocatière. *See* Pollet
Pochard, Alexandre, IV, 532, 534
Pocquet, Pierre, II, 629
Poignant, Jeanne (Giffard), I, 330
Poilly. *See* Grillot
Poincet, Martin, I, 460
Poinsu, François, IV, 239
Pointis. *See* Desjean
Poireaux, Marie-Françoise. *See* Morin
Poirel, Madeleine (Bourdon de Dombourg et de La Pinaudière), IV, 79

Poirier, Marie (Chouart), I, 223
Poisset, Françoise, III, 348
Poisson, Barbe (Barbeau, *dit* Lucault; Celles Duclos), I, 464; II, 164, 221
Poisson, François, I, 635
Poisson, Jeanne-Antoinette, Marquise de Pompadour (Le Normant d'Étioles), IV, 354, 467
Poitevin, Jeanne (Le Rouge), II, 418
Poitiers, Diane de, II, 328
Poitiers, Isabeau de (La Roque, *dit* Couillaud), I, 422
Poitiers Du Buisson, Élisabeth. *See* Jossard
Poitiers Du Buisson, Jean-Baptiste, III, 532
Poivre, Pierre, IV, 243, 752
Polemond, Jean-Baptiste, III, 18
Pollard*, Richard (1752–1824), IV, 118, 779
Pollet, Angélique. *See* Hamelin
Pollet, Arnould-Balthazar, III, **524**, 519
Pollet, Germain, III, 524
Pollet, Marguerite. *See* Harry
Pollet de La Combe de La Pocatière, Catherine. *See* Rossin
Pollet de La Combe de La Pocatière, François, I, 550
Pollet de La Combe-Pocatière, François, I, **550–51**; II, 391, 584, 586
Pollet de La Combe-Pocatière, Marie-Anne. *See* Juchereau de Saint-Denis
Pollet de La Combe-Pocatière, Marie-Louise (Rouer de Villeray et de La Cardonnière), I, 551; II, 584
Pollet de La Combe-Pocatière, Marie-Thérèse (Le Moyne d'Iberville et d'Ardillières; Béthune, Comtesse de Béthune), I, 551; II, 391, 399
Pollexfen, Henry, III, 151
Polo, Marco, I, 147, 150
Polonceau, Henry, IV, 206
Pometacom (King Philip), II, xxxv, 6, 145; III, 265
Pommereau, Catherine-Élisabeth (Bruyères), III, 525; IV, 109
Pommereau, Claire-Françoise. *See* Boucher de Boucherville
Pommereau, Françoise. *See* Nafrechoux
Pommereau, Françoise-Renée (Gough), III, 525
Pommereau, Gilles-François, III, 525
Pommereau, Jean-Baptiste, III, **524–25**, 339, 429; IV, 91, 109, 263, 447
Pommereau, Jean-François, III, 525
Pommereau, Pierre-Jacques, III, 524
Pommier, Hugues, I, **551**, 314, 359; II, 19
Pomoacan (Half-King), IV, 302
Pompadour, Marquise de. *See* Poisson
Ponce de Léon, Rodrigo, Duke of Arcos, II, 633
Poncet, Joseph-Antoine, I, 551
Poncet de La Rivière, Joseph-Antoine, I, **551–52**, 205, 208, 216, 217, 352, 563, 610, 645, 665; II, 535, 624
Poncet de La Rivière et de Brétigny, Jean, I, 551
Poncet de La Rivière et de Brétigny, Marguerite. *See* Thiersault
Poncin*, Claude (1725–1811), IV, 508
Pond*, Peter (b. 1740, d. *c.* 1807), II, xxviii; III, xxxiii; IV, 245, 262, 310, 365, 403, 585, 741, 757
Pondiac (Pondiak, Pondiag). *See* Pontiac
Pons, Antoinette de, Marquise de Guercheville (Du Plessis de Liancourt), I, 67, 68, 69, 94, 95, 98, 100, 101, 294, 299, 367, 441, 521, 560
Pontarion. *See* Castagnac
Pontbriand. *See also* Dubreil

221

Pontbriand, Comtesse de. *See* Marot de La Garaye
Pontbriand, Claude de, I, 167
Pontchartrain. *See* Phélypeaux
Pontchartrain, Comtesse de. *See* La Rochefoucauld-Roye
Pontevès, Elzéar de, Marquis de Pontevès, III, 188
Pontevès, Marguerite-Charlotte-Baptistine de (Doreil), III, 188
Pontgibaud. *See* Vicq
Pont-Gravé. *See* Gravé Du Pont
Pontiac, II, 316; III, **525–31**, xxxiv, xxxvi, xxxvii, xxxviii, xxxix, 13, 95, 159, 167, 256, 262, 306, 410, 451, 452, 495, 559, 652; IV, xxxv, xxxvi, xlix, lii, liv, lv, lvi, lvii, 24, 39, 85, 150, 174, 241, 260, 294, 297, 301, 316, 337, 347, 384, 396, 397, 408, 427, 487, 506, 552, 573, 575, 576, 580, 587, 634, 675, 680, 722, 734, 761, 762, 768
Pontif, Jeanne. *See* Saint-Étienne de La Tour
Pontleroy. *See* Sarrebource
Pontonnier, Marie (Gadois), II, 234
Poole, Sir William, I, 93
Pope, Alexander, IV, 554
Popham, Sir John, I, 69
Popincourt de Roberval, Alix de, I, 422
Popple, Alured, II, 591
Poquelin, Jean-Baptiste (Molière), I, 139, 141, 607; II, 76; III, 639
Porc-épic, Le. *See* Noro
Porlier, Angélique. *See* Cuillerier
Porlier, Catherine, III, 167
Porlier, Claude, II, 256
Porlier, Claude-Cyprien-Jacques, IV, 270, 638
Porlier, Marie. *See* Bissot
Porlier, Pierre-Antoine, IV, **638–39**, 100
Porrée, Pélagie (Magon de La Balluë), IV, 506
Portanier, Claire (Beaussier), III, 54
Porten, Robert, I, 107
Porteous, John, IV, 58, 261, 311, 592, 722, 732
Porter, Aaron, III, 125
Porter, Susannah (Cleveland), III, 125
Porteret, Pierre, I, 491; II, 144
Portland, Duke of. *See* Cavendish
Portlock*, Nathaniel (d. 1817), IV, 166, 218, 244, 744
Portneuf. *See* Robinau
Portneuf, Baronne de. *See* Legardeur de Villiers
Portneuf, Baronne de. *See* Leneuf de La Poterie
Portugais. *See* Dasilva
Possel, Ursule-Thérèse (Duquesne), IV, 255
Post, Christian Frederick, III, 212
Pote, Dorothy. *See* Gatchell
Pote, William (father), III, 531
Pote, William, III, **531–32**, 650
Potel, Jacqueline (Bourdon), I, 113, 114, 430, 480; II, 91, 92
Potentien, Father. *See* Houdin, Jean-Michel
Potevin, François, III, 144
Pothier, Mgr, I, 534
Pothier, Anne-Françoise. *See* Bruyères
Pothier, Claude, II, 105
Pothier*, Jean-Baptiste-Toussaint (1771–1845), IV, 109
Pothier, Louise (Couagne), III, 145; IV, 173
Pothier, Marie (Rocbert), III, 562
Pothier, Toussaint, II, 376
Pothorst, Hans, I, 679
Potier. *See also* Poitiers

Potier, Jacques, IV, 640
Potier, Marie. *See* Duchatelet
Potier, Marie (Devau), IV, 216
Potier, Pierre-Philippe, III, 355, 528; IV, **640–41**, 370
Potier de Courcy, Madeleine (Callières), II, 112
Potier de Saint-Denis, Jacques, I, 25, 63
Potier Dubuisson, Marie-Charlotte. *See* Arnaud
Potier Dubuisson, Robert, II, 35, 220; III, **532–33**
Potot de Montbeillard, Claude. *See* Orbigny
Potot de Montbeillard, Fiacre-François, III, 672; IV, **641–42**, 243, 382, 460, 620
Potot de Montbeillard, François-Augustin, IV, 640
Potot de Montbeillard, Jean, IV, 641
Potot de Montbeillard, Louise, IV, 641
Potot de Montbeillard, Marie-Claude. *See* Carlet de La Rozière
Potter, Nathaniel, IV, 675, 680, 681
Pottié (Pottier). *See* Potier
Pottier, Étiennette. *See* Beauvais
Pottier, Jean, II, 527
Pottier, Jean-Baptiste, II, **527–28**, xxiv, 16, 163, 562; III, 537
Pottier, Marguerite. *See* Sainctes
Pottle, Thomas, IV, 177
Potts, Elizabeth (wife of JOHN), III, 534
Potts, George, III, 304; IV, 46
Potts, James, IV, 398
Potts, John, III, **533–34**, 151
Potts, John (son), III, 534
Pouchet, Marie (Lévesque), IV, 476
Pouchot (Pouchot de Maupas), Pierre, III, **534–37**, 378; IV, 24, 27, 54, 211, 396, 487, 587, 637, 773
Poudre Chaude. *See* Ogenheratarihiens
Poudret, François, III, 598
Poudret, Marie-Apolline. *See* Spagniolini
Pouget*, Jean-Baptiste-Noël (1745–1818), IV, 190
Pouilliot, Marie (Larue), II, 348
Poulain, Guillaume, I, **552**, 379
Poulain, Madeleine (Maufils), II, 466
Poulard, Louis, III, 377
Poulet, Captain, I, 626
Poulet, Georges-François, known as M. Dupont, II, **528–29**, 629; III, 223
Poulin, Guillot, IV, 386
Poulin, Jeanne. *See* Ploumelle
Poulin, Madeleine-Louise. *See* Le Boulanger
Poulin, Marie. *See* Jutra
Poulin, Michel, I, 553; II, 529; III, 537
Poulin, Pierre (great-grandfather), I, 552
Poulin, Pierre, II, 530; III, **537–38**, 146, 153; IV, 284
Poulin de Courval, François, IV, 618
Poulin de Courval, Françoise. *See* Foucault
Poulin de Courval, François-Louis, III, **538–39**; IV, 31, 729, 733
Poulin de Courval, Jean-Baptiste, I, 553; II, **529**; III, 539
Poulin de Courval, Louise. *See* Cressé
Poulin de Courval, Louis-Jean, II, 529; III, **539**, 63, 538; IV, 263, 391
Poulin de Courval, Marguerite. *See* Leneuf de Beaubassin
Poulin de Courval, Marie-Madeleine. *See* Forestier
Poulin de Courval, Michel, III, 537
Poulin de Courval, Thérèse. *See* Bouat
Poulin de Courval Cressé. *See also* Cressé

Poulin de Courval Cressé, Charlotte-Louise. *See* Lambert Dumont
Poulin de Courval Cressé, Claude, III, 433, 538, 539
Poulin de Courval-Cressé, Jean-Baptiste, IV, 332
Poulin de Courval Cressé, Louis-Pierre, III, **539–40**; IV, 474
Poulin de Courval Cressé, Marie-Anne. *See* Lefebvre
Poulin de Francheville, François, I, 553; II, **529–30**, 153, 236, 457; III, 146, 153, 154, 239, 402, 537; IV, 167, 284, 358, 590
Poulin de Francheville, Marie-Angélique, II, 529
Poulin de Francheville, Thérèse. *See* Couagne
Poulin de La Fontaine, Catherine (Godefroy de Vieuxpont), I, 553; II, 254
Poulin de La Fontaine, Jeanne. *See* Jallot
Poulin de La Fontaine, Marguerite (Lemaître Lamorille), I, 553
Poulin de La Fontaine, Maurice, I, **552–53**; II, xvi, xvii, 16, 254, 529
Poullet, Jehan, I, 167, 170
Poulous. *See* Sahonwagy
Pound, Arthur, IV, 86
Poupart, Pierre, II, 517
Pourchaut. *See* Pouchot
Pournin, Marie (Testard de La Forest; La Marque), I, 641; II, 421, 626
Pourroy de Lauberivière, Claude-Joseph de, II, 530
Pourroy de Lauberivière, François-Louis de, II, **530–31**, 60; III, 193, 223, 263, 285, 344, 422, 481, 487, 545; IV, 221, 509, 521, 539, 601
Pourroy de Lauberivière, Marie-Anne de. *See* Saint-Germain
Poussans, Antoinette de (Chavigny Lachevrotière), II, 142
Poussin, Nicolas, I, 313
Pouteret de Bellecourt, *dit* Colombier, Jean-François, I, 225
Poutrincourt. *See* Biencourt
Pouy, Georgette (Monbeton de Brouillan), II, 478
Powel, David, I, 678
Powell, Daniel, I, 162, 672
Powell*, Henry Watson (1733–1814), IV, 48
Powell, John, II, 293
Powell*, William Dummer (1755–1834), IV, 6, 7, 162, 229, 777, 778, 779
Power, Richard, I, **553**, 324, 476
Power, Thomas, IV, 470
Powhatan, I, 67
Powless. *See* Sahonwagy
Powlett. *See* Paulet
Powlett, Katherine, Duchess of Bolton. *See* Lowther
Pownall*, Sir George (1755–1834), IV, 477
Pownall, John, IV, 452
Pownall, Thomas, III, 509, 654
Poyer, Françoise (Grisé), IV, 315
Poytiers, Marie-Charlotte (Hébert), I, 367
Pradel, Jean-Charles de, III, 36
Pradines, Élisabeth de (Jordy), II, 186
Praslin. *See* Choiseul-Chevigny
Prat, Claude (Giard), III, 258
Prat, Jeanne-Angélique. *See* Gobeil
Prat, Louis, II, **531–32**, xxiv, 387, 430; III, 180, 621
Prat, Marie-Joseph (Denys de Saint-Simon), III, 180; IV, 207
Prato, Albertus de, I, 586
Pratt, Charles, 1st Earl of Camden, IV, 571

Pratt, James, I, 369
Pratt, Matthew, IV, 397
Pratte, Marguerite (Badeaux), IV, 40
Preaux, Marie (L'Hermitte), II, 435
Preble, Jedediah, III, 129, 257
Preissac, Anne de. *See* Dupré
Preissac, Lambert de, IV, 642
Preissac, Paul de, IV, 642
Preissac d'Arlens, Jean-Gérard de, IV, 642
Preissac d'Arlens, Paul de, IV, 642
Preissac de Bonneau, Louis de, IV, **642**
Prentice, Anna (Willard), IV, 769
Prentice, Miles, IV, 556
Pré-Ravillon. *See* La Court
Prescott, Elizabeth (Willard), IV, 769
Prescott, Jonathan, IV, 696
Pressart, Angélique. *See* Lorans
Pressart, Colomban-Sébastien, III, 203; IV, **642–43**, 74, 183, 370, 387, 388, 755
Pressart, François, IV, 642
Pressé, Hyacinthe-Olivier, II, 523; III, **540–41**, 67
Preston, Viscount. *See* Graham
Preston, Amias (Amyas), I, 278, 279
Preston, Charles, IV, 546
Prévert. *See* Sarcel
Prévost. *See also* Provost
Prévost, Charlotte. *See* Vien
Prévost, Marie. *See* Abancourt
Prévost, Marie. *See* Manitouabeouich
Prevost, Marie-Gabrielle-Élisabeth. *See* L'Estobec de Langristain
Prévost, Martin, I, **553–54**, 392
Prevost, Philippe, IV, 643
Prévost, Pierre, I, 553
Prevost, Robert, IV, 643
Prévost de Fontenay, M., II, 154
Prevost de La Croix, Charles-Auguste, IV, 646
Prevost de La Croix, Jacques, III, 72, 73, 79, 184, 185, 188, 230, 231, 367, 389, 440; IV, **643–47**, 56, 60, 61, 401, 421, 422, 438, 443, 455, 558, 605, 630, 631, 656
Prevost de La Croix, Jacques-Marie-André, IV, 646
Prevost de La Croix, Louis-Anne, IV, 646
Prevost de La Croix, Marguerite-Thérèse. *See* Carrerot
Prevost de La Croix, Pierre-François, IV, 644
Priat, Yves, II, 142; III, 612
Price, Benjamin, III, **541–42**; IV, 243, 570, 576, 618
Price, Charles. *See* Isham, Charles Thomas
Price, James, III, 541
Price, Walter, IV, 438
Pricket, Abacuk, I, 144, 145, 374, 375, 376, 377, 378
Prideaux, John, IV, 23, 396, 586, 733
Prieur, Marguerite (Verreau; Gravelle), II, 648
Prieur, Marie (Chambalon), II, 129
Prieur, Perrette (François), I, 312
Primault, Joachim, III, 547
Primeau, Joseph, IV, 647
Primeau, Louis, IV, **647**, 47, 160
Primot, Antoine, I, 465, 507; II, 469
Primot, Catherine. *See* Thierry
Primot, Martine. *See* Messier
Prince, Elizabeth (Higgins), IV, 352
Prince, Job, IV, 352
Pring, Martin, I, 75

Pringle, Mrs. *See* Balneavis
Pringle, Elizabeth Susanna. *See* Wenman
Pringle, Robert, IV, **647–48**, 259, 402, 707
Pringle, William, IV, 764
Printemps. *See* Dupont
Proulx, Basile, IV, 556
Proust, Marie (Hazeur), II, 275
Prouvereau, Sébastien, I, 60, 387; II, 159
Prouville, Alexandre de, Marquis de Tracy, I, **554–57**, 11, 33, 40, 41, 47, 48, 62, 74, 108, 113, 185, 202, 221, 245, 277, 308, 322, 353, 355, 393, 398, 400, 401, 402, 409, 416, 418, 442, 464, 511, 516, 547, 570, 571, 580, 584, 589, 602, 616, 617, 624, 627, 630, 635, 650; II, xix, 5, 59, 61, 85, 106, 107, 141, 191, 252, 282, 367, 385, 488, 540, 592; III, 201
Prouville, Louise de, Marquise de Tracy. *See* Fouilleuse
Prouville, Marie de. *See* Bochart de Champigny
Prouville, Pierre de, I, 554
Prouville de Tracy, Charles-Henri de, I, 557
Provencher, Sébastien, I, 49
Provost. *See also* Prévost
Provost, Catherine (Barbel), II, 42
Provost, Charles, II, 532
Provost, François, I, 85, 664; II, **532–33**, 16, 162, 163, 458
Provost, Geneviève. *See* Macard
Provost, Jeanne. *See* Gousset
Prowse*, Daniel Woodley (1834–1914), IV, 599, 600, 771, 785
Prud'homme, Claude, I, 557
Prud'homme, François, I, 557
Prud'homme, Isabelle. *See* Aliomet
Prud'homme, Louis, I, **557**, 177, 230, 319; II, 466
Prud'homme, Louis (grandson), I, 557
Prud'homme, Louise (Le Moyne de Longueuil; Bonne de Missègle), III, 70
Prud'homme, Marguerite (Martinet de Fonblanche; Latour), II, 466
Prud'homme, Marie-Amable (Coulon de Villiers), III, 148
Prud'homme, Marie-Anne (Landriaux), IV, 434
Prud'homme, Paul, II, 466
Prud'homme, Pierre, I, 177, 557
Prud'homme, Roberte. *See* Gadoys
Pruneau, Pierre, II, 273
Prunier, Honorade (Vachon de Belmont), II, 641
Puebla, Gonsalez de, I, 148
Pufendorf, Samuel, Baron von Pufendorf, IV, 230
Puget*, Peter John (d. 1822), IV, 768
Puiseaux, Pierre de, I, **557–58**, 215, 216, 217, 401, 485, 640
Purcell, Martin, II, 250, 487
Purchas, Samuel, I, 74, 75, 101, 158, 329, 349, 360, 379, 471, 586, 677, 678
Purss*, John (1732–1803), IV, 399, 618
Puybarau de Maisonneuve, Jean, II, 617
Puybarau de Maisonneuve, Madeleine. *See* Baudry
Puybareau, Pierre, III, 220
Puygibault. *See* Hingue
Puyperouse, Anne (Pascaud), IV, 605
Puyperoux de La Fosse, Marie-Angélique (Goutin), III, 264
Puysieux, Marquis de. *See* Bruslart
Pyke, Anne. *See* Scroope
Pyke*, George (1775–1851), IV, 502
Pyke*, John George (d. 1828), IV, 763

Pyle, William, I, 652
Pyne. *See also* Pynne
Pyne, Thomas, IV, 784
Pynne, John, II, 533
Pynne, Robert, II, 533, 534
Pynne, William, II, **533–34**, 395
Pynne, William (son), II, 534
Pytheas of Massilia, I, 17
Pyvart (Pinard) de Chastullé, Marguerite-Françoise (Beauharnois de La Boische), II, 52; III, 41, 51
Pyvart de Chastullé, Marie-Anne (Beauharnois de La Boische et de La Chaussée), III, 50

QINOUSAKI. *See* Kinousaki
Quadra. *See* Bodega
Quaife, Milo Milton, IV, 322
Quant, Mary. *See* Webber
Quarante Sols. *See* Michipichy
Quary, Robert, III, 65
Quéan (Quen), Eustache (Boullongue), I, 43, 110
Quémar, Jacquette, IV, 95
Quémar, Jacquette (Burel), IV, 95
Quen, Jean de, I, **558–59**, 48, 341, 404, 459, 552, 645, 646
Quenet (Guénet), Jean-Baptiste, II, 215
Quenneville. *See* Quesneville
Quentin, Claude, I, **560**, 214, 560
Quentin, Jacques, I, **560**, 68, 95, 299, 560
Quer (Querque). *See* Kirke
Querbonyer (commandant), I, 210, 422
Querdisien. *See* Pichot
Quéré de Tréguron, Maurice, II, 241; III, **542–43**, 268, 269
Quesnel, Jacques, II, 230; III, 290
Quesnel*, Jules-Maurice (1786–1842), IV, 172
Quesnel, Louise (Hervieux), III, 290
Quesnel, Marie-Anne. *See* Franquelin
Quesnel, Marie-Josephte. *See* Cotté
Quesnel, Pasquier, II, 528
Quesnel Fonblanche, Jacques, IV, 312
Quesnel Fonblanche, Marie-Joseph (Grasset de Saint-Sauveur), IV, 312
Quesneville, Denise. *See* Marié
Quesneville, Jean, II, **534**
Quesneville, Jeanne. *See* Saye
Quesneville, Pierre, II, 534
Questach (Cockeye), IV, 389, 518
Quevillon, Catherine (Lacombe; Papineau, *dit* Montigny; Daniel; Verac), II, 507
Queylus. *See* Thubières
Quiala. *See* Kiala
Quiasutha. *See* Kayahsota?
Quider. *See* Schuyler, Peter
Quigg, Dr, III, 504
Quignon, François, I, 314
Quimper, Manuel, IV, 568
Quindre. *See* Dagneau
Quiniard, Antoine, II, 534
Quiniard, Jeanne. *See* Branquais
Quiniard, *dit* Duplessis, Antoine-Olivier, II, **534–35**, xxiii
Quiniard, *dit* Duplessis, Marie-Louise. *See* Bolper
Quinousaquy. *See* Kinousaki
Quintal. *See also* Quittel
Quintal, Augustin (baptized Joseph), I, 312; II, 200; III, 67; IV, **649–50**

Quintal, François, IV, 649
Quintal, Marie. *See* Gaultier
Quiquinanis. *See* Wikinanish
Quisence, Jeanne (Barrat), II, 45, 481
Quittel (Quitter, Quintal), Marthe (Verreau), II, 648

RABELAIS, François, I, 170, 365, 424; IV, xxiii
Rabutin-Chantal, Marie de, Marquise de Sévigné, I, 117;
    IV, 656
Raby, Augustin, IV, **650**, 210, 700
Raby, Françoise. *See* Delisle
Raby, Marie-Anne (Moreau), IV, 402
Raby, Marie-Françoise. *See* Morin
Raby, Mathieu, IV, 650
Racine, Étienne, I, 495
Racine, Louise (Guyon), I, 359; III, 681
Racine, Marguerite. *See* Martin
Raclot, Ildebon, II, 517
Raclot, Madeleine (Perrot), II, 517
Raclot, Marie. *See* Viennot
Racsenagate, IV, 368
Radcliffe-Brown, Alfred Reginald, III, 338
Radisson. *See also* Volant
Radisson, Elizabeth (wife of PIERRE-ESPRIT), II, 539
Radisson, Françoise (Volant de Saint-Claude), II, 655
Radisson, Madeleine. *See* Hénaut
Radisson, Margaret Charlotte. *See* Godet
Radisson, Pierre (father), II, 535
Radisson, Pierre-Esprit, I, 16, 20, 35, 39, 42, 48, 49, 56, 82,
    83, 129, 130, 223, 226, 227, 228, 270, 271, 273, 274,
    282, 337, 338, 377, 397, 406, 464, 509, 518, 528, 529,
    578, 602, 625, 653; II, **535–40**, 31, 247, 298, 391, 647
Radisson, *dit* Duplessis, Marguerite. *See* Duplessis
Raffeix, Pierre, I, 48, 108, 321, 651; II, **540**, 19; III, 104,
    335, 649
Raffetot. *See* Deschamps
Rageot, François, I, 561; II, 58, 325, 541, 576
Rageot, Gilles, I, **560–61**, 394, 474, 550; II, xix, 129, 133,
    242, 325, 347, 540, 541, 576
Rageot, Isaac, I, 560
Rageot, Jean-Baptiste, I, 561
Rageot, Louise. *See* Duret
Rageot, Marie-Madeleine. *See* Morin
Rageot, Marie-Madeleine (Rivet Cavelier), II, 576
Rageot, Philippe, I, 561; II, 238
Rageot de Beaurivage, Gilles, I, 561
Rageot de Saint-Luc, Charles, I, 561; II, **540–41**, 138, 576
Rageot de Saint-Luc, Marie-Geneviève. *See* Gauvreau
Rageot de Saint-Luc, Marie-Madeleine-Geneviève, II, 541
Rageot de Saint-Luc, Nicolas, I, 561; II, **541**, 576
Ragueneau, François, I, 214, 453, 561
Ragueneau, Paul, I, **561–64**, 44, 64, 71, 123, 125, 128, 143,
    184, 185, 186, 205, 206, 214, 225, 296, 328, 412, 414,
    455, 459, 460, 461, 489, 607, 608, 609, 610, 637, 640; II,
    xvi, 85, 536, 537
Raguet, Gilles-Bernard, III, 40
Raimbault, Charlotte. *See* Damours
Raimbault, Claude, II, 541
Raimbault, Jeanne-Françoise. *See* Simblin
Raimbault, Louise. *See* Nafrechoux
Raimbault, Marguerite (Boucher de Boucherville), II, 542;
    III, 80
Raimbault, Marie-Thérèse. *See* Sallé

Raimbault, Pierre (trader), IV, 647
Raimbault, Pierre, II, **541–42**, 111, 617, 618; III, 44, 80,
    205, 270, 340, 422, 450, 520
Raimbault de Piedmont, Joseph-Charles, II, **542**, 627; III,
    164
Raimbault de Saint-Blaint, Charlotte-Gabrielle. *See* Jarret de
    Verchères
Raimbault de Saint-Blaint (Simblin), Paul-François, II, 542
Raimbault de Saint-Blaint, Pierre-Marie-Joseph, III, 611;
    IV, 344
Rainborow. *See* Rainsborough
Rainer, Dr, I, 553
Rainsborough, William, I, 407
Rainsthorpe, Esther (Morris), IV, 559
Rainville, Charlotte (Corbin), IV, 167
Raisin, Anne. *See* Collet
Raisin, Edmé, I, 564
Raisin, Marie, I, **564**, 116
Raisin, Nicolas, I, 564
Raizenne, Amable-Simon, IV, 188
Rale, Sébastien, II, **542–45**, xxxvi, 64, 287, 476, 477, 668,
    669; III, xxxvii, 104, 330, 476, 477, 584
Raleigh, Sir Carew, I, 279, 331
Raleigh, Sir Walter, I, 251, 278, 331, 332, 333, 335, 363,
    364, 668, 669
Ralluau, Jean, I, **564–65**, 292, 293
Rameau* de Saint-Père, François-Edme (1820–99), IV,
    xviii, xx, 239
Ramezay, Catherine de. *See* Tribouillard
Ramezay, Charlotte-Marguerite de (Bellot), IV, 652
Ramezay, Claude de, I, 602; II, **545–49**, xxi, 25, 33, 47, 81,
    87, 162, 181, 186, 354, 389, 402, 409, 436, 497, 533,
    569, 571, 589, 606, 626, 645; III, 22, 81, 146, 190, 247,
    543, 563, 579; IV, 41, 235, 650, 653, 690
Ramezay, Claude de (son), II, 548
Ramezay, Élisabeth de (La Corne), IV, 224
Ramezay, Jean-Baptiste-Nicolas-Roch de, II, 548; III, xxii,
    xxv, 49, 110, 255, 256, 378, 417, 438, 467, 483, 484,
    511, 538, 578, 608, 650; IV, **650–53**, 10, 33, 34, 63, 143,
    213, 296, 319, 361, 382, 446, 454, 459, 480, 602, 633,
    672, 728, 783
Ramezay, Louise de. *See* Godefroy de Tonnancour
Ramezay, Louise de, II, 548; IV, **653–55**, 650
Ramezay, Louise-Geneviève de (Deschamps de
    Boishébert), II, 181; IV, 212, 654
Ramezay, Marie-Charlotte de. *See* Denys de La Ronde
Ramezay, Marie-Charlotte de, *dite* de Saint-Claude de la
    Croix, III, **543–44**, 319; IV, 650, 653
Ramezay, Timothé de, II, 545
Ramezay de La Gesse, Charles-Hector de, II, 547, 548; IV,
    650
Ramezay de Monnoir, Louis de, II, 548
Ramón, Diego, III, 317
Ramón de Navarro, Emanuela (Juchereau de Saint-Denis),
    III, 317
Ramondine, Marie-Josèphe (Rodrigue), IV, 679
Ramsey, Martha. *See* Burch
Ramusio, Giovanni Battista, I, 151, 153, 154, 170, 235,
    658, 660
Ranc, Blanche (Mathevet), IV, 521
Rancin, Madeleine-Ursule (Hedouin; Janson, *dit* Lapalme),
    III, 306
Rancour, Joseph, III, 138

Randall, Benjamin, IV, 20
Randin, Hugues, I, **565**; II, 59, 262
Randolph, Edward, II, 247
Rankin, James, IV, 162
Rankin, John, III, **544**, 449, 663
Rankin, Mary. *See* Collins
Ransonnet, Sylvestre-François-Michel, III, **544–45**, 630
Ranuyer, Mathieu, II, 130
Ranville. *See* Baby
Ranvoyzé*, Étienne (1776–1826), IV, 332
Ranvoyzé*, François (1739–1819), III, 346; IV, 205, 206
Raoul, Jeanne (Savonnières de La Troche), I, 603
Raphaël, Father, II, 41
Raphaël de Luxembourg, III, 40, 41
Rapine de Boisvert, Charles, I, 219, 484, 485
Rashleigh, Robert, IV, 58
Rasilly. *See* Launay-Rasilly; Razilly
Rastel* de Rocheblave, Philippe-François (1727–1802), IV, 322
Rastell, Elizabeth. *See* More
Rastell, John (father), I, 565, 566
Rastell, John, I, **565–66**, 371
Rat, Le. *See* Kondiaronk
Rateau, Marie (Létourneau; Guillot, *dit* Larose; Sicard), IV, 320
Rathery, Louise de (Jordy), II, 185
Rattier, Catherine. *See* Rousseau
Rattier, Jean, II, **549**, xxiv
Rattier, Marie. *See* Rivière
Rattier, Pierre, II, 549; III, 398
Raudin. *See* Randin
Raudot, Antoine-Denis, II, **549–54**, 7, 9, 48, 120, 121, 125, 242, 270, 286, 301, 555, 556, 559, 560, 570, 587, 608, 632; III, 57, 88, 104, 112, 563
Raudot, Françoise. *See* Gioux
Raudot, Jacques, I, 452; II, **554–61**, 13, 41, 42, 52, 57, 58, 111, 120, 121, 131, 132, 139, 147, 155, 173, 201, 223, 224, 234, 252, 276, 277, 283, 286, 301, 305, 325, 327, 372, 375, 381, 384, 402, 406, 413, 430, 432, 448, 465, 484, 508, 526, 535, 541, 550, 551, 552, 562, 566, 569, 574, 576, 587, 597, 604, 632, 672; III, 53, 57, 81, 83, 104, 112, 190, 191, 205, 220, 233, 234, 498, 520, 523, 563, 570
Raudot, Jean, II, 549, 555
Raudot, Jean-Baptiste, II, 555
Raudot, Louis-François, II, 555
Raudot, Marguerite. *See* Talon
Raudot, Marguerite-Françoise, II, 555
Raudot de Chalus, Jacques-Denis, II, 555, 558, 560; III, 104
Ravillon. *See* La Court
Raye, Pierre, I, 493
Raymbaut, Charles, I, **566–67**, 388, 549; II, 157
Raymond, Étienne, III, 617
Raymond, George, I, 279, 499
Raymond, Jean-Louis de, Comte de Raymond, III, 6, 50, 136, 183, 229, 231, 417, 498, 616; IV, **655–57**, 28, 401, 438, 439, 443, 444, 630, 631, 644, 645
Raymond, Joseph-Marie, III, 617
Raymond, Marie-Cécile. *See* Mignot
Raymond*, William Odber (1853–1923), IV, 723
Raymond Des Rivières, Charles de, IV, 655, 657
Rayner, John, I, **567**
Raynsforde, Thomas, I, 279

Razilly. *See also* Launay-Rasilly
Razilly, Catherine de. *See* Valliers
Razilly, François de (father), I, 567
Razilly, François de, I, 209, 567
Razilly, Gabriel de, I, 567
Razilly, Isaac de, I, **567–69**, 25, 32, 54, 63, 196, 234, 247, 256, 258, 311, 442, 471, 482, 490, 502, 503, 593, 594, 642; II, 480
Ré. *See* Derré
Read, John, IV, 559
Read, Mary (Morris), IV, 559
Reade, Sarah (De Peyster), IV, 210
Réaume, Sieur, III, 145
Réaume, Alexis, IV, 592, 593
Réaume, Charles, IV, 697
Réaume, Julie-Marie (Hay), IV, 336
Réaume, Marguerite (Howard), IV, 369
Réaume, Marguerite (Welles), IV, 697
Réaume, Marie-Luce-Amable. *See* Orillat
Réaume, Marie-Madeleine (Larchevesque; Chevallier), III, 122
Réaume, Marie-Renée (Renaud, *dit* Cannard), IV, 658
Réaume, Thérèse (Sanguinet), IV, 697
Réaume (Rhéaume), *dit* La Croix, Susanne (Baby, *dit* Dupéront), IV, 38
Réaumur. *See* Ferchault
Rebourceau, Marie (Groston), II, 267
Rêche (Reiche, Reische). *See* Resche
Récher, Jean-Félix, III, **545–47**, 11, 194, 198, 199, 259, 554; IV, 100, 387
Reconciled. *See* Cherououny
Red Head. *See* Kakᴕenthiony; Ononwarogo
Redwood, Nicholas, I, 652
Reeves*, John (d. 1829), IV, 713
Régemortes, Noël de, III, 229, 230, 700
Regnard Duplessis, François, II, 156
Regnard Duplessis, François-Xavier, II, 561; III, 549
Regnard Duplessis, Geneviève, *dite* de l'Enfant-Jésus, III, 547
Regnard Duplessis, Georges, II, **561**, 14, 138, 214, 485; III, 547, 549
Regnard Duplessis, Marie. *See* Le Roy
Regnard Duplessis, Marie-Andrée, *dite* de Sainte-Hélène, II, 304, 333, 460, 561; III, **547–49**, 625, 690, 711; IV, 189
Regnard Duplessis, Marie-Madeleine. *See* Coulon de Villiers
Regnard Duplessis de Morampont, Charles-Denis, III, **549**, 64
Regnard Duplessis de Morampont, Geneviève-Élisabeth. *See* Guillimin
Regnault, Christophe, I, 124, 562
Regnouard, Marie (Giffard), I, 329, 330
Reiche (Reische). *See* Resche
Reid, John, IV, 385
Reinel, Pedro, I, 235, 303, 304
Reis, Thérèse (Gugi), IV, 316
Rembaud, François-Joseph, III, 8
Remogis, Françoise (Ameau), II, 16
Rémus. *See* Romieux
Rémy, Élisabeth. *See* Le Moyne
Rémy, Marie (Céloron), II, 125
Rémy, Michel, II, 561
Rémy (de Saint-Rémy), Pierre, II, **561–62**, 125, 195, 528

Rémy de Courcelle, Daniel de, I, **569–72**, 33, 40, 48, 55, 62, 80, 108, 111, 120, 135, 174, 204, 308, 322, 327, 355, 393, 400, 402, 416, 452, 464, 539, 540, 543, 555, 556, 581, 599, 615, 616, 617, 624, 625, 627, 629, 630; II, xix, 85, 106, 136, 141, 192, 195, 282, 385, 540, 579; III, 201

Renard, Marie (Bigot), IV, 59

Renardin de La Blanchetière, Françoise. *See* Ouary

Renardin de La Blanchetière, Marie (Le Vieux de Hauteville), I, 475

Renardin de La Blanchetière, Vincent, I, 475

Renaud. *See also* Desferières

Renaud, Jean, IV, **657–58**

Renaud, John Lewis, IV, 658

Renaud, Louis, III, 494

Renaud, Louise. *See* Bizard

Renaud, Marie. *See* Noyon

Renaud, Martha. *See* Sheldon

Renaud, Paul-Émile, IV, 376

Renaud, *dit* Cannard, Marie. *See* Gariépy

Renaud, *dit* Cannard, Marie-Renée. *See* Réaume

Renaud, *dit* Cannard, Michel, IV, 658

Renaud, *dit* Cannard, Pierre, IV, **658–59**, 202

Renaud d'Avène de Desmeloizes, Françoise-Thérèse. *See* Dupont de Neuville

Renaud d'Avène de Desmeloizes, François-Marie, I, **572–73**; II, 205; III, 112, 549

Renaud d'Avène de Desmeloizes, Marie-Françoise (Chartier de Lotbinière), III, 112; IV, 141, 143

Renaud d'Avène de Des Méloizes et de Berges, Adrienne. *See* Montsaulnin

Renaud d'Avène de Des Méloizes et de Berges, Edmé (Aimé), I, 572

Renaud d'Avène Des Méloizes, Angélique. *See* Chartier de Lotbinière

Renaud d'Avène Des Méloizes, Angélique (Péan), III, 551; IV, **659–60**, 66, 459, 614, 615, 616, 621, 642

Renaud d'Avène Des Méloizes, Catherine-Madeleine, II, 129

Renaud d'Avène Des Méloizes, Marie-Jeanne, II, 463

Renaud* d'Avène Des Méloizes, Nicolas (1729–1803), III, 550; IV, 88

Renaud d'Avène Des Méloizes, Nicolas-Marie, I, 572; II, 463; III, **549–51**, 5, 112; IV, 173, 358, 659

Renaud Dubuisson, Gabrielle. *See* Pinet

Renaud Dubuisson, Jacques-Charles, II, **562–63**, 68, 122, 128, 515, 627, 645; III, 491, 551, 576, 577

Renaud Dubuisson, Louise (Tonty de Liette), III, 627

Renaud Dubuisson, Louis-Jacques-Charles, III, **551–52**

Renaud Dubuisson, Madeleine (Chabert de Joncaire), III, 101

Renaud Dubuisson, Marie-Charlotte (Catalogne), II, 122

Renaud Dubuisson, Thérèse. *See* Godefroy

Renau d'Éliçagaray, Bernard, III, 117

Renaudot, Eusèbe, I, 174, 175, 179; II, 517

Rende. *See* Larrante

Renden (Rendin). *See* Randin

Render, Thomas, II, **563–64**, 10, 62

René, Patrice, III, **552**, 681, 682

Renon. *See* Du Pont

Renou, *dit* La Chapelle, François, I, 321, 578

Renou, *dit* La Chapelle, Marguerite. *See* Crevier

Renswore, Dame, II, 279

Renty, Gaston, Baron de Renty, I, 214, 219

Renvoizé. *See* Ranvoyzé

Repentigny. *See also* Legardeur; Terrier

Repentigny, Mme de, II, 187

Resche, François, III, 553

Resche, Marguerite. *See* Pinard

Resche, Pierre-Joseph, III, **553–54**, 223; IV, 535

Rességuier, Marguerite de (Galaup), IV, 282

Retor. *See* Devau

Retz, François, III, 360

Reventa. *See* Eliza

Revilla Gigedo, Count de. *See* Güemes

Révol, Hélène. *See* Bastard

Révol, Jacques, III, 554

Révol, Marie-Charlotte. *See* Roy

Révol, Pierre, III, **554–55**; IV, 243, 386, 729

Rey Gaillard, Françoise. *See* Gailleteau

Rey Gaillard, Pierre, I, 261; II, 106, 129, 256; III, 509

Reymer, Nicholas, II, 264

Reyner. *See also* Rayner

Reyner, William, I, 567

Reynolds, Sir Joshua, IV, 26, 122, 702

Rhéaume. *See* Réaume

Rhoades, John, I, **573**, 39, 40, 185

Rhodes, Alexandre de, II, 360

Ribaut (Ribault), Jean, I, 333, 469

Ribero, Pedro, I, 342

Riberpré, M. de, I, 88

Ricard, Françoise (Forestier), II, 226

Ricci, Lorenzo, III, 580

Riccoboni, Marie-Jeanne, IV, 553

Rice, Henry, III, 615

Rice, Jacob, II, **564**, 163, 291, 534, 636; III, 219

Rice, Mary (Button), I, 144

Rice, Thomas, II, 564

Rice, Sir Walter, I, 144

Rich, Henry, Earl of Holland, I, 369, 405

Rich, Robert, 1st Earl of Warwick, I, 67, 69

Richard III, King of England, I, 120, 239

Richard, André, I, 266, 477, 539

Richard, Anne. *See* Meusnier

Richard, Anne (Lascoret; Lannelongue), III, 350

Richard, Catherine (Brossard), II, 105; III, 87

Richard, Édouard, III, 34

Richard, Jean (father of Guillaume RICHARD, *dit* Lafleur), I, 573

Richard, Jean (interpreter), I, 573

Richard, Jean-Baptiste, I, 573; II, 673

Richard, Jeanne. *See* Bonnet

Richard, Madeleine. *See* Blanchard

Richard, Marguerite (Dugas), IV, 239

Richard, Marguerite (Levasseur, *dit* Lavigne), I, 473

Richard, Marie-Anne. *See* You de La Découverte

Richard, Michel, II, 105

Richard, Suzanne (Parant), I, 573

Richard, *dit* Lafleur, Guillaume, I, **573–74**

Richard, *dit* Lafond, Michel, III, 173

Richard de Goigni, Anne (Blaise Des Bergères de Rigauville), II, 68, 69

Richardie. *See* La Richardie

Richards, Francis, II, 93

Richards, Jacob, II, 564

Richards, John (ancestor of Guillaume RICHARD, *dit* Lafleur), I, 573

Richards, John (HBC employee), IV, 727
Richards, Michael, II, **564–65**, 260, 261, 274, 290, 293, 373, 438, 486, 534, 582; III, 488
Richards, William (grandfather), III, 124
Richards*, William (d. 1811), IV, 33
Richardson, Cécile (Cecilia) (Moore), II, 487
Richardson*, John (d. 1831), IV, 39, 261
Richardson, Matthew, IV, 111
Richardson, Samuel, IV, 553
Richaume, Marie-Madeleine (Brunet, *dit* La Sablonnière), III, 87
Richebourg, Chavagne de, II, 203
Richelieu. *See* Vignerot
Richelieu, Cardinal de. *See* Du Plessis
Richer, Edmond, I, 629
Richer, Jean, I, 225
Richer, Pierre-Daniel, III, 360
Richerville. *See also* Drouet
Richerville, M., III, 399
Richeterre. *See* Dessailliant
Richmond, Duke of. *See* Lennox
Richmond, Isabella (Gledhill), II, 250
Richmond, Silvester, II, 671
Richomme, Françoise (Sarcel de Prévert), I, 602
Rickard, Elizabeth (Doggett), IV, 219
Ridday, *dit* Beauceron, Jean, III, 472, 473
Riddell*, William Renwick (1852–1945), IV, 230
Rider, Elizabeth (Cobb), III, 128
Rider, Lydia (Cobb), III, 128
Riedesel, Friedrich Adolphus von, Baron von Riedesel, IV, 589
Rieutord*, Jean-Baptiste (d. 1818), IV, 385
Rieutord, Marie-Josette. *See* Audette, *dit* Lapointe
Rifos, Miguel, I, 156
Rigaud, Françoise (Maugue), I, 498
Rigaud de Vaudreuil, Anne de (Adhémar de Lantagnac), II, 565; III, 5
Rigaud de Vaudreuil, Antoine de, II, 565
Rigaud de Vaudreuil, Antoinette de. *See* Colombet
Rigaud de Vaudreuil, Arnaud de, Baron de Vaudreuil, II, 566, 571
Rigaud de Vaudreuil, Élisabeth-Catherine de, Marquise de Vaudreuil. *See* Le Moyne de Serigny et de Loire
Rigaud de Vaudreuil, François-Aimé de, II, 565
Rigaud de Vaudreuil, François-Pierre de, II, 301, 574; III, 48, 162, 181, 215, 217, 459, 461, 557, 578; IV, **660–62**, 54, 145, 146, 242, 256, 265, 363, 459, 464, 478, 512, 517, 663, 667, 686
Rigaud de Vaudreuil, Jean de, Vicomte de Vaudreuil, II, 573; IV, 243, 669, 673
Rigaud de Vaudreuil, Jean-Louis de, III, 557
Rigaud de Vaudreuil, Jean-Louis de, Baron de Vaudreuil, II, 565
Rigaud de Vaudreuil, Joseph-Hyacinthe de, II, 574; III, **555–56**
Rigaud de Vaudreuil, Joseph-Hyacinthe-François de Paule de, III, 556
Rigaud de Vaudreuil, Louise de. *See* Fleury de La Gorgendière
Rigaud de Vaudreuil, Louise-Élisabeth de, II, 574
Rigaud de Vaudreuil, Louise-Élisabeth de, Marquise de Vaudreuil. *See* Joybert de Soulanges et de Marson

Rigaud de Vaudreuil, Louis-Philippe de, Marquis de Vaudreuil, II, 374, 573; III, **556–57**, 104, 621; IV, 256, 673
Rigaud de Vaudreuil, Louis-Philippe de, Marquis de Vaudreuil (son), III, 557; IV, 303
Rigaud de Vaudreuil, Marie de, Baronne de Vaudreuil. *See* Chateauverdun
Rigaud de Vaudreuil, Marie-Claire-Françoise de. *See* Guyot de Lamirande
Rigaud de Vaudreuil, Marie-Josèphe de, II, 574
Rigaud de Vaudreuil, Marie-Louise de (Villeneuve), II, 574
Rigaud de Vaudreuil, Philippe de, II, 566
Rigaud de Vaudreuil, Philippe de, Marquis de Vaudreuil, I, 138, 139, 140, 239, 399, 463, 634; II, **565–74**, 4, 12, 13, 17, 26, 36, 37, 39, 41, 42, 48, 68, 70, 74, 77, 79, 81, 87, 96, 103, 110, 111, 113, 114, 126, 128, 132, 139, 143, 147, 150, 162, 163, 167, 169, 173, 180, 186, 198, 203, 223, 224, 252, 256, 264, 268, 276, 283, 285, 286, 287, 301, 302, 303, 304, 316, 317, 318, 323, 324, 327, 333, 338, 346, 353, 354, 383, 384, 386, 387, 389, 401, 402, 403, 404, 405, 406, 409, 410, 414, 415, 428, 432, 433, 435, 437, 441, 446, 447, 448, 449, 453, 456, 457, 464, 475, 476, 477, 480, 484, 492, 495, 497, 502, 503, 504, 505, 509, 515, 516, 519, 523, 527, 528, 543, 544, 546, 547, 548, 552, 553, 555, 558, 559, 560, 561, 562, 563, 576, 580, 581, 585, 587, 588, 589, 597, 606, 622, 623, 626, 627, 632, 651, 653, 667, 668, 669, 672; III, xli, 3, 5, 15, 23, 42, 44, 50, 51, 53, 56, 57, 58, 59, 60, 61, 62, 81, 83, 86, 87, 89, 104, 112, 113, 118, 159, 176, 178, 190, 191, 200, 217, 224, 233, 245, 248, 289, 299, 330, 360, 402, 410, 428, 429, 431, 486, 503, 512, 550, 555, 556, 563, 564, 576, 603, 632, 682; IV, 235, 510, 660, 662, 663
Rigaud de Vaudreuil, Philippe-Antoine de, Baron de Vaudreuil, II, 573
Rigaud de Vaudreuil de Cavagnial, Jeanne-Charlotte de, Marquise de Vaudreuil. *See* Fleury Deschambault
Rigaud de Vaudreuil de Cavagnial, Pierre de, Marquis de Vaudreuil, I, 345, 399; II, 224, 301, 433, 573, 574; III, xix, xx, xxi, xxii, 8, 12, 21, 22, 47, 85, 101, 149, 161, 185, 188, 198, 215, 255, 256, 259, 289, 300, 332, 361, 373, 376, 383, 402, 408, 418, 424, 425, 445, 459, 460, 461, 462, 463, 464, 465, 466, 467, 468, 469, 510, 534, 535, 536, 540, 549, 555, 557, 560, 570, 578, 579, 588, 591, 601, 617, 626; IV, **662–74**, xxxiii, 3, 23, 24, 27, 28, 54, 57, 63, 76, 79, 88, 125, 138, 143, 146, 147, 183, 201, 207, 221, 227, 242, 250, 256, 257, 265, 268, 286, 289, 307, 311, 312, 368, 382, 408, 426, 435, 448, 449, 453, 460, 464, 465, 467, 476, 478, 479, 480, 481, 482, 512, 514, 517, 563, 587, 588, 595, 612, 614, 616, 617, 620, 633, 634, 636, 637, 641, 651, 652, 660, 661, 685, 729, 734, 739, 751, 764, 765, 770
Rigault, Geneviève (Testu Du Tilly), III, 620
Rigault, Pierre-François, III, 541
Rigauville. *See* Blaise
Rinault. *See* Gaultier
Rinfret, *dit* Malouin, Thérèse (Deguise, *dit* Flamand), IV, 203
Riot, Marguerite (Lauzon), III, 360
Rioux, Jean, II, 179
Rioux, Nicolas, II, 528; III, 572
Risbé, Jean-François, IV, 205, 629
Rishworth, Mary (Sayward), II, 601
Rising, John, IV, 30

Riss, François, I, 170
Ritchie, Alicia Maria. *See* Le Cain
Ritchie, Andrew, IV, 674
Ritchie, Jennet (Janet) (wife of JOHN), IV, 674
Ritchie, John, IV, **674–75**
Ritchie*, Sir William Johnstone (1813–92), IV, 675
Rivard (Pinard), Marie (Maillet), I, 480
Rivard, Nicolas, II, 446
Rivard, *dit* Lanouette, Marie-Joseph (Perrault), III, 510
Rivard, *dit* Loranger, Robert, II, 584
Riverin, Angélique. *See* Gaultier de Comporté
Riverin, Denis, I, 326, 402: II, **574–76**, 32, 179, 214, 275, 276, 302, 338, 526, 556; III, 15, 52, 153, 557, 681
Riverin, Joseph (father), II, 235; III, 22, 557
Riverin, Joseph, III, **557–58**; IV, 248, 249
Riverin, Madeleine. *See* Mahyet
Riverin, Marie-Charlotte. *See* Guillimin
Riverin, Marie-Joseph. *See* Perthuis
Riverin, Marie-Joseph (Du Pont Duchambon de Vergor), IV, 248, 249
Riverin, Michelle. *See* Mars
Riverin, Pierre, II, 574
Rivers, Mary (Payne), II, 513
Rivet, Marie-Madeleine (Lestage), III, 394
Rivet Cavelier, Marie-Madeleine. *See* Rageot
Rivet Cavelier, Pierre, II, **576–77**, xxiv, 485; III, 35
Rivière, François, III, 168
Rivière, François de, Marquis de Giscaro, II, 513
Rivière, Marie. *See* Mars
Rivière, Marie (Rattier), II, 549
Rivière, Marie-Josèphe de, Marquise de Giscaro. *See* Pastour de Costebelle
Rivington, James, IV, 105
Rizy. *See* Perrot
Robaille, Jean, IV, 205
Robaud, Jacques, II, 161
Robereau, *dit* Duplessis, Pierre, IV, 654
Roberge, Denis, II, 19, 520, 639
Roberge, Geneviève. *See* Auber
Roberge, Marie-Anne (Guion), II, 271
Roberge, Marie-Madeleine (Perthuis), II, 520; III, 511; IV, 624
Roberol, *dit* Morin, Pierre, II, 637
Robert, Antoine, IV, 505
Robert, Cécile (MacLeod), IV, 505
Robert, Clément, II, **577**; III, 413
Robert, David ap, I, 655
Robert, Edme-Nicolas, II, 208; III, 62, 427
Robert, Elizabeth (Vaughan), I, 655
Robert, Guillemette (Bizard), I, 102
Robert, Nicolas-François, IV, 200
Robert de Fortel, Louis, I, 32, 615; II, xvii
Robert Jasne, Marie-Angélique (Godin, *dit* Chatillon, et *dit* Bellefontaine), IV, 305
Roberts, Ann (mother of LEWIS), I, 574
Roberts, Ann (wife of LEWIS), I, 574
Roberts, Benjamin, IV, **675–76**, 582, 681
Roberts, Gabriel, I, 574
Roberts, Henry, IV, 218, 744, 745
Roberts, Hugh, IV, 176
Roberts, Kenneth Lewis, III, xxix; IV, 683
Roberts, Lewis, I, **574**

Robertson, Charles, III, **558–59**, 95, 167, 306, 528; IV, 761
Robertson, Daniel, III, 542
Robertson, James (officer), IV, 686
Robertson*, James (fl. 1766–1810), IV, 482
Roberval. *See* La Rocque
Roberval, Dame de. *See* Popincourt
Robeshaw. *See* Robichaux
Robichaud, Marie, *dite* Saint-Vincent-de-Paul, III, 18; IV, 638
Robichaux, Henriette. *See* Petitpas
Robichaux, Jeanne. *See* Bourgeois
Robichaux, Louis, III, 418; IV, **676–77**
Robichaux*, Otho (1742–1824), IV, 677
Robichaux, Prudent, II, 23; III, 418; IV, 676
Robichaux*, Vénérande (1753–1839), IV, 677
Robidoux, Anne. *See* Lehoux
Robidoux, Charles, III, 278, 279
Robin*, Charles (1743–1824), IV, 79, 180
Robin, Claude (Fredin), III, 14
Robin, Isabeau (Babie), I, 74
Robin, Jacques, IV, xxvii
Robin, Mathurine (Guyon Du Buisson), I, 359
Robin, *dit* Des Forges, Étienne, I, 267
Robin de Coulogne, Thomas, I, 97, 100
Robinau, Marie-Anne (Martel de Magos), I, 577; II, 459; III, 433; IV, 517
Robinau de Bécancour, François-Alexandre, II, 578
Robinau de Bécancour, Louise-Catherine (Desjordy Moreau de Cabanac), II, 186; III, 171
Robinau de Bécancour, Marie-Anne, Baronne de Portneuf. *See* Leneuf de La Poterie
Robinau de Bécancour, Marie-Anne-Geneviève (Legardeur de Croisille), II, 577; III, 374; IV, 446
Robinau de Bécancour, Marie-Charlotte, Baronne de Portneuf. *See* Legardeur de Villiers
Robinau de Bécancour, Marie-Marguerite-Renée, II, 577; III, 245
Robinau de Bécancour, Pierre, I, 349, 574
Robinau de Bécancour, Pierre, Baron de Portneuf, I, 575; II, **577–79**, xxiii, 242; III, 74, 105, 245, 350, 374, 420
Robinau de Bécancour, René, Baron de Portneuf, I, **574–76**, 582; II, 27, 48, 186, 577, 578, 579
Robinau de Bécancour, Renée. *See* Marteau
Robinau de Fortelle, François, I, 575
Robinau de Neuvillette, Daniel, II, **579**, 3, 145, 578
Robinau de Portneuf, Jacques, II, 577, 578
Robinau de Portneuf, Marguerite. *See* Daneau de Muy
Robinau de Portneuf, Marie-Louise. *See* Dandonneau Du Sablé
Robinau de Portneuf, Philippe-René, III, **559–60**; IV, 74
Robinau de Portneuf, Pierre, III, **560–61**
Robinau de Portneuf, René, II, **579–80**, 6, 172, 283, 383, 578; III, 168, 273, 476, 596, 681; IV, xxiv, 305
Robinau de Villebon, Joseph, I, **576–78**, 26, 80, 246, 250, 338, 426, 427, 436, 510, 529, 542, 575, 586, 649, 654; II, 14, 46, 47, 109, 145, 166, 167, 177, 183, 257, 271, 394, 449, 450, 459, 464, 479, 578, 579, 605, 626, 630, 654; III, 7, 170, 273, 476, 596, 681; IV, xxiv, 305
Robinson, Christopher, IV, **677–78**, 777
Robinson, Esther. *See* Sayre
Robinson, John, IV, 677
Robinson, Sir John, I, 82

229

Robinson*, Sir John Beverley (1791–1863), IV, 677
Robinson, Mary. See Darby
Robinson, Mary (Palliser), IV, 597
Robinson, Nicholas, IV, 597
Robinson, Peter, IV, 677
Robinson*, Peter (1785–1838), IV, 677
Robinson, Sir Robert, I, 93, 370; II, **580–81**
Robinson, Sarah. See Lister
Robinson, Thomas, IV, 118
Robinson, Thomas, 1st Baron Grantham, III, 362
Robinson*, William Benjamin (1797–1873), IV, 677
Robitaille, Philippe, III, 424
Robreau, dit Leroux-Duplessis, Pierre, III, 88
Robson, Joseph, II, 309, 310, 312, 314; III, **561–62**, 214, 490, 521; IV, 740
Robutel de La Noue, Anne (Le Marchand de Lignery), II, 390; III, 378
Robutel de La Noue, Catherine. See Le Moyne de Sainte-Hélène
Robutel de La Noue, Catherine. See Le Moyne de Sainte-Marie
Robutel de La Noue, Claude, II, 581
Robutel de La Noue, Marie-Anne, IV, 238
Robutel de La Noue, Suzanne. See Gabrielle
Robutel de La Noue, Thomas, III, 561
Robutel de La Noue, Zacharie, II, **581**, 13, 523, 603; III, 105, 248, 414
Rocbert, Abel, III, 562
Rocbert, Marie. See Pothier
Rocbert de La Morandière, Anne-Geneviève (Legardeur de Tilly), III, 376
Rocbert de La Morandière, Élisabeth. See Duverger
Rocbert de La Morandière, Étienne, II, 47, 160, 672; III, **562–63**, 56, 445, 564
Rocbert de La Morandière, Étienne (son), III, 563; IV, 618
Rocbert de La Morandière, Jacques-Urbain, II, 47; III, 563
Rocbert de La Morandière, Louis-Joseph, III, 445, 563; IV, 41, 359, 461
Rocbert de La Morandière, Marguerite-Barbe. See Hingue de Puygibault
Rocbert de La Morandière, Marguerite-Charlotte (Lemoine Despins), IV, 461
Rocbert de La Morandière, Marguerite-Élisabeth-Ursule (Chabert de Joncaire de Clausonne), IV, 137
Rocbert de La Morandière, Marie-Élisabeth (Bégon de La Cour), III, **563–65**, 16, 30, 56, 158, 170, 240, 295, 296, 316, 376, 377, 445; IV, 250, 265, 268, 461
Rochambeau, Comte de. See Vimeur
Roch* de Saint-Ours, Paul (1747–1814), IV, 716
Rocheblave. See Rastel
Rochechouart de Mortemart, Françoise-Athénaïs de, Marquise de Montespan, II, 328; III, 106
Rochechouart de Mortemart, Gabrielle-Victor de, Duchesse de Lesdiguières, III, 106
Rochechouart de Mortemart, Louis-Victor de, Duc de Vivonne, II, 162; III, 106
Rochefort. See Lamouraux
Rochemonteix, Camille de, II, 161, 259, 607, 608; III, 689
Rochemore, Vincent de, IV, 65
Rocheron, Marie (Gaulin), II, 238
Rockingham, Marquess of. See Watson-Wentworth
Rocquant, dit La Ville, Pierre, III, 96
Rodas, Miguel de, I, 156

Roddam, Lucy Mary. See Clinton
Roddam, Robert, III, 127
Rodgers. See Rogers
Rodney, George Brydges, 1st Baron Rodney, III, 283; IV, 223, 226, 282
Rodrigue, Anne. See Le Borgne de Belle-Isle
Rodrigue, Antoine, III, 236; IV, **678–79**, 28, 245, 246, 439, 470
Rodrigue, Antoine (son), IV, 678, 679
Rodrigue, Claude, IV, 679
Rodrigue, Jean-Baptiste, II, **581–82**; IV, 678
Rodrigue, Jeanne-Françoise. See Jacau
Rodrigue, Jeanne-Françoise (L'Espérance), IV, 470, 679
Rodrigue, Joseph-Baptiste, IV, 678
Rodrigue, Marguerite-Josephte (Du Pont Duchambon), IV, 249
Rodrigue, Marie-Josèphe. See Ramondine
Rodrigue, Michel (uncle), II, 582; III, 236, 357; IV, 128, 249, 422, 678
Rodrigue, Michel, IV, 679
Rodrigue, Pierre (merchant), IV, 421
Rodrigue, Pierre (son of JEAN-BAPTISTE), II, 582; IV, 136, 678
Rodrigue, Rose. See Castaing
Roe, Sir Thomas, I, 144, 312
Roger. See also Caissy
Roger, M., II, 187
Roger, Élisabeth. See Oussaye
Roger, Guillaume (father), II, 582
Roger, Guillaume, II, **582**; III, 344
Roger, Madeleine-Renée (Gagnon), I, 319
Roger, Marie-Louise (Lajus), III, 344
Roger, Ursule. See Levasseur
Rogers, Arthur, IV, 682
Rogers, Elizabeth. See Browne
Rogers, James (father), IV, 679
Rogers, James, IV, 682
Rogers, Jonathan, IV, 675
Rogers, Mary (mother of ROBERT), IV, 679
Rogers, Richard, IV, 679
Rogers, Robert, III, xxix, 95, 452, 525, 526; IV, **679–83**, li, 3, 174, 241, 278, 294, 297, 309, 335, 423, 513, 563, 582, 583, 606, 634, 675, 676, 685
Rohan, Charles de, Prince de Soubise, IV, 481
Rohan, Louis de, Prince de Guémenée, I, 533
Rohan, Pierre de, Sire de Gié, I, 423
Rojas, Francisco de, I, 156
Roland, Angélique-Françoise (Coron), III, 140, 141
Rolfe, Benjamin, II, 285
Rolland. See Lenoir
Rollet, Marie (Hébert; Hubou), I, **578**, 110, 222, 302, 366, 367, 368, 509
Rollin, Charles, III, 26
Rollo, Andrew, 5th Baron Rollo, III, **565**, 668; IV, 22, 688
Rollo, Catharine, Baroness Rollo. See Murray
Rollo, Cecilia. See Johnstone
Rollo, Elizabeth, Baroness Rollo. See Moray
Rollo, John, III, 565
Rollo, Mary (Rollo, Baroness Rollo), III, 565
Rollo, Robert, 4th Baron Rollo, III, 565
Roma, Jean-Pierre, II, 219; III, **566–67**, 533; IV, 249
Roma, Jean-Pierre-Michel, IV, 248
Roma, Marie-Anne (Du Pont Duchambon), IV, 249

Roma, Marie-Madeleine. *See* Moreau
Romagnac, François, III, 571
Romain, Marthe (Marguerie), I, 489
Romainville. *See* Bourdon
Romanet de Briderie, M., III, 481
Romby, Marie-Marguerite de (Franquet), III, 228
Romieux, Pierre, I, **578–79**
Rompré, Marquis de. *See* Fleutelot
Romulus. *See* Romieux
Ronceray, Andrée de, II, 490
Rondeau, Étienne, II, 273
Rondeau, Françoise. *See* Baudry
Rondeau, Jacques, III, 567, 568
Rondeau, Jacques-Philippe-Urbain, III, **567–68**, 389; IV, 60, 421, 783
Rondeau, Marie-Josephe. *See* Le Borgne de Belle-Isle
Rondoenie. *See* Orontony
Rondort, Jacques, II, 516
Ronsard, Pierre, I, 425
Rooke, Sir George, II, 226, 260, 373, 659
Roome. *See* Le Chevalier
Roope, John, II, **582–83**, 117
Rooseboom. *See* Roseboom
Roquebrune. *See* La Roque
Roquefeuil, Jacques, Comte de Roquefeuil, III, 27
Roquemont de Brison, Claude, I, **578**, 59, 263, 330, 402, 405, 411, 521, 561, 593, 596
Rosanvern, M. *See* Le Loutre, Jean-Louis
Rosé, Sieur de, I, 538
Rose, Nicolas, III, 580
Rose, Toussaint, II, 112
Roseboom, Gerritje. *See* Coster
Roseboom Gysbertje. *See* Lansing
Roseboom, Hendrick, III, 568
Roseboom, Johannes, III, **568–69**
Roselli, Francesco, I, 148
Rosier, James, I, 667
Rosny, Baron de. *See* Béthune
Ross, Catherine (Kalm), IV, 406
Ross, Charles, IV, 685
Ross, George, IV, 685
Ross, John, IV, **683–84**, 121, 505, 710
Ross*, Sir John (1777–1856), I, 75
Ross, Malchom, IV, **684–85**, 157, 741, 742
Ross, William, IV, 71
Rossay, Angélique. *See* Cadet
Rossay, Jérôme, IV, 124
Rossignol, Jean, I, 292
Rossin, Catherine (Pollet de La Combe de La Pocatière), I, 550
Rostan, Anne de (Michel de Villebois), III, 444
Rostan, Henri de, III, 444
Rottot. *See* Trefflé
Roubaud, Marguerite. *See* Tressol
Roubaud, Pierre-Joseph-Antoine, III, 296; IV, **685–87**, 7, 98, 231, 294, 298, 299, 423, 574, 788
Roubaud, Pierre-Pascal, IV, 685
Roubillac, Louis-François, III, 658
Roucy. *See* La Rochefoucauld
Rouer d'Artigny, Louis, I, 583; II, 152, 235, 583; III, **569–70**, 45; IV, 624
Rouer de Villeray, Benjamin, III, **570–71**; IV, 250, 541, 631
Rouer de Villeray, Catherine. *See* Sevestre

Rouer de Villeray, Charles, I, 583
Rouer de Villeray, Jacques, I, 579
Rouer de Villeray, Louis, I, **579–83**, 91, 112, 202, 288, 448, 538, 584, 587, 588, 589, 606; II, xvi, xvii, 137, 138, 508, 583; III, 569
Rouer de Villeray, Marie. *See* Perthuis
Rouer de Villeray, Marie-Anne. *See* Du Saussay
Rouer de Villeray, Marie-Catherine (Sallaberry), III, 582
Rouer de Villeray, Marie-Joseph. *See* Pépin, *dit* Laforce
Rouer de Villeray et de La Cardonnière, Augustin, I, 551, 583; II, **583–84**, 277; III, 569, 570
Rouer de Villeray et de La Cardonnière, Marie-Louise. *See* Legardeur de Tilly
Rouer de Villeray et de La Cardonnière, Marie-Louise. *See* Pollet de La Combe-Pocatière
Rouffio, Dominique, III, 571
Rouffio, Étienne, III, 571
Rouffio, François, III, 571
Rouffio, Jean, III, 571
Rouffio, Jean-Jacques, III, 571
Rouffio, Joseph, III, **571–72**; IV, 123
Rouffio, Louise. *See* Cadet
Rouffio, Marquèze. *See* Nègre
Rouffio, Pierre, III, 571
Rouffray, Pierre, I, 479
Rougemont, Philippe, I, 168
Rouillard, Ambroise (baptized Louis-Joseph), III, **572**, 99
Rouillard, Jean, III, 572
Rouillard, Jean-Baptiste, IV, 203
Rouillard, Jeanne. *See* Levasseur
Rouillard, Marie-Anne (Deguise, *dit* Flamand), III, 170
Rouillard, Marie-Charlotte. *See* Trotain, *dit* Saint-Seürin
Rouillard, *dit* Fondville, Joseph, II, 637
Rouillé, Antoine-Louis, Comte de Jouy, III, 31, 117, 124, 184, 245, 246, 253, 385, 435, 486, 540, 556, 561, 578, 608, 616; IV, 64, 67, 146, 249, 254, 256, 258, 438, 443, 456, 467, 615, 655, 656, 657, 665, 666, 667
Rouillé, Mathurin, II, 335
Roulleaux de La Vente, Henri, II, 260, 349; III, 380, 381
Rous, John, III, **572–74**, 70, 128, 209, 293, 362, 363, 628; IV, 110, 213, 242, 249, 700
Rous, Joseph, III, 573
Rous, Mary (Bulkeley), IV, 109
Rous, Rachel (wife of JOHN), III, 573
Rousseau, Catherine (Rattier), II, 549
Rousseau, Charlotte. *See* Foureur, *dit* Champagne
Rousseau*, Dominique (1755–1825), IV, 206, 272, 629
Rousseau, François-Dominique, IV, 71
Rousseau*, Jacques (1905–70), III, 677, 678, 679
Rousseau, Jean-Jacques, II, 444; IV, 44, 92
Rousseau, Marie. *See* Gournay
Rousseau, Pierre (Sulpician), IV, 637
Rousseau, Pierre (watchmaker), III, 410
Rousseau, *dit* Larose, Laurent, II, 127
Rousseau de Souvigny, Jeanne. *See* Saint-Étienne de La Tour
Rousseau de Souvigny, Marie-Josephte (Chassin de Thierry), III, 115
Rousseau de Souvigny, Pierre, III, 115
Rousseau de Villejouin, Anne. *See* Gannes de Falaise
Rousseau de Villejouin, Barbe. *See* Leneuf de La Vallière et de Beaubassin
Rousseau de Villejouin, Gabriel (father), III, 6, 368; IV, 688

Rousseau de Villejouin, Gabriel, III, 176, 615; IV, **688–89**
Rousseau de Villejouin, Marguerite (Tarride Duhaget), III, 615
Rousseau de Villejouin, Marie-Anne (Le Coutre de Bourville), III, 368
Rousseau de Villlejouin, Marie-Josephte. *See* Bertrand
Rousseau de Villejouin, Michel, IV, 688
Roussel, Catherine. *See* Fournier
Roussel, Catherine, I, 583
Roussel, Étienne, I, 583
Roussel, Françoise (Villedonné), II, 653
Roussel, Geneviève (Chambalon), I, 583; II, 129, 130
Roussel, Jeanne. *See* Bouette
Roussel, Louise, I, 583
Roussel, Louise (Grasset de Saint-Sauveur), IV, 311
Roussel, Louise-Catherine (Saillant), IV, 692
Roussel, Madeleine. *See* Du Mortier
Roussel, Marguerite (Chabrand), IV, 138
Roussel, Marie-Anne (Baudouin; Dusautoy), III, 35
Roussel, Marie-Louise (Pagé, *dit* Carcy), III, 498
Roussel, Marie-Renée (Lambert), II, 274
Roussel, Timothée, I, **583**; II, 653; III, 237, 305
Rousselot, Marie. *See* Hurault
Roussol, Edmée (La Chasse), III, 329
Rousson. *See* Le Verrier
Routier, Marie-Jeanne (Voyer, *dit* Le Jardinier; Dubreuil), II, 201
Rouville. *See* Hertel
Rouvray. *See* Lenoir
Rouvroy, Louis de, Duc de Saint-Simon, I, 135; II, 57; III, 64
Roux*, Jean-Henri-Auguste (1760–1831), IV, 90
Rowley, Roger, I, 584
Rowley, Thomas, I, **584**, 241, 350, 497
Roy, Angélique (Batailler), II, 508
Roy, Catherine. *See* Ducharme
Roy, Charles, IV, 690
Roy, François, IV, 689
Roy, Jean, IV, 702
Roy, Jean-Joseph, IV, 424
Roy, Joseph, III, 142, 554
Roy, Joseph-Marie, IV, 689, 690
Roy, Louis, IV, **689–90**
Roy, Louise. *See* Chevalier
Roy, Louise-Olive, *dite* de Saint-Paul, IV, 690
Roy, Marguerite, *dite* de la Conception, III, **574–75**, 17, 191, 630
Roy, Marie (Lépine, *dit* Lalime; Corpron), III, 142
Roy, Marie-Charlotte (Révol), III, 554
Roy, Marie-Louise. *See* Lapérade
Roy, Mathurin, II, 639
Roy, Michel (father of Michel Roy, *dit* Châtellerault), II, 584
Roy, Michel (silversmith), IV, 206
Roy, Pierre, III, 574
Roy*, Pierre-Georges (1870–1953), III, 19, 143, 312, 434, 616, 721; IV, 461, 509, 517, 755
Roy, *dit* Châtellerault, Françoise. *See* Hobbé
Roy, *dit* Châtellerault, Michel, II, **584**
Roy, *dit* Desjardins, Antoine, II, 466
Roybon d'Allonne, Jacques de, II, 584
Roybon d'Allonne, Madeleine de, II, **584–85**
Roy-Desjardins, Agathe (Cotté), IV, 171

Roye. *See* La Rochefoucauld
Roye, Marquise de. *See* Ducasse
Rozinoghyata. *See* Hotsinoñhyahta?
Rozoy. *See* Dugey
Ruau, Perrine (Terriot), II, 625
Rubelles. *See* Bonneau
Rudduck, Sarah (Cleveland; Fillis), IV, 267
Rudolf, Leonard Christian, III, 212
Ruehegan, III, 520
Ruette d'Auteuil, Claire-Françoise. *See* Clément Du Vuault de Monceaux
Ruette d'Auteuil, Denis-Joseph, I, **584–85**, 136, 202, 288, 289, 580, 581, 582, 587, 588, 589; II, 137, 585
Ruette d'Auteuil, Louise-Geneviève (Daneau de Muy), III, 162
Ruette d'Auteuil, Marie-Anne. *See* Juchereau de Saint-Denis
Ruette d'Auteuil, Marie-Claire (Crisafy, Marquise de Crisafy), II, 163
Ruette d'Auteuil de La Malotière, Marie-Charlotte. *See* Piot de Langloiserie
Ruette d'Auteuil de La Malotière, Pierre, II, 527
Ruette d'Auteuil de Monceaux, François-Madeleine-Fortuné, I, 289, 551, 585; II, **585–88**, 42, 90, 134, 149, 163, 302, 303, 305, 325, 354, 448, 527, 546, 547, 557, 558, 569, 571, 575; III, 51, 52, 58, 104, 201, 202, 410
Ruggles, Timothy, IV, 769
Ruis-Embito de La Chesnardière, Charles-Claude de, IV, 91
Rupert, Prince, Count Palatine, I, 281, 406, 604, 642
Rushworth, Bryan, II, 610
Rushworth, George, III, 123
Russell, Captain, I, 93
Russell, Mr, I, 567
Russell, Anne (Dudley, Countess of Warwick), I, 318
Russell, Elizabeth, Lady Russell. *See* Cooke
Russell, Elizabeth (Hicks), IV, 350
Russell*, Elizabeth (1754–1822), IV, 766
Russell, Jeremy Condy, IV, 414
Russell, John, IV, 536
Russell, John, 4th Duke of Bedford, III, 261, 362, 659; IV, 168, 169, 559, 571
Russell*, Peter (1733–1808), IV, 12, 756, 766, 767
Rust, Rebecca (Danks), IV, 193
Rut, John, I, **585–86**, 19, 301
Rutherford, John, III, 167; IV, 761
Rutherford, Walter, III, 537
Ruysch, Johannes, I, 148, 678
Ruyter, Michiel Adriaanszoon de, I, 25, 443, 496
Ruzé. *See* Coiffier
Ryall, George, IV, 83
Ryan*, John (d. 1847), IV, 483, 721
Rybot, Francis, III, 620

Saarom. *See* Atecouando (Jérôme)
Sabatier, Antoine, III, **575–76**, 98, 387, 396; IV, 60, 420, 644
Sabatier, François, I, 514
Sabatier, François de Paule, III, 576
Sabatier, Joseph, III, 575
Sabatier, Madeleine. *See* Arnauld
Sabatis. *See* Gill, Antoine
Sabourin, Marie-Madeleine (Tonty de Liette), III, 627
Sabourin, *dit* Chauniers, Catherine (Foucault), III, 226

Sabrevois, Charles de, II, 589; III, 258; IV, 690, 691
Sabrevois, Jacques-Charles de, II, **588–89**, 563, 580; III, 105; IV, 690
Sabrevois, Jeanne de. *See* Boucher
Sabrevois de Bleury, Charlotte de. *See* Guichard
Sabrevois de Bleury, Clément de, II, 548, 589; III, 412; IV, **690–91**, 362, 653
Sabrevois de Bleury, Jean-Clément de (baptized Jean), IV, 691
Sabrevois de Bleury, Marguerite de (Dandonneau Du Sablé; Lorimier de Verneuil), IV, 691
Sabrevois de Sermonville, Christophe de, II, 589; IV, 690
Sabrevois de Sermonville, Gabrielle de. *See* Martin
Sabrevois de Sermonville, Henri de, II, 588
Saccardy, Vincent, I, **586–87**, 533, 576; II, 183
Sackville, Viscount. *See* Germain
Sackville, Lionel Cranfield, 1st Duke of Dorset, IV, 20
Saffray de Mézy, Augustin de, I, **587–90**, 32, 47, 113, 146, 202, 203, 221, 245, 323, 325, 400, 448, 467, 537, 542, 543, 549, 556, 570, 580, 584, 592; II, xvii, xix, 85, 365, 366, 367
Sagard, Gabriel (baptized Théodat), I, **590–92**, 70, 73, 121, 123, 125, 130, 132, 133, 160, 211, 222, 233, 263, 265, 346, 368, 382, 417, 419, 433, 437, 509, 511, 546, 578, 639, 663; II, 281, 429
Sagean, Jean, II, 589
Sagean, Marie. *See* Larrante
Sagean, Mathieu, II, **589–90**
Sageot, Geneviève (Adhémar de Saint-Martin), II, 11
Sageot, *dit* Laforge, Marie-Madeleine. *See* Sasseville
Sagouarrab (Sagouarrat, Saguaarum). *See* Sauguaaram
Saguima, II, 324, 515; III, **576–77**, xxxix
Sahonwagy (Sahonwadi), IV, **691–92**
Saillans, Anne de. *See* Mius d'Entremont de Pobomcoup
Saillans, Antoine de, II, 38, 512
Saillant, Anne. *See* Laurent
Saillant, Jacques, IV, 692
Saillant (Saillant de Collégien), Jean-Antoine, III, 142, 397; IV, **692–93**
Saillant, Louise-Catherine. *See* Roussel
Saillant, Véronique. *See* Pépin, *dit* Laforce
Saille, Mary (Outlaw), I, 529
Sailly, Anne-Françoise de. *See* Bourduceau
Sailly, Louis-Arthus de, I, **592**, 47
Sainctar, Catherine (Baillif), I, 76
Sainctes, Marguerite de (Pottier), II, 527
Saint-Aignan. *See* Marsolet
Saint-Aignan, Duc de. *See* Beauvillier
Saint-Amant. *See* Pélerin
Saint-Amour. *See* Payet
Saint-André. *See* Besnard
Saint-André. *See* Monbeton de Brouillan, Jacques-François de
Saint-Ange. *See* Charly; Groston
Saint-Antoine. *See* Martel
Saint-Arsène. *See* Arnaud
Saint-Aubin. *See also* Le Poupet; Serreau
Saint-Aubin, Ambroise, IV, **693**, 13, 30, 736
Saint-Auron. *See* Maugenest
Saint-Barnabé. *See* Lepage
Saint-Benoît. *See* Lefebvre Belle-Isle
Saint-Bernard, Raymond de, I, 352, 357
Saint-Blaint. *See* Raimbault

Saint-Castin. *See* Abbadie
Saint-Castin, Baronne de. *See* Béarn-Bonasse; Damours de Chauffours; Pidianske
Saint-Chéran. *See* Saint-Thairau
Saint-Clair, Pierre de, II, **590**, 434, 479
Saint-Claude. *See* Volant
Saint-Columbe, M., II, 184
Saint-Cosme. *See also* Buisson
Saint-Cosme (Natchez chief), II, 110
Saint-Cyrque (Saint-Sircq), M. de, II, 603
Saint-Denis. *See* Potier
Saint-Denis (Saint-Denys). *See* Juchereau
Saint-Dizier. *See* Nivard
Sainte, Claude de (Monseignat), II, 483
Sainte-Agnès. *See* Tibierge
Sainte-Barbe. *See* Guillet
Sainte-Claire. *See* Lepage
Sainte-Croix. *See* Brice
Sainte-Gertrude. *See* Hervieux
Sainte-Hélène. *See* Le Moyne
Sainte-Henriette. *See* Lemire-Marsolais
Sainte-James, Baron de. *See* Baudart
Sainte-Madelcinc. *See* Longley
Sainte-Marie. *See* Allard; Gastineau; Le Moyne
Sainte-Marie-Médiatrice. *See* Lambert
Sainte-Rosalie. *See* Piot de Langloiserie
Saint-Esprit. *See* Le Moyne de Sainte-Marie
Saint-Étienne. *See also* Dinan
Saint-Étienne de La Tour, Agathe de (Bradstreet; Campbell), II, **590–91**; IV, xix, 83
Saint-Étienne de La Tour, Angélique de. *See* Loreau
Saint-Étienne de La Tour, Anne de. *See* Melanson
Saint-Étienne de La Tour, Anne de (Mius d'Entremont, Baronne de Pobomcoup), I, 510, 514; II, 206, 512
Saint-Étienne de La Tour, Charles de (father), I, **592–96**, 25, 32, 51, 53, 54, 62, 66, 90, 97, 102, 223, 234, 241, 248, 257, 258, 311, 323, 383, 433, 434, 435, 436, 469, 471, 476, 490, 495, 503, 504, 510, 514, 567, 569, 597, 604, 605, 636; II, 206, 460, 590, 591; IV, xviii, xix, xxiii
Saint-Étienne de La Tour, Charles de (son), I, 436, 514; II, **591–92**, 39; III, 503
Saint-Étienne de La Tour, Charles de (3rd), II, 592
Saint-Étienne de La Tour, Claude de, I, **596–98**, 25, 53, 54, 77, 503, 579, 592, 593, 594, 605; IV, xix
Saint-Étienne de La Tour, Françoise-Marie de. *See* Jacquelin
Saint-Étienne de La Tour, Jacques de, I, 514; II, 590; IV, xix
Saint-Étienne de La Tour, Jeanne de. *See* Motin
Saint-Étienne de La Tour, Jeanne de (Aprendestiguy), I, 66, 595
Saint-Étienne de La Tour, Jeanne de (Pontif; Rousseau de Souvigny), III, 115
Saint-Étienne de La Tour, Marguerite de (Mius de Plemazais), I, 510, 514
Saint-Étienne de La Tour, Marie de (Le Borgne de Belle-Isle), I, 436, 514; II, 581
Saint-Eugène, Sieur de, III, 135
Saint-Ferréol. *See* Lyon
Saint-Florentin, Comte de. *See* Phélypeaux
Saint-Flour, Chevalier de, II, 446
Saint-François. *See* Crevier; François; Hertel; Trottier
Saint-François, Sieur de. *See* Bourdon
Saint-Front. *See* Duclos
Saint-Georges, Adrien de, II, 381

Saint-Georges, Jeanne de. *See* Guernon
Saint-Georges, Marie-Catherine de (Le Conte Dupré), II, 81, 381; III, 367
Saint-Georges Dupré. *See* Le Comte Dupré, Georges-Hippolyte
Saint-Germain. *See also* Audouart; Cureux; Diverny; Lamoureux; Lemaire; Mangeant
Saint-Germain, Sieur, III, 377
Saint-Germain-Beaupré. *See also* Foucault
Saint-Germain de Mérieux, Marie-Anne de (Pourroy de Lauberivière), II, 530
Saint-Hilaire. *See* Hillaire
Saint-Hippolyte. *See* Piot de Langloiserie
Saint-Horan (Saint-Jorand). *See also* Maugenest
Saint-Horan (Saint-Jorand), Marie-Anne (Maugenest), IV, 524
Saint-Jacques. *See* Cheval
Saint-Jean. *See* Bourdon
Saint-Jérôme, Mother, I, 353
St John, Henry, 1st Viscount Bolingbroke, II, 286, 497, 659, 660, 662; III, 200
St John, Oliver, Viscount Grandison, I, 94
St John of Basing, Lord. *See* Paulet
Saint-Joseph. *See* Leduc; Trottier
Saint-Julhien. *See* Mascle
Saint-Jure, Jean-Baptiste de, I, 484, 485
Saint-Just. *See* Biencourt
Saint-Lambert. *See* Philippe
Saint-Laurent, Comte de. *See* Berthelot
Saint-Laurent, Comtesse de. *See* Juchereau de Saint-Denis
St Leger, Mrs. *See* Bayly
St Leger, Sir Anthony, I, 82
St Leger, Barrimore Matthew, IV, **694–95**, 114, 118, 120, 155, 323, 324, 367, 405, 410, 417, 710, 731
St Leger, Sir John, IV, 694
St Leger, Lavina, Lady St Leger. *See* Pennefather
St Leger, Mary (Sutton, Baroness Lexington), I, 82
St Lo, George, II, 659
St Lo, John, II, 89
Saint-Louis. *See* Hertel; Plichon
Saint-Louis-des-Anges. *See* Paré
Saint-Luc. *See* La Corne; Rageot
Saint-Luc, Marquis de. *See* Espinay
Saint-Lusson. *See* Daumont
Saint-Mars (Saint-Marc), Jean-Baptiste, II, 513
Saint-Martin. *See* Adhémar; Baudry; Boschet; Boutet; Dumas; Lestringant
Saint-Martin, Joannis (Jean) de, III, 157
Saint-Mas (agent), I, 433
Saint-Maur. *See* Dupré
Saint-Maurice. *See* Dubois; Olivier
Saint-Médard. *See* Le Mercier
Saint-Méry. *See* Moreau
Saint-Michel. *See* Messier
Saint-Nectaire. *See* Senneterre
Saint-Olive, Claude de, II, 54
Saint-Olon. *See* Pidou
Saint-Onge. *See* Garreau
Saint-Ours. *See also* Roch
Saint-Ours, Élisabeth de (Le Roy de La Potherie), II, 422, 593
Saint-Ours, François-Xavier de, III, **577–78**, 34

Saint-Ours, Hélène de. *See* Céloron de Blainville
Saint-Ours, Henri de, II, 592
Saint-Ours, Jeanne de. *See* Calignon
Saint-Ours, Jeanne de (Pécaudy de Contrecœur), I, 535; II, 593; III, 503, 505; IV, 617
Saint-Ours, Marguerite de. *See* Legardeur de Tilly
Saint-Ours, Marie de. *See* Mullois
Saint-Ours, Marie-Anne de (Mine), II, 593
Saint-Ours, Marie-Barbe de (Legardeur de Beauvais), III, 374
Saint-Ours, Pierre de, I, 418; II, **592–93**, 105, 203, 323, 403, 616; III, 233, 374, 385, 505, 577, 578
Saint-Ours, Pierre de (son), II, 125, 593; III, 577
Saint-Ours, Thérèse de. *See* Hertel de Cournoyer
Saint-Ours Deschaillons, Jean-Baptiste de, II, 285, 296, 495, 593; III, **578–79**, 104, 450
Saint-Ours Deschaillons, Marguerite de. *See* Legardeur de Repentigny
Saint-Ours Deschaillons, Pierre-Roch de, III, 183, 332, 579; IV, xliii, 455, 634
Saint-Ovide. *See* Monbeton
Saint-Paul. *See also* Godefroy; Lambert; Lamotte; Le Ber
Saint-Paul, Claude de, I, 313
Saint-Pé, Jean-Baptiste de, II, 40; III, **579–80**, 204, 361, 428; IV, 240, 298, 685
Saint-Père, Agathe de (Legardeur de Repentigny), II, 385, 386, 552, 597; III, **580–81**, 579
Saint-Père, Étienne de, I, 598
Saint-Père, Étiennette de. *See* Julian
Saint-Père, Jean de, I, **598–99**, 79, 218, 230, 231; II, xvi, 386; III, 580
Saint-Père, Mathurine de. *See* Godé
Saint-Pierre. *See* Denys; Du Pont; Jussaume; Legardeur
Saint-Pierre, Comte de. *See* Castel
Saint-Pierre, Comtesse de. *See* Kerven
Saint-Placide. *See* Boucher de Montbrun
Saint-Pol, Comte de. *See* Orléans
Saint-Poncy. *See* La Vernède
Saint-Quentin. *See* Moral
Saint-Rémy. *See* Rémy
Saint-Romain. *See* Chorel
Saint-Sacrement. *See* Bourgeoys; La Corne de Chaptes
Saint-Sauveur. *See* Grasset
Saint-Sauveur, Abbé de. *See* Le Sueur
Saint-Sceine. *See* Petitot
Saint-Seürin. *See* Trotain
Saint-Séverin. *See* Ameau
Saint-Simon. *See also* Denis; Denys; Lefebvre Angers
Saint-Simon, Duc de. *See* Rouvroy
Saint-Simon, Claude-Anne de, Duc de Saint-Simon, IV, 208
Saint-Sircq. *See* Saint-Cyrque
Saint-Terone. *See* Maugenest
Saint-Thairau (Saint-Turine, Saint-Chéran), Antoinette de (Tarride Duhaget), III, 615
Saint-Vallier. *See* La Croix
Saint-Vilmé. *See* Ailleboust
St Vincent, Earl of. *See* Jervis
Saint-Vincent, Abbé de, III, 415; IV, 453
Saint-Vincent, Henri-Albert de, IV, 263
Saint-Vincent-de-Paul. *See* Robichaud
Sajan. *See* Sagean
Sakima. *See* Saguima

Sakonentsiask, III, 615
Sakumow Sagma. *See* Segipt
Salaberry. *See* Irumberry
Saladin, Simon, II, 283
Salavy, Margaret de (Mascarene), III, 435
Salazar, Jeanne de (Biencourt), I, 96
Sales, François de, I, 91; II, 34
Salières, Marquis de. *See* Chastelard
Salignac de La Mothe-Fénelon, François de (archbishop), I, 599; II, 330; IV, 467
Salignac de La Mothe-Fénelon, François de, I, **599–601**, 127, 136, 175, 270, 287, 297, 410, 539, 584, 613, 647; II, 45, 130, 193, 194, 195, 227, 349, 350, 514, 561, 582, 637
Salignac de La Mothe-Fénelon, Marie-Louise-Augustine de (Le Normant de Mézy), IV, 467
Salisbury. *See* Salusbury
Salisbury, Earl of. *See* Cecil
Sall (slave), IV, 779
Sallaberry, Angélique de, III, 582
Sallaberry, Madeleine-Louise de. *See* Juchereau Duchesnay de Saint-Denis
Sallaberry, Marie de. *See* Michelance
Sallaberry, Marie-Catherine de. *See* Rouer de Villeray
Sallaberry, Marsans de, III, 582
Sallaberry, Michel de, III, **582–83**, 377
Sallé, Marie-Thérèse (Raimbault), II, 541
Salleneuve, Jean-Baptiste de, III, 347; IV, 640
Salmon, Edme-Gatien, III, 40, 382
Salmon, Thomas, II, 251
Salomon. *See also* Allemewi
Salomon, Elias, IV, 332, 385
Salter, Malachy (father), IV, 695
Salter, Malachy, IV, **695–97**, 29, 52, 110, 116, 273, 291, 313, 562
Salter, Sarah. *See* Holmes
Salter, Susanna. *See* Mulberry
Saltonstall, Dudley, IV, 504
Saltonstall, Gurdon, II, 498
Salusbury, Sir Henry, I, 656
Salusbury, Hester. *See* Cotton
Salusbury, Hester Lynch (Thrale; Piozzi), III, 583
Salusbury, John, III, **583–84**
Salusbury, Lucy (wife of Thomas, father), III, 583
Salusbury, Thomas (father), III, 583
Salusbury, Thomas, III, 583
Salvaye, (Pierre?) de, III, 65
Salvert. *See* Perier
Samalins, Jeanne de (Lanouguère), I, 417
Sampson, Richard, II, 118
Sancé, Michel de, I, 229
Sandersleben, Henriette-Edwige. *See* Curie
Sanderson, Robert, IV, 313
Sanderson, William, I, 251, 252
Sandford. *See* Sanford
Sandin, Anna Magaretha. *See* Sjöman
Sandray, M. de, IV, 686
Sandrier. *See* Imbert
Sandwich, Earl of. *See* Montagu
Sandys, Sir Edwin, I, 69
Sanford, Bridget. *See* Hutchinson
Sanford, Esbon, I, **601**, 129, 337, 338
Sanford, John, I, 601

Sanford, Sarah (wife of EsBON), I, 601
Sangouessy. *See* Chingouessi
Sanguinet, Angélique. *See* Lefebvre, *dit* Duchouquet
Sanguinet, Christophe, IV, 592, 697, 698
Sanguinet, Joseph, IV, 592, 697, 698
Sanguinet, Marie-Jeanne. *See* Hervieux
Sanguinet, Simon (father), III, 522; IV, 204, 697
Sanguinet, Simon, IV, **697–98**, 72, 373, 547, 549
Sanguinet, Thérèse. *See* Réaume
Sanlerg, Gabrielle. *See* Senler
Sanson, Moullart, II, 121
Santa Cruz, Alonso de, I, 156, 157, 304, 342
Saossarinon, I, 634
Sapaillé. *See* Taschereau
Saquima (Saquin). *See* Saguima
Sarah. *See also* Shanawdithit
Sarah, III, 322
Sarasin Depelteau, Angélique (Cartier), IV, 709
Saravia. *See* Peña
Sarcel de Prévert, Françoise. *See* Richomme
Sarcel de (Du) Prévert, Jean, I, **601–2**, 188, 189, 292, 507
Sareau, Catherine. *See* Brossard
Sareau, Jean, II, 105
Sareillier (Sarcelié, Lecarulier), Isabau (Élisabeth), (Castaing), IV, 135
Sarney, Margaret Irene (Harcourt; Shuldham, Baroness Shuldham), IV, 707
Sarraute-Marjolet, Jacques de, II, 4
Sarrazin, Charlotte-Louise-Angélique (Gaultier de Varennes), II, 598; III, 246
Sarrazin, Claude (father), II, 593
Sarrazin, Claude, II, 598
Sarrazin, Claude-Michel, II, 598; III, 184; IV, 338, 339
Sarrazin, Joseph-Michel, II, 598; III, 675; IV, 339
Sarrazin, Madeleine. *See* Bonnefoy
Sarrazin, Marie-Anne-Ursule. *See* Hazeur
Sarrazin, Marie-Jeanne, II, 598
Sarrazin, Michel, I, 107; II, **593–600**, 44, 47, 48, 60, 212, 276, 307, 533; III, 67, 285, 315, 334, 344, 353, 369, 410, 603, 675, 677, 678, 679, 680; IV, 338, 357
Sarrazin, Nicolas, II, 239; IV, 77
Sarreau. *See also* Serreau
Sarreau, Sieur, III, 398
Sarrebource* Maladre de Pontleroy, Nicolas (1717–1802), III, xix, 229, 464; IV, 143, 144, 146, 211, 672
Sartine, Antoine de, Comte d'Alby, III, 141, 441, 442; IV, 69, 243, 422, 646
Sasoonan. *See* Allumapees
Sasousmat (François Marsolet), I, 164, 533
Sasseville, Joseph, IV, 702
Sasseville, Marie-Madeleine (Normandeau, *dit* Deslauriers; Sageot, *dit* Laforge; Parent), IV, 204
Sastaretsi. *See* Kondiaronk
Satouta, I, 637
Sattin, Abbé, II, 378
Sauer. *See* Sower
Sauguaaram, II, 665, 669; III, **584–85**, xxxix, 136
Saul, George, III, 586
Saul, Thomas, III, **585–86**, 365; IV, 695, 696
Saulcier, Charles, II, 201
Saulnier, Étienne, I, 264
Saumarez, Madeline (Durell), III, 208

Saunders, Mr, I, 370
Saunders, Lady. *See* Buck
Saunders, Sir Charles, III, xxv, 132, 209, 210, 293, 465, 573, 592, 606, 669, 671; IV, **698–702**, 163, 210, 223, 250, 460, 597, 600, 601, 650, 652, 751
Saunders, James, IV, 698
Saur. *See* Sower
Saurel, Catherine de. *See* Legardeur de Tilly
Saurel, Jeanne de. *See* Giraud
Saurel, Mathieu de, I, 602
Saurel, Pierre de, I, **602–3**, 308, 418, 555; II, 11, 59, 60, 592
Sauvaget, Jean, I, 553
Sauveterre. *See* Aussillon
Sauvole, Ensign, III, 380
Savage, Arthur, II, **600–1**; III, 518
Savage, Elizabeth. *See* Scottow
Savage, Faith. *See* Hutchinson
Savage, Perez, II, 601
Savage, Thomas (father), II, 601
Savage, Thomas, I, 545; II, **601**, 532
Savard, M., IV, 650
Savari. *See* Du Plessis-Savari
Savignac, Antoinette-Charlotte de (Maurès de Malartic, Comtesse de Montricoux), IV, 530
Savignon, I, **603**, 131, 190, 381
Savigny, Marie-Anne de. *See* Aubert de Courserac
Savile, Henry, I, 82
Savoie-Lascaris, Renée de, II, 349
Savonnières de La Troche, Jeanne de. *See* Raoul
Savonnières de La Troche, Marie de, *dite* de Saint-Joseph (de Saint-Bernard), I, **603–4**, 108, 352
Savonnières de La Troche, Simon de, I, 603
Savoy, Duke of. *See* Charles Emmanuel
Savoy, Marquis of. *See* Easton, Peter
Savoye, Marie, IV, 81
Saxe, Maurice de, Comte de Saxe, known as Maréchal de Saxe, III, xv, xvi, 185, 186, 458, 466, 535; IV, 443
Sayde Pasha, III, 62
Saye, Jeanne (Quesneville), II, 534
Saye and Sele, Viscount of. *See* Fiennes
Sayenqueraghta. *See* Kaieñ?kwaahtoñ
Sayer. *See also* Sayward
Sayer*, John (d. 1818), IV, 369
Saymond, Daniel, I, 590
Sayre, Esther (Robinson; Beman), IV, 677
Sayve, Marie de (La Croix de Chevrières de Saint-Vallier), II, 328
Sayward (Sayer), Esther (rebaptized Marie-Joseph) (Lestage), II, 601, 602; III, 253, 393, 394; IV, 765
Sayward, Mary. *See* Rishworth
Sayward, Mary (rebaptized Marie-Geneviève), *dite* Marie des Anges, II, **601–2**; III, 394, 407
Sayward, William, II, 601
Scamen (Scammon), Mary (rebaptized Marie) (Godefroy de Tonnancour), IV, 305
Scarroyady, III, xl, 320, 607, 613, 614; IV, lvi
Scatchamisse, II, **602**, 492
Scatts Eye. *See* Scorch Eye
Schank*, John (1740–1823), IV, 231
Schimmelpinck, Lydia (Douglas), IV, 223
Schindler, Frédéric, IV, 702
Schindler, Geneviève. *See* Maranda

Schindler, Joseph (father), IV, 702
Schindler, Joseph (Jonas), IV, **702–3**
Schindler, Marguerite. *See* Gaspar
Schloezer, Christian Andrew, III, 411
Schmid, Luc III, 307
Schmid, Luke, IV, 294
Schmid, Madeleine. *See* Trefflé, *dit* Rottot
Schomberg, Sir Alexander, III, 606
Schomberg, Henry (Sir Alexander?), III, 417, 418, 425
Schomberg, Jeanne de (Du Plessis, Marquise de Liancourt, Duchesse de La Roche-Guyon), I, 484
Schoolcraft, Henry Rowe, III, 660
Schrimshire. *See* Skrimsher
Schuyler, Abraham, II, 341, 402; III, 428
Schuyler, Alida (Van Rensselaer; Livingston), II, 436
Schuyler, Arent, III, 587
Schuyler, Elizabeth. *See* Staats
Schuyler, Engeltie. *See* Van Schaick
Schuyler, Hester. *See* Walter
Schuyler, Johannes, III, **586–87**, 265; IV, 770
Schuyler, Margarita. *See* Van Slichtenhorst
Schuyler, Maria. *See* Van Rensselaer
Schuyler, Mary (wife of PETER, d. 1762), III, 587
Schuyler, Peter, I, 239; II, **602–4**, 21, 112, 148, 168, 237, 474, 502, 523, 624; III, 428, 568, 586, 622, 623
Schuyler, Peter, III, **587–89**; IV, 612
Schuyler, Philip John, III, 587; IV, 545, 546, 694, 730
Schuyler, Philip Pieterse, II, 602; III, 586
Schuyler, Swantie. *See* Dyckhuyse
Schwartz, Anna Justina (Liebrich; wife of OTTO WILLIAM), IV, 703
Schwartz, Otto William, IV, **703–4**, 110
Scolvus, John, I, **679**
Scorch Eye, IV, 420
Scot, Dominique, I, 495
Scot, Sir John, I, 496
Scott, Captain, III, 663
Scott, Mrs, III, 589
Scott, Abigail (wife of GEORGE), III, 590
Scott, George, III, 589
Scott, George, III, **589–90**, xxvi, xxvii, xxviii, 87, 667, 671; IV, 21, 193, 308, 630, 631, 705
Scott, John Morin, IV, 715
Scott*, Jonathan (1744–1819), IV, 18, 19, 565
Scott, Joseph (brother of GEORGE), III, 590; IV, 705
Scott, Joseph, IV, **704–5**, 199
Scott, Margaret (Montgomery, Lady Montgomery), IV, 550
Scott, Margaret Ramsey. *See* Cottnam
Scott, Mary (Argall; Washington), I, 67
Scott, Sir Reginald, I, 67
Scott, Thomas (naval officer), II, 153; III, 323
Scott*, Thomas (d. 1810), IV, 89
Scottee, Joshua, I, 242
Scottow, Elizabeth (Savage), II, 601
Scratchemisse. *See* Scatchamisse
Scrimshire. *See* Skrimsher
Scroggs, John, II, **604**, 313, 320, 493, 658; III, 447, 448, 489, 599
Scroope, Ann (Pyke; Wenman), IV, 763, 764
Scull, Gideon Delaplaine, IV, 553
Seabury, Samuel, IV, 327
Sébille, Jean, II, 275
Sébille, Marie-Anne. *See* Hazeur

Seccomb, Hannah. *See* Willis
Seccomb, Peter, IV, 705
Seccombe, John, IV, **705–6**, 490
Seccombe, Mercy. *See* Williams
Séchelles. *See* Moreau
Secondat, Charles de, Baron de La Brède et de Montesquieu, III, 334
Secoudon (Secondon), I, **604**, 96, 507, 526, 529, 564
Sedgwick, Elizabeth. *See* Howe
Sedgwick, Robert, I, **604–5**, 25, 39, 241, 259, 434, 435, 469, 474, 595; II, 94
Sedgwick, Sarah (Leverett), I, 475
Sedgwick, William, I, 604
Sédilot, Marie (Blanchet; Adhémar de Saint-Martin), II, 11
Segipt, I, **605**, 53
Segris, Barbe (Jacquiés), II, 294
Seguaron. *See* Sauguaaram
Seguenot, François, II, 376
Séguier, Pierre, Comte de Gien, Duc de Villemor, I, 214, 484, 505
Séguin, M., IV, 558, 644, 645
Ségure (Chignac), Jeanne (Maisonnat), II, 449
Seignelay, Marquis de. *See* Colbert
Seigneur, Marie-Josephe (Loppinot de La Frésillière; Claparède), III, 123
Seigneuret, Étienne, II, 647
Seigneuret, Marguerite (Godefroy de Normanville; Boudor), II, 252, 253
Selby*, George (1759–1835), IV, 82, 434
Selkirk, Earl of. *See* Douglas
Seller, John, I, 337
Sempkins, Sarah (Kilby), III, 326
Sénat, Antoine, II, 67
Senat, Françoise. *See* Phélypeaux
Senau, *dit* La Viazère, Michel, I, 524
Seneca King. *See* Kaieñ?kwaahtoñ
Senet, Gertrude. *See* Daunet
Senet, Pierre, II, 604
Senet, Suzanne. *See* Vanier
Senet, *dit* Laliberté, Nicolas, II, **604**
Senex, John, III, 325
Senezergues, Louis de, III, 590
Senezergues de La Rodde, Étienne-Guillaume de, III, **590–91**, xx
Senler, Gabrielle (Fillion), I, 305
Senneterre (Saint-Nectaire), Jean-Charles de, III, xxii
Senneville. *See* Le Ber
Sequaresera, III, 321
Sequidonquee (Little Beard), IV, 121
Séré. *See* Cerré
Sergeant, Mrs (wife of HENRY), I, 657
Sergeant, Henry, I, **605–6**, 130, 315, 329, 519, 657, 666; II, 49, 231, 265, 318
Sergeant, Thomas, I, 606
Serigny. *See* Le Moyne
Sérindac, Antoine, III, 637
Serkoak, IV, 536
Sermonville. *See* Sabrevois
Seroin, Claudine (Muiron), III, 478
Serquigny. *See* Aché
Serré, Jean-Baptiste, III, 144
Serreau de Saint-Aubin, Jean, II, **604–5**, 6; III, 111
Serreau de Saint-Aubin, Marguerite. *See* Boileau

Serres, Dominique, III, 592
Sertrouville. *See* La Salle
Servian. *See* Alquier
Servien, Bishop, II, 360
Settle, Dionise, I, 670
Sevestre, Catherine (Rouer de Villeray), I, 580, 583; II, 583; III, 569
Sevestre, Charles (father), I, 606
Sevestre, Charles, I, **606**, 145, 429, 580, 583; II, xvi, 426
Sevestre, Étienne, I, 606
Sevestre, Ignace, I, 606
Sevestre, Louis, I, 606
Sevestre, Marguerite. *See* Petitpas
Sevestre, Marguerite (Lessard), II, 426
Sevestre, Marie. *See* Pichon
Sevestre, Marie-Denise (Neveu), III, 482
Sevestre, Thomas, I, 606
Sévigné, Marquise de. *See* Rabutin-Chantal
Sewall, Hannah (Moody), III, 470, 471
Sewall, Samuel, III, 470, 505
Sewall, Stephen, IV, 51
Sewel, William, I, 81
Sewell, Harriet. *See* Smith
Sewell, Jonathan (father), IV, 292
Sewell*, Jonathan (1766–1839), IV, 502, 718
Seygris. *See* Segris
Seymour, Francis, Viscount Beauchamp and Earl of Hertford, IV, 146
Seymour, Sarah (Mathews), IV, 522
Sforza, Gian Galeazzo, Duke of Milan, I, 164
Sforza, Ludovico (il Moro), Duke of Milan, I, 22, 148, 150, 164
Shaftesbury, Earl of. *See* Cooper
Shanap, III, 654
Shanks. *See* Schank
Shannon, Viscount. *See* Boyle
Shanson, Gilliom. *See* Jeanson, Guillaume
Shapleigh, Alexander, I, 652
Shapleigh, Catherine (Treworgie), I, 652
Sharkee, M. *See* Chartier, Michel
Sharp, Granville, IV, 627
Sharpe, Hannah, I, 338
Sharpnack, Catharine (Sower), IV, 721
Shaw*, Angus (d. 1832), IV, 727
Shaw, Jane. *See* Wood
Shaw, William, IV, **706–7**, 674, 776
Shawandithit* (d. 1829), II, 8
Shee, Hélène (Latouche MacCarthy), III, 357
Sheehan, Walter Butler, IV, 119
Sheepscot Jo. *See* Wowurna
Shelburne, Earl of. *See* Petty
Sheldon, Martha (Renaud), IV, 657, 658
Shepard, Thomas, I, **607**, 343, 642
Sheperd, Suzanna (Gibbons), IV, 292
Shepherd, Elizabeth. *See* White
Shepherd, Sir Samuel, IV, 766, 767
Sherard, William, II, 596
Sherlock, Thomas, IV, 775
Sherman, Prudence (Denison), III, 174
Sherwood*, Justus (1752–1836), IV, 153
Shewescome, III, 151
Shikellimy. *See also* Swatana
Shikellimy, John, III, 607

Shilling, Andrew, I, 75

Shirley, William, II, 524; III, xxiv, xxv, xxix, xxx, 9, 10, 30, 32, 33, 87, 101, 126, 255, 260, 261, 274, 275, 288, 322, 325, 326, 362, 363, 365, 403, 404, 438, 439, 483, 507, 512, 572, 585, 588, 628, 641, 653, 654, 655, 657; IV, 52, 83, 84, 281, 314, 395, 487, 489, 540, 559, 560, 588, 679, 769, 774, 775

Shirreff, William, III, 143, 276, 518

Short, Richard (naval officer), I, 546

Short, Richard, I, 76; II, 200, 452; III, **591–92**

Shortt*, Adam (1859–1931), IV, xlv, 128

Shovell, Sir Cloudesley, II, 636; III, 488

Shuldham, Elizabeth. *See* Molyneux

Shuldham, Lemuel, IV, 707

Shuldham, Margaret Irene, Baroness Shuldham. *See* Sarney

Shuldham, Molyneux, 1st Baron Shuldham, IV, **707–8**, 122, 176

Shute, Samuel, II, 476, 543, 544, 609, 610, 668

Sicard, Augustin, IV, 320

Sicard, Barthélemi, II, 340

Sicard, Marie. *See* Rateau

Sicard, Marie-Catherine. *See* Lamarre, *dit* Bélisle

Sicard, *dit* Marseille, Barthélemy, IV, 618

Sicot, Madeleine (Navières), III, 481

Sidney, Sir Henry, I, 331

Sierra. *See* Martínez

Sifert, M., II, 424

Sifert, Sébastienne. *See* Curie

Siginakee (Blackbird, Letourneau), IV, 233

Signay*, Joseph (1778–1850), III, 99

Sigogne*, Jean-Mandé (1763–1844), IV, xxix, 81

Sikes, Walter, I, 652

Silhouette, Étienne de, III, 30

Sillery. *See* Brulart

Silly, Jean-Baptiste de, II, **605–6**; III, 444

Silva. *See* Luján

Silvain. *See* Dupleix

Silvain, Timothée. *See* Sullivan, Timothy

Silver, Catherine. *See* Zouberbuhler

Silver, Mary. *See* Williams

Silver, Mary (rebaptized Adélaïde), II, **606–7**; IV, 765

Silver, Thomas, II, 606

Silver Heels. *See* Aroas

Silvy, Antoine, I, 56, 244, 653; II, **607–9**, 94; III, 104, 204; IV, 424

Simblin. *See also* Raimbault

Simblin, Jeanne-Françoise (Raimbault), II, 541, 542

Simcoe, Elizabeth Posthuma. *See* Gwillim

Simcoe, John, III, 210; IV, 163

Simcoe*, John Graves (1752–1806), IV, 12, 119, 198, 260, 418, 445, 499, 567, 677, 682, 689, 766

Simms, Pamela (Fitzgerald), IV, 159

Simon. *See* Pieskaret

Simon, Marie-Madeleine. *See* Lefebvre

Simon de Longpré, Françoise de. *See* Jourdan

Simon de Longpré, Jacques de, I, 607

Simon de Longpré, Marie-Catherine de, *dite* de Saint-Augustin, I, **607–10**, 31, 204, 310, 314, 457, 472, 551, 563; II, 84, 161

Simonds*, James (1735–1830), IV, 329, 389, 723

Simonet, Élisabeth. *See* Bériault

Simonet, Jean-Baptiste, III, 592

Simonet d'Abergemont, Geneviève. *See* Boucher de Grandpré

Simonet d'Abergemont, Jacques, III, **592–93**, 153, 351, 617; IV, 284, 362, 590

Simonet d'Abergemont, Jean-Baptiste, III, 593

Simonet d'Abergemont, Marie. *See* Foissey

Simonin, Maurice, III, 350; IV, 124

Simonnet, François, IV, **708–10**, 148, 270

Simonnet, Marguerite. *See* Bougret Dufort

Simonnet, Marguerite. *See* Neveu

Simonnet, Marie. *See* Boismenay

Simonnet, Marie-Louise, IV, 709

Simmonet, Philippe, IV, 708

Simons, Levy, IV, 332

Simpson, John, I, 107, 361, 493, 673

Simpson, Mary (Ellice), IV, 261

Sincennes. *See* Petitot

Sinclair, Andrew, I, 243

Sinclair, Henry, 1st Earl of Orkney, I, 680

Sinclair, Stephen, II, 231

Singleton, George, IV, **710–11**

Singleton, Henry, IV, 223

Singleton, John, IV, 710

Singleton, Mary. *See* Moore, Frances

Singleton, Nancy. *See* Ferguson

Sintré. *See* Legrand

Siongorochti. *See* Kaieñ?kwaahtoñ

Sirier. *See* Cirier

Sivadier, Marie (Horné, *dit* Laneuville), II, 292

Sivert. *See* L'Espérance

Sivot, Marie (Perrot), II, 517

Sjöman, Anna Magaretha (Sandin; Kalm), IV, 406

Skanudharoua (Skannud-Haroï) (Geneviève-Agnès de Tous-les-Saints), I, **610–11**

Skatzi. *See* Scorch Eye

Skeffington, George, II, **609**, 89, 626

Skene, William, III, 143, 276, 514

Skey, Miss (Durell), III, 208

Skidegate, IV, 420

Skillen, Sarah (Lyon), IV, 490

Skolvsson. *See* Scolvus

Skrimsher, Samuel (father), III, 593

Skrimsher, Samuel, III, **593–94**, 483

Skrimshire, Ann (Isham), III, 301

Skulkinanse, IV, 419, 420

Slade, Ann (mother of JOHN), IV, 711

Slade, David, IV, 713

Slade, John (father), IV, 711

Slade, John, IV, **711–14**

Slade, John, known as John Slade Jr, IV, 713

Slade, John Haitor, IV, 713

Slade, Martha. *See* Haitor

Slade, Robert (uncle), IV, 711, 713

Slade, Robert, IV, 713

Slade, Thomas (uncle), IV, 711

Slade, Thomas, IV, 713

Slany (Slaney), John, I, 233, 349, 350, 650

Slater, John, III, 277

Slave Woman. *See* Thanadelthur

Slichtenhorst. *See* Van Slichtenhorst

Sloane, Sir Hans, I, 669; II, 444

Small, Eliza. *See* Goldsmith

Small*, John (1746–1831), IV, 766
Small, Patrick, IV, 366, 741
Smart, Thomas, II, **609–10**, 15, 22, 198, 288, 524; III, 182, 456, 512, 597
Smith, Charlotte. *See* Brant
Smith*, Sir David William (1764–1837), IV, 766, 767
Smith, Francis, III, **594**, 303, 472
Smith, Harriet (Sewell), IV, 718
Smith, James (Newfoundland resident), II, 611
Smith, James, II, **610–11**
Smith, Janet. *See* Livingston
Smith, Jedidah (Osborn), IV, 593
Smith, John, I, 67, 101, 132, 262, 650
Smith, Joseph, III, **594–95**, 171, 287, 304; IV, 47
Smith, Kitty (wife of FRANCIS), III, 594
Smith, Mary. *See* Het
Smith*, Peter (d. 1826), IV, 494
Smith, Sir Thomas, I, 331, 335, 374
Smith, William (clergyman), III, 125
Smith, William (father of WILLIAM), IV, 714
Smith, William (merchant), IV, 266
Smith, William, IV, **714–18**, 37, 42, 299, 324, 345, 367, 372, 373, 400, 485, 493, 537, 576, 698
Smith*, William (1769–1847), III, 254; IV, 718
Smiths John. *See* Flemish Bastard
Smithsend, John, I, 612
Smithsend, Nicholas, I, **611**, 308; II, 266
Smithsend, Richard, I, **611–12**; II, 487
Smits Jan. *See* Flemish Bastard
Smollett, Tobias George, III, 370, 601; IV, 416
Smyth. *See also* Smith
Smyth*, Hervey (1734–1811), III, 592
Snell, Mary (Wheelwright), IV, 764
Sneppy. *See* Atkinson, George
Snorri Thorfinnsson, I, **612**, 5, 643
Snow Tail. *See* Waxaway
Snuff the Blanket, III, 654
Soiaga, Gaspard. *See* Kondiaronk
Soines, I, 66
Soissons, Comte de. *See* Bourbon
Solander, Daniel Carl, IV, 762
Solís. *See* Díaz
Solo, Henri, III, 410
Solomon, IV, 57
Solomons, Ezekiel, IV, 332, 524, 525, 718, 719, 726
Solomons, Lucius Levy, IV, **718–19**, 332, 725
Solomons, Rebecca. *See* Franks
Sombrun, Jean-Baptiste, III, 13
Sommerive, Comte de. *See* Lascaris
Sommillard, Catherine, I, 116
Sommillard, Louise (Fortin), I, 116
Sommillard, Marguerite, I, 116, 117
Soncino, Raimondo de, I, 22, 148, 149, 150, 164
Sondes, Baron. *See* Monson
Sononchiez. *See* Chabert de Joncaire, Louis-Thomas
Soranhes, I, 58, 59
Sorbier de Villars, François, IV, **719–20**, 189, 234, 510, 642
Sorel. *See* Saurel
Sores (Sors, Soré), Marie (Caën), I, 159
Sorester. *See* Forrester
Sosawaket. *See* Nissowaquet

Soto, Hernando de, I, 171
Souart, Gabriel, I, **612–13**, 108, 206, 220, 273, 508, 539, 592, 644, 647, 648; II, 46, 194, 335, 376, 401, 490; III, 612
Souart d'Adoucourt, Claude-Élisabeth (Le Moyne de Longueuil, Baronne de Longueuil), II, 401; III, 384; IV, 463
Soubiron, Judith (Maisonnat), II, 449; III, 421
Soubise, Prince de. *See* Rohan
Soubras, Pierre-Auguste de, II, **611–12**, 106, 219, 336, 339; III, 264, 389, 396, 475, 512, 576
Souhet, Marthe. *See* Bélanger
Soulage, Catherine (Boutet de Saint-Martin), I, 119
Soulanges. *See* Joybert
Soulard. *See also* Baudry
Soulard, Mathurin, I, 271
Soulard, Pascal, IV, 241
Soulègre, M. de, II, 182, 352
Soulier Rouge. *See* Matahachitoux
Soulignié (Souligny), Marie (Leduc), III, 369
Soullard, Catherine. *See* Boutet
Soullard, Jean (father), II, 612
Soullard, Jean, II, **612**
Soullard, Jean-Baptiste, II, 612
Soullard, Jeanne. *See* Couvreur
Soullard, Jeanne (Baudry, *dit* Des Butes), II, 48; III, 37
Soumande, Anne (Hazeur), II, 275, 277; III, 284; IV, 337
Soumande, Jean, II, 111, 598
Soumande, Louis, II, **612–13**; III, 397
Soumande, Louise, *dite* de Saint-Augustin, II, **613**, 93, 612; III, 330
Soumande, Marie-Anne-Marguerite (Coulon de Villiers de Jumonville), III, 150
Soumande, Pierre, II, 275, 612, 613; III, 153
Soumande, Simone. *See* Coté
Souoias. *See* Kondiaronk
Soupiran, Antoine, II, 613
Soupiran, Catherine. *See* Laborde
Soupiran, Charles-Simon, II, 614; III, 596
Soupiran, Charlotte (Hiché; Arnoux), III, 292
Soupiran, Louis-François, III, 553; IV, 539
Soupiran, Marie-Anne. *See* Gaultier
Soupiran, Marie-Jeanne. *See* Avisse
Soupiran, Marthe. *See* Bélanger
Soupiran, Simon (father), II, **613–14**; III, 595; IV, 178
Soupiran, Simon (son), II, 614; III, **595–96**
Sourdeval. *See* Le Gouès
Souste, Sieur, II, 134
Souste, André, III, 633; IV, **720–21**
Souste, Jean-Marie, IV, 720
Souste, Marguerite. *See* Vulliermet
Souste, Marie-Louise. *See* Estienne Du Bourgué de Clérin
Southack, Cyprian (father), III, 596
Southack, Cyprian, I, 90, 250, 299; II, 14, 46, 409; III, **596–97**, 635
Southack, Elizabeth. *See* Foy
Southack, Elizabeth. *See* Oakley
Southack, Elizabeth (Parnel; Tyng), III, 635
Southampton, Earl of. *See* Wriothesley
Southmayd, Allen, II, 152
Southouse, Edward, IV, 229, 345, 391
Southworth, Alice (Church), II, 145, 146
Southworth, Constant, II, 145

Southworth, Elizabeth. *See* Collier
Souvigny. *See* Rousseau
Sower, Catharine. *See* Sharpnack
Sower, Christopher (father), IV, 721
Sower, Christopher, IV, **721–22**, 483, 626
Sower, Hannah. *See* Knorr
Sozap (Suzack), II, 26
Spada, Cardinal, II, 280
Spagniolini, Catherine. *See* Bénard, *dit* Carignan
Spagniolini, Charlotte. *See* Bourleton
Spagniolini, Domenico, III, 597
Spagniolini, Françoise. *See* Boucher de Niverville
Spagniolini, Jean-Baptiste, III, 598
Spagniolini, Jean-Fernand, III, **597–98**
Spagniolini, Margherita. *See* Tussichi
Spagniolini, Marie-Apolline (Poudret), III, 598
Spagniolini, Marie-Élisabeth (Gamelin), III, 598
Spangenberg, Augustus Gottlieb (Bishop Joseph), III, 607
Spark*, Alexander (1762–1819), IV, 580, 581
Spence, George, III, 600, 654
Spence, James, IV, 48
Spence, John, III, 123, 124
Spencer, Miss (Treworgie), I, 652
Spencer, Mary (Hull; Phips), I, 544
Spencer, Robert, 1st Baron Spencer, I, 632
Spencer, William, I, 239, 240
Spert, Sir Thomas, I, 155, 371, 565
Spicer, Grace (Hayman), I, 365
Spicer, Richard, I, 565
Spinula, Agostino de, I, 150, 164
Spöring, Herman Diedrich, IV, 406
Spragge, William Prosperous, IV, 154
Spring, Barbara. *See* Henry
Sproule*, George (1743–1817), IV, 81
Spry, Anne (Goreham), IV, 308
Spry, Sir Richard, III, 293
Spry, William, IV, 108, 552, 561
Spurrell, George, II, 10; III, **598–99**, 483, 490, 593; IV, 583
Spurrell, Joseph, III, 598
Squando (Squanto), I, 650
Squanto (Squantum). *See* Tisquantum
Squash Cutter. *See* Yaghkaposin
Staats, Barent, III, 428
Staats, Elizabeth (Schuyler), III, 587
Staats, Isabella. *See* Lÿdius
Stach, Matthew, III, 212
Staffe, Philip, I, 375, 376, 378
Stainville, Comte de. *See* Choiseul
Stanhope, James, 1st Earl Stanhope, II, 250, 286
Stanley, Lady Charlotte (Burgoyne), IV, 113
Stanley, Edward, 11th Earl of Derby, III, 425; IV, 113
Stanley, James, known as Lord Strange, IV, 113
Stannard, William, I, 343
Stanser*, Robert (1760–1828), IV, 94
Stanton, Joanna (Denison), III, 174
Stanton, William, IV, 115
Stanyan, Catherine (Hardy, Lady Hardy), IV, 326
Staunton, Richard, II, 51, 62, 65, 312, 319, 492; III,
  599–600, 414, 489, 624
Stayner, Thomas, IV, 685
Stebbins, Abigail (rebaptized Marguerite) (Noyon), III, 493;
  IV, 765

Steed, Isabella (Mason), I, 496
Steel, Thomas, II, 497
Steele. *See also* Still
Steele, John, III, 405
Steele, Richard, IV, 553
Steele, William, IV, 526, 527
Steenoven, Cornelius, III, 640
Steenwijck, Cornelis van, I, 573
Steinmeyer, Ferdinand, known as Ferdinand Farmer, IV,
  270
Steinner, Jacob, IV, 386
Sterling, Angélique. *See* Cuillerier, *dit* Beaubien
Sterling, James, IV, **722**
Sterling (Stirling), Thomas, IV, 316
Sterns, Jonathan, IV, 604
Stevens, Ann. *See* Glasier
Stevens, Phineas, III, 21
Stevenson, Sarah (Christie), IV, 151
Stewart. *See also* Stuart
Stewart, Lady Elizabeth, I, 613
Stewart, James, Earl of Arran, I, 613
Stewart, James, 4th Lord Ochiltree, I, **613–14**, 25, 53, 54,
  248, 305, 482
Stewart, Jane. *See* Douglas
Stewart, John, IV, 401
Stewart, John, 4th Earl of Atholl, I, 613
Stewart*, John (d. 1834), IV, 129, 609, 610
Stewart, John James, III, 91
Stewart, Margaret. *See* Macdowall
Stewart, Mary. *See* Livingstone
Stewart*, Peter (1725–1805), IV, 129, 551, 608, 609, 610
Stewart, William, I, 613
Still (Steele), Murphy, IV, 626
Stirling. *See also* Sterling
Stirling, Countess of. *See* Erskine
Stirling, Earl of. *See* Alexander
Stirling, Elizabeth (Murray, Baroness Murray), IV, 569
Stobo, Robert, III, **600–2**, 149, 588; IV, 425, 709
Stobo, William, III, 600
Stockton, Rebecca (Cuthbert), IV, 190
Stoddard, Elizabeth (Fillis), IV, 267
Stoddard, John, II, 667
Stofflemire. *See* Tufflemire
Stokes, Jane, I, 81
Storer, Jeremiah, II, 54
Storer, Mary, II, 54
Storer, Priscilla, II, 54
Storer, Rachel (rebaptized Marie-Françoise) (Berger), II, 54
Storer, Ruth. *See* Masters
Stoughton, William, II, 452, 494
Stourton, Edward, I, 614
Stourton, Elizabeth. *See* Gravenor
Stourton, Erasmus, I, **614**, 163
Stourton, Mary, (wife of Edward), I, 614
Stout*, Richard (fl. 1791–1817), IV, 523
Stow, John, I, 151
Strachan, James, IV, 330
Strange, Lord. *See* Stanley
Strange*, James Charles Stuart (1753–1840), IV, 325, 498
Strange*, Sir Thomas Andrew Lumisden (1756–1841), IV,
  112
Stratham, Catherina (Bagshawe; Philipps), III, 518

Straunge, Robert, I, 239, 240
Street, Robert, I, 652
Street*, Samuel (1750–1815), IV, 113, 119
Stretton, John, IV, 176, 177
Stricklar, Oliver, II, 233
Strong, Richard, I, 306
Strouds, Gilles William (rebaptized Louis-Claude-Joseph), III, **602**, 340
Strouds, Marie-Josephte. *See* Morisseau
Strouds, Pierre, III, 602
Strouds, Rachel Relind. *See* Baionas
Strouds, William, III, 602
Strowbridge, Elizabeth (Bushell), III, 90
Strozzi, Philippe, I, 87
Stuart. *See also* Stewart
Stuart, Charles. *See* Charles Edward, the Young Pretender
Stuart, Henry Coleridge, IV, 811
Stuart, James. *See* James, the Old Pretender
Stuart, John, IV, xxxviii, 450
Stuart, John, 3rd Earl of Bute, IV, 571
Stuart*, John (1740–1811), IV, 418, 495, 692, 710, 730
Stuart, Mary. *See* Mary Stuart, Queen of Scots
Stuart, Peter, IV, 107, 324
Stuart, William, II, **614–16**, xxvii, xxviii, 171, 310, 319, 627, 628, 658; III, xxxii, 285
Studholme, Gilfred, IV, **723–24**, 80, 161
Studley, Daniel, I, 390, 392, 450
Subercase. *See* Auger
Sublet de Noyers, François, I, 313
Suckling, Frances. *See* Duport
Suckling, George, III, 130; IV, **724–26**, 37, 399, 415, 570
Suève, Edmond de, I, 321, 418; II, **616–17**; III, 311, 312
Sullivan, Daniel, III, 602
Sullivan, John, IV, 118, 405, 484, 549, 735
Sullivan (Silvain), Marie-Renée. *See* Gaultier de Varennes
Sullivan, Mary Elizabeth. *See* MacCarthy
Sullivan, Timothy, known as Timothée Silvain, III, **602–4**, 246, 271, 373, 675; IV, 235
Sully, Duc de. *See* Béthune
Sulte*, Benjamin (1841–1923), III, 305, 629; IV, 168, 232
Surlaville. *See* Le Courtois
Surrey, Earl of. *See* Howard
Sutherland*, Daniel (d. 1832), IV, 311
Sutherland, George (HBC employee), IV, 727
Sutherland, George, IV, **726–27**, 524
Sutherland, James, IV, **727–28**
Sutherland, John, IV, 727
Sutherland, Patrick, III, **604–5**, 295, 513; IV, 780
Sutton, Mary, Baroness Lexington. *See* St Leger
Suzack. *See* Sozap
Suzanne. *See* Gouentagrandi
Swaine, Charles, III, 502
Swan, II, **617**
Swanley, Robert, I, 567
Swanton, Emma (wife of ROBERT), III, 606
Swanton, Robert, III, **605–6**, xxv, 132; IV, 210
Swart, Claudius Clavus, I, 18, 680
Swatana, III, **606–8**, xxxviii, xl; IV, lvi
Sweetland, Henry, IV, 784
Swett, Sarah (Marston), IV, 516
Swift, Jonathan, II, 444
Swiggett, Howard, IV, 121

Sydenham, Thomas, III, 677
Sydney, Viscount. *See* Townshend
Sylvain, Isabelle. *See* Veau, *dit* Sylvain, Élisabeth-Marguerite
Sylvain, Mathurine (Talbot), III, 612
Sym, Robert, IV, 82
Symes, Susanna Catharine (Ogilvie), IV, 586
Syrier. *See* Cirier
Szkolny. *See* Scolvus

TACHÉ*, Alexandre-Antonin (1823–94), III, 609
Taché, Étienne, III, 608
Taché*, Sir Étienne-Paschal (1795–1865), III, 609
Taché, Jean, III, **608–9**, 76, 160, 340; IV, 67, 306, 362
Taché*, Jean-Baptiste (1786–1849), III, 609
Taché*, Joseph-Charles (1820–94), III, 609
Taché, Marguerite. *See* Dauzet
Taché, Marie-Anne. *See* Jolliet de Mingan
Taffanel de La Jonquière, Catherine de. *See* Bonnes
Taffanel de La Jonquière, Jacques-Pierre de, Marquis de La Jonquière, III, **609–12**, 6, 22, 27, 29, 30, 69, 100, 148, 169, 183, 204, 214, 243, 246, 255, 289, 320, 329, 356, 357, 375, 378, 385, 400, 428, 435, 451, 484, 486, 496, 502, 561, 570, 628, 629; IV, 15, 35, 45, 63, 66, 79, 91, 145, 173, 174, 202, 213, 236, 237, 254, 256, 271, 289, 311, 382, 407, 449, 454, 455, 459, 470, 512, 514, 614, 615, 623, 633, 651, 666, 667, 688, 692, 728
Taffanel de La Jonquière, Jean de, III, 609
Taffanel de La Jonquière, Marie-Angélique de, Marquise de La Jonquière. *See* La Valette
Tagancout. *See* Tekanoet
Tagaskouïta. *See* Tekakwitha
Tagawirunte. *See* Tekawirofite
Tahahaiadoris, III, 95, 652; IV, 408
Taiearonk, I, 354
Taignoagny, I, 11, 166, 167, 275, 276
Tailer, Elizabeth (Nelson), III, 494
Tailhandier, Antoine, II, 617
Tailhandier, Jeanne (Tétro), II, 627
Tailhandier, *dit* La Beaume, Madeleine. *See* Baudry
Tailhandier, *dit* La Beaume, Marien, II, **617–18**, 470, 627; III, 397, 598
Také, III, 527, 529
Talbot, Jacques (father), III, 612
Talbot, Jacques, III, **612–13**, 221
Talbot, Mathurine. *See* Sylvain
Talon, Le. *See* Le Talon
Talon, Anne. *See* Bury
Talon, Artus, I, 614
Talon, Denis, I, 629
Talon, Jean, II, 555
Talon (Talon Du Quesnoy), Jean, I, **614–32**, 29, 32, 34, 35, 36, 47, 48, 55, 60, 62, 63, 85, 86, 111, 116, 119, 120, 127, 135, 146, 174, 175, 185, 193, 198, 203, 226, 237, 238, 248, 260, 261, 287, 297, 313, 315, 326, 327, 340, 345, 355, 393, 394, 399, 400, 416, 418, 464, 494, 534, 535, 536, 539, 540, 550, 553, 555, 556, 560, 565, 570, 571, 580, 581, 582, 592, 600, 602, 648; II, xviii, xix, 17, 28, 59, 85, 86, 141, 179, 181, 242, 295, 338, 344, 347, 367, 368, 369, 378, 380, 418, 467, 488, 508, 517, 531, 533, 559, 592, 653; III, 60, 62, 201, 202, 247, 308, 311, 548, 581, 648; IV, 356, 360

Talon, Marguerite (Raudot), II, 555
Talon, Marie-Louise, Marquise de Boulay. *See* Molé
Talon, Marie-Suzanne (Phélypeaux), II, 555
Talon, Omèr, I, 629
Talon, Omer, Marquis de Boulay, III, 458
Talon, Phillippe, I, 614
Talon de Boulay, Angélique-Louise (Montcalm, Marquise de Montcalm), III, 458, 467
Talus, *dit* Vendamont, Julien, II, 465
Tamburini, Michelangelo, III, 335, 336
Tanaghrisson, III, **613–15**, xxxvi, 101, 148, 150, 319, 320
Tancré, Antoine, II, 374
Tancré, Jean, II, 374
Tandihetsi, I, 71, 404; II, 83
Tanfield, Anne (wife of Clement), I, 632
Tanfield, Clement, I, 632
Tanfield, Elizabeth, I, 632
Tanfield, Sir Francis, I, **632**, 669
Tanfield, Sir Lawrence, I, 632
Tangeux. *See* Courtin
Tanguay*, Cyprien (1819–1902), III, 122, 125, 140, 141, 391, 410, 602, 629
Tantouin de La Touche, Louis, II, **618–19**, 36, 114, 147, 353, 574; III, 563
Tantouin de La Touche, Madeleine. *See* Girard
Taondechoren, I, **632–33**, 11
Taouestaouis. *See* Le Moyne de Maricourt, Paul
Taratouan (Taratwane), I, **633**, 637, 639
Tarbell, Elizabeth. *See* Wood
Tarbell, John, III, **615**
Tarbell, Sarah (rebaptized Marguerite), III, 615
Tarbell, Thomas (father), III, 615
Tarbell, Thomas, III, 615
Tarbell, Zachariah, III, 615
Tard. *See* Du Tartre
Tardy, François, II, 466
Tardy, Marie, II, 326
Tareha, I, **633–34**; II, 255
Targis. *See* Pinguet
Tarieu de Lanaudière, Catherine (Aubert de Gaspé), IV, 34
Tarieu de La Naudière, Charles-François, III, 312; IV, **728–30**, xliii, 91
Tarieu* de Lanaudière, Charles-Louis (1743–1811), IV, 43, 50, 427, 547, 716, 729
Tarieu de La Naudière, Louise-Geneviève. *See* Deschamps de Boishébert
Tarieu de La Naudière, Marie-Catherine. *See* Le Moyne de Longueuil
Tarieu* de Lanaudière, Xavier-Roch (1771–1813), IV, 729
Tarieu de La Pérade, Madeleine-Marie-Anne (Testu de La Richardière; Coulon de Villiers; Gaultier), III, 150, 620, 676
Tarieu de La Pérade, Marie-Madeleine. *See* Jarret de Verchères
Tarieu de La Pérade, Pierre-Thomas, I, 418; II, 547; III, 311, 312, 313, 519, 676; IV, 216, 728
Tarihia (Christine), I, 652
Tarride Duhaget, Antoinette. *See* Saint-Thairau
Tarride Duhaget, Charles, III, 615
Tarride Duhaget, Marguerite. *See* Rousseau de Villejouin
Tarride Duhaget, Robert, II, 220; III, **615–16**, 533; IV, 15, 444, 644, 688
Tarrigha (Tarsha). *See* Tareha

Taschereau*, Elzéar-Alexandre (1820–98), III, 617
Taschereau*, Gabriel-Elzéar (1745–1809), III, 617; IV, 72, 549
Taschereau, Marie-Anne-Louise, *dite* de Saint-François-Xavier, III, 617
Taschereau, Marie-Claire. *See* Fleury de La Gorgendière
Taschereau, Thomas-Jacques, III, **616–17**, 69, 154, 179, 217, 300, 353, 592; IV, 284, 359, 361, 362, 363, 421, 590
Taschereau de Sapaillé, Christophe, III, 616
Taschereau de Sapaillé, Renée. *See* Boutin
Tasquantum. *See* Tisquantum
Tassé*, Joseph (1848–95), IV, 637
Tassy, Félix de, I, 81; III, 237
Tatamy, Tunda (baptized Moses), IV, 27
Tate, Mary (Hardy, Lady Hardy), IV, 326
Tatnam, James, I, 553, 666
Taudet. *See* Tollet
Taverner, Abraham, III, 618
Taverner, Rachel (wife of WILLIAM), III, 618
Taverner, William (father), III, 618
Taverner, William, II, 118, 439, 487, 583, 611; III, **617–20**
Taverner, William (3rd), III, 619
Tavernier de La Forest, *dit* La Lochetière, Jean, I, 267, 269; II, 234
Tawmaugh, IV, 57
Taxous, II, 475
Tayler, Henry, I, 228, 229
Taylor, Mrs. *See* Durell
Taylor, Henry (father), IV, 399
Taylor, Henry, IV, 400
Taylor, James, II, 56
Taylor, John, IV, 400
Taylor, Nathaniel, IV, 89
Taylor, Sarah (Mitchell), III, 453
Taylor, William, IV, 604
Taylor, Wittewronge, III, 208
Taylour, Joseph, II, **619**, 152, 291, 439
Taylour, Thomas, II, 619
Tayorheasere. *See* Teiorhénhsere?
Téata, III, 528, 529
Techenet, Mme. *See* Couc, Elizabeth
Tecumseh* (1768–1813), II, 316
Teedyuscung, III, 323; IV, 27
Tee Yee Neen Ho Ga Row. *See* Theyanoguin
Tegakwitha. *See* Tekakwitha
Tegancourt (Tegancout, Tegancouti, Teganeout). *See* Tekanoet
Teganissorens, I, 445, 634; II, **619–23**, xxx, xxxi, xxxvi, 169, 321, 401, 502, 631; III, 321, 622
Tegannehout. *See* Tekanoet
Tegarihogen (Tegariouguen, Teharihogen). *See* Tekarihoken
Tegaskouïta. *See* Tekakwitha
Tegonhatsiongo (Anastasie), I, 635
Teharonhiagannra, I, 460
Tehastakout. *See* Tonatakout
Tehoragwanegen* (d. 1849), IV, 770
Tehorenhaegnon, I, **634–35**
Teiorhénhsere?, IV, **730–31**
Teissier, Jean, IV, 386
Teiyoquande. *See* Teyohaqueande
Tekakwitha (Kateri), I, **635–36**, 522; II, 139, 144, 341
Tekanoet, II, **623–24**, xxxix, 256; III, xl

Tekarihoken, II, **624–25**, xxxiv
Tekawironte, IV, **731**
Tekouerimat. *See* Negabamat
Telari-o-lin. *See* Vincent, Zacharie
Temple, Dorothy. *See* Lee
Temple, Sir John, I, 636
Temple, Mary (Nelson), II, 494
Temple, Robert, III, 123, 662
Temple, Sir Thomas (grandfather), I, 636
Temple, Sir Thomas, I, **636–37**, 25, 62, 63, 241, 399, 407, 434, 435, 436, 475, 500, 513, 595, 605, 654, 666, 667; II, 459, 494; III, 653; IV, xvii, xxiv
Tenanguer. *See* Duparc
Teondechoren (Joseph), I, 42, 212, 344, 523
Teoniahigarawe. *See* Theyanoguin
Teouatiron, I, **637–38**, 633
Terlaye. *See* Magon
Terme, Jean, II, 604, 605
Termont. *See* Demay
Ternay. *See* Arsac
Ternay, Marquise de. *See* Lefebvre de Laubrière
Terriau (Terriault). *See* Terriot
Terrick, Richard, IV, 104
Terrier de Francheville et de Repentigny, Jeanne. *See* Jallot
Terrier de Francheville et de Repentigny, Marin, I, 553; II, 227
Terriot, Cécile. *See* Landry
Terriot, Jeanne (Tibaudeau), II, 257, 629
Terriot, Jehan, II, 625
Terriot, Marie (Cormier; Landry), IV, 436
Terriot, Perrine. *See* Ruau
Terriot, Pierre, II, **625**
Terron. *See* Colbert
Terroux, François, III, 620; IV, 731
Terroux, Jacques, III, **620**; IV, **731**, 629
Tessier, Élisabeth (Damours), I, 245
Tessier, Jacques, II, 11
Tessier, Laurent, I, 452
Tessier, Marie (Maleray de La Périne), II, 450
Tessier, *dit* Chaumine, Paul, IV, 732
Tessier (Texier), *dit* Lavigne, Jacques (father), IV, 732
Tessier, *dit* Lavigne, Jacques, IV, 732
Tessier, *dit* Lavigne, Jean, II, 133
Tessier, *dit* Lavigne, Jeanne. *See* Lefebvre
Tessier, *dit* Lavigne, Marie. *See* Adhémar, *dit* Saint-Martin
Tessier, *dit* Lavigne, Paul, IV, **731–33**
Tessier, *dit* Lavigne, Urbain, I, 427; II, 164
Tessouat (fl. 1603–13), I, **638–39**, 6, 192, 662
Tessouat (d. 1636), I, **639**, 10, 222, 489, 516, 633
Tessouat (Tesswehas) (d. 1654), I, **640–41**, 548, 558
Testard de La Forest, Gabriel, I, **641**, 180; II, 298, 394, 406, 626
Testard de La Forest, Jacques, I, 641; II, 626
Testard de La Forest, Marie. *See* Pournin
Testard de Montigny, Jacques, II, **625–27**, 36, 37, 118, 252, 395, 495, 534, 563, 609, 653; III, 81, 105, 238, 243, 278, 488, 505; IV, 733
Testard de Montigny, Jean-Baptiste-Philippe, IV, **733–34**, 449
Testard de Montigny, Marguerite. *See* Damours de Chauffours
Testard de Montigny, Marie-Amable (Gaultier de La Vérendrye), III, 243

Testard de Montigny, Marie-Anne. *See* La Porte de Louvigny
Testard de Montigny, Marie-Charlotte. *See* Trottier Desrivières
Testu, Captain, I, 300
Testu, Guillaume, I, 679
Testu de La Richardière, Madeleine-Marie-Anne. *See* Tarieu de La Pérade
Testu de La Richardière, Marie. *See* Hurault
Testu de La Richardière, Richard, II, 520; III, **620–22**, 22, 150, 676; IV, 10, 360, 619
Testu Du Tilly, Geneviève. *See* Rigault
Testu Du Tilly, Pierre, III, 620
Tête Blanche, La. *See* Gray Lock
Tetesigaguoy (Marie-Madeleine) (Jérémie, *dit* Lamontagne), II, 256, 296
Tétro, Jean-Baptiste, II, **627**, 617
Tétro, Jeanne. *See* Tailhandier
Tétro, Louis, II, 627
Tétro, Marie-Noëlle. *See* Landeau
Têtu*, Henri (1849–1915), III, 546, 712; IV, 95
Teuleron, Pierre, I, 401
Tewathiron. *See* Teouatiron
Texier. *See also* Tessier
Texier de La Touche, Marie-Reine. *See* Berbudeau
Texier de La Touche, Pierre-Alexis, IV, 56
Teyarhasere. *See* Teiorhéñhsere?
Teyohaqueande, IV, **734–35**, 596
Teyoninhokarawen. *See* Norton, John
Thacter, Mary (Gorham), III, 260; IV, 308
Thanadelthur, II, **627–28**, xxvii, 319, 614, 615; III, xxxii
Thanayieson. *See* Tanaghrisson
Thaonawyuthe* (d. 1859), IV, 404, 406
Tharbell. *See* Tarbell
Tharca. *See* Tareha
Thaumur de La Source, Dominique, II, 628
Thaumur de La Source, Dominique-Antoine-René, II, **628**, 117; III, 105, 443, 640
Thaumur de La Source, Jeanne. *See* Bonhomme
Thaumur de La Source, Marie-Louise, IV, 235
Thavenet, Élisabeth de. *See* Mancelin
Thavenet, Marguerite de (Hertel de La Fresnière), I, 185; II, **628–29**, 284; III, 7, 83, 288
Thavenet, Marie-Françoise de, I, 185; II, 628, 629
Thavenet, Raymond de, II, 628
Thaxter, Samuel, III, 200
Thayendanegea* (d. 1807), III, xxxvii, 323; IV, liv, lv, lvi, lvii, 119, 121, 130, 149, 155, 405, 406, 416, 613, 692, 710, 731, 756
Thayer, Simeon, IV, 550
Thearihogen. *See* Tekarihoken
Théberge. *See* Thiberge
Thémines, Marquis de. *See* Lauzières
Thérèse. *See* Oionhaton
Thériaud (Thériault, Thério). *See* Terriot
Théry, Antoine, II, 161
Théry, Marguerite (Crespieul), II, 161
Thevet, André, I, **679–80**, 88, 170, 276, 423, 424, 425, 426; III, 337
Thévin, Judith (Champion de Cicé), II, 130
Thewathiron. *See* Teouatiron
Theyanoguin, III, **622–24**, 185, 186, 322, 331; IV, lvii, 154, 395, 416, 691

Thibaudeau (Thibodeau). *See* Tibaudeau
Thibault (Tibault), Charles, I, 246; III, 681
Thibault, Claude, II, 457
Thibault, Louise. *See* Guyon
Thibault, Marie-Madeleine (Verrier), III, 646
Thiberge (Théberge), Jean, I, 394
Thibierge, Élisabeth-Cécile (Estèbe), IV, 263
Thibierge, Étienne, IV, 263
Thibierge, Jacques, III, 523
Thibodeau, Agnès. *See* Dugas
Thibodeau, Agnès (Brossard, *dit* Beausoleil), III, 87
Thibodeau, Michel, III, 87
Thiboult, Thomas, II, **629**, 90, 528
Thierry. *See also* Chassin
Thierry, M., II, 155
Thierry (Primot), Catherine (Le Moyne de Longueuil et de
    Châteauguay), I, 463, 465, 507; II, 133, 390, 401, 403,
    406, 469, 508; III, 379
Thierry, Catherine (Louet), II, 447
Thierry, Élisabeth. *See* Messier
Thierry, Guillaume, II, 469
Thiersant, François-Gabriel de, II, 221
Thiersant, François-Henri de, II, 221
Thiersant, Marie-Josephe de. *See* Fézeret
Thiersant, Pierre-François de, II, 221
Thiersault, Marguerite (Poncet de La Rivière et de Brétigny),
    I, 551
Thiollière, Simon-Pierre, IV, 306
Thirel. *See* Pichon
Thirement, Anne (Peiras), II, 514
Thirement, Jacques, II, 514
Thirement, Marie. *See* Hubert
Thirkill, Lancelot, I, **641**, 120, 150, 164
Thoizy. *See* Petit
Thomas, George, IV, 600
Thomas, Isaiah, III, 91, 267; IV, 342, 343
Thomas, Jean, I, **642**, 442, 490, 569
Thomas, John (bishop), III, 634
Thomas, John (general), IV, 548, 549
Thomas, John (HBC employee), IV, 525
Thomas, John (merchant), I, 343
Thomé, Antoinette (Collet), II, 149
Thomelin, Ambroise. *See* Aulquoy
Thomelin, Jean de, I, 213
Thomelin, Marie de (Chomedey), I, 213
Thomey, Arthur, IV, 177
Thompson*, David (1770–1857), IV, 647, 685, 741
Thompson, Edward, III, **624–25**, 449, 544, 663
Thompson, Henrietta (Wolfe), III, 666
Thompson, Joseph, I, **642**, 232, 281, 607, 666
Thompson, William, IV, 320, 549
Thomson, Archibald, IV, 494
Thomson, J., IV, 295
Thomson, James, IV, 491, 554
Thorbjörn, I, 612
Thordarson. *See* Thorfinnr
Thorfinnr *karlsefni* Thordarson, I, **642–43**, 5, 448, 449, 612
Thorfinnsson. *See* Snorri
Thorgerdr, I, 103
Thorne, Robert (father), I, **643–44**, 302
Thorne, Robert (son), I, **643–44**, 21, 148, 302
Thorne, William, I, 302

Thornton, Joshua, IV, 487
Thorsteinn, I, 448, 449, 612, 642
Thorvaldr, I, 449, 612, 643
Thorvaldr Asvaldsson, I, 676
Thorvaldsson. *See* Eirikr
Thrale, Hester Lynch. *See* Salusbury
Thu a higon. *See* Ruehegan
Thubières de Levy de Queylus, Gabriel, I, **644–49**, 46, 56,
    57, 78, 126, 220, 310, 486, 552, 559, 599, 612, 662; II,
    45, 191, 192, 194, 247, 360, 361, 364, 370, 637
Thunay, *dit* Dufresne, Catherine (Demers Monfort;
    Houdin), III, 295, 296
Thunay, *dit* Dufresne, Madeleine (Pelletier; Mallet), III, 423
Thuot Duval, Pierre, III, 581
Thurlow, Edward, IV, xlvi
Thury, Louis-Pierre, I, **649**, 309, 577; II, 238, 630; III, 476
Thyerry, Charlotte (Chassin), III, 115
Tiahogwando. *See* Teyohaqueande
Tibaudeau. *See also* Thibodeau
Tibaudeau, Agnès (Brossard), II, 105
Tibaudeau, Jeanne. *See* Terriot
Tibaudeau, Jeanne (Goutin), II, 205, 257, 630; III, 264
Tibaudeau, Marguerite (Brossard), II, 105
Tibaudeau, Pierre, II, **629–30**, 71, 105, 257, 410, 654
Tibault. *See* Thibault
Tibierge, M., I, **630**
Tibierge, Angélique, *dite* de Sainte-Agnès, III, 625
Tibierge, Hippolyte, III, 625
Tibierge, Marie-Catherine, *dite* de Saint-Joachim, III,
    625–26
Tibierge, Renée. *See* Hervé
Tiblemont, Nicolas, I, 267
Tigoransera. *See* Teiorhénhsereʔ
Tilliard, Henry, I, 369
Tilly. *See* Legardeur
Timothée, Captain, I, 292
Tin, Antoinette (Chaudillon), II, 140
Ting. *See* Tyng
Tinling, William, IV, 684
Tionnotoguen. *See* Togouiroui
Tipton, John, I, 85
Tirel. *See* Pichon
Tisnet (Tissenay). *See* Dutisné
Tison, Jean-Baptiste, IV, 533
Tison, Marie-Anne (Mesplet), IV, 533
Tisquantum (Squanto, Squantum), I, **649–50**, 262
Tisserant de Moncharvaux, François, III, 626
Tisserant de Moncharvaux, Jean-Baptiste, III, 626
Tisserant de Moncharvaux, Jean-Baptiste-François, III,
    626–27
Tisserant de Moncharvaux, Marie-Agnès. *See* Chassin
Tisserant de Moncharvaux, Marie-Louise. *See* Vienne
Tisserant de Moncharvaux, Marie-Thérèse. *See* L'Arche-
    vêque
Titailt. *See* Blarye
Tiwatacout. *See* Tonatakout
Tiyanoga. *See* Theyanoguin
Tiyerhasere. *See* Teiorhénhsereʔ
Toby, Maurice, I, 148, 149
Todd, Elizabeth (Patterson), IV, 606
Todd*, Isaac (d. 1819), IV, 184, 277, 703
Tofflemire. *See* Tufflemier
Togouiroui (Togoniron), I, **650–51**, 322; II, 107

Tohaswuchdoniunty. *See* Kaghswaghtaniunt

Tohonsiowanne. *See* Ohonsiowanne

Tokhrahenehiaron, I, 370, 403

Tollendal, Baron de. *See* Lally

Tollet (Taudet), Marie (Lanoullier), III, 352

Tomah (Tomas, Tomer, Tomma), Pierre, IV, **735–36**, 13, 30, 196, 389, 693

Tombelles. *See* Marquette

Tomison*, William (1739–1829), IV, 47, 366, 518, 684, 726, 727, 742, 743, 760

Tonatakout, II, **631**, xxxix, 20, 323, 502; III, xl

Tonge, Martha Grace. *See* Cottnam

Tonge*, William Cottnam (b. 1764, d. in or after 1825), IV, 737

Tonge, Winckworth, IV, **736–38**, 93, 451

Tonnancour. *See* Godefroy

Tonnetuit. *See* Chauvin

Tonsahoten, I, **651**, 321; II, 107

Tonty, Alphonse, II, 219, 632; III, 627

Tonty, Alphonse (de), Baron de Paludy, I, 416, 547; II, **631–33**, 48, 81, 300, 306, 353, 355, 435, 508, 645; III, 45, 96, 105, 288, 289, 485, 493, 627; IV, 634

Tonty, Claude-Joseph, III, 627

Tonty, Henri (de), I, 79, 114, 175, 176, 177, 178, 444; II, **633–36**, xxxii, 49, 76, 110, 124, 169, 170, 171, 173, 181, 306, 320, 397, 435, 443, 450, 488, 508, 589, 624, 631, 672; III, 65, 380, 469

Tonty, Isabelle de. *See* Liette

Tonty, Laurent (Lorenzo) de, Baron de Paludy, II, 631, 633

Tonty, Marie-Anne. *See* Picoté de Belestre

Tonty, Marie-Anne (de). *See* La Marque

Tonty, Marie-Françoise, II, 632

Tonty, Marie-Josette (Damours de Louvières), II, 633

Tonty, Pierre-Antoine, II, 632; III, 627

Tonty, Thérèse (Desjordy), II, 633

Tonty de Liette, Charles-Henri-Joseph de, II, 436, 632; III, **627**

Tonty de Liette, Louise de. *See* Renaud Dubuisson

Tonty de Liette, Marie-Madeleine de. *See* Sabourin

Toosey, James, IV, 738

Toosey, John, IV, 738

Toosey, Philip, IV, **738–39**

Toosey, Sarah. *See* Denton

Tootac (Palliser), IV, 536, 537

Torakaron. *See* Tarbell, Zachariah

Torcapel, Jean, I, 91

Torrington, Viscount. *See* Byng

Torrington, Viscountess. *See* Masters

Totiri (Totihri), I, **651–52**, 42, 523

Tottenham, Synge, IV, 388

Touaniscou, I, 69

Touchet, Geneviève. *See* Gagnier

Touchet, Simon, III, 377

Touchet, Thomas, II, 90

Toulouse, Comte de. *See* Bourbon

Toupin, Louise-Renée (Barbel), II, 42

Toupin, Marguerite. *See* Boucher

Toupin, Toussaint, I, 404; II, 82

Toupin, *dit* Dussault, Françoise. *See* Delisle

Tour, Anne de (Pastour de Costebelle), II, 389, 511

Tour, Catherine de. *See* Le Baudy

Tour, Germain de, II, 389, 511

Tour, Marie-Anne de (Allard de Sainte-Marie), II, 15; IV, 14

Tourblanche. *See* Martinet de Fonblanche

Toureault, Françoise (Archambault), I, 427

Tournefort. *See* Pitton

Tourneuve. *See* Loubinois

Tournois, Jean-Baptiste, III, **627–28**, 329, 361, 428, 481, 611; IV, 36

Tourville. *See* Duteau

Toussaint, Jeanne (Carpentier), II, 528

Toussiqui. *See* Tussichi

Townsend, Elizabeth. *See* Larcum

Townsend, Isaac, III, **628–29**

Townsend, Sir Isaac, III, 628

Townshend, Charles, IV, 84, 147, 571

Townshend, Charles, 2nd Viscount Townshend, IV, 168

Townshend, Charles, 3rd Viscount Townshend, III, 669

Townshend*, George, 4th Viscount and 1st Marquess Townshend (1723/24–1807), III, xxvi, 172, 365, 466, 669, 670, 672, 674; IV, 109, 147, 308, 541, 570, 608, 609, 610, 652, 700, 701

Townshend, Mary (Cornwallis), IV, 168

Townshend, Thomas, 1st Viscount Sydney, IV, 6, 230, 293, 367, 371, 485, 687, 707

Tracy. *See* Prouville

Tracy, Marquise de. *See* Fouilleuse

Trahan, Guillaume, II, 94

Trahan, Jeanne (Bourgeois), II, 94

Tranchant, Antoine, III, 398

Tranchant, Élisabeth. *See* Contant

Traquair*, Ramsay (1874–1952), III, 118, 346

Traversy, Captain de, I, 40, 308

Travis, Esther (Barnard), III, 25

Trefflé, *dit* Rottot, Agathe (Imbert), III, 299

Trefflé, *dit* Rottot, François, III, 135, 596

Trefflé, *dit* Rottot, Madeleine (Schmid; Janson, *dit* Lapalme), III, 307

Trefflé, *dit* Rottot, Marie-Jeanne. *See* Avisse

Trefflé, *dit* Rottot, Pierre, III, 135, 348

Tregouaroti, I, 603

Trégu de Langon, Madeleine-Angélique (Verville), II, 648

Tréguron. *See* Quéré

Trelawny, Edward, III, 316

Trémais. *See* Pichot

Tremblay, Henri-Jean, II, 79, 80, 109, 117, 134, 171, 207, 227, 341; III, **683–85**, 51, 52, 413, 470, 636

Tressol, Marguerite (Roubaud), IV, 685

Tressonville. *See* Chardon

Trevanion, Sir Nicholas, II, **636–37**, 152, 164, 564

Trevanion, Richard, II, 636

Trevannion, Sophia (Byron), IV, 121

Trevenen, James, IV, 413

Trevet, Françoise de (Benoist), IV, 54

Trevor, Frances Hornby (Barkley), IV, 498

Trevor, Sir John, I, 144

Trevor, Richard, III, 275

Trewerghy. *See* Treworgie

Treworgie, Mrs. *See* Spencer

Treworgie, Catherine. *See* Shapleigh

Treworgie, James, I, 652

Treworgie, John, I, **652–53**, 24, 406

Treworgie, John (son), I, 652

Treytorrens, Marie-Madeleine de (Haldimand), IV, 793

Tribouillard, Catherine (Ramezay), II, 545

Tribouillard, Hilaire, II, 545

Tronjoly. *See* L'Ollivier
Tronquet, Guillaume, I, 557, 558; II, 82
Tronson, Louis, I, 80, 117, 134, 180, 244; II, 44, 124, 128, 175, 191, 194, 195, 196, 241, 245, 272, 326, 336, 467, 594, 638, 641; III, 542
Trotain, François, II, 637
Trotain, Jeanne. *See* Gribond
Trotain, *dit* Saint-Seürin, François, II, **637**
Trotain, *dit* Saint-Seürin, Jeanne. *See* Hardy
Trotain, *dit* Saint-Seürin, Marie-Charlotte (Rouillard), II, 637
Trottier, Dom, III, 161
Trottier, Catherine (Lefebvre, *dit* Laciseraye), II, 382
Trottier, Catherine, *dite* Saint-François, III, 629
Trottier, Geneviève. *See* La Fond
Trottier, Jean-Baptiste, III, 629
Trottier, Jules, III, 629
Trottier, Marguerite, *dite* Saint-Joseph, III, **629–30**, 17, 574, 575
Trottier, *dit* Beaubien, Michel, II, 380
Trottier Desauniers, Catherine. *See* Charest
Trottier Desauniers, Jacques, III, 632
Trottier Desauniers, Marguerite. *See* Chéron
Trottier Desauniers, Marguerite (Charest), IV, 141
Trottier Desauniers, Marie-Catherine (Charest), IV, 141
Trottier Desauniers, Pierre (father), III, 631; IV, 739
Trottier Desauniers, Pierre, II, 43, 66, 125; III, **631–32**, 111, 434, 509; IV, 10, 141, 362, 650, 739
Trottier Desauniers, Pierre-François, III, 632
Trottier Desauniers Beaubien, Catherine (Lévesque), IV, 476
Trottier Desrivières, Catherine (Dejordy de Villebon), III, 171
Trottier Desrivières, Julien, IV, 178
Trottier Desrivières, Marie-Charlotte (Testard de Montigny), IV, 733
Trottier-Desrivières, Pierre-Julien, IV, 284
Trottier Desrivières-Beaubien, Eustache Ignace, IV, 318, 508
Trottier Desrivières-Beaubien, Marguerite-Alexis. *See* Malhiot
Trottier Des Ruisseaux, Antoine, II, 533
Trottier Des Ruisseaux, Marie-Anne (Martel), II, 459
Trottier Desruisseaux. Marie-Catherine (Cuillerier, *dit* Beaubien; Picoté de Belestre), IV, 632
Trottier Dufy Desauniers, Marie-Thomas. *See* Fleury de La Gorgendière
Trottier Dufy Desauniers, Thomas-Ignace, IV, **739–40**, 549
Trouin. *See* Duguay-Trouin
Trout, Nehemiah, I, 496
Trouvé, Claude, I, 82, 544, 599, 647; II, **637–39**, 45, 130, 184, 410, 522
Troyes, Madeleine de. *See* Alard
Troyes, Marie de. *See* Petit de L'Estang
Troyes, Michel de, I, 653
Troyes, Pierre de, known as Chevalier de Troyes, I, **653–54**, 39, 56, 107, 130, 315, 324, 329, 361, 417, 465, 509, 529, 537, 606, 611, 657, 672; II, 49, 62, 69, 101, 102, 120, 231, 267, 284, 307, 319, 390, 391, 392, 393, 405, 412, 445, 563, 581, 607, 608
Truchi (Truchy), Jeanne-Antoinette de (Adhémar de Lantagnac), III, 5
Trudelle, Charles, IV, 9

True, Jemima (March), II, 452
True, Ruth (Gyles), III, 273
Truillier, *dit* Lacombe, Jeanne (Guy), III, 271
Trumbull, Jonathan, IV, 527
Truteau, Marie (Arnaud), III, 17
Trye, James, IV, 262
Tryggvesson. *See* Olaf I
Tryon, William, IV, 427, 613
Tsawouenhouhi*, known as Nicolas Vincent (d. 1830), III, 650
Tsondatsaa (Charles), I, 42, 523
Tsondoutannen (Thomas), I, 143
Tucker, Frances (Montresor), IV, 552
Tuckey, Jack, II, 233
Tuffet, Jean, I, 248, 490, 593
Tufflemier (Tufflemear), Jacob, IV, 778
Tufflemier (Stofflemire), Ruth (wife of Jacob), IV, 777, 778
Tufton Mason, Anna Elizabeth (Livius), IV, 484
Tufton Mason, John, IV, 484
Tuglavina (Tuglawina, Tukelavinia), IV, **740**, 536, 537
Tunstall*, James Marmaduke (1760–1840), IV, 139, 151
Tunstall, Sarah. *See* Christie
Turc de Castelveyre, Claude, III, 632
Turc de Castelveyre, Louis, known as Brother Chrétien, II, 135, 378; III, **632–34**, 76, 292; IV, 237, 720
Turc de Castelveyre, Marie. *See* Bonnel
Turcot, Marie-Renée (You de La Découverte), II, 672
Turenne, Vicomte de. *See* La Tour
Turgeon, Jean, IV, 64
Turgeon, Marie (Bilodeau), III, 519
Turgis. *See* Saint-Étienne de La Tour
Turin, Marie (André), III, 14
Turmenys, Phillipe de, I, 221
Turner, Lieutenant, I, 68
Turner, Ephraim, I, 337
Turnor, Elizabeth (wife of PHILIP), IV, 742
Turnor, Philip, IV, **740–42**, 310, 365, 366, 389, 525, 684, 758
Turpin, Alexandre, II, 134
Turpin, Marie-Madeleine (Levasseur), II, 430, 431; IV, 471, 475
Tussichi (Toussiqui), Margherita (Spagniolini), III, 597
Tute, James, III, 452; IV, 681
Tutty, Catherine (wife of WILLIAM; widow of Hollows), III, 635
Tutty, Gruzzel. *See* Drew
Tutty, William (father), III, 634
Tutty, William, III, **634–35**, 125, 275, 473; IV, 94, 775
Tuvache, Captain, I, 208
Tüyaguande. *See* Teyohaqueande
Twatt, Magnus, IV, 366
Tweeddale, Marchioness of. *See* Hamilton
Tweeddale, Marquis of. *See* Hay
Twide, Richard, I, 380
Tyng, Anne. *See* Waldo
Tyng, Edward (father of EDWARD, father), I, 654
Tyng, Edward (father), I, **654**, 426, 576; II, 14, 25, 177, 494; III, 635
Tyng, Edward (son), I, 654; III, **635–36**; IV, 588
Tyng, Elizabeth. *See* Clarke
Tyng, Elizabeth. *See* Southack
Tyng, Rebecca (Dudley), III, 200
Tyorhansera. *See* Teiorhénhsere?

Tyrell, Thomas. *See* Pichon
Tyrkir, I, 449
Tyrrell*, Joseph Burr (1858–1957), IV, 342

UBALDINI, Roberto, I, 97, 307
Ulpius, Euphrosynus, I, 659
Umfreville, Edward, IV, **742–43**, 277, 518, 684
Underdown, John, II, 152, 439
Ungquaterughiathe. *See* Swatana
Unton, Henry, I, 531
Upton, John, II, 672
Upton, Mary (Yonge), II, 672
Urfé. *See* Lascaris
Urfé, Marquise d'. *See* Allègre
Ursúa. *See* Bucareli
Urtebise, Élisabeth (Barsalou), IV, 46
Urville. *See* Dumont

VACHON, Louise-Marie (Paillard), II, 506
Vachon, Marguerite. *See* Langlois
Vachon, Marguerite (Duprac), II, 206, 639
Vachon, Paul (father), II, **639–40**, xxiii, 206
Vachon, Paul (son), II, **640–41**
Vachon, Sapience. *See* Vateau
Vachon, Vincent, II, 639
Vachon de Belmont, François, I, 116, 273, 274, 445, 598;
    II, **641–42**, 134, 241, 562; III, 180, 486, 649
Vachon de Belmont, Jean-Baptiste, II, 641
Vachon de Belmont, Jean-François, II, 641
Vachon de Belmont et de Crapanoz, Ennemond, II, 641
Vachon de Belmont et de Crapanoz, Honorade. *See* Prunier
Vaillant, Marguerite-Ursule. *See* Lajus
Vaillant, Marie-Ursule-Antoinette (Vienne), IV, 754
Vaillant, Sébastien, II, 188, 595, 596, 597, 599, 600; III,
    675, 678
Vaillant de Gueslis, François, II, **642–43**, 237, 502, 585
Valbelle, Chevalier de, I, 443
Valbringue, Robert. *See* La Rocque de Roberval, Jean-
    François de
Valentine, Thomas, IV, 162
Valerianos, Apostolos. *See* Fuca, Juan de
Valets, Jean, I, 201, 267, 269, 270, 273
Vallée, Charles, III, 478
Vallée, François-Madeleine, III, **636–37**
Vallée, Laurence. *See* Casselle
Vallée, Louis-Félix, III, 637
Vallée, Madeleine (Brassard Deschenaux), IV, 89
Vallée, Marie (Varlet), III, 639
Vallette de Chévigny, Charles, III, 637
Vallette de Chévigny, Marguerite. *See* Maillou, *dit*
    Desmoulins
Vallette de Chévigny, Marie-Anne. *See* Deschamps de
    Fellière
Vallette de Chévigny, Médard-Gabriel, III, **637–38**, 373;
    IV, 473
Vallier, François-Elzéar, III, **638–39**, 11, 192, 194, 413,
    545; IV, 387, 429, 719
Vallière, Louis-Florent de, Marquis de Vallière, IV, 208
Valliers, Catherine de (Razilly), I, 567
Valmur. *See* Bricault
Valois-Villette, Philippe de, Comte de Murcé (Mursay), II,
    98
Valpergue, Françoise de (Lescarbot), I, 471

Valrennes. *See* Clément
Vanacott, Hatty (Darby), IV, 194
Van Blacklandt. *See* Blacklandt
Van Braam, Jacob, III, 149, 600, 601; IV, 227
Vanbrugh, Philip, IV, 226
Vancouver, Bridget. *See* Berners
Vancouver, George, IV, **743–48**, 73, 166, 218, 244, 325,
    411, 568, 768
Vancouver, John, IV, 747
Vancouver, John Jasper, IV, 743
Van Curler. *See* Curler
Vandémont, Philippe-Emmanuel de, Duc de Mercœur et de
    Penthièvre, I, 421
Vandeput, George, IV, 112
Van der Donck. *See* Donck
Van der Dostyne. *See* Dostyne
Vandry, Marie (Couillard de Lespinay), II, 156
Vane, Lady Anne (Hope Weir), IV, 366
Vane, George, II, **643–44**, 22, 351, 439, 651, 652
Vaner (Vannier), Hans, I, 383
Van Felson, William, IV, 79
Van Gennep, Arnold, III, 337
Van Harwick. *See* Harwick
Vanier, Suzanne (Senet), II, 604
Vannasse, François, II, 166
Vanneck, Sophie (Lambert Dumont), II, 82
Vannier, Catherine (Pelletier), I, 536
Van Rensselaer, Alida. *See* Schuyler
Van Rensselaer, Jeremiah, II, 342, 602
Van Rensselaer, Kiliaen, I, 527
Van Rensselaer, Maria (Schuyler), II, 602
Van Rensselaer, Nicholas, II, 436
Van Schaick, Engeltie (Schuyler), II, 602
Van Schaick, Goose, IV, lv
Van Slichtenhorst (Van Slichtarhorst), Margarita (Schuy-
    ler), II, 602; III, 586
Van Steenwijck. *See* Steenwijck
Vantelon. *See* Esprit
Var. *See* Saint-Aubin
Varennes. *See* Gaultier
Varin, *dit* La Pistole, Jacques (uncle), IV, 748
Varin, *dit* La Pistole, Jacques, IV, **748–49**
Varin, *dit* La Pistole, Louis-Joseph, IV, 748
Varin, *dit* La Pistole, Marie-Josette. *See* Périnault
Varin, *dit* La Pistole, Marie-Louise (Joram Chappuis, *dit*
    Comtois), IV, 748
Varin, *dit* La Pistole, Marie-Renée. *See* Gautier
Varin, *dit* La Pistole, Nicolas (father), IV, 748
Varin, *dit* La Pistole, Nicolas, IV, 748
Varin de La Marre, Charlotte. *See* Liénard de Beaujeu
Varin de La Marre, Jean-Baptiste-François-Marie, IV, 750
Varin de La Marre, Jean-Victor, II, 95; III, 64, 74, 124, 225,
    300, 402, 647; IV, **749–51**, 66, 67, 68, 91, 187, 216, 265,
    356, 359, 461, 517, 615, 616, 644, 728
Varin de La Sablonnière, Jean, IV, 749
Varlet, Achille, Sieur de Verneuil, III, 639
Varlet, Charles, Sieur de La Grange, III, 639
Varlet, Dominique-Marie, III, **639–41**
Varlet, Jean-Achille, III, 639
Varlet, Marie. *See* Vallée
Varlet, Marie-Anne (Olivier), III, 639
Vassall, John, IV, 677
Vassall, William, IV, 677

Vassan. *See* Mutigny

Vasse, Anne (Becquet), I, 86

Vasseur. *See* Levasseur

Vateau, Sapience (Vachon), II, 639

Vauban. *See* Le Prestre

Vaubougon. *See* Chauvigny

Vaucour. *See* Pinguet

Vaudésir. *See* Baudart

Vaudive, Nicolas-Félix, IV, 69

Vaudreuil. *See* Rigaud

Vaudreuil, Baronne de. *See* Chateauverdun

Vaudreuil, Marquise de. *See* Fleury Deschambault; Joybert de Soulanges et de Marson

Vaughan, Anne. *See* Christmas

Vaughan, David, II, **644**, 56, 267, 319, 320

Vaughan, Elizabeth. *See* Elliot

Vaughan, Elizabeth. *See* Robert

Vaughan, Francis, I, 655

Vaughan, George, II, **644–45**; III, 641

Vaughan, John, 1st Earl of Carbery, I, 655

Vaughan, Katherine (wife of Walter), I, 654

Vaughan, Margaret. *See* Cutt

Vaughan, Mary. *See* Belcher

Vaughan, Walter, I, 654

Vaughan, William (father of GEORGE), II, 644

Vaughan, William, II, 644; III, **641–42**, 116, 507, 508, 653; IV, 83

Vaughan, Sir William, I, **654–57**, 162, 365, 496, 632, 668, 672

Vaulezar. *See* Juchereau

Vaulthier, Perrette (Gloria), I, 339

Vaultier (servant), I, 105

Vaulx, Jacques de, I, 88, 89

Vauquelin, Jean, III, 73, 321, 322, 606, 667; IV, **751–52**, 22, 589

Vause, Edward, IV, 199

Vautrollier, Thomas, I, 531

Vauvilliers, Jeanne de (Basset Des Lauriers), I, 79

Vauvril, Françoise. *See* Lepellé

Vauvril de Blason, Marguerite (Boucher de Grandpré; Blaise Des Bergères de Rigauville), I, 109; II, 70

Vavasor, Elizabeth. *See* Lane

Vavasor, Henry, II, 291

Vavasor, Roger, II, 291

Vaz Dourado, Fernan, I, 304

Veau, *dit* Sylvain, Élisabeth-Marguerite (Isabelle) (Grossin), III, 142, 143

Veaux. *See* Devau

Veitch. *See also* Vetch

Veitch, Marion. *See* Fairly

Veitch, William (father), II, 650

Veitch, William, II, 650

Vélez Cachupín, Tomás, III, 424

Venables, Robert, I, 605

Vendamont. *See* Talus

Vendôme, Duc de. *See* Bourbon

Véniard de Bourgmond, Étienne de, II, **645–47**, xxix, xxxi, xxxiv, 267, 414, 475, 632; III, xxxiv, 147; IV, 315

Véniard de Bourgmond, Jacqueline de. *See* Jean

Véniard Du Vergier, Charles de, II, 645

Ventadour, Duc de. *See* Lévis

Verac, Catherine de. *See* Quevillon

Verchères. *See* Jarret

Verdon, Vincent, II, 382

Verdun, Sieur de. *See* Dupuy

Vere, Baron. *See* Beauclerk

Verelst, John, III, 624

Vergennes, Comte de. *See* Gravier

Vergil, Polydore, I, 151

Vergor. *See* Du Pont

Verhoune, Scholastique-Geneviève (Huguet), IV, 375

Verier. *See* Verrier

Verner, Elinor (wife of HUGH), I, 657

Verner, Hugh, I, **657**; II, 231

Verneuil. *See* Bochart; Chaspoux; Lorimier; Petit

Verneuil, Sieur de. *See* Varlet

Vernhes, Jeanne-Marie (Aleyrac), IV, 14

Vernon, Edward, III, 136, 628, 655, 662

Vernon, Gillette de (Gaultier de Rinault), I, 326

Véron de Grandmesnil, Catherine (Fleury Deschambault), IV, 268

Véron de Grandmesnil, Étienne (father), I, 223; II, **647–48**, 522, 523; III, 642, 643

Véron de Grandmesnil, Étienne (son), II, 648; III, **642–43**; IV, 268

Véron de Grandmesnil, Guillaume, I, 223; II, 647

Véron de Grandmesnil, Jean, I, 223; II, 535, 647

Véron de Grandmesnil, Madeleine. *See* Hertel de La Fresnière

Véron de Grandmesnil, Marguerite. *See* Hayet

Véron de Grandmesnil, Marguerite (Petit), II, 522; IV, 167

Véron de Grandmesnil, Marie-Catherine. *See* Le Picard

Véron de Grandmesnil, Marie-Thérèse. *See* Moral de Saint-Quentin

Véronneau, Agathe, III, **643**

Véronneau, Louis, III, 643

Véronneau, Marguerite. *See* Maugras

Verrazzano, Bernardo da, I, 657

Verrazzano, Fiametta da. *See* Capelli

Verrazzano, Gerolamo da, I, 657, 659, 660

Verrazzano, Giovanni da, I, **657–60**, 19, 21, 27, 72, 165, 187, 188, 332, 333, 342, 374, 469, 585, 586; III, 248

Verrazzano, Nicolo da, I, 657

Verrazzano, Piero da, I, 657

Verrazzano, Piero Andrea da, I, 657

Verreau, Barthélemy, II, **648**

Verreau*, Hospice-Anthelme-Jean-Baptiste (1828–1901), III, 691, 695; IV, 41, 698, 801

Verreau, Marguerite. *See* Prieur

Verreau, Marthe. *See* Quittel

Verreau, *dit* Le Bourguignon, Barthélemy, II, 648

Verrier, Christophe, III, 643

Verrier, Claude-Étienne, III, 79, 646

Verrier, Étienne, II, 154, 648, 649, 650; III, **643–46**, 79, 80, 116, 118, 191, 235, 389, 455, 478; IV, 15, 62, 248, 253

Verrier, Guillaume, III, 646

Verrier, Hélène. *See* Papin

Verrier, Louis-Guillaume, II, 150, 152; III, **646–48**, 4, 64, 74, 164, 203, 225, 228, 491, 511, 675; IV, 182, 186, 318, 343, 359, 624

Verrier, Marguerite. *See* Ferrant

Verrier, Marie-Madeleine. *See* Thibault

Verrier, Pierre, I, 557

Verrier, Roberte. *See* Gadoys

Verron, Renée (Maumousseau), II, 466

Vertefeuille. *See* Bachand

Verville. *See also* Gautier

Verville, Guillaume de, II, 648

Verville, Jean-François de, II, **648–50**, 154, 292, 611; III, 79, 80, 117, 118, 191, 234, 389, 455, 575, 644

Verville, Louis de, II, 648

Verville, Madeleine-Angélique de. *See* Trégu de Langon

Vésin. *See* Olivier

Vesins, Élisabeth de (Couillard), I, 236

Vespucci, Amerigo, I, 151, 155, 658

Vetch, Alida, II, 652

Vetch, Margaret. *See* Livingston

Vetch, Samuel, II, **650–52**, 21, 22, 38, 39, 122, 123, 167, 238, 287, 289, 436, 437, 461, 497, 498, 508, 546, 643, 644, 660; III, 200, 207, 208, 276, 436, 515

Vetch, William, II, 652

Veyrac. *See* Chabrand

Veysey, John, IV, 700

Veyssière, M., III, 481

Veyssière, Christiana (Gotson; wife of LEGER-JEAN-BAPTISTE-NOËL), IV, 752

Veyssière, Elizabeth. *See* Lawrear

Veyssière, Jean, IV, 565

Veyssière, Leger-Jean-Baptiste-Noël, known as Father Emmanuel, III, 296; IV, **752–54**, 104, 139, 140

Veyssière, Pierre, IV, 565

Veyssières, Étienne, IV, 752

Veyssières, Françoise. *See* Fraysse

Vézier, François, II, 159

Vézier, Marie. *See* Couture

Vézin (Vézain). *See* Olivier

Vézina, Charles, II, 378, 379; III, **648–49**

Vézina, François, III, 648

Vézina, Louise. *See* Godin

Vézina, Marie. *See* Clément

Vezins, Marie (Villedonné), II, 652

Vialars, Antoine, IV, 35, 461

Vialars, Daniel, IV, 35, 286, 461

Vibraye, Marquis de. *See* Hurault

Vicq de Pontgibaud, Marie-Claude de (Guillouet d'Orvilliers), II, 269

Victoria, Queen of Great Britain and Ireland, IV, 628

Vidal, Jean, III, 596

Vidalle, Anne (Chaussegros), III, 116

Vieille Robe de Castor. *See* Chomina

Viel, Marie (Jolliet; Petit de Verneuil; Des Forges), II, 521

Viel, Nicolas, I, **661**, 58, 263, 420, 437, 440, 590, 639

Viele, Aernout Cornelissen, I, 526

Vien, Charlotte (Prévost), I, 553

Viennay-Pachot, Charlotte-Françoise. *See* Juchereau de Saint-Denis

Viennay-Pachot, François, I, **661**, 56, 397; II, 69, 276, 305

Viennay-Pachot, Jean-Daniel-Marie, III, 105

Viennay-Pachot, Jeanne. *See* Avamy

Viennay-Pachot, Marie-Françoise (Berthier; Blaise Des Bergères de Rigauville), II, 60, 69

Vienne, Françoise de. *See* Perdrigean

Vienne, François-Joseph de, IV, **754–55**, 263, 271

Vienne, Jean de, IV, 754

Vienne, Marguerite, I, 233

Vienne, Marie-Louise de (Tisserant de Moncharvaux), III, 626

Vienne, Marie-Ursule-Antoinette de. *See* Vaillant

Viennot, Marie (Raclot), II, 517

Vieux Crapaud, III, 248

Vieuxpont. *See also* Godefroy

Vieuxpont, Alexandre de, I, 453, 665

Viger, Angélique, *dite* de Saint-Martin, IV, 190

Viger*, Denis (1741–1805), IV, 148

Viger*, Denis-Benjamin (1774–1861), IV, 148

Viger, Jacques, III, 473

Viger*, Jacques (1787–1858), II, 259, 378; III, 691; IV, 427, 509, 510, 801

Viger, Marie-Françoise (Hantraye), IV, 326

Viger, Marie-Marguerite. *See* La Corne

Viger, Périne-Charles. *See* Cherrier

Viger, Thérèse-Amable (Orillat), IV, 591

Vignal, Guillaume, I, **661–62**, 46, 130, 458, 612; II, 164, 426

Vignau. *See also* Maurice

Vignau, Jean-Raymond, IV, 123

Vignau, Marie-Joseph. *See* Cadet

Vignau, Nicolas de, I, **662–63**, 191, 192, 638

Vigneau, Anne (Lajus), III, 344

Vigneau, Catherine (Martin), II, 462

Vigneault, Stanislas, IV, 385

Vignerot, Marie-Madeleine de, Duchesse d'Aiguillon (Beauvoir Du Roure de Combalet), I, 203, 297, 347, 348, 373, 483, 484

Vignerot Du Plessis, Armand-Jean, Duc de Richelieu, I, 483

Vignerot Du Plessis, Louis-François-Armand de, Duc de Richelieu, III, 31; IV, 468, 469

Vignerot Du Plessis de Richelieu, Emmanuel-Armand de, Duc d'Aiguillon, III, 111; IV, 739

Vilain, Jeanne (Chevalier), II, 142

Vildaigre. *See* Perrot

Vilermaula, Louis-Michel de, II, 164, 562; III, **649**

Vilers, Madeleine (Levasseur), II, 430

Villain, Jean (master jeweller), I, 663

Villain, Jean (uncle of JEAN-BAPTISTE), I, 663

Villain, Jean-Baptiste, I, **663**

Villain, Jeanne. *See* Barbé

Villain, Jeanne (Bernier), I, 663

Villaine, Louis de, I, 425

Villars. *See also* Sorbier

Villars, Mme de, I, 58

Villazur, Pedro de, II, xxxvii, 646

Ville. *See also* Villes

Ville, Sieur de, II, 82

Villebois. *See also* Michel

Villebois, M. de, III, 51

Villebon. *See* Dejordy; Robinau

Villechauve. *See* Beauharnois

Villedonné, Étienne de (father), II, 652

Villedonné, Étienne de, II, **652–53**, 626

Villedonné, Françoise de. *See* Roussel

Villedonné, Marie de. *See* Damours de Chaffours

Villedonné, Marie de. *See* Vezins

Villefranche. *See* Grisé

Villegaignon. *See* Durand

Villejouin (Villejoin, Villejoint). *See* Rousseau

Villemenon, Sieur, I, 433

Villemomble. *See* Liénard

Villemor, Duc de. *See* Séguier

Villeneuve. *See also* Amiot

Villeneuve, Marquis de. *See* Duret

Villeneuve, Domitilde. *See* Domitilde

Villeneuve, Gaspard de, II, 574
Villeneuve, Marie de (Bonne de Missègle), III, 69
Villeneuve, Marie-Louise de. *See* Rigaud de Vaudreuil
Villeneuve, Robert de, I, **663–64**; II, 229, 432, 532; III, 190
Villeray. *See* Rouer
Villermaula (Villermola). *See* Vilermaula
Villermont. *See* Cabart
Villers, Jean de, IV, 124
Villes, Jean-Marie de, II, **653**, 455, 645; III, 66
Villesavin. *See* Phélypeaux
Villette. *See* Valois
Villiers. *See also* Coulon; Legardeur; Neyon
Villiers, Barbara, Countess of Castlemaine and Duchess of
    Cleveland (Palmer), III, 369
Villiers, Christopher, 1st Earl of Anglesey, I, 614
Villiers, George, 1st Duke of Buckingham, I, 365, 419, 669
Villieu, Claude-Sébastien de (father), II, 653
Villieu, Claude-Sébastien de, I, 426, 427, 578; II, **653–54**,
    47, 71, 185, 257, 410, 626, 629, 664; III, 190
Villieu, Jeanne de. *See* Lebreton
Villieu, Judith de. *See* Leneuf de La Vallière
Villieu, Sébastien de, II, **654–55**, 238
Vimeur, Jean-Baptiste de, Comte de Rochambeau, IV, 32,
    212
Vimont, Barthélemy, I, **665**, 124, 205, 215, 216, 248, 348,
    382, 389, 404, 430, 453, 516; III, 310
Vincelotte. *See* Amiot
Vincenne. *See* Bissot
Vincent. *See also* Clément
Vincent, III, **650**
Vincent, Joseph, III, 650
Vincent, Matthew, IV, 527
Vincent, Nicolas. *See* Tsawouenhouhi
Vincent, Prosper, III, 650
Vincent, Robert, III, **650–51**, 474
Vincent, Stanislas, III, 650
Vincent*, Zacharie (1815–86), III, 650
Vincent de Paul, I, 91, 208
Vinsenne. *See* Bissot
Virazel. *See* Belrieux
Virot, Claude-François-Louis, III, 21
Visscher, N. J., I, 525
Visseri. *See* Dutisné
Vitally, Antoine, IV, 286
Vitré. *See* Denys
Vitry, Jean, I, 108
Vivonne, Duc de. *See* Rochechouart
Volant, Anne-Marie (Cailly), III, 93
Volant, François, II, 529
Volant, Marguerite (Legardeur de Tilly), II, 387
Volant, Nicolas, II, 43
Volant d'Haudebourg, Jean-Louis, II, 66, 301; III, 579; IV,
    181
Volant d'Haudebourg, Marie. *See* Mars
Volant de Radisson, Étienne, II, **655**, 505; III, 205, 372
Volant de Radisson, Geneviève. *See* Letendre
Volant de Saint-Claude, Claude (father), II, 655
Volant de Saint-Claude, Claude, II, **655–56**
Volant de Saint-Claude, Françoise. *See* Radisson
Volant de Saint-Claude, Pierre, II, **655–56**
Voltaire. *See* Arouet, François-Marie
Vondenvelden*, William (d. 1809), IV, 154, 502
Von Galen, Christoph Bernhard, I, 142

Von Linné. *See* Linnaeus
Von Wallmoden, Amalie Sophie Marianne. *See* Von Wendt
Von Wendt, Amalie Sophie Marianne, Countess of Yar-
    mouth (Von Wallmoden), IV, 21
Vouet, Simon, I, 214, 313
Vox. *See* Devau
Voyer, Antoine-René de, Marquis de Paulmy d'Argenson,
    IV, 655
Voyer, Joseph, III, 312, 518
Voyer, Marc-Pierre de, Comte d'Argenson, III, 458, 459;
    IV, 175, 478
Voyer, Marie-Madeleine (Bernard de La Rivière), II, 59
Voyer, Michel, IV, 125
Voyer, *dit* Le Jardinier, Jacques, II, 201
Voyer, *dit* Le Jardinier, Marie-Jeanne. *See* Routier
Voyer d'Argenson, Marc de, II, 656
Voyer d'Argenson, Pierre de, I, 46, 48, 206, 224, 225, 269,
    270, 283, 288, 330, 431, 538, 563, 580, 588, 645, 646,
    665; II, **656–58**, 136, 158, 363, 364, 536
Voyer d'Argenson, René de, II, 656
Vuadens. *See also* Waddens
Vuadens. Adam Samuel, IV, 757
Vuadens, Marie-Bernardine. *See* Ormond
Vuil, Daniel, I, **665–66**, 284
Vulliermet, Marguerite (Souste), IV, 720
Vuyart, Nicolas, III, 221
Vyner, Sir Robert, I, 83

WABAKININE (Wabacoming), IV, **755–56**
Wabasha (Wabashar). *See* Wahpasha
Wabbicommicot (Wabacumaga), III, **651–52**, xxxvii, 215;
    IV, 174
Wäber. *See also* Webber
Waber, Marie-Élisabeth, II, 526
Wäber, Rosina, IV, 762
Wabicanine. *See* Wabakinine
Wabunmashue. *See* Wapinesiw
Waddens, Jean-Étienne, IV, **757**, 592
Waddens, Marguerite (McKay; McLoughlin), IV, 757
Waddens, Marie-Josephte. *See* Deguire
Waddens, Véronique (Bethune), IV, 757
Wade, Cooper, II, 666
Wadsworth, Benjamin, II, 25
Wager, Sir Charles, III, 447, 448, 659
Waggoner, Joseph, III, 304, 595; IV, 47
Waggoner, Rowland, II, **658**, 65; III, 595; IV, 380
Wahawanulet, Louis, III, 266
Wahpasha* (d. 1805 or 1806), IV, 486
Wainwright, Francis, II, 38, 452
Wainwright, Lucy (Waldo), III, 652
Wainwright, Mary. *See* Williams
Wainwright, Simon, II, 606
Waipykanine. *See* Wabakinine
Walbank, Thomas, III, 504
Waldo, Ann (Tyng), III, 635
Waldo, Hannah. *See* Mason
Waldo, Jonathan, III, 652
Waldo, Lucy. *See* Wainwright
Waldo, Samuel, II, 494; III, **652–54**, 6, 128, 259, 483, 635,
    642, 645; IV, 780
Wales, Prince of. *See* Frederick Louis; George IV
Wales, William, IV, **757–58**, 339, 341, 377, 740, 741, 744
Walker*, Alexander (1764–1831), IV, 498, 499

Walker, Anne (wife of Nehemiah, mariner), I, 666
Walker, Elizabeth. *See* Chamberlen
Walker, Fowler, IV, 574
Walker, George, IV, 436
Walker, Hannah (mother of WILLIAM), IV, 760
Walker, Harriet. *See* McLean
Walker, Sir Hovenden, I, 36, 76; II, **658–62**, 21, 52, 80, 122, 246, 250, 254, 286, 287, 289, 304, 384, 437, 485, 490, 497, 508, 511, 569, 643, 651, 667; III, 177, 178, 200, 429, 596, 662
Walker, James, I, 666
Walker, John (merchant), IV, 682
Walker, John (shipowner), IV, 163
Walker, John (traveller), I, 333
Walker, Nehemiah (mariner), I, 666
Walker, Nehemiah, I, **666**, 39, 84, 232, 324, 417, 476, 518, 519, 528, 543, 605, 606, 657; II, 231, 264
Walker, Obediah, I, 667
Walker, Richard, I, **666–67**, 62, 399, 637
Walker, Sarah (wife of RICHARD), I, 667
Walker, Thomas, IV, **758–60**, 130, 184, 270, 295, 345, 348, 369, 379, 380, 546, 576, 634
Walker, William (brother of NEHEMIAH), I, 666
Walker, William (father of Sir HOVENDEN), II, 658
Walker, William (father of NEHEMIAH), I, 84, 666
Walker, William, IV, **760–61**, 157, 740
Walker, William (son of WILLIAM), IV, 760
Wall, Rachel. *See* Butler
Walley, John, I, 466, 545; II, **662**, 601
Wallis, Benjamin, II, 265
Walmesley, Sara (Parr), IV, 603
Walpole, Horatio (Horace), 4th Earl of Orford, III, 92, 150, 166; IV, 114, 571
Walpole, Robert, 1st Earl of Oxford, II, 24; III, 283, 447
Walsh, Thomas, I, 329; II, 42, 177, 311, 393, 394, 407, 454
Walsingham, Baron. *See* Grey
Walsingham, Sir Francis, I, 251, 252, 332, 333, 363, 380
Walter, Hester (Schuyler), III, 587
Walters. *See also* Palliser
Walters, William, III, 320
Wanduny. *See* Orontony
Wanton*, William (d. 1816), IV, 769
Wanungonet. *See* Wenemouet
Wapackcamigat (Wapaumagen). *See* Wabbicommicot
Wapasha. *See* Wahpasha
Wapinesiw (Wappenessew), IV, **761**, 47
Wappisis, III, **654–55**, 123; IV, 381, 518
Ward, Edward, IV, 617
Ward, Richard, II, **662–63**, 51, 65, 267, 493
Warde, Richard, I, 343
Warden, Matthew, III, 151
Warner, John, II, 265
Warrancansit (Warracunsit, Warrawcuset). *See* Mog
Warren, Anne (Johnson), IV, 394
Warren, Catherine. *See* Aylmer
Warren, Elizabeth (Church), II, 145
Warren, Hester (Patterson), IV, 606
Warren, Michael, III, 655
Warren, Sir Peter, III, **655–59**, 6, 49, 91, 209, 294, 345, 356, 507, 508, 572, 610, 628, 636, 642, 644, 653, 654; IV, 62, 83, 168, 239, 248, 363, 394, 417, 420, 454, 783
Warren, Susannah. *See* De Lancey
Warwick, Countess of. *See* Russell

Warwick, Earl of. *See* Dudley; Rich
Washiabitt, III, 595
Washington, George, III, 148, 149, 150, 151, 320, 375, 376, 587, 600, 601, 614; IV, 34, 177, 178, 227, 229, 256, 257, 322, 408, 459, 490, 522, 547, 617, 667, 681, 736
Washington, John, II, **663**, 601; III, 277
Washington, Mary. *See* Scott
Wasson (Ojibwa chief), IV, 762
Wasson (Warsong, Wassong), III, 95, 96; IV, **761–62**, lv
Waters, Abigail (Cleveland), III, 125
Watson*, Sir Brook (1735–1807), IV, 53, 57, 58, 112, 244, 273, 313, 369, 528, 592, 618, 696, 717, 721
Watson, Caroline, III, 592
Watson, Charles, III, **659**
Watson, John, III, 659
Watson, Rebecca. *See* Buller
Watson-Wentworth, Charles, 2nd Marquess of Rocking-ham, IV, xli, 348, 571
Watteville, John de (Bishop Johannes), III, 212
Watts, Agnes. *See* Mackworth
Watts, John, I, 241
Watts, Margaret (wife of RICHARD), II, 663
Watts, Richard, I, 241
Watts, Richard, II, **663–64**, 275
Wawanesse, IV, 133
Wawanolewat (Wawenorrawot). *See* Gray Lock
Wawatam, III, **659–60**
Waxaway, II, **664**
Waymouth, George, I, **667–68**, 20, 189, 318, 375, 397, 650
Wayne, Anthony, IV, 260, 410, 499
Webb, Daniel, III, 460
Webb, Grace (wife of JAMES), III, 661
Webb, James, III, **660–61**; IV, 259
Webber (Wäber), Abraham, IV, 762
Webber, John, IV, **762–63**
Webber, Mary (Quant; mother of JOHN), IV, 762
Webster*, John Clarence (1863–1950), III, 667; IV, 458
Wedderburn, Alexander, 1st Baron Loughborough, IV, xlv, xlvi, xlvii, xlviii, 349
Wedel, Miss (Mabane), IV, 491
Wegg, George Samuel, IV, 758
Weir. *See* Hope Weir
Weiser, Johann Conrad, III, 496, 606, 607, 613, 614; IV, 154
Weissenberg (Weisenburg, Wisenberg), Catherine (John-son), IV, 155, 397, 417
Weld*, Isaac (1774–1856), IV, 738
Well, Bernard, II, 337; IV, 135, 299
Welles, John, IV, 140, 277, 697
Welles, Marguerite. *See* Réaume
Wellesley, Arthur, 1st Duke of Wellington, IV, 26
Wendell, Jacob, II, 26
Wenemouet (Wenemowet, Wenemuit), II, **664–66**, xxxvii, 495, 669; III, 584
Wenman, Amos, IV, 763
Wenman, Ann. *See* Scroope
Wenman, Elizabeth Susanna (Pringle), IV, 764
Wenman, Richard, IV, **763–64**, 451
Wenman, Susanna (Green), IV, 764
Wenongonet (Wenoggenet). *See* Wenemouet
Wensley, Sarah (Winslow), IV, 774
Wentworth. *See also* Watson-Wentworth
Wentworth, Benning (uncle), III, 453

Wentworth, Benning, IV, 112
Wentworth*, Sir John (1737–1820), IV, 111, 112, 484, 485, 516, 605
Wenungenit. *See* Wenemouet
Wesley, John, IV, 19, 175, 176, 776
West, Benjamin, III, 670; IV, 394
West, Thomas, 3rd Baron De La Warr, I, 67
Westbrook, Thomas, II, 544; III, 359
Westfield, Judith (Irving), IV, 379
Westfield, William, IV, 379
Wewonorawed. *See* Gray Lock
Wexar. *See* Waxaway
Weymouth. *See* Waymouth
Whalley. *See* Walley
Wharton, John, IV, 634
Wheelock, Eleazar, IV, 416, 731
Wheelwright, Esther (rebaptized Marie-Joseph), *dite* de l'Enfant-Jésus, II, 65; IV, **764–66**, 536, 554
Wheelwright, John (grandfather), IV, 764
Wheelwright, John, IV, 764
Wheelwright, Mary. *See* Snell
Wheelwright, Samuel, IV, 764
Wheler, Sir Francis, I, 546; II, 478, 510
Whetstone, John, II, 666
Whetstone, Maria (wife of Sir WILLIAM), II, 666
Whetstone, Sir William, II, **666**, 260
Whitbourne, Sir Richard, I, **668–69**, 229, 278, 279, 300, 362, 632, 655, 656
Whitcomb, Benjamin, IV, 294
White, Elizabeth (Shepherd), IV, 766
White, James, IV, 196, 389, 736
White, John (father of JOHN, d. 1800), IV, 766
White, John, I, **669–70**, 5
White, John, IV, **766–67**
White, Joseph, IV, 711
White, Marrianne. *See* Lynne
White, Richard, III, **661**
White, Thomas, III, **661–62**, 301, 302, 342, 521, 593, 654
White Eyes, IV, 301
Whitefield, George, III, 125; IV, 402, 494, 514
Whitefield, Mrs Martha, IV, 208
Whitehead. *See* Gray Lock
White Head. *See* Theyanoguin
White Mingo, III, 320
White Thunder. *See* Kaghswaghtaniunt
Whitham. *See* Witham
Whitmore, Arthur, III, 662
Whitmore, Edward, III, **662–63**, 601, 666, 667; IV, 21, 22
Whitmore, Edward (son), III, 663
Whittington, George, I, 350
Widmerpole, Dorothy. *See* Frobisher
Widmerpole, Sir William, I, 318
Wigate, John, III, **663**, 449, 544, 594
Wikinanish (fl. 1788–1818), IV, 767
Wikinanish (Wickananish), IV, **767–68**, lv, 244, 568, 569
Wilamak. *See* Ouenemek
Wilberforce, William, IV, 413
Wilkes, John, IV, 571, 619
Wilkins, John, III, 262, 530; IV, **768–69**
Wilkinson*, Elizabeth (fl. 1783–1806), IV, 317
Wilkinson, Moses, IV, 515
Willard, Abel (nephew of ABIJAH), IV, 769
Willard, Abel (prisoner), IV, 432

Willard, Abijah, IV, **769–70**
Willard, Anna. *See* Prentice
Willard, Elizabeth. *See* Prescott
Willard, Mary (McKown; wife of ABIJAH), IV, 769
Willard, Samuel, IV, 769
Willard, Susanna (Johnson; Hastings), IV, 294
Willcocks*, William (1736–1813), IV, 677
Wille, Johann Georg, IV, 762
Willes, Richard, I, 154
William. *See* Tuglavina
William I, King of England (William the Conqueror), I, 121
William III, King of Great Britain and Ireland (William of Orange), I, 92, 329, 426, 544, 545; II, 103, 183, 246, 262, 279, 280, 497, 601, 650; III, 515; IV, xxiv
William IV, King of Great Britain and Ireland, IV, 556
William, Duke of Gloucester, II, 286
William Augustus, Duke of Cumberland, III, 218, 362, 666; IV, 21
William Henry, Prince. *See* William IV
William of Canajoharie. *See* Tekawironte
Williams, Commodore. *See* Gillam, Thomas
Williams, Abigail. *See* Allen
Williams, Ann. *See* Fothersall
Williams, Ephraim, III, 186
Williams, Eunice. *See* Mather
Williams, Eunice (Marie, Marguerite), II, 667; IV, **770–71**
Williams, Griffith, IV, **771–72**
Williams*, Jenkin (d. 1819), IV, 72, 549
Williams, John (brother of GRIFFITH), IV, 771
Williams, John (gunner), I, 376
Williams, John (minister), II, **667**, 80, 285, 437, 450; III, 200, 493; IV, 770
Williams, John (officer), II, **667–68**
Williams, Mary (Silver; Wainwright), II, 606
Williams, Mercy (Seccombe), IV, 705
Williams, Robert, II, 667
Williams, Samuel, II, 667
Williams, Stephen, IV, 770
Williams, Theoda. *See* Park
Williams, Thomas. *See also* Tehoragwanegen
Williams, Thomas, IV, 674
Williams, Warham, III, 581; IV, 770
Williams, William, IV, 705
Williamson, Sir Adam, IV, 768, 772
Williamson, David, IV, 302
Williamson, George, III, xxv; IV, **772–73**, 22, 24
Willis, Hannah (Seccomb), IV, 705
Willis, Marie (Arnaud; Perrot de Rizy; Cotton), II, 520; IV, 173
Willoughby, Bridget (wife of Sir Percival), I, 670
Willoughby, Edward, I, 670
Willoughby, Sir Hugh, I, 158
Willoughby, Sir Percival, I, 240, 351, 534, 535, 584, 670
Willoughby, Thomas, I, **670–71**, 240, 584
Willoughby, William, I, 443
Willson, Beckles, III, 589
Wilmot, Anne. *See* Montagu
Wilmot, Christopher, III, 663
Wilmot, Montagu, III, **663–65**, 365; IV, xxvii, 51, 110, 131, 193, 274, 291, 292, 308, 313, 528, 562, 695, 781
Wilson, Ann (Hilton), II, 287
Wilson, Edward, I, 374, 375, 378
Wilson, Humphrey, II, 287

Wilson, William, I, 374, 376, 377
Winchelsea, Earl of. *See* Finch
Winchester, Marquis of. *See* Paulet
Winchester, Charles, IV, 401
Winman. *See* Wenman
Winne. *See* Wynne
Winnekee. *See* Caupemartissue
Winnenimmit. *See* Wenemouet
Winniett, Anne (Cosby), III, 143, 421, 665
Winniett, Elizabeth (Handfield), III, 277, 421, 665
Winniett, Joseph, III, 277, 665
Winniett, Marie-Madeleine. *See* Maisonnat
Winniett, Marie-Madeleine (How), III, 297, 421, 665
Winniett, William, II, 22; III, **665–66**, 3, 143, 277, 297, 421
Winninnewaycappo, IV, **773–74**
Winslow, Bethiah. *See* Barker
Winslow*, Edward (1746/47–1815), IV, xxviii, 55, 328, 516, 677, 723
Winslow, Elizabeth (Marston), IV, 516
Winslow, Isaac, IV, 774
Winslow, John, III, xxviii, xxix, 129, 260, 275, 277, 362, 363, 572, 589; IV, **774–75**, xxviii, 314, 540, 679
Winslow, Mary. *See* Little
Winslow, Sarah. *See* Wensley
Winter, William, I, 229, 333, 532
Winthrop, Fitz-John, II, 436, 603; III, 586, 587
Winthrop, John, II, 287
Winthrop, Mary (Livingston), II, 436
Wisenberg (Wisenburg). *See* Weissenberg
Witham (Whitham), Anne (Murray), IV, 569
Withipoll, John, I, 386
Witzel. *See* Miçel
Wiwurna. *See* Wowurna
Wolcott, Roger, III, 645
Wolfall, Robert, I, 85
Wolfe, Edward, III, 666
Wolfe, Henrietta. *See* Thompson
Wolfe, James, I, 76; III, **666–74**, xvii, xviii, xx, xxi, xxv, xxvi, xxvii, xxix, xxx, 33, 71, 72, 85, 89, 129, 172, 173, 209, 210, 289, 293, 296, 364, 372, 440, 464, 465, 466, 468, 480, 509, 544, 559, 589, 590, 592, 601, 662, 663; IV, 3, 14, 21, 22, 23, 34, 37, 93, 109, 112, 134, 163, 168, 193, 224, 250, 278, 279, 308, 314, 316, 327, 332, 379, 415, 446, 448, 476, 479, 500, 503, 531, 541, 552, 563, 569, 570, 579, 603, 641, 651, 671, 674, 680, 694, 697, 700, 737, 772, 773
Wolfe, Walter, III, 668
Wollaston, John, IV, 397
Wolsey, Thomas, Cardinal Wolsey, I, 155
Wolstenholme, Sir John, I, 362, 374
Wood, Elizabeth (Tarbell), III, 615
Wood, Jane (Shaw), IV, 706
Wood, Mary. *See* Myers
Wood, Sarah (Douglas, Lady Douglas), IV, 223
Wood, Thomas (father), IV, 775
Wood, Thomas, III, 418; IV, **775–76**, 94, 674, 706
Woodbee. *See* Wappisis
Woodbury (Woodberry), Anna (Barnard), III, 25
Woodhouse. *See* Wydowse
Wooster, David, IV, 345, 390, 427, 442, 547, 548, 549, 697
Wooster, Edward, IV, 776
Wooster, Hezekiah Calvin, IV, **776–77**
Worcester, William, I, 386

Worsley, Henry, III, 405
Worthington, William, I, 158
Woudby. *See* Wappisis
Wowurna, II, **668–70**, xxxvi, 476, 477, 543; III, xxxvii
Wraxall, Sir Nathaniel William, IV, 26
Wright, Benjamin, III, 266
Wright, Edward, I, 144, 252
Wright*, Thomas (d. 1812), IV, 128, 607, 610
Wriothesley, Henry, 3rd Earl of Southampton, I, 667
Wroth, Robert, II, **670**, 23; III, 276, 517
Württemberg, Duke of. *See* Friedrich I
Wyatt. *See also* Wyet
Wyatt, Sir Thomas, I, 157
Wydowse (Woodhouse), Thomas, I, 374, 377, 378
Wyet, Sylvester, I, **671–72**, 5, 306, 364, 451
Wyndham, Charles, 2nd Earl of Egremont, IV, xxxiii, xxxv, xxxviii, 571, 572
Wyndham, Thomas, I, 316
Wynne, Edward, I, **672**, 162, 614

Xavier, François, IV, 13

Yaghkaposin (Squash Cutter), IV, 27
Yarmouth, Countess of. *See* Von Wendt
Yates, Mary Ann, IV, 555
Yong; Yonge. *See also* Young
Yonge, James, II, **670–72**
Yonge, James (son), II, 672
Yonge, Jane. *See* Crampporn
Yonge, Joanna. *See* Blackaller
Yonge, John, II, 670
Yonge, Mary. *See* Upton
York, Duke of. *See* Edward IV; Frederick Augustus; James II
York, Jack, IV, **777–79**
York, Sir John, I, 316
Yorke, Charles, IV, xxxiii, xli, xlii, xlvii, 348
Yorke, Gilbert, I, 85, 317
Yorke, John, IV, 293, 522
Yorke, Joseph, 1st Baron Dover, IV, 686
Yorke, Philip, 1st Earl of Hardwicke, IV, 50, 348
You, Marie-Renée. *See* Turcot
You, Pierre, II, 672
You de La Découverte, Élisabeth. *See* Élisabeth
You de La Découverte, Madeleine. *See* Just
You de La Découverte, Marie-Anne (Richard), I, 573; II, 673
You de La Découverte, Philippe, II, 673; III, 450, 520
You de La Découverte, Pierre, I, 573; II, **672–73**, 125, 160; IV, 235
Young, Arthur, IV, 738
Young, James, I, **672–73**; II, 266, 308
Young, Thomas, I, **673**
Young, Walter, IV, 165
Youville, Charles-Marie-Madeleine d', II, 673; IV, **779–80**, 235
Youville, François-Madeleine d', II, 673; IV, 235, 779
Youville, Joseph-François d', II, 673; IV, 235, 779
Youville, Marie-Marguerite d'. *See* Dufrost de Lajemmerais
Youville Dufrost, Charles. *See* Youville, Charles-Marie-Madeleine d'
Yroquet. *See* Iroquet
Yvon. *See* Phlem

ZAMET, Sébastien, I, 483
Zeisberger*, David (1721–1808), III, 319, 607; IV, 260, 301, 302
Zemballe, Marie-Louise (Lemoine), III, 379
Zeno, Antonio, I, **680–81**, 316
Zeno, Nicolò, I, **680–81**, 316

Zichmni (potentate), I, 680
Zinzendorf, Nicolaus Ludwig, Count von, III, 147, 607
Zorn, Jacques, IV, 618
Zouberbuhler, Catherine (Silver), IV, 781
Zouberbuhler, Sebastian, III, 513; IV, **780–81**, 526